WEBSTER'S
UNIVERSAL
ENGLISH
THESAURUS

WEBSTER'S
UNIVERSAL
ENGLISH
THESAURUS

**GEDDES&
GROSSET**

This edition published 2004
by Geddes & Grosset,
David Dale House, New Lanark,
ML11 9DJ, Scotland

Copyright © 2004 Geddes & Grosset

ISBN 1 84205 442 2

Printed and bound in Canada

A

aback *adv* back, backward, rearward, regressively.

abaft *prep* (*naut*) aft, astern, back of, behind.

abandon *vb* abdicate, abjure, desert, drop, evacuate, forsake, forswear, leave, quit, relinquish, yield; cede, forgo, give up, let go, renounce, resign, surrender, vacate, waive.
• *n* careless freedom, dash, impetuosity, impulse, wildness.

abandoned *adj* depraved, derelict, deserted, discarded, dropped, forsaken, left, outcast, rejected, relinquished; corrupt, demoralized, depraved, dissolute, graceless, impenitent, irreclaimable, lost, obdurate, profligate, reprobate, shameless, sinful, unprincipled, vicious, wicked.

abandonment *n* desertion, dereliction, giving up, leaving, relinquishment, renunciation, surrender.

abase *vb* depress, drop, lower, reduce, sink; debase, degrade, disgrace, humble, humiliate.

abasement *n* abjection, debasement, degradation, disgrace, humbleness, humiliation, shame.

abash *vb* affront, bewilder, confound, confuse, dash, discompose, disconcert, embarrass, humiliate, humble, shame, snub.

abashment *n* confusion, embarrassment, humiliation, mortification, shame.

abate *vb* diminish, decrease, lessen, lower, moderate, reduce, relax, remove, slacken; allow, bate, deduct, mitigate, rebate, remit; allay, alleviate, appease, assuage, blunt, calm, compose, dull, mitigate, moderate, mollify, pacify, qualify, quiet, quell, soften, soothe, tranquillize.

abatement *n* alleviation, assuagement, decrement, decrease, extenuation, mitigation, moderation, remission; cessation, decline, diminution, ebb, fading, lowering, sinking, settlement; allowance, deduction, rebate, reduction.

abbey *n* convent, monastery, priory.

abbreviate *vb* abridge, compress, condense, contract, cut, curtail, epitomize, reduce, retrench, shorten.

abbreviation *n* abridgment, compression, condensation, contraction, curtailment, cutting, reduction, shortening.

abdicate *vb* abandon, cede, forgo, forsake, give up, quit, relinquish, renounce, resign, retire, surrender.

abdication *n* abandonment, abdicating, relinquishment, renunciation, resignation, surrender.

abdomen *n* belly, gut, paunch, stomach.

abduct *vb* carry off, kidnap, spirit away, take away.

abduction *n* carrying off, kidnapping, removal, seizure, withdrawal.

aberrant *adj* deviating, devious, divergent, diverging, erratic, rambling, wandering; abnormal, anomalistic, anomalous, disconnected, eccentric, erratic, exceptional, inconsequent, peculiar, irregular, preternatural, singular, strange, unnatural, unusual.

aberration *n* departure, deviation, divergence, rambling, wandering; abnormality, anomaly, eccentricity, irregularity, peculiarity, singularity, unconformity; delusion, disorder, hallucination, illusion, instability.

abet *vb* aid, assist, back, help, support, sustain, uphold; advocate, condone, countenance, encourage, favor, incite, sanction.

abettor *n* ally, assistant; adviser, advocate, promoter; accessory, accomplice, associate, confederate.

abeyance *n* anticipation, calculation, expectancy, waiting; dormancy, inactivity, intermission, quiescence, remission, reservation, suppression, suspension.

abhor *vb* abominate, detest, dislike intensely, execrate, hate, loathe, nauseate, view with horror.

abhorrence *n* abomination, antipathy, aversion, detestation, disgust, hatred, horror, loathing.

abhorrent *adj* abominating, detesting, hating, loathing; hateful, horrifying, horrible, loathsome, nauseating, odious, offensive, repellent, repugnant, repulsive, revolting, shocking.

abide *vb* lodge, rest, sojourn, stay, wait; dwell, inhabit, live, reside; bear, continue, persevere, persist, remain; endure, last, suffer, tolerate; (*with* **by**) act up to, conform to, discharge, fullfil, keep, persist in.

abiding *adj* changeless, constant, continuing, durable, enduring, immutable, lasting, permanent, stable, unchangeable.

ability *n* ableness, adroitness, aptitude,

aptness, cleverness, dexterity, efficacy, efficiency, facility, might, ingenuity, knack, power, readiness, skill, strength, talent, vigor; competency, qualification; caliber, capability, capacity, expertness, faculty, gift, parts.

abject *adj* base, beggarly, contemptible, cringing, degraded, despicable, dirty, groveling, ignoble, low, mean, menial, miserable, paltry, pitiful, poor, servile, sneaking, slavish, vile, worthless, wretched.

abjectness *n* abasement, abjection, baseness, contemptibleness, meanness, pitifulness, servility, vileness.

abjuration *n* abandonment, abnegation, discarding, disowning, rejection, relinquishment, renunciation, repudiation; disavowal, disclaimer, disclaiming, recall, recantation, repeal, retraction, reversal, revocation.

abjure *vb* abandon, discard, disclaim, disown, forgo, forswear, give up, reject, relinquish, renounce, repudiate; disavow, disclaim, recall, recant, renounce, repeal, retract, revoke, withdraw.

able *adj* accomplished, adroit, apt, clever, expert, ingenious, practical, proficient, qualified, quick, skillful, talented, versed; competent, effective, efficient, fitted, quick; capable, gifted, mighty, powerful, talented; athletic, brawny, muscular, robust, stalwart, strong, vigorous.

ablution *n* baptism, bathing, cleansing, lavation, purification, washing.

abnegation *n* abandonment, denial, renunciation, surrender.

abnormal *adj* aberrant, anomalous, divergent, eccentric, exceptional, peculiar, odd, singular, strange, uncomfortable, unnatural, unusual, weird.

abnormality *n* abnormity, anomaly, deformity, idiosyncrasy, irregularity, monstrosity, peculiarity, oddity, singularity, unconformity.

aboard *adv* inside, within, on.

abode *n* domicile, dwelling, habitation, home, house, lodging, quarters, residence, residency, seat.

abolish *vb* abrogate, annul, cancel, eliminate, invalidate, nullify, quash, repeal, rescind, revoke; annihilate, destroy, end, eradicate, extirpate, extinguish, obliterate, overthrow, suppress, terminate.

abolition *n* abrogation, annulling, annulment, cancellation, canceling, nullification, repeal, rescinding, rescission, revocation; annihilation, destruction, eradication,

extinction, extinguishment, extirpation, obliteration, overthrow, subversion, suppression.

abominable *adj* accursed, contemptible, cursed, damnable, detestable, execrable, hellish, horrid, nefarious, odious; abhorrent, detestable, disgusting, foul, hateful, loathsome, nauseous, obnoxious, shocking, revolting, repugnant, repulsive; shabby, vile, wretched.

abominate *vb* abhor, detest, execrate, hate, loathe, recoil from, revolt at, shrink from, shudder at.

abomination *n* abhorrence, antipathy, aversion, detestation, disgust, execration, hatred, loathing, nauseation; contamination, corruption, corruptness, defilement, foulness, impurity, loathsomeness, odiousness, pollution, taint, uncleanness; annoyance, curse, evil, infliction, nuisance, plague, torment.

aboriginal *adj* autochthonal, autochthonous, first, indigenous, native, original, primary, prime, primeval, primitive, pristine.

abortion *n* miscarriage, premature labor; disappointment, failure.

abortive *adj* immature, incomplete, rudimental, rudimentary, stunted, untimely; futile, fruitless, idle, ineffectual, inoperative, nugatory, profitless, unavailing, unsuccessful, useless, vain.

abound *vb* flow, flourish, increase, swarm, swell; exuberate, luxuriate, overflow, proliferate, swarm, teem.

about *prep* around, encircling, surrounding, round; near; concerning, referring to, regarding, relating to, relative to, respecting, touching, with regard to, with respect to; all over, over, through. • *adv* around, before; approximately, near, nearly.

above *adj* above-mentioned, aforementioned, aforesaid, foregoing, preceding, previous, prior. • *adv* aloft, overhead; before, previously; of a higher rank. • *prep* higher than, on top of; exceeding, greater than, more than, over; beyond, superior to.

above-board *adj* candid, frank, honest, open, straightforward, truthful, upright. • *adv* candidly, fairly, openly, sincerely.

abrade *vb* erase, erode, rub off, scrape out, wear away.

abrasion *n* attrition, disintegration, friction, wearing down; scrape, scratch.

abreast *adv* aligned, alongside.

abridge *vb* abbreviate, condense, compress,

shorten, summarize; contract, diminish, lessen, reduce.

abridgment n compression, condensation, contraction, curtailment, diminution, epitomizing, reduction, shortening; abstract, brief, compendium, digest, epitome, outline, précis, summary, syllabus, synopsis; deprivation, limitation, restriction.

abroad adv expansively, unrestrainedly, ubiquitously, widely; forth, out of doors; overseas; extensively, publicly.

abrogate vb abolish, annul, cancel, invalidate, nullify, overrule, quash, repeal, rescind, revoke, set aside, vacate, void.

abrogation n abolition, annulling, annulment, cancellation, canceling, repeal rescinding, rescission, revocation, voidance, voiding.

abrupt adj broken, craggy, jagged, rough, rugged; acclivous, acclivitous, precipitous, steep; hasty, ill-timed, precipitate, sudden, unanticipated, unexpected; blunt, brusque, curt, discourteous; cramped, harsh, jerky, stiff.

abscess n boil, fester, pustule, sore, ulcer.

abscond vb bolt, decamp, elope, escape, flee, fly, retreat, run off, sneak away, steal away, withdraw.

absence n nonappearance, nonattendance; abstraction, distraction, inattention, musing, preoccupation, reverie; default, defect, deficiency, lack, privation.

absent adj abroad, away, elsewhere, gone, not present, otherwhere; abstracted, dreaming, inattentive, lost, musing, napping, preoccupied.

absolute adj complete, ideal, independent, perfect, supreme, unconditional, unconditioned, unlimited, unqualified, unrestricted; arbitrary, authoritative, autocratic, despotic, dictatorial, imperious, irresponsible, tyrannical, tyrannous; actual, categorical, certain, decided, determinate, genuine, positive, real, unequivocal, unquestionable, veritable.

absolutely adv completely, definitely, unconditionally; actually, downright, indeed, indubitably, infallibly, positively, really, truly, unquestionably.

absoluteness n actuality, completeness, ideality, perfection, positiveness, reality, supremeness; absolutism, arbitrariness, despotism, tyranny.

absolution n acquittal, clearance, deliverance, discharge, forgiveness, liberation, pardon, release, remission, shrift, shriving.

absolutism n absoluteness, arbitrariness, autocracy, despotism, tyranny.

absolve vb acquit, clear, deliver, discharge, exculpate, excuse, exonerate, forgive, free, liberate, loose, pardon, release, set free, shrive.

absorb vb appropriate, assimilate, drink in, imbibe, soak up; consume, destroy, devour, engorge, engulf, exhaust, swallow up, take up; arrest, engage, engross, fix, immerse, occupy, rivet.

absorbent adj absorbing, imbibing, penetrable, porous, receptive.

absorption adj appropriation, assimilation, imbibing, osmosis, soaking up; consumption, destroying, devouring, engorgement, engulfing, exhaustion, swallowing up; concentration, engagement, engrossment, immersion, occupation, preoccupation.

abstain vb avoid, cease, deny oneself, desist, forbear, refrain, refuse, stop, withhold.

abstemious adj abstinent, frugal, moderate, self-denying, sober, temperate.

abstinence n abstemiousness, avoidance, forbearance, moderation, self-restraint, soberness, sobriety, teetotalism, temperance.

abstinent adj abstaining, fasting; abstemious, restraining, self-denying, self-restraining, sober, temperate.

abstract vb detach, disengage, disjoin, dissociate, disunite, isolate, separate; appropriate, purloin, seize, steal, take; abbreviate, abridge, epitomize. • adj isolated, separate, simple, unrelated; abstracted, occult, recondite, refined, subtle, vague; nonobjective, nonrepresentational. • n abridgment, condensation, digest, excerpt, extract, précis, selection, summary, synopsis.

abstracted adj absent, absent-minded, dreaming, inattentive, lost, musing, preoccupied; abstruse, refined, subtle.

abstraction n absence, absent-mindedness, brown study, inattention, muse, musing, preoccupation, reverie; disconnection, disjunction, isolation, separation; abduction, appropriation, pilfering, purloining, seizure, stealing, taking.

abstruse adj abstract, attenuated, dark, difficult, enigmatic, hidden, indefinite, mysterious, mystic, mystical, obscure, occult, profound, recondite, remote, subtle, transcendental, vague.

absurd adj egregious, fantastic, foolish, incongruous, ill-advised, ill-judged, irrational, ludicrous, nonsensical, nugatory, preposterous, ridiculous, self-annulling, senseless, silly, stupid, unreasonable.

absurdity *n* drivel, extravagance, fatuity, folly, foolery, foolishness, idiocy, nonsense.

abundance *n* affluence, amplitude, ampleness, copiousness, exuberance, fertility, flow, flood, largeness, luxuriance, opulence, overflow, plenitude, profusion, richness, store, wealth.

abundant *adj* abounding, ample, bountiful, copious, exuberant, flowing, full, good, large, lavish, rich, liberal, much, overflowing, plentiful, plenteous, replete, teeming, thick.

abuse *vb* betray, cajole, deceive, desecrate, dishonor, misapply, misemploy, misuse, pervert, pollute, profane, prostitute, violate, wrong; harm, hurt, ill-use, ill-treat, injure, maltreat, mishandle; asperse, berate, blacken, calumniate, defame, disparage, lampoon, lash, malign, revile, reproach, satirize, slander, traduce, upbraid, vilify. • *n* desecration, dishonor, ill-use, misuse, perversion, pollution, profanation; ill-treatment, maltreatment, outrage; malfeasance, malversation; aspersion, defamation, disparagement, insult, invective, obloquy, opprobrium, railing, rating, reviling, ribaldry, rudeness, scurrility, upbraiding, vilification, vituperation.

abusive *adj* calumnious, carping, condemnatory, contumelious, damnatory, denunciatory, injurious, insolent, insulting, offensive, opprobrious, reproachful, reviling, ribald, rude, scurrilous, vilificatory, vituperative.

abut *vb* adjoin, border, impinge, meet, project.

abutment *n* bank, bulwark, buttress, embankment, fortification; abutting, abuttal, adjacency, contiguity, juxtaposition.

abuttal *n* adjacency, boundary, contiguity, juxtaposition, nearness, next, terminus.

abyss *n* abysm, chasm, gorge, gulf, pit.

academic *adj* collegiate, lettered, scholastic. • *n* academician, classicist, doctor, fellow, pundit, savant, scholar, student, teacher.

academy *n* college, high school, institute, school.

accede *vb* accept, acquiesce, agree, assent to, comply with, concur, consent, yield.

accelerate *vb* dispatch, expedite, forward, hasten, hurry, precipitate, press on, quicken, speed, urge on.

acceleration *n* expedition, hastening, hurrying, quickening, pickup, precipitation, speeding up, stepping up.

accent *vb* accentuate, emphasize, stress. • *n* cadence, inflection, intonation, tone; beat, emphasis, ictus.

accentuate *vb* accent, emphasize, mark, point up, punctuate, stress; highlight, overemphasize, overstress, underline, underscore.

accept *vb* acquire, derive, get, gain, obtain, receive, take; accede to, acknowledge, acquiesce in, admit, agree to, approve, assent to, avow, embrace; estimate, construe, interpret, regard, value.

acceptable *adj* agreeable, gratifying, pleasant, pleasing, pleasurable, welcome.

acceptance *n* accepting, acknowledgment, receipt, reception, taking; approbation, approval, gratification, satisfaction.

acceptation *n* construction, import, interpretation, meaning, sense, significance, signification, understanding; adoption, approval, currency, vogue.

access *vb* broach, enter, open, open up. • *n* approach, avenue, entrance, entry, passage, way; admission, admittance, audience, interview; addition, accession, aggrandizement, enlargement, gain, increase, increment; (*med*) attack, fit, onset, recurrence.

accession *n* addition, augmentation, enlargement, extension, increase; succession.

accessory *adj* abetting, additional, additive, adjunct, aiding, ancillary, assisting, contributory, helping, subsidiary, subordinate, supplemental. • *n* abettor, accomplice, assistant, associate, confederate, helper; accompaniment, attendant, concomitant, detail, subsidiary.

accident *n* calamity, casualty, condition, contingency, disaster, fortuity, incident, misadventure, miscarriage, mischance, misfortune, mishap; affection, alteration, chance, contingency, mode, modification, property, quality, state.

accidental *adj* casual, chance, contingent, fortuitous, undesigned, unintended; adventitious, dispensable, immaterial, incidental, nonessential.

acclamation *n* acclaim, applause, cheer, cry, plaudit, outcry, salutation, shouting.

acclimatization, acclimation *n* adaptation, adjustment, conditioning, familiarization, habituation, inurement, naturalization.

acclimatize, acclimate *vb* accustom, adapt, adjust, condition, familiarize, habituate, inure, naturalize, season.

acclivity *n* ascent, height, hill, rising ground, steep, upward slope.

accommodate *vb* contain, furnish, hold, oblige, serve, supply; adapt, fit, suit; adjust, compose, harmonize, reconcile, settle.

accommodation *n* advantage, convenience, privilege; adaptation, agreement, conformity, fitness, suitableness; adjustment, harmonization, harmony, pacification, reconciliation, settlement.

accompaniment *n* adjunct, appendage, attachment, attendant, concomitant.

accompany *vb* attend, chaperon, convoy, escort, follow, go with.

accomplice *n* abettor, accessory, ally, assistant, associate, confederate, partner.

accomplish *vb* achieve, bring about, carry, carry through, complete, compass, consummate, do, effect, execute, perform, perfect; conclude, end, finish, terminate.

accomplished *adj* achieved, completed, done, effected, executed, finished, fulfilled, realized; able, adroit, apt, consummate, educated, experienced, expert, finished, instructed, practiced, proficient, qualified, ripe, skillful, versed; elegant, fashionable, fine, polished, polite, refined.

accomplishment *n* achievement, acquirement, attainment, qualification; completion, fullfilment.

accord *vb* admit, allow, concede, deign, give, grant, vouchsafe, yield; agree, assent, concur, correspond, harmonize, quadrate, tally. • *n* accordance, agreement, concord, concurrence, conformity, consensus, harmony, unanimity, unison.

accordant *adj* agreeable, agreeing, congruous, consonant, harmonious, suitable, symphonious.

accordingly *adv* agreeably, conformably, consistently, suitably; consequently, hence, so, thence, therefore, thus, whence, wherefore.

accost *vb* address, confront, greet, hail, salute, speak to, stop.

account *vb* assess, appraise, estimate, evaluate, judge, rate; (*with* **for**) assign, attribute, explain, expound, justify, rationalize, vindicate. • *n* inventory, record, register, score; bill, book, charge; calculation, computation, count, reckoning, score, tale, tally; chronicle, detail, description, narration, narrative, portrayal, recital, rehearsal, relation, report, statement, tidings, word; elucidation, explanation, exposition; consideration, ground, motive, reason, regard, sake; consequence, consideration, dignity, distinction, importance, note, repute, reputation, worth.

accountable *adj* amenable, answerable, duty-bound, liable, responsible.

accouter *vb* arm, dress, equip, fit out, furnish.

accredit *vb* authorize, depute, empower, entrust.

accrue *vb* arise, come, follow, flow, inure, issue, proceed, result.

accumulate *vb* agglomerate, aggregate, amass, bring together, collect, gather, grow, hoard, increase, pile, store.

accumulation *n* agglomeration, aggregation, collection, heap, hoard, mass, pile, store.

accuracy *n* carefulness, correctness, exactness, fidelity, precision, strictness.

accurate *adj* close, correct, exact, faithful, nice, precise, regular, strict, true, truthful.

accusation *n* arraignment, charge, incrimination, impeachment, indictment.

accuse *vb* arraign, charge, censure, impeach, indict, tax.

accustom *vb* discipline, drill, familiarize, habituate, harden, inure, train, use.

ace *n* (*cards, dice*) one spot, single pip, single point; atom, bit, grain, iota, jot, particle, single, unit, whit; expert, master, virtuoso. • *adj* best, expert, fine, outstanding, superb.

acerbity *n* acidity, acridity, acridness, astringency, bitterness, roughness, sourness, tartness; acrimony, bitterness, harshness, severity, venom.

achieve *vb* accomplish, attain, complete, do, effect, execute, finish, fullfil, perform, realize; acquire, gain, get, obtain, win.

achievement *n* accomplishment, acquirement, attainment, completion, consummation, performance, realization; deed, exploit, feat, work.

acid *adj* pungent, sharp, sour, stinging, tart, vinegary.

acknowledge *vb* recognize; accept, admit, accept, allow, concede, grant; avow, confess, own, profess.

acme *n* apex, climax, height, peak, pinnacle, summit, top, vertex, zenith.

acquaint *vb* familiarize; announce, apprise, communicate, enlighten, disclose, inform, make aware, make known, notify, tell.

acquaintance *n* companionship, familiarity, fellowship, intimacy, knowledge; associate, companion, comrade, friend.

acquiesce *vb* bow, comply, consent, give way, rest, submit, yield; agree, assent, concur, consent.

acquire *vb* achieve, attain, earn, gain, get, have, obtain, procure, realize, secure, win; learn thoroughly, master.

acquirement *n* acquiring, gaining, gathering, mastery; acquisition, accomplishment, attainment.

acquit *vb* absolve, clear, discharge, exculpate, excuse, exonerate, forgive, liberate, pardon, pay, quit, release, set free, settle.

acquittal *n* absolution, acquittance, clearance, deliverance, discharge, exoneration, liberation, release.

acquittance *n* discharge; quittance, receipt.

acrid *adj* biting, bitter, caustic, pungent, sharp.

acrimonious *adj* acrid, bitter, caustic, censorious, crabbed, harsh, malignant, petulant, sarcastic, severe, testy, virulent.

acrimony *n* causticity, causticness, corrosiveness, sharpness; abusiveness, acridity, asperity, bitterness, churlishness, harshness, rancor, severity, spite, venom.

act *vb* do, execute, function, make, operate, work; enact, feign, perform, play. • *n* achievement, deed, exploit, feat, performance, proceeding, turn; bill, decree, enactment, law, ordinance, statute; actuality, existence, fact, reality.

acting *adj* interim, provisional, substitute, temporary. • *n* enacting, impersonation, performance, portrayal, theater; counterfeiting, dissimulation, imitation, pretence.

action *n* achievement, activity, agency, deed, exertion, exploit, feat; battle, combat, conflict, contest, encounter, engagement, operation; lawsuit, prosecution.

active *adj* effective, efficient, influential, living, operative; assiduous, bustling, busy, diligent, industrious, restless; agile, alert, brisk, energetic, lively, nimble, prompt, quick, smart, spirited, sprightly, supple; animated, ebullient, fervent, vigorous.

actual *adj* certain, decided, genuine, objective, real, substantial, tangible, true, veritable; perceptible, present, sensible, tangible; absolute, categorical, positive.

actuate *vb* impel, incite, induce, instigate, move, persuade, prompt.

acumen *n* acuteness, astuteness, discernment, ingenuity, keenness, penetration, sagacity, sharpness, shrewdness.

acute *adj* pointed, sharp; astute, bright, discerning, ingenious, intelligent, keen, quick, penetrating, piercing, sagacious, sage, sharp, shrewd, smart, subtle; distressing, fierce, intense, piercing, pungent, poignant, severe, violent; high, high-toned, sharp, shrill; (*med*) sudden, temporary, violent.

adage *n* aphorism, dictum, maxim, proverb, saw, saying.

adapt *vb* accommodate, adjust, conform, coordinate, fit, qualify, proportion, suit, temper.

add *vb* adjoin, affix, annex, append, attach, join, tag; sum, sum up, total.

addict *vb* accustom, apply, dedicate, devote, habituate. • *n* devotee, enthusiast, fan; head, junkie, user.

addicted *adj* attached, devoted, given up to, inclined, prone, wedded.

addition *n* augmentation, accession, enlargement, extension, increase, supplement; adjunct, appendage, appendix, extra.

address *vb* accost, apply to, court, direct. • *n* appeal, application, entreaty, invocation, memorial, petition, request, solicitation, suit; discourse, oration, lecture, sermon, speech; ability, adroitness, art, dexterity, expertness, skill; courtesy, deportment, demeanor, tact.

adduce *vb* advance, allege, assign, offer, present; cite, mention, name.

adept *adj* accomplished, experienced, practiced, proficient, skilled. • *n* expert, master, virtuoso.

adequate *adj* able, adapted, capable, competent, equal, fit, requisite, satisfactory, sufficient, suitable.

adhere *vb* cling, cleave, cohere, hold, stick; appertain, belong, pertain.

adherent *adj* adhering, clinging, sticking. • *n* acolyte, dependant, disciple, follower, partisan, supporter, vassal.

adhesion *n* adherence, attachment, clinging, coherence, sticking.

adhesive *adj* clinging, sticking; glutinous, gummy, sticky, tenacious, viscous. • *n* binder, cement, glue, paste.

adieu *n* farewell, goodbye, parting, valediction.

adipose *adj* fat, fatty, greasy, oily, oleaginous, sebaceous.

adjacent *adj* adjoining, bordering, conterminous, contiguous, near, near to, neighboring, touching.

adjoin *vb* abut, add, annex, append, border, combine, neighbor, unite, verge.

adjourn vb defer, delay, postpone, procrastinate; close, dissolve, end, interrupt, prorogue, suspend.

adjudge vb allot, assign, award; decide, decree, determine, settle.

adjunct n addition, advantage, appendage, appurtenance, attachment, attribute, auxiliary, dependency, help.

adjure vb beg, beseech, entreat, pray, supplicate.

adjust vb adapt, arrange, dispose, rectify; regulate, set right, settle, suit; compose, harmonize, pacify, reconcile, settle; accommodate, adapt, fit, suit.

administer vb contribute, deal out, dispense, supply; conduct, control, direct, govern, manage, oversee, superintend; conduce, contribute.

admirable adj astonishing, striking, surprising, wonderful; excellent, fine, rare, superb.

admiration n affection, approbation, approval, astonishment, delight, esteem, pleasure, regard.

admirer n beau, gallant, suitor, sweetheart; fan, follower, supporter.

admissible adj allowable, lawful, permissible, possible.

admission n access, admittance, entrance, introduction; acceptance, acknowledgement, allowance, assent, avowal, concession.

admit vb give access to, let in, receive; agree to, accept, acknowledge, concede, confess; allow, bear, permit, suffer, tolerate.

admonish vb censure, rebuke, reprove; advise caution, counsel, enjoin, forewarn, warn; acquaint, apprise, inform, instruct, notify, remind.

admonition n censure, rebuke, remonstrance; advice, caution, chiding, counsel, instruction, monition.

adolescence n minority, nonage, teens, youth.

adolescent adj juvenile, young, youthful.
• n minor, teenager, youth.

adopt vb appropriate, assume; accept, approve, avow, espouse, maintain, support; affiliate, father, foster.

adore vb worship; esteem, honor, idolize, love, revere, venerate.

adorn vb beautify, decorate, embellish, enrich, garnish, gild, grace, ornament.

adroit adj apt, dextrous, expert, handy, ingenious, ready, skillful.

adulation n blandishment, cajolery, fawning, flattery, flummery, praise, sycophancy.

adult adj grown-up, mature, ripe, ripened.
• n grown-up person.

adulterate vb alloy, contaminate, corrupt, debase, deteriorate, vitiate.

advance adj beforehand, forward, leading.
• vb propel, push, send forward; aggrandize, dignify, elevate, exalt, promote; benefit, forward, further, improve, promote; adduce, allege, assign, offer, propose, propound; augment, increase; proceed, progress; grow, improve, prosper, thrive.
• n march, progress; advancement, enhancement, growth, promotion, rise; offer, overture, proffering, proposal, proposition, tender; appreciation, rise.

advancement n advance, benefit, gain, growth, improvement, profit.

advantage n ascendancy, precedence, pre-eminence, superiority, upper-hand; benefit, blessing, emolument, gain, profit, return; account, behalf, interest; accommodation, convenience, prerogative, privilege.

advantageous adj beneficial, favorable, profitable.

advent n accession, approach, arrival, coming, visitation.

adventitious adj accidental, extraneous, extrinsic, foreign, fortuitous, nonessential.

adventure vb dare, hazard, imperil, peril, risk, venture. • n chance, contingency, experiment, fortuity, hazard, risk, venture; crisis, contingency, event, incident, occurrence, transaction.

adventurous adj bold, chivalrous, courageous, daring, doughty; foolhardy, headlong, precipitate, rash, reckless; dangerous, hazardous, perilous.

adversary n antagonist, enemy, foe, opponent.

adverse adj conflicting, contrary, opposing; antagonistic, harmful, hostile, hurtful, inimical, unfavorable, unpropitious; calamitous, disastrous, unfortunate, unlucky, untoward.

adversity n affliction, calamity, disaster, distress, misery, misfortune, sorrow, suffering, woe.

advertise vb advise, announce, declare, inform, placard, proclaim, publish.

advertisement n announcement, information, notice, proclamation.

advice n admonition, caution, counsel, exhortation, persuasion, suggestion, recommendation; information, intelligence, notice, notification; care, counsel, deliberation, forethought.

advisable *adj* advantageous, desirable, expedient, prudent.

advise *vb* admonish, counsel, commend, recommend, suggest, urge; acquaint, apprise, inform, notify; confer, consult, deliberate.

adviser *n* counselor, director, guide, instructor.

advocate *vb* countenance, defend, favor, justify, maintain, support, uphold, vindicate. • *n* apologist, counselor, defender, maintainer, patron, pleader, supporter; attorney, barrister, counsel, lawyer, solicitor.

aegis *n* defense, protection, safeguard, shelter.

aesthetic *adj* appropriate, beautiful, tasteful.

affable *adj* accessible, approachable, communicative, conversable, cordial, easy, familiar, frank, free, sociable, social; complaisant, courteous, civil, obliging, polite, urbane.

affair *n* business, circumstance, concern, matter, office, question; event, incident, occurrence, performance, proceeding, transaction; battle, combat, conflict, encounter, engagement, skirmish.

affairs *npl* administration, relations; business, estate, finances, property.

affect *vb* act upon, alter, change, influence, modify, transform; concern, interest, regard, relate; improve, melt, move, overcome, subdue, touch; aim at, aspire to, crave, yearn for; adopt, assume, feign.

affectation *n* affectedness, airs, artificiality, foppery, pretension, simulation.

affected *adj* artificial, assumed, feigned, insincere, theatrical; assuming, conceited, foppish, vain.

affection *n* bent, bias, feeling, inclination, passion, proclivity, propensity; accident, attribute, character, mark, modification, mode, note, property; attachment, endearment, fondness, goodwill, kindness, partiality, love.

affectionate *adj* attached, devoted, fond, kind, loving, sympathetic, tender.

affiliate *vb* ally, annex, associate, connect, incorporate, join, unite. • *n* ally, associate, confederate.

affinity *n* connection, propinquity, relationship; analogy, attraction, correspondence, likeness, relation, resemblance, similarity, sympathy.

affirm *vb* allege, assert, asseverate, aver, declare, state; approve, confirm, establish, ratify.

affix *vb* annex, attach, connect, fasten, join, subjoin, tack.

afflict *vb* agonize, distress, grieve, pain, persecute, plague, torment, trouble, try, wound.

affliction *n* adversity, calamity, disaster, misfortune, stroke, visitation; bitterness, depression, distress, grief, misery, plague, scourge, sorrow, trial, tribulation, wretchedness, woe.

affluent *adj* abounding, abundant, bounteous, plenteous; moneyed, opulent, rich, wealthy.

afford *vb* furnish, produce, supply, yield; bestow, communicate, confer, give, grant, impart, offer; bear, endure, support.

affray *n* brawl, conflict, disturbance, feud, fight, quarrel, scuffle, struggle.

affright *vb* affray, alarm, appal, confound, dismay, shock, startle. • *n* alarm, consternation, fear, fright, panic, terror.

affront *vb* abuse, insult, outrage; annoy, chafe, displease, fret, irritate, offend, pique, provoke, vex. • *n* abuse, contumely, insult, outrage, vexation, wrong.

afraid *adj* aghast, alarmed, anxious, apprehensive, frightened, scared, timid.

after *prep* later than, subsequent to; behind, following; about, according to; because of, in imitation of. • *adj* behind, consecutive, ensuing, following, later, succeeding, successive, subsequent; aft, back, hind, rear, rearmost, tail. • *adv* afterwards, later, next, since, subsequently, then, thereafter.

again *adv* afresh, anew, another time, once more; besides, further, in addition, moreover.

against *prep* adverse to, contrary to, in opposition to, resisting; abutting, close up to, facing, fronting, off, opposite to, over; in anticipation of, for, in expectation of; in compensation for, to counterbalance, to match.

age *vb* decline, grow old, mature. • *n* aeon, date, epoch, period, time; decline, old age, senility; antiquity, oldness.

agency *n* action, force, intervention, means, mediation, operation, procurement; charge, direction, management, superintendence, supervision.

agent *n* actor, doer, executor, operator, performer; active element, cause, force; attorney, broker, commissioner, deputy, factor, intermediary, manager, middleman.

agglomeration *n* accumulation, aggregation, conglomeration, heap, lump, pile.

agglutinate vb cement, fasten, glue, unite.

aggrandize vb advance, dignify, elevate, enrich, exalt, promote.

aggravate vb heighten, increase, worsen; color, exaggerate, magnify, overstate; enrage, irritate, provoke, tease.

aggravation n exaggeration, heightening, irritation.

aggregate vb accumulate, amass, collect, heap, pile. • adj collected, total. • n amount, gross, total, whole.

aggressive adj assailing, assailant, assaulting, attacking, invading, offensive; pushing, self-assertive.

aggressor n assailant, assaulter, attacker, invader.

aggrieve vb afflict, grieve, pain; abuse, ill-treat, impose, injure, oppress, wrong.

aghast adj appalled, dismayed, frightened, horrified, horror-struck, panic-stricken, terrified; amazed, astonished, startled, thunderstruck.

agile adj active, alert, brisk, lively, nimble, prompt, smart, ready.

agitate vb disturb, jar, rock, shake, trouble; disquiet, excite, ferment, rouse, trouble; confuse, discontent, flurry, fluster, flutter; canvass, debate, discuss, dispute, investigate.

agitation n concussion, shake, shaking; commotion, convulsion, disturbance, ferment, jarring, storm, tumult, turmoil; discomposure, distraction, emotion, excitement, flutter, perturbation, ruffle, tremor, trepidation; controversy, debate, discussion.

agnostic n doubter, empiricist, sceptic.

agonize vb distress, excruciate, rack, torment, torture.

agony n anguish, distress, pangs.

agree vb accord, concur, harmonize, unite; accede, acquiesce, assent, comply, concur, subscribe; bargain, contract, covenant, engage, promise, undertake; compound, compromise; chime, cohere, conform, correspond, match, suit, tally.

agreeable adj charming, pleasant, pleasing.

agreement n accordance, compliance, concord, harmony, union; bargain, compact, contract, pact, treaty.

agriculture n cultivation, culture, farming, geoponics, husbandry, tillage.

aid vb assist, help, serve, support; relieve, succor; advance, facilitate, further, promote. • n assistance, cooperation, help, patronage; alms, subsidy, succor, relief.

ailment n disease, illness, sickness.

aim vb direct, level, point, train; design, intend, mean, purpose, seek. • n bearing, course, direction, tendency; design, object, view, reason.

air vb expose, display, ventilate. • n atmosphere, breeze; appearance, aspect, manner; melody, tune.

aisle n passage, walk.

akin adj allied, kin, related; analogous, cognate, congenial, connected.

alacrity n agility, alertness, activity, eagerness, promptitude; cheerfulness, gaiety, hilarity, liveliness, vivacity.

alarm vb daunt, frighten, scare, startle, terrify. • n alarm-bell, tocsin, warning; apprehension, fear, fright, terror.

alert adj awake, circumspect, vigilant, watchful, wary; active, brisk, lively, nimble, quick, prompt, ready, sprightly. • vb alarm, arouse, caution, forewarn, signal, warn. • n alarm, signal, warning.

alertness n circumspection, vigilance, watchfulness, wariness; activity, briskness, nimbleness, promptness, readiness, spryness.

alien adj foreign, not native; differing, estranged, inappropriate, remote, unallied, separated. • n foreigner, stranger.

alienate vb (legal) assign, demise, transfer; disaffect, estrange, wean, withdraw.

alienation n (legal) assignment, conveyance, transfer; breach, disaffection, division, estrangement, rupture; (med) aberration, delusion, derangement, hallucination, insanity, madness.

alike adj akin, analogous, duplicate, identical, resembling, similar. • adv equally.

aliment n diet, fare, meat, nutriment, provision, rations, sustenance.

alive adj animate, breathing, live; aware, responsive, sensitive, susceptible; brisk, cheerful, lively, sprightly.

allay vb appease, calm, check, compose; alleviate, assuage, lessen, moderate, solace, temper.

allege vb affirm, assert, declare, maintain, say; adduce, advance, assign, cite, plead, produce, quote.

allegiance n duty, homage, fealty, fidelity, loyalty, obligation.

allegory n apologue, fable, myth, parable, story, tale.

alleviate vb assuage, lighten, mitigate, mollify, moderate, quell, quiet, quieten, soften, soothe.

alliance n affinity, intermarriage, relation; coalition, combination, confederacy, league, treaty, union; affiliation, connection, relationship, similarity.

allot vb divide, dispense, distribute; assign, fix, prescribe, specify.

allow vb acknowledge, admit, concede, confess, grant, own; authorize, grant, let, permit; bear, endure, suffer, tolerate; grant, yield, relinquish, spare; approve, justify, sanction; abate, bate, deduct, remit.

allude vb glance, hint, mention, imply, insinuate, intimate, refer, suggest, touch.

allure vb attract, beguile, cajole, coax, entice, lure, persuade, seduce, tempt. • n appeal, attraction, lure, temptation.

allusion n hint, implication, intimation, insinuation, mention, reference, suggestion.

ally vb combine, connect, join, league, marry, unite. • n aider, assistant, associate, coadjutor, colleague, friend, partner.

almighty adj all-powerful, omnipotent.

alms npl benefaction, bounty, charity, dole, gift, gratuity.

alone adj companionless, deserted, forsaken, isolated, lonely, only, single, sole, solitary.

along adv lengthways, lengthwise; forward, onward; beside, together, simultaneously.

aloud adv audibly, loudly, sonorously, vociferously.

alter vb change, conform, modify, shift, turn, transform, transmit, vary.

altercation n bickering, contention, controversy, dispute, dissension, strife, wrangling.

alternating adj intermittent, interrupted.

alternative adj another, different, second, substitute. • n choice, option, preference.

although conj albeit, even if, for all that, notwithstanding, though.

altitude n elevation, height, loftiness.

altogether adv completely, entirely, totally, utterly.

always adv continually, eternally, ever, evermore, perpetually, unceasingly.

amalgamate vb blend, combine, commingle, compound, incorporate, mix.

amass vb accumulate, aggregate, collect, gather, heap, scrape together.

amateur n dilettante, nonprofessional.

amaze vb astonish, astound, bewilder, confound, confuse, dumbfound, perplex, stagger, stupefy.

amazement n astonishment, bewilderment, confusion, marvel, surprise, wonder.

ambassador n deputy, envoy, legate, minister, plenipotentiary.

ambiguous adj dubious, doubtful, enigmatic, equivocal, uncertain, indefinite, indistinct, obscure, vague.

ambition n aspiration, emulation, longing, yearning.

ambitious adj aspiring, avid, eager, intent.

ameliorate vb amend, benefit, better, elevate, improve, mend.

amenability n amenableness, responsiveness; accountability, liability, responsibility.

amenable adj acquiescent, agreeable, persuadable, responsive, susceptible; accountable, liable, responsible.

amend vb better, correct, improve, mend, redress, reform.

amends npl atonement, compensation, expiation, indemnification, recompense, reparation, restitution.

amenity n agreeableness, mildness, pleasantness, softness; affability, civility, courtesy, geniality, graciousness, urbanity.

amiable adj attractive, benign, charming, genial, good-natured, harmonious, kind, lovable, lovely, pleasant, pleasing, sweet, winning, winsome.

amicable adj amiable, cordial, friendly, harmonious, kind, kindly, peaceable.

amiss adj erroneous, inaccurate, incorrect, faulty, improper, wrong. • adv erroneously, inaccurately, incorrectly, wrongly.

amnesty n absolution, condonation, dispensation, forgiveness, oblivion.

amorous adj ardent, enamored, fond, longing, loving, passionate, tender; erotic, impassioned.

amorphous adj formless, irregular, shapeless, unshapen; noncrystalline, structureless; chaotic, characterless, clumsy, disorganized, misshapen, unorganized, vague.

amount n aggregate, sum, total.

ample adj broad, capacious, extended, extensive, great, large, roomy, spacious; abounding, abundant, copious, generous, liberal, plentiful; diffusive, unrestricted.

amputate vb clip, curtail, prune, lop, remove, separate, sever.

amuse vb charm, cheer, divert, enliven, entertain, gladden, relax, solace; beguile, cheat, deceive, delude, mislead.

amusement n diversion, entertainment, frolic, fun, merriment, pleasure.

analeptic adj comforting, invigorating, restorative.

analogy *n* correspondence, likeness, parallelism, parity, resemblance, similarity.

analysis *n* decomposition, dissection, resolution, separation.

anarchy *n* chaos, confusion, disorder, misrule, lawlessness, riot.

anathema *n* ban, curse, denunciation, excommunication, execration, malediction, proscription.

anatomy *n* dissection; form, skeleton, structure.

ancestor *n* father, forebear, forefather, progenitor.

ancestry *n* family, house, line, lineage; descent, genealogy, parentage, pedigree, stock.

anchor *vb* fasten, fix, secure; cast anchor, take firm hold. • *n (naut)* ground tackle; defense, hold, security, stay.

ancient *adj* old, primitive, pristine; antiquated, antique, archaic, obsolete.

ancillary *adj* accessory, auxiliary, contributory, helpful, instrumental.

angelic *adj* adorable, celestial, cherubic, heavenly, saintly, seraphic; entrancing, enrapturing, rapturous, ravishing.

anger *vb* chafe, displease, enrage, gall, infuriate, irritate, madden. • *n* choler, exasperation, fury, gall, indignation, ire, passion, rage, resentment, spleen, wrath.

angle *vb* fish. • *n* divergence, flare, opening; bend, corner, crotch, cusp, point; fishhook, hook.

angry *adj* chafed, exasperated, furious, galled, incensed, irritated, nettled, piqued, provoked, resentful.

anguish *n* agony, distress, grief, pang, rack, torment, torture.

anile *adj* aged, decrepit, doting, imbecile, senile.

animadversion *n* comment, notice, observation, remark; blame, censure, condemnation, reproof, stricture.

animate *vb* inform, quicken, vitalize, vivify; fortify, invigorate, revive; activate, enliven, excite, heat, impel, kindle, rouse, stimulate, stir, waken; elate, embolden, encourage, exhilarate, gladden, hearten. • *adj* alive, breathing, live, living, organic, quick.

animosity *n* bitterness, enmity, grudge, hatred, hostility, rancor, rankling, spleen, virulence.

annals *npl* archives, chronicles, records, registers, rolls.

annex *vb* affix, append, attach, subjoin, tag, tack; connect, join, unite.

annihilate *vb* abolish, annul, destroy, dissolve, exterminate, extinguish, kill, obliterate, raze, ruin.

annotation *n* comment, explanation, illustration, note, observation, remark.

announce *vb* advertise, communicate, declare, disclose, proclaim, promulgate, publish, report, reveal, trumpet.

announcement *n* advertisement, annunciation, bulletin, declaration, manifesto, notice, notification, proclamation.

annoy *vb* badger, chafe, disquiet, disturb, fret, hector, irk, irritate, molest, pain, pester, plague, trouble, vex, worry, wound.

annul *vb* abolish, abrogate, cancel, countermand, nullify, overrule, quash, repeal, recall, reverse, revoke.

anoint *vb* consecrate, oil, sanctify, smear.

anonymous *adj* nameless, unacknowledged, unsigned.

answer *vb* fulfil, rejoin, reply, respond, satisfy. • *n* rejoinder, reply, response, retort; confutation, rebuttal, refutation.

answerable *adj* accountable, amenable, correspondent, liable, responsible, suited.

antagonism *n* contradiction, discordance, disharmony, dissonant, incompatibility, opposition.

antecedent *adj* anterior, foregoing, forerunning, precedent, preceding, previous. • *n* forerunner, precursor.

anterior *adj* antecedent, foregoing, preceding, previous, prior; fore, front.

anticipate *vb* antedate, forestall, foretaste, prevent; count upon, expect, forecast, foresee.

anticipation *n* apprehension, contemplation, expectation, hope, prospect, trust; expectancy, forecast, foresight, foretaste, preconception, presentiment.

antidote *n* corrective, counteractive, counterpoison; cure, remedy, restorative, specific.

antipathy *n* abhorrence, aversion, disgust, detestation, hate, hatred, horror, loathing, repugnance.

antique *adj* ancient, archaic, bygone, old, old-fashioned.

anxiety *n* apprehension, care, concern, disquiet, fear, foreboding, misgiving, perplexity, trouble, uneasiness, vexation, worry.

anxious *adj* apprehensive, restless, solicitous, uneasy, unquiet, worried.

apart *adv* aloof, aside, separately; asunder.

apathetic *adj* cold, dull, impassive, inert, listless, obtuse, passionless, sluggish, torpid, unfeeling.

ape *vb* counterfeit, imitate, mimic; affect.
• *n* simian, troglodyte; imitator, mimic;
image, imitation, likeness, type.

aperture *n* chasm, cleft, eye, gap, opening,
hole, orifice, passage.

aphorism *n* adage, apothegm, byword,
maxim, proverb, saw, saying.

apish *adj* imitative, mimicking; affected,
foppish, trifling.

aplomb *n* composure, confidence, equanimity, self-confidence.

apocryphal *adj* doubtful, fabulous, false,
legendary, spurious, uncanonical.

apologetic *adj* exculpatory, excusatory; de-
fensive, vindictive.

apology *n* defense, justification, vindication; acknowledgement, excuse, explanation, plea, reparation.

apostate *adj* backsliding, disloyal, faithless,
false, perfidious, recreant, traitorous, untrue. • *n* backslider, deserter, pervert, renegade, turncoat.

apostle *n* angel, herald, messenger, mis-
sionary, preacher; advocate, follower, supporter.

apothegm *n* aphorism, byword, dictum,
maxim, proverb, saw, saying.

appal *vb* affright, alarm, daunt, dismay,
frighten, horrify, scare, shock.

apparel *n* attire, array, clothes, clothing,
dress, garments, habit, raiment, robes,
suit, trappings, vestments.

apparent *adj* discernible, perceptible, visible; conspicuous, evident, legible, manifest, obvious, open, patent, plain, unmistakable; external, ostensible, seeming, superficial.

apparition *n* appearance, appearing,
epiphany, manifestation; being, form;
ghost, phantom, spectre, spirit, vision.

appeal *vb* address, entreat, implore, invoke,
refer, request, solicit. • *n* application, entreaty, invocation, solicitation, suit.

appear *vb* emerge, loom; break, open; arise,
occur, offer; look, seem, show.

appearance *n* advent, arrival, apparition,
coming; form, shape; color, face, fashion,
feature, guise, pretence, pretext; air, aspect, complexion, demeanor, manner,
mien.

appease *vb* abate, allay, assuage, calm, ease,
lessen, mitigate, pacify, placate, quell,
soothe, temper, tranquillize.

appellation *n* address, cognomen, denomination, epithet, style, title.

append *vb* attach, fasten, hang; add, annex,
subjoin, tack, tag.

appendix *n* addition, adjunct, appurtenance, codicil; excursus, supplement.

appetite *n* craving, desire, longing, lust,
passion; gusto, relish, stomach, zest; hunger.

applaud *vb* acclaim, cheer, clap, compliment, encourage, extol, magnify.

applause *n* acclamation, approval, cheers,
commendation, plaudit.

applicable *adj* adapted, appropriate, apt,
befitting, fitting, germane, pertinent,
proper, relevant.

application *n* emollient, lotion, ointment,
poultice, wash; appliance, exercise, practice, use; appeal, petition, request;
solicitation, suit; assiduity, constancy, diligence, effort, industry.

apply *vb* bestow, lay upon; appropriate, convert, employ, exercise, use; addict, address,
dedicate, devote, direct, engage.

appoint *vb* determine, establish, fix, prescribe; bid, command, decree, direct, order, require; allot, assign, delegate, depute,
detail, destine, settle; constitute, create,
name, nominate; equip, furnish, supply.

apportion *vb* allocate, allot, allow, assign,
deal, dispense, divide, share.

apposite *adj* apt, fit, germane, pertinent,
relevant, suitable, pertinent.

appraise *vb* appreciate, estimate, prize,
rate, value.

appreciate *vb* appreciate, esteem, estimate,
rate, realize, value.

apprehend *vb* arrest, catch, detain, seize,
take; conceive, imagine, regard, view; appreciate, perceive, realize, see, take in; fear,
forebode; conceive, fancy, hold, imagine,
presume, understand.

apprehension *n* arrest, capture, seizure;
intellect, intelligence, mind, reason; discernment, intellect, knowledge, perception, sense; belief, fancy, idea, notion, sentiment, view; alarm, care, dread, distrust,
fear, misgiving, suspicion.

apprise *vb* acquaint, inform, notify, tell.

approach *vb* advance, approximate, come
close; broach; resemble. • *n* advance, advent; approximation, convergence, nearing, tendency; entrance, path, way.

approbation *n* approval, commendation, liking, praise; assent, concurrence, consent,
endorsement, ratification, sanction.

appropriate *vb* adopt, arrogate, assume, set

apart; allot, apportion, assign, devote; apply, convert, employ, use. • *adj* adapted, apt, befitting, fit, opportune, seemly, suitable.

approve *vb* appreciate, commend, like, praise, recommend, value; confirm, countenance, justify, ratify, sustain, uphold.

approximate *vb* approach, resemble. • *adj* approaching, proximate; almost exact, inexact, rough.

apt *adj* applicable, apposite, appropriate, befitting, fit, felicitous, germane; disposed, inclined, liable, prone, subject; able, adroit, clever, dextrous, expert, handy, happy, prompt, ready, skillful.

aptitude *n* applicability, appropriateness, felicity, fitness, pertinence, suitability; inclination, tendency, turn; ability, address, adroitness, quickness, readiness, tact.

arbitrary *adj* absolute, autocratic, despotic, domineering, imperious, overbearing, unlimited; capricious, discretionary, fanciful, voluntary, whimsical.

arcade *n* colonnade, loggia.

arch[1] *adj* cunning, knowing, frolicsome, merry, mirthful, playful, roguish, shrewd, sly; consummate, chief, leading, pre-eminent, prime, primary, principal.

arch[2] *vb* span, vault; bend, curve. • *n* archway, span, vault.

archaic *adj* ancient, antiquated, antique, bygone, obsolete, old.

archives *npl* documents, muniments, records, registers, rolls.

ardent *adj* burning, fiery, hot; eager, earnest, fervent, impassioned, keen, passionate, warm, zealous.

ardor *n* glow, heat, warmth; eagerness, enthusiasm, fervor, heat, passion, soul, spirit, warmth, zeal.

arduous *adj* high, lofty, steep, uphill; difficult, fatiguing, hard, laborious, onerous, tiresome, toilsome, wearisome.

area *n* circle, circuit, district, domain, field, range, realm, region, tract.

argue *vb* plead, reason upon; debate, dispute; denote, evince, imply, indicate, mean, prove; contest, debate, discuss, sift.

arid *adj* barren, dry, parched, sterile, unfertile; dry, dull, jejune, pointless, uninteresting.

aright *adv* correctly, justly, rightly, truly.

arise *vb* ascend, mount, soar, tower; appear, emerge, rise, spring; begin, originate; rebel, revolt, rise; accrue, come, emanate,

ensue, flow, issue, originate, proceed, result.

aristocracy *n* gentry, nobility, noblesse, peerage.

arm[1] *n* bough, branch, limb; protection; cove, creek, estuary, firth, fjord, frith, inlet.

arm[2] *vb* array, equip, furnish; clothe, cover, fortify, guard, protect, strengthen.

arms *npl* accoutrements, armor, array, harness, mail, panoply, weapons; crest, escutcheon.

army *n* battalions, force, host, legions, troops; host, multitude, throng, vast assemblage.

around *prep* about, encircling, encompassing, round, surrounding. • *adv* about, approximately, generally, near, nearly, practically, round, thereabouts.

arouse *vb* animate, awaken, excite, incite, kindle, provoke, rouse, stimulate, warm, whet.

arraign *vb* accuse, censure, charge, denounce, impeach, indict, prosecute, tax.

arrange *vb* array, class, classify, dispose, distribute, group, range, rank; adjust, determine, fix upon, settle; concoct, construct, devise, plan, prepare, project.

arrant *adj* bad, consummate, downright, gross, notorious, rank, utter.

array *vb* arrange, dispose, place, range, rank; accoutre, adorn, attire, decorate, dress, enrobe, embellish, equip, garnish, habit, invest. • *n* arrangement, collection, disposition, marshaling, order; apparel, attire, clothes, dress, garments; army, battalions, soldiery, troops.

arrest *vb* check, delay, detain, hinder, hold, interrupt, obstruct, restrain, stay, stop, withhold; apprehend, capture, catch, seize, take; catch, engage, engross, fix, occupy, secure, rivet. • *n* check, checking, detention, hindrance, interruption, obstruction, restraining, stay, staying, stopping; apprehension, capture, detention, seizure.

arrive *vb* attain, come, get to, reach.

arrogance *n* assumption, assurance, disdain, effrontery, haughtiness, loftiness, lordliness, presumption, pride, scornfulness, superciliousness.

arrogate *vb* assume, claim unduly, demand, usurp.

arrow *n* bolt, dart, reed, shaft.

art *n* business, craft, employment, trade; address, adroitness, aptitude, dexterity, ingenuity, knack, readiness, sagacity, skill;

artfulness, artifice, astuteness, craft, deceit, duplicity, finesse, subtlety.

artful *adj* crafty, cunning, disingenuous, insincere, sly, tricky, wily.

article *n* branch, clause, division, head, item, member, paragraph, part, point, portion; essay, paper, piece; commodity, substance, thing.

artifice *n* art, chicanery, contrivance, cunning, deception, deceit, duplicity, effort, finesse, fraud, imposture, invention, stratagem, subterfuge, trick, trickery.

artificial *adj* counterfeit, sham, spurious; assumed, affected, constrained, fictitious, forced, labored, strained.

artless *adj* ignorant, rude, unskillful, untaught; natural, plain, simple; candid, fair, frank, guileless, honest, plain, unaffected, simple, sincere, truthful, unsuspicious.

ascend *vb* arise, aspire, climb, mount, soar, tower.

ascendancy, ascendency *n* authority, control, domination, mastery, power, predominance, sovereignty, superiority, sway.

ascertain *vb* certify, define, determine, establish, fix, settle, verify; discover, find out, get at.

ashamed *adj* abashed, confused.

ask *vb* interrogate, inquire, question; adjure, beg, conjure, crave, desire, dun, entreat, implore, invite, inquire, petition, request, solicit, supplicate, seek, sue.

aspect *n* air, bearing, countenance, expression, feature, look, mien, visage; appearance, attitude, condition, light, phase, position, posture, situation, state, view; angle, direction, outlook, prospect.

asperity *n* ruggedness, roughness, unevenness; acrimony, causticity, corrosiveness, sharpness, sourness, tartness; acerbity, bitterness, churlishness, harshness, sternness, sullenness, severity, virulence.

aspersion *n* abuse, backbiting, calumny, censure, defamation, detraction, slander, vituperation, reflection, reproach.

aspiration *n* aim, ambition, craving, hankering, hope, longing.

aspire *vb* desire, hope, long, yearn; ascend, mount, rise, soar, tower.

assail *vb* assault, attack, invade, oppugn; impugn, malign, maltreat; ply, storm.

assassinate *vb* dispatch, kill, murder, slay.

assault *vb* assail, attack, charge, invade. • *n* aggression, attack, charge, incursion, invasion, onset, onslaught; storm.

assemble *vb* call, collect, congregate, convene, convoke, gather, levy, muster; converge, forgather.

assembly *n* company, collection, concourse, congregation, gathering, meeting, rout, throng; caucus, congress, conclave, convention, convocation, diet, legislature, meeting, parliament, synod.

assent *vb* accede, acquiesce, agree, concur, subscribe, yield. • *n* accord, acquiescence, allowance, approval, approbation, consent.

assert *vb* affirm, allege, aver, asseverate, declare, express, maintain, predicate, pronounce, protest; claim, defend, emphasize, maintain, press, uphold, vindicate.

assertion *n* affirmation, allegation, asseveration, averment, declaration, position, predication, remark, statement, word; defense, emphasis, maintenance, pressing, support, vindication.

assess *vb* appraise, compute, estimate, rate, value; assign, determine, fix, impose, levy.

asseverate *vb* affirm, aver, avow, declare, maintain, protest.

assiduous *adj* active, busy, careful, constant, diligent, devoted, indefatigable, industrious, sedulous, unremitting, untiring.

assign *vb* allot, appoint, apportion, appropriate; fix, designate, determine, specify; adduce, advance, allege, give, grant, offer, present, show.

assist *vb* abet, aid, befriend, further, help, patronize, promote, second, speed, support, sustain; aid, relieve, succor; alternate with, relieve, spell.

associate *vb* affiliate, combine, conjoin, couple, join, link, relate, yoke; consort, fraternize, mingle, sort. • *n* chum, companion, comrade, familiar, follower, mate; ally, confederate, friend, partner, fellow.

association *n* combination, company, confederation, connection, partnership, society.

assort *vb* arrange, class, classify, distribute, group, rank, sort; agree, be adapted, consort, suit.

assuage *vb* allay, alleviate, appease, calm, ease, lessen, mitigate, moderate, mollify, pacify, quell, relieve, soothe, tranquillize.

assume *vb* take, undertake; affect, counterfeit, feign, pretend, sham; arrogate, usurp; beg, hypothesize, imply, postulate, posit, presuppose, suppose, simulate.

assurance n assuredness, certainty, conviction, persuasion, pledge, security, surety, warrant; engagement, pledge, promise; averment, assertion, protestation; audacity, confidence, courage, firmness, intrepidity; arrogance, brass, boldness, effrontery, face, front, impudence.

assure vb encourage, embolden, hearten; certify, insure, secure against loss, vouch for.

astonish vb amaze, astound, confound, daze, dumbfound, overwhelm, startle, stun, stupefy, surprise.

astute adj acute, cunning, deep, discerning, ingenious, intelligent, penetrating, perspicacious, quick, sagacious, sharp, shrewd.

asylum n refuge, retreat, sanctuary, shelter.

athletic adj brawny, lusty, muscular, powerful, robust, sinewy, stalwart, stout, strapping, strong, sturdy.

athletics npl acrobics, eurythmics, exercise, exercising, gymnastics, sports, track and field, workout.

atom n bit, molecule, monad, particle, scintilla.

atone vb answer, compensate, expiate, satisfy.

atonement n amends, expiation, propitiation, reparation, satisfaction.

atrocity n depravity, enormity, flagrancy, ferocity, savagery, villainy.

attach vb affix, annex, connect, fasten, join, hitch, tie; charm, captivate, enamor, endear, engage, win; (legal) distress, distrain, seize, take.

attack vb assail, assault, charge, encounter, invade, set upon, storm, tackle; censure, criticise, impugn. • n aggression, assault, charge, offence, onset, onslaught, raid, thrust.

attain vb accomplish, achieve, acquire, get, obtain, secure; arrive at, come to, reach.

attempt vb assail, assault, attack; aim, endeavor, seek, strive, try. • n effort, endeavor, enterprise, experiment, undertaking, venture; assault, attack, onset.

attend vb accompany, escort, follow; guard, protect, watch; minister to, serve, wait on; give heed, hear, harken, listen; be attendant, serve, tend, wait.

attention n care, circumspection, heed, mindfulness, observation, regard, watch, watchfulness; application, reflection, study; civility, courtesy, deference,

politeness, regard, respect; addresses, courtship, devotion, suit, wooing.

attentive adj alive, awake, careful, civil, considerate, courteous, heedful, mindful, observant, watchful.

attenuate vb contract, dilute, diminish, elongate, lengthen, lessen, rarefy, reduce, slim, thin, weaken.

attest vb authenticate, certify, corroborate, confirm, ratify, seal, vouch; adjure, call to witness, invoke; confess, display, exhibit, manifest, prove, show, witness.

attic n garret, loft, upper storey.

Attic adj delicate, subtle, penetrating, pointed, pungent; chaste, classic, correct, elegant, polished, pure.

attire vb accouter, apparel, array, clothe, dress, enrobe, equip, rig, robe. • n clothes, clothing, costume, dress, garb, gear, habiliment, outfit, toilet, trapping, vestment, vesture, wardrobe.

attitude n pose, position, posture; aspect, conjuncture, condition, phase, prediction, situation, standing, state.

attract vb draw, pull; allure, captivate, charm, decoy, enamour, endear, entice, engage, fascinate, invite, win.

attraction n affinity, drawing, pull; allurement, charm, enticement, fascination, magnetism, lure, seduction, witchery.

attribute vb ascribe, assign, impute, refer. • n characteristic, mark, note, peculiarity, predicate, property, quality.

attrition n abrasion, friction, rubbing.

attune vb accord, harmonize, modulate, tune; accommodate, adapt, adjust, attempt.

audacity n boldness, courage, daring, fearlessness, intrepidity; assurance, brass, effrontery, face, front, impudence, insolence, presumption, sauciness.

audience n assemblage, congregation; hearing, interview, reception.

augment vb add to, enhance, enlarge, increase, magnify, multiply, swell.

augmentation n accession, addition, enlargement, extension, increase.

augury n prediction, prognostication, prophecy, soothsaying; auspice, forerunner, harbinger, herald, omen, precursor, portent, sign.

august adj awe-inspiring, awful, dignified, grand, imposing, kingly, majestic, noble, princely, regal, solemn, stately, venerable.

auspicious *adj* fortunate, happy, lucky, prosperous, successful; bright, favorable, golden, opportune, promising, prosperous.

austere *adj* ascetic, difficult, formal, hard, harsh, morose, relentless, rigid, rigorous, severe, stern, stiff, strict, uncompromising, unrelenting.

authentic *adj* genuine, pure, real, true, unadulterated, uncorrupted, veritable; accurate, authoritative, reliable, true, trustworthy.

authority *n* dominion, empire, government, jurisdiction, power, sovereignty; ascendency, control, influence, rule, supremacy, sway; authorization, liberty, order, permit, precept, sanction, warranty; testimony, witness; connoisseur, expert, master.

authorize *vb* empower, enable, entitle; allow, approve, confirm, countenance, permit, ratify, sanction.

auxiliary *adj* aiding, ancillary, assisting, helpful, subsidiary. • *n* ally, assistant, confederate, help.

avail *vb* assist, benefit, help, profit, use, service.

available *adj* accessible, advantageous, applicable, beneficial, profitable, serviceable, useful.

avarice *n* acquisitiveness, covetousness, greediness, penuriousness, rapacity.

avaricious *adj* grasping, miserly, niggardly, parsimonious.

avenge *vb* punish, retaliate, revenge, vindicate.

avenue *n* access, entrance, entry, passage; alley, path, road, street, walk; channel, pass, route, way.

aver *vb* allege, assert, asseverate, avouch, declare, pronounce, protest, say.

averse *adj* adverse, backward, disinclined, indisposed, opposed, unwilling.

aversion *n* abhorrence, antipathy, disgust, dislike, hate, hatred, loathing, reluctance, repugnance.

avid *adj* eager, greedy, voracious.

avocation *n* business, calling, employment, occupation, trade, vocation; distraction, hindrance, interruption.

avoid *vb* dodge, elude, escape, eschew, shun; forebear, refrain from.

avouch *vb* allege, assert, declare, maintain, say.

avow *vb* admit, acknowledge, confess, own.

awaken *vb* arouse, excite, incite, kindle, provoke, spur, stimulate; wake, waken; begin, be excited.

award *vb* adjudge, allot, assign, bestow, decree, grant. • *n* adjudication, allotment, assignment, decision, decree, determination, gift, judgement.

aware *adj* acquainted, apprised, conscious, conversant, informed, knowing, mindful, sensible.

away *adv* absent, not present. • *adj* at a distance; elsewhere; out of the way.

awe *vb* cow, daunt, intimidate, overawe. • *n* abashment, fear, reverence; dread, fear, fearfulness, terror.

awful *adj* august, awesome, dread, grand, inspired; abashed, alarming, appalled, dire, frightful, portentous, tremendous.

awkward *adj* bungling, clumsy, inept, maladroit, unskillful; lumbering, unfit, ungainly, unmanageable; boorish; inconvenient, unsuitable.

axiom *n* adage, aphorism, apothegm, maxim, postulation, truism.

axis *n* axle, shaft, spindle.

azure *adj* blue, cerulean, sky-colored.

B

babble *vb* blather, chatter, gibber, jabber, prate, prattle. • *n* chat, gossip, palaver, prate, tattle.

babel *n* clamor, confusion, din, discord, disorder, hubbub, jargon, pother.

baby *vb* coddle, cosset, indulge, mollycoddle, pamper, spoil. • *adj* babyish, childish, infantile, puerile; diminutive, doll-like, miniature, pocket, pocket-sized, small-scale. • *n* babe, brat, child, infant, suckling, nursling; chicken, coward, milksop, namby-pamby, sad sack, weakling; miniature; innocent.

bacchanal *n* carouse, debauchery, drunkenness, revelry, roisterousness.

back *vb* abet, aid, countenance, favor, second, support, sustain; go back, move back, retreat, withdraw. • *adj* hindmost. • *adv* in return, in consideration; ago, gone, since; aside, away, behind, by; abaft, astern, backwards, hindwards, rearwards. • *n* end, hind part, posterior, rear.

backbite *vb* abuse, asperse, blacken, defame, libel, malign, revile, scandalize, slander, traduce, vilify.

backbone *n* chine, spine; constancy, courage, decision, firmness, nerve, pluck, resolution, steadfastness.

backslider n apostate, deserter, renegade.

backward adj disinclined, hesitating, indisposed, loath, reluctant, unwilling, wavering; dull, slow, sluggish, stolid, stupid. • adv aback, behind, rearward.

bad adj baleful, baneful, detrimental, evil, harmful, hurtful, injurious, noxious, pernicious, unwholesome, vicious; abandoned, corrupt, depraved, immoral, sinful, unfair, unprincipled, wicked; unfortunate, unhappy, unlucky, miserable; disappointing, discouraging, distressing, sad, unwelcoming; abominable, mean, shabby, scurvy, vile, wretched; defective, inferior, imperfect, incompetent, poor, unsuitable; hard, heavy, serious, severe.

badge n brand, emblem, mark, sign, symbol, token.

badger vb annoy, bait, bother, hector, harry, pester, persecute, tease, torment, trouble, vex, worry.

baffle vb balk, block, check, circumvent, defeat, foil, frustrate, mar, thwart, undermine, upset; bewilder, confound, disconcert, perplex.

bait vb harry, tease, worry. • n allurement, decoy, enticement, lure, temptation.

balance vb equilibrate, pose, (naut) trim; compare, weigh; compensate, counteract, estimate; adjust, clear, equalize, square. • n equilibrium, liberation; excess, remainder, residue, surplus.

bald adj bare, naked, uncovered, treeless; dull, inelegant, meager, prosaic, tame, unadorned, vapid.

baleful adj baneful, deadly, calamitous, hurtful, injurious, mischievous, noxious, pernicious, ruinous.

balk vb baffle, defeat, disappoint, disconcert, foil, frustrate, thwart.

ball n drop, globe, orb, pellet, marble, sphere; bullet, missile, projectile, shot; assembly, dance.

balmy adj aromatic, fragrant, healing, odorous, perfumed.

ban vb anathematize, curse, execrate; interdict, outlaw. • n edict, proclamation; anathema, curse, denunciation, execration; interdiction, outlawry, penalty, prohibition

band[1] vb belt, bind, cinch, encircle, gird, girdle; ally, associate, combine, connect, join, league; bar, marble, streak, stripe, striate, vein. • n crew, gang, horde, society, troop; ensemble, group, orchestra.

band[2] n ligament, ligature, tie; bond, chain, cord, fetter, manacle, shackle, trammel; bandage, belt, binding, cincture, girth, tourniquet.

bandit n brigand, freebooter, footpad, gangster, highwayman, outlaw, robber.

baneful adj poisonous, venomous; deadly, destructive, hurtful, mischievous, noxious, pernicious.

bang vb beat, knock, maul, pommel, pound, strike, thrash, thump; slam; clatter, rattle, resound, ring. • n clang, clangor, whang; blow, knock, lick, thump, thwack, whack.

banish vb exile, expatriate, ostracize; dismiss, exclude, expel.

bank[1] vb incline, slope, tilt; embank. • n dike, embankment, escarpment, heap, knoll, mound; border, bound, brim, brink, margin, rim, strand; course, row, tier.

bank[2] vb deposit, keep, save. • n depository, fund, reserve, savings, stockpile.

banner n colors, ensign, flag, standard, pennon, standard, streamer.

banter vb chaff, deride, jeer, joke, mock, quiz, rally, ridicule. • n badinage, chaff, derision, jesting, joking, mockery, quizzing, raillery, ridicule.

bar vb exclude, hinder, obstruct, prevent, prohibit, restrain, stop. • n grating, pole, rail, rod; barricade, hindrance, impediment, obstacle, obstruction, stop; bank, sand bar, shallow, shoal, spit; (legal) barristers, counsel, court, judgement, tribunal.

barbarian adj brutal, cruel, ferocious, fierce, fell, inhuman, ruthless, savage, truculent, unfeeling. • n brute, ruffian, savage.

barbaric adj barbarous, rude, savage, uncivilized, untamed; capricious, coarse, gaudy, riotous, showy, outlandish, uncouth, untamed, wild.

bare vb denude, depilate, divest, strip, unsheathe; disclose, manifest, open, reveal, show. • adj denuded, exposed, naked, nude, stripped, unclothed, uncovered, undressed, unsheltered; alone, mere, sheer, simple; bald, meagre, plain, unadorned, uncovered, unfurnished; empty, destitute, indigent, poor.

bargain vb agree, contract, covenant, stipulate; convey, sell, transfer. • n agreement, compact, contract, covenant, convention, indenture, transaction, stipulation, treaty; proceeds, purchase, result.

barren adj childless, infecund, sterile; (bot)

acarpous, sterile; bare, infertile, poor, sterile, unproductive; ineffectual, unfruitful, uninstructive.

barricade vb block up, fortify, protect, obstruct. • n barrier, obstruction, palisade, stockade.

barrier n bar, barricade, hindrance, impediment, obstacle, obstruction, stop.

barter vb bargain, exchange, sell, trade, traffic.

base[1] adj cheap, inferior, worthless; counterfeit, debased, false, spurious; baseborn, humble, lowly, mean, nameless, plebeian, unknown, untitled, vulgar; abject, beggarly, contemptible, degraded, despicable, low, menial, pitiful, servile, sordid, sorry, worthless.

base[2] vb establish, found, ground. • n foundation, fundament, substructure, underpinning; pedestal, plinth, stand; center, headquarters, HQ, seat; starting point; basis, cause, grounds, reason, standpoint; bottom, foot, foundation, ground.

bashful adj coy, diffident, shy, timid.

basis n base, bottom, foundation, fundament, ground, groundwork.

bastard adj adulterated, baseborn, counterfeit, false, illegitimate, sham. • n love child.

batch vb assemble, bunch, bundle, collect, gather, group. • n amount, collection, crowd, lot, quantity.

bathe vb immerse, lave, wash; cover, enfold, enwrap, drench, flood, infold, suffuse. • n bath, shower, swim.

batter[1] vb beat, pelt, smite; break, bruise, demolish, destroy, shatter, shiver, smash; abrade, deface, disfigure, indent, mar; incline, recede, retreat, slope. • n batsman, striker.

batter[2] n dough, goo, goop, gunk, paste, pulp.

battle vb contend, contest, engage, fight, strive, struggle. • n action, affair, brush, combat, conflict, contest, engagement, fight, fray.

bauble n gewgaw, gimcrack, knick-knack, plaything, toy, trifle, trinket.

bawdy adj obscene, filthy, impure, indecent, lascivious, lewd, smutty, unchaste.

bawl vb clamor, cry, hoot, howl, roar, shout, squall, vociferate, yell.

bay[1] vb bark, howl, wail, yell, yelp.

bay[2] n alcove, compartment, niche, nook, opening, recess.

bay[3] n bight, cove, gulf, inlet.

bays npl applause, chaplet, fame, garland, glory, honor, plaudits, praise, renown.

beach vb ground, maroon, strand. • n coast, margin, rim, sands, seashore, seaside, shore, shoreline, strand, waterfront.

beacon vb brighten, flame, shine, signal; enlighten, illuminate, illumine, guide, light, signal. • n lighthouse, pharos, watchtower; sign, signal.

beadle n apparitor, church officer, crier, servitor, summoner.

beak n bill, mandible, (sl) nose; (naut) bow, prow, stem.

beam vb beacon, gleam, glisten, glitter, shine. • n balk, girder, joist, scantling, stud; gleam, pencil, ray, streak.

bear vb support, sustain, uphold; carry, convey, deport, transport, waft; abide, brook, endure, stand, suffer, tolerate, undergo; carry on, keep up, maintain; cherish, entertain, harbor; produce; cast, drop, sustain; endure, submit, suffer; act, operate, work. • n growler, grumbler, moaner, snarler; speculator.

bearable adj endurable, sufferable, supportable, tolerable.

bearing n air, behavior, demeanor, deportment, conduct, carriage, conduct, mien, port; connection, dependency, relation; endurance, patience, suffering; aim, course, direction; bringing forth, producing; bed, receptacle, socket.

beastly adj abominable, brutish, ignoble, low, sensual, vile.

beat vb bang, baste, belabor, buffet, cane, cudgel, drub, hammer, hit, knock, maul, pound, pummel, punch, strike, thrash, thump, thwack, whack, whip; bray, bruise, pound, pulverize; batter, pelt; conquer, defeat, overcome, rout, subdue, surpass, vanquish; pulsate, throb; dash, strike. • adj baffled, bamboozled, confounded, mystified, nonplused, perplexed, puzzled, stumped; done, dog-tired, exhausted, tired out, worn out; beaten, defeated, licked, worsted. • n blow, striking, stroke; beating, pulsation, throb; accent, meter, rhythm; circuit, course, round.

beatific adj ecstatic, enchanting, enraptured, ravishing, rapt.

beatitude n blessing, ecstasy, felicity, happiness.

beau n coxcomb, dandy, exquisite, fop, popinjay; admirer, lover, suitor, sweetheart.

beautiful adj charming, comely, fair, fine, exquisite, handsome, lovely, pretty.

beautify vb adorn, array, bedeck, deck,

decorate, embellish, emblazon, garnish, gild, grace, ornament, set.

beauty n elegance, grace, symmetry; attractiveness, comeliness, fairness, loveliness, seemliness; belle.

become vb change to, get, go, wax; adorn, befit, set off, suit.

becoming adj appropriate, apt, congruous, decent, decorous, due, fit, proper, right, seemly, suitable; comely, graceful, neat, pretty.

bed vb embed, establish, imbed, implant, infix, inset, plant; harbor, house, lodge. • n berth, bunk, cot, couch; channel, depression, hollow; base, foundation, receptacle, support, underlay; accumulation, layer, seam, stratum, vein.

bedim vb cloud, darken, dim, obscure.

befall vb betide, overtake; chance, happen, occur, supervene.

befitting adj appropriate, apt, becoming, decorous, fit, proper, right, suitable, seemly.

befool vb bamboozle, beguile, cheat, circumvent, delude, deceive, dupe, fool, hoax, hoodwink, infatuate, stupefy, trick.

befriend vb aid, benefit, countenance, encourage, favor, help, patronize.

beg vb adjure, ask, beseech, conjure, crave, entreat, implore, importune, petition, pray, request, solicit, supplicate.

beggarly adj destitute, needy, poor; abject, base, despicable, groveling, low, mean, miserable, miserly, paltry, pitiful, scant, servile, shabby, sorry, stingy, vile, wretched.

begin vb arise, commence, enter, open; inaugurate, institute, originate, start.

beginning n arising, commencement, dawn, emergence, inauguration, inception, initiation, opening, outset, start, rise; origin, source.

beguile vb cheat, deceive, delude; amuse, cheer, divert, entertain, solace.

behaviour n air, bearing, carriage, comportment, conduct, demeanor, deportment, manner, manners, mien.

behest n bidding, charge, command, commandment, direction, hest, injunction, mandate, order, precept.

behind prep abaft, after, following. • adv abaft, aft, astern, rearward. • adj arrested, backward, checked, detained, retarded; after, behind. • n afterpart, rear, stern, tail; back, back side, reverse; bottom, buttocks, posterior, rump.

behold vb consider, contemplate, eye, observe, regard, see, survey, view.

behoove vb become, befit, suit; be binding, be obligatory.

being n actuality, existence, reality, subsistence; core, essence, heart, root.

beleaguer vb besiege, blockade, invest; beset, block, encumber, encompass, encounter, obstruct, surround.

belief n assurance, confidence, conviction, persuasion, trust; acceptance, assent, credence, credit, currency; creed, doctrine, dogma, faith, opinion, tenet.

bellow vb bawl, clamor, cry, howl, vociferate, yell.

belt n band, cincture, girdle, girth, zone; region, stretch, strip.

bemoan vb bewail, deplore, lament, mourn.

bemused adj bewildered, confused, fuddled, muddled, muzzy, stupefied, tipsy.

bend vb bow, crook, curve, deflect, draw; direct, incline, turn; bend, dispose, influence, mold, persuade, subdue; (naut) fasten, make fast; crook, deflect, deviate, diverge, swerve; bow, lower, stoop; condescend, deign. • n angle, arc, arcuation, crook, curvature, curve, elbow, flexure, turn.

beneath prep below, under, underneath; unbecoming, unbefitting, unworthy. • adv below, underneath.

benediction n beatitude, benefit, benison, blessing, boon, grace, favor.

benefaction n alms, boon, charity, contribution, donation, favor, gift, grant, gratuity, offering, present.

beneficent adj benevolent, bounteous, bountiful, charitable, generous, kind, liberal.

beneficial adj advantageous, favorable, helpful, profitable, salutary, serviceable, useful, wholesome.

benefit vb befriend, help, serve; advantage, avail, profit. • n favor, good turn, kindness, service; account, advantage, behalf, gain, good, interest, profit, utility.

benevolence n beneficence, benignity, generosity, goodwill, humanity, kindliness, kindness.

benevolent adj altruistic, benign, charitable, generous, humane, kind, kindhearted, liberal, obliging, philanthropic, tender, unselfish.

benign adj amiable, amicable, beneficent, benevolent, complaisant, friendly, gentle, good, gracious, humane, kind, kindly, obliging.

bent *adj* angled, angular, bowed, crooked, curved, deflected, embowed, flexed, hooked, twisted; disposed, inclined, prone, minded; *(with* **on**) determined, fixed on, resolved, set on. • *n* bias, inclination, leaning, partiality, penchant, predilection, prepossession, proclivity, propensity.

bequeath *vb* devise, give, grant, leave, will; impart, transmit.

berate *vb* chide, rate, reprimand, reprove, scold.

bereave *vb* afflict, deprive of, despoil, dispossess, divest, rob, spoil, strip.

beseech *vb* beg, conjure, entreat, implore, importune, petition, supplicate; ask, beg, crave, solicit.

beset *vb* besiege, encompass, enclose, environ, encircle, hem in, surround; decorate, embarrass, embellish, entangle, garnish, ornament, perplex, set.

beside *prep* at the side of, by the side of, close to, near; aside from, not according to, out of the course of, out of the way of; not in possession of, out of.

besides[1] *prep* barring, distinct from, excluding, except, excepting, in addition to, other than, over and above, save.

beside[2], **besides**[2] *adv* additionally, also, further, furthermore, in addition, more, moreover, over and above, too, yet.

besiege *vb* beset, blockade, encircle, encompass, environ, invest, surround.

besot *vb* drench, intoxicate, soak, steep; befool, delude, infatuate, stultify, stupefy.

bespatter *vb* bedaub, befoul, besmirch, smear, spatter.

bespeak *vb* accost, address, declare, evince, forestall, imply, indicate, prearrange, predict, proclaim, solicit.

best *vb* better, exceed, excel, predominate, rival, surpass; beat, defeat, outdo, worst. • *adj* chief, first, foremost, highest, leading, utmost. • *adv* advantageously, excellently; extremely, greatly. • *n* choice, cream, flower, pick.

bestial *adj* beast-like, beastly, brutal, degraded, depraved, irrational, low, vile; sensual.

bestow *vb* deposit, dispose, put, place, store, stow; accord, give, grant, impart.

bet *vb* gamble, hazard, lay, pledge, stake, wage, wager. • *n* gamble, hazard, stake, wager.

bethink *vb* cogitate, consider, ponder, recall, recollect, reflect, remember.

betide *vb* befall, happen, occur, overtake.

betimes *adv* beforehand, early, forward, soon.

betoken *vb* argue, betray, denote, evince, imply, indicate, prove, represent, show, signify, typify.

betray *vb* be false to, break, violate; blab, discover, divulge, expose, reveal, show, tell; argue, betoken, display, evince, expose, exhibit, imply, indicate, manifest, reveal; beguile, delude, ensnare, lure, mislead; corrupt, ruin, seduce, undo.

betroth *vb* affiance, engage to marry, pledge in marriage, plight.

better *vb* advance, amend, correct, exceed, improve, promote, rectify, reform. • *adj* bigger, fitter, greater, larger, less ill, preferable. • *n* advantage, superiority, upper hand, victory; improvement, greater good.

between *prep* amidst, among, betwixt.

bewail *vb* bemoan, deplore, express, lament, mourn over, rue, sorrow.

beware *vb* avoid, heed, look out, mind.

bewilder *vb* confound, confuse, daze, distract, embarrass, entangle, muddle, mystify, nonplus, perplex, pose, puzzle, stagger.

bewitch *vb* captivate, charm, enchant, enrapture, entrance, fascinate, spellbind, transport.

beyond *prep* above, before, farther, over, past, remote, yonder.

bias *vb* bend, dispose, incline, influence, predispose, prejudice. • *n* bent, inclination, leaning, partiality, penchant, predilection, prepossession, proclivity, propensity, slant, tendency, turn.

bicker *vb* argue, dispute, jangle, quarrel, spar, spat, squabble, wrangle.

bid *vb* charge, command, direct, enjoin, order, require, summon; ask, call, invite, pray, request, solicit; offer, propose, proffer, tender. • *n* bidding, offer, proposal.

big *adj* bumper, bulking, bulky, great, huge, large, massive, monstrous; important, imposing; distended, inflated, full, swollen, tumid; fecund, fruitful, productive, teeming.

bigoted *adj* dogmatic, hidebound, intolerant, obstinate, narrow-minded, opinionated, prejudiced.

bill[1] *vb* charge, dun, invoice; program, schedule; advertise, boost, plug, promote, publicize. • *n* account, charges, reckoning, score; advertisement, banner, hoarding, placard, poster; playbill, program, schedule; bill of exchange, certificate, money; account, reckoning, statement.

bill[2] *n* beak, mandible, (*sl*) nose; billhook, brush-cutter, hedge-bill, hedging knife; caress, fondle, kiss, toy.

billet *vb* allot, apportion, assign, distribute, quarter, station. • *n* accommodation, lodgings, quarters.

billow *vb* surge, wave; heave, roll; bag, baloon, bulge, dilate, swell. • *n* roller, surge, swell, wave.

bin *n* box, bunker, crib, frame, receptacle.

bind *vb* confine, enchain, fetter, restrain, restrict; bandage, tie up, wrap; fasten, lash, pinion, secure, tie, truss; engage, hold, oblige, obligate, pledge; contract, harden, shrink, stiffen.

birth *n* ancestry, blood, descent, extraction, lineage, race; being, creation, creature, offspring, production, progeny.

bit *n* crumb, fragment, morsel, mouthful, piece, scrap; atom, grain, jot, mite, particle, tittle, whit; instant, minute, moment, second.

bite *vb* champ, chew, crunch, gnaw; burn, make smart, sting; catch, clutch, grapple, grasp, grip; bamboozle, cheat, cozen, deceive, defraud, dupe, gull, mislead, outwit, overreach, trick. • *n* grasp, hold; punch, relish, spice, pungency, tang, zest; lick, morsel, sip, taste; crick, nip, pain, pang, prick, sting.

bitter *adj* acrid; dire, fell, merciless, relentless, ruthless; harsh, severe, stern; afflictive, calamitous, distressing, galling, grievous, painful, poignant, sore, sorrowful.

black *adj* dark, ebony, inky, jet, sable, swarthy; dingy, dusky, lowering, murky, pitchy; calamitous, dark, depressing, disastrous, dismal, doleful, forbidding, gloomy, melancholy, mournful, somber, sullen.

blacken *vb* darken; deface, defile, soil, stain, sully; asperse, besmirch, calumniate, defame, malign, revile, slander, traduce, vilify.

blamable *adj* blameable, blameworthy, censurable, culpable, delinquent, faulty, remiss, reprehensible.

blame *vb* accuse, censure, condemn, disapprove, reflect upon, reprehend, reproach, reprove, upbraid. • *n* animadversion, censure, condemnation, disapproval, dispraise, disapprobation, reprehension, reproach, reproof; defect, demerit, fault, guilt, misdeed, shortcoming, sin, wrong.

blameless *adj* faultless, guiltless, inculpable, innocent, irreproachable, unblemished, undefiled, unimpeachable, unspotted, unsullied, spotless, stainless.

blanch *vb* bleach, fade, etiolate, whiten.

bland *adj* balmy, demulcent, gentle, mild, soothing, soft; affable, amiable, complaisant, kindly, mild, suave.

blandishment *n* cajolery, coaxing, compliment, fascination, fawning, flattery, wheedling.

blank *adj* bare, empty, vacuous, void; amazed, astonished, confounded, confused, dumbfounded, nonplussed; absolute, complete, entire, mere, perfect, pure, simple, unabated, unadulterated, unmitigated, unmixed, utter, perfect.

blare *vb* blazon, blow, peal, proclaim, trumpet. • *n* blast, clang, clangor, peal.

blasphemy *n* impiousness, sacrilege; cursing, profanity, swearing.

blast *vb* annihilate, blight, destroy, kill, ruin, shrivel, wither; burst, explode, kill. • *n* blow, gust, squall; blare, clang, peal; burst, discharge, explosion.

blaze *vb* blazon, proclaim, publish; burn, flame, glow. • *n* flame, flare, flash, glow, light.

bleach *vb* blanch, etiolate, render white, whiten.

bleak *adj* bare, exposed, unprotected, unsheltered, storm-beaten, windswept; biting, chill, cold, piercing, raw; cheerless, comfortless, desolate, dreary, uncongenial.

blemish *vb* blur, injure, mar, spot, stain, sully, taint, tarnish; asperse, calumniate, defame, malign, revile, slander, traduce, vilify. • *n* blot, blur, defect, disfigurement, fault, flaw, imperfection, soil, speck, spot, stain, tarnish; disgrace, dishonor, reproach, stain, taint.

blend *vb* amalgamate, coalesce, combine, commingle, fuse, mingle, mix, unite. • *n* amalgamation, combination, compound, fusion, mix, mixture, union.

bless *vb* beatify, delight, gladden; adore, celebrate, exalt, extol, glorify, magnify, praise.

blessedness *n* beatitude, bliss, blissfulness, felicity, happiness, joy.

blight *vb* blast, destroy, kill, ruin, shrivel, wither; annihilate, annul, crush, disappoint, frustrate. • *n* blast, mildew, pestilence.

blind *vb* blear, darken, deprive of sight; blindfold, hoodwink. • *adj* eyeless, sightless, stone-blind, unseeing; benighted, ignorant, injudicious, purblind, undiscerning, unenlightened; concealed, confused, dark, dim, hidden, intricate, involved, labyrinthine, obscure, private, remote; careless, headlong, heedless, inconsiderate, indiscriminate, thoughtless; blank, closed, shut. • *n* cover, curtain, screen, shade, shutter; blinker; concealment, disguise, feint, pretence, pretext, ruse, stratagem, subterfuge.

blink *vb* nictate, nictitate, wink; flicker, flutter, gleam, glitter, intermit, twinkle; avoid, disregard, evade, gloss over, ignore, overlook, pass over. • *n* glance, glimpse, sight, view, wink; gleam, glimmer, sheen, shimmer, twinkle.

bliss *n* beatification, beatitude, blessedness, blissfulness, ecstasy, felicity, happiness, heaven, joy, rapture, transport.

blithe *adj* airy, animated, blithesome, buoyant, cheerful, debonair, elated, happy, jocund, joyful, joyous, lively, mirthful, sprightly, vivacious.

bloat *vb* dilate, distend, inflate, swell.

block *vb* arrest, bar, blockade, check, choke, close, hinder, impede, jam, obstruct, stop; form, mold, shape; brace, stiffen. • *n* lump, mass; blockhead, dunce, fool, simpleton; pulley, tackle; execution, scaffold; jam, obstruction, pack, stoppage.

blood *n* children, descendants, offspring, posterity, progeny; family, house, kin, kindred, line, relations; consanguinity, descent, kinship, lineage, relationship; courage, disposition, feelings, mettle, passion, spirit, temper.

bloom *vb* blossom, blow, flower; thrive, prosper. • *n* blossom, blossoming, blow, efflorescence, florescence, flowering; delicacy, delicateness, flush, freshness, heyday, prime, vigor; flush, glow, rose.

blossom *vb* bloom, blow, flower. • *n* bloom, blow, efflorescence, flower.

blot *vb* cancel, efface, erase, expunge, obliterate, rub out; blur, deface, disfigure, obscure, spot, stain, sully; disgrace, dishonor, tarnish. • *n* blemish, blur, erasure, spot, obliteration, stain; disgrace, dishonor, stigma.

blow[1] *n* bang, beat, buffet, dab, impact, knock, pat, punch, rap, slam, stroke, thump, wallop, buffet, impact; affliction, calamity, disaster, misfortune, setback.

blow[2] *vb* breathe, gasp, pant, puff; flow, move, scud, stream, waft. • *n* blast, gale, gust, squall, storm, wind.

blue *adj* azure, cerulean, cobalt, indigo, sapphire, ultramarine; ghastly, livid, pallid; dejected, depressed, dispirited, downcast,

gloomy, glum, mopey, melancholic, melancholy, sad.

bluff[1] *adj* abrupt, blunt, blustering, coarse, frank, good-natured, open, outspoken; abrupt, precipitous, sheer, steep. • *n* cliff, headland, height.

bluff[2] *vb* deceive, defraud, lie, mislead. • *n* deceit, deception, feint, fraud, lie.

blunder *vb* err, flounder, mistake; stumble. • *n* error, fault, howler, mistake, solecism.

blunt *adj* dull, edgeless, obtuse, pointless, unsharpened; insensible, stolid, thickwitted; abrupt, bluff, downright, plain-spoken, outspoken, unceremonious, uncourtly. • *vb* deaden, dull, numb, weaken.

blur *vb* bedim, darken, dim, obscure; blemish, blot, spot, stain, sully, tarnish. • *n* blemish, blot, soil, spot, stain, tarnish; disgrace, smear.

blush *vb* color, flush, glow, redden. • *n* bloom, flush, glow, color, reddening, suffusion.

bluster *vb* boast, brag, bully, domineer, roar, swagger, swell, vaunt. • *n* boisterousness, noise, tumult, turbulence; braggadocio, bravado, boasting, gasconade, swaggering.

board *n* deal, panel, plank; diet, entertainment, fare, food, meals, provision, victuals; cabinet, conclave, committee, council; directorate; panel.

boast *vb* bluster, brag, crack, flourish, crow, vaunt. • *n* blustering, boasting, bombast, brag, braggadocio, bravado, swaggering, vaunt.

bode *vb* augur, betoken, forebode, foreshadow, foretell, portend, predict, prefigure, presage, prophesy.

bodily *adj* carnal, corporeal, fleshly, physical. • *adv* altogether, completely, entirely, wholly.

body *n* carcass, corpse, remains; stem, torso, trunk; aggregate, bulk, corpus, mass; being, individual, mortal creature, person; assemblage, association, band, company, corporation, corps, coterie, force, party, society, troop; consistency, substance, thickness.

boggle *vb* demur, falter, hang fire, hesitate, shrink, vacillate, waver.

boil[1] *vb* agitate, bubble, foam, froth, rage, seethe, simmer. • *n* ebullience, ebullition.

boil[2] (*med*) gathering, pimple, pustule, swelling, tumor.

boisterous *adj* loud, roaring, stormy; clamoring, loud, noisy, obstreperous, tumultuous, turbulent.

bold *adj* adventurous, audacious, courageous; brave, daring, dauntless, doughty, fearless, gallant, hardy, heroic, intrepid, mettlesome, manful, manly, spirited, stouthearted, undaunted, valiant, valorous; assured, confident, self-reliant; assuming, forward, impertinent, impudent, insolent, push, rude, saucy; conspicuous, projecting, prominent, striking; abrupt, precipitous, prominent, steep.

bolster *vb* aid, assist, defend, help, maintain, prop, stay, support. • *n* cushion, pillow; prop, support.

bolt *vb* abscond, flee, fly. • *n* arrow, dart, missile, shaft; thunderbolt.

bombast *n* bluster, brag, braggadocio, fustian, gasconade, mouthing, pomposity, rant.

bond *vb* bind, connect, fuse, glue, join. • *adj* captive, enslaved, enthralled, subjugated. • *n* band, cord, fastening, ligament, ligature, link, nexus; bondage, captivity, chains, constraint, fetters, prison, shackle; attachment, attraction, connection, coupling, link, tie, union; compact, obligation, pledge, promise.

bondage *n* captivity, confinement, enslavement, enthralment, peonage, serfdom, servitude, slavery, thraldom, vassalage.

bonny *adj* beautiful, handsome, fair, fine, pretty; airy, blithe, buoyant, buxom, cheerful, jolly, joyous, merry. playful, sporty, sprightly, winsome.

bonus *n* gift, honorarium, premium, reward, subsidy.

booby *n* blockhead, dunce, fool, idiot, simpleton.

book *vb* bespeak, engage, reserve; program, schedule; list, log, record, register. • *n* booklet, brochure, compendium, handbook, manual, monograph, pamphlet, textbook, tract, treatise, volume, work.

bookish *adj* erudite, learned, literary, scholarly, studious.

boon *adj* convivial, jolly, jovial, hearty; close, intimate. • *n* benefaction, favor, grant, gift, present; advantage, benefit, blessing, good, privilege.

boor *n* bumpkin, clodhopper, clown, lout, lubber, peasant, rustic, swain.

boorish *adj* awkward, bearish, clownish, course, gruff, ill-bred, loutish, lubberly, rude, rustic, uncivilized, uncouth, uneducated.

bootless *adj* abortive, fruitless, futile, profitless, vain, worthless, useless.

booty *n* loot, pillage, plunder, spoil.

border *vb* bound, edge, fringe, line, march, rim, skirt, verge; abut, adjoin, butt, conjoin, connect, neighbor. • *n* brim, brink, edge, fringe, hem, margin, rim, skirt, verge; boundary, confine, frontier, limit, march, outskirts.

bore[1] *vb* annoy, fatigue, plague, tire, trouble, vex, weary, worry. • *n* bother, nuisance, pest, worry.

bore[2] *vb* drill, perforate, pierce, sink, tunnel. • *n* caliber, hole, shaft, tunnel.

borrow *vb* take and return, use temporarily; adopt, appropriate, imitate; dissemble, feign, simulate.

boss[1] *vb* emboss, stud; • *n* knob, protuberance, stud.

boss[2] *vb* command, direct, employ, run. • *n* employer, foreman, master, overseer, superintendent.

botch *vb* blunder, bungle, cobble, mar, mend, mess, patch, spoil. • *n* blotch, pustule, sore; failure, miscarriage.

bother *vb* annoy, disturb, harass, molest, perplex, pester, plague, tease, trouble, vex, worry. • *n* annoyance, perplexity, plague, trouble, vexation.

bottom *vb* build, establish, found. • *adj* base, basic, ground, lowermost, lowest, nethermost, undermost. • *n* base, basis, foot, foundation, groundwork; dale, meadow, valley; buttocks, fundament, seat; dregs, grounds, lees, sediment.

bounce *vb* bound, jump, leap, rebound, recoil, spring. • *n* knock, thump; bound, jump, leap, spring, vault.

bound[1] *adj* assured, certain, decided, determined, resolute, resolved; confined, hampered, restricted, restrained; committed, contracted, engaged, pledged, promised; beholden, duty-bound, obligated, obliged.

bound[2] *vb* border, delimit, circumscribe, confine, demarcate, limit, restrict, terminate. • *n* boundary, confine, edge, limit, march, margin, periphery, term, verge.

bound[3] *vb* jump, leap, spring. • *n* bounce, jump, leap, spring, vault.

boundary *n* border, bourn, circuit, circumference, confine, limit, march, periphery, term, verge.

boundless *adj* endless, immeasurable, infinite, limitless, unbounded, unconfined, undefined, unlimited, vast.

bountiful *adj* beneficent, bounteous, generous, liberal, munificent, princely.

bounty *n* beneficence, benevolence, charity, donation, generosity, gift, kindness, premium, present, reward.

bourn *n* border, boundary, confine, limit; brook, burn, rill, rivulet, stream, torrent.

bow[1] *n* (*naut*) beak, prow, stem.

bow[2] *vb* arc, bend, buckle, crook, curve, droop, flex, yield; crush, depress, subdue; curtsy, genuflect, kowtow, submit. • *n* arc, bend, bilge, bulge, convex, curve, flexion; bob, curtsy, genuflection, greeting, homage, obeisance; coming out, debut, introduction; curtain call, encore.

bowels *npl* entrails, guts, insides, viscera; compassion, mercy, pity, sympathy, tenderness.

box[1] *vb* fight, hit, mill, spar. • *n* blow, buffet, fight, hit, spar.

box[2] *vb* barrel, crate, pack, parcel. • *n* case, chest, container, crate, portmanteau, trunk.

boy *n* lad, stripling, youth.

brace *vb* make tight, tighten; buttress, fortify, reinforce, shore, strengthen, support, truss. • *n* couple, pair; clamp, girder, prop, shore, stay, support, tie, truss.

brag *vb* bluster, boast, flourish, gasconade, vaunt.

branch *vb* diverge, fork, bifurcate, ramify, spread. • *n* bough, offset, limb, shoot, sprig, twig; arm, fork, ramification, spur; article, department, member, part, portion, section, subdivision.

brand *vb* denounce, stigmatize, mark. • *n* firebrand, torch; bolt, lightning flash; cachet, mark, stamp, tally; blot, reproach, stain, stigma.

brave *vb* dare, defy. • *adj* bold, courageous, fearless, heroic, intrepid, stalwart.

bravery *n* courage, daring, fearlessness, gallantry, valor.

brawl *vb* bicker, dispute, jangle, quarrel, squabble. • *n* broil, dispute, feud, fracas, fray, jangle, quarrel, row, scuffle, squabble, uproar, wrangle.

brawny *adj* athletic, lusty, muscular, powerful, robust, sinewy, stalwart, strapping, strong, sturdy.

bray *vb* clamor, hoot, roar, trumpet, vociferate. • *n* blare, crash, roar, shout.

breach *n* break, chasm, crack, disruption, fissure, flaw, fracture, opening, rent, rift, rupture; alienation, difference, disaffection, disagreement, split.

bread *n* aliment, diet, fare, food, nourishment, nutriment, provisions, regimen, victuals.

break *vb* crack, disrupt, fracture, part, rend, rive, sever; batter, burst, crush, shatter, smash, splinter; cashier, degrade, discard, discharge, dismiss; disobey, infringe, transgress, violate; intermit, interrupt, stop; disclose, open, unfold. • *n* aperture, breach, chasm, fissure, gap, rent, rip, rupture; break-up, crash, debacle.

breast *vb* face, oppose, resist, stem, withstand. • *n* bosom, chest, thorax; affections, conscience, heart; mammary gland, mammary organ, pap, udder.

breath *n* exhaling, inhaling, pant, sigh, respiration, whiff; animation, existence, life; pause, respite, rest; breathing space, instant, moment.

breathe *vb* live, exist; emit, exhale, give out; diffuse, express, indicate, manifest, show.

breed *vb* bear, beget, engender, hatch, produce; bring up, foster, nourish, nurture, raise, rear; discipline, educate, instruct, nurture, rear, school, teach, train; generate, originate. • *n* extraction, family, lineage, pedigree, progeny, race, strain.

brevity *n* briefness, compression, conciseness, curtness, pithiness, shortness, terseness, transiency.

brew *vb* concoct, contrive, devise, excite, foment, instigate, plot. • *n* beverage, concoction, drink, liquor, mixture, potation.

bribe *vb* buy, corrupt, influence, pay off, suborn. • *n* allurement, corruption, enticement, graft, pay-off, subornation.

bridle *vb* check, curb, control, govern, restrain. • *n* check, control, curb.

brief *vb* direct, give directions, instruct; capsulate, summarize, delineate, describe, draft, outline, sketch; (*law*) retain. • *adj* concise, curt, inconsiderable, laconic, pithy, short, succinct, terse; fleeting, momentary, short, temporary, transient. • *n* abstract, breviary, briefing, epitome, compendium, summary, syllabus; (*law*) precept, writ.

brigand *n* bandit, footpad, freebooter, gangster, highwayman, marauder, outlaw, robber, thug.

bright *adj* blazing, brilliant, dazzling, gleaming, glowing, light, luminous, radiant, shining, sparkling, sunny; clear, cloudless, lambent, lucid, transparent; famous, glorious, illustrious; acute, discerning, ingenious, intelligent, keen; auspicious, cheering, encouraging, exhilarating, favorable, inspiring, promising, propitious; cheerful, genial, happy, lively, merry, pleasant, smiling, vivacious.

brilliant adj beaming, bright, effulgent, gleaming, glistening, glittering, lustrous, radiant, resplendent, shining, sparkling splendid; admirable, celebrated, distinguished, famous, glorious, illustrious, renowned; dazzling, decided, prominent, signal, striking, unusual.

brim n border, brink, edge, rim, margin, skirt, verge; bank, border, coast, margin, shore.

bring vb bear, convey, fetch; accompany, attend, conduct, convey, convoy, guide, lead; gain, get, obtain, procure, produce.

brisk adj active, alert, agile, lively, nimble, perky, quick, smart, spirited, spry.

brittle adj brash, breakable, crisp, crumbling, fragile, frangible, frail, shivery.

broach vb open, pierce, set; approach, break, hint, suggest; proclaim, publish, utter.

broad adj ample, expansive, extensive, large, spacious, sweeping, vast, wide; enlarged, hospitable, liberal, tolerant; diffused, open, spread; coarse, gross, indecent, indelicate, unrefined, vulgar.

broaden vb augment, enlarge, expand, extend, increase, spread, stretch, widen.

broken adj fractured, rent, ruptured, separated, severed, shattered, shivered, torn; exhausted, feeble, impaired, shaken, shattered, spent, wasted; defective, halting, hesitating, imperfect, stammering, stumbling; contrite, humble, lowly, penitent; abrupt, craggy, precipitous, rough.

broker n agent, factor, go-between, middleman.

brood vb incubate, sit. • n issue, offspring, progeny; breed, kind, line, lineage, sort, strain.

brook vb abide, bear, endure, suffer, tolerate. • n burn, beck, creek, rill, rivulet, run, streamlet.

brotherhood n association, clan, clique, coterie, fraternity, junta, society.

brotherly adj affectionate, amicable, cordial, friendly, kind.

browbeat vb bully, intimidate, overawe, overbear.

bruise vb contuse, crunch, squeeze; batter, break, maul, pound, pulverize; batter,

deface, indent. • n blemish, contusion, swelling.

brush¹ n brushwood, bush, scrub, scrubwood, shrubs, thicket, wilderness.

brush² vb buff, clean, polish, swab, sweep, wipe; curry, groom, rub down; caress, flick, glance, graze, scrape, skim, touch. • n besom, broom; action, affair, collision, contest, conflict, encounter, engagement, fight, skirmish.

brutal adj barbaric, barbarous, brutish, cruel, ferocious, inhuman, ruthless, savage; bearish, brusque, churlish, gruff, impolite, harsh, rude, rough, truculent, uncivil.

brute n barbarian, beast, monster, ogre, savage; animal, beast, creature. • adj carnal, mindless, physical; bestial, coarse, gross.

bubble vb boil, effervesce, foam. • n bead, blob, fluid, globule; bagatelle, trifle; cheat, delusion, hoax.

buccaneer n corsair, freebooter, pirate.

buck vb jump, leap. • n beau, blade, blood, dandy, fop, gallant, spark; male.

bud vb burgeon, germinate, push, shoot, sprout, vegetate. • n burgeon, gem, germ, gemmule, shoot, sprout.

budget vb allocate, cost, estimate. • n account, estimate, financial statement; assets, finances, funds, means, resources; bag, bundle, pack, packet, parcel, roll; assortment, batch, collection, lot, set, store.

buffet¹ vb beat, box, cuff, slap, smite, strike; resist, struggle against, • n blow, box, cuff, slap, strike;

buffet² n cupboard, sideboard; refreshment counter.

buffoon n antic, clown, droll, fool, harlequin, jester, mountebank.

build vb construct, erect, establish, fabricate, fashion, model, raise, rear. • n body, figure, form, frame, physique; construction, shape, structure.

building n construction, erection, fabrication; edifice, fabric, house, pile, substructure, structure,

bulk n dimension, magnitude, mass, size, volume; amplitude, bulkiness, massiveness; body, majority, mass.

bully vb browbeat, bulldoze, domineer, haze, hector, intimidate, overbear. • n blusterer, browbeater, bulldozer, hector, swaggerer, roisterer, tyrant.

bulwark n barrier, fortification, parapet,

rampart, wall; palladium, safeguard, security.

bump *vb* collide, knock, strike, thump. • *n* blow, jar, jolt, knock, shock, thump; lump, protuberance, swelling.

bunch *vb* assemble, collect, crowd, group, herd, pack. • *n* bulge, bump, bundle, hump, knob, lump, protuberance; cluster, hand, fascicle; assortment, batch, collection, group, lot, parcel, set; knot, tuft.

bundle *vb* bale, pack, package, parcel, truss, wrap. • *n* bale, batch, bunch, collection, heap, pack, package, packet, parcel, pile, roll, truss.

bungler *n* botcher, duffer, fumbler, lout, lubber, mis-manager, muddler.

burden *vb* encumber, grieve, load, oppress, overlay, overload, saddle, surcharge, try. • *n* capacity, cargo, freight, lading, load, tonnage, weight; affliction, charge, clog, encumbrance, impediment, grievance, sorrow, trial, trouble; drift, point, substance, tenor, surcharge.

bureau *n* chest of drawers, dresser; counting room, office.

burial *n* burying, entombment, inhumation, interment, sepulture.

burlesque *vb* ape, imitate, lampoon, mock, ridicule, satirize. • *n* caricature, extravaganza, parody, send-up, take-off, travesty.

burn[1] *n* beck, brook, gill, rill, rivulet, runnel, runlet, stream water

burn[2] *vb* blaze, conflagrate, enflame, fire, flame, ignite, kindle, light, smoulder; cremate, incinerate; scald, scorch, singe; boil, broil, cook, roast, seethe, simmer, stew, swelter, toast; bronze, brown, sunburn, suntan, tan; bake, desiccate, dry, parch, sear, shrivel, wither; glow, incandesce, tingle, warm. • *n* scald, scorch, singe; sunburn.

burning *adj* aflame, fiery, hot, scorching; ardent, earnest, fervent, fervid, impassioned, intense.

burnish *vb* brighten, buff, furbish, polish, shine. • *n* glaze, gloss, patina, polish, shine.

burst *vb* break open, be rent, explode, shatter, split open. • *adj* broken, kaput, punctured, ruptured, shattered, split. • *n* break, breakage, breach, fracture, rupture; blast, blowout, blowup, discharge, detonation, explosion; spurt; blaze, flare, flash; cloudburst, downpour; bang, crack, crash, report, sound; fusillade, salvo, spray,

volley, outburst, outbreak flare-up, blaze, eruption.

bury *vb* entomb, inearth, inhume, inter; conceal, hide, secrete, shroud.

business *n* calling, employment, occupation, profession, pursuit, vocation; commerce, dealing, trade, traffic; affair, concern, engagement, matter, transaction, undertaking; duty, function, office, task, work.

bustle *vb* fuss, hurry, scurry. • *n* ado, commotion, flurry, fuss, hurry, hustle, pother, stir, tumult.

busy *vb* devote, employ, engage, occupy, spend, work. • *adj* employed, engaged, occupied; active, assiduous, diligent, engrossed, industrious, sedulous, working; agile, brisk, nimble, spry, stirring; meddling, officious.

but *conj* except, excepting, further, howbeit, moreover, still, unless, yet. • *adv* all the same, even, notwithstanding, still, yet.

butchery *n* massacre, murder, slaughter.

butt[1] *vb* bunt, push, shove, shunt, strike; encroach, impose, interfere, intrude, invade, obtrude. • *n* buck, bunt, push, shove, shunt, thrust.

butt[2] *n* barrel, cask.

butt[3] *n* aim, goal, mark, object, point, target; dupe, gull, victim.

butt[4] *vb* abut, adjoin, conjoin, connect, neighbor. • *n* end, piece, remainder, stub, stump; buttocks, posterior, rump.

buttonhole *vb* bore, catch, detain in conversation, importune.

buttress *vb* brace, prop, shore, stay, support. • *n* brace, bulwark, prop, stay, support.

buxom *adj* comely, fresh, healthy, hearty, plump, rosy, ruddy, vigorous.

byword *n* adage, aphorism, apothegm, dictum, maxim, proverb, saying, saw.

C

cabal *vb* conspire, intrigue, machinate, plot. • *n* clique, combination, confederacy, coterie, faction, gang, junta, league, party, set; conspiracy, intrigue, machination, plot.

cabbalistic, cabalistic *adj* dark, fanciful, mysterious, mystic, occult, secret.

cabaret *n* tavern, inn, public house, wine shop.

cabin *n* berth, bunk, cot, cottage, crib,

dwelling, hovel, hut, shack, shanty, shed.

cabinet *n* apartment, boudoir, chamber, closet; case, davenport, desk, escritoire; council, ministry.

cachinnation *n* guffaw, laugh, laughter.

cackle *vb* giggle, laugh, snicker, titter; babble, chatter, gabble, palaver, prate, prattle, titter. • *n* babble, chatter, giggle, prate, prattle, snigger, titter.

cacophonous *adj* discordant, grating, harsh, inharmonious, jarring, raucous.

cadaverous *adj* bloodless, deathlike, ghastly, pale, pallid, wan.

cage *vb* confine, immure, imprison, incarcerate. • *n* coop, pen, pound.

caitiff *adj* base, craven, pusillanimous, rascally, recreant. • *n* coward, knave, miscreant, rascal, rogue, scoundrel, sneak, traitor, vagabond, villain, wretch.

cajole *vb* blandish, coax, flatter, jolly, wheedle; beguile, deceive, delude, entrap, inveigle, tempt.

calamity *n* adversity, affliction, blow, casualty, cataclysm, catastrophe, disaster, distress, downfall, evil, hardship, mischance, misery, misfortune, mishap, reverse, ruin, stroke, trial, visitation.

calculate *vb* cast, compute, count, estimate, figure, rate, reckon, weigh; tell.

calculating *adj* crafty, designing, scheming, selfish; careful, cautious, circumspect, far-sighted, politic, sagacious, wary.

calefaction *n* heating, warming; hotness, incandescence, warmth.

calendar *n* almanac, ephemeris, register; catalog, list, schedule.

calibre *n* bore, capacity, diameter, gauge; ability, capacity, endowment, faculty, gifts, parts, scope, talent.

call *vb* christen, denominate, designate, dub, entitle, name, phrase, style, term; bid, invite, summons; assemble, convene, convoke, muster; cry, exclaim; arouse, awaken, proclaim, rouse, shout, waken; appoint, elect, ordain. • *n* cry, outcry, voice; appeal, invitation, summons; claim, demand, summons; appointment, election, invitation.

calling *n* business, craft, employment, occupation, profession, pursuit, trade.

callous *adj* hard, hardened, indurated; apathetic, dull, indifferent, insensible, inured, obdurate, obtuse, sluggish, torpid, unfeeling, unsusceptible.

callow *adj* naked, unfeathered, unfledged;

green, immature, inexperienced, sappy, silly, soft, unfledged, unsophisticated.

calm *vb* allay, becalm, compose, hush, lull, smooth, still, tranquillize; alleviate, appease, assuage, moderate, mollify, pacify, quiet, soften, soothe, tranquillize. • *adj* halcyon, mild, peaceful, placid, quiet, reposeful, serene, smooth, still, tranquil, unruffled; collected, cool, composed, controlled, impassive, imperturbable, sedate, self-possessed, undisturbed, unperturbed, unruffled, untroubled. • *n* lull; equanimity, peace, placidity, quiet, repose, serenity, stillness, tranquillity.

calorific *adj* heat, heat-producing.

calumniate *vb* abuse, asperse, backbite, blacken, blemish, defame, discredit, disparage, lampoon, libel, malign, revile, slander, traduce, vilify.

calumny *n* abuses, aspersion, backbiting, defamation, detraction, evil-speaking, insult, libel, lying, obloquy, slander, vilification, vituperation.

camarilla *n* cabal, clique, junta, ring.

camber *vb* arch, bend, curve. • *n* arch, arching, convexity.

camp[1] *vb* bivouac, encamp, lodge, pitch, tent. • *n* bivouac, cantonment, encampment, laager; cabal, circle, clique, coterie, faction, group, junta, party, ring, set.

camp[2] *adj* affected, artificial, effeminate, exaggerated, mannered, theatrical.

canaille *n* mob, populace, proletariat, rabble, ragbag, riffraff, scum.

canal *n* channel, duct, pipe, tube.

cancel *vb* blot, efface, erase, expunge, obliterate; abrogate, annul, countermand, nullify, quash, repeal, rescind, revoke.

candelabrum *n* candlestick, chandelier, luster.

candid *adj* fair, impartial, just, unbiased, unprejudiced; artless, frank, free, guileless, honest, honorable, ingenuous, naive, open, plain, sincere, straightforward.

candidate *n* applicant, aspirant, claimant, competitor, probationer.

candor *n* fairness, impartiality, justice; artlessness, frankness, guilelessness, honesty, ingenuousness, openness, simplicity, sincerity, straightforwardness, truthfulness.

canker *vb* corrode, erode, rot, rust, waste; blight, consume, corrupt, embitter, envenom, infect, poison, sour. • *n* gangrene, rot; bale, bane, blight, corruption, infection, irritation.

canon n catalog, criterion, formula, formulary, law, regulation, rule, standard, statute.

canorous adj musical, tuneful.

cant[1] vb whine. • adj current, partisan, popular, rote, routine, set; argotic, slangy. • n hypocrisy; argot, jargon, lingo, slang.

cant[2] vb bevel, incline, list, slant, tilt, turn. • n bevel, inclination, leaning, list, pitch, slant, tilt, turn.

cantankerous adj contumacious, crabbed, cross-grained, dogged, headstrong, heady, intractable, obdurate, obstinate, perverse, refractory, stiff, stubborn, willful, unyielding.

canting adj affected, pious, sanctimonious, whining.

canvas n burlap, scrim, tarpaulin.

canvass vb discuss, dispute; analyze, consider, examine, investigate, review, scrutinize, sift, study; campaign, electioneer, solicit votes. • n debate, discussion, dispute; examination, scrutiny, sifting.

canyon n gorge, gulch, ravine.

cap vb cover, surmount; complete, crown, finish; exceed, overtop, surpass, transcend; match, parallel, pattern. • n beret, head-cover, head-dress; acme, chief, crown, head, peak, perfection, pitch, summit, top.

capability n ability, brains, caliber, capableness, capacity, competency, efficiency, faculty, force, power, scope, skill.

capable adj adapted, fitted, qualified, suited; able, accomplished, clever, competent, efficient, gifted, ingenious, intelligent, sagacious, skillful.

capacious adj ample, broad, comprehensive, expanded, extensive, large, roomy, spacious, wide.

capacitate vb enable, qualify.

capacity n amplitude, dimensions, magnitude, volume; aptitude, aptness, brains, caliber, discernment, faculty, forte, genius, gift, parts, power, talent, turn, wit; ability, capability, caliber, cleverness, competency, efficiency, skill; character, charge, function, office, position, post, province, service, sphere.

caparison vb accouter, costume, equip, outfit, rig out. • n accouterments, armor, get-up, harness, housing, livery, outfit, panoply, tack, tackle, trappings, turnout.

caper vb bound, caracole, frisk, gambol, hop, leap, prank, romp, skip, spring. • n bound, dance, gambol, frisk, hop, jump, leap, prance, romp, skip.

capillary adj delicate, fine, minute, slender.

capital adj cardinal, chief, essential, important, leading, main, major, pre-eminent, principal, prominent; fatal; excellent, first-class, first-rate, good, prime, splendid. • n chief city, metropolis, seat; money, estate, investments, shares, stock.

caprice n crotchet, fancy, fickleness, freak, humor, inconstancy, maggot, phantasy, quirk, vagary, whim, whimsy.

capricious adj changeable, crotchety, fanciful, fantastical, fickle, fitful, freakish, humorsome, odd, puckish, queer, uncertain, variable, wayward, whimsical.

capsize vb overturn, upset.

capsule n case, covering, envelope, sheath, shell, wrapper: pericarp, pod, seed-vessel.

captain vb command, direct, head, lead, manage, officer, preside. • n chief, chieftain, commander, leader, master, officer, soldier, warrior.

captious adj carping, caviling, censorious, critical, fault-finding, hypercritical; acrimonious, cantankerous, contentious, crabbed, cross, snappish, snarling, splenetic, testy, touchy, waspish; ensnaring, insidious.

captivate vb allure, attract, bewitch, catch, capture, charm, enamor, enchant, enthral, fascinate, gain, hypnotize, infatuate, win.

captivity n confinement, durance, duress, imprisonment; bondage, enthralment, servitude, slavery, subjection, thraldom, vassalage.

capture vb apprehend, arrest, catch, seize. • n apprehension, arrest, catch, catching, imprisonment, seizure; bag, prize.

carcass n body, cadaver, corpse, corse, remains.

cardinal adj capital, central, chief, essential, first, important, leading, main, pre-eminent, primary, principal, vital.

care n anxiety, concern, perplexity, trouble, solicitude, worry; attention, carefulness, caution, circumspection, heed, regard, vigilance, wariness, watchfulness; charge, custody, guardianship, keep, oversight, superintendence, ward; burden, charge, concern, responsibility.

careful adj anxious, solicitous, concerned, troubled, uneasy; attentive, heedful, mindful, regardful, thoughtful; cautious, canny, circumspect, discreet, leery, vigilant, watchful.

careless adj carefree, nonchalant, unapprehensive, undisturbed, unperplexed, unsolicitous, untroubled; disregardful, heedless, inattentive, incautious, inconsiderate, neglectful, negligent, regardless, remiss, thoughtless, unobservant, unconcerned, unconsidered, unmindful, unthinking.

carelessness n heedlessness, inadvertence, inattention, inconsiderateness, neglect, negligence, remissness, slackness, thoughtlessness, unconcern.

caress vb coddle, cuddle, cosset, embrace, fondle, hug, kiss, pet. • n cuddle, embrace, fondling, hug, kiss.

caressing n blandishment, dalliance, endearment, fondling.

cargo n freight, lading load.

caricature vb burlesque, parody, send-up, take-off, travesty. • n burlesque, farce, ludicrous, parody, representation, take-off, travesty.

carious adj decayed, mortified, putrid, rotten, ulcerated.

cark vb annoy, fret, grieve, harass, perplex, worry.

carnage n bloodshed, butchery, havoc, massacre, murder, slaughter.

carnal adj animal, concupiscent, fleshly, lascivious, lecherous, lewd, libidinous, lubricous, lustful, salacious, sensual, voluptuous; bodily, earthy, mundane. natural, secular, temporal, unregenerate, unspiritual.

carol vb chant, hum, sing, warble. • n canticle, chorus, ditty, hymn, lay, song, warble.

carousal n banquet, entertainment, feast, festival, merry-making, regale; bacchanal, carouse, debauch, jamboree, jollification, orgy, revel, reveling, revelry, saturnalia, spree, wassail.

carp vb cavil, censure, criticize, fault.

carping adj captious, cavilling, censorious, hypercritical. • n cavil, censure, faultfinding, hypercriticism.

carriage n conveyance, vehicle; air, bearing, behavior, conduct, demeanor, deportment, front, mien, port.

carry vb bear, convey, transfer, transmit, transport; impel, push forward, urge; accomplish, compass, effect, gain, secure; bear up, support, sustain; infer, involve, imply, import, signify.

cart n conveyance, tumbril, van, vehicle, wagon.

carte-blanche n authority, power.

carve vb chisel, cut, divide, engrave, grave, hack, hew, indent, incise, sculpt, sculpture; fashion, form, mold, shape.

cascade vb cataract, descend, drop, engulf, fall, inundate, overflow, plunge, tumble. • n cataract, fall, falls, force, linn, waterfall.

case[1] vb cover, encase, enclose, envelop, protect, wrap; box, pack. • n capsule, covering, sheathe; box, cabinet, container, holder, receptacle.

case[2] n condition, plight, predicament, situation, state; example, instance, occurrence; circumstance, condition, contingency, event; action, argument, cause, lawsuit, process, suit, trial.

case-hardened adj hardened, indurated, steeled; brazen, brazen-faced, obdurate, reprobate.

cash n banknotes, bullion, coin, currency, money, payment, specie.

cashier vb break, discard, discharge, dismiss.

cast vb fling, hurl, pitch, send, shy, sling, throw, toss; drive, force, impel, thrust; lay aside, put off, shed; calculate, compute, reckon; communicate, diffuse, impart, shed, throw. • n fling, throw, toss; shade, tinge, tint, touch; air, character, look, manner, mien, style, tone, turn; form, mold.

castaway adj abandoned, cast-off, discarded, rejected. • n derelict, outcast, reprobate, vagabond.

caste n class, grade, lineage, order, race, rank, species, status.

castigate vb beat, chastise, flog, lambaste, lash, thrash, whip; chaste, correct, discipline, punish; criticize, flagellate, upbraid.

castle n citadel, fortress, stronghold.

castrate vb caponize, emasculate, geld; mortify, subdue, suppress, weaken.

casual adj accidental, contingent, fortuitous, incidental, irregular, occasional, random, uncertain, unforeseen, unintentional, unpremeditated; informal, relaxed.

casualty n chance, contingency, fortuity, mishap; accident, catastrophe, disaster, mischance, misfortune.

cat n grimalkin, kitten, puss, tabby, tomcat.

cataclysm n deluge, flood, inundation; disaster, upheaval.

catacomb n crypt, tomb, vault.

catalog vb alphabetize, categorize, chronicle, class, classify, codify, file, index, list, record, tabulate. • n enumeration, index, inventory, invoice, list, record, register, roll, schedule.

cataract n cascade, fall, waterfall.

catastrophe n conclusion, consummation,

denouement, end, finale, issue, termination, upshot; adversity, blow, calamity, cataclysm, debacle, disaster, ill, misfortune, mischance, mishap, trial, trouble.

catch vb clutch, grasp, gripe, nab, seize, snatch; apprehend, arrest, capture; overtake; enmesh, ensnare, entangle, entrap, lime, net; bewitch, captivate, charm, enchant, fascinate, win; surprise, take unawares. • n arrest, capture, seizure; bag, find, haul, plum, prize; drawback, fault, hitch, obstacle, rub, snag; captive, conquest.

catching adj communicable, contagious, infectious, pestiferous, pestilential; attractive, captivating, charming, enchanting, fascinating, taking, winning, winsome.

catechize adj examine, interrogate, question, quiz.

catechumen n convert, disciple, learner, neophyte, novice, proselyte, pupil, tyro.

categorical adj absolute, direct, downright, emphatic, explicit, express, positive, unconditional, unqualified, unreserved, utter.

category n class, division, head, heading, list, order, rank, sort.

catenation n conjunction, connection, union.

cater vb feed, provide, purvey.

cathartic adj abstergent, aperient, cleansing, evacuant, laxative, purgative. • n aperient, laxative, physic, purgative, purge.

catholic adj general, universal, world-wide; charitable, liberal, tolerant, unbigoted, unexclusive, unsectarian.

cause vb breed, create, originate, produce; effect, effectuate, occasion, produce. • n agent, creator, mainspring, origin, original, producer, source, spring; account, agency, consideration, ground, incentive, incitement, inducement, motive, reason; aim, end, object, purpose; action, case, suit, trial.

caustic adj acrid, cathartic, consuming, corroding, corrosive, eating, erosive, mordant, virulent; biting, bitter, burning, cutting, sarcastic, satirical, scalding, scathing, severe, sharp, stinging.

caution vb admonish, forewarn, warn. • n care, carefulness, circumspection, discretion, forethought, heed, heedfulness, providence, prudence, wariness, vigilance, watchfulness; admonition, advice, counsel, injunction, warning.

cautious adj careful, chary, circumspect,

discreet, heedful, prudent, wary, vigilant, wary, watchful.

cavalier adj arrogant, curt, disdainful, haughty, insolent, scornful, supercilious; debonair, gallant, gay. • n chevalier, equestrian, horseman, horse-soldier, knight.

cave n cavern, cavity, den, grot, grotto.

cavil vb carp, censure, hypercriticize, object.

caviling adj captious, carping, censorious, critical, hypercritical.

cavity n hollow, pocket, vacuole, void.

cease vb desist, intermit, pause, refrain, stay, stop; fail; discontinue, end, quit, terminate.

ceaseless adj continual, continuous, incessant, unceasing, unintermitting, uninterrupted, unremitting; endless, eternal, everlasting, perpetual.

cede vb abandon, abdicate, relinquish, resign, surrender, transfer, yield; convey, grant.

celebrate vb applaud, bless, commend, emblazon, extol, glorify, laud, magnify, praise, trumpet; commemorate, honor, keep, observe; solemnize.

celebrated adj distinguished, eminent, famed, famous, glorious, illustrious, notable, renowned.

celebrity n credit, distinction, eminence, fame, glory, honor, renown, reputation, repute; lion, notable, star.

celerity n fleetness, haste, quickness, rapidity, speed, swiftness, velocity.

celestial adj empyreal, empyrean; angelic, divine, god-like, heavenly, seraphic, supernal, supernatural.

celibate adj single, unmarried. • n bachelor, single, virgin.

cellular adj alveolate, honeycombed.

cement vb attach, bind, join, combine, connect, solder, unite, weld; cohere, stick. • n glue, paste, mortar, solder.

cemetery n burial-ground, burying-ground, churchyard, god's acre, graveyard, necropolis.

censor vb blue-pencil, bowdlerize, cut, edit, expurgate; classify, kill, quash, squash, suppress. • n caviller, censurer, faultfinder.

censorious adj captious, carping, caviling, condemnatory, faultfinding, hypercritical, severe.

censure vb abuse, blame, chide, condemn, rebuke, reprehend, reprimand, reproach, reprobate, reprove, scold, upbraid. • n animadversion, blame, condemnation, criticism, disapprobation, disapproval, rebuke, remonstrance, reprehension, reproach, reproof, stricture.

ceremonious adj civil, courtly, lofty, stately; formal, studied; exact, formal, punctilious, precise, starched, stiff.

ceremony n ceremonial, etiquette, form, formality, observance, solemnity, rite; parade, pomp, show, stateliness.

certain adj absolute, incontestable, incontrovertible, indisputable, indubitable, positive, undeniable, undisputed, unquestionable, unquestioned; assured, confident, sure, undoubting; infallible, neverfailing, unfailing; actual, existing, real; constant, determinate, fixed, settled, stated.

certainty n indubitability, indubitableness, inevitableness, inevitability, surety, unquestionability, unquestionableness; assurance, assuredness, certitude, confidence, conviction, surety.

certify vb attest, notify, testify, vouch; ascertain, determine, verify, show.

cerulean adj azure, blue, sky-blue.

cessation n ceasing, discontinuance, intermission, pause, remission, respite, rest, stop, stoppage, suspension.

cession n abandonment, capitulation, ceding, concession, conveyance, grant, relinquishement, renunciation, surrender, yielding.

chafe vb rub; anger, annoy, chagrin, enrage, exasperate, fret, gall, incense, irritate, nettle, offend, provoke, ruffle, tease, vex; fret, fume, rage.

chaff vb banter, deride, jeer, mock, rally, ridicule, scoff. • n glumes, hulls, husks; refuse, rubbish, trash, waste.

chaffer n bargain, haggle, higgle, negotiate.

chagrin vb annoy, chafe, displease, irritate, mortify, provoke, vex. • n annoyance, displeasure, disquiet, dissatisfaction, fretfulness, humiliation, ill-humor, irritation, mortification, spleen, vexation.

chain vb bind, confine, fetter, manacle, restrain, shackle, trammel; enslave. • n bond, fetter, manacle, shackle, union.

chalice n bowl, cup, goblet.

challenge vb brave, call out, dare, defy, dispute; demand, require. • n defiance, interrogation, question; exception, objection.

chamber n apartment, hall, room; cavity, hollow.

champion vb advocate, defend, uphold. • n

defender, promoter, protector, vindicator; belt-holder, hero, victor, warrior, winner.

chance vb befall, betide, happen, occur. • adj accidental, adventitious, casual, fortuitous, incidental, unexpected, unforeseen. • n accident, cast, fortuity, fortune, hap, luck; contingency, possibility; occasion, opening, opportunity; contingency, fortuity, gamble, peradventure, uncertainty; hazard, jeopardy, peril, risk.

change vb alter, fluctuate, modify, vary; displace, remove, replace, shift, substitute; barter, commute, exchange. • n alteration, mutation, revolution, transition, transmutation, turning, variance, variation; innovation, novelty, variety, vicissitude.

changeable adj alterable, inconstant, modifiable, mutable, uncertain, unsettled, unstable, unsteadfast, unsteady, variable, variant; capricious, fickle, fitful, flighty, giddy, mercurial, vacillating, volatile, wavering.

changeless adj abiding, consistent, constant, fixed, immutable, permanent, regular, reliable, resolute, settled, stationary, unalterable, unchanging.

channel vb chamfer, cut, flute, groove. • n canal, conduit, duct, passage; aqueduct, canal, chute, drain, flume, furrow; chamfer, groove, fluting, furrow, gutter.

chant vb carol, sing, warble; intone, recite; canticle, song.

chaos n anarchy, confusion, disorder.

chapfallen adj blue, crest-fallen, dejected, depressed, despondent, discouraged, disheartened, dispirited, downcast, downhearted, low-spirited, melancholy, sad.

chaplet n coronal, garland, wreath.

char vb burn, scorch.

character n emblem, figure, hieroglyph, ideograph, letter, mark, sign, symbol; bent, constitution, cast, disposition, nature, quality; individual, original, person, personage; reputation, repute; nature, traits; eccentric, trait.

characteristic adj distinctive, peculiar, singular, special, specific, typical. • n attribute, feature, idiosyncrasy, lineament, mark, peculiarity, quality, trait.

charge vb burden, encumber, freight, lade, load; entrust; ascribe, impute, lay; accuse, arraign, blame, criminate, impeach, inculpate, indict, involve; bid, command, exhort, enjoin, order, require, tax; assault, attack bear down. • n burden, cargo, freight, lading, load; care, custody, keeping, management, ward; commission, duty, employment, office, trust; responsibility, trust; command, direction, injunction, mandate, order, precept; exhortation, instruction; cost, debit, expense, expenditure, outlay; price, sum; assault, attack, encounter, onset, onslaught.

charger n dish, platter; mount, steed, war-horse.

charily adv carefully, cautiously, distrustfully, prudently, sparingly, suspiciously, warily.

charitable adj beneficial, beneficent, benignant, bountiful, generous, kind, liberal, open-handed; candid, considerate, lenient, mild.

charity n benevolence, benignity, fellow-feeling, good-nature, goodwill, kind-heartedness, kindness, tenderheartedness; beneficence, bounty, generosity, humanity, philanthropy liberality.

charlatan n cheat, empiric, impostor, mountebank, pretender, quack.

charm vb allure, attract, becharm, bewitch, captivate, catch, delight, enamor, enchain, enchant, enrapture, enravish, fascinate, transport, win. • n enchantment, incantation, magic, necromancy, sorcery, spell, witchery; amulet, talisman; allurement, attraction, attractiveness, fascination.

charming adj bewitching, captivating, delightful, enchanting, enrapturing, fascinating, lovely.

charter vb incorporate; hire, let. • n franchise, immunity, liberty, prerogation, privilege, right; bond, deed, indenture, instrument, prerogative.

chary adj careful, cautious, circumspect, shy, wary; abstemious, careful, choice, economical, frugal, provident, saving, sparing, temperate, thrifty, unwasteful.

chase vb follow, hunt, pursue, track; emboss. • n course, field-sport, hunt, hunting.

chasm n cavity, cleft, fissure, gap, hollow, hiatus, opening.

chaste adj clean, continent, innocent, modest, pure, pure-minded, undefiled, virtuous; chastened, pure, simple, unaffected, uncorrupt.

chasten vb correct, humble; purify, refine, render, subdue.

chastening n chastisement, correction, discipline, humbling.

chastise vb castigate, correct, flog, lash,

punish, whip; chasten, correct, discipline, humble, punish, subdue.

chastity n abstinence, celibacy, continence, innocence, modesty, pure-mindedness, purity, virtue; cleanness, decency; chasteness, refinement, restrainedness, simplicity, sobriety, unaffectedness.

chat vb babble, chatter, confabulate, gossip, prate, prattle. • n chit-chat, confabulation, conversation, gossip, prattle.

chatter vb babble, chat, confabulate, gossip, prate, prattle. • n babble, chat, gabble, jabber, patter, prattle.

cheap adj inexpensive, low-priced; common, indifferent, inferior, mean, meretricious, paltry, poor.

cheapen vb belittle, depreciate.

cheat vb cozen, deceive, dissemble, juggle, shuffle; bamboozle, befool, beguile, cajole, circumvent, deceive, defraud, chouse, delude, dupe, ensnare, entrap, fool, gammon, gull, hoax, hoodwink, inveigle, jockey, mislead, outwit, overreach, trick. • n artifice, beguilement, blind, catch, chouse, deceit, deception, fraud, imposition, imposture, juggle, pitfall, snare, stratagem, swindle, trap, trick, wile; counterfeit, deception, delusion, illusion, mockery, paste, sham, tinsel; beguiler, charlatan, cheater, cozener, impostor, jockey, knave, mountebank, trickster, rogue, render, sharper, seizer, shuffler, swindler, taker, tearer.

check vb block, bridle, control, counteract, curb, hinder, obstruct, repress, restrain; chide, rebuke, reprimand, reprove. • n bar, barrier, block, brake, bridle, clog, control, curb, damper, hindrance, impediment, interference, obstacle, obstruction, rebuff, repression, restraint, stop, stopper.

cheep vb chirp, creak, peep, pipe, squeak.

cheer vb animate, encourage, enliven, exhilarate, gladden, incite, inspirit; comfort, console, solace; applaud, clap. • n cheerfulness, gaiety, gladness, glee, hilarity, jollity, joy, merriment, mirth; entertainment, food, provision, repast, viands, victuals; acclamation, hurrah, huzza.

cheerful adj animated, airy, blithe, buoyant, cheery, gay, glad, gleeful, happy, joyful, jocund, jolly, joyous, light-hearted, lightsome, lively, merry, mirthful, sprightly, sunny; animating, cheering, cheery, encouraging, enlivening, glad, gladdening, gladsome, grateful, inspiriting, jocund, pleasant.

cheerless adj dark, dejected, desolate,

despondent, disconsolate, discouraged, dismal, doleful, dreary, forlorn, gloomy, joyless, low-spirited, lugubrious, melancholy, mournful, rueful, sad, somber, spiritless, woe-begone.

cherish *vb* comfort, foster, nourish, nurse, nurture, support, sustain; treasure; encourage, entertain, indulge, harbor.

chest *n* box, case, coffer; breast, thorax, trunk.

chew *vb* crunch, manducate, masticate, munch; bite, champ, gnaw; meditate, ruminate.

chicanery *n* chicane, deception, duplicity, intrigue, intriguing, sophistication, sophistry, stratagems, tergiversation, trickery, wiles, wire-pulling.

chide *vb* admonish, blame, censure, rebuke, reprimand, reprove, scold, upbraid; chafe, clamor, fret, fume, scold.

chief *adj* first, foremost, headmost, leading, master, supereminent, supreme, top; capital, cardinal, especial, essential, grand, great, main, master, paramount, prime, principal, supreme, vital. • *n* chieftain, commander; head, leader.

chiffonier *n* cabinet, sideboard.

child *n* babe, baby, bairn, bantling, brat, chit, infant, nursling, suckling, wean; issue, offspring, progeny.

childbirth *n* child-bearing, delivery, labor, parturition, travail.

childish *adj* infantile, juvenile, puerile, tender, young; foolish, frivolous, silly, trifling, weak.

childlike *adj* docile, dutiful, gentle, meek, obedient, submissive; confiding, guileless, ingenuous, innocent, simple, trustful, uncrafty.

chill *vb* dampen, depress, deject, discourage, dishearten. • *adj* bleak, chilly, cold, frigid, gelid. • *n* chilliness, cold, coldness, frigidity; ague, rigor, shiver; damp, depression.

chime *vb* accord, harmonize. • *n* accord, consonance.

chimera *n* crochet, delusion, dream, fantasy, hallucination, illusion, phantom.

chimerical *adj* delusive, fanciful, fantastic, illusory, imaginary, quixotic, shadowy, unfounded, visionary, wild.

chink[1] *vb* cleave, crack, fissure, crevasse, incise, split, slit. • *n* aperture, cleft, crack, cranny, crevice, fissure, gap, opening, slit.

chink[2] *vb, n* jingle, clink, ring, ting, tink, tinkle.

chip *vb* flake, fragment, hew, pare, scrape. • *n* flake, fragment, paring, scrap.

chirp *vb* cheep, chirrup, peep, twitter.

chirrup *vb* animate, cheer, encourage, inspirit.

chisel *vb* carve, cut, gouge, sculpt, sculpture.

chivalrous *adj* adventurous, bold, brave, chivalric, gallant, knightly, valiant, warlike; gallant, generous, high-minded, magnanimous.

chivalry *n* knighthood, knight-errantry; courtesy, gallantry, politeness; courage, valor.

choice *adj* excellent, exquisite, precious, rare, select, superior, uncommon, unusual, valuable; careful, chary, frugal, sparing. • *n* alternative, election, option, selection; favorite, pick, preference.

choke *vb* gag, smother, stifle, strangle, suffocate, throttle; overcome, overpower, smother, suppress; bar, block, close, obstruct, stop.

choleric *adj* angry, fiery, hasty, hot, fiery, irascible, irritable, passionate, petulant, testy, touchy, waspish.

choose *vb* adopt, co-opt, cull, designate, elect, pick, predestine, prefer, select.

chop *vb* cut, hack, hew; mince; shift, veer. • *n* slice; brand, quality; chap, jaw.

chouse *vb* bamboozle, beguile, cheat, circumvent, cozen, deceive, defraud, delude, dupe, gull, hoodwink, overreach, swindle, trick, victimize. • *n* cully, dupe, gull, simpleton, tool; artifice, cheat, circumvention, deceit, deception, delusion, double-dealing, fraud, imposition, imposture, ruse, stratagem, trick, wile.

christen *vb* baptize; call, dub, denominate, designate, entitle, name, style, term, title.

chronic *adj* confirmed, continuing, deep-seated, inveterate, rooted.

chronicle *vb* narrate, record, register. • *n* diary, journal, register; account, annals, history, narration, recital, record.

chuckle *vb* crow, exult, giggle, laugh, snigger, titter. • *n* giggle, laughter, snigger, titter.

chum *n* buddy, companion, comrade, crony, friend, mate, pal.

churl *n* boor, bumpkin, clodhopper, clown, countryman, lout, peasant, ploughman, rustic; curmudgeon, hunks, miser, niggard, scrimp, skinflint.

churlish *adj* brusque, brutish, cynical, harsh, impolite, rough, rude, snappish, snarling, surly, uncivil, waspish; crabbed, ill-tempered, morose, sullen; close, close-fisted, illiberal, mean, miserly, niggardly, penurious, stingy.

churn *vb* agitate, jostle.

cicatrice *n* cicatrix, mark, scar, seam.

cicesbeo *n* beau, escort, gallant, gigolo.

cincture *n* band, belt, cestos, cestus, girdle.

cipher *n* naught, nothing, zero; character, device, monogram, symbol; nobody, nonentity.

circle *vb* compass, encircle, encompass, gird, girdle, ring; gyrate, revolve, rotate, round, turn. • *n* circlet, corona, gyre, hoop, ring, rondure; circumference, cordon, periphery; ball, globe, orb, sphere; compass, enclosure; class, clique, company, coterie, fraternity, set, society; bounds, circuit, compass, field, province, range, region, sphere.

circuit *n* ambit, circumambience, circumambiency, cycle, revolution, turn; bounds, district, field, province, range, region, space, sphere, tract; boundary, compass; course, detour, perambulation, round, tour.

circuitous *adj* ambiguous, devious, indirect, roundabout, tortuous, turning, winding.

circulate *vb* diffuse, disseminate, promulgate, propagate, publish, spread.

circumference *n* bound, boundary, circuit, girth, outline, perimeter, periphery.

circumlocution *n* circuitousness, obliqueness, periphrase, periphrasis, verbosity, wordiness.

circumscribe *vb* bound, define, encircle, enclose, encompass, limit, surround; confine, restrict.

circumspect *adj* attentive, careful, cautious, considerate, discreet, heedful, judicious, observant, prudent, vigilant, wary, watchful.

circumstance *n* accident, incident; condition, detail, event, fact, happening, occurrence, position, situation.

circumstantial *adj* detailed, particular; indirect, inferential, presumptive.

circumvent *vb* check, checkmate, outgeneral, thwart; bamboozle, beguile, cheat, chouse, cozen, deceive, defraud, delude, dupe, gull, hoodwink, inveigle, mislead, outwit, overreach, trick.

circumvention *n* cheat, cheating, chicanery, deceit, deception, duplicity, fraud, guile, imposition, imposture, indirection, trickery, wiles.

cistern *n* basin, pond, reservoir, tank.

citation *n* excerpt, extract, quotation; enumeration, mention, quotation, quoting.

cite *vb* adduce, enumerate, extract, mention, name, quote; call, summon.

citizen *n* burgess, burgher, denizen, dweller, freeman, inhabitant, resident, subject, townsman.

civil *adj* civic, municipal, political; domestic; accommodating, affable, civilized, complaisant, courteous, courtly, debonair, easy, gracious, obliging, polished, polite, refined, suave, urbane, well-bred, well-mannered.

civility *n* affability, amiability, complaisance, courteousness, courtesy, good-breeding, politeness, suavity, urbanity.

civilize *vb* cultivate, educate, enlighten, humanize, improve, polish, refine.

claim *vb* ask, assert, challenge, demand, exact, require. • *n* call, demand, lien, requisition; pretension, privilege, right, title.

clammy *adj* adhesive, dauby, glutinous, gummy, ropy, smeary, sticky, viscid, viscous; close, damp, dank, moist, sticky, sweaty.

clamor *vb* shout, vociferate. • *n* blare, din, exclamation, hullabaloo, noise, outcry, uproar, vociferation.

clan *n* family, phratry, race, sect, tribe; band, brotherhood, clique, coterie, fraternity, gang, set, society, sodality.

clandestine *adj* concealed, covert, fraudulent, furtive, hidden, private, secret, sly, stealthy, surreptitious, underhand.

clap *vb* pat, slap, strike; force, slam; applaud, cheer. • *n* blow, knock, slap; bang, burst, explosion, peal, slam.

clarify *vb* cleanse, clear, depurate, purify, strain.

clash *vb* collide, crash, strike; clang, clank, clatter, crash, rattle; contend, disagree, interfere. • *n* collision; clang, clangor, clank, clashing, clatter, crash, rattle; contradiction, disagreement, interference, jar, jarring, opposition.

clasp *vb* clutch, entwine, grasp, grapple, grip, seize; embrace, enfold, fold, hug. • *n* buckle, catch, hasp, hook; embrace, hug.

class *vb* arrange, classify, dispose, distribute, range, rank. • *n* form, grade, order, rank, status; group, seminar; breed, kind, sort; category, collection, denomination, division, group, head.

classical *adj* first-rate, master, masterly, model, standard; Greek, Latin, Roman; Attic, chaste, elegant, polished, pure, refined.

classify *vb* arrange, assort, categorize, class,

dispose, distribute, group, pigeonhole, rank, systematize, tabulate.

clatter *vb* clash, rattle; babble, clack, gabble, jabber, prate, prattle. • *n* clattering, clutter, rattling.

clause *n* article, condition, provision, stipulation.

claw *vb* lacerate, scratch, tear. • *n* talon, ungula.

clean *vb* cleanse, clear, purge, purify, rinse, scour, scrub, wash, wipe. • *adj* immaculate, spotless, unsmirched, unsoiled, unspotted, unstained, unsullied, white; clarified, pure, purified, unadulterated, unmixed; adroit, delicate, dextrous, graceful, light, neat, shapely; complete, entire, flawless, faultless, perfect, unabated, unblemished, unimpaired, whole; chaste, innocent, moral, pure, undefiled. • *adv* altogether, completely, entirely, perfectly, quite, thoroughly, wholly.

cleanse *vb* clean, clear, elutriate, purge, purify, rinse, scour, scrub, wash, wipe.

clear *vb* clarify, cleanse, purify, refine; emancipate, disenthral, free, liberate, loose; absolve, acquit, discharge, exonerate, justify, vindicate; disembarrass, disengage, disentangle, extricate, loosen, rid; clean up, scour, sweep; balance; emancipate, free, liberate. • *adj* bright, crystalline, light, limpid, luminous, pellucid, transparent; pure, unadulterated, unmixed; free, open, unencumbered, unobstructed; cloudless, fair, serene, sunny, unclouded, undimmed, unobscured; net; distinct, intelligible, lucid, luminous, perspicuous; apparent, conspicuous, distinct, evident, indisputable, manifest, obvious, palpable, unambiguous, undeniable, unequivocal, unmistakable, unquestionable, visible; clean, guiltless, immaculate, innocent, irreproachable, sinless, spotless, unblemished, undefiled, unspotted, unsullied; unhampered, unimpeded, unobstructed; euphonious, fluty, liquid, mellifluous, musical, silvery, sonorous.

cleave[1] *vb* crack, divide, open, part, rend, rive, sever, split, sunder.

cleave[2] *vb* adhere, cling, cohere, hold, stick.

cleft *adj* bifurcated, cloven, forked. • *n* breach, break, chasm, chink, cranny, crevice, fissure, fracture, gap, interstice, opening, rent, rift.

clemency *n* mildness, softness; compassion, fellow-feeling, forgivingness, gentleness,

kindness, lenience, leniency, lenity, mercifulness, mercy, mildness, tenderness.

clement *adj* compassionate, forgiving, gentle, humane, indulgent, kind, kindhearted, lenient, merciful, mild, tender, tender-hearted.

clench *vb* close tightly, grip; fasten, fix, rivet, secure.

clergy *n* clergymen, the cloth, ministers.

clever *adj* able, apt, gifted, talented; adroit, capable, dextrous, discerning, expert, handy, ingenious, knowing, quick, ready, skillful, smart, talented.

click *vb* beat, clack, clink, tick. • *n* beat, clack, clink, tick; catch, detent, pawl, ratchet.

cliff *n* crag, palisade, precipice, scar, steep.

climate *n* clime, temperature, weather; country, region.

climax *vb* consummate, crown, culminate, peak. • *n* acme, consummation, crown, culmination, head, peak, summit, top, zenith.

clinch *vb* clasp, clench, clutch, grapple, grasp, grip; fasten, secure; confirm, establish, fix. • *n* catch, clutch, grasp, grip; clincher, clamp, cramp, holdfast.

cling *vb* adhere, clear, stick; clasp, embrace, entwine.

clink *vb*, *n* chink, jingle, ring, tinkle; chime, rhyme.

clip *vb* cut, shear, snip; curtail, cut, dock, pare, prune, trim. • *n* cutting, shearing; blow, knock, lick, rap, thump, thwack, thump.

clique *n* association, brotherhood, cabal, camarilla, clan, club, coterie, gang, junta, party, ring, set, sodality.

cloak *vb* conceal, cover, dissemble, hide, mask, veil. • *n* mantle, surcoat; blind, cover, mask, pretext, veil.

clock *vb* mark time, measure, stopwatch; clock up, record, register. • *n* chronometer, horologue, timekeeper, timepiece, timer, watch.

clog *vb* fetter, hamper, shackle, trammel; choke, obstruct; burden, cumber, embarrass, encumber, hamper, hinder, impede, load, restrain, trammel. • *n* dead-weight, drag-weight, fetter, shackle, trammel; check, drawback, encumbrance, hindrance, impediment, obstacle, obstruction.

cloister *n* abbey, convent, monastery, nunnery, priory; arcade, colonnade, piazza.

close[1] *adj* closed, confined, snug, tight; hidden, private, secret; incommunicative, reserved, reticent, secretive, taciturn; concealed, retired, secluded, withdrawn; confined, motionless, stagnant; airless, oppressive, stale, stifling, stuffy, sultry; compact, compressed, dense, form, solid, thick; adjacent, adjoining, approaching, immediately, near, nearly, neighboring; attached, dear, confidential, devoted, intimate; assiduous, earnest, fixed, intense, intent, unremitting; accurate, exact, faithful, nice, precise, strict; churlish, close-fisted, curmudgeonly, mean, illiberal, miserly, niggardly, parsimonious, penurious, stingy, ungenerous. • *n* courtyard, enclosure, grounds, precinct, yard.

close[2] *vb* occlude, seal, shut; choke, clog, estop, obstruct, stop; cease, complete, concede, end, finish, terminate; coalesce, unite; cease, conclude, finish, terminate; clinch, grapple; agree. • *n* cessation, conclusion, end, finish, termination.

closet *n* cabinet, retiring-room; press, store-room.

clot *vb* coagulate, concrete. • *n* coagulation, concretion, lump.

clothe *vb* array, attire, deck, dress, rig; cover, endow, envelop, enwrap, invest with, swathe.

clothes *n* apparel, array, attire, clothing, costume, dress, garb, garments, gear, habiliments, habits, raiment, rig, vestments, vesture.

cloud *vb* becloud, obnubilate, overcast, overspread; befog, darken, dim, obscure, shade, shadow. • *n* cirrus, cumulus, fog, haze, mist, nebulosity, scud, stratus, vapor; army, crowd, horde, host, multitude, swarm, throng; darkness, eclipse, gloom, obscuration, obscurity.

cloudy *adj* clouded, filmy, foggy, hazy, lowering, lurid, murky, overcast; confused, dark, dim, obscure; depressing, dismal, gloomy, sullen; clouded, mottled; blurred, dimmed, lusterless, muddy.

clown *n* churl, clod-breaker, clodhopper, hind, husbandman, lubber; boor, bumpkin, churl, fellow, lout; blockhead, dolt, clodpoll, dunce, dunderhead, numbskull, simpleton, thickhead; buffoon, droll, farceur, fool, harlequin, jack-a-dandy, jack-pudding, jester, merry-andrew, mime, pantaloon, pickle-herring, punch, scaramouch, zany.

clownish *adj* awkward, boorish, clumsy, coarse, loutish, ungainly, rough, rustic; churlish, ill-bred, ill-mannered, impolite, rude, uncivil.

cloy *vb* glut, pall, sate, satiate, surfeit.

club *vb* combine, unite; beat, bludgeon, cudgel. • *n* bat, bludgeon, cosh, cudgel, hickory, shillelagh, stick, truncheon; association, company, coterie, fraternity, set, society, sodality.

clump *vb* assemble, batch, bunch, cluster, group, lump; lumber, stamp, stomp, stump, trudge. • *n* assemblage, bunch, cluster, collection, group, patch, tuft.

clumsy *adj* botched, cumbrous, heavy, ill-made, ill-shaped, lumbering, ponderous, unwieldy; awkward, blundering, bungling, elephantine, heavy-handed, inapt, mal adroit, unhandy, unskilled.

cluster *vb* assemble, batch, bunch, clump, collect, gather, group, lump, throng. • *n* agglomeration, assemblage, batch, bunch, clump, collection, gathering, group, throng.

clutch[1] *vb* catch, clasp, clench, clinch, grab, grapple, grasp, grip, hold, seize, snatch, squeeze. • *n* clasp, clench, clinch, grasp, grip, hold, seizure, squeeze.

clutch[2] *n* aerie, brood, hatching, nest.

clutches *npl* claws, paws, talons; hands, power.

clutter *vb* confuse, disarrange, disarray, disorder, jumble, litter, mess, muss; clatter. • *n* bustle, clatter, clattering, racket; confusion, disarray, disorder, jumble, litter, mess, muss.

coadjutor *n* abettor, accomplice, aider, ally, assistant, associate, auxiliary, collaborator, colleague, cooperator, fellow-helper, helper, helpmate, partner.

coagulate *vb* clot, congeal, concrete, curdle, thicken.

coalesce *vb* amalgamate, blend, cohere, combine, commix, incorporate, mix, unite; concur, fraternize.

coalition *n* alliance, association, combination, compact, confederacy, confederation, conjunction, conspiracy, co-partnership, federation, league, union.

coarse *adj* crude, impure, rough, unpurified; broad, gross, indecent, indelicate, ribald, vulgar; bearish, bluff, boorish, brutish, churlish, clownish, gruff, impolite, loutish, rude, unpolished; crass, inelegant.

coast *vb* flow, glide, roll, skim, sail, slide,

sweep. • *n* littoral, seaboard, sea-coast, seaside, shore, strand; border.

coat *vb* cover, spread. • *n* cut-away, frock, jacket; coating, cover, covering; layer.

coax *vb* allure, beguile, cajole, cog, entice, flatter, persuade, soothe, wheedle.

cobble *vb* botch, bungle; mend, patch, repair, tinker.

cobweb *adj* flimsy, gauzy, slight, thin, worthless. • *n* entanglement, meshes, snare, toils.

cochleate *adj* cochlear, cochleary, cochleous, cochleated, spiral, spiry.

cockle *vb* corrugate, pucker, wrinkle.

coddle *vb* caress, cocker, fondle, humor, indulge, nurse, pamper, pet.

codger *n* churl, curmudgeon, hunks, lick-penny, miser, niggard, screw, scrimp, skin-flint.

codify *vb* condense, digest, summarize, systematize, tabulate.

coerce *vb* check, curb, repress, restrain, subdue; compel, constrain, drive, force, urge.

coercion *n* check, curb, repression, restraint; compulsion, constraint, force.

coeval *adj* coetaneous, coexistent, contemporaneous, contemporary, synchronous.

coexistent *adj* coetaneous, coeval, simultaneous, synchronous.

coffer *n* box, casket, chest, trunk; money-chest, safe, strongbox; caisson.

cogent *adj* compelling, conclusive, convincing, effective, forcible, influential, irresistible, persuasive, potent, powerful, resistless, strong, trenchant, urgent.

cogitate *vb* consider, deliberate, meditate, ponder, reflect, ruminate, muse, think, weigh.

cognate *adj* affiliated, affined, akin, allied, alike, analogous, connected, kindred, related, similar.

cognizance *n* cognition, knowing, knowledge, notice, observation.

cohere *vb* agree, coincide, conform, fit, square, suit.

coherence *n* coalition, cohesion, connection, dependence, union; agreement, congruity, consistency, correspondence, harmony, intelligibility, intelligible, meaning, rationality, unity.

coherent *adj* adherent, connected, united; congruous, consistent, intelligible, logical.

cohort *n* band, battalion, line, squadron.

coil *vb* curl, twine, twirl, twist, wind. • *n* convolution, curlicue, helix, knot, roll, spiral, tendril, twirl, volute, whorl; bustle, care, clamor, confusion, entanglements, perplexities, tumult, turmoil, uproar.

coin *vb* counterfeit, create, devise, fabricate, forge, form, invent, mint, originate, mold, stamp. • *n* coign, corner, quoin; key, plug, prop, wedge; cash, money, specie.

coincide *vb* cohere, correspond, square, tally; acquiesce, agree, harmonize, concur.

coincidence *n* corresponding, squaring, tallying; agreeing, concurrent, concurring.

cold *adj* arctic, biting, bleak, boreal, chill, chilly, cutting, frosty, gelid, glacial, icy, nipping, polar, raw, wintry; frost-bitten, shivering; apathetic, cold-blooded, dead, freezing, frigid, indifferent, lukewarm, passionless, phlegmatic, sluggish, stoical, stony, torpid, unconcerned, unfeeling, unimpressible, unresponsive, unsusceptible, unsympathetic; dead, dull, spiritless, unaffecting, uninspiring, uninteresting. • *n* chill, chilliness, coldness.

collapse *vb* break down, fail, fall. • *n* depression, exhaustion, failure, faint, prostration, sinking, subsidence.

collar *vb* apprehend, arrest, capture, grab, nab, seize. • *n* collarette, gorget, neckband, ruff, torque; band, belt, fillet, guard, ring, yoke.

collate *vb* adduce, collect, compare, compose.

collateral *adj* contingent, indirect, secondary, subordinate; concurrent, parallel; confirmatory, corroborative; accessory, accompanying, additional, ancillary, auxiliary, concomitant, contributory, simultaneous, supernumerary; consanguineous, related. • *n* guarantee, guaranty, security, surety, warranty; accessory, extra, nonessential, unessential; consanguinean, relative.

collation *n* luncheon, repast, meal.

colleague *n* aider, ally, assistant, associate, auxiliary, coadjutor, collaborator, companion, confederate, confrere, cooperator, helper, partner.

collect *vb* assemble, compile, gather, muster; accumulate, aggregate, amass, garner.

collected *adj* calm, composed, cool, placid, self-possessed, serene, unperturbed.

collection *n* aggregation, assemblage, cluster, crowd, drove, gathering, group, pack; accumulation, congeries, conglomeration, heap, hoard, lot, mass, pile, store; alms, contribution, offering, offertory.

colligate *vb* bind, combine, fasten, unite.

collision n clash, concussion, crash, encounter, impact, impingement, shock; conflict, crashing, interference, opposition.

collocate vb arrange, dispose, place, set.

colloquy n conference, conversation, dialogue, discourse, talk.

collude vb concert, connive, conspire.

collusion n connivance, conspiracy, coven, craft, deceit.

collusive adj conniving, conspiratorial, , dishonest, deceitful, deceptive, fraudulent.

colossal adj Cyclopean, enormous, gigantic, Herculean, huge, immense, monstrous, prodigious, vast.

color vb discolor, dye, paint, stain, tinge, tint; disguise, varnish; disguise, distort, garble, misrepresent, pervert; blush, flush, redden, show. • n hue, shade, tinge, tint, tone; paint, pigment, stain; redness, rosiness, ruddiness; complexion; appearance, disguise, excuse, guise, plea, pretence, pretext, semblance.

colorless adj achromatic, uncolored, untinged; blanched, hueless, livid, pale, pallid; blank, characterless, dull, expressionless, inexpressive, monotonous.

colours n banner, ensign, flag, standard.

column n pillar, pilaster; file, line, row.

coma n drowsiness, lethargy, somnolence, stupor, torpor; bunch, clump, cluster, tuft.

comatose adj drowsy, lethargic, sleepy, somnolent, stupefied.

comb vb card, curry, dress, groom, rake, unknot, untangle; rake, ransack, rummage, scour, search. • n card, hatchel, ripple; harrow, rake.

combat vb contend, contest, fight, struggle, war; battle, oppose, resist, struggle, withstand. • n action, affair, battle, brush, conflict, contest, encounter, fight, skirmish.

combative adj belligerent, contentious, militant, pugnacious, quarrelsome.

combination n association, conjunction, connection, union; alliance, cartel, coalition, confederacy, consolidation, league, merger, syndicate; cabal, clique, conspiracy, faction, junta, ring; amalgamation, compound, mixture.

combine vb cooperate, merge, pool, unite; amalgamate, blend, incorporate, mix.

combustible adj consumable, inflammable.

come vb advance, approach; arise, ensue, flow, follow, issue, originate, proceed, result; befall, betide, happen, occur.

comely adj becoming, decent, decorous, fitting, seemly, suitable; beautiful, fair, graceful, handsome, personable, pretty, symmetrical.

comfort vb alleviate, animate, cheer, console, encourage, enliven, gladden, inspirit, invigorate, refresh, revive, solace, soothe, strengthen. • n aid, assistance, countenance, help, support, succor; consolation, solace, encouragement, relief; ease, enjoyment, peace, satisfaction.

comfortable adj acceptable, agreeable, delightful, enjoyable, grateful, gratifying, happy, pleasant, pleasurable, welcome; commodious, convenient, easeful, snug; painless.

comfortless adj bleak, cheerless, desolate, drear, dreary, forlorn, miserable, wretched; broken-hearted, desolate, disconsolate, forlorn, heart-broken, inconsolable, miserable, woe-begone, wretched.

comical adj amusing, burlesque, comic, diverting, droll, farcical, funny, humorous, laughable, ludicrous, sportive, whimsical.

coming adj approaching, arising, arriving, ensuing, eventual, expected, forthcoming, future, imminent, issuing, looming, nearing, prospective, ultimate; emergent, emerging, successful; due, owed, owing. • n advent, approach, arrival; imminence, imminency, nearness; apparition, appearance, disclosure, emergence, manifestation, materialization, occurrence, presentation, revelation, rising.

comity n affability, amenity, civility, courtesy, politeness, suavity, urbanity.

command vb bid, charge, direct, enjoin, order, require; control, dominate, govern, lead, rule, sway; claim, challenge, compel, demand, exact. • n behest, bidding, charge, commandment, direction, hest, injunction, mandate, order, requirement, requisition; ascendency, authority, dominion, control, government, power, rule, sway, supremacy.

commander n captain, chief, chieftain, commandment, head, leader.

commemorate vb celebrate, keep, observe, solemnize.

commence vb begin, inaugurate, initiate, institute, open, originate, start.

commend vb assign, bespeak, confide, recommend, remit; commit, entrust, yield; applaud, approve, eulogize, extol, laud, praise.

commendation n approbation, approval,

good opinion, recommendation; praise, encomium, eulogy, panegyric.

commensurate *adj* commeasurable, commensurable; co-extensive, conterminous, equal; adequate, appropriate, corresponding, due, proportionate, proportioned, sufficient.

comment *vb* animadvert, annotate, criticize, explain, interpret, note, remark. • *n* annotation, elucidation, explanation, exposition, illustration, commentary, note, gloss; animadversion, observation, remark.

commentator *n* annotator, commentator, critic, expositor, expounder, interpreter.

commerce *n* business, exchange, dealing, trade, traffic; communication, communion, intercourse.

commercial *adj* mercantile, trading.

commination *n* denunciation, menace, threat, threatening.

commingle *vb* amalgamate, blend, combine, commix, intermingle, intermix, join, mingle, mix, unite.

comminute *vb* bray, bruise, grind, levigate, powder, pulverize, triturate.

commiserate *vb* compassionate, condole, pity, sympathize.

commiseration *n* compassion, pitying; condolence, pity, sympathy.

commission *vb* authorize, empower; delegate, depute. • *n* doing, perpetration; care, charge, duty, employment, errand, office, task, trust; allowance, compensation, fee, rake-off.

commissioner *n* agent, delegate, deputy.

commit *vb* confide, consign, delegate, entrust, remand; consign, deposit, lay, place, put, relegate, resign; do, enact, perform, perpetrate; imprison; engage, implicate, pledge.

commix *vb* amalgamate, blend, combine, commingle, compound, intermingle, mingle, mix, unite.

commodious *adj* advantageous, ample, comfortable, convenient, fit, proper, roomy, spacious, suitable, useful.

commodity *n* goods, merchandise, produce, wares.

common *adj* collective, public; general, useful; common-place, customary, everyday, familiar, frequent, habitual, usual; banal, hackneyed, stale, threadbare, trite; indifferent, inferior, low, ordinary, plebeian, popular, undistinguished, vulgar.

commonplace *adj* common, hackneyed, ordinary, stale, threadbare, trite. • *n*

banality, cliché, platitude; jotting, memoir, memorandum, note, reminder.

common-sense, common-sensical *adj* practical, sagacious, sensible, sober.

commotion *n* agitation, disturbance, ferment, perturbation, welter; ado, bustle, disorder, disturbance, hurly-burly, pother, tumult, turbulence, turmoil.

communicate *vb* bestow, confer, convey, give, impart, transmit; acquaint, announce, declare, disclose, divulge, publish, reveal, unfold; commune, converse, correspond.

communication *n* conveyance, disclosure, giving, imparting, transmittal; commence, conference, conversation, converse, correspondence, intercourse; announcement, dispatch, information, message, news.

communicative *adj* affable, chatty, conversable, free, open, sociable, unreserved.

communion *n* converse, fellowship, intercourse, participation; Eucharist, holy communion, Lord's Supper, sacrament.

community *n* commonwealth, people, public, society; association, brotherhood, college, society; likeness, participancy, sameness, similarity.

compact[1] *n* agreement, arrangement, bargain, concordant, contract, covenant, convention, pact, stipulation, treaty.

compact[2] *vb* compress, condense, pack, press; bind, consolidate, unite. • *adj* close, compressed, condensed, dense, firm, solid; brief, compendious, concise, laconic, pithy, pointed, sententious, short, succinct, terse.

companion *n* accomplice, ally, associate, comrade, compeer, confederate, consort, crony, friend, fellow, mate; partaker, participant, participator, partner, sharer.

companionable *adj* affable, conversable, familiar, friendly, genial, neighborly, sociable.

companionship *n* association, fellowship, friendship, intercourse, society.

company *n* assemblage, assembly, band, bevy, body, circle, collection, communication, concourse, congregation, coterie, crew, crowd, flock, gang, gathering, group, herd, rout, set, syndicate, troop; party; companionship, fellowship, guests, society, visitor, visitors; association, copartnership, corporation, firm, house, partnership.

compare *vb* assimilate, balance, collate, parallel; liken, resemble.

comparison n collation, compare, estimate; simile, similitude.

compartment n bay, cell, division, pigeon-hole, section.

compass vb embrace, encompass, enclose, encircle, environ, surround; beleaguer, beset, besiege, block, blockade, invest; accomplish, achieve, attain, carry, consummate, effect, obtain, perform, procure, realize; contrive, devise, intend, meditate, plot, purpose. • n bound, boundary, extent, gamut, limit, range, reach, register, scope, stretch; circuit, round.

compassion n clemency, commiseration, condolence, fellow-feeling, heart, humanity, kind-heartedness, kindness, kindliness, mercy, pity, rue, ruth, sorrow, sympathy, tenderheartedness, tenderness.

compassionate adj benignant, clement, commiserative, gracious, kind, merciful, pitying, ruthful, sympathetic, tender.

compatible adj accordant, agreeable to, congruous, consistent, consonant, reconcilable, suitable.

compeer n associate, comrade, companion, equal, fellow, mate, peer.

compel vb constrain, force, coerce, drive, necessitate, oblige; bend, bow, subdue, subject.

compend n abbreviation, abridgement, abstract, breviary, brief, compendium, conspectus, digest, epitome, précis, summary, syllabus, synopsis.

compendious adj abbreviated, abridged, brief, comprehensive, concise, short, succinct, summary.

compensate vb counterbalance, counterpoise, countervail; guerdon, recompense, reimburse, remunerate, reward; indemnify, reimburse, repay, requite; atone.

compensation n pay, payment, recompense, remuneration, reward, salary; amends, atonement, indemnification, indemnity, reparation, requital, satisfaction; balance, counterpoise, equalization, offset.

compete vb contend, contest, cope, emulate, rival, strive, struggle, vie.

competence n ability, capability, capacity, fitness, qualification, suitableness; adequacy, adequateness, enough, sufficiency.

competent adj able, capable, clever, equal, endowed, qualified; adapted, adequate, convenient, fit, sufficient, suitable.

competition n contest, emulation, rivalry, rivals.

competitor n adversary, antagonist, contestant, emulator, opponent.

compile vb compose, prepare, write; arrange, collect, select.

complacency n content, contentment, gratification, pleasure, satisfaction; affability, civility, complaisance, courtesy, politeness.

complacent adj contented, gratified, pleased, satisfied; affable, civil, complaisant, courteous, easy, gracious, grateful, obliging, polite, urbane.

complain vb bemoan, bewail, deplore, grieve, groan, grouch, grumble, lament, moan, murmur, repine, whine.

complainant n accuser, plaintiff.

complaining adj fault-finding, murmuring, querulous.

complaint n grievance, gripe, grumble, lament, lamentation, plaint, murmur, wail; ail, ailment, annoyance, disease, disorder, illness, indisposition, malady, sickness; accusation, charge, information

complete vb accomplish, achieve, conclude, consummate, do, effect, effectuate, end, execute, finish, fullfil, perfect, perform, realize, terminate. • adj clean, consummate, faultless, full, perfect, perform, thorough; all, entire, integral, total, unbroken, undiminished, undivided, unimpaired, whole; accomplished, achieved, completed, concluded, consummated, ended, finished.

completion n accomplishing, accomplishment, achieving, conclusion, consummation, effecting, effectuation, ending, execution, finishing, perfecting, performance, termination.

complex adj composite, compound, compounded, manifold, mingled, mixed; complicate, complicated, entangled, intricate, involved, knotty, mazy, tangled. • n complexus, complication, involute, skein, tangle; entirety, integration, network, totality, whole; compulsion, fixation, obsession, preoccupation, prepossession; prejudice.

complexion n color, hue, tint.

complexity n complication, entanglement, intricacy, involution.

compliance n concession, obedience, submission; acquiescence, agreement, assent, concurrence, consent, compliancy, yieldingness.

complicate vb confuse, entangle, interweave, involve.

complication n complexity, confusion, entanglement, intricacy; combination, complexus, mixture.

compliment *vb* commend, congratulate, eulogize, extol, flatter, laud, praise. • *n* admiration, commendation, courtesy, encomium, eulogy, favor, flattery, honor, laudation, praise, tribute.

complimentary *adj* commendatory, congratulatory, encomiastic, eulogistic, flattering, laudatory, panegyrical.

comply *vb* adhere to, complete, discharge, fullfil, meet, observe, perform, satisfy; accede, accord, acquiesce, agree to, assent, consent to, yield.

component *adj* composing, constituent, constituting. • *n* constituent, element, ingredient, part.

comport *vb* accord, agree, coincide, correspond, fit, harmonize, square, suit, tally.

compose *vb* build, compact, compound, constitute, form, make, synthesize; contrive, create, frame, imagine, indite, invent, write; adjust, arrange, regulate, settle; appease, assuage, calm, pacify, quell, quiet, soothe, still, tranquillize.

composed *adj* calm, collected, cool, imperturbable, placid, quiet, sedate, self-possessed, tranquil, undisturbed, unmoved, unruffled.

composite *adj* amalgamated, combined, complex, compounded, mixed; integrated, unitary. • *n* admixture, amalgam, blend, combination, composition, compound, mixture, unification.

composition *n* constitution, construction, formation, framing, making; compound, mixture; arrangement, combination, conjunction, make-up, synthesize, union; invention, opus, piece, production, writing; agreement, arrangement, compromise.

compost *n* fertilizer, fertilizing, manure, mixture.

composure *n* calmness, coolness, equanimity, placidity, sedateness, quiet, self-possession, serenity, tranquillity.

compotation *n* conviviality, frolicking, jollification, reveling, revelry, rousing, wassailling; bacchanal, carousal, carouse, debauch, orgy, revel, saturnalia, wassail.

compound[1] *vb* amalgamate, blend, combine, intermingle, intermix, mingle, mix, unite; adjust, arrange, compose, compromise, settle. • *adj* complex, composite. • *n* combination, composition, mixture; farrago, hodgepodge, jumble, medley, mess, olio.

compound[2] *n* enclosure, garden, yard.

comprehend *vb* comprise, contain, embrace, embody, enclose, include, involve; apprehend, conceive, discern, grasp, know, imagine, master, perceive, see, understand.

comprehension *n* comprising, embracing, inclusion; compass, domain, embrace, field, limits, province, range, reach, scope, sphere, sweep; connotation, depth, force, intention; conception, grasp, intelligence, understanding; intellect, intelligence, mind, reason, understanding.

comprehensive *adj* all-embracing, ample, broad, capacious, compendious, extensive, full, inclusive, large, sweeping, wide.

compress *vb* abbreviate, condense, constrict, contract, crowd, press, shorten, squeeze, summarize.

compression *n* condensation, confining, pinching, pressing, squeezing; brevity, pithiness, succinctness, terseness.

comprise *vb* comprehend, contain, embody, embrace, enclose, include, involve.

compromise *vb* adjust, arbitrate, arrange, compose, compound, settle; imperil, jeopardize, prejudice; commit, engage, implicate, pledge; agree, compound. • *n* adjustment, agreement, composition, settlement.

compulsion *n* coercion, constraint, force, forcing, pressure, urgency.

compulsory *adj* coercive, compelling, constraining; binding, enforced, imperative, necessary, obligatory, unavoidable.

compunction *n* contrition, misgiving, penitence, qualm, regret, reluctance, remorse, repentance, sorrow.

computable *adj* calculable, numerable, reckonable.

computation *n* account, calculation, estimate, reckoning, score, tally.

compute *vb* calculate, count, enumerate, estimate, figure, measure, number, rate, reckon, sum.

comrade *n* accomplice, ally, associate, chum, companion, compatriot, compeer, crony, fellow, mate, pal.

concatenate *vb* connect, join, link, unite.

concatenation *n* connection; chain, congeries, linking, series, sequence, succession.

concave *adj* depressed, excavated, hollow, hollowed, scooped.

conceal *vb* bury, cover, screen, secrete; disguise, dissemble, mask.

concede *vb* grant, surrender, yield; acknowledge, admit, allow, confess, grant.

conceit *n* belief, conception, fancy, idea,

image, imagination, notion, thought; caprice, illusion, vagary, whim; estimate, estimation, impression, judgement, opinion; conceitedness, egoism, self-complacency, priggishness, priggery, self-conceit, self-esteem, self-sufficiency, vanity; crotchet, point, quip, quirk.

conceited adj egotistical, opinionated, opinionative, overweening, self-conceited, vain,

conceivable adj imaginable, picturable; cogitable, comprehensible, intelligible, rational, thinkable.

conceive vb create, contrive, devise, form, plan, purpose; fancy, imagine; comprehend, fathom, think, understand; assume, imagine, suppose; bear, become pregnant.

concern vb affect, belong to, interest, pertain to, regard, relate to, touch; disquiet, disturb, trouble. • n affair, business, matter, transaction; concernment, consequence, importance, interest, moment, weight; anxiety, care, carefulness, solicitude, worry; business, company, establishment, firm, house.

concert vb combine, concoct, contrive, design, devise, invent, plan, plot, project. • n agreement, concord, concordance, cooperation, harmony, union, unison.

concession n acquiescence, assent, cessation, compliance, surrender, yielding; acknowledgement, allowance, boon, confession, grant, privilege.

conciliate vb appease, pacify, placate, propitiate, reconcile; engage, gain, secure, win, win over.

concise adj brief, compact, compendious, comprehensive, compressed, condensed, crisp, laconic, pithy, pointed, pregnant, sententious, short, succinct, summary, terse.

conclave n assembly, cabinet, council.

conclude vb close, end, finish, terminate; deduce, gather, infer, judge; decide, determine, judge; arrange, complete, settle; bar, hinder, restrain, stop; decide, determine, resolve.

conclusion n deduction, inference; decision, determination, judgement; close, completion, end, event, finale, issue, termination, upshot; arrangement, closing, effecting, establishing, settlement.

conclusive adj clinching, convincing, decisive, irrefutable, unanswerable; final, ultimate.

concoct vb brew, contrive, design, devise, frame, hatch, invent, mature, plan, plot, prepare, project.

concomitant adj accessory, accompanying, attendant, attending, coincident, concurrent, conjoined. • n accessory, accompaniment, attendant.

concord n agreement, amity, friendship, harmony, peace, unanimity, union, unison, unity; accord, adaptation, concordance, consonance, harmony.

concordant adj accordant, agreeable, agreeing, harmonious.

concordat n agreement, bargain, compact, convention, covenant, stipulation, treaty.

concourse n confluence, conflux, congress; assemblage, assembly, collection, crowd, gathering, meeting, multitude, throng.

concrete vb cake, congeal, coagulate, harden, solidify, thicken. • adj compact, consolidated, firm, solid, solidified; agglomerated, complex, conglomerated, compound, concreted; completely, entire, individualized, total. • n compound, concretion, mixture; cement.

concubine n hetaera, hetaira, mistress, paramour.

concupiscence n lasciviousness, lechery, lewdness, lust, pruriency.

concupiscent adj carnal, lascivious, lecherous, lewd, libidinous, lustful, prurient, rampant, salacious, sensual.

concur vb accede, acquiesce, agree, approve, assent, coincide, consent, harmonize; combine, conspire, cooperate, help.

concurrent adj agreeing, coincident, harmonizing, meeting, uniting; associate, associated, attendant, concomitant, conjoined, united.

concussion n agitation, shaking; clash, crash, shock.

condemn vb adjudge, convict, doom, sentence; disapprove, proscribe, reprobate; blame, censure, damn, deprecate, disapprove, reprehend, reprove, upbraid.

condemnation n conviction, doom, judgement, penalty, sentence; banning, disapproval, proscription; guilt, sin, wrong; blame, censure, disapprobation, disapproval, reprobation, reproof.

condemnatory adj blaming, censuring, damnatory, deprecatory, disapproving, reproachful.

condense vb compress, concentrate, consolidate, densify, thicken; abbreviate, abridge, contract, curtail, diminish, epitomize, reduce, shorten, summarize; liquefy.

condescend vb deign, vouchsafe; descend, stoop, submit.

condescension n affability, civility, courtesy, deference, favor, graciousness, obeisance.

condign adj adequate, deserved, just, merited, suitable.

condiment n appetizer, relish, sauce, seasoning.

condition vb postulate, specify, stipulate; groom, prepare, qualify, ready, train; acclimatize, accustom, adapt, adjust, familiarize, habituate, naturalize; attune, commission, fix, overhaul, prepare, recondition, repair, service, tune. • n case, circumstances, plight, predicament, situation, state; class, estate, grade, rank, station; arrangement, consideration, provision, proviso, stipulation; attendant, necessity, postulate, precondition, prerequisite.

condole vb commiserate, compassionate, console, sympathize.

condonation n forgiveness, overlooking, pardon.

condone vb excuse, forgive, pardon.

conduce vb contribute, lead, tend; advance, aid.

conducive adj conducting, contributing, instrumental, promotive, subservient, subsidiary.

conduct vb convoy, direct, escort, lead; administer, command, govern, lead, preside, superintend; manage, operate, regulate; direct, lead. • n administration, direction, guidance, leadership, management; convoy, escort, guard; actions, bearing, behavior, career, carriage, demeanor, deportment, manners.

conductor n guide, lead; director, leader, manager; propagator, transmitter.

conduit n canal, channel, duct, passage, pipe, tube.

confederacy n alliance, coalition, compact, confederation, covenant, federation, league, union.

confer vb advise, consult, converse, deliberate, discourse, parley, talk; bestow, give, grant, vouchsafe.

confess vb acknowledge, admit, avow, own; admit, concede, grant, recognize; attest, exhibit, manifest, prove, show; shrive.

confession n acknowledgement, admission, avowal.

confide vb commit, consign, entrust, trust.

confidence n belief, certitude, dependence, faith, reliance, trust; aplomb, assurance, boldness, cocksureness, courage, firmness, intrepidity, self-reliance; secrecy.

confident adj assured, certain, cocksure, positive, sure: bold, presumptuous. sanguine, undaunted.

confidential adj intimate, private, secret; faithful, trustworthy.

configuration n conformation, contour, figure, form, gestalt, outline, shape.

confine vb restrain, shut in, shut up; immure, imprison, incarcerate, impound, jail, mew; bound, circumscribe, limit, restrict. • n border, boundary, frontier, limit.

confinement n restraint; captivity, duress, durance, immurement, imprisonment, incarceration; childbed, childbirth, delivery, lying-in, parturition.

confines npl borders, boundaries, edges, frontiers, limits, marches, precincts.

confirm vb assure, establish, fix, settle; strengthen; authenticate, avouch, corroborate, countersign, endorse, substantiate, verify; bind, ratify, sanction.

confirmation n establishment, settlement; corroboration, proof, substantiation, verification.

confiscate vb appropriate, forfeit, seize.

conflict vb clash, combat, contend, contest, disagree, fight, interfere, strive, struggle. • n battle, collision, combat, contention, contest, encounter, fight, struggle; antagonism, clashing, disagreement, discord, disharmony, inconsistency, interference, opposition.

confluence n conflux, junction, meeting, union; army, assemblage, assembly, concourse, crowd, collection, horde, host, multitude, swarm.

confluent adj blending, concurring, flowing, joining, meeting, merging, uniting.

conform vb accommodate, adapt, adjust; agree, comport, correspond, harmonize, square, tally.

conformation n accordance, agreement, compliance, conformity; configuration, figure, form, manner, shape, structure.

confound vb confuse; baffle, bewilder, embarrass, flurry, mystify, nonplus, perplex, pose; amaze, astonish, astound, bewilder, dumfound, paralyse, petrify, startle, stun, stupefy, surprise; annihilate, demolish, destroy, overthrow, overwhelm, ruin; abash, confuse, discompose, disconcert, mortify, shame.

confront *vb* face; challenge, contrapose, encounter, oppose, threaten.

confuse *vb* blend, confound, intermingle, mingle, mix; derange, disarrange, disorder, jumble, mess, muddle; darken, obscure, perplex; befuddle, bewilder, embarrass, flabbergast, flurry, fluster, mystify, nonplus, pose; abash, confound, discompose, disconcert, mortify, shame.

confusion *n* anarchy, chaos, clutter, confusedness, derangement, disarrangement, disarray, disorder, jumble, muddle; agitation, commotion, ferment, stir, tumult, turmoil; astonishment, bewilderment, distraction, embarrassment, fluster, fuddle, perplexity; abashment, discomfiture, mortification, shame; annihilation, defeat, demolition, destruction, overthrow, ruin.

confute *vb* disprove, oppugn, overthrow, refute, silence.

congeal *vb* benumb, condense, curdle, freeze, stiffen, thicken.

congenial *adj* kindred, similar, sympathetic; adapted, agreeable, natural, suitable, suited; agreeable, favorable, genial.

congenital *adj* connate, connatural, inborn.

congeries *n* accumulation, agglomeration, aggregate, aggregation, collection, conglomeration, crowd, cluster, heap, mass.

congratulate *vb* compliment, felicitate, gratulate, greet, hail, salute.

congregate *vb* assemble, collect, convene, convoke, gather, muster; gather, meet, swarm, throng.

congregation *n* assemblage, assembly, collection, gathering, meeting.

congress *n* assembly, conclave, conference, convention, convocation, council, diet, meeting.

congruity *n* agreement, conformity, consistency, fitness, suitableness.

congruous *adj* accordant, agreeing, compatible, consistent, consonant, suitable; appropriate, befitting, fit, meet, proper, seemly.

conjecture *vb* assume, guess, hypothesize, imagine, suppose, surmise, suspect; dare say, fancy, presume. • *n* assumption, guess, hypothesis, supposition, surmise, theory.

conjoin *vb* associate, combine, connect, join, unite.

conjugal *adj* bridal, connubial, hymeneal, matrimonial, nuptial.

conjuncture *n* combination, concurrence, connection; crisis, emergency, exigency, juncture.

conjure *vb* adjure, beg, beseech, crave, entreat, implore, invoke, pray, supplicate; bewitch, charm, enchant, fascinate; juggle.

connect *vb* associate, conjoin, combine, couple, hyphenate, interlink, join, link, unite; cohere, interlock.

connected *adj* associated, coupled, joined, united; akin, allied, related; communicating.

connection *n* alliance, association, dependence, junction, union; commerce, communication, intercourse; affinity, relationship; kindred, kinsman, relation, relative.

connive *vb* collude, conspire, plot, scheme.

connoisseur *n* critic, expert, virtuoso.

connotation *n* comprehension, depth, force, intent, intention, meaning.

connubial *adj* bridal, conjugal, hymeneal, matrimonial, nuptial.

conquer *vb* beat, checkmate, crush, defeat, discomfit, humble, master, overcome, overpower, overthrow, prevail, quell, reduce, rout, subdue, subjugate, vanquish; overcome, surmount.

conqueror *n* humbler, subduer, subjugator, vanquisher; superior, victor, winner.

conquest *n* defeat, discomfiture, mastery, overthrow, reduction, subjection, subjugation; triumph, victor; winning.

consanguinity *n* affinity, kinship, blood-relationship, kin, kindred, relationship.

conscientious *adj* careful, exact, fair, faithful, high-principled, honest, honorable, incorruptible, just, scrupulous, straightforward, uncorrupt, upright.

conscious *adj* intelligent, knowing, percipient, sentient; intellectual, rational, reasoning, reflecting, self-conscious, thinking; apprised, awake, aware, cognizant, percipient, sensible; self-admitted, self-accusing.

consecrate *vb* dedicate, devote, ordain; hallow, sanctify, venerate.

consecutive *adj* following, succeeding.

consent *vb* agree, allow, assent, concur, permit, yield; accede, acquiesce, comply. • *n* approval, assent, concurrence, permission; accord, agreement, consensus, concord, cooperation, harmony, unison; acquiescence, compliance.

consequence *n* effect, end, event, issue, result; conclusion, deduction, inference; concatenation, connection, consecution; concern, distinction, importance, influence, interest, moment, standing, weight.

consequential *adj* consequent, following, resulting, sequential; arrogant, conceited, inflated, pompous, pretentious, self-important, self-sufficient, vainglorious.

conservation n guardianship, maintenance, preservation, protection.

conservative adj conservatory, moderate, moderationist; preservative; reactionary, unprogressive. • n die-hard, reactionary, redneck, rightist, right-winger; moderate; preservative.

conserve vb keep, maintain, preserve, protect, save, sustain, uphold. • n confit, confection, jam, preserve, sweetmeat.

consider vb attend, brood, contemplate, examine, heed, mark, mind, ponder, reflect, revolve, study, weigh; care for, consult, envisage, regard, respect; cogitate, deliberate, mediate, muse, ponder, reflect, ruminate, think; account, believe, deem, hold, judge, opine.

considerate adj circumspect, deliberate, discrete, judicious, provident, prudent, serious, sober, staid, thoughtful; charitable, forbearing, patient.

consideration n attention, cogitation, contemplation, deliberation, notice, heed, meditation, pondering, reflection, regard; consequence, importance, important, moment, significant, weight; account, cause, ground, motive, reason, sake, score.

consign vb deliver, hand over, remand, resign, transfer, transmit; commit, entrust; ship.

consignor n sender, shipper, transmitter.

consistency n compactness, consistence, density, thickness; agreement, compatibility, conformableness, congruity, consonance, correspondence, harmony.

consistent adj accordant, agreeing, comfortable, compatible, congruous, consonant, correspondent, harmonious, logical.

consolation n alleviation, comfort, condolence, encouragement, relief, solace.

console vb assuage, calm, cheer, comfort, encourage, solace, relieve, soothe.

consolidate vb cement, compact, compress, condense, conduce, harden, solidify, thicken; combine, conjoin, fuse, unite.

consolidation n solidification; combination, union.

consonance n accord, concord, conformity, harmony; accord, accordance, agreement, congruence, congruity, consistency, unison.

consonant adj accordant, according, harmonious; compatible, congruous, consistent. • n articulation, letter-sound.

consort vb associate, fraternize. • n associate, companion, fellow, husband, spouse, partner.

conspectus n abstract, brief, breviary, compend, compendium, digest, epitome, outline, precis, summary, syllabus, synopsis.

conspicuous adj apparent, clear, discernible, glaring, manifest, noticeable, perceptible, plain, striking, visible; celebrated, distinguished, eminent, famed, famous, illustrious, marked, noted, outstanding, pre-eminent, prominent, remarkable, signal.

conspiracy n cabal, collusion, confederation, intrigue, league, machination, plot, scheme.

conspire vb concur, conduce, cooperate; combine, compass, contrive, devise, project; confederate, contrive, hatch, plot, scheme.

constancy n immutability, permanence, stability, unchangeableness; regularity, unchangeableness; decision, determination, firmness, inflexibility, resolution, steadfastness, steadiness; devotion, faithfulness, fidelity, loyalty, trustiness, truth.

constant adj abiding, enduring, fixed, immutable, invariable, invariant, permanent, perpetual, stable, unalterable, unchanging, unvaried; certain, regular, stated, uniform; determined, firm, resolute, stanch, steadfast, steady, unanswering, undeviating, unmoved, unshaken, unwavering; assiduous, diligent, persevering, sedulous, tenacious, unremitting; continual, continuous, incessant, perpetual, sustained, unbroken, uninterrupted; devoted, faithful, loyal, true, trusty.

consternation n alarm, amazement, awe, bewilderment, dread, fear, fright, horror, panic, terror.

constituent adj component, composing, constituting, forming; appointing, electoral. • n component, element, ingredient, principal; elector, voter.

constitute vb compose, form, make; appoint, delegate, depute, empower; enact, establish, fix, set up.

constitution n establishment, formation, make-up, organization, structure; character, characteristic, disposition, form, habit, humor, peculiarity, physique, quality, spirit, temper, temperament.

constitutional adj congenital, connate, inborn, inbred, inherent, innate, natural, organic; lawful, legal, legitimate. • n airing, exercise, promenade, stretch, walk.

constrain *vb* coerce, compel, drive, force; chain, confine, curb, enthral, hold, restrain; draw, impel, urge.

constriction *n* compression, constraint, contraction.

construct *vb* build, fabricate, erect, raise, set up; arrange, establish, form, found, frame, institute, invent, make, organize, originate.

construction *n* building, erection, fabrication; configuration, conformation, figure, form, formation, made, shape, structure; explanation, interpretation, rendering, version.

construe *vb* analyze, explain, expound, interpret, parse, render, translate.

consult *vb* advise, ask, confer, counsel, deliberate, interrogate, question; consider, regard.

consume *vb* absorb, decay, destroy, devour, dissipate, exhaust, expend, lavish, lessen, spend, squander, vanish, waste.

consummate[1] *vb* accomplish, achieve, compass, complete, conclude, crown, effect, effectuate, end, execute, finish, perfect, perform.

consummate[2] *adj* complete, done, effected, finished, fulfilled, perfect, supreme.

consumption *n* decay, decline, decrease, destruction, diminution, expenditure, use, waste; atrophy, emaciation.

contact *vb* hit, impinge, touch; approach, be heard, communicate with, reach. • *n* approximation, contiguity, junction, juxtaposition, taction, tangency, touch.

contagion *n* infection; contamination, corruption, infection, taint.

contagious *adj* catching, epidemic, infectious; deadly, pestiferous, pestilential, poisonous.

contain *vb* accommodate, comprehend, comprise, embody, embrace, enclose, include; check, restrain.

contaminate *vb* corrupt, defile, deprave, infect, poison, pollute, soil, stain, sully, taint, tarnish, vitiate.

contamination *n* contaminating, defilement, defiling, polluting, pollution; abomination, defilement, impurity, foulness, infection, pollution, stain, taint, uncleanness.

contemn *vb* despise, disdain, disregard, neglect, scorn, scout, slight, spurn.

contemplate *vb* behold, gaze upon, observe, survey; consider, dwell on, meditate on, muse on, ponder, reflect upon, study,

survey, think about; design, intend, mean, plan, purpose.

contemplation *n* cogitation, deliberation, meditation, pondering, reflection, speculation, study, thought; prospect, prospective, view; expectation.

contemporaneous *adj* coetaneous, coeval, coexistent, coexisting, coincident, concomitant, contemporary, simultaneous, synchronous.

contemporary *adj* coetaneous, coeval, coexistent, coexisting, coincident, concomitant, concurrent, contemporaneous, current, present, simultaneous, synchronous; advanced, modern, modernistic, progressive, up-to-date. • *n* coeval, coexistent, compeer, fellow.

contempt *n* contumely, derision, despite, disdain, disregard, misprision, mockery, scorn, slight.

contemptible *adj* abject, base, despicable, haughty, insolent, insulting, low, mean, paltry, pitiful, scurvy, sorry, supercilious, vile, worthless.

contemptuous *adj* arrogant, contumelious, disdainful, haughty, insolent, insulting, scornful, sneering, supercilious.

contend *vb* battle, combat, compete, contest, fight, strive, struggle, vie; argue, debate, dispute, litigate; affirm, assert, contest, maintain.

content[1] *n* essence, gist, meaning, meat, stuff, substance; capacity, measure, space, volume.

content[2] *vb* appease, delight, gladden, gratify, humor, indulge, please, satisfy, suffice. • *adj* agreeable, contented, happy, pleased, satisfied. • *n* contentment, ease, peace, satisfaction.

contention *n* discord, dissension, feud, squabble, strife, quarrel, rapture, wrangle, wrangling; altercation, bickering, contest, controversy, debate, dispute, litigation, logomachy.

contentious *adj* belligerent, cross, litigious, peevish, perverse, petulant, pugnacious, quarrelsome, wrangling; captious, caviling, disputatious.

conterminous *adj* adjacent, adjoining, contiguous; co-extensive, coincident, commensurate.

contest *vb* argue, contend, controvert, debate, dispute, litigate, question; strive, struggle; compete, cope, fight, vie. • *n* altercation, contention, controversy, difference, dispute, debate, quarrel; affray, battle, bout, combat, conflict, encounter, fight, match, scrimmage, struggle, tussle; competition, contention, rivalry.

contexture *n* composition, constitution, framework, structure, texture.

contiguous *adj* abutting, adjacent, adjoining, beside, bordering, conterminous, meeting, near, neighboring, touching.

continent[1] *n* mainland, mass, tract.

continent[2] *adj* abstemious, abstinent, chaste, restrained, self-commanding, self-controlled, moderate, sober, temperate.

contingency *n* accidentalness, chance, fortuity, uncertainty; accident, casualty, event, incident, occurrence.

contingent *adj* accidental, adventitious, casual, fortuitous, incidental; conditional, dependent, uncertain. • *n* proportion, quota, share.

continual *adj* constant, perpetual, unceasing, uninterrupted, unremitting; endless, eternal, everlasting, interminable, perennial, permanent, perpetual, unending; constant, oft-repeated.

continuance *n* abiding, continuation, duration, endurance, lasting, persistence, stay; continuation, extension, perpetuation, prolongation, protraction; concatenation, connection, sequence, succession; constancy, endurance, perseverance, persistence.

continue *vb* endure, last, remain; abide, linger, remain, stay, tarry; endure, persevere, persist, stick; extend, prolong, perpetuate, protract.

continuous *adj* connected, continued, extended, prolonged, unbroken, unintermitted, uninterrupted.

contour *n* outline, profile.

contraband *adj* banned, forbidden, illegal, illicit, interdicted, prohibited, smuggled, unlawful.

contract *vb* abbreviate, abridge, condense, confine, curtail, diminish, epitomize, lessen, narrow, reduce, shorten; absorb, catch, incur, get, make, take; constrict, shrink, shrivel, wrinkle; agree, bargain, covenant, engage, pledge, stipulate. • *n* agreement, arrangement, bargain, bond, compact, concordat, covenant, convention, engagement, pact, stipulation, treaty.

contradict *vb* assail, challenge, controvert, deny, dispute, gainsay, impugn, traverse; abrogate, annul, belie, counter, disallow,

negative, contravene, counteract, oppose, thwart.

contradiction *n* controversion, denial, gainsaying; antinomy, clashing, contrariety, incongruity, opposition.

contradictory *adj* antagonistic, contrary, incompatible, inconsistent, negating, opposed, opposite, repugnant.

contrariety *n* antagonism, clashing, contradiction, contrast, opposition, repugnance.

contrary *adj* adverse, counter, discordant, opposed, opposing, opposite; antagonistic, conflicting, contradictory, repugnant, retroactive; forward, headstrong, obstinate, refractory, stubborn, unruly, wayward, perverse. • *n* antithesis, converse, obverse, opposite, reverse.

contrast *vb* compare, differentiate, distinguish, oppose. • *n* contrariety, difference, opposition; comparison, distinction.

contravene *vb* abrogate, annul, contradict, counteract, countervail, cross, go against, hinder, interfere, nullify, oppose, set aside, thwart.

contravention *n* abrogation, contradiction, interference, opposition, transgression, traversal, violation.

contretemps *n* accident, mischance, mishap.

contribute *vb* bestow, donate, give, grant, subscribe; afford, aid, furnish, supply; concur, conduce, conspire, cooperate, minister, serve, tend.

contribution *n* bestowal, bestowment, grant; donation, gift, offering, subscription.

contrite *adj* humble, penitent, repentant, sorrowful.

contrition *n* compunction, humiliation, penitence, regret, remorse, repentance, self-condemnation, self-reproach, sorrow.

contrivance *n* design, inventive, inventiveness; contraption, device, gadget, invention, machine; artifice, device, fabrication, machination, plan, plot, scheme, shift, stratagem.

contrive *vb* arrange, brew, concoct, design, devise, effect, form, frame, hatch, invent, plan, project; consider, plan, plot, scheme; manage, make out.

control *vb* command, direct, dominate, govern, manage, oversee, sway, regulate, rule, superintend; bridle, check, counteract, curb, check, hinder, repress, restrain. • *n* ascendency, command, direction, disposition, dominion, government, guidance, mastery, oversight, regiment, regulation, rule, superintendence, supremacy, sway.

controversy *n* altercation, argument, contention, debate, discussion, disputation, dispute, logomachy, polemics, quarrel, strife; lawsuit.

contumacious *adj* disobedient, cross-grained, disrespectful, haughty, headstrong, intractable, obdurate, obstinate, pertinacious, perverse, rebellious, refractory, stiff-necked, stubborn.

contumacy *n* doggedness, haughtiness, headiness, obduracy, obstinacy, pertinacity, perverseness, stubbornness; contempt, disobedience, disrespect, insolence, insubordination, rebelliousness.

contumelious *adj* abusive, arrogant, calumnious, contemptuous, disdainful, insolent, insulting, opprobrious, overbearing, rude, scornful, supercilious.

contumely *n* abuse, affront, arrogance, contempt, contemptuousness, disdain, indignity, insolence, insult, obloquy, opprobrium, reproach, rudeness, scorn, superciliousness.

contuse *vb* bruise, crush, injure, knock, squeeze, wound.

contusion *n* bruise, crush, injury, knock, squeeze, wound.

convalescence *n* recovery, recuperation.

convene *vb* assemble, congregate, gather, meet, muster; assemble, call, collect, convoke, muster, summon.

convenience *n* fitness, propriety, suitableness; accessibility, accommodation, comfort, commodiousness, ease, handiness, satisfaction, serviceability, serviceableness.

convenient *adj* adapted, appropriate, fit, fitted, proper, suitable, suited; advantageous, beneficial, comfortable, commodious, favorable, handy, helpful, serviceable, timely, useful.

convent *n* abbey, cloister, monastery, priory.

convention *n* assembly, congress, convocation, meeting; agreement, bargain, compact, contract, pact, stipulation, treaty; custom, formality, usage.

conventional *adj* agreed on, bargained for, stipulated; accustomed, approved, common, customary, everyday, habitual, ordinary, orthodox, regular, standard, traditional, usual, wonted.

conversable *adj* affable, communicative, free, open, sociable, social, unreversed.

conversation *n* chat, colloquy, communion,

confabulation, conference, converse, dialogue, discourse, intercourse, interlocution, parley, talk.

converse[1] *vb* commune; chat, confabulate, discourse, gossip, parley, talk. • *n* commerce, communication, intercourse; colloquy, conversation, talk.

converse[2] *adj* adverse, contradictory, contrary, counter, opposed, opposing, opposite; *n* antithesis, contrary, opposite, reverse.

conversion *n* change, reduction, resolution, transformation, transmutation; interchange, reversal, transposition.

convert *vb* alter, change, transform, transmute; interchange, reverse, transpose; apply, appropriate, convince. • *n* catechumen, disciple, neophyte, proselyte.

convey *vb* bear, bring, carry, fetch, transmit, transport, waft; abalienate, alienate, cede, consign, deliver, demise, devise, devolve, grant, sell, transfer.

conveyance *n* alienation, cession, transfer, transference, transmission; carriage, carrying, conveying, transfer, transmission.

convict *vb* condemn, confute, convince, imprison, sentence. • *n* criminal, culprit, felon, malefactor, prisoner.

convivial *adj* festal, festive, gay, jolly, jovial, merry, mirthful, social.

convocation *n* assembling, convening, convoking, gathering, summoning; assembly, congress, convention, council, diet, meeting, synod.

convoke *vb* assemble, convene, muster, summon.

convoy *vb* accompany, attend, escort, guard, protect. • *n* attendance, attendant, escort, guard, protection.

convulse *vb* agitate, derange, disorder, disturb, shake, shatter.

convulsion *n* cramp, fit, spasm; agitation, commotion, disturbance, shaking, tumult.

cook *vb* bake, boil, broil, fry, grill, microwave, roast, spit-roast, steam, stir-fry; falsify, garble.

cool *vb* chill, ice, refrigerate; abate, allay, calm, damp, moderate, quiet, temper. • *adj* calm, collected, composed, dispassionate, placid, sedate, self-possessed, quiet, staid, unexcited, unimpassioned, undisturbed, unruffled; cold-blooded, indifferent, lukewarm, unconcerned; apathetic, chilling, freezing, frigid, repellent; bold, impertinent, impudent, self-possessed, shameless. • *n* chill, chilliness, coolness; calmness, composure, coolheadedness, countenance, equanimity, poise, self-possession, self-restraint.

coop vb cage, confine, encage, immure, imprison. • n barrel, box, cage, pen.

cooperate vb abet, aid, assist, co-act, collaborate, combine, concur, conduce, conspire, contribute, help, unite.

cooperation n aid, assistance, co-action, concert, concurrence, collaboration, synergy.

coordinate vb accord, agree, arrange, equalize, harmonize, integrate, methodize, organize, regulate, synchronize, systematize. • adj coequal, equal, equivalent, tantamount; coincident, synchronous. • n complement, counterpart, like, pendant; companion, fellow, match, mate.

copartnership n association, fraternity, partnership; company, concern, establishment, firm, house.

cope vb combat, compete, contend, encounter, engage, strive, struggle, vie.

copious adj abundant, ample, exuberant, full, overflowing, plenteous, plentiful, profuse, rich.

copiousness n abundance, exuberance, fullness, plenty, profusion, richness.

copse n coppice, grove, thicket.

copulation n coition, congress, coupling.

copy vb duplicate, reproduce, trace, transcribe; follow, imitate, pattern. • n counterscript, duplicate, facsimile, offprint, replica, reproduction, transcript; archetype, model, original, pattern; manuscript, typescript.

cord n braid, gimp, line, string.

cordate adj cordiform, heart-shaped.

cordial adj affectionate, ardent, earnest, heartfelt, hearty, sincere, warm, warmhearted; grateful, invigorating, restorative, pleasant, refreshing. • n balm, balsam, elixir, tisane, tonic; liqueur.

core n center, essence, heart, kernel.

corner vb confound, confuse, nonplus, perplex, pose, puzzle. • n angle, bend, crutch, cusp, elbow, joint, knee; niche, nook, recess, retreat.

corollary n conclusion, consequence, deduction, induction, inference.

coronal n bays, chaplet, crown, garland, laurel, wreath.

corporal adj bodily; corporeal, material, physical.

corporeal adj bodily, fleshly, substantial; corporal, material, nonspiritual, physical.

corps n band, body, company, contingent, division, platoon, regiment, squad, squadron, troop.

corpse n body, carcass, corse, remains; ashes, dust.

corpulent adj big, burly, fat, fleshy, large, lusty, obese, plump, portly, pursy, rotund, stout.

corpuscle n atom, bit, grain, iota, jot, mite, molecule, monad, particle, scintilla, scrap, whit.

correct vb adjust, amend, cure, improve, mend, reclaim, rectify, redress, reform, regulate, remedy; chasten, discipline, punish. • adj accurate, equitable, exact, faultless, just, precise, proper, regular, right, true, upright.

correction n amendment, improvement, redress; chastening, discipline, punishment.

corrective adj alternative, correctory, counteractive, emendatory, improving, modifying, rectifying, reformative, reformatory.

correctness n accuracy, exactness, faultlessness, nicety, precision, propriety, rectitude, regularity, rightness, truth.

correlate n complement, correlative, counterpart.

correspond vb accord, agree, answer, comport, conform, fit, harmonize, match, square, suit, tally; answer, belong, correlate; communicate.

correspondence n accord, agreement, coincidence, concurrence, conformity, congruity, fitness, harmony, match; correlation, counterposition; communication, letters, writing.

corroborate vb confirm, establish, ratify, substantiate, support, sustain, strengthen.

corrode vb canker, erode, gnaw; consume, deteriorate, rust, waste; blight, embitter, envenom, poison.

corrosive adj acrid, biting, consuming, cathartic, caustic, corroding, eroding, erosive, violent; consuming, corroding, gnawing, mordant, wasting, wearing; blighting, cankerous, carking, embittering, envenoming, poisoning.

corrugate vb cockle, crease, furrow, groove, pucker, rumple, wrinkle.

corrupt vb putrefy, putrid, render; contaminate, defile, infect, pollute, spoil, taint, vitiate; degrade, demoralize, deprave, pervert; adulterate, debase, falsify, sophisticate; bribe, entice. • adj contaminated, corrupted, impure, infected, putrid, rotten, spoiled, tainted, unsound; abandoned, debauched, depraved, dissolute, profligate, reprobate, vicious, wicked; bribable, buyable.

corruption n putrefaction, putrescence, rottenness; adulteration, contamination, debasement, defilement, infection, perversion, pollution, vitiation; demoralization, depravation, depravity, immorality, laxity, sinfulness, wickedness; bribery, dishonesty.

corsair n buccaneer, picaroon, pirate, rover, sea-robber, sea-rover.

corset n bodice, girdle, stays.

cosmonaut n astronaut, spaceman.

cosmos n creation, macrocosm, universe, world; harmony, order, structure.

cost vb absorb, consume, require. • n amount, charge, expenditure, expense, outlay, price; costliness, preciousness, richness, splendor, sumptuousness; damage, detriment, loss, pain, sacrifice, suffering.

costly adj dear, expensive, high-priced; gorgeous, luxurious, precious, rich, splendid, sumptuous, valuable.

costume n apparel, attire, dress, robes, uniform.

cosy see cozy.

coterie n association, brotherhood, circle, club, set, society, sodality.

cottage n cabin, chalet, cot, hut, lodge, shack, shanty.

couch vb lie, recline; crouch, squat; bend down, stoop; conceal, cover up, hide; lay, level. • n bed, davenport, divan, lounge, seat, settee, settle, sofa.

council n advisers, cabinet, ministry; assembly, congress, conclave, convention, convocation, diet, husting, meeting, parliament, synod.

counsel vb admonish, advise, caution, recommend, warn. • n admonition, advice, caution, instruction, opinion, recommendation, suggestion; deliberation, forethought; advocate, barrister, counselor, lawyer.

count vb enumerate, number, score; calculate, cast, compute, estimate, reckon; account, consider, deem, esteem, hold, judge, regard, think; tell. • n reckoning, tally.

countenance vb abet, aid, approve, assist, befriend, encourage, favor, patronize, sanction, support. • n aspect, look, men; aid, approbation, approval, assistance, encouragement, favor, patronage, sanction, support.

counter[1] n abacus, calculator, computer, meter, reckoner, tabulator, totalizator; bar, buffet, shopboard, table; (naut) end, poop, stern, tail; chip, token.

counter[2] vb contradict, contravene, counteract, oppose, retaliate. • adj adverse, against, contrary, opposed, opposite. • adv contrariwise, contrary. • n antithesis, contrary, converse, opposite, reverse; counterblast, counterblow, retaliation.

counteract vb check, contrapose, contravene, cross, counter, counterpose, defeat, foil, frustrate, hinder, oppose, resist, thwart, traverse; annul, countervail, counterbalance, destroy, neutralize, offset.

counteractive adj antidote, corrective, counteragent, medicine, remedy, restorative.

counterbalance vb balance, counterpoise; compensate, countervail.

counterfeit vb forge, imitate; fake, feign, pretend, sham, simulate; copy, imitate. • adj fake, forged, fraudulent, spurious, supposititious; false, feigned, hypocritical, mock, sham, simulated, spurious; copied, imitated, resembling. • n copy, fake, forgery, sham.

countermand vb abrogate, annul, cancel, recall, repeal, rescind, revoke.

counterpane n coverlet, duvet, quilt.

counterpart n copy, duplicate; complement, correlate, correlative, reverse, supplement; fellow, mate, match, tally, twin.

counterpoise vb balance, counteract, countervail, counterbalance, equilibrate, offset. • n balance, counterweight.

countersign n password, watchword.

countervail vb balance, compensate, counterbalance.

country n land, region; countryside; fatherland, home, kingdom, state, territory; nation, people, population. • adj rural, rustic; countrified, rough, rude, uncultivated, unpolished, unrefined.

countryman n compatriot, fellow-citizen; boor, clown, farmer, hind, husbandman, peasant, rustic, swain.

couple vb pair, unite; copulate, embrace; buckle, clasp, conjoin, connect, join, link, pair, yoke. • n brace, pair, twain, two; bond, coupling, lea, link, tie.

courage n audaciousness, audacity, boldness, bravery, daring, derring-do, dauntlessness, fearlessness, firmness, fortitude, gallantry, hardihood, heroism, intrepidity, manhood, mettle, nerve, pluck, prowess, resolution, spirit, spunk, valorousness, valor.

courageous adj audacious, brave, bold, chivalrous, daring, dauntless, fearless, gallant, hardy, heroic, intrepid, lion-hearted, mettlesome, plucky, resolute, reliant, staunch, stout, undismayed, valiant, valorous.

course vb chase, follow, hunt, pursue, race, run. • n career, circuit, race, run; road, route, track, way; bearing, direction, path, tremor, track; ambit, beat, orbit, round; process, progress, sequence; order, regularity, succession, turn; behavior, conduct, deportment; arrangement, series, system.

court vb coddle, fawn, flatter, ingratiate; address, woo; seek; invite, solicit. • n area, courtyard, patio, quadrangle; addresses, civilities, homage, respects, solicitations; retinue, palace, tribunal.

courteous adj affable, attentive, ceremonious, civil, complaisant, courtly, debonair, elegant, gracious, obliging, polished, polite, refined, respected, urbane, well-bred, well-mannered.

courtesan n harlot, prostitute, strumpet, vamp, wanton, wench, whore.

courtesy n affability, civility, complaisance, courteousness, elegance, good-breeding, graciousness, polish, politeness, refine, urbanity.

courtly adj affable, ceremonious, civil, elegant, flattering, lordly, obliging, polished, polite, refined, urbane.

courtyard n area, court, patio, quadrangle, yard.

cove[1] n anchorage, bay, bight, creek, firth, fjord, inlet.

cove[2] n bloke, chap, character, customer, fellow, type.

covenant vb agree, bargain, contract, stipulate. • n bond, deed; arrangement, bargain, compact, concordat, contract, convention, pact, stipulation, treaty.

cover vb overlay, overspread; cloak, conceal, curtain, disguise, hide, mask, screen, secrete, shroud, veil; defend, guard, protect, shelter, shield; case, clothe, envelop, invest, jacket, sheathe; comprehend, comprise, contain, embody, embrace, include. • n capsule, case, covering, integument, tegument, top; cloak, disguise, screen, veil; guard, defense, protection, safeguard, shelter, shield; shrubbery, thicket,

underbrush, undergrowth, underwood, woods.

covert adj clandestine, concealed, disguised, hidden, insidious, private, secret, sly, stealthy, underhand. • n coppice, shade, shrubbery, thicket, underwood; asylum; defense, harbor, hiding-place, refuge, retreat, sanctuary, shelter.

covet vb aim after, desire, long for, yearn for; hanker after, lust after.

covetous adj acquisitive, avaricious, close-fisted, grasping, greedy, miserly, niggardly, parsimonious, penurious, rapacious.

cow[1] n bovine, heifer.

cow[2] vb abash, break, daunt, discourage, dishearten, frighten, intimidate, overawe, subdue.

coward adj cowardly, timid. • n caitiff, craven, dastard, milksop, poltroon, recreant, skulker, sneak, wheyface.

cowardly adj base, chicken-hearted, coward, craven, dastardly, faint-hearted, fearful, lily-livered, mean, pusillanimous, timid, timorous, white-livered, yellow.

cower vb bend, cringe, crouch, fawn, shrink, squat, stoop.

coxcomb n beau, dandy, dude, exquisite, fop, jackanapes, popinjay, prig.

coy adj backward, bashful, demure, diffident, distant, modest, reserved, retiring, self-effacing, shrinking, shy, timid.

coyness n affectation, archness, backwardness, bashfulness, coquettishness, demureness, diffidence, evasiveness, modesty, primness, reserve, shrinking, shyness, timidity.

cozen vb beguile, cheat, chouse, circumvent, deceive, defraud, diddle, dupe, gull, overreach, swindle, trick, victimize.

cozy, cosy adj comfortable, easy, snug; chatty, conversable, social, talkative.

crabbed adj acrid, rough, sore, tart; acrimonious, cantankerous, captious, caustic, censorious, churlish, cross, growling, harsh, ill-tempered, morose, peevish, petulant, snappish, snarling, splenetic, surly, testy, touchy, waspish; difficult, intractable, perplexing, tough, trying, unmanageable.

crabbedness n acridity, acridness, roughness, sourness, tartness; acerbity, acrimonious, asperity, churlishness, harshness, ill-tempered, moodiness, moroseness, sullenness; difficulty, intractability, perplexity.

crack *vb* break; chop, cleave, split; snap; craze, madden; boast, brag, bluster, crow, gasconade, vapor, vaunt. • *adj* capital, excellent, first-class, first-rate, tip-top. • *n* breach, break, chink, cleft, cranny, crevice, fissure, fracture, opening, rent, rift, split; burst, clap, explosion, pop, report; snap.

cracked *adj* broken, crackled, split; crack-brained, crazed, crazy, demented, deranged, flighty, insane.

crackle *vb* crepitate, decrepitate, snap.

craft *n* ability, aptitude, cleverness, dexterity, expertness, power, readiness, skill, tact, talent; artifice, artfulness, cunning, craftiness, deceitfulness, deception, guile, shrewdness, subtlety; art, avocation, business, calling, employment, handicraft, trade, vocation; vessel.

crafty *adj* arch, artful, astute, cunning, crooked, deceitful, designing, fraudulent, guileful, insidious, intriguing, scheming, shrewd, sly, subtle, tricky, wily.

crag *n* rock; neck, throat.

craggy *adj* broken, cragged, jagged, rough, rugged, scraggy, uneven.

cram *vb* fill, glut, gorge, satiate, stuff; compress, crowd, overcrowd, press, squeeze; coach, grind.

cramp *vb* convulse; check, clog, confine, hamper, hinder, impede, obstruct, restrain, restrict. • *n* convulsion, crick, spasm; check, restraint, restriction, obstruction

crank *vb* bend, crankle, crinkle, turn, twist, wind. • *n* bend, quirk, turn, twist, winding.

cranny *n* breach, break, chink, cleft, crack, crevice, fissure, gap, hole, interstice, nook, opening, rift.

crapulous *adj* crapulent, drunk, drunken, inebriated, intoxicated, tipsy.

crash *vb* break, shatter, shiver, smash, splinter. • *adj* emergency, fast, intensive, rushed, speeded-up. • *n* clang, clash, collision concussion, jar.

crass *adj* coarse, gross, raw, thick, unabated, unrefined.

cravat *n* neckcloth, neckerchief, necktie.

crave *vb* ask, beg, beseech, entreat, implore, petition, solicit, supplicate; desire, hanker after, long for, need, want, yearn for.

craven *n* coward, dastard, milk-sop, poltroon, recreant. • *adj* cowardly, chicken-hearted, lily-livered, pusillanimous, yellow.

craving *n* hankering, hungering, longing, yearning.

craw *n* crop, gullet, stomach, throat.

craze *vb* bewilder, confuse, dement, derange, madden; disorder, impair, weaken. • *n* fashion, mania, mode, novelty.

crazy *adj* broken, crank, rickety, shaky, shattered, tottering; crack-brained, delirious, demented, deranged, distracted, idiotic, insane, lunatic, mad, silly.

create *vb* originate, procreate; cause, design, fashion, form, invent, occasion, produce; appoint, constitute, make.

creation *n* formation, invention, origination, production; cosmos, universe; appointment, constitution, establishment, nomination.

creator *n* author, designer, inventor, fashioner, maker, originator; god.

creature *n* animal, beast, being, body, brute, man, person; dependant, hanger-on, minion, parasite, retainer, vassal; miscreant, wretch.

credence *n* acceptance, belief, confidence, credit, faith, reliance, trust.

credentials *npl* certificate, diploma, missive, passport, recommendation, testament, testimonial, title, voucher, warrant.

credibility *n* believability, plausibility, tenability, , trustworthiness.

credit *vb* accept, believe, trust; loan, trust. • *n* belief, confidence, credence, faith, reliance, trust; esteem, regard, reputableness, reputation; influence, power; honor, merit; loan, trust.

creditable *adj* estimable, honorable, meritorious, praiseworthy, reputable, respectable.

credulity *n* credulousness, gullibility, silliness, simplicity, stupidity.

credulous *adj* dupable, green, gullible, naive, over-trusting, trustful, uncritical, unsuspecting, unsuspicious.

creed *n* belief, confession, doctrine, dogma, opinion, profession, tenet.

creek *n* bay, bight, cove, fjord, inlet; rivulet, streamlet.

creep *vb* crawl; steal upon; cringe, fawn, grovel, insinuate. • *n* crawl, scrabble, scramble; fawner, groveler, sycophant, toady.

crenate *adj* indented, notched, scalloped.

crepitate *vb* crack, crackle, decrepitate, snap.

crest *n* comb, plume, topknot, tuft; apex,

crown, head, ridge, summit, top; arms, badge, bearings.

crestfallen *adj* chap-fallen, dejected, depressed, despondent, discouraged, disheartened, dispirited, downcast, downhearted, low-spirited, melancholy, sad.

crevice *n* chink, cleft, crack, cranny, fissure, fracture, gap, hole, interstice, opening, rent, rift.

crew *n* company, complement, hands; company, corps, gang, horde, mob, party, posse, set, squad, team, throng.

crib *vb* cage, confine, encage, enclose, imprison; pilfer, purloin. • *n* manger, rack; bin, bunker; plagiarism, plunder, theft.

crick *vb* jar, rick, wrench, wrick. • *n* convulsion, cramp, jarring, spasm, rick, wrench, wrick.

crime *n* felony, misdeed, misdemeanor, offence, violation; delinquency, fault, guilt, iniquity, sin, transgression, unrighteousness, wickedness, wrong.

criminal *adj* culpable, felonious, flagitious, guilty, illegal, immoral, iniquitous, nefarious, unlawful, vicious, wicked, wrong. • *n* convict, culprit, delinquent, felon, malefactor, offender, sinner, transgressor.

criminate *vb* accuse, arraign, charge, convict, impeach, indict; implicate, involve.

crimp *vb* crisp, curl.

cringe *vb* bend, bow, cower, crouch, fawn, grovel, kneel, sneak, stoop, truckle.

cripple *vb* cramp, destroy, disable, enfeeble, impair, lame, maim, mutilate, paralyse, ruin, weaken.

crisis *n* acme, climax, height; conjuncture, emergency, exigency, juncture, pass, pinch, push, rub, strait, urgency.

crisp *adj* brittle, curled, friable, frizzled.

criterion *n* canon, gauge, measure, principle, proof, rule, standard, test, touchstone.

critic *n* arbiter, caviler, censor, connoisseur, judge, nit-picker, reviewer.

critical *adj* accurate, exact, nice; captious, carping, caviling, censorious, exacting; crucial, decisive, determining, important, turning: dangerous, dubious, exigent, hazardous, imminent, momentous, precarious, ticklish.

criticism *n* analysis, animadversion, appreciation, comment, critique, evaluation, judgement, review, strictures.

criticize *vb* appraise, evaluate, examine, judge.

croak *vb* complain, groan, grumble, moan, mumble, repine; die.

crone *n* hag, witch.

crony *n* ally, associate, chum, friend, mate, mucker, pal.

crook *vb* bend, bow, curve, incurvate, turn, wind. • *n* bend, curvature, flexion; turn; artifice, machination, trick; criminal, thief, villain.

crooked *adj* angular, bent, bowed, curved, winding, zigzag; askew, aslant, awry, deformed, disfigured, distorted, twisted, wry; crafty, deceitful, devious, dishonest, dishonorable, fraudulent, insidious, intriguing, knavish, tricky, underhanded, unfair, unscrupulous.

crop *vb* gather, mow, pick, pluck, reap; browse, nibble; clip, curtail, lop, reduce, shorten. • *n* harvest, produce, yield.

cross *vb* intersect, pass over, traverse; hinder, interfere, obstruct, thwart; interbred, intermix. • *adj* transverse; cantankerous, captious, crabbed, churlish, crusty, cynical, fractious, fretful, grouchy, ill-natured, ill-tempered, irascible, irritable, morose, peevish, pettish, petulant, snappish, snarling, sour, spleeny, splenetic, sulky, sullen, surly, testy, touchy, waspish. • *n* crucifix, gibbet, rood; affliction, misfortune, trial, trouble, vexation; crossbreeding, hybrid, intermixture.

cross-grained *adj* cantankerous, headstrong, obdurate, peevish, perverse, refractory, stubborn, untractable, wayward.

crossing *n* intersection, overpass, traversing, under-pass.

crossways, crosswise *adv* across, over, transversely.

crotchet *n* caprice, fad, fancy, freak, quirk, vagary, whim, whimsy.

crouch *vb* cower, cringe, fawn, truckle; crouch, kneel, stoop, squat; bow, curtsy, genuflect.

croup *n* buttocks, crupper, rump.

crow *vb* bluster, boast, brag, chuckle, exult, flourish, gasconade, swagger, triumph, vapor, vaunt.

crowd *vb* compress, cram, jam, pack, press; collect, congregate, flock, herd, huddle, swarm. • *n* assembly, company, concourse, flock, herd, horde, host, jam, multitude, press, throng; mob, pack, populace, rabble, rout.

crown *vb* adorn, dignify, honor; recompense, requite, reward; cap, complete, consummate, finish, perfect. • *n* bays, chaplet, coronal, coronet, garland, diadem, laurel, wreath; monarchy, royalty, sovereignty; diadem; dignity, honor, recompense, reward; apex, crest, summit, top.

crowning adj completing, consummating, dignifying, finishing, perfecting.

crucial adj intersecting, transverse; critical, decisive, searching, severe, testing, trying.

crude adj raw, uncooked, undressed, unworked; harsh, immature, rough, unripe; crass, coarse, unrefined; awkward, immature, indigestible, rude, uncouth, unpolished, unpremeditated.

cruel adj barbarous, blood-thirsty, dire, fell, ferocious, inexorable, hard-hearted, inhuman, merciless, pitiless, relentless, ruthless, sanguinary, savage, truculent, uncompassionate, unfeeling, unmerciful, unrelenting; bitter, cold, hard, severe, sharp, unfeeling.

crumble vb bruise, crush, decay, disintegrate, perish, pound, pulverize, triturate.

crumple vb rumple, wrinkle.

crush vb bruise, compress, contuse, squash, squeeze; bray, comminute, crumble, disintegrate, mash; demolish, raze, shatter; conquer, overcome, overpower, overwhelm, quell, subdue.

crust n coat, coating, incrustation, outside, shell, surface.

crusty adj churlish, crabbed, cross, cynical, fretful, forward, morose, peevish, pettish, petulant, snappish, snarling, surly, testy, touchy, waspish; friable, hard, short.

cry vb call, clamor, exclaim; blubber, snivel, sob, wail, weep, whimper; bawl, bellow, hoot, roar, shout, vociferate, scream, screech, squawk, squall, squeal, yell; announce, blazon, proclaim, publish. • n acclamation, clamor, ejaculation, exclamation, outcry; crying, lament, lamentation, plaint, weeping; bawl, bellow, howl, roar, scream, screech, shriek, yell; announcement, proclamation, publication.

crypt n catacomb, tomb, vault.

cuddle vb cosset, nestle, snuggle, squat; caress, embrace, fondle, hug, pet. • n caress, embrace, hug.

cudgel vb bang, baste, batter, beat, cane, drub, thrash, thump. • n bastinado, baton, bludgeon, club, shillelagh, stick, truncheon.

cue vb intimate, prompt, remind, sign, signal. • n catchword, hint, intimation, nod, prompting, sign, signal, suggestion.

cuff vb beat, box, buffet, knock, pummel, punch, slap, smack, strike, thump. • n blow, box, punch, slap, smack, strike, thump.

cul-de-sac n alley, dead end, impasse, pocket.

cull vb choose, elect, pick, select; collect, gather, glean, pluck.

culmination n acme, apex, climax, completion, consummation, crown, summit, top, zenith.

culpability n blame, blameworthiness, criminality, culpableness, guilt, remissness, sinfulness.

culpable adj blameable, blameworthy, censurable, faulty, guilty, reprehensible, sinful, transgressive, wrong.

culprit n delinquent, criminal, evil-doer, felon, malefactor, offender.

cultivate vb farm, fertilize, till, work; civilize, develop, discipline, elevate, improve, meliorate, refine, train; investigate, prosecute, pursue, search, study; cherish, foster, nourish, patronize, promote.

culture n agriculture, cultivation, farming, husbandry, tillage; cultivation, elevation, improvement, refinement.

cumber vb burden, clog, encumber, hamper, impede, obstruct, oppress, overload; annoy, distract, embarrass, harass, perplex, plague, torment, trouble, worry.

cumbersome adj burdensome, clumsy, cumbrous, embarrassing, heavy, inconvenient, oppressive, troublesome, unmanageable, unwieldy, vexatious.

cuneiform adj cuneate, wedge-shaped.

cunning adj artful, astute, crafty, crooked, deceitful, designing, diplomatic, foxy, guileful, intriguing, machiavellian, sharp, shrewd, sly, subtle, tricky, wily; curious, ingenious. • n art, artfulness, artifice, astuteness, craft, shrewdness, subtlety; craftiness, chicane, chicanery, deceit, deception, intrigue, slyness.

cup n beaker, bowl, chalice, goblet, mug; cupful, draught, potion.

cupboard n buffet, cabinet, closet.

cupidity n avidity, greed, hankering, longing, lust; acquisitiveness, avarice, covetousness, greediness, stinginess.

curative adj healing, medicinal, remedial, restorative.

curator n custodian, guardian, keeper, superintendent.

curb vb bridle, check, control, hinder, moderate, repress, restrain. • n bridle, check, control, hindrance, rein, restraint.

cure *vb* alleviate, correct, heal, mend, remedy, restore; kipper, pickle, preserve. • *n* antidote, corrective, help, remedy, reparative, restorative, specific; alleviation, healing, restorative.

curiosity *n* interest, inquiringness, inquisitiveness; celebrity, curio, marvel, novelty, oddity, phenomenon, rarity, sight, spectacle, wonder.

curious *adj* interested, inquiring, inquisitive, meddling, peering, prying, scrutinizing; extraordinary, marvellous, novel, queer, rare, singular, strange, unique, unusual; cunning, elegant, fine, finished, neat, skillful, well-wrought.

curl *vb* coil, twist, wind, writhe; bend, buckle, ripple, wave. • *n* curlicue, lovelock, ringlet; flexure, sinuosity, undulation, wave, waving, winding.

curmudgeon *n* churl, lick-penny, miser, niggard, screw, scrimp, skinflint.

currency *n* publicity; acceptance, circulation, transmission; bills, coins, money, notes.

current *adj* common, general, popular, rife; circulating, passing; existing, instant, present, prevalent, widespread. • *n* course, progression, river, stream, tide, undertow. • *adv* commonly, generally, popularly, publicly.

curry *vb* comb, dress; beat, cudgel, drub, thrash.

curse *vb* anathematize, damn, denounce, execrate, imprecate, invoke, maledict; blast, blight, destroy, doom; afflict, annoy, harass, injure, plague, scourge, torment, vex; blaspheme, swear. • *n* anathema, ban, denunciation, execration, fulmination, imprecation, malediction, malison; affliction, annoyance, plague, scourge, torment, trouble, vexation; ban, condemnation, penalty, sentence.

cursed *adj* accursed, banned, blighted, curse-laden, unholy; abominable, detestable, execrable, hateful, villainous; annoying, confounded, plaguing, scourging, tormenting, troublesome, vexatious.

cursory *adj* brief, careless, desultory, hasty, passing, rapid, slight, summary, superficial, transient, transitory.

curt *adj* brief, concise, laconic, short, terse; crusty, rude, snappish, tart.

curtail *vb* abridge, dock, lop, retrench, shorten; abbreviate, contract, decrease, diminish, lessen.

curtain *vb* cloak, cover, drape, mantle, screen, shade, shield, veil. • *n* arras, drape, drop, portiÈre, screen, shade.

curvature *n* arcuation, bend, bending, camber, crook, curve, flexure, incurvation.

curve *vb* bend, crook, inflect, turn, twist, wind. • *n* arcuation, bend, bending, camber, crook, flexure, incurvation.

curvet *vb* bound, leap, vault; caper, frisk.

cushion *vb* absorb, damp, dampen, deaden, dull, muffle, mute, soften, subdue, suppress; cradle, pillow, support. • *n* bolster, hassock, pad, pillow, woolsack.

cusp *n* angle, horn, point.

custodian *n* curator, guardian, keeper, sacristan, superintendent, warden.

custody *n* care, charge, guardianship, keeping, safe-keeping, protection, watch, ward; confinement, durance, duress, imprisonment, prison.

custom *n* consuetude, convention, fashion, habit, manner, mode, practice, rule, usage, use, way; form, formality, observation; patronage; duty, impost, tax, toll, tribute.

customary *adj* accustomed, common, consuetudinary, conventional, familiar, fashionable, general, habitual, gnomic, prescriptive, regular, usual, wonted.

cut *vb* chop, cleave, divide, gash, incise, lance, sever, slice, slit, wound; carve, chisel, sculpture; hurt, move, pierce, touch; ignore, slight; abbreviate, abridge, curtail, shorten. • *n* gash, groove, incision, nick, slash, slice, slit; channel, passage; piece, slice; fling, sarcasm, taunt; fashion, form, mode, shape, style.

cutthroat *adj* barbarous, cruel, ferocious, murderous; competitive, exacting, exorbitant, extortionate, rivalling, ruthless, usurious, vying. • *n* assassin, murderer, ruffian.

cutting *adj* keen, sharp; acid, biting, bitter, caustic, piercing, sarcastic, sardonic, satirical, severe, trenchant, wounding.

cycle *n* age, circle, era, period, revolution, round.

Cyclopean *adj* colossal, enormous, gigantic, Herculean, immense, vast.

cynical *adj* captious, carping, censorious, churlish, crabbed, cross, crusty, fretful, ill-natured, ill-tempered, morose, peevish, pettish, petulant, sarcastic, satirical, snappish, snarling, surly, testy, touchy, waspish; contemptuous, derisive, misanthropic, pessimistic, scornful.

cynosure *n* attraction, center.

cyst *n* pouch, sac.

D

dab *vb* box, rap, slap, strike, tap touch; coat, daub, smear. • *adj* adept, expert, proficient; pat. • *n* lump, mass, pat.

dabble *vb* dip, moisten, soak, spatter, splash, sprinkle, wet; meddle, tamper, trifle.

daft *adj* absurd, delirious, foolish, giddy, idiotic, insane, silly, simple, stupid, witless; frolicsome, merry, mirthful, playful, sportive.

dagger *n* bayonet, dirk, poniard, stiletto.

dainty *adj* delicate, delicious, luscious, nice, palatable, savoury, tender, toothsome; beautiful, charming, choice, delicate, elegant, exquisite, fine, neat; fastidious, finical, finicky, over-nice, particular, scrupulous, squeamish. • *n* delicacy, titbit, treat.

dale *n* bottom, dell, dingle, glen, vale, valley.

dalliance *n* caressing, endearments, flirtation, fondling.

dally *vb* dawdle, fritter, idle, trifle, waste time; flirt, fondle, toy.

damage *vb* harm, hurt, impair, injure, mar. • *n* detriment, harm, hurt, injury, loss, mischief.

damages *npl* compensation, fine, forfeiture, indemnity, reparation, satisfaction.

dame *n* babe, baby, broad, doll, girl; lady, madam, matron, mistress.

damn *vb* condemn, doom, kill, ruin. • *n* bean, curse, fig, hoot, rap, sou, straw, whit.

damnable *adj* abominable, accursed, atrocious, cursed, detestable, hateful, execrable, odious, outrageous.

damp *vb* dampen, moisten; allay, abate, check, discourage, moderate, repress, restrain; chill, cool, deaden, deject, depress, dispirit. • *adj* dank, humid, moist, wet. • *n* dampness, dank, fog, mist, moisture, vapor; chill, dejection, depression.

damper *n* check, hindrance, impediment, obstacle; damp, depression, discouragement, wet blanket.

dandle *vb* amuse, caress, fondle, pet, toss; dance.

danger *n* jeopardy, insecurity, hazard, peril, risk, venture.

dangerous *adj* critical, hazardous, insecure, perilous, risky, ticklish, unsafe.

dangle *vb* drape, hang, pend, sway, swing; fawn.

dank *adj* damp, humid, moist, wet.

dapper *adj* active, agile, alert, brisk, lively, nimble, quick, ready, smart, spry; neat, nice, pretty, spruce, trim.

dapple *vb* diversify, spot, variegate. • *adj* dappled, spotted, variegated.

dare *vb* challenge, defy, endanger, hazard, provoke, risk. • *n* challenge, defiance, gage.

daring *adj* adventurous, bold, brave, chivalrous, courageous, dauntless, doughty, fearless, gallant, heroic, intrepid, valiant, valorous. • *n* adventurousness, boldness, bravery, courage, dauntlessness, doughtiness, fearlessness, intrepidity, undauntedness, valor.

dark *adj* black, cloudy, darksome, dusky, ebon, inky, lightless, lurid, moonless, murky, opaque, overcast, pitchy, rayless, shady, shadowy, starless, sunless, swart, tenebrous, umbrageous, unenlightened, unilluminated; abstruse, cabbalistic, enigmatical, incomprehensible, mysterious, mystic, mystical, obscure, occult, opaque, recondite, transcendental, unillumined, unintelligible; cheerless, discouraging, dismal, disheartening, funereal, gloomy; benighted, darkened, ignorant, rude, unlettered, untaught; atrocious, damnable, infamous, flagitious, foul, horrible, infernal, nefarious, vile, wicked. • *n* darkness, dusk, murkiness, obscurity; concealment, privacy, secrecy; blindness, ignorance.

darken *vb* cloud, dim, eclipse, obscure, shade, shadow; chill, damp, depress, gloom, sadden; benight, stultify, stupefy; obscure, perplex; defile, dim, dull, stain, sully.

darkness *n* blackness, dimness, gloom, obscurity; blindness, ignorance; cheerlessness, despondency, gloom, joylessness; privacy, secrecy.

darling *adj* beloved, cherished, dear, loved, precious, treasured. • *n* dear, favorite, idol, love, sweetheart.

dart *vb* ejaculate, hurl, launch, propel, sling, throw; emit, shoot; dash, rush, scoot, spring.

dash *vb* break, destroy, disappoint, frustrate, ruin, shatter, spoil, thwart; abash, confound, disappoint, surprise; bolt, dart, fly, run, speed, rush. • *n* blow, stroke; advance, onset, rush; infusion, smack, spice, sprinkling, tincture, tinge, touch; flourish, show.

dashing adj headlong, impetuous, precipitate, rushing; brilliant, gay, showy, spirited.

dastardly adj base, cowardly, coward, cowering, craven, pusillanimous, recreant. • n coward, craven, milksop, poltroon, recreant.

data npl conditions, facts, information, premises.

date n age, cycle, day, generation, time; epoch, era, period; appointment, arrangement, assignation, engagement, interview, rendezvous, tryst; catch, steady, sweetheart.

daub vb bedaub, begrime, besmear, blur, cover, deface, defile, grime, plaster, smear, smudge, soil, sully. • n smear, smirch, smudge.

daunt vb alarm, appal, check, cow, deter, discourage, frighten, intimate, scare, subdue, tame, terrify, thwart.

dauntless adj bold, brave, chivalrous, courageous, daring, doughty, gallant, heroic, indomitable, intrepid, unaffrighted, unconquerable, undaunted, undismayed, valiant, valorous.

dawdle vb dally, delay, fiddle, idle, lag, loiter, potter, trifle.

dawn vb appear, begin, break, gleam, glimmer, open, rise. • n daybreak, dawning, cockcrow, sunrise, sun-up.

day n daylight, sunlight, sunshine; age, epoch, generation, lifetime, time.

daze vb blind, dazzle; bewilder, confound, confuse, perplex, stun, stupefy. • n bewilderment, confusion, discomposure, perturbation, pother; coma, stupor, swoon, trance.

dazzle vb blind, daze; astonish, confound, overpower, surprise. • n brightness, brilliance, splendor.

dead adj breathless, deceased, defunct, departed, gone, inanimate, lifeless; apathetic, callous, cold, dull, frigid, indifferent, inert, lukewarm, numb, obtuse, spiritless, torpid, unfeeling; flat, insipid, stagnant, tasteless, vapid; barren, inactive, sterile, unemployed, unprofitable, useless. • adv absolutely, completely, downright, fundamentally, quite; direct, directly, due, exactly, just, right, squarely, straight. • n depth, midst; hush, peace, quietude, silence, stillness.

deaden vb abate, damp, dampen, dull, impair, muffle, mute, restrain, retard, smother, weaken; benumb, blunt, hebetate, obtund, paralyse.

deadly adj deleterious, destructive, fatal, lethal, malignant, mortal, murderous, noxious, pernicious, poisonous, venomous; implacable, mortal, rancorous, sanguinary.

deal vb allot, apportion, assign, bestow, dispense, distribute, divide, give, reward, share; bargain, trade, traffic, treat with. • n amount, degree, distribution, extent, lot, portion, quantity, share; bargain, transaction.

dear adj costly, expensive, high-priced; beloved, cherished, darling, esteemed, precious, treasured. • n beloved, darling, deary, honey, love, precious, sweet, sweetie, sweetheart.

dearth n deficiency, insufficiency, scarcity; famine, lack, need, shortage, want.

death n cessation, decease, demise, departure, destruction, dissolution, dying, end, exit, mortality, passing.

deathless adj eternal, everlasting, immortal, imperishable, undying; boring, dull, turgid.

debacle n breakdown, cataclysm, collapse; rout, stampede.

debar vb blackball, deny, exclude, hinder, prevent, prohibit, restrain, shut out, stop, withhold.

debase vb adulterate, alloy, depress, deteriorate, impair, injure, lower, pervert, reduce, vitiate; abase, degrade, disgrace, dishonor, humble, humiliate, mortify, shame; befoul, contaminate, corrupt, defile, foul, pollute, soil, taint.

debate vb argue, canvass, contest, discuss, dispute; contend, deliberate, wrangle. • n controversy, discussion, disputation; altercation, contention, contest, dispute, logomachy.

debauch vb corrupt, deprave, pollute, vitiate; deflower, ravish, seduce, violate. • n carousal, orgy, revel, saturnalia.

debauchery n dissipation, dissoluteness, excesses, intemperance; debauch, excess, intemperance, lewdness, licentiousness, lust; bacchanal, carousal, compotation, indulgence, orgies, potation, revelry, revels, saturnalia, spree.

debilitate vb enervate, enfeeble, exhaust, prostrate, relax, weaken.

debility n enervation, exhaustion, faintness, feebleness, frailty, imbecility, infirmity, languor, prostration, weakness.

debonair adj affable, civil, complaisant, courteous, easy, gracious, kind, obliging, polite, refined, urbane, well-bred.

debris n detritus, fragments, remains, rubbish, rubble, ruins, wreck, wreckage.

debt n arrears, debit, due, liability,

obligation; fault, misdoing, offence, short-coming, sin, transgression, trespass.

decadence n caducity, decay, declension, decline, degeneracy, degeneration, deterioration, fall, retrogression.

decamp vb abscond, bolt, escape, flee, fly.

decapitate vb behead, decollate, guillotine.

decay vb decline, deteriorate, disintegrate, fail, perish, wane, waste, wither; decompose, putrefy, rot. • n caducity, decadence, declension, decline, decomposition, decrepitude, degeneracy, degeneration, deterioration, dilapidation, disintegration, fading, failing, perishing, putrefaction, ruin, wasting, withering.

deceased adj dead, defunct, departed, gone, late, lost.

deceit n artifice, cheating, chicanery, cozenage, craftiness, deceitfulness, deception, double-dealing, duplicity, finesse, fraud, guile, hypocrisy, imposition, imposture, pretence, sham, treachery, tricky, underhandedness, wile.

deceitful adj counterfeit, deceptive, delusive, fallacious, hollow, illusive, illusory, insidious, misleading; circumventive, cunning, designing, dissembling, dodgy, double-dealing, evasive, false, fraudulent, guileful, hypocritical, insincere, tricky, underhanded, wily.

deceive vb befool, beguile, betray, cheat, chouse, circumvent, cozen, defraud, delude, disappoint, double-cross, dupe, ensnare, entrap, fool, gull, hoax, hoodwink, humbug, mislead, outwit, overreach, trick.

deceiver n charlatan, cheat, humbug, hypocrite, knave, impostor, pretender, rogue, sharper, trickster.

decent adj appropriate, becoming, befitting, comely, seemly, decorous, fit, proper, seemly; chaste, delicate, modest, pure; moderate, passable, respectable, tolerable.

deception n artifice, cheating, chicanery, cozenage, craftiness, deceitfulness, deception, double-dealing, duplicity, finesse, fraud, guile, hoax, hypocrisy, imposition, imposture, pretence, sham, treachery, trick, underhandedness, wile; cheat, chouse, ruse, stratagem, wile.

deceptive adj deceitful, deceiving, delusive, disingenuous, fallacious, false, illusive, illusory, misleading.

decide vb close, conclude, determine, end, settle, terminate; resolve; adjudge, adjudicate, award.

decided adj determined, firm, resolute, unhesitating, unwavering; absolute, categorical, positive, unequivocal; certain, clear, indisputable, undeniable, unmistakable, unquestionable.

deciduous adj caducous, nonperennial, temporary.

decipher vb explain, expound, interpret, reveal, solve, unfold, unravel; read.

decision n conclusion, determination, judgement, settlement; adjudication, award, decree, pronouncement, sentence; firmness, resolution.

decisive adj conclusive, determinative, final.

deck vb adorn, array, beautify, decorate, embellish, grace, ornament; apparel, attire, bedeck, clothe, dress, robe.

declaim vb harangue, mouth, rant, speak, spout.

declamation n declaiming, haranguing, mouthing, ranting, spouting.

declamatory adj bombastic, discursive, fustian, grandiloquent, high-flown, high-sounding, incoherent, inflated, pompous, pretentious, rhetorical, swelling, turgid.

declaration n affirmation, assertion, asseveration, averment, avowal, protestation, statement; announcement, proclamation, publication.

declaratory adj affirmative, annunciatory, assertive, declarative, definite, enunciative, enunciatory, expressive; explanatory, expository.

declare vb advertise, affirm, announce, assert, asseverate, aver, blazon, bruit, proclaim, promulgate, pronounce, publish, state, utter.

declension n decadence, decay, decline, degeneracy, deterioration, diminution; inflection, variation; declination, nonacceptance, refusal.

declination n bending, descent, inclination; decadence, decay, decline, degeneracy, degeneration, degradation, deterioration, diminution; aberration, departure, deviation, digression, divagation, divergence; declinature, nonacceptance, refusal.

decline vb incline, lean, slope; decay, droop, fail, flag, languish, pine, sink; degenerate, depreciate, deteriorate; decrease, diminish, dwindle, fade, ebb, lapse, lessen, wane; avoid, refuse, reject; inflect, vary. • n decadence, decay, declension, declination, degeneracy, deterioration, diminution, wane;

atrophy, consumption, marasmus, phthisis; declivity, hill, incline, slope.

declivity n declination, descent, incline, slope.

decompose vb analyze, disintegrate, dissolve, distil, resolve, separate; corrupt, decay, putrefy, rot.

decomposition n analysis, break-up, disintegration, resolution; caries, corruption, crumbling, decay, disintegration, dissolution, putrescence, rotting.

decorate vb adorn, beautify, bedeck, deck, embellish, enrich, garnish, grace, ornament.

decoration n adorning, beautifying, bedecking, decking, enriching, garnishing, ornamentation, ornamenting; adornment, enrichment, embellishment, ornament.

decorous adj appropriate, becoming, befitting, comely, decent, fit, suitable, proper, sedate, seemly, staid.

decorum n appropriate behavior, courtliness, decency, deportment, dignity, gravity, politeness, propriety, sedateness, seemliness.

decoy vb allure, deceive, ensnare, entice, entrap, inveigle, lure, seduce, tempt. • n allurement, lure, enticement.

decrease vb abate, contract, decline, diminish, dwindle, ebb, lessen, subside, wane; curtail, diminish, lessen, lower, reduce, retrench. • n abatement, contraction, declension, decline, decrement, diminishing, diminution, ebb, ebbing, lessening, reduction, subsidence, waning.

decree vb adjudge, appoint, command, decide, determine, enact, enjoin, order, ordain. • n act, command, edict, enactment, fiat, law, mandate, order, ordinance, precept, regulation, statute.

decrement n decrease, diminution, lessening, loss, waste.

decrepit adj feeble, effete, shattered, wasted, weak; aged, crippled, superannuated.

decry vb abuse, belittle, blame, condemn, denounce, depreciate, detract, discredit, disparage, run down, traduce, underrate, undervalue.

dedicate vb consecrate, devote, hallow, sanctify; address, inscribe.

deduce vb conclude, derive, draw, gather, infer.

deducible adj derivable, inferable.

deduct vb remove, subtract, withdraw; abate, detract.

deduction n removal, subtraction, withdrawal; abatement, allowance, defalcation, discount, rebate, reduction, reprise; conclusion, consequence, corollary, inference.

deed n achievement, act, action, derring-do, exploit, feat, performance; fact, truth, reality; charter, contract, document, indenture, instrument, transfer.

deem vb account, believe, conceive, consider, count, estimate, hold, imagine, judge, regard, suppose, think; fancy, opine.

deep adj abysmal, extensive, great, profound; abstruse, difficult, hard, intricate, knotty, mysterious, recondite, unfathomable; astute, cunning, designing, discerning, intelligent, insidious, penetrating, sagacious, shrewd; absorbed, engrossed; bass, grave, low; entire, great, heartfelt, thorough. • n main, ocean, water, sea; abyss, depth, profundity; enigma, mystery, riddle; silence, stillness.

deeply adv profoundly; completely, entirely, extensively, greatly, thoroughly; affectingly, distressingly, feelingly, mournfully, sadly.

deface vb blotch, deform, disfigure, injure, mar, mutilate, obliterate, soil, spoil, sully, tarnish.

de facto adj actual, real. • adv actually, in effect, in fact, really, truly.

defalcate vb abate, curtail, retrench, lop.

defalcation n abatement, deduction, diminution, discount, reduction; default, deficiency, deficit, shortage, shortcoming; embezzlement, fraud.

defamation n abuse, aspersion, back-biting, calumny, detraction, disparagement, libel, obloquy, opprobrium, scandal, slander.

defamatory adj abusive, calumnious, libellous, slanderous.

defame vb abuse, asperse, blacken, belie, besmirch, blemish, calumniate, detract, disgrace, dishonor, libel, malign, revile, slander, smirch, traduce, vilify.

default vb defalcate, dishonor, fail, repudiate, welsh. • n defalcation, failure, lapse, neglect, offence, omission, oversight, shortcoming; defect, deficiency, deficit, delinquency, destitution, fault, lack, want.

defaulter n delinquent, embezzler, offender, peculator.

defeat vb beat, checkmate, conquer, discomfit, overcome, overpower, overthrow, repulse, rout, ruin, vanquish; baffle, balk, block, disappoint, disconcert, foil, frustrate, thwart. • n discomfiture, downfall, overthrow, repulse, rout, vanquishment; bafflement, checkmate, frustration.

defect *vb* abandon, desert, rebel, revolt. • *n* default, deficiency, destitution, lack, shortcoming, spot, taint, want; blemish, blotch, error, flaw, imperfection, mistake; failing, fault, foible.

defection *n* abandonment, desertion, rebellion, revolt; apostasy, backsliding, dereliction.

defective *adj* deficient, inadequate, incomplete, insufficient, scant, short; faulty, imperfect, marred.

defend *vb* cover, fortify, guard, preserve, protect, safeguard, screen, secure, shelter, shield; assert, espouse, justify, maintain, plead, uphold, vindicate.

defender *n* asserter, maintainer, pleader, upholder; champion, protector, vindicator.

defense *n* defending, guarding, holding, maintaining, maintenance, protection; buckler, bulwark, fortification, guard, protection, rampart, resistance, shield; apology, excuse, justification, plea, vindication.

defenseless *adj* exposed, helpless, unarmed, unprotected, unguarded, unshielded, weak.

defer[1] *vb* adjourn, delay, pigeonhole, procrastinate, postpone, prorogue, protract, shelve, table.

defer[2] *vb* abide by, acknowledge, bow to, give way, submit, yield; admire, esteem, honor, regard, respect.

deference *n* esteem, homage, honor, obeisance, regard, respect, reverence, veneration; complaisance, consideration; obedience, submission.

deferential *adj* respectful, reverential.

defiance *n* challenge, daring; contempt, despite, disobedience, disregard, opposition, spite.

defiant *adj* contumacious, recalcitrant, resistant; bold, courageous, resistant.

deficiency *n* dearth, default, deficit, insufficiency, lack, meagerness, scantiness, scarcity, shortage, shortness, want; defect, error, failing, falling, fault, foible, frailty, imperfection, infirmity, weakness.

deficient *adj* defective, faulty, imperfect, inadequate, incomplete, insufficient, lacking, scant, scanty, scarce, short, unsatisfactory, wanting.

deficit *n* deficiency, lack, scarcity, shortage, shortness.

defile[1] *vb* dirty, foul, soil, stain, tarnish; contaminate, debase, poison, pollute, sully,

taint, vitiate; corrupt, debauch, deflower, ravish, seduce, violate.

defile[2] *vb* file, march, parade, promenade. • *n* col, gorge, pass, passage, ravine, strait.

define *vb* bound, circumscribe, designate, delimit, demarcate, determine, explain, limit, specify.

definite *adj* defined, determinate, determined, fixed, restricted; assured, certain, clear, exact, explicit, positive, precise, specific, unequivocal.

definitive *adj* categorical, determinate, explicit, express, positive, unconditional; conclusive, decisive, final.

deflect *vb* bend, deviate, diverge, swerve, turn, twist, waver, wind.

deflower *vb* corrupt, debauch, defile, seduce.

deform *vb* deface, disfigure, distort, injure, mar, misshape, ruin, spoil.

deformity *n* abnormality, crookedness, defect, disfigurement, distortion, inelegance, irregularity, malformation, misproportion, misshapenness, monstrosity, ugliness.

defraud *vb* beguile, cheat, chouse, circumvent, cozen, deceive, delude, diddle, dupe, embezzle, gull, overreach, outwit, pilfer, rob, swindle, trick.

defray *vb* bear, discharge, liquidate, meet, pay, settle.

deft *adj* adroit, apt, clever, dab, dextrous, expert, handy, ready, skillful.

defunct *adj* dead, deceased, departed, extinct, gone; abrogated, annulled, canceled, inoperative.

defy *vb* challenge, dare; brave, contemn, despise, disregard, face, flout, provoke, scorn, slight, spurn.

degeneracy *n* abasement, caducity, corruption, debasement, decadence, decay, declension, decline, decrease, degenerateness, degeneration, degradation, depravation, deterioration; inferiority, meanness, poorness.

degenerate *vb* decay, decline, decrease, deteriorate, retrograde, sink. • *adj* base, corrupt, decayed, degenerated, deteriorated, fallen, inferior, low, mean, perverted.

degeneration *n* debasement, decline, degeneracy, deterioration.

degradation *n* deposition, disgrace, dishonor, humiliation, ignominy; abasement, caducity, corruption, debasement, decadence, decline, degeneracy, degeneration, deterioration, perversion, vitiation.

degrade *vb* abase, alloy, break, cashier, corrupt, debase, demote, discredit, disgrace, dishonor, disparage, downgrade, humiliate, humble, lower, pervert, vitiate; deteriorate, impair, lower, sink.

degree *n* stage, step; class, grade, order, quality, rank, standing, station; extent, measure; division, interval, space.

deify *vb* apotheosize, idolize, glorify, revere; elevate, ennoble, exalt.

deign *vb* accord, condescend, grant, vouchsafe.

deject *vb* depress, discourage, dishearten, dispirit, sadden.

dejected *adj* blue, chapfallen, crestfallen, depressed, despondent, disheartened, dispirited, doleful, downcast, down-hearted, gloomy, low-spirited, miserable, sad, wretched.

delay *vb* defer, postpone, procrastinate; arrest, detain, check, hinder, impede, retard, stay, stop; prolong, protract; dawdle, linger, loiter, tarry. • *n* deferment, postponement, procrastination; check, detention, hindrance, impediment, retardation, stoppage; prolonging, protraction; dallying, dawdling, lingering, tarrying, stay, stop.

delectable *adj* agreeable, charming, delightful, enjoyable, gratifying, pleasant, pleasing.

delectation *n* delight, ecstasy, gladness, joy, rapture, ravishment, transport.

delegate *vb* appoint, authorize, mission, depute, deputize, transfer; commit, entrust. • *n* ambassador, commissioner, delegate, deputy, envoy, representative.

delete *vb* cancel, efface, erase, expunge, obliterate, remove.

deleterious *adj* deadly, destructive, lethal, noxious, poisonous; harmful, hurtful, injurious, pernicious, unwholesome.

deliberate *vb* cogitate, consider, consult, meditate, muse, ponder, reflect, ruminate, think, weigh. • *adj* careful, cautious, circumspect, considerate, heedful, purposeful, methodical, thoughtful, wary; well-advised, well-considered; aforethought, intentional, premeditated, purposed, studied.

deliberation *n* caution, circumspection, cogitation, consideration, coolness, meditation, prudence, reflection, thought, thoughtfulness, wariness; purpose.

delicacy *n* agreeableness, daintiness, deliciousness, pleasantness, relish, savoriness; bonne bouche, dainty, tidbit; elegance, fitness, lightness, niceness, nicety, smoothness, softness, tenderness; fragility, frailty, slenderness, slightness, tenderness, weakness; carefulness, discrimination, fastidiousness, finesse, nicety, scrupulousness, sensitivity, subtlety, tact; purity, refinement, sensibility.

delicate *adj* agreeable, delicious, pleasant, pleasing, palatable, savory; elegant, exquisite, fine, nice; careful, dainty, discriminating, fastidious, scrupulous; fragile, frail, slender, slight, tender, delicate; pure, refined.

delicious *adj* dainty, delicate, luscious, nice, palatable, savory; agreeable, charming, choice, delightful, exquisite, grateful, pleasant.

delight *vb* charm, enchant, enrapture, gratify, please, ravish, rejoice, satisfy, transport. • *n* charm, delectation, ecstasy, enjoyment, gladness, gratification, happiness, joy, pleasure, rapture, ravishment, satisfaction, transport.

delightful *adj* agreeable, captivating, charming, delectable, enchanting, enjoyable, enrapturing, rapturous, ravishing, transporting.

delineate *vb* design, draw, figure, paint, sketch, trace; depict, describe, picture, portray.

delineation *n* design, draught, drawing, figure, outline, sketch; account, description, picture, portrayal.

delinquency *n* crime, fault, misdeed; misdemeanor, offence, wrong-doing.

delinquent *adj* negligent, offending. • *n* criminal, culprit, defaulter, malefactor, miscreant, misdoer, offender, transgressor, wrong-doer.

delirious *adj* crazy, demented, deranged, frantic, frenzied, light-headed, mad, insane, raving, wandering.

delirium *n* aberration, derangement, frenzy, hallucination, incoherence, insanity, lunacy, madness, raving, wandering.

deliver *vb* emancipate, free, liberate, release; extricate, redeem, rescue, save; commit, give, impart, transfer; cede, grant, relinquish, resign, yield; declare, emit, promulgate, pronounce, speak, utter; deal, discharge.

deliverance *n* emancipation, escape, liberation, redemption, release.

delivery *n* conveyance, surrender; commitment, giving, rendering, transference, transferral, transmission; elocution, enunciation, pronunciation, speech, utterance; childbirth, confinement, labor, parturition, travail.

dell *n* dale, dingle, glen, valley, ravine.

delude *vb* beguile, cheat, chouse, circumvent, cozen, deceive, dupe, gull, misguide, mislead, overreach, trick.

deluge *vb* drown, inundate, overflow, overwhelm, submerge. • *n* cataclysm, downpour, flood, inundation, overflow, rush.

delusion *n* artifice, cheat, clap-trap, deceit, dodge, fetch, fraud, imposition, imposture, ruse, snare, trick, wile; deception, error, fallacy, fancy, hallucination, illusion, mistake, mockery, phantasm.

delusive *adj* deceitful, deceiving, deceptive, fallacious, illusional, illusionary, illusive.

demand *vb* challenge, exact, require; claim, necessitate, require; ask, inquire. • *n* claim, draft, exaction, requirement, requisition; call, want; inquiry, interrogation, question.

demarcation *n* bound, boundary, confine, distinction, division, enclosure, limit, separation.

demeanor *n* air, bearing, behavior, carriage, deportment, manner, mien.

demented *adj* crack-brained, crazed, crazy, daft, deranged, dotty, foolish, idiotic, infatuated, insane, lunatic.

dementia *n* idiocy, insanity, lunacy.

demerit *n* delinquency, fault, ill-desert.

demise *vb* alienate, consign, convey, devolve, grant, transfer; bequeath, devise, leave, will. • *n* alienation, conveyance, transfer, transference, transmission; death, decease.

demolish *vb* annihilate, destroy, dismantle, level, over-throw, overturn, pulverize, raze, ruin.

demon *n* devil, fiend, kelpie, goblin, troll.

demoniac, demoniacal *adj* demonic, demonical, devilish, diabolic, diabolical, fiendish, hellish, infernal, Mephistophelean, Mephistophelian, satanic; delirious, distracted, frantic, frenzied, feverish, hysterical, mad, overwrought, rabid.

demonstrate *vb* establish, exhibit, illustrate, indicate, manifest, prove, show.

demonstration *n* display, exhibition, manifestation, show.

demonstrative *adj* affectionate, communicative, effusive, emotional, expansive, expressive, extroverted, open, outgoing, passionate, sentimental, suggestive, talkative, unreserved; absolute, apodictic, certain, conclusive, probative; exemplificative, illustrative.

demoralize *vb* corrupt, debase, debauch, deprave, vitiate; depress, discourage, dishearten, weaken.

demulcent *adj* emollient, lenitive, mild, mollifying, sedative, soothing.

demur *vb* halt, hesitate, pause, stop, waver; doubt, object, scruple. • *n* demurral, hesitance, hesitancy, hesitation, objection, pause, qualm, scruple.

demure *adj* prudish; coy, decorous, grave, modest, priggish, prudish, sedate, sober, staid.

den *n* cavern, cave; haunt, lair, resort, retreat.

denial *n* contradiction, controverting, negation; abjuration, disavowal, disclaimer, disowning; disallowance, refusal, rejection.

denizen *n* citizen, dweller, inhabitant, resident.

denominate *vb* call, christen, designate, dub, entitle, name, phrase, style, term.

denomination *n* appellation, designation, name, style, term, title; class, kind, sort; body, persuasion, school, sect.

denote *vb* betoken, connote, designate, imply, indicate, mark, mean, note, show, signify, typify.

dénouement *n* catastrophe, unraveling; consummation, issue, finale, upshot, conclusion, termination.

denounce *vb* menace, threaten; arraign, attack, brand, censure, condemn, proscribe, stigmatize, upbraid; accuse, inform, denunciate.

dense *adj* close, compact, compressed, condensed, thick; dull, slow, stupid.

dent *vb* depress, dint, indent, pit. • *n* depression, dint, indentation, nick, notch.

dentate *adj* notched, serrate, toothed.

denude *vb* bare, divest, strip.

denunciation *n* menace, threat; arraignment, censure, fulmination, invective; exposure.

deny *vb* contradict, gainsay, oppose, refute, traverse; abjure, abnegate, disavow, disclaim, disown, renounce; disallow, refuse, reject, withhold.

depart *vb* absent, disappear, vanish; abandon, decamp, go, leave, migrate, quit, remove, withdraw; decease, die; deviate, diverge, vary.

department *n* district, division, part, portion, province; bureau, function, office, province, sphere, station; branch, division, subdivision.

departure *n* exit, leaving, parting, removal, recession, removal, retirement, withdrawal; abandonment, forsaking; death, decease, demise, deviation, exit.

depend *vb* hang, hinge, turn.

dependant *n* client, hanger-on, henchman, minion, retainer, subordinate, vassal; attendant, circumstance, concomitant, consequence, corollary.

dependence *n* concatenation, connection, interdependence; confidence, reliance, trust; buttress, prop, staff, stay, support, sup-porter; contingency, need, subjection, subordination.

dependency *n* adjunct, appurtenance; colony, province.

dependent *adj* hanging, pendant; conditioned, contingent, relying, subject, subordinate.

depict *vb* delineate, limn, outline, paint, pencil, portray, sketch; describe, render, represent.

deplete *vb* drain, empty, evacuate, exhaust, reduce.

deplorable *adj* calamitous, distressful, distressing, grievous, lamentable, melancholy, miserable, mournful, pitiable, regrettable, sad, wretched.

deplore *vb* bemoan, bewail, grieve for, lament, mourn, regret.

deploy *vb* display, expand, extend, open, unfold.

deportment *n* air, bearing, behaviour, breeding, carriage, comportment, conduct, demeanor, manner, mien, port.

depose *vb* break, cashier, degrade, dethrone, dismiss, displace, oust, reduce; avouch, declare, depone, testify.

deposit *vb* drop, dump, precipitate; lay, put; bank, hoard, lodge, put, save, store; commit, entrust. • *n* diluvium, dregs, lees, precipitate, precipitation, sediment, settlement, settlings, silt; money, pawn, pledge, security, stake.

depositary *n* fiduciary, guardian, trustee.

deposition *n* affidavit, evidence, testimony; deposit, precipitation, settlement; dethroning, displacement, removal.

depository *n* deposit, depot, storehouse, warehouse.

depot *n* depository, magazine, storehouse, warehouse.

depravation *n* abasement, corruption, deterioration, impairing, injury, vitiation; debasement, degeneracy, degeneration, depravity, impairment.

depraved *adj* abandoned, corrupt, corrupted, debased, debauched, degenerate, dissolute, evil, graceless, hardened, immoral, lascivious, lewd, licentious, lost, perverted, profligate, reprobate, shameless, sinful, vicious, wicked.

depravity *n* corruption, degeneracy, depravedness; baseness, contamination, corruption, corruptness, criminality, demoralization, immorality, iniquity, license, perversion, vice, viciousness, wickedness.

depreciate *vb* underestimate, undervalue, underrate; belittle, censure, decry, degrade, disparage, malign, traduce.

depreciation *n* belittling, censure, derogation, detraction, disparagement, maligning, traducing.

depredation *n* despoiling, devastation, pilfering, pillage, plunder, rapine, robbery, spoliation, theft.

depress *vb* bow, detrude, drop, lower, reduce, sink; abase, abash, degrade, debase, disgrace, humble, humiliate; chill, damp, dampen, deject, discourage, dishearten, dispirit, sadden; deaden, lower.

depression *n* cavity, concavity, dent, dimple, dint, excavation, hollow, hollowness, indentation, pit; blues, cheerlessness, dejection, dejectedness, despondency, disconsolateness, disheartenment, dispiritedness, dole, dolefulness, downheartedness, dumps, gloom, gloominess, hypochondria, melancholy, sadness, vapors; inactivity, lowness, stagnation; abasement, debasement, degradation, humiliation.

deprivation *n* bereavement, dispossession, loss, privation, spoliation, stripping.

deprive *vb* bereave, denude, despoil, dispossess, divest, rob, strip.

depth *n* abyss, deepness, drop, profundity; extent, measure; middle, midst, stillness; astuteness, discernment, penetration, perspicacity, profoundness, profundity, sagacity, shrewdness.

deputation *n* commission, delegation; commissioners, deputies, delegates, delegation, embassies, envoys, legation.

depute *vb* accredit, appoint, authorize, charge, commission, delegate, empower, entrust.

deputy *adj* acting, assistant, vice, subordinate.

• *n* agent, commissioner, delegate, envoy, factor, legate, lieutenant, proxy, representative, substitute, viceregent.

derange *vb* confound, confuse, disarrange, disconcert, disorder, displace, madden, perturb, unsettle; discompose, disconcert, disturb, perturb, ruffle, upset; craze, madden, unbalance, unhinge.

derangement *n* confusion, disarrangement, disorder, irregularity; discomposure, disturbance, perturbation; aberration, alienation, delirium, dementia, hallucination, insanity, lunacy, madness, mania.

derelict *adj* abandoned, forsaken, left, relinquished; delinquent, faithless, guilty, neglectful, negligent, unfaithful. • *n* castaway, castoff, outcast, tramp, vagrant, wreck, wretch.

dereliction *n* abandonment, desertion, relinquishement, renunciation; delinquency, failure, faithlessness, fault, neglect, negligence.

deride *vb* chaff, flout, gibe, insult, jeer, lampoon, mock, ridicule, satirize, scoff, scorn, sneer, taunt.

derision *n* contempt, disrespect, insult, laughter, mockery, ridicule, scorn.

derisive *adj* contemptuous, contumelious, mocking, ridiculing, scoffing, scornful.

derivation *n* descent, extraction, genealogy; etymology; deducing, deriving, drawing, getting, obtaining; beginning, foundation, origination, source.

derive *vb* draw, get, obtain, receive; deduce, follow, infer, trace.

derogate *vb* compromise, depreciate, detract, diminish, disparage, lessen.

derogatory *adj* belittling, depreciative, deprecatory, detracting, dishonoring, disparaging, injurious.

descant *vb* amplify, animadvert, dilate, discourse, discuss, enlarge, expatiate. • *n* melody, soprano, treble; animadversion, commentary, remarks; discourse, discussion.

descend *vb* drop, fall, pitch, plunge, sink, swoop; alight, dismount; go, pass, proceed, devolve; derive, issue, originate.

descendants *npl* offspring, issue, posterity, progeny.

descent *n* downrush, drop, fall; descending; decline, declivity, dip, pitch, slope; ancestry, derivation, extraction, genealogy, lineage, parentage, pedigree; assault, attack, foray, incursion, invasion, raid.

describe *vb* define, delineate, draw, illustrate, limn, sketch, specify, trace; detail; depict, explain, narrate, portray, recount, relate, represent; characterize.

description *n* delineation, tracing; account, depiction, explanation, narration, narrative, portrayal, recital, relation, report, representation; class, kind, sort, species.

descry *vb* behold, discover, discern, distinguish, espy, observe, perceive, see; detect, recognize.

desecrate *vb* abuse, pervert, defile, pollute, profane, violate.

desert[1] *n* due, excellence, merit, worth; punishment, reward.

desert[2] *vb* abandon, abscond, forsake, leave, quit, relinquish, renounce, resign, quit, vacate.

desert[3] *adj* barren, desolate, forsaken, lonely, solitary, uncultivated, uninhabited, unproductive, untilled, waste, wild.

deserted *adj* abandoned, forsaken, relinquished.

deserter *n* abandoner, forsaker, quitter, runaway; apostate, backslider, fugitive, recreant, renegade, revolter, traitor, turncoat.

desertion *n* abandonment, dereliction, recreancy, relinquishment.

deserve *vb* earn, gain, merit, procure, win.

desiderate *vb* desire, lack, miss, need, want.

design *vb* brew, concoct, contrive, devise, intend, invent, mean, plan, project, scheme; intend, mean, purpose; delineate, describe, draw, outline, sketch, trace. • *n* aim, device, drift, intent, intention, mark, meaning, object, plan, proposal, project, purport, purpose, scheme, scope; delineation, draught, drawing, outline, plan, sketch; adaptation, artifice, contrivance, invention, inventiveness.

designate *vb* denote, distinguish, indicate, particularize, select, show, specify, stipulate; characterize, define, describe; call, christen, denominate, dub, entitle, name, style; allot, appoint, christen.

designation *n* indication, particularization, selection, specification; class, description, kind; appellation, denomination, name, style, title.

designing *adj* artful, astute, crafty, crooked, cunning, deceitful, insidious, intriguing, Machiavellian, scheming, sly, subtle, treacherous, trickish, tricky, unscrupulous, wily.

desirable *adj* agreeable, beneficial, covetable, eligible, enviable, good, pleasing, preferable.

desire *vb* covet, crave, desiderate, fancy, hanker after, long for, lust after, want, wish, yearn for; ask, entreat, request, solicit. • *n* eroticism, lasciviousness, libidinousness, libido, lust, lustfulness, passion; eagerness, fancy, hope, inclination, mind, partiality, penchant, pleasure, volition, want, wish.

desirous *adj* avid, eager, desiring, longing, solicitous, wishful.

desist *vb* cease, discontinue, forbear, pause, stay, stop.

desolate *vb* depopulate, despoil, destroy, devastate, pillage, plunder, ravage, ruin, sack. • *adj* bare, barren, bleak, desert, forsaken, lonely, solitary, unfrequented, uninhabited, waste, wild; companionable, lonely, lonesome, solitary; desolated, destroyed, devastated, ravaged, ruined; cheerless, comfortless, companionless, disconsolate, dreary, forlorn, forsaken, miserable, wretched.

desolation *n* destruction, devastation, havoc, ravage, ruin; barrenness, bleakness, desolateness, dreariness, loneliness, solitariness, solitude, wildness; gloom, gloominess, misery, sadness, unhappiness, wretchedness.

despair *vb* despond, give up, lose hope. • *n* dejection, desperation, despondency, disheartenment, hopelessness.

despatch *see* **dispatch**.

desperado *n* daredevil, gangster, marauder, ruffian, thug, tough.

desperate *adj* despairing, despondent, desponding, hopeless; forlorn, irretrievable; extreme; audacious, daring, foolhardy, frantic, furious, headstrong, precipitate, rash, reckless, violent, wild, wretched; extreme, great, monstrous, prodigious, supreme.

desperation *n* despair, hopelessness; fury, rage.

despicable *adj* abject, base, contemptible, degrading, low, mean, paltry, pitiful, shameful, sordid, slight, vile, worthless.

despise *vb* contemn, disdain, disregard, neglect, scorn, slight, spurn, undervalue.

despite *n* malevolence, malice, malignity, spite; contempt, contumacy, defiance. • *prep* notwithstanding.

despoil *vb* bereave, denude, deprive, dispossess, divest, strip; devastate, fleece, pillage, plunder, ravage, rifle, rob.

despond *vb* despair, give up, lose hope, mourn, sorrow.

despondency *n* blues, dejection, depression, discouragement, gloom, hopelessness, melancholy, sadness.

despondent *adj* dejected, depressed, discouraged, disheartened, dispirited, low-spirited, melancholy.

despot *n* autocrat, dictator; oppressor, tyrant.

despotic *adj* absolute, arrogant, autocratic, dictatorial, imperious; arbitrary, oppressive, tyrannical, tyrannous.

despotism *n* absolutism, autocracy, dictatorship; oppression, tyranny.

destination *n* appointment, decree, destiny, doom, fate, foreordainment, foreordination, fortune, lot, ordination, star; aim, design, drift, end, intention, object, purpose, scope; bourne, goal, harbor, haven, journey's end, resting-place, terminus.

destine *vb* allot, appoint, assign, consecrate, devote, ordain; design, intend, predetermine; decree, doom, foreordain, predestine.

destitute *adj* distressed, indigent, moneyless, necessitous, needy, penniless, penurious, pinched, poor, reduced, wanting.

destitution *n* indigence, need, penury, poverty, privation, want.

destroy *vb* demolish, overthrow, overturn, subvert, raze, ruin; annihilate, dissolve, efface, quench; desolate, devastate, devour, ravage, waste; eradicate, extinguish, extirpate, kill, uproot, slay.

destruction *n* demolition, havoc, overthrow, ruin, subversion; desolation, devastation, holocaust, ravage; annihilation, eradication, extinction, extirpation; death, massacre, murder, slaughter.

destructive *adj* baleful, baneful, deadly, deleterious, detrimental, fatal, hurtful, injurious, lethal, mischievous, noxious, pernicious, ruinous; annihilatory, eradicative, exterminative, extirpative.

desultory *adj* capricious, cursory, discursive, erratic, fitful, inconstant, inexact, irregular, loose, rambling, roving, slight, spasmodic, unconnected, unmethodical, unsettled, unsystematic, vague, wandering.

detach *vb* disengage, disconnect, disjoin, dissever, disunite, divide, part, separate, sever, unfix; appoint, detail, send.

detail *vb* delineate, depict, describe, enumerate, narrate, particularize, portray, recount, rehearse, relate, specify; appoint, detach, send. • *n* account, narration, narrative, recital, relation; appointment, detachment; item, part.

details *npl* facts, minutiae, particulars, parts.

detain *vb* arrest, check, delay, hinder, hold, keep, restrain, retain, stay, stop; confine.

detect *vb* ascertain, catch, descry, disclose, discover, expose, reveal, unmask.

detention *n* confinement, delay, hindrance, restraint, withholding.

deter *vb* debar, discourage, frighten, hinder, prevent, restrain, stop, withhold.

deteriorate *vb* corrupt, debase, degrade, deprave, disgrace, impair, spoil, vitiate; decline, degenerate, depreciate, worsen.

deterioration *n* corruption, debasement, degradation, depravation, vitiation, perversion; caducity, decadence, decay, decline, degeneracy, degeneration, impairment.

determinate *adj* absolute, certain, definite, determined, established, explicit, express, fixed, limited, positive, settled; conclusive, decided, decisive, definitive.

determination *n* ascertainment, decision, deciding, determining, fixing, settlement, settling; conclusion, judgment, purpose, resolution, resolve, result; direction, leaning, tendency; firmness, constancy, effort, endeavor, exertion, grit, persistence, stam-ina, resoluteness; definition, limitation, qualification.

determine *vb* adjust, conclude, decide, end, establish, fix, resolve, settle; ascertain, certify, check, verify; impel, incline, induce, influence, lead, turn; decide, resolve; condition, define, limit; compel, necessitate.

detest *vb* abhor, abominate, despise, execrate, hate, loathe, nauseate, recoil from.

detestable *adj* abhorred, abominable, accursed, cursed, damnable, execrable, hateful, odious; disgusting, loathsome, nauseating, offensive, repulsive, sickening, vile.

dethrone *vb* depose, uncrown.

detract *vb* abuse, asperse, belittle, calumniate, debase, decry, defame, depreciate, derogate, disparage, slander, traduce, vilify; deprecate, deteriorate, diminish, lessen.

detraction *n* abuse, aspersion, calumny, censure, defamation, depreciation, derogation, disparagement, slander.

detriment *n* cost, damage, disadvantage, evil, harm, hurt, injury, loss, mischief, prejudice.

detrimental *adj* baleful, deleterious, destructive, harmful, hurtful, injurious, mischievous, pernicious, prejudicial.

devastate *vb* desolate, despoil, destroy, lay waste, harry, pillage, plunder, ravage, sack, spoil, strip, waste.

devastation *n* despoiling, destroying, harrying, pillaging, plundering, ravaging, sacking, spoiling, stripping, wasting; desolation, destruction, havoc, pillage, rapine, ravage, ruin, waste.

develop *vb* disentangle, disclose, evolve, exhibit, explicate, uncover, unfold, unravel; cultivate, grow, mature, open, progress.

development *n* disclosure, disentanglement, exhibition, unfolding, unraveling; growth, increase, maturation, maturing; evolution, growth, progression; elaboration, expansion, explication.

deviate *vb* alter, deflect, digress, diverge, sheer off, slew, tack, turn aside, wheel, wheel about; err, go astray, stray, swerve, wander; differ, vary.

deviation *n* aberration, departure, depression, divarication, divergence, turning; alteration, change, difference, variance, variation.

device *n* contraption, contrivance, gadget, invention; design, expedient, plan, project, resort, resource, scheme, shift; artifice, evasion, fraud, maneuvre, ruse, stratagem, trick, wile; blazon, emblazonment, emblem, sign, symbol, type.

devil *n* archfiend, demon, fiend, goblin; Apollyon, Belial, Deuce, Evil One, Lucifer, Old Harry, Old Nick, Old Serpent, Prince of Darkness, Satan.

devilish *adj* demon, demonic, demonical, demoniac, demoniacal, diabolic, diabolical, fiendish, hellish, infernal, Mephistophelean, Mephistophelian, satanic; atrocious, barbarous, cruel, malevolent, malicious, malign, malignant, wicked.

devilry *n* devilment, diablerie, mischief; devilishness, fiendishness, wickedness.

devious *adj* deviating, erratic, roundabout, wandering; circuitous, confusing, crooked, labyrinthine, mazy, obscure; crooked, disingenuous, misleading, treacherous.

devise *vb* brew, compass, concert, concoct, contrive, dream up, excogitate, imagine, invent, plan, project, scheme; bequeath, demise, leave, will.

devoid *adj* bare, destitute, empty, vacant, void.

devolve vb alienate, consign, convey, deliver over, demise, fall, hand over, make over, pass, transfer.

devote vb appropriate, consecrate, dedicate, destine; set apart; addict, apply, give up, resign; consign, doom, give over.

devoted adj affectionate, attached, loving; ardent, assiduous, earnest, zealous.

devotee n bigot, enthusiast, fan, fanatic, zealot.

devotion n consecration, dedication, duty; devotedness, devoutness, fidelity, godliness, holiness, piety, religion, religiousness, saintliness, sanctity; adoration, prayer, worship; affection, attachment, love; ardour, devotedness, eagerness, earnestness, fervour, passion, spirit, zeal.

devotional adj devout, godly, pious, religious, saintly.

devour vb engorge, gorge, gulp down, raven, swallow eagerly, wolf; annihilate, consume, destroy, expend, spend, swallow up, waste.

devout adj devotional, godly, holy, pious, religious, saint-like, saintly; earnest, grave, serious, sincere, solemn.

dexterity n ability, address, adroitness, aptitude, aptness, art, cleverness, expertness, facility, knack, quickness, readiness, skillfulness, skill, tact.

dexterous, dextrous adj able, adept, adroit, apt, deft, clever, expert, facile, handy, nimble-fingered, quick, ready, skillful.

diabolic, diabolical adj atrocious, barbarous, cruel, devilish, fiendish, hellish, impious, infernal, malevolent, malign, malignant, satanic, wicked.

diagram n chart, delineation, figure, graph, map, outline, plan, sketch.

dialect n idiom, localism, provincialism; jargon, lingo, patois, patter; language, parlance, phraseology, speech, tongue.

dialectal adj idiomatic, local, provincial.

dialectic, dialectical adj analytical, critical, logical, rational, rationalistic.

dialogue n colloquy, communication, conference, conversation, converse, intercourse, interlocution; playbook, script, speech, text, words.

diaphanous adj clear, filmy, gossamer, pellucid, sheer, translucent, transparent.

diarrhea n (med) flux, looseness, purging, relaxation.

diary n chronicle, daybook, journal, register.

diatribe n disputation, disquisition, dissertation; abuse, harangue, invective, philippic, reviling, tirade.

dictate vb bid, direct, command, decree, enjoin, ordain, order, prescribe, require. • n bidding, command, decree, injunction, order; maxim, precept, rule.

dictation n direction, order, prescription.

dictator n autocrat, despot, tyrant.

dictatorial adj absolute, unlimited, unrestricted; authoritative, despotic, dictatory; domineering, imperious, overbearing, peremptory, tyrannical.

dictatorship n absolutism, authoritarianism, autocracy, despotism, iron rule, totalitarianism, tyranny.

diction n expression, language, phraseology, style, vocabulary, wording.

dictionary n glossary, lexicon, thesaurus, vocabulary, wordbook; cyclopedia, encyclopedia.

dictum n affirmation, assertion, saying; (law) award, arbitrament, decision, opinion.

didactic, didactical adj educational, instructive, pedagogic, preceptive.

die vb decease, demise, depart, expire, pass on; decay, decline, fade, fade out, perish, wither; cease, disappear, vanish; faint, fall, sink.

diet[1] vb eat, feed, nourish; abstain, fast, regulate, slim. • n aliment, fare, food, nourishment, nutriment, provision, rations, regimen, subsistence, viands, victuals.

diet[2] n assembly, congress, convention, convocation, council, parliament.

differ vb deviate, diverge, vary; disagree, dissent; bicker, contend, dispute, quarrel, wrangle.

difference n contrariety, contrast, departure, deviation, disagreement, disparity, dissimilarity, dissimilitude, divergence, diversity, heterogeneity, inconformity, nuance, opposition, unlikeness, variation; alienation, altercation, bickering, breach, contention, contest, controversy, debate, disaccord, disagreement, disharmony, dispute, dissension, embroilment, falling out, irreconcilability, jarring, misunderstanding, quarrel, rupture, schism, strife, variance, wrangle; discrimination, distinction.

different adj distinct, nonidentical, separate, unlike; contradistinct, contrary, contrasted, deviating, disagreeing, discrepant, dissimilar, divergent, diverse, incompatible, incongruous, unlike, variant, various; divers, heterogeneous, manifold, many, sundry.

difficult *adj* arduous, exacting, hard, Herculean, stiff, tough, uphill; abstruse, complex, intricate, knotty, obscure, perplexing; austere, rigid, unaccommodating, uncompliant, unyielding; dainty, fastidious, squeamish.

difficulty *n* arduousness, laboriousness; bar, barrier, crux, deadlock, dilemma, embarrassment, emergency, exigency, fix, hindrance, impediment, knot, obstacle, obstruction, perplexity, pickle, pinch, predicament, stand, standstill, thwart, trial, trouble; cavil, objection, complication, controversy, difference, embarrassment, embroilment, imbroglio, misunderstanding.

diffidence *n* distrust, doubt, hesitance, hesitancy, hesitation, reluctance; bashfulness, modesty, sheepishness, shyness, timidity.

diffident *adj* distrustful, doubtful, hesitant, hesitating, reluctant; bashful, modest, over-modest, sheepish, shy, timid.

diffuse[1] *vb* circulate, disperse, disseminate, distribute, intermingle, propagate, scatter, spread, strew.

diffuse[2] *adj* broadcast, dispersed, scattered, sparse, sporadic, widespread; broad, extensive, liberal, profuse, wide; copious, loose, prolix, rambling, verbose, wordy.

diffusion *n* circulation, dispersion, dissemination, distribution, extension, propagation, spread, strewing.

diffusive *adj* expansive, permeating, wide-reaching; spreading, dispersive, disseminative, distributive, distributory.

dig *vb* channel, delve, excavate, grub, hollow out, quarry, scoop, tunnel. • *n* poke, punch, thrust.

digest[1] *vb* arrange, classify, codify, dispose, methodize, systemize, tabulate; concoct; assimilate, consider, contemplate, meditate, ponder, reflect upon, study; master; macerate, soak, steep.

digest[2] *n* code, system; abridgement, abstract, brief, breviary, compend, compendium, conspectus, epitome, summary, synopsis.

dignified *adj* august, courtly, decorous, grave, imposing, majestic, noble, stately.

dignify *vb* advance, aggrandize, elevate, ennoble, exalt, promote; adorn, grace, honor.

dignity *n* elevation, eminence, exaltation, excellence, glory, greatness, honor, place,

rank, respectability, standing, station; decorum, grandeur, majesty, nobleness, stateliness; preferment; dignitary, magistrate; elevation, height.

digress *vb* depart, deviate, diverge, expatiate, wander.

digression *n* departure, deviation, divergence; episode, excursus.

dilapidate *vb* demolish, destroy, disintegrate, ruin, waste.

dilapidated *adj* decayed, ruined, run down, wasted.

dilapidation *n* decay, demolition, destruction, disintegration, disrepair, dissolution, downfall, ruin, waste.

dilate *vb* distend, enlarge, expand, extend, inflate, swell, tend, widen; amplify, descant, dwell, enlarge, expatiate.

dilation *n* amplification, bloating, distension, enlargement, expanding, expansion, spreading, swelling.

dilatory *adj* backward, behind-hand, delaying, laggard, lagging, lingering, loitering, off-putting, procrastinating, slack, slow, sluggish, tardy.

dilemma *n* difficulty, fix, plight, predicament, problem, quandary, strait.

diligence *n* activity, application, assiduity, assiduousness, attention, care, constancy, earnestness, heedfulness, industry, laboriousness, perseverance, sedulousness.

diligent *adj* active, assiduous, attentive, busy, careful, constant, earnest, hardworking, indefatigable, industrious, laborious, notable, painstaking, persevering, persistent, sedulous, tireless.

dilly-dally *vb* dally, dawdle, delay, lag, linger, loiter, saunter, trifle.

dilute *vb* attenuate, reduce, thin, weaken. • *adj* attenuated, diluted, thin, weak, wishy-washy.

dim *vb* blur, cloud, darken, dull, obscure, sully, tarnish. • *adj* cloudy, dark, dusky, faint, ill-defined, indefinite, indistinct, mysterious, obscure, shadowy; dull, obtuse; clouded, confused, darkened, faint, obscured; blurred, dulled, sullied, tarnished.

dimension *n* extension, extent, measure.

dimensions *npl* amplitude, bigness, bulk, capacity, greatness, largeness, magnitude, mass, massiveness, size, volume; measurements.

diminish *vb* abate, belittle, contract, decrease, lessen, reduce; curtail, cut, dwindle, melt, narrow, shrink, shrivel, subside, taper off, weaken.

diminution n abatement, abridgement, attenuation, contraction, curtailment, decrescendo, cut, decay, decrease, deduction, lessening, reduction, retrenchment, weakening.

diminutive adj contracted, dwarfish, little, minute, puny, pygmy, small, tiny.

din vb beat, boom, clamor, drum, hammer, pound, repeat, ring, thunder. • n bruit, clamor, clash, clatter, crash, crashing, hubbub, hullabaloo, hurly-burly, noise, outcry, racket, row, shout, uproar.

dingle n dale, dell, glen, vale, valley.

dingy adj brown, dun, dusky; bedimmed, colorless, dimmed, dulled, faded, obscure, smirched, soiled, sullied.

dint n blow, stroke; dent, indentation, nick, notch; force, power.

diocese n bishopric, charge, episcopate, jurisdiction, see.

dip vb douse, duck, immerse, plunge, souse; bail, ladle; dive, pitch; bend, incline, slope. • n decline, declivity, descent, drop, fall; concavity, depression, hole, hollow, pit, sink; bathe, dipping, ducking, sousing, swim.

diplomat n diplomatist, envoy, legate, minister, negotiator.

dire adj alarming, awful, calamitous, cruel, destructive, disastrous, dismal, dreadful, fearful, gloomy, horrible, horrid, implacable, inexorable, portentous, shocking, terrible, terrific, tremendous, woeful.

direct vb aim. cast, level, point, turn; advise, conduct, control, dispose, guide, govern, manage, regulate, rule; command, bid, enjoin, instruct, order; lead, show; address, superscribe. • adj immediate, straight, undeviating; absolute, categorical, express, plain, unambiguous; downright, earnest, frank, ingenuous, open, outspoken, sincere, straightforward, unequivocal.

direction n aim; tendency; bearing, course; administration, conduct, control, government, management, oversight, superintendence; guidance, lead; command, order, prescription; address, superscription.

directly adv absolutely, expressly, openly, unambiguously; forthwith, immediately, instantly, quickly, presently, promptly, soon, speedily.

director n boss, manager, superintendent;

adviser, counselor, guide, instructor, mentor, monitor.

direful adj awful, calamitous, dire, dreadful, fearful, gloomy, horrible, shocking, terrible, terrific, tremendous.

dirge n coronach, elegy, lament, monody, requiem, threnody.

dirty vb befoul, defile, draggle, foul, pollute, soil, sully. • adj begrimed. defiled, filthy, foul, mucky, nasty, soiled, unclean; clouded, cloudy, dark, dull, muddy, sullied; base, beggarly, contemptible, despicable, groveling, low, mean, paltry, pitiful, scurvy, shabby, sneaking, squalid; disagreeable, rainy, sloppy, uncomfortable.

disability n disablement, disqualification, impotence, impotency, inability, incapacity, incompetence, incompetency, unfitness, weakness.

disable vb cripple, enfeeble, hamstring, impair, paralyse, unman, weaken; disenable, disqualify, incapacitate, unfit.

disabuse vb correct, undeceive.

disadvantage n disadvantageousness, inconvenience, unfavorableness; damage, detriment, disservice, drawback, harm, hindrance, hurt, injury, loss, prejudice.

disadvantageous adj inconvenient, inexpedient, unfavorable; deleterious, detrimental, harmful, hurtful, injurious, prejudicial.

disaffect vb alienate, disdain, dislike, disorder, estrange.

disaffected adj alienated, disloyal, dissatisfied, estranged.

disaffection n alienation, breach, disagreement, dislike, disloyalty, dissatisfaction, estrangement, repugnance, ill will, unfriendliness.

disagree vb deviate, differ, diverge, vary; dissent; argue, bicker, clash, debate, dispute, quarrel, wrangle.

disagreeable adj contrary, displeasing, distasteful, nasty, offensive, unpleasant, unpleasing, unsuitable.

disagreement n deviation, difference, discrepancy, dissimilarity, dissimilitude, divergence, diversity, incongruity, unlikeness; disaccord, dissent; argument, bickering, clashing, conflict, contention, dispute, dissension, disunion, disunity, jarring, misunderstanding, quarrel, strife, variance, wrangle.

disallow vb forbid, prohibit; disapprove, reject; deny, disavow, disclaim, dismiss, disown, repudiate.

disappear vb depart, fade, vanish; cease, dissolve.

disappoint vb baffle, balk, deceive, defeat, delude, disconcert, foil, frustrate, mortify, tantalize, thwart, vex.

disappointment n baffling, balk, failure, foiling, frustration, miscarriage, mortification, unfullfilment.

disapprobation n blame, censure, condemnation, disapproval, dislike, displeasure, reproof.

disapprove vb blame, censure, condemn, deprecate, dislike; disallow, reject.

disarrange vb agitate, confuse, derange, disallow, dishevel, dislike, dislocate, disorder, disorganize, disturb, jumble, reject, rumple, tumble, unsettle.

disarray n confusion, disorder; dishabille.

disaster n accident, adversity, blow, calamity, casualty, catastrophe, misadventure, mischance, misfortune, mishap, reverse, ruin, stroke.

disastrous adj adverse, calamitous, catastrophic, destructive, hapless, ill-fated, ill-starred, ruinous, unfortunate, unlucky, unpropitious, unprosperous, untoward.

disavow vb deny, disallow, disclaim, disown.

disband vb break up, disperse, scatter, separate.

disbelief n agnosticism, doubt, nonconviction, rejection, unbelief.

disburden vb alleviate, diminish, disburden, discharge, disencumber, ease, free, relieve, rid.

disbursement n expenditure, spending.

discard vb abandon, cast off, lay aside, reject; banish, break, cashier, discharge, dismiss, remove, repudiate.

discern vb differentiate, discriminate, distinguish, judge; behold, descry, discover, espy, notice, observe, perceive, recognize, see.

discernible adj detectable, discoverable, perceptible.

discerning adj acute, astute, clear-sighted, discriminating, discriminative, eagle-eyed, ingenious, intelligent, judicious, knowing, perspicacious, piercing, sagacious, sharp, shrewd.

discernment n acumen, acuteness, astuteness, brightness, cleverness, discrimination, ingenuity, insight, intelligence, judgement, penetration, perspicacity, sagacity, sharpness, shrewdness; beholding, descrying, discerning, discovery, espial, notice, perception.

discharge vb disburden, unburden, unload; eject, emit, excrete, expel, void; cash, liquidate, pay; absolve, acquit, clear, exonerate, free, release, relieve; cashier, discard, dismiss, sack; destroy, remove; execute, perform, fulfill, observe; annul, cancel, invalidate, nullify, rescind. • n disburdening, unloading; acquittal, dismissal, displacement, ejection, emission, evacuation, excretion, expulsion, vent, voiding; blast, burst, detonation, explosion, firing; execution, fulfillment, observance; annulment, clearance, liquidation, payment, satisfaction, settlement; exemption, liberation, release; flow, flux, execration.

disciple n catechumen, learner, pupil, scholar, student; adherent, follower, partisan, supporter.

discipline vb breed, drill, educate, exercise, form, instruct, teach, train; control, govern, regulate, school; chasten, chastise, punish. • n culture, drill, drilling, education, exercise, instruction, training; control, government, regulation, subjection; chastisement, correction, punishment.

disclaim vb abandon, disallow, disown, disavow; reject, renounce, repudiate.

disclose vb discover, exhibit, expose, manifest, uncover; bare, betray, blab, communicate, divulge, impart, publish, reveal, show, tell, unfold, unveil, utter.

disclosure n betrayal, discovery, exposé, exposure, revelation, uncovering. discolor vb stain, tarnish, tinge.

discomfit vb beat, checkmate, conquer, defeat, overcome, overpower, overthrow, rout, subdue, vanquish, worst; abash, baffle, balk, confound, disconcert, foil, frustrate, perplex, upset.

discomfiture n confusion, defeat, frustration, overthrow, rout, vexation.

discomfort n annoyance, disquiet, distress, inquietude, malaise, trouble, uneasiness, unpleasantness, vexation.

discommode vb annoy, disquiet, disturb, harass, incommode, inconvenience, molest, trouble.

discompose vb confuse, derange, disarrange, disorder, disturb, embroil, jumble, unsettle; agitate, annoy, chafe, displease, disquiet, fret, harass, irritate, nettle, plague, provoke, ruffle, trouble, upset, vex, worry; abash, bewilder, disconcert, embarrass, fluster, perplex.

disconcert vb baffle, balk, contravene,

defeat, disarrange, frustrate, interrupt, thwart, undo, upset; abash, agitate, bewilder, confuse, demoralize, discompose, disturb, embarrass, faze, perplex, perturb, unbalance, worry.

disconnect vb detach, disengage, disjoin, dissociate, disunite, separate, sever, uncouple, unlink.

disconsolate adj broken-hearted, cheerless, comfortless, dejected, desolate, forlorn, gloomy, heartbroken, inconsolable, melancholy, miserable, sad, sorrowful, unhappy, woeful, wretched.

discontent n discontentment, displeasure, dissatisfaction, inquietude, restlessness, uneasiness.

discontinuance n cessation, discontinuation, disjunction, disruption, intermission, interruption, separation, stop, stoppage, stopping, suspension.

discontinue vb cease, intermit, interrupt, quit, stop.

discord n contention, difference, disagreement, dissension, opposition, quarreling, rupture, strife, variance, wrangling; cacophony, discordance, dissonance, harshness, jangle, jarring.

discordance n conflict, disagreement, incongruity, inconsistency, opposition, repugnance; discord, dissonance.

discordant adj contradictory, contrary, disagreeing, incongruous, inconsistent, opposite, repugnant; cacophonous, dissonant, harsh, inharmonious, jangling, jarring.

discount vb allow for, deduct, lower, rebate, reduce, subtract; disregard, ignore, overlook. • n abatement, drawback; allowance, deduction, rebate, reduction.

discourage vb abase, awe, damp, daunt, deject, depress, deject, dismay, dishearten, dispirit, frighten, intimidate; deter, dissuade, hinder; disfavor, discountenance.

discouragement n disheartening; dissuasion; damper, deterrent, embarrassment, hindrance, impediment, obstacle, wet blanket.

discourse vb expiate, hold forth, lucubrate, sermonize, speak; advise, confer, converse, parley, talk; emit, utter. • n address, disquisition, dissertation, homily, lecture, preachment, sermon, speech, treatise; colloquy, conversation, converse, talk.

discourteous adj abrupt, brusque, curt, disrespectful, ill-bred, ill-mannered, impolite, inurbane, rude, uncivil, uncourtly, ungentlemanly, unmannerly.

discourtesy n abruptness, brusqueness, ill-breeding, impoliteness, incivility, rudeness.

discover vb communicate, disclose, exhibit, impart, manifest, show, reveal, tell; ascertain, behold, discern, espy, see; descry, detect, determine, discern; contrive, invent, originate.

discredit vb disbelieve, doubt, question; depreciate, disgrace, dishonor, disparage, reproach. • n disbelief, distrust; disgrace, dishonor, disrepute, ignominy, notoriety, obloquy, odium, opprobrium, reproach, scandal.

discreditable adj derogatory, disgraceful, disreputable, dishonorable, ignominious, infamous, inglorious, scandalous, unworthy.

discreet adj careful, cautious, circumspect, considerate, discerning, heedful, judicious, prudent, sagacious, wary, wise.

discrepancy n contrariety, difference, disagreement, discordance, dissonance, divergence, incongruity, inconsistency, variance, variation.

discrete adj discontinuous, disjunct, distinct, separate; disjunctive.

discretion n care, carefulness, caution, circumspection, considerateness, consideration, heedfulness, judgement, judicious, prudence, wariness; discrimination, maturity, responsibility; choice, option, pleasure, will.

discrimination n difference, distinction; acumen, acuteness, discernment, in-sight, judgement, penetration, sagacity.

discriminatory adj characteristic, characterizing, discriminating, discriminative, distinctive, distinguishing.

discursive adj argumentative, reasoning; casual, cursory, desultory, digressive, erratic, excursive, loose, rambling, roving, wandering, wave.

discus n disk, quoit.

discuss vb agitate, argue, canvass, consider, debate, deliberate, examine, sift, ventilate.

disdain vb contemn, deride, despise, disregard, reject, scorn, slight, scout, spurn. • n arrogance, contempt, contumely, haughtiness, hauteur, scorn, sneer, superciliousness.

disdainful adj cavalier, contemptuous, contumelious, haughty, scornful, supercilious.

disease n affection, affliction, ail, ailment, complaint, disorder, distemper, illness, indisposition, infirmity, malady, sickness.

disembarrass vb clear, disburden, disencumber, disengage, disentangle, extricate, ease, free, release, rid.

disembodied adj bodiless, disincarnate, immaterial, incorporeal, spiritual, unbodied.

disembowel vb degut, embowel, eviscerate.

disengage vb clear, deliver, discharge, disembarrass, disembroil, disencumber, disentangle, extricate, liberate, release; detach, disjoin, dissociate, disunite, divide, separate; wean, withdraw.

disentangle vb loosen, separate, unfold, unravel, untwist; clear, detach, disconnect, disembroil, disengage, extricate, liberate, loose, unloose.

disfavor n disapproval, disesteem, dislike, disrespect; discredit, disregard, disrepute, unacceptableness; disservice, unkindness. • vb disapprove, dislike, object, oppose.

disfigure vb blemish, deface, deform, injure, mar, spoil.

disfigurement n blemishing, defacement, deforming, disfiguration, injury, marring, spoiling; blemish, defect, deformity, scar, spot, stain.

disgorge vb belch, cast up, spew, throw up, vomit; discharge, eject; give up, relinquish, surrender, yield.

disgrace vb degrade, humble, humiliate; abase, debase, defame, discredit, disfavor, dishonor, disparage, reproach, stain, sully, taint, tarnish. • n abomination, disrepute, humiliation, ignominy, infamy, mortification, shame, scandal.

disgraceful adj discreditable, dishonorable, disreputable, ignominious, infamous, opprobrious, scandalous, shameful.

disguise vb cloak, conceal, cover, dissemble, hide, mask, muffle, screen, secrete, shroud, veil. • n concealment, cover, mask, veil; blind, cloak, masquerade, pretence, pretext, veneer.

disguised adj cloaked, masked, veiled.

disgust vb nauseate, sicken; abominate, detest, displease, offend, repel, repulse, revolt. • n disrelish, distaste, loathing, nausea; abhorrence, abomination, antipathy, aversion, detestation, dislike, repugnance, revulsion.

dish vb deal out, give, ladle, serve; blight, dash, frustrate, mar, ruin, spoil. • n bowl, plate, saucer, vessel.

dishearten vb cast down, damp, dampen, daunt, deject, depress, deter, discourage, dispirit.

dished adj baffled, balked, disappointed, disconcerted, foiled, frustrated, upset.

disheveled adj disarranged, disordered, messed, tousled, tumbled, unkempt, untidy, untrimmed.

dishonest adj cheating, corrupt, crafty, crooked, deceitful, deceiving, deceptive, designing, faithless, false, falsehearted, fraudulent, guileful, knavish, perfidious, slippery, treacherous, unfair, unscrupulous.

dishonesty n deceitfulness, faithlessness, falsehood, fraud, fraudulence, fraudulency, improbity, knavery, perfidious, treachery, trickery.

dishonor vb abase, defame, degrade, discredit, disfavour, dishonor, disgrace, disparage, reproach, shame, taint. • n abasement, basement, contempt, degradation, discredit, disesteem, disfavor, disgrace, dishonor, disparagement, disrepute, ignominy, infamy, obloquy, odium, opprobrium, reproach, scandal, shame.

dishonorable adj discreditable, disgraceful, disreputable, ignominious, infamous, scandalous, shameful; base, false, falsehearted, shameless.

disinclination n alienation, antipathy, aversion, dislike, indisposition, reluctance, repugnance, unwillingness.

disinfect vb cleanse, deodorize, fumigate, purify, sterilize.

disingenuous adj artful, deceitful, dishonest, hollow, insidious, insincere, uncandid, unfair, wily.

disintegrate vb crumble, decompose, dissolve, disunite, pulverize, separate.

disinter vb dig up, disentomb, disinhume, exhume, unbury.

disinterested adj candid, fair, high-minded, impartial, indifferent, unbiased, unselfish, unprejudiced; generous, liberal, magnanimous.

disjoin vb detach, disconnect, dissever, dissociate, disunite, divide, part, separate, sever, sunder.

disjointed adj desultory, disconnected, incoherent, loose.

disjunction n disassociation, disconnection, disunion, isolation, parting, separation, severance.

dislike vb abominate, detest, disapprove, disrelish, hate, loathe. • n antagonism, antipathy, aversion, disapproval, disfavor, disgust, disinclination, displeasure, disrelish, distaste, loathing, repugnance.

dislocate vb disarrange, displace, disturb; disarticulate, disjoint, luxate, slip.

dislodge vb dismount, dispel, displace, eject, expel, oust, remove.

disloyal adj disaffected, faithless, false, perfidious, traitorous, treacherous, treasonable, undutiful, unfaithful, unpatriotic, untrue.

disloyalty n faithlessness, perfidy, treachery, treason, undutifulness, unfaithfulness.

dismal adj cheerless, dark, dreary, dull, gloomy, lonesome; blue, calamitous, doleful, dolorous, funereal, lugubrious, melancholy, mournful, sad, somber, sorrowful.

dismantle vb divest, strip, unrig.

dismay vb affright, alarm, appal, daunt, discourage, dishearten, frighten, horrify, intimidate, paralyse, scare, terrify. • n affright, alarm, consternation, fear, fright, horror, terror.

dismember vb disjoint, dislimb, dislocate, mutilate; divide, separate, rend, sever.

dismiss vb banish, cashier, discard, discharge, disperse, reject, release, remove.

dismount vb alight, descend, dismantle, unhorse; dislodge, displace.

disobedient adj froward, noncompliant, noncomplying, obstinate, rebellious, refractory, uncomplying, undutiful, unruly, unsubmissive.

disobey vb infringe, transgress, violate.

disobliging adj ill-natured, unaccommodating, unamiable, unfriendly, unkind.

disorder vb confound, confuse, derange, disarrange, discompose, disorganize, disturb, unsettle, upset. • n confusion, derangement, disarrangement, disarray, disorganization, irregularity, jumble, litter, mess, topsy-turvy; brawl, commotion, disturbance, fight, quarrel, riot, tumult; riotousness, tumultuousness, turbulence; ail, ailment, complaint, distemper, illness, indisposition, malady, sickness.

disorderly adj chaotic, confused, intemperate, irregular, unmethodical, unsystematic, untidy; lawless, rebellious, riotous, tumultuous, turbulent, ungovernable, unmanageable, unruly.

disorganization n chaos, confusion, demoralization, derangement, disorder.

disorganize vb confuse, demoralize, derange, disarrange, discompose, disorder, disturb, unsettle, upset.

disown vb disavow, disclaim, reject, renounce, repudiate; abnegate, deny, disallow.

disparage vb belittle, decry, depreciate, derogate from, detract from, doubt, question, run down, underestimate, underpraise, underrate, undervalue; asperse, defame, inveigh against, reflect on, reproach, slur, speak ill of, traduce, vilify.

disparagement n belittlement, depreciation, derogation, detraction, underrating, undervaluing; derogation, detraction, diminution, harm, impairment, injury, lessening, prejudice, worsening; aspersion, calumny, defamation, reflection, reproach, traduction, vilification; blackening, disgrace, dispraise, indignity, reproach.

disparity n difference, disproportion, inequality; dissimilarity, dissimilitude, unlikeness.

dispassionate adj calm, collected, composed, cool, imperturbable, inexcitable, moderate, quiet, serene, sober, staid, temperate, undisturbed, unexcitable, unexcited, unimpassioned, unruffled; candid, disinterested, fair, impartial, neutral, unbiased.

dispatch, despatch vb assassinate, kill, murder, slaughter, slay; accelerate, conclude, dismiss, expedite, finish, forward, hasten, hurry, quicken, speed. • n dispatching, sending; diligence, expedition, haste, rapidity, speed; completion, conduct, doing, transaction; communication, document, instruction, letter, message, missive, report.

dispel vb banish, disperse, dissipate, scatter.

dispensation n allotment, apportioning, apportionment, dispensing, distributing, distribution; administration, stewardship; economy, plan, scheme, system; exemption, immunity, indulgence, license, privilege.

dispense vb allot, apportion, assign, distribute; administer, apply, execute; absolve, excuse, exempt, exonerate, release, relieve.

disperse vb dispel, dissipate, dissolve, scatter, separate; diffuse, disseminate, spread; disappear, vanish.

dispirit vb damp, dampen, depress, deject, discourage, dishearten.

dispirited adj chapfallen, dejected, depressed, discouraged, disheartened, down-cast, down-hearted.

displace vb dislocate, mislay, misplace, move; dislodge, remove; cashier, depose, discard, discharge, dismiss, oust, replace, unseat.

display vb expand, extend, open, spread, unfold; exhibit, show; flaunt, parade. • n exhibition, manifestation, show; flourish, ostentation, pageant, parade, pomp.

displease vb disgruntle, disgust, disoblige, dissatisfy, offend; affront, aggravate, anger, annoy, chafe, chagrin, fret, irritate, nettle, pique, provoke, vex.

displeasure n disaffection, disapprobation, disapproval, dislike, dissatisfaction, distaste; anger, annoyance, indignation, irritation, pique, resentment, vexation, wrath; injury, offence.

disport vb caper, frisk, frolic, gambol, play, sport, wanton; amuse, beguile, cheer, divert, entertain, relax, solace.

disposal n arrangement, disposition; conduct, control, direction, disposure, government, management, ordering, regulation; bestowment, dispensation, distribution.

dispose vb arrange, distribute, marshal, group, place, range, rank, set; adjust, determine, regulate, settle; bias, incline, induce, lead, move, predispose; control, decide, regulate, rule, settle; arrange, bargain, compound; alienate, convey, demise, sell, transfer.

disposed adj apt, inclined, prone, ready, tending.

disposition n arrangement, arranging, classification, disposing, grouping, location, placing; adjustment, control, direction, disposure, disposal, management, ordering, regulation; aptitude, bent, bias, inclination, nature, predisposition, proclivity, proneness, propensity, tendency; character, constitution, humor, native, nature, temper, temperament, turn; inclination, willingness; bestowal, bestowment, dispensation, distribution.

dispossess vb deprive, divest, expropriate, strip; dislodge, eject, oust; disseise, disseize, evict, oust.

dispraise n blame, censure; discredit, disgrace, dishonor, disparagement, opprobrium, reproach, shame.

disproof n confutation, rebuttal, refutation.

disproportion n disparity, inadequacy, inequality, insufficiency, unsuitableness; incommensurateness.

disprove vb confute, rebel, rebut.

disputable adj controvertible, debatable, doubtful, questionable.

disputation n argumentation, controversy, debate, dispute.

disputatious adj argumentative, bickering, captious, caviling, contentious, dissentious, litigious, polemical, pugnacious, quarrelsome.

dispute vb altercate, argue, debate, litigate, question; bicker, brawl, jangle, quarrel, spar, spat, squabble, tiff, wrangle; agitate, argue, debate, ventilate; challenge, contradict, controvert, deny, impugn; contest, struggle for. • n controversy, debate, discussion, disputation; altercation, argument, bickering, brawl, disagreement, dissension, spat, squabble, tiff, wrangle.

disqualification n disability, incapitation.

disqualify vb disable, incapacitate, unfit; disenable, preclude, prohibit.

disquiet vb agitate, annoy, bother, discompose, disturb, excite, fret, harass, incommode, molest, plague, pester, trouble, vex, worry. • n anxiety, discomposure, disquietude, disturbance, restlessness, solicitude, trouble, uneasiness, unrest, vexation, worry.

disquisition n dissertation, discourse, essay, paper, thesis, treatise.

disregard vb contemn, despise, disdain, disobey, disparage, ignore, neglect, overlook, slight. • n contempt, ignoring, inattention, neglect, pretermit, oversight, slight; disesteem, disfavor, indifference.

disrelish vb dislike, loathe. • n dislike, distaste; flatness, insipidity, insipidness, nauseousness; antipathy, aversion, repugnance.

disreputable adj derogatory, discreditable, dishonorable, disgraceful, infamous, opprobrious, scandalous, shameful; base, contemptible, low, mean, vicious, vile, vulgar.

disrepute n abasement, degradation, derogation, discredit, disgrace, dishonor, ill-repute, odium.

disrespect n disesteem, disregard, irreverence, neglect, slight.

disrespectful adj discourteous, impertinent, impolite, rude, uncivil, uncourteous.

dissatisfaction n discontent, disquiet, inquietude, uneasiness; disapprobation, disapproval, dislike, displeasure.

dissect vb analyze, examine, explore, investigate, scrutinize, sift; cut apart.

dissemble vb cloak, conceal, cover, disguise, hide; counterfeit, dissimulate, feign, pretend.

dissembler n dissimulator, feigner, hypocrite, pretender, sham.

disseminate vb circulate, diffuse, disperse, proclaim, promulgate, propagate, publish, scatter, spread.

dissension n contention, difference, disagreement, discord, quarrel, strife, variance.

dissent vb decline, differ, disagree, refuse. • n difference, disagreement, nonconformity, opposition, recusancy, refusal.

dissentient adj disagreeing, dissenting, dissident, factious.

dissertation n discourse, disquisition, essay, thesis, treatise.

disservice n disadvantage, disfavor, harm, hurt, ill-turn, injury, mischief.

dissidence n disagreement, dissent, nonconformity, sectarianism.

dissimilar adj different, divergent, diverse, heterogeneous, unlike, various.

dissimilarity n dissimilitude, disparity, divergent, diversity, unlikeness, variation.

dissimulation n concealment, deceit, dissembling, double-dealing, duplicity, feigning, hypocrisy, pretence.

dissipate vb dispel, disperse, scatter; consume, expend, lavish, spend, squander, waste; disappear, vanish.

dissipation n dispersion, dissemination, scattering, vanishing; squandering, waste; crapulence, debauchery, dissoluteness, drunkenness, excess, profligacy.

dissociate vb disjoin, dissever, disunite, divide, separate, sever, sunder.

dissolute adj abandoned, corrupt, debauched, depraved, disorderly, dissipated, graceless, lax, lewd, licentious, loose, profligate, rakish, reprobate, shameless, vicious, wanton, wild.

dissolution n liquefaction, melting, solution; decomposition, putrefaction; death, disease; destruction, overthrow, ruin; termination.

dissolve vb liquefy, melt; disorganize, disunite, divide, loose, separate, sever; destroy, ruin; disappear, fade, scatter, vanish; crumble, decompose, disintegrate, perish.

dissonance n cacophony, discord, discordance, harshness, jarring; disagreement, discrepancy, incongruity, inconsistency.

dissonant adj discordant, grating, harsh,

jangling, jarring, unharmonious; contradictory, disagreeing, discrepant, incongruous, inconsistent.

distance vb excel, outdo, outstrip, surpass. • n farness, remoteness; aloofness, coldness, frigidity, reserve, stiffness, offishness; absence, separation, space.

distant adj far, far-away, remote; aloof, ceremonious, cold, cool, frigid, haughty, reserved, stiff, uncordial; faint, indirect, obscure, slight.

distaste n disgust, disrelish; antipathy, aversion, disinclination, dislike, displeasure, dissatisfaction, repugnance.

distasteful adj disgusting, loathsome, nauseating, nauseous, unpalatable, unsavory; disagreeable, displeasing, offensive, repugnant, repulsive, unpleasant.

distemper n ail, ailment, complaint, disease, disorder, illness, indisposition, malady, sickness.

distempered adj diseased, disordered; immoderate, inordinate, intemperate, unregulated.

distend vb bloat, dilate, enlarge, expand, increase, inflate, puff, stretch, swell, widen.

distil vb dribble, drip, drop; extract, separate.

distinct adj definite, different, discrete, disjunct, individual, separate, unconnected; clear, defined, manifest, obvious, plain, unconfused, unmistakable, well-defined.

distinction n discernment, discrimination, distinguishing; difference; account, celebrity, credit, eminence, fame, name, note, rank, renown, reputation, repute, respectability, superiority.

distinctive adj characteristic, differentiating, discriminating, distinguishing.

distinctness n difference, separateness; clearness, explicitness, lucidity, lucidness, perspicuity, precision.

distinguish vb characterize, mark; differentiate, discern, discriminate, perceive, recognize, see, single out, tell; demarcate, divide, separate; celebrate, honor, signalize.

distinguished adj celebrated, eminent, famous, illustrious, noted; conspicuous, extraordinary, laureate, marked, shining, superior, transcendent.

distort vb contort, deform, gnarl, screw, twist, warp, wrest; falsify, misrepresent, pervert.

distortion *n* contortion, deformation, deformity, twist, wryness; falsification, misrepresentation, perversion, wresting.

distract *vb* divert, draw away; bewilder, confound, confuse, derange, discompose, disconcert, disturb, embarrass, harass, madden, mystify, perplex, puzzle.

distracted *adj* crazed, crazy, deranged, frantic, furious, insane, mad, raving, wild.

distraction *n* abstraction, bewilderment, confusion, mystification, embarrassment, perplexity; agitation, commotion, discord, disorder, disturbance, division, perturbation, tumult, turmoil; aberration, alienation, delirium, derangement, frenzy, hallucination, incoherence, insanity, lunacy, madness, mania, raving, wandering.

distress *vb* afflict, annoy, grieve, harry, pain, perplex, rack, trouble; distrain, seize, take. • *n* affliction, calamity, disaster, misery, misfortune, adversity, hardship, perplexity, trial, tribulation; agony, anguish, dolor, grief, sorrow, suffering; gnawing, gripe, griping, pain, torment, torture; destitution, indigence, poverty, privation, straits, want.

distribute *vb* allocate, allot, apportion, assign, deal, dispense, divide, dole out, give, mete, partition, prorate, share; administer, arrange, assort, class, classify, dispose.

distribution *n* allocation, allotment, apportionment, assignment, assortment, dispensation, dispensing; arrangement, disposal, disposition, classification, division, dole, grouping, partition, sharing.

district *n* circuit, department, neighbourhood, province, quarter, region, section, territory, tract, ward.

distrust *vb* disbelieve, discredit, doubt, misbelieve, mistrust, question, suspect. • *n* doubt, misgiving, mistrust, question, suspicion.

distrustful *adj* doubting, dubious, suspicious.

disturb *vb* agitate, shake, stir; confuse, derange, disarrange, disorder, unsettle, upset; annoy, discompose, disconcert, disquiet, distract, fuss, incommode, molest, perturb, plague, trouble, ruffle, vex, worry; impede, interrupt, hinder.

disturbance *n* agitation, commotion, confusion, convulsion, derangement, disorder, perturbation, unsettlement; annoyance, discomposure, distraction, excitement, fuss; hindrance, interruption, molestation; brawl, commotion, disorder, excitement,

fracas, hubbub, riot, rising, tumult, turmoil, uproar.

disunion *n* disconnection, disjunction, division, separation, severance; breach, feud, rupture, schism.

disunite *vb* detach, disconnect, disjoin, dissever, dissociate, divide, part, rend, separate, segregate, sever, sunder; alienate, estrange.

disuse *n* desuetude, discontinuance, disusage, neglect, nonobservance.

ditch *vb* canalize, dig, excavate, furrow, gouge, trench; abandon, discard, dump, jettison, scrap. • *n* channel, drain, fosse, moat, trench.

divagation *n* deviation, digression, rambling, roaming, straying, wandering.

divan *n* bed, chesterfield, couch, settee, sofa.

divaricate *vb* diverge, fork, part.

dive *vb* explore, fathom, penetrate, plunge, sound. • *n* drop, fall, header, plunge; bar, den, dump, joint, saloon.

diverge *vb* divide, radiate, separate; divaricate, separate; deviate, differ, disagree, vary.

divers *adj* different, manifold, many, numerous, several, sundry, various.

diverse *adj* different, differing, disagreeing, dissimilar, divergent, heterogeneous, multifarious, multiform, separate, unlike, variant, various, varying.

diversion *n* deflection, diverting; amusement, delight, distraction, enjoyment, entertainment, game, gratification, pastime, play, pleasure, recreation, sport; detour, digression.

diversity *n* difference, dissimilarity, dissimilitude, divergence, unlikeness, variation; heterogeneity, manifoldness, multifariousness, multiformity, variety.

divert *vb* deflect, distract, disturb; amuse, beguile, delight, entertain, exhilarate, give pleasure, gratify, recreate, refresh, solace.

divest *vb* denude, disrobe, strip, unclothe, undress; deprive, dispossess, strip.

divide *vb* bisect, cleave, cut, dismember, dissever, disunite, open, part, rend, segregate, separate, sever, shear, split, sunder; allocate, allot, apportion, assign, dispense, distribute, dole, mete, portion, share; compartmentalize, demarcate, partition; alienate, disunite, estrange.

divination *n* augury, divining, foretelling, incantation, magic, sooth-saying, sorcery; prediction, presage, prophecy.

divine vb foretell, predict, presage, prognosticate, vaticinate, prophesy; believe, conjecture, fancy, guess, suppose, surmise, suspect, think. • adj deiform, godlike, superhuman, supernatural; angelic, celestial, heavenly, holy, sacred, seraphic, spiritual; exalted, exalting, rapturous, supreme, transcendent. • n churchman, clergyman, ecclesiastic, minister, parson, pastor, priest.

division n compartmentalization, disconnection, disjunction, dismemberment, segmentation, separation, severance; category, class, compartment, head, parcel, portion, section, segment; demarcation, partition; alienation, allotment, apportionment, distribution; breach, difference, disagreement, discord, disunion, estrangement, feud, rupture, variance.

divorce vb disconnect, dissolve, disunite, part, put away, separate, sever, split up, sunder, unmarry. • n disjunction, dissolution, disunion, division, divorcement, parting, separation, severance.

divulge vb communicate, declare, disclose, discover, exhibit, expose, impart, proclaim, promulgate, publish, reveal, tell, uncover.

dizzy adj giddy, vertiginous; careless, heedless, thoughtless.

do vb accomplish, achieve, act, commit, effect, execute, perform; complete, conclude, end, finish, settle, terminate; conduct, transact; observe, perform, practice; translate, render; cook, prepare; cheat, chouse, cozen, hoax, swindle; serve, suffice. • n act, action, adventure, deed, doing, exploit, feat, thing; banquet, event, feast, function, party.

docile adj amenable, obedient, pliant, teachable, tractable, yielding.

dock¹ vb clip, curtail, cut, deduct, truncate; lessen, shorten.

dock² vb anchor, moor; join, meet. • n anchorage, basin, berth, dockage, dockyard, dry dock, harbor, haven, marina, pier, shipyard, wharf.

doctor vb adulterate, alter, cook, falsify, manipulate, tamper with; attend, minister to, cure, heal, remedy, treat; fix, mend, overhaul, repair, service. • n general practitioner, GP, healer, leech, medic, physician; adept, savant.

doctrinaire adj impractical, theoretical. • n ideologist, theorist, thinker.

doctrine n article, belief, creed, dogma,

opinion, precept, principle, teaching, tenet.

dodge vb equivocate, evade, prevaricate, quibble, shuffle. • n artifice, cavil, evasion, quibble, subterfuge, trick.

dogged adj cantankerous, headstrong, inflexible, intractable, mulish, obstinate, pertinacious, perverse, resolute, stubborn, tenacious, unyielding, willful; churlish, morose, sour, sullen, surly.

dogma n article, belief, creed, doctrine, opinion, precept, principle, tenet.

dogmatic adj authoritative, categorical, formal, settled; arrogant, confident, dictatorial, imperious, magisterial, opinionated, oracular, overbearing, peremptory, positive; doctrinal.

dole vb allocate, allot, apportion, assign, deal, distribute, divide, share. • n allocation, allotment, apportionment, distribution; part, portion, share; alms, donation, gift, gratuity, pittance; affliction, distress, grief, sorrow, woe.

doleful adj lugubrious, melancholy, piteous, rueful, sad, somber, sorrowful, woebegone, woeful; cheerless, dark, dismal, dolorous, dreary, gloomy.

dolorous adj cheerless, dark, dismal, gloomy; doleful, lugubrious, mournful, piteous, rueful, sad, sorrowful, woeful.

dolt n blockhead, booby, dullard, dunce, fool, ignoramus, simpleton.

domain n authority, dominion, jurisdiction, province, sway; empire, realm, territory; lands, estate; branch, department, region.

domestic n charwoman, help, home help, maid, servant. • adj domiciliary, family, home, household, private; domesticated; internal, intestine.

domesticate vb tame; adopt, assimilate, familiarize, naturalize.

domicile vb domiciliate, dwell, inhabit, live, remain, reside. • n abode, dwelling, habitation, harbor, home, house, residence.

dominant adj ascendant, ascending, chief, controlling, governing, influential, outstanding, paramount, predominant, preeminent, preponderant, presiding, prevailing, ruling.

dominate vb control, rule, sway; command, overlook, overtop, surmount.

domineer vb rule, tyrannize; bluster, bully, hector, menace, swagger, swell, threaten.

dominion n ascendancy, authority, command, control, domain, domination, government, jurisdiction, mastery, rule, sovereign, sovereignty, supremacy, sway; country, kingdom, realm, region, territory.

donation *n* alms, benefaction, boon, contribution, dole, donative, gift, grant, gratuity, largesse, offering, present, subscription.

done *adj* accomplished, achieved, effected, executed, performed; completed, concluded, ended, finished, terminated; carried on, transacted; rendered, translated; cooked, prepared; cheated, cozened, hoaxed, swindled; (*with* **for**) damned, dished, *hors de combat*, ruined, shelved, spoiled, wound up.

donkey *n* ass, mule; dunce, fool, simpleton.

donor *n* benefactor, bestower, giver; donator.

double *vb* fold, plait; duplicate, geminate, increase, multiply, repeat; return. • *adj* binary, coupled, geminate, paired; dual, twice, twofold; deceitful, dishonest, double-dealing, false, hollow, insincere, knavish, perfidious, treacherous, two-faced. • *adv* doubly, twice, twofold. • *n* doubling, fold, plait; artifice, maneuvre, ruse, shift, stratagem, trick, wile; copy, counterpart, twin.

doublet *n* jacket, jerkin.

doubt *vb* demur, fluctuate, hesitate, vacillate, waver; distrust, mistrust, query, question, suspect. • *n* dubiety, dubiousness, dubitation, hesitance, hesitancy, hesitation, incertitude, indecision, irresolution, question, suspense, uncertainty, vacillation; distrust, misgiving, mistrust, scepticism, suspicion.

doubtful *adj* dubious, hesitating, sceptical, undecided, undetermined, wavering; ambiguous, dubious, enigmatical, equivocal, hazardous, obscure, problematical, unsure; indeterminate, questionable, undecided, unquestioned.

doubtless *adv* certainly, unquestionably; clearly, indisputably, precisely.

doughty *adj* adventurous, bold, brave, chivalrous, courageous, daring, dauntless, fearless, gallant, heroic, intrepid, redoubtable, valiant, valorous.

douse *see* **dowse**.

dowdy *adj* awkward, dingy, ill-dressed, shabby, slatternly, slovenly; old-fashioned, unfashionable.

dowel *n* peg, pin, pinion, tenon.

dower *n* endowment, gift; dowry; portion, share.

downcast *adj* chapfallen, crestfallen, dejected, depressed, despondent, discouraged, disheartened, dispirited, downhearted, low-spirited, sad, unhappy.

downfall *n* descent, destruction, fall, ruin.

downhearted *adj* chapfallen, crestfallen, dejected, depressed, despondent, discouraged, disheartened, dispirited, downcast, low-spirited, sad, unhappy.

downright *adj* absolute, categorical, clear, explicit, plain, positive, sheer, simple, undisguised, unequivocal, utter; aboveboard, artless, blunt, direct, frank, honest, ingenuous, open, sincere, straightforward, unceremonious.

downy *adj* lanate, lanated, lanose.

dowse, douse *vb* dip, immerse, plunge, souse, submerge.

doxy *n* mistress, paramour; courtesan, drab, harlot, prostitute, strumpet, streetwalker, whore.

doze *vb* drowse, nap, sleep, slumber. • *n* drowse, forty-winks, nap.

dozy *adj* drowsy, heavy, sleepy, sluggish.

draft *vb* detach, select; commandeer, conscript, impress; delineate, draw, outline, sketch. • *n* conscription, drawing, selection; delineation, outline, sketch; bill, check, order.

drag *vb* draw, haul, pull, tow, tug; trail; linger, loiter. • *n* favor, influence, pull; brake, check, curb, lag, resistance, retardation, scotch, skid, slackening, slack-off, slowing.

draggle *vb* befoul, bemire, besmirch, dangle, drabble, trail.

dragoon *vb* compel, drive, force, harass, harry, persecute. • *n* cavalier, equestrian, horse-soldier.

drain *vb* milk, sluice, tap; empty, evacuate, exhaust; dry. • *n* channel, culvert, ditch, sewer, sluice, trench, watercourse; exhaustion, withdrawal.

draught *n* current, drawing, pulling, traction; cup, dose, drench, drink, potion; delineation, design, draft, outline, sketch.

draw *vb* drag, haul, tow, tug, pull; attract; drain, suck, syphon; extract, extort; breathe in, inhale, inspire; allure, engage, entice, induce, influence, lead, move, persuade; extend, protract, stretch; delineate, depict, sketch; deduce, derive, infer; compose, draft, formulate, frame, prepare; blister, vesicate, write.

drawback *n* defect, deficiency, detriment,

disadvantage, fault, flaw, imperfection, injury; abatement, allowance, deduction, discount, rebate, reduction.

drawing *n* attracting, draining, inhaling, pulling, traction; delineation, draught, outline, picture, plan, sketch.

dread *vb* apprehend, fear. • *adj* dreadful, frightful, horrible, terrible; awful, venerable. • *n* affright, alarm, apprehension, fear, terror; awe, veneration.

dreadful *adj* alarming, appalling, awesome, dire, direful, fearful, formidable, frightful, horrible, horrid, terrible, terrific, tremendous; awful, venerable.

dream *vb* fancy, imagine, think. • *n* conceit, day-dream, delusion, fancy, fantasy, hallucination, illusion, imagination, reverie, vagary, vision.

dreamer *n* enthusiast, visionary.

dreamy *adj* absent, abstracted, fanciful, ideal, misty, shadowy, speculative, unreal, visionary.

dreary *adj* cheerless, chilling, comfortless, dark, depressing, dismal, drear, gloomy, lonely, lonesome, sad, solitary, sorrowful; boring, dull, monotonous, tedious, tiresome, uninteresting, wearisome.

dregs *npl* feculence, grounds, lees, offscourings, residuum, scourings, sediment, waste; draff, dross, refuse, scum, trash.

drench *vb* dowse, drown, imbrue, saturate, soak, souse, steep, wet; physic, purge.

dress *vb* align, straighten; adjust, arrange, dispose; fit, prepare; accouter, apparel, array, attire, clothe, robe, rig; adorn, bedeck, deck, decorate, drape, embellish, trim. • *n* apparel, attire, clothes, clothing, costume, garb, guise, garments, habiliment, habit, raiment, suit, toilet, vesture; bedizenment, bravery; frock, gown, rob.

dressing *n* compost, fertilizer, manure; forcemeat, stuffing.

dressy *adj* flashy, gaudy, showy.

driblet *n* bit, drop, fragment, morsel, piece, scrap.

drift *vb* accumulate, drive, float, wander. • *n* bearing, course, direction; aim, design, intent, intention, mark, object, proposal, purpose, scope, tendency; detritus, deposit, diluvium; gallery, passage, tunnel; current, rush, sweep; heap, pile.

drill[1] *vb* bore, perforate, pierce; discipline, exercise, instruct, teach, train. • *n* borer; discipline, exercise, training.

drill[2] *n* channel, furrow, trench.

drink *vb* imbibe, sip, swill; carouse, indulge, revel, tipple, tope; swallow, quaff; absorb. • *n* beverage, draught, liquid, potation, potion; dram, nip, sip, snifter, refreshment.

drip *vb* dribble, drop, leak, trickle; distil, filter, percolate; ooze, reek, seep, weep. • *n* dribble, drippings, drop, leak, leakage, leaking, trickle, tricklet; bore, nuisance, wet blanket.

drive *vb* hurl, impel, propel, send, shoot, thrust; actuate, incite, press, urge; coerce, compel, constrain, force, harass, oblige, overburden, press, rush; go, guide, ride, travel; aim, intend. • *n* effort, energy, pressure; airing, ride; road.

drivel *vb* babble, blether, dote, drool, slaver, slobber. • *n* balderdash, driveling, fatuity, nonsense, prating, rubbish, slaver, stuff, twaddle.

drizzle *vb* mizzle, rain, shower, sprinkle. • *n* haar, mist, mizzle, rain, sprinkling.

droll *adj* comic, comical, farcical, funny, jocular, ludicrous, laughable, ridiculous; amusing, diverting, facetious, odd, quaint, queer, waggish. • *n* buffoon, clown, comedian, fool, harlequin, jester, punch, Punchinello, scaramouch, wag, zany.

drollery *n* archness, buffoonery, fun, humor, jocularity, pleasantry, waggishness, whimsicality.

drone *vb* dawdle, drawl, idle, loaf, lounge; hum. • *n* idler, loafer, lounger, sluggard.

drool *vb* drivel, slaver.

droop *vb* fade, wilt, wither; decline, fail, faint, flag, languish, sink, weaken; bend, hang.

drop *vb* distil, drip, shed; decline, depress, descend, dump, lower, sink; abandon, desert, forsake, forswear, leave, omit, relinquish, quit; cease, discontinue, intermit, remit; fall, precipitate. • *n* bead, droplet, globule; earring, pendant.

dross *n* cinder, lees, recrement, scoria, scum, slag; refuse, waste.

drought *n* aridity, drouth, dryness, thirstiness.

drove *n* flock, herd; collection, company, crowd.

drown *vb* deluge, engulf, flood, immerse, inundate, overflow, sink, submerge, swamp; overcome, overpower, overwhelm.

drowse *vb* doze, nap, sleep, slumber, snooze. • *n* doze, forty winks, nap, siesta, sleep, snooze.

drowsy *adj* dozy, sleepy; comatose, lethargic, stupid; lulling, soporific.

drub *vb* bang, beat, cane, cudgel, flog, hit, knock, pommel, pound, strike, thrash, thump, whack.

drubbing *n* beating, caning, cudgeling, flagellation, flogging, pommelling, pounding, thrashing, thumping, whacking.

drudge *vb* grub, grind, plod, slave, toil, work. • *n* grind, hack, hard worker, menial, plodder, scullion, servant, slave, toiler, worker.

drug *vb* dose, medicate; disgust, surfeit. • *n* medicine, physic, remedy; poison.

drunk *adj* boozed, drunken, inebriated, intoxicated, maudlin, soaked, tipsy; ablaze, aflame, delirious, fervent, suffused. • *n* alcoholic, boozer, dipsomaniac, drunkard, inebriate, lush, soak; bacchanal, bender, binge.

drunkard *n* alcoholic, boozer, carouser, dipsomaniac, drinker, drunk, inebriate, reveler, sot, tippler, toper.

dry *vb* dehydrate, desiccate, drain, exsiccate, parch. • *adj* desiccated, dried, juiceless, sapless, unmoistened; arid, droughty, parched; drouthy, thirsty; barren, dull, insipid, jejune, plain, pointless, tame, tedious, tiresome, unembellished, uninteresting, vapid; cutting, keen, sarcastic, severe, sharp, sly.

dub *vb* call, christen, denominate, designate, entitle, name, style, term.

dubious *adj* doubtful, fluctuating, hesitant, irresolute, skeptical, uncertain, undecided, unsettled, wavering; ambiguous, doubtful, equivocal, improbable, questionable, uncertain.

duck *vb* dip, dive, immerse, plunge, submerge, souse; bend, bow, dodge, stoop.

duct *n* canal, channel, conduit, pipe, tube; blood-vessel.

ductile *adj* compliant, docile, facile, tractable, yielding; flexible, malleable, pliant; extensible, tensile.

dudgeon *n* anger, indignation, ill will, ire, malice, resentment, umbrage, wrath.

due *adj* owed, owing; appropriate, becoming, befitting, bounden, fit, proper, suitable, right. • *adv* dead, direct, directly, exactly, just, right, squarely, straight. • *n* claim, debt, desert, right.

dulcet *adj* delicious, honeyed, luscious, sweet; harmonious, melodious; agreeable, charming, delightful, pleasant, pleasing.

dull *vb* blunt; benumb, besot, deaden, hebetate, obtund, paralyse, stupefy; dampen, deject, depress, discourage, dishearten, dispirit; allay, alleviate, assuage, mitigate, moderate, quiet, soften; deaden, dim, sully, tarnish. • *adj* blockish, brutish, doltish, obtuse, stolid, stupid, unintelligent; apathetic, callous, dead, insensible, passionless, phlegmatic, unfeeling, unimpassioned, unresponsive; heavy, inactive, inanimate, inert, languish, lifeless, slow, sluggish, torpid; blunt, dulled, hebetate, obtuse; cheerless, dismal, dreary, gloomy, sad, sombre; dim, lack-luster, lusterless, mart, obscure, opaque, tarnished; dry, flat, insipid, irksome, jejune, prosy, tedious, tiresome, uninteresting, wearisome.

duly *adv* befittingly, decorously, fitly, properly, rightly; regularly.

dumb *adj* inarticulate, mute, silent, soundless, speechless, voiceless.

dumbfound, dumfound *vb* amaze, astonish, astound, bewilder, confound, confuse, nonplus, pose.

dumps *npl* blues, dejection, depression, despondency, gloom, gloominess, melancholy, sadness.

dun[1] *adj* grayish-brown, brown, drab.

dun[2] *vb* beset, importune, press, urge.

dunce *n* ass, block, blockhead, clodpole, dolt, donkey, dullard, dunderhead, fool, goose, halfwit, ignoramus, jackass, lackwit, loon, nincompoop, numskull, oaf, simpleton, thickhead, witling.

dupe *vb* beguile, cheat, chouse, circumvent, cozen, deceive, delude, gull, hoodwink, outwit, overreach, swindle, trick. • *n* gull, simpleton.

duplicate *vb* copy, double, repeat, replicate, reproduce. • *adj* doubled, twofold. • *n* copy, counterpart, facsimile, replica, transcript.

duplicity *n* artifice, chicanery, circumvention, deceit, deception, dishonesty, dissimulation, double-dealing, falseness, fraud, guile, hypocrisy, perfidy.

durable *adj* abiding, constant, continuing, enduring, firm, lasting, permanent, persistent, stable.

duration *n* continuance, continuation, permanency, perpetuation, prolongation; period, time.

duress *n* captivity, confinement, constraint, durance, hardship, imprisonment, restraint; compulsion.

dusky *adj* cloudy, darkish, dim, murky,

obscure, overcast, shady, shadowy; dark, swarthy, tawny.

dutiful *adj* duteous, obedient, submissive; deferential, respectful, reverential.

duty *n* allegiance, devoirs, obligation, responsibility, reverence; business, engagement, function, office, service; custom, excise, impost, tariff, tax, toll.

dwarf *vb* lower, stunt. • *n* bantam, homunculus, manikin, midget, pygmy.

dwarfish *adj* diminutive, dwarfed, little, low, pygmy, small, stunted, tiny, undersized.

dwell *vb* abide, inhabit, live, lodge, remain, reside, rest, sojourn, stay, stop, tarry, tenant.

dwelling *n* abode, cot, domicile, dugout, establishment, habitation, home, house, hutch, lodging, mansion, quarters, residence.

dwindle *vb* decrease, diminish, lessen, shrink; decay, decline, deteriorate, pine, sink, waste away.

dye *vb* color, stain, tinge. • *n* cast, color, hue, shade, stain, tinge, tint.

dying *adj* expiring; mortal, perishable. • *n* death, decease, demise, departure, dissolution, exit.

dynasty *n* dominion, empire, government, rule, sovereignty.

dyspepsia *n* indigestion.

E

eager *adj* agog, avid, anxious, desirous, fain, greedy, impatient, keen, longing, yearning; animated, ardent, earnest, enthusiastic, fervent, fervid, forward, glowing, hot, impetuous, sanguine, vehement, zealous.

eagerness *n* ardor, avidity, earnestness, enthusiasm, fervor, greediness, heartiness, hunger, impatience, impetuosity, intentness, keenness, longing, thirst, vehemence, yearning, zeal.

eagle-eyed *adj* discerning, hawk-eyed, sharp-sighted.

ear[1] *n* attention, hearing, heed, regard.

ear[2] *n* head, spike.

early *adj* opportune, seasonable, timely; forward, premature; dawning, matutinal. • *adv* anon, beforehand, betimes, ere, seasonably, shortly, soon.

earn *vb* acquire, gain, get, obtain, procure, realize, reap, win; deserve, merit.

earnest *adj* animated, ardent, eager, cordial, fervent, fervid, glowing, hearty, impassioned, importune, warm, zealous; fixed, intent, steady; sincere, true, truthful; important, momentous, serious, weighty. • *n* reality, seriousness, truth; foretaste, pledge, promise; handsel, payment.

earnings *npl* allowance, emoluments, gains, income, pay, proceeds, profits, remuneration, reward, salary, stipend.

earth *n* globe, orb, planet, world; clay, clod, dirt, glebe, ground, humus, land, loam, sod, soil, turf; mankind, world.

earthborn *adj* abject, base, earthly, groveling, low, mean, unspiritual.

earthly *adj* terrestrial; base, carnal, earthborn, low, gross, groveling, sensual, sordid, unspiritual, worldly; bodily, material, mundane, natural, secular, temporal.

earthy *adj* clayey, earth-like, terrene; earthly, terrestrial; coarse, gross, material, unrefined.

ease *vb* disburden, disencumber, pacify, quiet, relieve, still; abate, allay, alleviate, appease, assuage, diminish, mitigate, soothe; loosen, release; facilitate, favor. • *n* leisure, quiescence, repose, rest; calmness, content, contentment, enjoyment, happiness, peace, quiet, quietness, quietude, relief, repose, satisfaction, serenity, tranquillity; easiness, facility, readiness; flexibility, freedom, liberty, lightness, naturalness, unconcern, unconstraint; comfort, elbowroom.

easy *adj* light; careless, comfortable, contented, effortless, painless, quiet, satisfied, tranquil, untroubled; accommodating, complaisant, compliant, complying, facile, indolent, manageable, pliant, submissive, tractable, yielding; graceful, informal, natural, unconstrained; flowing, ready, smooth, unaffected; gentle, lenient, mild, moderate; affluent, loose, unconcerned, unembarrassed.

eat *vb* chew, consume, devour, engorge, ingest, ravage, swallow; corrode, demolish, erode; breakfast, dine, lunch, sup.

eatable *adj* edible, esculent, harmless, wholesome.

ebb *vb* abate, recede, retire, subside; decay, decline, decrease, degenerate, deteriorate, sink, wane. • *n* refluence, reflux, regress, regression, retrocedence, retrocession, retrogression, return; caducity, decay, decline, degeneration, deterioration, wane, waning;

abatement, decrease, decrement, diminution.

ebullience n ebullition, effervescence; burst, bursting, overenthusiasm, overflow, rush, vigor.

ebullition n boiling, bubbling; effervescence, fermentation; burst, fit, outbreak, outburst, paroxysm.

eccentric adj decentered, parabolic; aberrant, abnormal, anomalous, cranky, erratic, fantastic, irregular, odd, outlandish, peculiar, singular, strange, uncommon, unnatural, wayward, whimsical. • n crank, curiosity, original.

eccentricity n ellipticity, flattening, flatness, oblateness; aberration, irregularity, oddity, oddness, peculiarity, singularity, strangeness, waywardness.

ecclesiastic[1], **ecclesiastical** adj churchish, churchly, clerical, ministerial, nonsecular, pastoral, priestly, religious, sacerdotal.

ecclesiastic[2] n chaplain, churchman, clergyman, cleric, clerk, divine, minister, parson, pastor, priest, reverend, shepherd.

echo vb reply, resound, reverberate, ring; re-echo, repeat. • n answer, repetition, reverberation; imitation.

éclat n acclamation, applause, brilliancy, effect, glory, luster, pomp, renown, show, splendor.

eclipse vb cloud, darken, dim, obscure, overshadow, veil; annihilate, annul, blot out, extinguish. • n clouding, concealment, darkening, dimming, disappearance, hiding, obscuration, occultation, shrouding, vanishing, veiling; annihilation, blotting out, destruction, extinction, extinguishment, obliteration.

eclogue n bucolic, idyl, pastoral.

economize vb husband, manage, save; retrench.

economy n frugality, husbandry, parsimony, providence, retrenchment, saving, skimping, stinginess, thrift, thriftiness; administration, arrangement, management, method, order, plan, regulation, system; dispensation.

ecstasy n frenzy, madness, paroxysm, trance; delight, gladness, joy, rhapsody, rapture, ravishment, transport.

eddy vb gurgle, surge, spin, swirl, whirl. • n countercurrent; swirl, vortex, whirlpool.

edge vb sharpen; border, fringe, rim. • n border, brim, brink, bound, crest, fringe, hem, lip, margin, rim, verge; animation,

intensity, interest, keenness, sharpness, zest; acrimony, bitterness, gall, sharpness, sting.

edging n border, frill, fringe, trimming.

edible adj eatable, esculent, harmless, wholesome.

edict n act, command, constitution, decision, decree, law, mandate, manifesto, notice, order, ordinance, proclamation, regulation, rescript, statute.

edifice n building, fabric, habitation, house, structure.

edify vb educate, elevate, enlightenment, improve, inform, instruct, nurture, teach, upbuild.

edition n impression, issue, number.

educate vb breed, cultivate, develop, discipline, drill, edify, exercise, indoctrinate, inform, instruct, mature, nurture, rear, school, teach, train.

educated adj cultured, lettered, literate.

education n breeding, cultivation, culture, development, discipline, drilling, indoctrination, instruction, nurture, pedagogics, schooling, teaching, training, tuition.

educe vb bring out, draw out, elicit, evolve, extract.

eerie adj awesome, fearful, frightening, strange, uncanny, weird.

efface vb blot, blot out, cancel, delete, destroy, erase, expunge, obliterate, remove, sponge.

effect vb cause, create, effectuate, produce; accomplish, achieve, carry, compass, complete, conclude, consummate, contrive, do, execute, force, negotiate, perform, realize, work. • n consequence, event, fruit, issue, outcome, result; efficiency, fact, force, power, reality; validity, weight; drift, import, intent, meaning, purport, significance, tenor.

effective adj able, active, adequate, competent, convincing, effectual, sufficient; cogent, efficacious, energetic, forcible, potent, powerful.

effects npl chattels, furniture, goods, movables, property.

effectual adj operative, successful; active, effective, efficacious, efficient.

effectuate vb accomplish, achieve, complete, do, effect, execute, fulfil, perform, secure.

effeminate adj delicate, feminine, soft, tender, timorous, unmanly, womanish, womanlike, womanly; camp.

effervesce *vb* bubble, ferment, foam, froth.

effete *adj* addle, barren, fruitless, sterile, unfruitful, unproductive, unprolific; decayed, exhausted, spent, wasted.

efficacious *adj* active, adequate, competent, effective, effectual, efficient, energetic, operative, powerful.

efficacy *n* ability, competency, effectiveness, efficiency, energy, force, potency, power, strength, vigor, virtue.

efficient *adj* active, capable, competent, effective, effectual, efficacious, operative, potent; able, energetic, ready, skillful.

effigy *n* figure, image, likeness, portrait, representation, statue.

effloresce *vb* bloom, flower.

efflorescence *n* blooming, blossoming, flowering.

offluence *n* discharge, efflux, effluvium, emanation, emission, flow, outflow, outpouring.

effort *n* application, attempt, endeavor, essay, exertion, pains, spurt, strain, strife, stretch, struggle, trial, trouble.

effrontery *n* assurance, audacity, boldness, brass, disrespect, hardihood, impudence, incivility, insolence, presumption, rudeness, sauciness, shamelessness.

effulgent *adj* burning, beaming, blazing, bright, brilliant, dazzling, flaming, glowing, lustrous, radiant, refulgent, resplendent, shining, splendid.

effusion *n* discharge, efflux, emission, gush, outpouring; shedding, spilling, waste; address, speech, talk, utterance.

egg *vb* (*with* **on**) encourage, incite, instigate, push, stimulate, urge; harass, harry, provoke.

ego *n* id, self, me, subject, superego.

egotism *n* self-admiration, self-assertion, self-commendation, self-conceit, self-esteem, self-importance, self-praise; egoism, selfishness.

egotistic, egotistical *adj* bumptious, conceited, egoistical, opinionated, self-asserting, self-admiring, self-centered, self-conceited, self-important, self-loving, vain.

egregious *adj* conspicuous, enormous, extraordinary, flagrant, great, gross, huge, monstrous, outrageous, prodigious, remarkable, tremendous.

egress *n* departure, emergence, exit, outlet, way out.

eject *vb* belch, discharge, disgorge, emit, evacuate, puke, spew, spit, spout, spurt, void, vomit; bounce, cashier, discharge, dismiss, disposes, eliminate, evict, expel, fire, oust; banish, reject, throw out.

elaborate *vb* develop, improve, mature, produce, refine, ripen. • *adj* complicated, decorated, detailed, dressy, labored, laborious, ornate, perfected, studied.

elapse *vb* go, lapse, pass.

elastic *adj* rebounding, recoiling, resilient, springy; buoyant, recuperative.

elated *adj* animated, cheered, elate, elevated, excited, exhilarated, exultant, flushed, puffed up, roused.

elbow *vb* crowd, force, hustle, jostle, nudge, push, shoulder. • *n* angle, bend, corner, flexure, joining, turn.

elder *adj* older, senior; ranking; ancient, earlier, older. • *n* ancestor, senior; presbyter, prior, senator.

elect *vb* appoint, choose, cull, designate, pick, prefer, select. • *adj* choice, chosen, picked, selected; appointed, elected; predestinated, redeemed.

election *n* appointment, choice, preference, selection; alternative, freedom, freewill, liberty; predestination.

elector *n* chooser, constituent, selector, voter.

electrify *vb* charge, galvanize; astonish, enchant, excite, rouse, startle, stir, thrill.

elegance, elegancy *n* beauty, grace, propriety, symmetry; courtliness, daintiness, gentility, nicety, polish, politeness, refinement, taste.

elegant *adj* beautiful, chaste, classical, dainty, graceful, fine, handsome, neat, symmetrical, tasteful, trim, well-made, well-proportioned; accomplished, courtly, cultivated, fashionable, genteel, polished, polite, refined.

elegiac *adj* dirgeful, mournful, plaintive, sorrowful.

elegy *n* dirge, epicedium, lament, ode, threnody.

element *n* basis, component, constituent, factor, germ, ingredient, part, principle, rudiment, unit; environment, milieu, sphere.

elementary *adj* primordial, simple, uncombined, uncomplicated, uncompounded; basic, component, fundamental, initial, primary, rudimental, rudimentary.

elevate *vb* erect, hoist, lift, raise; advance, aggrandize, exalt, promote; dignify, ennoble, exalt, greaten, improve, refine; animate, cheer, elate, excite, exhilarate, rouse.

elfin *adj* elflike, elvish, mischievous, weird.

elicit *vb* draw out, educe, evoke, extort, fetch, obtain, pump, wrest, wring; deduce, educe.

eligible *adj* desirable, preferable; qualified, suitable, worthy.

eliminate *vb* disengage, eradicate, exclude, expel, remove, separate; ignore, omit, reject.

ellipsis *n* gap, hiatus, lacuna, omission.

elliptical *adj* oval; defective, incomplete.

elocution *n* declamation, delivery, oratory, rhetoric, speech, utterance.

elongate *vb* draw, draw out, extend, lengthen, protract, stretch.

elope *vb* abscond, bolt, decamp, disappear, leave.

eloquence *n* fluency, oratory, rhetoric.

else *adv* besides, differently, otherwise.

elucidate *vb* clarify, demonstrate, explain, expound, illuminate, illustrate, interpret, unfold.

elucidation *n* annotation, clarification, comment, commentary, elucidating, explaining, explanation, exposition, gloss, scholium.

elude *vb* avoid, escape, evade, shun, slip; baffle, balk, disappoint, disconcert, escape, foil, frustrate, thwart.

elusive *adj* deceptive, deceitful, delusive, evasive, fallacious, fraudulent, illusory; equivocatory, equivocating, shuffling.

Elysian *adj* blissful, celestial, delightful, enchanting, heavenly, ravishing, seraphic.

emaciation *n* attenuation, lankness, leanness, meagerness, tabes, tabescence, thinness.

emanate *vb* arise, come, emerge, flow, issue, originate, proceed, spring.

emancipate *vb* deliver, discharge, disenthral, enfranchise, free, liberate, manumit, release, unchain, unfetter, unshackle.

emancipation *n* deliverance, enfranchisement, deliverance, freedom, liberation, manumission, release.

emasculate *vb* castrate, geld; debilitate, effeminize, enervate, unman, weaken.

embalm *vb* cherish, consecrate, conserve, enshrine, preserve, store, treasure; perfume, scent.

embargo *vb* ban, bar, blockade, debar, exclude, prohibit, proscribe, restrict, stop, withhold. • *n* ban, bar, blockade, exclusion, hindrance, impediment, prohibition,

prohibitory, proscription, restraint, restriction, stoppage.

embark *vb* engage, enlist.

embarrass *vb* beset, entangle, perplex; annoy, clog, bother, distress, hamper, harass, involve, plague, trouble, vex; abash, confound, confuse, discomfit, disconcert, dumbfound, mortify, nonplus, pose, shame.

embellish *vb* adorn, beautify, bedeck, deck, decorate, emblazon, enhance, enrich, garnish, grace, ornament.

embellishment *n* adornment, decoration, enrichment, ornament, ornamentation.

embezzle *vb* appropriate, defalcate, filch, misappropriate, peculate, pilfer, purloin, steal.

embitter *vb* aggravate, envenom, exacerbate; anger, enrage, exasperate, madden.

emblem *n* badge, cognizance, device, mark, representation, sign, symbol, token, type.

embody *vb* combine, compact, concentrate, incorporate; comprehend, comprise, contain, embrace, include; codify, methodize, systematize.

embolden *vb* animate, cheer, elate, encourage, gladden, hearten, inspirit, nerve, reassure.

embosom *vb* bury, cherish, clasp, conceal, enfold, envelop, enwrap, foster, hide, nurse, surround.

embrace *vb* clasp; accept, seize, welcome; comprehend, comprise, contain, cover, embody, encircle, enclose, encompass, enfold, hold, include. • *n* clasp, fold, hug.

embroil *vb* commingle, encumber, ensnarl, entangle, implicate, involve; confuse, discompose, disorder, distract, disturb, perplex, trouble.

embryo *n* beginning, germ, nucleus, root, rudiment.

embryonic *adj* incipient, rudimentary, undeveloped.

emendation *n* amendment, correction, improvement, rectification.

emerge *vb* rise; emanate, escape, issue; appear, arise, outcrop.

emergency *n* crisis, difficulty, dilemma, exigency, extremity, necessity, pass, pinch, push, strait, urgency; conjuncture, crisis, juncture, pass.

emigration *n* departure, exodus, migration, removal.

eminence *n* elevation, hill, projection, prominence, protuberance; celebrity, conspicuousness, distinction, exaltation, fame, loftiness, note, preferment, reputation, repute, renown.

eminent *adj* elevated, high, lofty; celebrated, conspicuous, distinguished, exalted, famous, illustrious, notable, prominent, remarkable, renowned.

emissary *n* messenger, scout, secret agent, spy.

emit *vb* breathe out, dart, discharge, eject, emanate, exhale, gust, hurl, jet, outpour, shed, shoot, spurt, squirt.

emollient *adj* relaxing, softening. soothing.
• *n* softener.

emolument *n* compensation, gain, hire, income, lucer, pay, pecuniary, profits, salary, stipend, wages; advantage, benefit, profit, perquisites.

emotion *n* agitation, excitement, feeling, passion, perturbation, sentiment, sympathy, trepidation.

emphasis *n* accent, stress; force, importance, impressiveness, moment, significance, weight.

emphatic *adj* decided, distinct, earnest, energetic, expressive, forcible, impressive, intensive, positive, significant, strong, unequivocal.

empire *n* domain, dominion, sovereignty, supremacy; authority, command, control, government, rule, sway.

empirical, empiric *adj* experimental, experiential; hypothetical, provisional, tentative; charlatanic, quackish.

employ *vb* busy, devote, engage, engross, enlist, exercise, occupy, retain; apply, commission, use. • *n* employment, service.

employee *n* agent, clerk, employee, hand, servant, workman.

employment *n* avocation, business, calling, craft, employ, engagement, occupation, profession, pursuit, trade, vocation, work.

emporium *n* market, mart, shop, store.

empower *vb* authorize, commission, permit, qualify, sanction, warrant; enable.

empty *vb* deplete, drain, evacuate, exhaust; discharge, disembogue; flow, embogue.
• *adj* blank, hollow, unoccupied, vacant, vacuous, void; deplete, destitute, devoid, hungry; unfilled, unfurnished, unsupplied; unsatisfactory, unsatisfying, unsubstantial, useless, vain; clear, deserted, desolate, exhausted, free, unburdened, unloaded, waste; foolish, frivolous, inane, senseless, silly, stupid, trivial, weak.

empyrean, empyreal *adj* aerial, airy, ethereal, heavenly, refined, sublimated, sublimed.

emulation *n* competition, rivalry, strife, vying; contention, envy, jealousy.

enable *vb* authorize, capacitate, commission, empower, fit, permit, prepare, qualify, sanction, warrant.

enact *vb* authorize, command, decree, establish, legislate, ordain, order, sanction; act, perform, personate, play, represent.

enactment *n* act, decree, law, edict, ordinance.

enamor *vb* bewitch, captivate, charm, enchant, endear, fascinate.

enchain *vb* bind, confine, enslave, fetter, hold, manacle, restrain, shackle.

enchant *vb* beguile, bewitch, charm, delude, fascinate; captivate, catch, enamor, win; beatify, delight, enrapture, rapture, ravish, transport.

enchanting *adj* bewitching, blissful, captivating, charming, delightful, enrapturing, fascinating, rapturous, ravishing.

enchantment *n* charm, conjuration, incantation, magic, necromancy, sorcery, spell, witchery; bliss, delight, fascination, rapture, ravishment, transport.

encase *vb* encircle, enclose, incase, infix, set; chase, emboss, engrave, inlay, ornament.

encage *vb* confine, coop up, impound, imprison, shut up.

encircle *vb* belt, circumscribe, encompass, enclose, engird, enring, environ, gird, ring, span, surround, twine; clasp, embrace, enfold, fold.

enclose, inclose *vb* circumscribe, corral, coop, embosom, encircle, encompass, environ, fence in, hedge, include, pen, shut in, surround; box, cover, encase, envelop, wrap.

encomium *n* applause, commendation, eulogy, laudation, panegyric, praise.

encompass *vb* belt, compass, encircle, enclose, engird, environ, gird, surround; beset, besiege, hem in, include, invest, surround.

encounter *vb* confront, face, meet; attack, combat, contend, engage, strive, struggle.
• *n* assault, attack, clash, collision, meeting, onset; action, affair, battle, brush, combat, conflict, contest, dispute, engagement, skirmish.

encourage *vb* animate, assure, cheer,

comfort, console, embolden, enhearten, fortify, hearten, incite, inspirit, instigate, reassure, stimulate, strengthen; abet, aid, advance, approve, countenance, favor, foster, further, help, patronize, promote, support.

encroach *vb* infringe, invade, intrude, tench, trespass, usurp.

encumber *vb* burden, clog, hamper, hinder, impede, load, obstruct, overload, oppress, retard; complicate, embarrass, entangle, involve, perplex.

encumbrance *n* burden, clog, deadweight, drag, embarrassment, hampering, hindrance, impediment, incubus, load; claim, debt, liability, lien.

end *vb* abolish, close, conclude, discontinue, dissolve, drop, finish, stop, terminate; annihilate, destroy, kill; cease, terminate. • *n* extremity, tip; cessation, close, denouement, ending, expiration, finale, finis, finish, last, period, stoppage, windup; completion, conclusion, consummation; annihilation, catastrophe, destruction, dissolution; bound, limit, termination, terminus; consequence, event, issue, result, settlement, sequel, upshot; fragment, remnant, scrap, stub, tag, tail; aim, design, goal, intent, intention, object, objective, purpose.

endanger *vb* compromise, hazard, imperil, jeopardize, peril, risk.

endear *vb* attach, bind, captivate, charm, win.

endearment *n* attachment, fondness, love, tenderness; caress, blandishment, fondling.

endeavor *vb* aim, attempt, essay, labor, seek, strive, struggle, study, try. • *n* aim, attempt, conatus, effort, essay, exertion, trial, struggle, trial.

endless *adj* boundless, illimitable, immeasurable, indeterminable, infinite, interminable, limitless, unlimited; dateless, eternal, everlasting, never-ending, perpetual, unending; deathless, ever-enduring, everliving, immortal, imperishable, undying.

endorse, indorse *vb* approve, back, confirm, guarantee, ratify, sanction, superscribe, support, visé, vouch for, warrant; superscribe.

endow *vb* bequeath, clothe, confer, dower, endue, enrich, gift, indue, invest, supply.

endowment *n* bequest, boon, bounty, gift, grant, largesse, present; foundation, fund, property, revenue; ability, aptitude, capability, capacity, faculty, genius, gift, parts, power, qualification, quality, talent.

endurance *n* abiding, bearing, sufferance, suffering, tolerance, toleration; backbone, bottom, forbearance, fortitude, guts, patience, resignation.

endure *vb* bear, support, sustain; experience, suffer, undergo, weather; abide, brook, permit, pocket, swallow, tolerate, stomach, submit, withstand; continue, last, persist, remain, wear.

enemy *n* adversary, foe; antagonist, foeman, opponent, rival.

energetic *adj* active, effective, efficacious, emphatic, enterprising, forceful, forcible, hearty, mettlesome, potent, powerful, strenuous, strong, vigorous.

energy *n* activity, dash, drive, efficacy, efficiency, force, go, impetus, intensity, mettle, might, potency, power, strength, verve, vim; animation, life, manliness, spirit, spiritedness, stamina, vigor, zeal.

enervate *vb* break, debilitate, devitalize, emasculate, enfeeble, exhaust, paralyse, relax, soften, unhinge, unnerve, weaken.

enfeeble *vb* debilitate, devitalize, enervate, exhaust, relax, unhinge, unnerve, weaken.

enfold, infold *vb* enclose, envelop, fold, enwrap, wrap; clasp, embrace.

enforce *vb* compel, constrain, exact, force, oblige, require, urge.

enfranchise *vb* emancipate, free, liberate, manumit, release.

engage *vb* bind, commit, obligate, pledge, promise; affiance, betroth, plight; book, brief, employ, enlist, hire, retain; arrest, allure, attach, draw, entertain, fix, gain, win; busy, commission, contract, engross, occupy; attack, encounter; combat, contend, contest, fight, interlock, struggle; embark, enlist; agree, promise, stipulate, undertake, warrant.

engagement *n* appointment, assurance, contract, obligation, pledge, promise, stipulation; affiancing, betrothment, betrothal, plighting; avocation, business, calling, employment, enterprise, occupation; action, battle, combat, encounter, fight.

engender *vb* bear, beget, breed, create, generate, procreate, propagate; cause, excite, incite, occasion, produce.

engine *n* invention, machine; agency, agent, device, implement, instrument, means, method, tool, weapon.

engorge *vb* bolt, devour, eat, gobble, gorge, gulp, swallow; glut, obstruct, stuff.

engrave *vb* carve, chisel, cut, etch, grave, hatch, incise, sculpt; grave, impress, imprint, infix.

engross *vb* absorb, engage, occupy, take up; buy up, forestall, monopolize.

engrossment *n* absorption, forestalling, monopoly.

engulf, ingulf *vb* absorb, overwhelm, plunge, swallow up.

enhance *vb* advance, aggravate, augment, elevate, heighten, increase, intensify, raise, swell.

enhearten *vb* animate, assure, cheer, comfort, console, embolden, encourage, hearten, incite, inspirit, reassure, stimulate.

enigma *n* conundrum, mystery, problem, puzzle, riddle.

enigmatic, enigmatical *adj* ambiguous, dark, doubtful, equivocal, hidden, incomprehensible, mysterious, mystic, obscure, occult, perplexing, puzzling, recondite, uncertain, unintelligible.

enjoin *vb* admonish, advise, urge; bid, command, direct, order, prescribe, require; prohibit, restrain.

enjoy *vb* like, possess, relish.

enjoyment *n* delight, delectation, gratification, happiness, indulgence, pleasure, satisfaction; possession.

enkindle *vb* inflame, ignite, kindle; excite, incite, instigate, provoke, rouse, stimulate.

enlarge *vb* amplify, augment, broaden, develop, dilate, distend, expand, extend, grow, increase, magnify, widen; aggrandize, engreaten, ennoble, expand, exaggerate, greaten; swell.

enlighten *vb* illume, illuminate, illumine; counsel, educate, civilize, inform, instruct, teach.

enlist *vb* enrol, levy, recruit, register; enrol, list; embark, engage.

enliven *vb* animate, invigorate, quicken, reanimate, rouse, wake; exhilarate, cheer, brighten, delight, elate, gladden, inspire, inspirit, rouse.

enmity *n* animosity, aversion, bitterness, hate, hatred, hostility, ill-will, malevolence, malignity, rancor.

ennoble *vb* aggrandize, dignify, elevate, engreaten, enlarge, exalt, glorify, greaten, raise.

ennui *n* boredom, irksomeness, languor, lassitude, listlessness, tedium, tiresomeness, weariness.

enormity *n* atrociousness, atrocity, depravity, flagitiousness, heinousness, nefariousness, outrageousness, villainy, wickedness.

enormous *adj* abnormal. exceptional, inordinate, irregular; colossal, Cyclopean, elephantine, Herculean, huge, immense, monstrous, vast, gigantic, prodigious, titanic, tremendous.

enough *adj* abundant, adequate, ample, plenty, sufficient. • *adv* satisfactorily, sufficiently. • *n* abundance, plenty, sufficiency.

enquire *see* **inquire.**

enrage *vb* anger, chafe, exasperate, incense, inflame, infuriate, irritate, madden, provoke.

onrapture *vb* beatify, bewitch, delight, enchant, enravish, entrance, surpassingly, transport.

enrich *vb* endow; adorn, deck, decorate, embellish, grace, ornament.

enrobe *vb* clothe, dress, apparel, array, attire, invest, robe.

enrol *vb* catalog, engage, engross, enlist, list, register; chronicle, record.

ensconce *vb* conceal, cover, harbor, hide, protect, screen, secure, settle, shelter, shield, snugly.

enshrine *vb* embalm, enclose, entomb; cherish, treasure.

ensign *n* banner, colors, eagle, flag, gonfalcon, pennon, standard, streamer; sign, signal, symbol; badge, hatchment.

enslave *vb* captivate, dominate, master, overmaster, overpower, subjugate.

ensnare *vb* catch, entrap; allure, inveigle, seduce; bewilder, confound, embarrass, encumber, entangle, perplex

ensue *vb* follow, succeed; arise, come, flow, issue, proceed, result, spring.

entangle *vb* catch, ensnare, entrap; confuse, enmesh, intertwine, intertwist, interweave, knot, mat, ravel, tangle; bewilder, embarrass, encumber, ensnare, involve, nonplus, perplex, puzzle.

enterprise *n* adventure, attempt, cause, effort, endeavor, essay, project, undertaking, scheme, venture; activity, adventurousness, daring, dash, energy, initiative, readiness, push.

enterprising *adj* adventurous, audacious, bold, daring, dashing, venturesome, venturous; active, adventurous, alert, efficient, energetic, prompt, resourceful, smart, spirited, stirring, strenuous, zealous.

entertain vb fete, receive, regale, treat; cherish, foster, harbor, hold, lodge, shelter; admit, consider; amuse, cheer, divert, please, recreate.

entertainment n hospitality; banquet, collation, feast, festival, reception, treat; amusement, diversion, pastime, recreation, sport.

enthusiasm n ecstasy, exaltation, fanaticism; ardor, earnestness, devotion, eagerness, fervor, passion, warmth, zeal.

enthusiast n bigot, devotee, fan, fanatic, freak, zealot; castle-builder, dreamer, visionary.

entice vb allure, attract, bait, cajole, coax, decoy, inveigle, lure, persuade, prevail on, seduce, tempt, wheedle, wile.

enticement n allurement, attraction, bait, blandishment, inducement, inveiglement, lure, persuasion, seduction.

entire adj complete, integrated, perfect, unbroken, undiminished, undivided, unimpaired, whole; complete, full, plenary, thorough; mere, pure, sheer, unalloyed, unmingled, unmitigated, unmixed.

entitle vb call, characterize, christen, denominate, designate, dub, name, style; empower, enable, fit for, qualify for.

entomb vb bury, inhume, inter.

entrails npl bowels, guts, intestines, inwards, offal, viscera.

entrance[1] n access, approach, avenue, incoming, ingress; adit, avenue, aperture, door, doorway, entry, gate, hallway, inlet, lobby, mouth, passage, portal, stile, vestibule; beginning, commencement, debut, initiation, introduction; admission, entrée.

entrance[2] vb bewitch, captivate, charm, delight, enchant, enrapture, fascinate, ravish, transport.

entrap vb catch, ensnare; allure, entice, inveigle, seduce; embarrass, entangle, involve, nonplus, perplex, pose, stagger.

entreat vb adjure, beg, beseech, crave, enjoin, implore, importune, petition, pray, solicit, supplicate.

entreaty n adjuration, appeal, importunity, petition, prayer, request, solicitation, suit, supplication.

entrée n access, admission, admittance.

entrench, intrench vb furrow; circumvallate, fortify; encroach, infringe, invade, trench, trespass.

entrenchment, intrenchment n entrenching; earthwork, fortification; defense, protection, shelter; encroachment, inroad, invasion.

entrust vb commit, confide, consign.

entwine vb entwist, interlace, intertwine, interweave, inweave, twine, twist, weave; embrace, encircle, encumber, interlace, surround.

enumerate vb calculate, cite, compute, count, detail, mention, number, numerate, reckon, recount, specify, tell.

enunciate vb articulate, declare, proclaim, promulgate, pronounce, propound, publish, say, speak, utter.

envelop vb encase, enfold, enwrap, fold, pack, wrap; cover, encircle, encompass, enshroud, hide, involve, surround.

envelope n capsule, case, covering, integument, shroud, skin, wrapper, veil, vesture, wrap.

envenom vb poison, taint; embitter, malign; aggravate, enrage, exasperate, incense, inflame, irritate, madden, provoke.

environ n begird, belt, embrace, encircle, encompass, enclose, engrid, envelop, gird, hedge, hem, surround; beset, besiege, encompass, invest.

environs npl neighborhood, vicinage, vicinity.

envoy n ambassador, legate, minister, plenipotentiary; courier, messenger.

envy vb hate; begrudge, grudge; covet, emulate, desire. • n enviousness, hate, hatred, ill-will, jealousy, malice, spite; grudge, grudging.

enwrap vb absorb, cover, encase, engross, envelop, infold, involve, wrap, wrap up.

ephemeral adj brief, diurnal, evanescent, fleeting, flitting, fugacious, fugitive, momentary, occasional, short-lived, transient, transitory.

epic adj Homeric, heroic, narrative.

epicure n gastronome, glutton, gourmand, gourmet; epicurean, sensualist, Sybarite, voluptuary.

epidemic adj general, pandemic, prevailing, prevalent. • n outbreak, pandemia, pestilence, plague, spread, wave.

epidermis n cuticle, scarf-skin.

epigrammatic adj antithetic, concise, laconic, piquant, poignant, pointed, pungent, sharp, terse.

episcopal adj Episcopalian, pontifical, prelatic.

epistle n communication, letter, missive, note.

epithet n appellation, description, designation, name, predicate, title.

epitome n abbreviation, abridgement, abstract, breviary, brief, comment, compendium, condensation, conspectus, digest, summary, syllabus, synopsis.

epitomize vb abbreviate, abridge, abstract, condense, contract, curtail, cut, reduce, shorten, summarize.

epoch n age, date, era, period, time.

equable adj calm, equal, even, even-tempered, regular, steady, uniform, serene, tranquil, unruffled.

equal vb equalize, even, match. • adj alike, coordinate, equivalent, like, tantamount; even, level, equable, regular, uniform; equitable, even-handed, fair, impartial, just, unbiased; co-extensive, commensurate, corresponding, parallel, proportionate; adequate, competent, fit, sufficient. • n compeer, fellow, match, peer; rival.

equanimity n calmness, composure, coolness, peace, regularity, self-possession, serenity, steadiness.

equestrian adj equine, horse-like, horsy. • n horseman, rider; cavalier, cavalryman, chevalier, horse soldier, knight.

equilibrist n acrobat, balancer, funambulist, rope-walker.

equip vb appoint, arm, furnish, provide, rig, supply; accouter, array, dress.

equipage n accouterments, apparatus, baggage, effects, equipment, furniture; carriage, turnout, vehicle; attendance, procession, retinue, suite, train.

equipment n accouterment, apparatus, baggage, equipage, furniture, gear, outfit, rigging.

equipoise n balance, equilibrium.

equitable adj even handed, candid, honest, impartial, just, unbiased, unprejudiced, upright; adequate, fair, proper, reasonable, right.

equity n just, right; fair play, fairness, impartiality, justice, rectitude, reasonableness, righteousness, uprightness.

equivalent adj commensurate, equal, equipollent, tantamount; interchangeable, synonymous. • n complement, coordinate, counterpart, double, equal, fellow, like, match, parallel, pendant, quid pro quo.

equivocal adj ambiguous; doubtful, dubious, enigmatic, indeterminate, problematical, puzzling, uncertain.

equivocate vb dodge, evade, fence, palter, prevaricate, shuffle, quibble.

equivocation n evasion, paltering, prevarication, quibbling, shuffling; double entendre, double meaning, quibble.

era n age, date, epoch, period, time.

eradicate vb extirpate, root, uproot; abolish, annihilate, destroy, obliterate.

erase vb blot, cancel, delete, efface, expunge, obliterate, scrape out.

erasure n cancellation, canceling, effacing, expunging, obliteration.

erect vb build, construct, raise, rear; create, establish, form, found, institute, plant. • adj standing, unrecumbent, uplifted, upright; elevated, vertical, perpendicular, straight; bold, firm, undaunted, undismayed, unshaken, unterrified.

erelong adv early, quickly, shortly, soon, speedily.

eremite n anchoret, anchorite, hermit, recluse, solitary.

ergo adv consequently, hence, therefore.

erode vb canker, consume, corrode, destroy, eat away, fret, rub.

erosive adj acrid, cathartic, caustic, corroding, corrosive, eating, virulent.

erotic adj amorous, amatory, arousing, seductive, stimulating, titillating.

err vb deviate, ramble, rove, stray, wander; blunder, misjudge, mistake; fall, lapse, nod, offend, sin, stumble, trespass, trip.

errand n charge, commission, mandate, message, mission, purpose.

errant adj adventurous, rambling, roving, stray, wandering.

erratic adj nomadic, rambling, roving, wandering; moving, planetary; abnormal, capricious, deviating, eccentric, irregular, odd, queer, strange.

erratum n correction, corrigendum, error, misprint, mistake.

erroneous adj false, incorrect, inaccurate, inexact, mistaken untrue, wrong.

error n blunder, fallacy, inaccuracy, misapprehension, mistake, oversight; delinquency, fault, iniquity, misdeed, misdoing, misstep, obliquity, offence, shortcoming, sin, transgression, trespass, wrongdoing.

erudition n knowledge, learning, lore, scholarship.

eruption n explosion, outbreak, outburst; sally; rash.

escape vb avoid, elude, evade, flee from, shun; abscond, bolt, decamp, flee, fly; slip.

• *n* flight; release; passage, passing; leakage.

eschew *vb* abstain, avoid, elude, flee from, shun.

escort *vb* convey, guard, protect; accompany, attend, conduct. • *n* attendant, bodyguard, cavalier, companion, convoy, gallant, guard, squire; protection, safe conduct, safeguard; attendance, company.

esculent *adj* eatable, edible, wholesome.

esoteric *adj* hidden, inmost, inner, mysterious, private, recondite, secret.

especial *adj* absolute, chief, distinct, distinguished, marked, particular, peculiar, principal, singular, special, specific, uncommon, unusual; detailed, minute, noteworthy.

espousal *n* affiancing, betrothing, espousing, plighting; adoption, defense, maintenance, support.

espouse *vb* betroth, plight, promise; marry, wed; adopt, champion, defend, embrace, maintain, support.

espy *vb* descry, detect, discern, discover, observe, perceive, spy, watch.

esquire *n* armiger, attendant, escort, gentleman, squire.

essay[1] *vb* attempt, endeavor, try. • *n* aim, attempt, effort, endeavor, exertion, struggle, trial.

essay[2] *n* article, composition, disquisition, dissertation, paper, thesis.

essence *n* nature, quintessence, substance; extract, part; odor, perfume, scent; being, entity, existence, nature.

essential *adj* fundamental, indispensable, important, inward, intrinsic, necessary, requisite, vital; diffusible, pure, rectified, volatile.

establish *vb* fix, secure, set, settle; decree, enact, ordain; build, constitute, erect, form, found, institute, organize, originate, pitch, plant, raise; ensconce, ground, install, place, plant, root, secure; approve, confirm, ratify, sanction; prove, substantiate, verify.

estate *n* condition, state; position, rank, standing; division, order; effects, fortune, possessions, property; interest.

esteem *vb* appreciate, estimate, rate, reckon, value; admire, honor, like, prize, respect, revere, reverence, value, venerate, worship; account, believe, consider, deem, fancy, hold, imagine, suppose, regard, think. • *n* account, appreciation, consideration, estimate, estimation, judgement, opinion, reckoning, valuation; credit, honor, regard, respect, reverence.

estimable *adj* appreciable, calculable, computable; admirable, credible, deserving, excellent, good, meritorious, precious, respectful, valuable, worthy.

estimate *vb* appraise, appreciate, esteem, prise, rate, value; assess, calculate, compute, count, gauge, judge, reckon. • *n* estimation, judgement, valuation; calculation, computation.

estimation *n* appreciation, estimate, valuation; esteem, estimate, judgement, opinion; honor, reckoning, regard, respect, reverence.

estop *vb* bar, impede, preclude, stop.

estrange *vb* withdraw, withhold; alienate, divert; disaffect, destroy.

estuary *n* creek, inlet, fiord, firth, frith, mouth.

etch *vb* corrode, engrave.

eternal *adj* absolute, inevitable, necessary, self-active, self-existent, self-originated; abiding, ceaseless, endless, ever-enduring, everlasting, incessant, interminable, never-ending, perennial, permanent, perpetual, sempiternal, unceasing, unending; deathless, immortal, imperishable, incorruptible, indestructible, never-dying, undying; immutable, unchangeable; constant, continual, continuous, incessant, persistent, unbroken, uninterrupted.

ethereal *adj* aerial, airy, celestial, empyreal, heavenly, unworldly; attenuated, light, subtle, tenuous, volatile; delicate, fairy, flimsy, fragile, rare, refined, subtle.

eulogize *vb* applaud, commend, extol, laud, magnify, praise.

eulogy *n* discourse, eulogium, panegyric, speech; applause, encomium, commendation, laudation, praise.

euphonious *adj* clear, euphonic, harmonious, mellifluous, mellow, melodious, musical, silvery, smooth, sweet-toned.

evacuant *adj* abstergent, cathartic, cleansing, emetic, purgative. • *n* cathartic, purgative.

evacuate *vb* empty; discharge, clean out, clear out, eject, excrete, expel, purge, void; abandon, desert, forsake, leave, quit, relinquish, withdraw.

evade *vb* elude, escape; avoid, decline, dodge, funk, shun; baffle, elude, foil; dodge, equivocate, fence, palter, prevaricate, quibble, shuffle.

evanescence n disappearance, evanishing, evanishment, vanishing; transience, transientness, transitoriness.

evanescent adj ephemeral, fleeting, flitting, fugitive, passing, short-lived, transient, transitory, vanishing.

evaporate vb distil, volatilize; dehydrate, dry, vaporize; disperse, dissolve, fade, vanish.

evaporation n distillation, volatilization; dehydration, drying, vaporization; disappearance, dispersal, dissolution.

evasion n artifice, avoidance, bluffing, deceit, dodge, equivocation, escape, excuse, funking, prevarication, quibble, shift, subterfuge, shuffling, sophistical, tergiversation.

evasive adj elusive, elusory, equivocating, prevaricating, shuffling, slippery, sophistical.

even vb balance, equalize, harmonize, symmetrize; align, flatten, flush, level, smooth, square. • adj flat, horizontal, level, plane, smooth; calm, composed, equable, equal, peaceful, placid, regular, steady, uniform, unruffled; direct, equitable, fair, impartial, just, straightforward. • adv exactly, just, verily; likewise. • n eve, evening, eventide, vesper.

evening n dusk, eve, even, eventide, nightfall, sunset, twilight.

event n circumstance, episode, fact, happening, incident, occurrence; conclusion, consequence, end, issue, outcome, result, sequel, termination; adventure, affair.

eventful adj critical, important, memorable, momentous, remarkable, signal, stirring.

eventual adj final, last, ultimate; conditional, contingent, possible. • adv always, aye, constantly, continually, eternally, ever evermore, forever, incessantly, perpetually, unceasingly.

everlasting adj ceaseless, constant, continual, endless, eternal, ever-during, incessant, interminable, never-ceasing, neverending, perpetual, unceasing, unending, unintermitting, uninterrupted; deathless, ever-living, immortal, imperishable, never-dying, undying.

evermore adv always, constantly, continually, eternally, ever, forever, perpetually.

everyday adj accustomed, common, commonplace, customary, habitual, routine, usual, wonted.

evict vb dispossess, eject, thrust out.

evidence vb evince, make clear, manifest, prove, show, testify, vouch. • n affirmation, attestation, averment, confirmation, corroboration, deposition, grounds, indication, proof, testimony, token, trace, voucher, witness.

evident adj apparent, bald, clear, conspicuous, distinct, downright, incontestable, indisputable, manifest, obvious, open, overt, palpable, patent, plain, unmistakable.

evil adj bad, ill; base, corrupt, malicious, malevolent, malign, nefarious, perverse, sinful, vicious, vile, wicked, wrong; bad, deleterious, baleful, baneful, destructive, harmful, hurtful, injurious, mischievous, noxious, pernicious, profane; adverse, calamitous, diabolic, disastrous, unfortunate, unhappy, unpropitious, woeful. • n calamity, disaster, ill, misery, misfortune, pain, reverse, sorrow, suffering, woe; badness, baseness, corruption, depravity, malignity, sin, viciousness, wickedness; bale, bane, blast, canker, curse, harm, injury, mischief, wrong.

evince vb establish, evidence, manifest, prove, show; disclose, display, exhibit, indicate, reveal.

eviscerate vb disembowel, embowel, gut.

evoke vb arouse, elicit, excite, provoke, rouse.

evolve vb develop, educe, exhibit, expand, open, unfold, unroll.

exacerbate vb aggravate, embitter, enrage, exasperate, excite, inflame, infuriate, irritate, provoke, vex.

exact vb elicit, extort, mulch, require, squeeze; ask, claim, compel, demand, enforce, requisition, take. • adj rigid, rigorous, scrupulous, severe, strict; diametric, express, faultless, precise, true; accurate, close, correct, definite, faithful, literal, undeviating; accurate, critical, delicate, fine, nice, sensitive; careful, methodical, punctilious, orderly, punctual, regular.

exacting adj critical, difficult, exactive, rigid, extortionary.

exaction n contribution, extortion, oppression, rapacity, tribute.

exactness n accuracy, correctness, exactitude, faithfulness, faultlessness, fidelity, nicety, precision, rigor; carefulness, method, precision, regularity, rigidness, scrupulousity, scrupulousness, strictness.

exaggerate vb enlarge, magnify, overcharge, overcolor, overstate, romance, strain, stretch.

exalt *vb* elevate, erect, heighten, lift up, raise; aggrandize, dignify, elevate, ennoble; bless, extol, glorify, magnify, praise.

exalted *adj* elated, elevated, high, highflown, lofty, lordly, magnificent.

examination *n* inspection, observation; exploration, inquiry, inquisition, investigation, perusal, research, search, scrutiny, survey; catechism, probation, review, test, trial.

examine *vb* inspect, observe; canvass, consider, explore, inquire, investigate, scrutinize, study, test; catechize, interrogate.

example *n* archetype, copy, model, pattern, piece, prototype, representative, sample, sampler, specimen, standard; exemplification, illustration, instance, precedent, warning.

exanimate *adj* dead, defunct, inanimate, lifeless; inanimate, inert, sluggish, spiritless, torpid.

exasperate *vb* affront, anger, chafe, enrage, incense, irritate, nettle, offend, provoke, vex; aggravate, exacerbate, inflame, rouse.

exasperation *n* annoyance, exacerbation, irritation, provocation; anger, fury, ire, passion, rage, wrath; aggravation, heightening, increase, worsening.

excavate *vb* burrow, cut, delve, dig, hollow, hollow out, scoop, trench.

exceed *vb* cap, overstep, surpass, transcend; excel, outdo, outstrip, outvie, pass.

excel *vb* beat, eclipse, outdo, outrival, outstrip, outvie, surpass; cap, exceed, transcend.

excellence *n* distinction, eminence, preeminence, superiority, transcendence; fineness, fitness, goodness, perfection, purity, quality, superiority; advantage; goodness, probity, uprightness, virtue, worth.

excellent *adj* admirable, choice, crack, eminent, first-rate, prime, sterling, superior, tiptop, transcendent; deserving, estimable, praiseworthy, virtuous, worthy.

except *vb* exclude, leave out, omit, reject. • *conj* unless. • *prep* bar, but, excepting, excluding, save.

exceptional *adj* aberrant, abnormal, anomalous, exceptive, irregular, peculiar, rare, special, strange, superior, uncommon, unnatural, unusual.

excerpt *vb* cite, cull, extract, quote, select, take. • *n* citation, extract, quotation, selection.

excess *adj* excessive, unnecessary, redundant, spare, superfluous, surplus. • *n* disproportion, fulsomeness, glut, oversupply, plethora, redundance, redundancy, surfeit, superabundance, superfluity; overplus, remainder, surplus; debauchery, dissipation, dissoluteness, intemperance, immoderation, overindulgence, unrestraint; extravagance, immoderation, overdoing.

excessive *adj* disproportionate, exuberant, superabundant, superfluous, undue; extravagant, enormous, inordinate, outrageous, unreasonable; extreme, immoderate, intemperate; vehement, violent.

exchange *vb* barter, change, commute, shuffle, substitute, swap, trade, truck; bandy, interchange. • *n* barter, change, commutation, dealing, shuffle, substitution, trade, traffic; interchange, reciprocity; bazaar, bourse, fair, market.

excise[1] *n* capitation, customs, dues, duty, tariff, tax, taxes, toll.

excise[2] *vb* cancel, cut, delete, edit, efface, eradicate, erase, expunge, extirpate, remove, strike out.

excision *n* destruction, eradication, extermination, extirpation.

excitable *adj* impressible, nervous, sensitive, susceptible; choleric, hasty, hotheaded, hot-tempered, irascible, irritable, passionate, quick-tempered.

excite *vb* animate, arouse, awaken, brew, evoke, impel, incite, inflame, instigate, kindle, move, prompt, provoke, rouse, spur, stimulate; create, elicit, evoke, raise; agitate, discompose, disturb, irritate.

excitement *n* excitation, exciting; incitement, motive, stimulus; activity, agitation, bustle, commotion, disturbance, ferment, flutter, perturbation, sensation, stir, tension; choler, heat, irritation, passion, violence, warmth.

exclaim *vb* call, cry, declare, ejaculate, shout, utter, vociferate.

exclude *vb* ban, bar, blackball, debar, ostracize, preclude, reject; hinder, prevent, prohibit, restrain, withhold; except, omit; eject, eliminate, expel, extrude.

exclusive *adj* debarring, excluding; illiberal, narrow, narrow-minded, selfish, uncharitable; aristocratic, choice, clannish, cliquish, fastidious, fashionable, select, snobbish; only, sole, special.

excommunicate *vb* anathematize, ban, curse, denounce, dismiss, eject, exclude, expel, exscind, proscribe, unchurch.

excoriate *vb* abrade, flay, gall, scar, scarify, score, skin, strip.

excrement n dejections, dung, feces, excreta, excretion, ordure, stool.

excrescence n fungus, growth, knob, lump, outgrowth, protuberance, tumor, wart.

excrete vb discharge, eject, eliminate, separate.

excruciate vb agonize, rack, torment, torture.

exculpate vb absolve, acquit, clear, discharge, exonerate, free, justify, release, set right, vindicate.

excursion n drive, expedition, jaunt, journey, ramble, ride, sally, tour, trip, voyage, walk; digression, episode.

excursive adj devious, diffuse, digressive, discursive, erratic, rambling, roaming, roving, wandering.

excusable adj allowable, defensible, forgivable, justifiable, pardonable, venial, warrantable.

excursus n discussion, disquisition, dissertation.

excuse vb absolve, acquit, exculpate, exonerate, forgive, pardon, remit; extenuate, justify; exempt, free, release; overlook. • n absolution, apology, defense, extenuation, justification, plea; color, disguise, evasion, guise, pretence, pretext, makeshift, semblance, subterfuge.

execrable adj abhorrent, abominable, accursed, cursed, damnable, detestable, hateful, odious; disgusting, loathsome, nauseating, nauseous, obnoxious, offensive, repulsive, revolting, sickening, vile.

execrate vb curse, damn, imprecate; abhor, abominate, detest, hate, loathe.

execute vb accomplish, achieve, carry out, complete, consummate, do, effect, effectuate, finish, perform, perpetrate; administer, enforce, seal, sign; behead, electrocute, guillotine, hang.

execution n accomplishment, achievement, completion, consummation, operation, performance; warrant, writ; beheading, electrocution, hanging.

executive adj administrative, commanding, controlling, directing, managing, ministerial, officiating, presiding, ruling. • n administrator, director, manager.

exegetic, exegetical adj explanatory, explicative, explicatory, expository, hermeneutic, interpretative.

exemplary adj assiduous, close, exact, faithful, punctual, punctilious, rigid, rigorous, scrupulous; commendable, correct, good, estimable, excellent, praiseworthy, virtuous; admonitory, condign, monitory, warning.

exemplify vb evidence, exhibit, illustrate, manifest, show.

exempt vb absolve, except, excuse, exonerate, free, release, relieve. • adj absolved, excepted, excused, exempted, free, immune, liberated, privileged, released.

exemption n absolution, dispensation, exception, immunity, privilege, release.

exercise vb apply, busy, employ, exert, praxis, use; effect, exert, produce, wield; break in, discipline, drill, habituate, school, train; practice, prosecute, pursue; task, test, try; afflict, agitate, annoy, burden, pain, trouble. • n appliance, application, custom, employment, operation, performance, play, plying, practice, usage, use, working; action, activity, effort, exertion, labor, toil, work; discipline, drill, drilling, schooling, training; lesson, praxis, study, task, test, theme.

exert vb employ, endeavor, exercise, labor, strain, strive, struggle, toil, use, work.

exertion n action, exercise, exerting, use; attempt, effort, endeavour, labour, strain, stretch, struggle, toil, trial.

exhalation n emission, evaporation; damp, effluvium, fog, fume, mist, reek, smoke, steam, vapor.

exhale vb breathe, discharge, elect, emanate, emit, evaporate, reek; blow, expire, puff.

exhaust vb drain, draw, empty; consume, destroy, dissipate, expend, impoverish, lavish, spend, squander, waste; cripple, debilitate, deplete, disable, enfeeble, enervate, overtire, prostrate, weaken.

exhaustion n debilitation, enervation, fatigue, lassitude, weariness.

exhibit vb demonstrate, disclose, display, evince, expose, express, indicate, manifest, offer, present, reveal, show; offer, present, propose.

exhibition n demonstration, display, exposition, manifestation, representation, spectacle, show; allowance, benefaction, grant, pension, scholarship.

exhilarate vb animate, cheer, elate, enliven, gladden, inspire, inspirit, rejoice, stimulate.

exhilaration n animating, cheering, elating, enlivening, gladdening, rejoicing, stimulating; animation, cheer, cheerfulness, gaiety, gladness, glee, good spirits, hilarity, joyousness.

exhort vb advise, caution, encourage, incite, persuade, stimulate, urge, warm; preach.

exhume vb disentomb, disinhume, disinter, unbury, unearth.

exigency, exigence n demand, necessity, need, requirement, urgency, want; conjuncture, crisis, difficulty, distress, emergency, extremity, juncture, nonplus, quandary, pass, pinch, pressure, strait.

exiguous adj attenuated, diminutive, fine, small, scanty, slender, tiny.

exile vb banish, expatriate, expel, ostracize, proscribe. • n banishment, expatriation, expulsion, ostracism, proscription, separation; outcast, refugee.

exist vb be, breathe, live; abide, continue, endure, last, remain.

existence n being, subsisting, subsistence; being, creature, entity, essence, thing; animation, continuation, life, living, vitality, vivacity.

exit vb depart, egress, go, leave. • n departure, withdrawal; death, decrease, demise, end; egress, outlet.

exonerate vb absolve, acquit, clear, exculpate, justify, vindicate; absolve, discharge, except, exempt, free, release.

exorbitant adj enormous, excessive, extravagant, inordinate, unreasonable.

exorcise vb cast out, drive away, expel; deliver, purify; address, conjure.

exordium n introduction, opening, preamble, preface, prelude, proem, prologue.

exotic adj extraneous, foreign; extravagant.

expand vb develop, open, spread, unfold, unfurl; diffuse, enlarge, extend, increase, stretch; dilate, distend, enlarge.

expanse n area, expansion, extent, field, stretch.

expansion n expansion, opening, spreading; diastole, dilation, distension, swelling; development, diffusion, enlargement, increase; expanse, extent, stretch.

ex parte adj biased, one-sided, partisan.

expatiate vb amplify, decant, dilate, enlarge, range, rove.

expatriate vb banish, exile, expel, ostracize, proscribe. • adj banished, exiled, refugee. • n displaced person, emigrant, exile.

expect vb anticipate, await, calculate, contemplate, forecast, foresee, hope, reckon, rely.

expectancy n expectance, expectation; abeyance, prospect.

expectation n anticipation, expectance, expectancy, hope, prospect; assurance, confidence, presumption, reliance, trust.

expedient adj advisable, appropriate, convenient, desirable, fit, proper, politic, suitable; advantageous, profitable, useful. • n contrivance, device, means, method, resort, resource, scheme, shift, stopgap, substitute.

expedite vb accelerate, advance, dispatch, facilitate, forward, hasten, hurry, precipitate, press, quicken, urge.

expedition n alacrity, alertness, celerity, dispatch, haste, promptness, quickness, speed; enterprise, undertaking; campaign, excursion, journey, march, quest, voyage.

expeditious adj quick, speedy, swift, rapid; active, alert, diligent, nimble, prompt, punctual, swift.

expel vb dislodge, egest, eject, eliminate, excrete; discharge, eject, evacuate, void; bounce, discharge, exclude, exscind, fire, oust, relegate, remove; banish, disown, excommunicate, exile, expatriate, ostracize, proscribe, unchurch.

expend vb disburse, spend; consume, employ, exert, use; dissipate, exhaust, scatter, waste.

expenditure n disbursement, outlay, outlaying, spending; charge, cost, expenditure, outlay.

expensive adj costly, dear, high-priced; extravagant, lavish, wasteful.

experience vb endure, suffer; feel, know; encounter, suffer, undergo. • n endurance, practice, trial; evidence, knowledge, proof, test, testimony.

experienced adj able, accomplished, expert, instructed, knowing, old, practiced, qualified, skillful, trained, thoroughbred, versed, veteran, wise.

experiment vb examine, investigate, test, try. • n assay, examination, investigation, ordeal, practice, proof, test, testimony, touchstone, trial.

expert adj able, adroit, apt, clever, dextrous, proficient, prompt, quick, ready, skillful. • n adept, authority, connoisseur, crack, master, specialist.

expertise n adroitness, aptness, dexterity, facility, promptness, skillfulness, skill.

expiate vb atone, redeem, satisfy.

expiration n death, decease, demise, departure, exit; cessation, close, conclusion, end, termination.

expire vb cease, close, conclude, end, stop, terminate; emit, exhale; decease, depart, die, perish.

explain vb demonstrate, elucidate, expound, illustrate, interpret, resolve, solve, unfold, unravel; account for, justify, warrant.

explanation n clarification, description, elucidation, exegesis, explication, exposition, illustration, interpretation; account, answer, deduction, justification, key, meaning, secret, solution, warrant.

explicit adj absolute, categorical, clear, definite, determinate, exact, express, plain, positive, precise, unambiguous, unequivocal, unreserved.

explode vb burst, detonate, discharge, displode, shatter, shiver; contemn, discard, repudiate, scorn, scout.

exploit vb befool, milk, use, utilize. • n achievement, act, deed, feat.

explore vb examine, fathom, inquire, inspect, investigate, prospect, scrutinize, seek.

explosion n blast, burst, bursting, clap, crack, detonation, discharge, displosion, fulmination, pop.

exponent n example, illustration, index, indication, specimen, symbol, type; commentator, demonstrator, elucidator, expounder, illustrator, interpreter.

expose vb bare, display, uncover; descry, detect, disclose, unearth; denounce, mask; subject; endanger, jeopardize, risk, venture.

exposé n exhibit, exposition, manifesto; denouncement, divulgement, exposure, revelation.

exposition n disclosure, interpretation; commentary, critique, elucidation, exegesis, explanation, explication, interpretation; display, show.

expound vb develop, present, rehearse, reproduce, unfold; clear, elucidate, explain, interpret.

express vb air, assert, asseverate, declare, emit, enunciate, manifest, utter, vent, signify, speak, state, voice; betoken, denote, equal, exhibit, indicate, intimate, present, represent, show, symbolize. • adj categorical, clear, definite, determinate, explicit, outspoken, plain, positive, unambiguous; accurate, close, exact, faithful, precise, true; particular, special; fast, nonstop, quick, rapid, speedy, swift. • n dispatch, message.

expression n assertion, asseveration, communication, declaration, emission, statement, utterance, voicing; language, locution, phrase, remark, saying, term, word; air, aspect, look, mien.

expressive adj indicative, meaningful, significant; demonstrative, eloquent, emphatic, energetic, forcible, lively, strong, vivid; appropriate, sympathetic, well-modulated.

expulsion n discharge, eviction, expelling, ousting; elimination, evacuation, excretion; ejection, excision, excommunication, extrusion, ostracism, separation.

expunge vb annihilate, annul, cancel, delete, destroy, efface, erase, obliterate, wipe out.

expurgate vb clean, cleanse, purge, purify; bowdlerize, emasculate.

exquisite adj accurate, delicate, discriminating, exact, fastidious, nice, refined; choice, elect, excellent, precious, rare, valuable; complete, consummate, matchless, perfect; acute, keen, intense, poignant. • n beau, coxcomb, dandy, fop, popinjay.

extant adj existent, existing, present, surviving, undestroyed, visible.

extempore adj extemporaneous, extemporary, impromptu, improvised. • adv offhand, suddenly, unpremeditatedly, unpreparedly.

extend vb reach, stretch; continue, elongate, lengthen, prolong, protract, widen; augment, broaden, dilate, distend, enlarge, expand, increase; diffuse, spread; give, impart, offer, yield; lie, range.

extensible adj ductile, elastic, extendible, extensile, protractible, protractile.

extension n augmentation, continuation, delay, dilatation, dilation, distension, enlargement, expansion, increase, prolongation, protraction.

extensive adj broad, capacious, comprehensive, expanded, extended, far-reaching, large, wide, widespread.

extent n amplitude, expanse, expansion; amount, bulk, content, degree, magnitude, size, volume; compass, measure, length, proportions, reach, stretch; area, field, latitude, range, scope; breadth, depth, height, width.

extenuate vb diminish, lessen, reduce, soften, weaken; excuse, mitigate, palliate, qualify.

exterior *adj* external, outer, outlying, outside, outward, superficial, surface; extrinsic, foreign. • *n* outside, surface; appearance.

exterminate *vb* abolish, annihilate, destroy, eliminate, eradicate, extirpate, uproot.

external *adj* exterior, outer, outside, outward, superficial; extrinsic, foreign; apparent, visible.

extinct *adj* extinguished, quenched; closed, dead, ended, lapsed, terminated, vanished.

extinction *n* death, extinguishment; abolishment, abolition, annihilation, destruction, excision, extermination, extirpation.

extinguish *vb* choke, douse, put out, quell, smother, stifle, suffocate, suppress; destroy, nullify, subdue; eclipse, obscure.

extirpate *vb* abolish, annihilate, deracinate, destroy, eradicate, exterminate, uproot, weed.

extol *vb* celebrate, exalt, glorify, laud, magnify, praise; applaud, commend, eulogize, panegyrize.

extort *vb* elicit, exact, extract, force, squeeze, wrench, wrest, wring.

extortion *n* blackmail, compulsion, demand, exaction, oppression, overcharge, rapacity, tribute; exorbitance.

extortionate *adj* bloodsucking, exacting, hard, harsh, oppressive, rapacious, rigorous, severe; exorbitant, unreasonable.

extra *adj* accessory, additional, auxiliary, collateral; another, farther, fresh, further, more, new, other, plus, ulterior; side, spare, supernumerary, supplemental, supplementary, surplus; extraordinary, extreme, unusual. • *adv* additionally, also, beyond, farthermore, furthermore, more, moreover, plus. • *n* accessory, appendage, collateral, nonessential, special, supernumerary, supplement; bonus, premium; balance, leftover, remainder, spare, surplus.

extract *vb* extort, pull out, remove, withdraw; derive, distil, draw, express, squeeze; cite, determine, derive, quote, select. • *n* citation, excerpt, passage, quotation, selection; decoction, distillation, essence, infusion, juice.

extraction *n* drawing out, derivation, distillation, elicitation, essence, pulling out; birth, descent, genealogy, lineage, origin, parentage.

extraneous *adj* external, extrinsic, foreign; additional, adventitious, external, superfluous, supplementary, unessential.

extraordinary *adj* abnormal, amazing, distinguished, egregious, exceptional, marvellous, monstrous, particular, peculiar, phenomenal, prodigious, rare, remarkable, signal, singular, special, strange, uncommon, unprecedented, unusual, unwonted, wonderful.

extravagance *n* excess, enormity, exorbitance, preposterousness, unreasonableness; absurdity, excess, folly, irregularity, wildness; lavishness, prodigality, profuseness, profusion, superabundance; waste.

extravagant *adj* excessive, exorbitant, inordinate, preposterous, unreasonable; absurd, foolish, irregular, wild; lavish, prodigal, profuse, spendthrift.

extreme *adj* farthest, outermost, remotest, utmost, uttermost; greatest, highest; final, last, ultimate; drastic, egregious, excessive, extravagant, immoderate, intense, outrageous, radical, unreasonable. • *n* end, extremity, limit; acme, climax, degree, height, pink; danger, distress.

extremity *n* border, edge, end, extreme, limb, termination, verge.

extricate *vb* clear, deliver, disembarrass, disengage, disentangle, liberate, release, relieve.

extrinsic *adj* external, extraneous, foreign, outside, outward, superabundance, superfluity.

exuberance *n* abundance, copiousness, flood, luxuriance, plenitude; excess, lavishness, overabundance, overflow, overgrowth, over-luxuriance, profusion, rankness, redundancy, superabundance, superfluity.

exuberant *adj* abounding, abundant, copious, fertile, flowing, luxuriant, prolific, rich; excessive, lavish, overabundant, overflowing, over-luxuriant, profuse, rank, redundant, superabounding, superabundant, wanton.

exude *vb* discharge, excrete, secrete, sweat; infiltrate, ooze, percolate.

exult *vb* gloat, glory, jubilate, rejoice, transport, triumph, taunt, vault.

exultation *n* delight, elation, joy, jubilation, transport, triumph.

eye *vb* contemplate, inspect, ogle, scrutinize, survey, view, watch. • *n* estimate, judgement, look, sight, vision, view; inspection, notice, observation, scrutiny, sight, vigilance, watch; aperture, eyelet, peephole, perforation; bud, shoot.

F

fable *n* allegory, legend, myth, parable, story, tale; fabrication, falsehood, fiction, figment, forgery, untruth.

fabric *n* building, edifice, pile, structure; conformation, make, texture, workmanship; cloth, material, stuff, textile, tissue, web.

fabricate *vb* build, construct, erect, frame; compose, devise, fashion, make, manufacture; coin, fake, feign, forge, invent.

fabrication *n* building, construction, erection; manufacture; fable, fake, falsehood, fiction, figment, forgery, invention, lie.

fabulous *adj* amazing, apocryphal, coined, fabricated, feigned, fictitious, forged, imaginary, invented, legendary, marvellous, mythical, romancing, unbelievable, unreal.

façade *n* elevation, face, front.

face *vb* confront; beard, buck, brave, dare, defy, front, oppose; dress, level, polish, smooth; cover, incrust, veneer. • *n* cover, facet, surface; breast, escarpment, front; countenance, features, grimace, physiognomy, visage; appearance, expression, look, semblance; assurance, audacity, boldness, brass, confidence, effrontery, impudence.

facet *n* cut, face, lozenge, surface.

facetious *adj* amusing, comical, droll, funny, humorous, jocose, jocular, pleasant, waggish, witty; entertaining, gay, lively, merry, sportive, sprightly.

facile *adj* easy; affable, approachable, complaisant, conversable, courteous, mild; compliant, ductile, flexible, fluent, manageable, pliable, pliant, tractable, yielding; dextrous, ready, skillful.

facilitate *vb* expedite, help.

facility *n* ease, easiness; ability, dexterity, expertness, knack, quickness, readiness; ductility, flexibility, pliancy; advantage, appliance, convenience, means, resource; affability, civility, complaisance, politeness.

facsimile *n* copy, duplicate, fax, reproduction.

fact *n* act, circumstance, deed, event, incident, occurrence, performance; actuality, certainty, existence, reality, truth.

faction *n* cabal, clique, combination, division, junta, party, side; disagreement, discord, disorder, dissension, recalcitrance, recalcitrancy, refractoriness, sedition, seditiousness, tumult, turbulence, turbulency.

factious *adj* litigious, malcontent, rebellious, recalcitrant, refractory, seditious, turbulent.

factitious *adj* artful, artificial, conventional, false, unnatural, unreal.

factor *n* agent, bailiff, broker, consignee, go-between, steward, component, element, ingredient; influence, reason.

factory *n* manufactory, mill, work, workshop.

faculty *n* ability, capability, capacity, endowment, power, property, quality; ableness, address, adroitness, aptitude, aptness, clearness, competency, dexterity, efficiency, expertness, facility, forte, ingenuity, knack, qualification, quickness, readiness, skill, skillfulness, talent, turn; body, department, profession; authority, prerogative, license, privilege, right.

fade *vb* disappear, die, evanesce, fall, faint, perish, vanish; decay, decline, droop, fall, languish, wither; bleach, blanch, pale; disperse, dissolve.

fag *vb* droop, flag, sink; drudge, toil; fatigue, jade, tire, weary. • *n* drudgery, fatigue, work; drudge, grub, hack; cigarette, smoke.

fail *vb* break, collapse, decay, decline, fade, sicken, sink, wane; cease, disappear; fall, miscarry, miss; neglect, omit; bankrupt, break.

failing *adj* deficient, lacking, needing, wanting; declining, deteriorating, fading, flagging, languishing, sinking, waning, wilting; unsuccessful. • *prep* lacking, needing, wanting. • *n* decay, decline; failure, miscarriage; defect, deficiency, fault, foible, frailty, imperfection, infirmity, shortcoming, vice, weakness; error, lapse, slip; bankruptcy, insolvency.

failure *n* defectiveness, deficiency, delinquency, shortcoming; fail, miscarriage, negligence, neglect, nonobservance, nonperformance, omission, slip; abortion, botch, breakdown, collapse, fiasco, fizzle; bankruptcy, crash, downfall, insolvency, ruin; decay, declension, decline, loss.

fain *adj* anxious, glad, inclined, pleased, rejoiced, well-pleased. • *adv* cheerfully, eagerly, gladly, joyfully, willingly.

faint *vb* swoon; decline, fade, fail, languish, weaken. • *adj* swooning; drooping, exhausted, feeble, languid, listless, sickly, weak; gentle, inconsiderable, little, slight, small, soft, thin; dim, dull, indistinct, perceptible, scarce, slight; cowardly, dastardly, faint-hearted, fearful, timid, timorous; dejected, depressed, discouraged, disheartened, dispirited. • *n* blackout, swoon.

faint-hearted *adj* cowardly, dastardly, faint, fearful, timid, timorous.

fair[1] *adj* spotless, unblemished, unspotted, unstained, untarnished; blond, light, white; beautiful, comely, handsome, shapely; clear, cloudless, pleasant, unclouded; favorable, prosperous; hopeful, promising, propitious; clear, distinct, open, plain, unencumbered, unobstructed; candid, frank, honest, honorable, impartial, ingenuous, just, unbiased, upright; equitable, proper; average, decent, indifferent, mediocre, moderate, ordinary, passable, reasonable, respectful, tolerable.

fair[2] *n* bazaar, carnival, exposition, festival, fete, funfair, gala, kermess.

fairy *n* brownie, elf, demon, fay, sprite.

faith *n* assurance, belief, confidence, credence, credit, dependence, reliance, trust; creed, doctrine, dogma, persuasion, religion, tenet; constancy, faithfulness, fidelity, loyalty, truth, truthfulness.

faithful *adj* constant, devoted, loyal, staunch, steadfast, true; honest, upright, reliable, trustworthy, trusty; reliable, truthful; accurate, close, conscientiousness, exact, nice, strict.

faithless *adj* unbelieving; dishonest, disloyal, false, fickle, fluctuating, inconstant, mercurial, mutable, perfidious, shifting, treacherous, truthless, unsteady, untruthful, vacillating, variable, wavering.

fall *vb* collapse, depend, descend, drop, sink, topple, tumble; abate, decline, decrease, depreciate, ebb, subside; err, lapse, sin, stumble, transgress, trespass, trip; die, perish; befall, chance, come, happen, occur, pass; become, get; come, pass. • *n* collapse, comedown, descent, downcome, dropping, falling, flop, plop, tumble; cascade, cataract, waterfall; death, destruction, downfall, overthrow, ruin, surrender; comeuppance, degradation; apostasy, declension, failure, lapse, slip; decline, decrease, depreciation, diminution, ebb, sinking, subsidence; cadence, close; declivity, inclination, slope.

fallacious *adj* absurd, deceptive, deceiving, delusive, disappointing, erroneous, false, illusive, illusory, misleading; paralogistic, sophistical, worthless.

fallacy *n* aberration, deceit, deception, delusion, error, falsehood, illusion, misapprehension, misconception, mistake, untruth; non sequitur, paralogism, sophism, sophistry.

fallibility *n* frailty, imperfection, uncertainty.

fallible *adj* erring, frail, ignorant, imperfect, uncertain, weak.

fallow *adj* left, neglected, uncultivated, unsowed, untilled; dormant, inactive, inert.

false *adj* lying, mendacious, truthless, untrue, unveracious; dishonest, dishonorable, disingenuous, disloyal, double-faced, double-tongued, faithless, false-hearted, perfidious, treacherous, unfaithful; fictitious, forged, made-up, unreliable, untrustworthy; artificial, bastard, bogus, counterfeit, factitious, feigned, forged, hollow, hypocritical, make-believe, pretended, pseudo, sham, spurious, supposititious; erroneous, improper, incorrect, unfounded, wrong; deceitful, deceiving, deceptive, disappointing, fallacious, misleading.

false-hearted *adj* dishonorable, disloyal, double, double-tongued, faithless, false, perfidious, treacherous.

falsehood *n* falsity; fabrication, fib, fiction, lie, untruth; cheat, counterfeit, imposture, mendacity, treachery.

falsify *vb* alter, adulterate, belie, cook, counterfeit, doctor, fake, falsely, garble, misrepresent, misstate, represent; disprove; violate.

falsity *n* falsehood, untruth, untruthfulness.

falter *vb* halt, hesitate, lisp, quaver, stammer, stutter; fail, stagger, stumble, totter, tremble, waver; dodder.

fame *n* bruit, hearsay, report, rumor; celebrity, credit, eminence, glory, greatness, honor, illustriousness, kudos, luster, notoriety, renown, reputation, repute.

familiar *adj* acquainted, aware, conversant, well-versed; amicable, close, cordial, domestic, fraternal, friendly, homely, intimate, near; affable, accessible, companionable, conversable, courteous, civil, friendly, kindly, sociable, social; easy, free and easy, unceremonious, unconstrained; common, frequent, well-known. • *n* acquaintance, associate, companion, friend, intimate.

familiarity *n* acquaintance, knowledge, understanding; fellowship, friendship, intimacy; closeness, friendliness, sociability; freedom, informality, liberty; disrespect, overfreedom, presumption; intercourse.

familiarize *vb* accustom, habituate, inure, train, use.

family *n* brood, household, people; ancestors, blood, breed, clan, dynasty, kindred, house, lineage, race, stock, strain, tribe; class, genus, group, kind, subdivision.

famine *n* dearth, destitution, hunger, scarcity, starvation.

famish *vb* distress, exhaust, pinch, starve.

famous *adj* celebrated, conspicuous, distinguished, eminent, excellent, fabled, famed, far-famed, great, glorious, heroic, honored, illustrious, immortal, notable, noted, notorious, remarkable, renowned, signal.

fan[1] *vb* agitate, beat, move, winnow; blow, cool, refresh, ventilate; excite, fire, increase, rouse, stimulate. • *n* blower, cooler, punkah, ventilator.

fan[2] *n* admirer, buff, devotee, enthusiast, fancier, follower, pursuer, supporter.

fanatic *n* bigot, devotee, enthusiast, visionary, zealot.

fanatical *adj* bigoted, enthusiastic, frenzied, mad, rabid, visionary, wild, zealous.

fanciful *adj* capricious, crotchety, imaginary, visionary, whimsical; chimerical, fantastical, ideal, imaginary, wild.

fancy *vb* apprehend, believe, conjecture, imagine, suppose, think; conceive, imagine. • *adj* elegant, fine, nice, ornamented; extravagant, fanciful, whimsical. • *n* imagination; apprehension, conceit, conception, impression, idea, image, notion, thought; approval, fondness, inclination, judgement, liking, penchant, taste; caprice, crotchet, fantasy, freak, humor, maggot, quirk, vagary, whim, whimsy; apparition, chimera, daydream, delusion, hallucination, megrim, phantasm, reverie, vision.

fanfaron *n* blatherskite, blusterer, braggadocio, bully, hector, swaggerer, vaporer.

fang *n* claw, nail, talon, tooth; tusk.

fantastic *adj* chimerical, fanciful, imaginary, romantic, unreal, visionary; bizarre, capricious, grotesque, odd, quaint, queer, strange, whimsical, wild.

far *adj* distant, long, protracted, remote; farther, remoter; alienated, estranged, hostile. • *adv* considerably, extremely, greatly, very much; afar, distantly, far away, remotely.

farce *n* burlesque, caricature, parody, travesty; forcemeat, stuffing.

farcical *adj* absurd, comic, droll, funny, laughable, ludicrous, ridiculous.

fardel *n* bundle, burden, load, pack; annoyance, burden, ill, trouble.

fare *vb* go, journey, pass, travel; happen, prosper, prove; feed, live, manage, subsist. • *n* charge, price, ticket money; passenger, traveler; board, commons, food, table, victuals, provisions; condition, experience, fortune, luck, outcome.

farewell *n* adieu, leave-taking, valediction; departure, leave, parting, valedictory.

far-fetched *adj* abstruse, catachrestic, forced, recondite, strained.

farrago *n* gallimaufry, hodgepodge, hotchpotch, jumble, medley, miscellany, mixture, potpourri, salmagundi.

farther *adj* additional, further, remoter, ulterior. • *adv* beyond, further; besides, furthermore, moreover.

farthingale *n* crinoline, hoop, hoop skirt.

fascinate *vb* affect, bewitch, overpower, spellbind, stupefy, transfix; absorb, captivate, catch, charm, delight, enamor, enchant, enrapture, entrance.

fascination *n* absorption, charm, enchantment, magic, sorcery, spell, witchcraft, witchery.

fash *vb* harass, perplex, plague, torment, trouble, vex, worry. • *n* anxiety, care, trouble, vexation.

fashion *vb* contrive, create, design, forge, form, make, mold, pattern, shape; accommodate, adapt, adjust, fit, suit. • *n* appearance, cast, configuration, conformation, cut, figure, form, make, model, mold, pattern, shape, stamp; manner, method, sort, wake; conventionalism, conventionality, custom, fad, mode, style, usage, vogue; breeding, gentility; quality.

fashionable *adj* modish, stylish; current, modern, prevailing, up-to-date; customary, usual; genteel, well-bred.

fast[1] *adj* close, fastened, firm, fixed, immovable, tenacious, tight; constant, faithful, permanent, resolute, staunch, steadfast, unswerving, unwavering, fortified, impregnable, strong; deep, profound, sound; fleet, quick, rapid, swift; dissipated, dissolute, extravagant, giddy, reckless, thoughtless, thriftless, wild. • *adv* firmly, immovably, tightly; quickly, rapidly, swiftly; extravagantly, prodigally, reckless, wildly.

fast[2] *vb* abstain, go hungry, starve. • *n* abstention, abstinence, diet, fasting, starvation.

fasten *vb* attach, bind, bolt, catch, chain, cleat, fix, gird, lace, lock, pin, secure, strap, tether, tie; belay, bend; connect, hold, join, unite.

fastidious *adj* critical, dainty, delicate, difficult, exquisite, finical, hypercritical, meticulous, overdelicate, overnice, particular, precise, precious, punctilious, queasy, squeamish.

fat *adj* adipose, fatty, greasy, oily, oleaginous, unctuous; corpulent, fleshy, gross, obese, paunchy, portly, plump, pudgy, pursy; coarse, dull, heavy, sluggish, stupid; lucrative, profitable, rich; fertile, fruitful, productive, rich. • *n* adipose tissue, ester, grease, oil; best part, cream, flower; corpulence, fatness, fleshiness, obesity, plumpness, stoutness.

fatal *adj* deadly, lethal, mortal; baleful, baneful, calamitous, catastrophic, destructive, mischievous, pernicious, ruinous; destined, doomed, foreordained, inevitable, predestined.

fatality *n* destiny, fate; mortality; calamity, disaster.

fate *n* destination, destiny, fate; cup, die, doom, experience, lot, fortune, portion, weird; death, destruction, ruin.

fated *adj* appointed, destined, doomed, foredoomed, predetermined, predestinated, predestined, preordained.

fatherly *adj* benign, kind, paternal, protecting, tender.

fathom *vb* comprehend, divine, penetrate, reach, understand; estimate, gauge, measure, plumb, probe, sound.

fathomless *adj* abysmal, bottomless, deep, immeasurable, profound; impenetrable, incomprehensible, obscure.

fatigue *vb* exhaust, fag, jade, tire, weaken, weary. • *n* exhaustion, lassitude, tiredness, weariness; hardship, labor, toil.

fatuity *n* foolishness, idiocy, imbecility, stupidity; absurdity, folly, inanity, infatuation, madness.

fatuous *adj* dense, drivelling, dull, foolish, idiotic, stupid, witless; infatuated, mad, senseless, silly, weak.

fault *n* blemish, defect, flaw, foible, frailty, imperfection, infirmity, negligence, obliquity, offence, shortcoming, spot, weakness; delinquency, error, indiscretion, lapse, misdeed, misdemeanor, offence, peccadillo, slip, transgression, trespass, vice, wrong; blame, culpability.

faultless *adj* blameless, guiltless, immaculate, innocent, sinless, spotless, stainless; accurate, correct, perfect, unblemished.

faulty *adj* bad, defective, imperfect, incorrect; blameable, blameworthy, censurable, culpable, reprehensible.

faux pas *n* blunder, indiscretion, mistake.

favor *vb* befriend, countenance, encourage, patronize; approve; ease, facilitate; aid, assist, help, oblige, support; extenuate, humor, indulge, palliate, spare. • *n* approval, benignity, countenance, esteem, friendless, goodwill, grace, kindness; benefaction, benefit, boon, dispensation, kindness; championship, patronage, popularity, support; gift, present, token; badge, decoration, knot, rosette; leave, pardon, permission; advantage, cover, indulgence, protection; bias, partiality, prejudice.

favorable *adj* auspicious, friendly, kind, propitious, well-disposed, willing; conductive, contributing, propitious; adapted, advantage, beneficial, benign, convenient, fair, fit, good, helpful, suitable.

favorite *adj* beloved, darling, dear; choice, fancied, esteemed, pet, preferred.

fawn *vb* bootlick, bow, creep, cringe, crouch, dangle, kneel, stoop, toady, truckle.

fealty *n* allegiance, homage, loyalty, obeisance, submission; devotion, faithfulness, fidelity, honor, loyalty.

fear *vb* apprehend, dread; revere, reverence, venerate. • *n* affright, alarm, apprehension, consternation, dismay, dread, fright, horror, panic, phobia, scare, terror; disquietude, flutter, perturbation, palpitation, quaking, quivering, trembling, tremor, trepidation; anxiety, apprehension, concern, misdoubt, misgiving, qualm, solicitude; awe, dread, reverence, veneration.

fearful *adj* afraid, apprehensive, haunted; chicken-hearted, chicken-livered, cowardly, faint-hearted, lily-livered, nervous, pusillanimous, timid, timorous; dire, direful, dreadful, frightful, ghastly, horrible, shocking, terrible.

fearless *adj* bold, brave, courageous, daring, dauntless, doughty, gallant, heroic, intrepid, unterrified, valiant, valorous.

feasible *adj* achievable, attainable, possible, practicable, suitable.

feast *vb* delight, gladden, gratify, rejoice. • *n* banquet, carousal, entertainment, regale, repast, revels, symposium, treat; celebration, festival, fete, holiday; delight, enjoyment, pleasure.

feat *n* accomplishment, achievement, act, deed, exploit, performance, stunt, trick.

feather *n* plume; kind, nature, species.

featly *adv* adroitly, dextrously, nimbly, skilfully.

feature *vb* envisage, envision, picture, visualize; imagine; specialize; appear in, headline, star. • *n* appearance, aspect, component; conformation, fashion, make; characteristic, item, mark, particularity, peculiarity, property, point, trait, leader, lead item, special; favor, expression, lineament; article, film, motion picture, movie, story; highlight, high spot.

feces *npl* dregs, lees, sediment, settlings; dung, excrement, ordure, settlings.

fecund *adj* fruitful, impregnated, productive, prolific, rich.

fecundity *n* fertility, fruitfulness, productiveness.

federation *n* alliance, allying, confederation, federating, federation, leaguing, union, uniting; affiliation, coalition, combination, compact, confederacy, entente, federacy, league, copartnership.

fee *vb* pay, recompense, reward. • *n* account, bill, charge, compensation, honorarium, remuneration, reward, tip; benefice, fief, feud.

feeble *adj* anemic, debilitated, declining, drooping, enervated, exhausted, frail, infirm, languid, languishing, sickly; dim, faint, imperfect, indistinct.

feed *vb* contribute, provide, supply; cherish, eat, nourish, subsist, sustain. • *n* fodder, food, foodstuff, forage, provender.

feel *vb* apprehend, intuit, perceive, sense; examine, handle, probe, touch; enjoy, experience, suffer; prove, sound, test, try; appear, look, seem; believe, conceive, deem, fancy, infer, opine, suppose, think. • *n* atmosphere, feeling, quality; finish, surface, texture.

feeling *n* consciousness, impression, notion, perception, sensation; atmosphere, sense, sentience, touch; affecting, emotion, heartstrings, impression, passion, soul, sympathy; sensibility, sentiment, susceptibility, tenderness; attitude, impression, opinion.

feign *vb* devise, fabricate, forge, imagine, invent; affect, assume, counterfeit, imitate, pretend, sham, simulate.

feint *n* artifice, blind, expedient, make-believe, pretence, stratagem, trick.

felicitate *vb* complicate, congratulate; beatify, bless, delight.

felicitous *adj* appropriate, apt, fit, happy, ingenious, inspired, opportune, pertinent, seasonable, skillful, well-timed; auspicious, fortunate, prosperous, propitious, successful.

felicity *n* blessedness, bliss, blissfulness, gladness, happiness, joy; appropriateness, aptitude, aptness, felicitousness, fitness, grace, propriety, readiness, suitableness, fortune, luck, success.

fell[1] *vb* beat, knock down, level, prostrate; cut, demolish, hew.

fell[2] *adj* barbarous, bloodthirsty, bloody, cruel, ferocious, fierce, implacable, inhuman, malicious, malign, malignant, pitiless, relentless, ruthless, sanguinary, savage, unrelenting, vandalistic; deadly, destructive.

fellow *adj* affiliated, associated, joint, like, mutual, similar, twin. • *n* associate, companion, comrade; compeer, equal, peer; counterpart, mate, match, partner; member; boy, character, individual, man, person.

fellowship *n* brotherhood, companionship, comradeship, familiarity, intimacy; participation; partnership; communion, converse, intercourse; affability, kindliness, sociability, sociableness.

felon *n* convict, criminal, culprit, delinquent, malefactor, outlaw; inflammation, whitlow.

felonious *adj* atrocious, cruel, felon, heinous, infamous, malicious, malign, malignant, nefarious, perfidious, vicious, villainous.

female *adj* delicate, gentle, ladylike, soft; fertile, pistil-bearing, pistillate.

feminine *adj* affectionate, delicate, gentle, graceful, modest, soft, tender; female, ladylike, maidenly, womanish, womanly; effeminateness, effeminacy, softness, unmanliness, weakness, womanliness.

fen *n* bog, marsh, moor, morass, quagmire, slough, swamp.

fence *vb* defend, enclose, fortify, guard, protect, surround; circumscribe, evade, equivocate, hedge, prevaricate; guard, parry. • *n* barrier, hedge, hoarding, palings, palisade, stockade, wall; defence, protection, guard, security, shield; fencing, swordplay, swordsmanship; receiver.

fenny *adj* boggy, fennish, swampy, marshy.

feral, ferine *adj* ferocious, fierce, rapacious, ravenous, savage, untamed, wild.

ferment *vb* agitate, excite, heat; boil, brew, bubble, concoct, heat, seethe. • *n* barm, leaven, yeast; agitation, commotion, fever, glow, heat, tumult.

ferocious *adj* feral, fierce, rapacious, ravenous, savage, untamed, wild; barbarous, bloody, bloodthirsty, brutal, cruel, fell, inhuman, merciless, murderous, pitiless, remorseless, ruthless, sanguinary, truculent, vandalistic, violent.

ferocity *n* ferociousness, ferocity, fierceness, rapacity, savageness, wildness; barbarity, cruelty, inhumanity.

fertile *adj* bearing, breeding, fecund, prolific; exuberant, fruitful, luxuriant, plenteous, productive, rich, teeming; female, fruit-bearing, pistillate.

fertility *n* fertileness, fertility; abundance, exuberant, fruitfulness, luxuriance, plenteousness, productiveness, richness.

fervent *adj* burning, hot, glowing, melting, seething; animated, ardent, earnest, enthusiastic, fervid, fierce, fiery, glowing, impassioned, intense, passionate, vehement, warm, zealous.

fervour *n* heat, warmth; animation, ardor, eagerness, earnestness, excitement, fervency, intensity, vehemence, zeal.

fester *vb* corrupt, rankle, suppurate, ulcerate; putrefy, rot. • *n* abscess, canker, gathering, pustule, sore, suppination; festering, rankling.

festival *n* anniversary, carnival, feast, fete, gala, holiday, jubilee; banquet, carousal, celebration, entertainment, treat.

festive *adj* carnival, convivial, festal, festival, gay, jolly, jovial, joyful, merry, mirthful, uproarious.

festivity *n* conviviality, festival, gaiety, jollity, joviality, joyfulness, joyousness, merrymaking, mirth.

festoon *vb* adorn, decorate, embellish, garland, hoop, ornament. • *n* decoration, embellishment, garland, hoop, ornament, ornamentation.

fetch *vb* bring, elicit, get; accomplish, achieve, effect, perform; attain, reach. • *n* artifice, dodge, ruse, stratagem, trick.

fetid *adj* foul, malodorous, mephitic, noisome, offensive, rancid, rank, rank-smelling, stinking, strong-smelling.

fetish *n* charm, medicine, talisman.

fetter *vb* clog, hamper, shackle, trammel; bind, chain, confine, encumber, hamper, restrain, tie, trammel. • *n* bond, chain, clog, hamper, shackle.

feud *vb* argue, bicker, clash, contend, dispute, quarrel. • *n* affray, argument, bickering, broil, clashing, contention, contest, discord, dissension, enmity, fray, grudge, hostility, jarring, quarrel, rupture, strife, vendetta.

fever *n* agitation, excitement, ferment, fire, flush, heat, passion.

fey *adj* clairvoyant, ethereal, strange, unusual, whimsical; death-smitten, doomed.

fiasco *n* failure, fizzle.

fiat *n* command, decree, order, ordinance.

fiber *n* filament, pile, staple, strand, texture, thread; stamina, strength, toughness.

fickle *adj* capricious, changeable, faithless, fitful, inconstant, irresolute, mercurial, mutable, shifting, unsettled, unstable, unsteady, vacillating, variable, veering, violate, volatile, wavering.

fiction *n* fancy, fantasy, imagination, invention; novel, romance; fable, fabrication, falsehood, figment, forgery, invention, lie.

fictitious *adj* assumed, fabulous, fanciful, feigned, imaginary, invented, mythical, unreal; artificial, counterfeit, dummy, false, spurious, suppositious.

fiddle *vb* dawdle, fidget, interfere, tinker, trifle; cheat, swindle, tamper. • *n* fraud, swindle; fiddler, violin, violinist.

fiddle-de-dee *interj* fudge, moonshine, nonsense, stuff.

fiddle-faddle *n* frivolity, gabble, gibberish, nonsense, prate, stuff, trifling, trivia, twaddle.

fidelity *n* constancy, devotedness, devotion, dutifulness, faithfulness, fealty, loyalty, true-heartedness, truth; accuracy, closeness, exactness, faithfulness, precision.

fidget *vb* chafe, fret, hitch, twitch, worry. • *n* fidgetiness, impatience, restlessness, uneasiness.

fiduciary *adj* confident, fiducial, firm, steadfast, trustful, undoubting, unwavering; reliable, trustworthy. • *n* depositary, trustee.

field *n* clearing, glebe, meadow; expanse, extent, opportunity, range, room, scope, surface; department, domain, province, realm, region.

fiendish *adj* atrocious, cruel, demoniac, devilish, diabolical, hellish, implacable, infernal, malevolent, malicious, malign, malignant.

fierce *adj* barbarous, brutal, cruel, fell, ferocious, furious, infuriate, ravenous, savage; fiery, impetuous, murderous, passionate, tearing, tigerish, truculent, turbulent, uncurbed, untamed, vehement, violent.

fiery *adj* fervent, fervid, flaming, heated, hot, glowing, lurid; ardent, fierce, impassioned, impetuous, inflamed, passionate, vehement.

fight *vb* battle, combat, war; contend, contest, dispute, feud, oppose, strive, struggle, wrestle; encounter, engage; handle, manage, maneuvre. • *n* affair, affray, action, battle, brush, combat, conflict, confrontation, contest, duel, encounter, engagement, melée, quarrel, struggle, war; brawl, broil, riot, row, skirmish; fighting, pluck, pugnacity, resistance, spirit, temper.

figment *n* fable, fabrication, falsehood, fiction, invention.

figurative *adj* emblematical, representative, symbolic, representative, typical; metaphorical, tropical; florid, flowery, ornate, poetical.

figure *vb* adorn, diversify, ornament, variegate; delineate, depict, represent, signify, symbolize, typify; conceive, image, imagine, picture; calculate, cipher, compute; act, appear, perform. • *n* configuration, conformation, form, outline, shape; effigy, image, likeness, representative; design, diagram, drawing, pattern; image, metaphor, trope; emblem, symbol, type; character, digit, number, numeral.

filament *n* cirrus, fiber, fibril, gossamer, hair, strand, tendril, thread.

filch *vb* crib, nick, pilfer, purloin, rob, snitch, seal, thieve.

file[1] *vb* order, pigeonhole, record, tidy. • *n* data, dossier, folder, portfolio; column, line, list, range, rank, row, series, tier.

file[2] *vb* burnish, furbish, polish, rasp, refine, smooth.

filibuster *vb* delay, frustrate, obstruct, play for time, stall, temporize. • *n* frustrater, obstructionist, thwarter; adventurer, buccaneer, corsair, freebooter, pirate.

fill *vb* occupy, pervade; dilate, distend,

expand, stretch, trim; furnish, replenish, stock, store, supply; cloy, congest, content, cram, glut, gorge, line, pack, pall, sate, satiate, satisfy, saturate, stuff, suffuse, swell; engage, fulfill, hold, occupy, officiate, perform.

film *vb* becloud, cloud, coat, cover, darken, fog, mist, obfuscate, obscure, veil; photograph, shoot, take. • *n* cloud, coating, gauze, membrane, nebula, pellicle, scum, skin, veil; thread.

filter *vb* filtrate, strain; exude, ooze, percolate, transude. • *n* diffuser, colander, riddle, sieve, sifter, strainer.

filth *n* dirt, nastiness, ordure; corruption, defilement, foulness, grossness, impurity, obscenity, pollution, squalor, uncleanness, vileness.

filthy *adj* defiled, dirty, foul, licentious, nasty, obscene, pornographic, squalid, unclean; corrupt, gross, impure, unclean; miry, mucky, muddy.

final *adj* eventual, extreme, last, latest, terminal, ultimate; conclusive, decisive, definitive, irrevocable.

finale *n* conclusion, end, termination.

finances *npl* funds, resources, revenues, treasury; income, property.

find *vb* discover, fall upon; gain, get, obtain, procure; ascertain, notice, observe, perceive, remark; catch, detect; contribute, furnish, provide, supply. • *n* acquisition, catch, discovery, finding, plum, prize, strike.

fine[1] *vb* filter, purify, refine. • *adj* comminuted, little, minute, small; capillary, delicate, small; choice, light; exact, keen, sharp; attenuated, subtle, tenuous, thin; exquisite, fastidious, nice, refined, sensitive, subtle; dandy, excellent, superb, superior; beautiful, elegant, handsome, magnificent, splendid; clean, pure, unadulterated.

fine[2] *vb* amerce, mulct, penalize, punish. • *n* amercement, forfeit, forfeiture, mulct, penalty, punishment.

finery *n* decorations, frippery, gewgaws, ornaments, splendor, showiness, trappings, trimmings, trinkets.

finesse *vb* manipulate, maneuvre. • *n* artifice, contrivance, cunning, craft, manipulation, maneuvre, maneuvring, ruses, stratagems, strategy, wiles.

finger *vb* handle, manipulate, play, purloin.

finical *adj* critical, dainty, dapper, fastidious,

foppish, jaunty, overnice, overparticular, scrupulous, spruce, squeamish, trim.

finish vb accomplish, achieve, complete, consummate, execute, fulfill, perform; elaborate, perfect, polish; close, conclude, end, terminate. • n elaboration, elegance, perfection, polish; close, end, death, termination, wind-up.

finite adj bounded, circumscribed, conditioned, contracted, definable, limited, restricted, terminable.

fire vb ignite, kindle, light; animate, enliven, excite, inflame, inspirit, invigorate, rouse, stir up; discharge, eject, expel, hurl. • n combustion; blaze, conflagration; discharge, firing; animation, ardor, enthusiasm, fervor, fervency, fever, force, heat, impetuosity, inflammation, intensity, passion, spirit, vigor, violence; light, luster, radiance, splendor; imagination, imaginativeness, inspiration, vivacity; affliction, persecution, torture, trouble.

firm[1] adj established, coherent, confirmed, consistent, fast, fixed, immovable, inflexible, rooted, secure, settled, stable; compact, compressed, dense, hard, solid; constant, determined, resolute, staunch, steadfast, steady, unshaken; loyal, robust, sinewy, stanch, stout, sturdy, strong.

firm[2] n association, business, company, concern, corporation, house, partnership.

firmament n heavens, sky, vault, welkin.

firmness n compactness, fixedness, hardness, solidity; stability, strength; constancy, soundness, steadfastness, steadiness.

first adj capital, chief, foremost, highest, leading, prime, principal; earliest, eldest, original; maiden; elementary, primary, rudimentary; aboriginal, primal, primeval, primitive, pristine. • adv chiefly, firstly, initially, mainly, primarily, principally; before, foremost, headmost; before, rather, rather than, sooner, sooner than. • n alpha, initial, prime.

first-rate adj excellent, prime, superior.

fissure n breach, break, chasm, chink, cleft, crack, cranny, crevice, fracture, gap, hole, interstice, opening, rent, rift.

fit[1] vb adapt, adjust, suit; become, conform; accommodate, equip, prepare, provide, qualify. • adj capacitated, competent, fitted; adequate, appropriate, apt, becoming, befitting, consonant, convenient, fitting, good, meet, pertinent, proper, seemly, suitable.

fit[2] n convulsion, fit, paroxysm, qualm, seizure, spasm, spell; fancy, humor, whim; mood, pet, tantrum; interval, period, spell, turn.

fitful adj capricious, changeable, convulsive, fanciful, fantastic, fickle, humorsome, impulsive, intermittent, irregular, odd, spasmodic, unstable, variable, whimsical; checkered, eventful.

fitness n adaptation, appropriateness, aptitude, aptness, pertinence, propriety, suitableness; preparation, qualification.

fix vb establish, fasten, place, plant, set; adjust, correct, mend, repair; attach, bind, clinch, connect, fasten, lock, rivet, stay, tie; appoint, decide, define, determine, limit, seal, settle; consolidate, harden, solidify; abide, remain, rest; congeal, stiffen. • n difficulty, dilemma, quandary, pickle, plight, predicament.

flabbergast vb abash, amaze, astonish, astound, confound, confuse, disconcert, dumbfound, nonplus.

flabby adj feeble, flaccid, inelastic, limp, soft, week, yielding.

flaccid adj baggy, drooping, flabby, inelastic, lax, limber, limp, loose, pendulous, relaxed, soft, weak, yielding.

flag[1] vb droop, hang, loose; decline, droop, fail, faint, lag, languish, pine, sink, succumb, weaken, weary; stale, pall.

flag[2] vb indicate, mark, semaphore, sign, signal. • n banner, colours, ensign, gonfalon, pennant, pennon, standard, streamer.

flagellate vb beat, castigate, chastise, cudgel, drub, flog, scourge, thrash, whip.

flagitious adj abandoned, atrocious, corrupt, flagrant, heinous, infamous, monstrous, nefarious, profligate, scandalous, villainous, wicked.

flagrant adj burning, flaming, glowing, raging; crying, enormous, flagitious, glaring, monstrous, nefarious, notorious, outrageous, shameful, wanton, wicked.

flake vb desquamate, scale. • n lamina, layer, scale.

flamboyant adj bright, gorgeous, ornate, rococo.

flame vb blaze, shine; burn, flash, glow, warm. • n blaze, brightness, fire, flare, vapor; affection, ardor, enthusiasm, fervency, fervor, keenness, warmth.

flaming adj blazing; burning, bursting, exciting, glowing, intense, lambent, vehement, violent.

flap *vb* beat, flutter, shake, vibrate, wave. • *n* apron, fly, lap, lappet, tab; beating, flapping, flop, flutter, slap, shaking, swinging, waving.

flare *vb* blaze, flicker, flutter, waver; dazzle, flame, glare; splay, spread, widen. • *n* blaze, dazzle, flame, glare.

flash *vb* blaze, glance, glare, glisten, light, shimmer, scintillate, sparkle, twinkle. • *n* instant, moment, twinkling.

flashy *adj* flaunting, gaudy, gay, loud, ostentatious, pretentious, showy, tawdry, tinsel.

flat *adj* champaign, horizontal, level; even, plane, smooth, unbroken; low, prostrate, overthrow; dull, frigid, jejune, lifeless, monotonous, pointless, prosaic, spiritless, tame, unanimated, uniform, uninteresting; dead, flashy, insipid, mawkish, stale, tasteless, vapid; absolute, clear, direct, downright, peremptory, positive. • *adv* flatly, flush, horizontally, level. • *n* bar, sandbank, shallow, shoal, strand; champaign, lowland, plain; apartment, floor, lodging, storey.

flatter *vb* compliment, gratify, praise; blandish, blarney, butter up, cajole, coax, coddle, court, entice, fawn, humor, inveigle, wheedle.

flattery *n* adulation, blandishment, blarney, cajolery, fawning, obsequiousness, servility, sycophancy, toadyism.

flaunt *vb* boast, display, disport, flourish, parade, sport, vaunt; brandish.

flaunting *adj* flashy, garish, gaudy, ostentatious, showy, tawdry.

flavor *n* gust, gusto, relish, savor, seasoning, smack, taste, zest; admixture, lacing, seasoning; aroma, essence, soul, spirit.

flaw *n* break, breach, cleft, crack, fissure, fracture, gap, rent, rift; blemish, defect, fault, fleck, imperfection, speck, spot.

flay *vb* excoriate, flay; criticize.

fleck *vb* dapple, mottle, speckle, spot, streak, variegate. • *n* speckle, spot, streak.

flecked *adj* dappled, mottled, piebald, spotted, straked, striped, variegated.

flee *vb* abscond, avoid, decamp, depart, escape, fly, leave, run, skedaddle.

fleece *vb* clip, shear; cheat, despoil, pluck, plunder, rifle, rob, steal, strip.

fleer *vb* mock, jeer, gibe, scoff, sneer.

fleet[1] *n* armada, escadrille, flotilla, navy, squadron; company, group.

fleet[2] *adj* fast, nimble, quick, rapid, speedy, swift.

fleeting *adj* brief, caducous, ephemeral, evanescent, flitting, flying, fugitive, passing, short-lived, temporary, transient, transitory.

fleetness *n* celerity, nimbleness, quickness, rapidity, speed, swiftness, velocity.

flesh *n* food, meat; carnality, desires; kindred, race, stock; man, mankind, world.

fleshly *adj* animal, bodily, carnal, lascivious, lustful, lecherous, sensual.

fleshy *adj* corpulent, fat, obese, plump, stout.

flexibility *n* flexibleness, limbersome, lithesome, pliability, pliancy, suppleness; affability, complaisance, compliance, disposition, ductility, pliancy, tractableness, tractability, yielding.

flexible *adj* flexible, limber, lithe, pliable, pliant, supple, willowy; affable, complaisant, ductile, docile, gentle, tractable, tractile, yielding.

flexose, flexuous *adj* bending, crooked, serpentine, sinuate, sinuous, tortuous, waxy, winding.

flibbertigibbet *n* demon, imp, sprite.

flight[1] *n* flying, mounting, soaring, volition; shower, flight; steps, stairs.

flight[2] *n* departure, fleeing, flying, retreat, rout, stampede; exodus, hegira.

flighty *adj* capricious, deranged, fickle, frivolous, giddy, light-headed, mercurial, unbalanced, volatile, wild, whimsical.

flimsy *adj* slight, thin, unsubstantial; feeble, foolish, frivolous, light, puerile, shallow, superficial, trashy, trifling, trivial, weak; insubstantial, sleazy.

flinch *vb* blench, flee, recoil, retreat, shirk, shrink, swerve, wince, withdraw.

fling *vb* cast, chuck, dart, emit, heave, hurl, pitch, shy, throw, toss; flounce, wince. • *n* cast, throw, toss.

flippancy *n* volubility; assuredness, glibness, pertness.

flippant *adj* fluent, glib, talkative, voluble; bold, forward, frivolous, glib, impertinent, inconsiderate, irreverent, malapert, pert, saucy, trifling.

flirt *vb* chuck, fling, hurl, pitch, shy, throw, toss; flutter, twirl, whirl, whisk; coquet, dally, philander. • *n* coquette, jilt, philanderer; jerk.

flirtation *n* coquetry, dalliance, philandering.

flit *vb* flicker, flutter, hover; depart, hasten, pass.

flitting *adj* brief, ephemeral, evanescent, fleeting, fugitive, passing, short, transient, transitory.

float *vb* drift, glide, hang, ride, sail, soar, swim, waft; launch, support.

flock *vb* collect, congregate, gather, group, herd, swarm, throng. • *n* collection, group, multitude; bevy, company, convoy, drove, flight, gaggle, herd, pack, swarm, team, troupe; congregation.

flog *vb* beat, castigate, chastise, drub, flagellate, lash, scourge, thrash, whip.

flood *vb* deluge, inundate, overflow, submerge, swamp. • *n* deluge, freshet, inundation, overflow, tide; bore, downpour, eagre, flow, outburst, spate, rush; abundance, excess.

floor *vb* deck, pave; beat, confound, conquer, overthrow, prevail, prostrate, puzzle; disconcert, nonplus. • *n* storey; bottom, deck, flooring, pavement, stage.

florid *adj* bright-colored, flushed, red-faced, rubicund; embellished, figurative, luxuriant, ornate, rhetorical, rococo.

flounce[1] *vb* fling, jerk, spring, throw, toss, wince. • *n* jerk, spring.

flounce[2] *n* frill, furbelow, ruffle.

flounder *vb* blunder, flop, flounce, plunge, struggle, toss, tumble, wallow.

flourish *vb* grow, thrive; boast, bluster, brag, gasconade, show off, vaunt, vapor; brandish, flaunt, swing, wave. • *n* dash, display, ostentation, parade, show; bombast, fustian, grandiloquence; brandishing, shake, waving; blast, fanfare, tantivy.

flout *vb* chaff, deride, fleer, gibe, insult, jeer, mock, ridicule, scoff, sneer, taunt. • *n* gibe, fling, insult, jeer, mock, mockery, mocking, scoff, scoffing, taunt.

flow *vb* pour, run, stream; deliquesce, liquefy, melt; arise, come, emanate, follow, grow, issue, proceed, result, spring; glide; float, undulate, wave, waver; abound, run. • *n* current, discharge, flood, flux, gush, rush, stream, trickle; abundance, copiousness.

flower *vb* bloom, blossom, effloresce; develop. • *n* bloom, blossom; best, cream, elite, essence, pick; freshness, prime, vigor.

flowery *adj* bloomy, florid; embellished, figurative, florid, ornate, overwrought.

flowing *adj* abundant, copious, fluent, smooth.

fluctuate *vb* oscillate, swing, undulate, vibrate, wave; change, vary; vacillate, waver.

flue *n* chimney, duct; flew, fluff, nap, floss, fur.

fluency *n* liquidness, smoothness; affluence, copiousness; ease, facility, readiness.

fluent *adj* current, flowing, gliding, liquid; smooth; affluent, copious, easy, facile, glib, ready, talkative, voluble.

fluff *vb* blunder, bungle, forget, fumble, mess up, miscue, misremember, muddle, muff. • *n* down, flew, floss, flue, fur, lint, nap; cobweb, feather, gossamer, thistledown; blunder, bungle, fumble, muff.

flume *n* channel, chute, mill race, race.

flummery *n* chaff, frivolity, froth, moonshine, nonsense, trash, trifling; adulation, blandishment, blarney, flattery; brose, porridge, sowens.

flunky, flunkey *n* footman, lackey, livery servant, manservant, valet; snob, toady.

flurry *vb* agitate, confuse, disconcert, disturb, excite, fluster, hurry, perturb. • *n* gust, flaw, squall; agitation, bustle, commotion, confusion, disturbance, excitement, flutter, haste, hurry, hurry-scurry, perturbation, ruffle, scurry.

flush[1] *vb* flow, rush, start; glow, mantle, redden; animate, elate, elevate, erect, excite; cleanse, drench. • *adj* bright, fresh, glowing, vigorous; abundant, affluent, exuberant, fecund, fertile, generous, lavish, liberal, prodigal, prolific, rich, wealthy, wellsupplied; even, flat, level, plane. • *adv* evenly, flat, level; full, point-blank, right, square, squarely, straight. • *n* bloom, blush, glow, redness, rosiness, ruddiness; impulse, shock, thrill.

flush[2] *vb* disturb, rouse, start, uncover.

fluster *vb* excite, flush, heat; agitate, disturb, flurry, hurry, perturb, ruffle; confound, confuse, discompose, disconcert. • *n* glow, heat; agitation, flurry, flutter, hurry, hurry-scurry, perturbation, ruffle.

fluted *adj* channeled, corrugated, grooved.

flutter *vb* flap, hover; flirt, flit; beat, palpitate, quiver, tremble; fluctuate, oscillate, vacillate, waver. • *n* agitation, tremor; hurry, commotion, confusion, excitement, flurry, fluster, hurry-scurry, perturbation, quivering, tremble, tumult, twitter.

flux *n* flow, flowing; change, mutation, shifting, transition; diarrhea, dysentery, looseness; fusing, melting, menstruum, solvent.

fly[1] *vb* aviate, hover, mount, soar; flap, float, flutter, play, sail, soar, undulate, vibrate, wave; burst, explode; abscond, decamp, depart, flee, vanish; elapse, flit, glide, pass, slip.

fly[2] *adj* alert, bright, sharp, smart, wide-awake; astute, cunning, knowing, sly; agile, fleet, nimble, quick, spry.

foal *n* colt, filly.

foam *vb* cream, froth, lather, spume; boil, churn, ferment, fume, seethe, simmer, stew. • *n* bubbles, cream, froth, scum, spray, spume, suds.

fodder *n* feed, food, forage, provender, rations.

foe *n* adversary, antagonist, enemy, foeman, opponent.

fog *vb* bedim, bemist, blear, blur, cloud, dim, enmist, mist; addle, befuddle, confuse, fuddle, muddle. • *n* blear, blur, dimness, film, fogginess, haze, haziness, mist, smog, vapor; befuddlement, confusion, fuddle, maze, muddle.

foggy *adj* blurred, cloudy, dim, dimmed, hazy, indistinct, misty, obscure; befuddled, bewildered, confused, dazed, muddled, muddy, stupid.

foible *n* defect, failing, fault, frailty, imperfection, infirmity, penchant, weakness.

foil[1] *vb* baffle, balk, check, checkmate, circumvent, defeat, disappoint, frustrate, thwart.

foil[2] *n* film, flake, lamina; background, contrast.

foist *vb* impose, insert, interpolate, introduce, palm off, thrust.

fold[1] *vb* bend, cover, double, envelop, wrap; clasp, embrace, enfold, enwrap, gather, infold, interlace; collapse, fail. • *n* double, doubling, gather, plait, plicature.

fold[2] *n* cot, enclosure, pen.

foliaceous *adj* foliate, leafy; flaky, foliated, lamellar, lamellate, lamellated, laminated, scaly, schistose.

folk *n* kindred, nation, people.

follow *vb* ensue, succeed; chase, dog, hound, pursue, run after, trail; accompany, attend; conform, heed, obey, observe; cherish, cultivate, seek; practice, pursue; adopt, copy, imitate; arise, come, flow, issue, proceed, result, spring.

follower *n* acolyte, attendant, associate, companion, dependant, retainer, supporter; adherent, admirer, disciple, partisan, pupil; copier, imitator.

folly *n* doltishness, dullness, imbecility, levity, shallowness; absurdity, extravagance, fatuity, foolishness, imprudence, inanity,

indiscretion, ineptitude, nonsense, senselessness; blunder, faux pas, indiscretion, unwisdom.

foment *vb* bathe, embrocate, stupe; abet, brew, encourage, excite, foster, instigate, promote, stimulate.

fond *adj* absurd, baseless, empty, foolish, senseless, silly, vain, weak; affectionate, amorous, doting, loving, overaffectionate, tender.

fondle *vb* blandish, caress, coddle, cosset, dandle, pet.

fondness *n* absurdity, delusion, folly, silliness, weakness; liking, partiality, predilection, preference, propensity; appetite, relish, taste.

food *n* aliment, board, bread, cheer, commons, diet, fare, meat, nourishment, nutriment, nutrition, pabulum, provisions, rations, regimen, subsistence, sustenance, viands, victuals; feed, fodder, forage, provender.

fool *vb* jest, play, toy, trifle; beguile, cheat, circumvent, cozen, deceive, delude, dupe, gull, hoodwink, overreach, trick. • *n* blockhead, dolt, driveller, idiot, imbecile, nincompoop, ninny, nitwit, simpleton; antic, buffoon, clown, droll, harlequin, jester, merry-andrew, punch, scaramouch, zany; butt, dupe.

foolery *n* absurdity, folly, foolishness, nonsense; buffoonery, mummery, tomfoolery.

foolhardy *adj* adventurous, bold, desperate, harebrained, headlong, hot-headed, incautious, precipitate, rash, reckless, venturesome, venturous.

foolish *adj* brainless, daft, fatuous, idiotic, inane, inept, insensate, irrational, senseless, shallow, silly, simple, thick-skulled, vain, weak, witless; absurd, ill-judged, imprudent, indiscreet, nonsensical, preposterous, ridiculous, unreasonable, unwise; childish, contemptible, idle, puerile, trifling, trivial, vain.

foolishness *n* doltishness, dullness, fatuity, folly, imbecility, shallowness, silliness, stupidity; absurdity, extravagance, imprudence, indiscretion, nonsense; childishness, puerility, triviality.

footing *n* foothold, purchase; basis, foundation, groundwork, installation; condition, grade, rank, standing, state, status; settlement, establishment.

footman *n* footboy, menial, lackey, runner, servant.

footpad n bandit, brigand, freebooter, high-wayman, robber.

footpath n footway, path, trail.

footprint n footfall, footmark, footstep, trace, track.

footstep n footmark, footprint, trace, track; footfall, step, tread; mark, sign, token, trace, vestige.

fop n beau, coxcomb, dandy, dude, exquisite, macaroni, popinjay, prig, swell.

foppish adj coxcombical, dandified, dandyish, dressy, finical, spruce, vain.

forage vb feed, graze, provender, provision, victual; hunt for, range, rummage, search, seek; maraud, plunder, raid. • n feed, fodder, food, pasturage, provender; hunt, rummage, search.

foray n descent, incursion, invasion, inroad, irruption, raid.

forbear vb cease, desist, hold, pause, stop, stay; abstain, refrain; endure, tolerate; avoid, decline, shun; abstain, omit, withhold.

forbearance n abstinence, avoidance, forbearing, self-restraint, shunning, refraining; indulgence, lepiency, long-suffering, mildness, moderation, patience.

forbid vb ban, debar, disallow, embargo, enjoin, hinder, inhibit, interdict, prohibit, proscribe, taboo, veto.

forbidding adj abhorrent, disagreeable, displeasing, odious, offensive, repellant, repulsive, threatening, unpleasant.

force vb coerce, compel, constrain, necessitate, oblige; drive, impel, overcome, press, urge; ravish, violate. • n emphasis, energy, head, might, pith, power, strength, stress, vigor, vim; agency, efficacy, efficiency, cogency, potency, validity, virtue; coercion, compulsion, constraint, enforcement, vehemence, violence; army, array, battalion, host, legion, phalanx, posse, soldiery, squadron, troop.

forcible adj all-powerful, cogent, impressive, irresistible, mighty, potent, powerful, strong, weighty; impetuous, vehement, violent, unrestrained; coerced, coercive, compulsory; convincing, energetic, effective, efficacious, telling, vigorous.

forcibly adv mightily, powerfully; coercively, compulsorily, perforce, violently; effectively, energetically, vigorously.

ford n current, flood, stream; crossing, wading place.

fore adj anterior, antecedent, first, foregoing, former, forward, preceding, previous, prior; advanced, foremost, head, leading.

forebode vb augur, betoken, foreshow, foretell, indicate, portend, predict, prefigure, presage, prognosticate, promise, signify.

foreboding n augury, omen, prediction, premonition, presage, presentiment, prognostication.

forecast vb anticipate, foresee, predict; calculate, contrive, devise, plan, project, scheme. • n anticipation, foresight, forethought, planning, prevision, prophecy, provident.

foreclose vb debar, hinder, preclude, prevent, stop.

foredoom vb foreordain, predestine, preordain.

forego see **forgo**.

foregoing adj antecedent, anterior, fore, former, preceding, previous, prior.

foregone adj bygone, former, past, previous.

foreign adj alien, distant, exotic, exterior, external, outward, outlandish, remote, strange, unnative; adventitious, exterior, extraneous, extrinsic, inappropriate, irrelevant, outside, unnatural, unrelated.

foreknowledge n foresight, prescience, prognostication.

foremost adj first, front, highest, leading, main, principal.

foreordain vb appoint, foredoom, predestinate, predetermine, preordain.

forerunner n avant-courier, foregoer, harbinger, herald, precursor, predecessor; omen, precursor, prelude, premonition, prognosticate, sign.

foresee vb anticipate, forebode, forecast, foreknow, foretell, prognosticate, prophesy.

foreshadow vb forebode, predict, prefigure, presage, presignify, prognosticate, prophesy.

foresight n foreknowledge, prescience, prevision; anticipation, care, caution, forecast, forethought, precaution, providence, prudence.

forest n wood, woods, woodland.

forestall vb hinder, frustrate, intercept, preclude, prevent, thwart; antedate, anticipate, foretaste; engross, monopolize, regrate.

foretaste n anticipation, forestalling, prelibation.

foretell vb predict, prophesy; augur, betoken, forebode, forecast, foreshadow, foreshow, portend, presage, presignify, prognosticate, prophesy.

forethought n anticipation, forecast, foresight, precaution, providence, prudence.

forever adv always, constantly, continually, endlessly, eternally, ever, evermore, everlastingly, perpetually, unceasingly.

forewarn vb admonish, advise, caution, dissuade.

forfeit vb alienate, lose. • n amercement, damages, fine, forfeiture, mulct, penalty.

forfend vb avert, forbid, hinder, prevent, protect.

forge vb beat, fabricate, form, frame, hammer; coin, devise, frame, invent; counterfeit, falsify, feign. • n furnace, ironworks, smithy.

forgery n counterfeit, fake, falsification, imitation.

forgetful adj careless, heedless, inattentive, mindless, neglectful, negligent, oblivious, unmindful.

forgive vb absolve, acquit, condone, excuse, exonerate, pardon, remit.

forgiveness n absolution, acquittal, amnesty, condoning. exoneration, pardon, remission, reprieve.

forgiving adj absolutory, absolvatory, acquitting, clearing, excusing, pardoning, placable, releasing.

forgo vb abandon, cede, relinquish, renounce, resign, surrender, yield.

fork vb bifurcate, branch, divaricate, divide. • n bifurcation, branch, branching, crotch, divarication, division.

forked adj bifurcated, branching, divaricated, furcate, furcated.

forlorn adj abandoned, deserted, forsaken, friendless, helpless, lost, solitary; abject, comfortless, dejected, desolate, destitute, disconsolate, helpless, hopeless, lamentable, pitiable, miserable, woebegone, wretched.

form vb fashion model, mold, shape; build, conceive, construct, create, fabricate, make, produce; contrive, devise, frame, invent; compose, constitute, develop, organize; discipline, educate, teach, train. • n body, build, cast, configuration, conformation, contour, cut, fashion, figure, format, mold, outline, pattern, shape; formula, formulary, method, mode, practice, ritual; class, kind, manner, model, order, sort, system, type; arrangement, order, regularity, shapeliness; ceremonial, ceremony, conventionality, etiquette, formality, observance, ordinance, punctilio, rite, ritual; bench, seat; class, rank; arrangement, combination, organization.

formal adj explicit, express, official, positive, strict; fixed, methodical, regular, rigid, set, stiff; affected, ceremonious, exact, precise, prim, punctilious, starchy, starched; constitutive, essential; external, outward, perfunctory; formative, innate, organic, primordial.

formality n ceremonial, ceremony, conventionality, etiquette, punctilio, rite, ritual.

formation n creation, genesis, production; composition, constitution; arrangement, combination, disposal, disposition.

formative adj creative, determinative, plastic, shaping; derivative, inflectional, nonradical.

former adj antecedent, anterior, earlier, foregoing, preceding, previous, prior; late, old-time, quondam; by, bygone, foregone, gone, past.

formidable adj appalling, dangerous, difficult, dreadful, fearful, frightful, horrible, menacing, redoubtable, shocking, terrible, terrific, threatening, tremendous.

forsake vb abandon, desert, leave, quit; drop, forgo, forswear, relinquish, renounce, surrender, yield.

forsooth adv certainly, indeed, really, surely, truly.

forswear vb abandon, desert, drop, forsake, leave, quit, reject, renounce; abjure, deny, eschew, perjure, recant, repudiate, retract.

fort n bulwark, castle, citadel, defense, fastness, fortification, fortress, stronghold.

forthwith adv directly, immediately, instantly, quickly, straightaway.

fortification n breastwork, bulwark, castle, citadel, defense, earthwork, fastness, fort, keep, rampart, redoubt, stronghold, tower.

fortify vb brace, encourage, entrench, garrison, protect, reinforce, stiffen, strengthen; confirm, corroborate.

fortitude n braveness, bravery, courage, determination, endurance, firmness, hardiness, patience, pluck, resolution, strength, valor.

fortuitous adj accidental, casual, chance, contingent, incidental.

fortunate adj favored, happy, lucky, prosperous, providential, successful; advantageous, auspicious, favorable, happy, lucky, propitious, timely.

fortune *n* accident, casualty, chance, contingency, fortuity, hap, luck; estate, possessions, property, substance; affluence, felicity, opulence, prosperity, riches, wealth; destination, destiny, doom, fate, lot, star; event, issue, result; favour, success.

forward *vb* advance, aid, encourage, favor, foster, further, help, promote, support; accelerate, dispatch, expedite, hasten, hurry, quicken, speed; dispatch, post, send, ship, transmit. • *adj* ahead, advanced, onward; anterior, front, fore, head; prompt, eager, earnest, hasty, impulsive, quick, ready, willing, zealous; assuming, bold, brazen, brazen-faced, confident, flippant, impertinent, pert, presumptuous, presuming; advanced, early, premature. • *adv* ahead, onward.

foster *vb* cosset, feed, nurse, nourish, support, sustain; advance, aid, breed, cherish, cultivate, encourage, favor, foment, forward, further, harbor, patronize, promote, rear, stimulate.

foul *vb* besmirch, defile, dirty, pollute, soil, stain, sully; clog, collide, entangle, jam. • *adj* dirty, fetid, filthy, impure, nasty, polluted, putrid, soiled, stained, squalid, sullied, rank, tarnished, unclean; disgusting, hateful, loathsome, noisome, odious, offensive; dishonorable, underhand, unfair, sinister; abominable, base, dark, detestable, disgraceful, infamous, scandalous, scurvy, shameful, wile, wicked; coarse, low, obscene, vulgar; abusive, foul-mouthed, foul-spoken, insulting, scurrilous; cloudy, rainy, rough, stormy, wet; feculent, muddy, thick, turbid; entangled, tangled.

foul-mouthed *adj* abusive, blackguardly, blasphemous, filthy, foul, indecent, insolent, insulting, obscene, scurrilous.

found *vb* base, fix, ground, place, rest, set; build, construct, erect, raise; colonize, establish, institute, originate, plant; cast, mold.

foundation *n* base, basis, bed, bottom, footing, ground, groundwork, substructure, support; endowment, establishment, settlement.

founder[1] *n* author, builder, establisher, father, institutor, originator, organizer, planter.

founder[2] *n* caster, molder.

founder[3] *vb* sink, swamp, welter; collapse, fail, miscarry; fall, stumble, trip.

fountain *n* fount, reservoir, spring, well; jet, upswelling; cause, fountainhead, origin, original, source.

foxy *adj* artful, crafty, cunning, sly, subtle, wily.

fracas *n* affray, brawl, disturbance, outbreak, quarrel, riot, row, uproar, tumult.

fractious *adj* captious, cross, fretful, irritable, peevish, pettish, perverse, petulant, querulous, snappish, splenetic, touchy, testy, waspish.

fracture *vb* break, crack, split. • *n* breaking, rupture; breach, break, cleft, crack, fissure, flaw, opening, rift, rent.

fragile *adj* breakable, brittle, delicate, frangible; feeble, frail, infirm, weak.

fragility *n* breakability, breakableness, brittleness, frangibility, frangibleness; feebleness, frailty, infirmity, weakness.

fragment *vb* atomize, break, fracture, pulverize, splinter. • *n* bit, chip, fraction, fracture, morsel, part, piece, remnant, scrap.

fragrance *n* aroma, balminess, bouquet, odor, perfume, redolence, scent, smell.

fragrant *adj* ambrosial, aromatic, balmy, odoriferous, odorous, perfumed, redolent, spicy, sweet, sweet-scented, sweet-smelling.

frail *adj* breakable, brittle, delicate, fragile, frangible, slight; feeble, infirm, weak.

frailty *n* feebleness, frailness, infirmity, weakness; blemish, defect, failing, fault, foible, imperfection, peccability, shortcoming.

frame *vb* build, compose, constitute, construct, erect, form, make, mold, plan, shape; contrive, devise, fabricate, fashion, forge, invest, plan. • *n* body, carcass, framework, framing, shell, skeleton; constitution, fabric, form, structure, scheme, system; condition, humor, mood, state, temper.

franchise *n* privilege, right; suffrage, vote; exemption, immunity.

frangible *adj* breakable, brittle, fragile.

frank *adj* artless, candid, direct, downright, frank-hearted, free, genuine, guileless, ingenuous, naive, open, outspoken, outright, plain, plain-spoken, point-blank, sincere, straightforward, truthful, unequivocal, unreserved, unrestricted.

frankness *n* candor, ingenuousness, openness, outspokenness, plain speaking, truth, straightforwardness.

frantic *adj* crazy, distracted, distraught,

frenzied, furious, infuriate, mad, outrageous, phrenetic, rabid, raging, raving, transported, wild.

fraternity n association, brotherhood, circle, clan, club, company, fellowship, league, set, society, sodality; brotherliness.

fraternize vb associate, coalesce, concur, consort, cooperate, harmonize, sympathize, unite.

fraud n artifice, cheat, craft, deception, deceit, duplicity, guile, hoax, humbug, imposition, imposture, sham, stratagem, treachery, trick, trickery, wile.

fraudulent adj crafty, deceitful, deceptive, dishonest, false, knavish, treacherous, trickish, tricky, wily.

fraught adj abounding, big, burdened, charged, filled, freighted, laden, pregnant, stored, weighted.

fray[1] n affray, battle, brawl, broil, combat, fight, quarrel, riot.

fray[2] vb chafe, fret, rub, wear; ravel, shred.

freak adj bizarre, freakish, grotesque, monstrous, odd, unexpected, unforeseen. • n caprice, crotchet, fancy, humor, maggot, quirk, vagary, whim, whimsey; antic, caper, gambol; abnormality, abortion, monstrosity.

freakish adj capricious, changeable, eccentric, erratic, fanciful, humorsome, odd, queer, whimsical.

free vb deliver, discharge, disenthral, emancipate, enfranchise, enlarge, liberate, manumit, ransom, release, redeem, rescue, save; clear, disencumber, disengage, extricate, rid, unbind, unchain, unfetter, unlock; exempt, immunize, privilege. • adj bondless, independent, loose, unattached, unconfined, unentangled, untrammeled; autonomous, delivered, emancipated, freeborn, liberated, manumitted, ransomed, released, self-governing; clear, exempt, immune, privileged; allowed, permitted; devoid, empty, open, unimpeded, unobstructed, unrestricted; affable, artless, candid, frank, ingenuous, sincere, unreserved; bountiful, charitable, free-hearted, generous, hospitable, liberal, munificent, openhanded; immoderate, lavish, prodigal; eager, prompt, ready, willing; available, gratuitous, spontaneous; careless, lax, loose; bold, easy, familiar, informal, overfamiliar, unconstrained. • adv openly, outright, unreservedly, unrestrainedly, unstintingly; freely, gratis, gratuitously.

freebooter n bandit, brigand, despoiler, footpad, gangster, highwayman, marauder, pillager, plunderer, robber; buccaneer, pirate, rover.

freedom n emancipation, independence, liberation, liberty, release; elbowroom, margin, play, range, scope, swing; franchise, immunity, privilege; familiarity, laxity, license, looseness.

freethinker n agnostic, deist, doubter, infidel, sceptic, unbeliever.

freeze vb congeal, glaciate, harden, stiffen; benumb, chill.

freight vb burden, charge, lade, load. • n burden, cargo, lading, load.

frenzy n aberration, delirium, derangement, distraction, fury, insanity, lunacy, madness, mania, paroxysm, rage, raving, transport.

frequent vb attend, haunt, resort, visit. • adj iterating, oft-repeated; common, customary, everyday, familiar, habitual, persistent, usual; constant, continual, incessant.

fresh adj new, novel, recent; renewed, revived; blooming, flourishing, green, undecayed, unimpaired, unfaded, unobliterated, unwilted, unwithered, well-preserved; sweet; delicate, fair, fresh-colored, ruddy, rosy; florid, hardy, healthy, vigorous, strong; active, energetic, unexhausted, unfatigued, unwearied, vigorous; keen, lively, unabated, undecayed, unimpaired, vivid, additional, further; uncured, undried, unsalted, unsmoked; bracing, health-giving, invigorating, refreshing, sweet; brink, stiff, strong; inexperienced, raw, uncultivated, unpracticed, unskilled, untrained, unused.

freshen vb quicken, receive, refresh, revive.

fret[1] vb abrade, chafe, fray, gall, rub, wear; affront, agitate, annoy, gall, harass, irritate, nettle, provoke, ruffle, tease, vex, wear, worry; ripple, roughen; corrode; fume, peeve, rage, stew. • n agitation, fretfulness, fretting, irritation, peevishness, vexation.

fret[2] vb diversify, interlace, ornament, variegate. • n fretwork, interlacing, ornament; ridge, wale, whelk.

fretful adj captious, cross, fractious, ill-humored, ill-tempered, irritable, peevish, pettish, petulant, querulous, short-tempered, snappish, spleeny, splenetic, testy, touchy, uneasy, waspish.

friable adj brittle, crisp, crumbling, powdery, pulverable.

friction *n* abrasion, attrition, grating, rubbing; bickering, disagreement, dissension, wrangling.

friend *adj* benefactor, chum, companion, comrade, crony, confidant, intimate; adherent, ally, associate, confrere, partisan; advocate, defender, encourager, favorer, patron, supporter, well-wisher.

friendly *adj* affectionate, amiable, benevolent, favorable, kind, kind-hearted, kindly, well-disposed; amicable, cordial, fraternal, neighborly; conciliatory, peaceable, unhostile.

friendship *n* affection, attachment, benevolence, fondness, goodness, love, regard; fellowship, intimacy; amicability, amicableness, amity, cordiality, familiarity, fraternization, friendliness, harmony.

fright *n* affright, alarm, consternation, dismay, funk, horror, panic, scare, terror.

frighten *vb* affright, alarm, appal, daunt, dismay, intimidate, scare, stampede, terrify.

frightful *adj* alarming, awful, dire, direful, dread, dreadful, fearful, horrible, horrid, shocking, terrible, terrific; ghastly, grim, grisly, gruesome, hideous.

frigid *adj* cold, cool, gelid; dull, lifeless, spiritless, tame, unanimated, uninterested, uninteresting; chilling, distant, forbidding, formal, freezing, prim, repellent, repelling, repulsive, rigid, stiff.

frill *n* edging, frilling, furbelow, gathering, ruche, ruching, ruffle; affectation, mannerism.

fringe *vb* border, bound, edge, hem, march, rim, skirt, verge. • *n* border, edge, edging, tassel, trimming. • *adj* edging, extra, unofficial.

frisk *vb* caper, dance, frolic, gambol, hop, jump, play, leap, romp, skip, sport, wanton.

frisky *adj* frolicsome, coltish, gay, lively, playful, sportive.

frivolity *n* flummery, folly, fribbling, frippery, frivolousness, levity, puerility, trifling, triviality.

frivolous *adj* childish, empty, flighty, flimsy, flippant, foolish, giddy, idle, light, paltry, petty, puerile, silly, trashy, trifling, trivial, unimportant, vain, worthless.

frolic *vb* caper, frisk, gambol, lark, play, romp, sport. • *n* escapade, gambol, lark, romp, skylark, spree, trick; drollery, fun, play, pleasantry, sport.

frolicsome *adj* coltish, fresh, frolic, gamesome, gay, lively, playful, sportive.

front *vb* confront, encounter, face, oppose. • *adj* anterior, forward; foremost, frontal, headmost. • *n* brow, face, forehead; assurance, boldness, brass, effrontery, impudence; breast, head, van, vanguard; anterior, face, forepart, obverse; facade, frontage.

frontier *n* border, boundary, coast, confine, limits, marches.

frosty *adj* chill, chilly, cold, icy, stinging, wintry; cold, cold-hearted, frigid, indifferent, unaffectionate, uncordial, unimpassioned, unloving; dull-hearted, lifeless, spiritless, unanimated; frosted, gray-haired, hoary, white.

froth *vb* bubble, cream, foam, lather, spume. • *n* bubbles, foam, lather, spume; balderdash, flummery, nonsense, trash, triviality.

frothy *adj* foamy, spumy; empty, frivolous, light, trifling, trivial, unsubstantial, vain.

froward *adj* captious, contrary, contumacious, cross, defiant, disobedient, fractious, impudent, intractable, obstinate, peevish, perverse, petulant, refractory, stubborn, ungovernable, untoward, unyielding, wayward, willful.

frown *vb* glower, lower, scowl.

frowzy, frowsy *adj* fetid, musty, noisome, rancid, rank, stale; disordered, disorderly, dowdy, slatternly, slovenly.

frugal *adj* abstemious, careful, chary, choice, economical, provident, saving, sparing, temperate, thrifty, unwasteful.

fruit *n* crop, harvest, produce, production; advantage, consequence, effect, good, outcome, product, profit, result; issue, offspring, young.

fruitful *adj* abounding, productive; fecund, fertile, prolific; abundant, exuberant, plenteous, plentiful, rich, teeming.

fruition *n* completion, fulfillment, perfection; enjoyment.

fruitless *adj* acarpous, barren, sterile, infecund, unfertile, unfruitful, unproductive, unprolific; abortive, bootless, futile, idle, ineffectual, profitless, unavailing, unprofitable, useless, vain.

frumpish, frumpy *adj* cross, cross-grained, cross-tempered, dowdy, grumpy, irritable, shabby, slatternly, snappish.

frustrate *vb* baffle, balk, check, circumvent, defeat, disappoint, disconcert, foil, thwart; cross, hinder, outwit.

frustrated adj balked, blighted, dashed, defeated, foiled, thwarted; ineffectual, null, useless, vain.

fuddled adj befuddled, boozy, corned, crapulous, drunk, groggy, high, inebriated, intoxicated, muddled, slewed, tight, tipsy.

fugacious adj evanescent, fleeting, fugitive, transient, transitory.

fugitive adj escaping, fleeing, flying; brief, ephemeral, evanescent, fleeting, flitting, fugacious, momentary, short, short-lived, temporal, temporary, transient, transitory, uncertain, unstable, volatile. • n émigré, escapee, evacuee, fleer, outlaw, refugee, runaway.

fulfill vb accomplish, complete, consummate, effect, effectuate, execute, realize; adhere, discharge, do, keep, obey, observe, perform; answer, fill, meet, satisfy.

full adj brimful, filled, flush, replete, abounding, replete, well-stocked; bagging, flowing, loose, voluminous; chock-full, cloyed, crammed, glutted, gorged, overflowing, packed, sated, satiated, saturated, soaked, stuffed, swollen; adequate, complete, entire, mature, perfect; abundant, ample, copious, plenteous, plentiful, sufficient; clear, deep, distinct, loud, rounded, strong; broad, large, capacious, comprehensive, extensive, plump; circumstantial, detailed, exhaustive. • adv completely, fully; directly, exactly, precisely.

fullness n abundance, affluence, copiousness, plenitude, plenty, profusion; glut, satiety, sating, repletion; completeness, completion, entireness, perfection; clearness, loudness, resonance, strength; dilation, distension, enlargement, plumpness, rotundity, roundness, swelling.

fully adv abundantly, amply, completely, copiously, entirely, largely, plentifully, sufficiently.

fulminate vb detonate, explode; curse, denounce, hurl, menace, threaten, thunder.

fulsome adj excessive, extravagant, fawning; disgusting, nauseous, nauseating, offensive, repulsive; coarse, gross, lustful, questionable.

fumble vb bungle, grope, mismanage, stumble; mumble, stammer, stutter.

fume vb reek, smoke, vaporize. • n effluvium exhalation, reek, smell, smoke, steam, vapor; agitation, fret, fry, fury, passion, pet, rage, storm.

fun adj amusing, diverting, droll, entertaining.
• n amusement, diversion, drollery, frolic, gaiety, humor, jesting, jocularity, jollity, joy, merriment, mirth, play, pranks, sport, pleasantry, waggishness.

function vb act, discharge, go, operate, officiate, perform, run, serve, work. • n discharge, execution, exercise, operation, performance, purpose, use; activity, business, capacity, duty, employment, occupation, office, part, province, role; ceremony, rite; dependant, derivative.

fund vb afford, endow, finance, invest, provide, subsidise, support; garner, hoard, stock, store. • n accumulation, capital, endowment, reserve, stock; store, supply; foundation.

fundament n bottom, buttocks, seat.

fundamental adj basal, basic, bottom, cardinal, constitutional, elementary, essential, indispensable, organic, principal, primary, radical. • n essential, principal, rule.

funeral n burial, cremation, exequies, interment, obsequies.

funereal adj dark, dismal, gloomy, lugubrious, melancholy, mournful, sad, sepulchral, sombre, woeful.

funk vb blanch, shrink, quail. • n stench, stink; fear, fright, panic.

funny adj amusing, comic, comical, diverting, droll, facetious, farcical, humorous, jocose, jocular, laughable, ludicrous, sportive, witty; curious, odd, queer, strange.
• n jest, joke; cartoon, comic.

furbish vb burnish, brighten, polish, renew, renovate, rub, shine.

furious adj angry, fierce, frantic, frenzied, fuming, infuriated, mad, raging, violent, wild; boisterous, fierce, impetuous, stormy, tempestuous, tumultuous, turbulent, vehement.

furnish vb appoint, endow, provide, supply; decorate, equip, fit; afford, bestow, contribute, give, offer, present, produce, yield.

furniture n chattels, effects, household goods, movables; apparatus, appendages, appliances, equipment, fittings, furnishings; decorations, embellishments, ornaments.

furore n commotion, craze, enthusiasm, excitement, fad, fury, madness, mania, rage, vogue.

furrow vb chamfer, channel, cleave, corrugate, cut, flute, groove, hollow; pucker, seam, wrinkle. • n chamfer, channel, cut, depression, fluting, groove, hollow, line, seam, track, trench, rot, wrinkle.

further *vb* advance, aid, assist, encourage, help, forward, promote, succor, strengthen. • *adj* additional. • *adv* also, besides, farther, furthermore, moreover.

furtive *adj* clandestine, hidden, secret, sly, skulking, sneaking, sneaky, stealthy, stolen, surreptitious.

fury *n* anger, frenzy, fit, furore, ire, madness, passion, rage; fierceness, impetuosity, turbulence, turbulency, vehemence; bacchant, bacchante, bedlam, hag, shrew, termagant, virago, vixen.

fuse *vb* dissolve, melt, liquefy, smelt; amalgamate, blend, coalesce, combine, commingle, intermingle, intermix, merge, unite. • *n* match.

fusion *n* liquefaction, melting; amalgamation, blending, commingling, commixture, intermingling, intermixture, union; coalition, merging.

fuss *vb* bustle, fidget, fret, fume, worry. • *n* ado, agitation, bother, bustle, commotion, disturbance, excitement, fidget, flurry, fluster, fret, hurry, pother, stir, worry.

fustian *n* bombast, claptrap, rant, rodomontade; balderdash, inanity, nonsense, stuff, trash, twaddle.

fusty *adj* ill-smelling, malodorous, mildewed, moldy, musty, rank.

futile *adj* frivolous, trifling, trivial; bootless, fruitless, idle, ineffectual, profitless, unavailing, unprofitable, useless, vain, valueless, worthless.

futility *n* frivolousness, triviality; bootlessness, fruitlessness, uselessness, vanity, worthlessness.

future *adj* coming, eventual, forthcoming, hereafter, prospective, subsequent. • *n* hereafter, outlook, prospect.

G

gabble *vb* babble, chatter, clack, gibber, gossip, prate, prattle. • *n* babble, chatter, clack, gap, gossip, jabber, palaver, prate, prattle, twaddle.

gadabout *n* idler, loafer, rambler, rover, vagrant; gossip, talebearer, vagrant.

gaffer *n* boss, foreman, overseer, supervisor.

gag[1] *n* jape, jest, joke, stunt, wisecrack.

gag[2] *vb* muffle, muzzle, shackle, silence, stifle, throttle; regurgitate, retch, throw up, vomit; choke, gasp, pant. • *n* muzzle.

gage *n* pawn, pledge, security, surety; challenge, defiance, gauntlet, glove.

gaiety *n* animation, blithesomeness, cheerfulness, glee, hilarity, jollity, joviality, merriment, mirth, vivacity.

gain *vb* achieve, acquire, earn, get, obtain, procure, reap, secure; conciliate, enlist, persuade, prevail, win; arrive, attain, reach; clear, net, profit. • *n* accretion, addition, gainings, profits, winnings; acquisition, earnings, emolument, lucre; advantage, benefit, blessing, good, profit.

gainful *adj* advantageous, beneficial, profitable; lucrative, paying, productive, remunerative.

gainsay *vb* contradict, controvert, deny, dispute, forbid.

gait *n* carriage, pace, step, stride, walk.

galaxy *n* assemblage, assembly, cluster, collection, constellation, group.

gale *n* blast, hurricane, squall, storm, tempest, tornado, typhoon.

gall[1] *n* effrontery, impudence; bile; acerbity, bitterness, malice, maliciousness, malignity, rancor, spite.

gall[2] *vb* chafe, excoriate, fret, hurt; affront, annoy, exasperate, harass, incense, irritate, plague, provoke, sting, tease, vex.

gallant *adj* fine, magnificent, showy, splendid, well-dressed; bold, brave, chivalrous, courageous, daring, fearless, heroic, highspirited, intrepid, valiant, valorous; chivalrous, fine, honorable, high-minded, lofty, magnanimous, noble. • *n* beau, blade, spark; lover, suitor, wooer.

gallantry *n* boldness, bravery, chivalry, courage, courageousness, fearlessness, heroism, intrepidity, prowess, valor; courtesy, courteousness, elegance, politeness.

galling *adj* chafing, irritating, vexing.

gallop *vb* fly, hurry, run, rush, scamper, speed.

gamble *vb* bet, dice, game, hazard, plunge, speculate, wager. • *n* chance, risk, speculation; bet, punt, wager.

gambol *vb* caper, cut, frisk, frolic, hop, jump, leap, romp, skip. • *n* frolic, hop, jump, skip.

game[1] *vb* gamble, sport, stake. • *n* amusement, contest, diversion, pastime, play, sport; adventure, enterprise, measure, plan, project, scheme, stratagem, undertaking; prey, quarry, victim.

game[2] *adj* brave, courageous, dauntless, fearless, gallant, heroic, intrepid, plucky, unflinching, valorous; enduring, persevering, resolute, undaunted; ready, eager, willing.

game[1] *adj* crippled, disabled, halt, injured, lame.

gameness *n* bravery, courage, grit, heart, mettle, nerve, pith, pluck, pluckiness, spirit, stamina.

gamesome *adj* frisky, frolicsome, lively, merry, playful, sportive, sprightly, vivacious.

gammon *vb* bamboozle, beguile, cheat, circumvent, deceive, delude, dupe, gull, hoax, humbug, inveigle, mislead, overreach, outwit. • *n* bosh, hoax, humbug, imposition, nonsense.

gang *n* band, cabal, clique, company, coterie, crew, horde, party, set, troop.

gaol *see* jail.

gap *n* breach, break, cavity, chasm, chink, cleft, crack, cranny, crevice, hiatus, hollow, interval, interstice, lacuna, opening, pass, ravine, rift, space, vacancy.

gape *vb* burst open, dehisce, open, stare, yawn.

garb *vb* attire, clothe, dress. • *n* apparel, attire, clothes, costume, dress, garments, habiliment, habit, raiment, robes, uniform, vestment.

garbage *n* filth, offal, refuse, remains, rubbish, trash, waste.

garble *vb* corrupt, distort, falsify, misquote, misrepresent, mutilate, pervert.

gargantuan *adj* big, Brobdingnagian, colossal, enormous, gigantic, huge, prodigious, tremendous.

garish *adj* bright, dazzling, flashy, flaunting, gaudy, glaring, loud, showy, staring, tawdry.

garland *vb* adorn, festoon, wreathe. • *n* chaplet, coronal, crown, festoon, wreath.

garment *n* clothes, clothing, dress, habit, vestment.

garner *vb* accumulate, collect, deposit, gather, hoard, husband, reserve, save, store, treasure.

garnish *vb* adorn, beautify, bedeck, decorate, deck, embellish, grace, ornament, prank, trim. • *n* decoration, enhancement, ornament, trimming.

garrulous *adj* babbling, loquacious, prating, prattling, talkative.

gasconade *n* bluster, boast, brag, bravado, swagger, vaunt, vaporing.

gasp *vb* blow, choke, pant, puff. • *n* blow, exclamation, gulp, puff.

gather *vb* assemble, cluster, collect, convene, group, muster, rally; accumulate, amass, garner, hoard, huddle, lump; bunch, crop, cull, glean, pick, pluck, rake, reap, shock, stack; acquire, gain, get, win; conclude, deduce, derive, infer; fold, plait, pucker, shirr, tuck; condense, grow, increase, thicken.

gathering *n* acquisition, collecting, earning, gain, heap, pile, procuring; assemblage, assembly, collection, company, concourse, congregation, meeting, muster; abscess, boil, fester, pimple, pustule, sore, suppuration, tumor, ulcer.

gauche *adj* awkward, blundering, bungling, clumsy, inept, tactless, uncouth.

gaudy *adj* bespangled, brilliant, brummagem, cheap, flashy, flaunting, garish, gimcrack, glittering, loud, ostentatious, overdecorated, sham, showy, spurious, tawdry, tinsel.

gauge *vb* calculate, check, determine, weigh; assess, estimate, guess, reckon. • *n* criterion, example, indicator, measure, meter, touchstone, yardstick; bore, depth, height, magnitude, size, thickness, width.

gaunt *adj* angular, attenuated, emaciated, haggard, lank, lean, meager, scraggy, skinny, slender, spare, thin.

gawky *adj* awkward, boorish, clownish, clumsy, green, loutish, raw, rustic, uncouth, ungainly.

gay *adj* bright, brilliant, dashing, fine, showy; flashy, flaunting, garish, gaudy, glittering, loud, tawdry, tinsel; airy, blithe, blithesome, cheerful, festive, frivolous, frolicsome, gladsome, gleeful, hilarious, jaunty, jolly, jovial, light-hearted, lively, merry, mirthful, sportive, sprightly, vivacious.

gear *vb* adapt, equip, fit, suit, tailor. • *n* apparel, array, clothes, clothing, dress, garb; accouterments, appliances, appointments, appurtenances, array, harness, goods, movables, subsidiaries; harness, rigging, tackle, trappings; apparatus, machinery, mechanics.

gelid *adj* chill, chilly, cold, freezing, frigid, icy.

gem *n* jewel, stone, treasure.

genealogy *n* ancestry, descent, lineage, pedigree, stock.

general *adj* broad, collective, generic, popular, universal, widespread; catholic, ecumenical; common, current, ordinary, usual; inaccurate, indefinite, inexact, vague.

generally *adv* commonly, extensively, universally, usually.

generate *vb* beget, breed, engender, procreate, propagate, reproduce, spawn; cause, form, make, produce.

generation *n* creation, engendering, formation, procreation, production; age, epoch, era, period, time; breed, children, family, kind, offspring, progeny, race, stock.

generosity *n* disinterestedness, high-mindedness, magnanimity, nobleness; bounteousness, bountifulness, bounty, charity, liberality, openhandedness.

generous *adj* high-minded, honorable, magnanimous, noble; beneficent, bountiful, charitable, free, hospitable, liberal, munificent, open-handed; abundant, ample, copious, plentiful, rich.

genial *adj* cheering, encouraging, enlivening, fostering, inspiring, mild, warm; agreeable, cheerful, cordial, friendly, hearty, jovial, kindly, merry, mirthful, pleasant.

genius *n* aptitude, aptness, bent, capacity, endowment, faculty, flair, gift, talent, turn; brains, creative power, ingenuity, inspiration, intellect, invention, parts, sagacity, wit; adeptness, master, master hand, proficiency; character, disposition, naturalness, nature; deity, demon, spirit.

genteel *adj* aristocratic, courteous, gentlemanly, lady-like, polished, polite, refined, well-bred; elegant, fashionable, graceful, stylish.

gentility *n* civility, courtesy, good breeding, politeness, refinement, urbanity.

gentle *adj* amiable, bland, clement, compassionate, humane, indulgent, kind, kindly, lenient, meek, merciful, mild, moderate, soft, tender, tender-hearted; docile, pacific, peaceable, placid, quiet, tame, temperate, tractable; bland, easy, gradual, light, slight; soft; high-born, noble, well-born; chivalrous, courteous, cultivated, knightly, polished, refined, well-bred.

gentlemanly *adj* civil, complaisant, courteous, cultivated, delicate, genteel, honorable, polite, refined, urbane, well-bred.

genuine *adj* authentic, honest, proper, pure, real, right, true, unadulterated, unalloyed, uncorrupted, veritable; frank, native, sincere, unaffected.

genus *n* class, group, kind, order, sort, type.

germ *n* embryo, nucleus, ovule, ovum, seed, seed-bud; bacterium, microbe, microorganism; beginning, cause, origin, rudiment, source.

germane *adj* akin, allied, cognate, related; apposite, appropriate, fitting, pertinent, relevant, suitable.

germinate *vb* bud, burgeon, develop, generate, grow, pollinate, push, shoot, sprout, vegetate.

gesture *vb* indicate, motion, signal, wave. • *n* action, attitude, gesticulation, gesturing, posture, sign, signal.

get *vb* achieve, acquire, attain, earn, gain, obtain, procure, receive, relieve, secure, win; finish, master, prepare; beget, breed, engender, generate, procreate.

gewgaw *n* bauble, gimcrack, gaud, kickshaw, knick-knack, plaything, trifle, toy, trinket.

ghastly *adj* cadaverous, corpse-like, death-like, deathly, ghostly, lurid, pale, pallid, wan; dismal, dreadful, fearful, frightful, grim, grisly, gruesome, hideous, horrible, shocking, terrible.

ghost *n* soul, spirit; apparition, phantom, revenant, shade, specter, spook, sprite, wraith.

giant *adj* colossal, enormous, Herculean, huge, large, monstrous, prodigious, vast. • *n* colossus, cyclops, Hercules, monster.

gibberish *n* babble, balderdash, drivel, gabble, gobbledygook, jabber, nonsense, prate, prating.

gibe, jibe *vb* deride, fleer, flout, jeer, mock, ridicule, scoff, sneer, taunt. • *n* ridicule, sneer, taunt.

giddiness *n* dizziness, head-spinning, vertigo.

giddy *adj* dizzy, head-spinning, vertiginous; careless, changeable, fickle, flighty, frivolous, hare-brained, headlong, heedless, inconstant, irresolute, light-headed, thoughtless, unsteady, vacillating, wild.

gift *n* alms, allowance, benefaction, bequest, bonus, boon, bounty, contribution, donation, dowry, endowment, favor, grant, gratuity, honorarium, largesse, legacy, offering, premium, present, prize, subscription, subsidy, tip; faculty, talent.

gifted *adj* able, capable, clever, ingenious, intelligent, inventive, sagacious, talented.

gigantic *adj* colossal, Cyclopean, enormous,

giant, herculean, huge, immense, prodigious, titanic, tremendous, vast.

giggle *vb, n* cackle, grin, laugh, snigger, snicker, titter.

gild *vb* adorn, beautify, bedeck, brighten, decorate, embellish, grace, illuminate.

gimcrack *adj* flimsy, frail, puny; base, cheap, paltry, poor. • *n* bauble, knick-knack, toy, trifle.

gird *vb* belt, girdle; begird, encircle, enclose, encompass, engird, environ, surround; brace, support. • *n* band, belt, cincture, girdle, girth, sash, waistband.

gist *n* basis, core, essence, force, ground, marrow, meaning, pith, point, substance.

give *vb* accord, bequeath, bestow, confer, devise, entrust, present; afford, contribute, donate, furnish, grant, proffer, spare, supply; communicate, impart; deliver, exchange, pay, requite; allow, permit, vouchsafe; emit, pronounce, render, utter; produce, yield; cause, occasion; apply, devote, surrender; bend, sink, recede, retire, retreat, yield.

glad *adj* delighted, gratified, happy, pleased, rejoicing, well-contented; animated, blithe, cheerful, cheery, elated, gladsome, jocund, joyful, joyous, light, light-hearted, merry, playful, radiant; animating, bright, cheering, exhilarating, gladdening, gratifying, pleasing.

gladden *vb* bless, cheer, delight, elate, enliven, exhilarate, gratify, please, rejoice.

gladiator *n* prize-fighter, sword-player, swordsman.

gladness *n* animation, cheerfulness, delight, gratification, happiness, joy, joyfulness, joyousness, pleasure.

gladsome *adj* airy, blithe, blithesome, cheerful, delighted, frolicsome, glad, gleeful, jocund, jolly, jovial, joyful, joyous, lighthearted, lively, merry, pleased, sportive, sprightly, vivacious.

glamor *n* bewitchment, charm, enchantment, fascination, spell, witchery.

glance *vb* coruscate, gleam, glisten, glister, glitter, scintillate, shine; dart, flit; gaze, glimpse, look, view. • *n* gleam, glitter; gleam, look, view.

glare *vb* dazzle, flame, flare, gleam, glisten, glitter, sparkle; frown, gaze, glower. • *n* flare, glitter.

glaring *adj* dazzling, gleaming, glistening, glittering; barefaced, conspicuous, extreme, manifest, notorious, open.

glassy *adj* brilliant, crystal, crystalline, gleaming, lucent, shining, transparent.

glaze *vb* burnish, calender, furbish, gloss, polish. • *n* coat, enamel, finish, glazing, polish, varnish.

gleam *vb* beam, coruscate, flash, glance, glimmer, glitter, shine, sparkle. • *n* beam, flash, glance, glimmer, glimmering, glow, ray; brightness, coruscation, flashing, gleaming, glitter, glittering, luster, splendor.

glean *vb* collect, cull, gather, get, harvest, pick, select.

glee *n* exhilaration, fun, gaiety, hilarity, jocularity, jollity, joviality, joy, liveliness, merriment, mirth, sportiveness, verve.

glib *adj* slippery, smooth; artful, facile, flippant, fluent, ready, talkative, voluble.

glide *vb* float, glissade, roll on, skate, skim, slide, slip; flow, lapse, run, roll. • *n* gliding, lapse, sliding, slip.

glimmer *vb* flash, flicker, gleam, glitter, shine, twinkle. • *n* beam, gleam, glimmering, ray; glance, glimpse.

glimpse *vb* espy, look, spot, view. • *n* flash, glance, glimmering, glint, look, sight.

glitter *vb* coruscate, flare, flash, glance, glare, gleam, glisten, glister, scintillate, shine, sparkle. • *n* beam, beaming, brightness, brilliancy, coruscation, gleam, glister, luster, radiance, scintillation, shine, sparkle, splendor.

gloaming *n* dusk, eventide, nightfall, twilight.

gloat *vb* exult, gaze, rejoice, stare, triumph.

globe *n* ball, earth, orb, sphere.

globular *adj* globate, globated, globeshaped, globose, globous, round, spheral, spheric, spherical.

globule *n* bead, drop, particle, spherule.

gloom *n* cloud, darkness, dimness, gloominess, obscurity, shade, shadow; cheerlessness, dejection, depression, despondency, downheartedness, dullness, melancholy, sadness.

gloomy *adj* dark, dim, dusky, obscure; cheerless, dismal, lowering, lurid; crestfallen, dejected, depressed, despondent, disheartened, dispirited, downcast, downhearted, glum, melancholy, morose, sad, sullen; depressing, disheartening, dispiriting, heavy, saddening.

glorify *vb* adore, bless, celebrate, exalt, extol, honor, laud, magnify, worship; adorn, brighten, elevate, ennoble, make bright.

glorious *adj* celebrated, conspicuous, distinguished, eminent, excellent, famed, famous, illustrious, pre-eminent, renowned; brilliant, bright, grand, magnificent, radiant, resplendent, splendid; consummate, exalted, high, lofty, noble, supreme.

glory *vb* boast, exult, vaunt. • *n* celebrity, distinction, eminence, fame, honor, illustriousness, praise, renown; brightness, brilliancy, effulgence, luster, pride, resplendence, splendor; exaltation, exceeding, gloriousness, greatness, grandeur, nobleness; bliss, happiness.

gloss[1] *vb* coat, color, disguise, extenuate, glaze, palliate, varnish, veneer, veil. • *n* coating, luster, polish, sheen, varnish, veneer; pretence, pretext.

gloss[2] *vb* annotate, comment, elucidate, explain, interpret. • *n* annotation, comment, commentary, elucidation, explanation, interpretation, note.

glove *n* gantlet, gauntlet, handwear, mitt, mitten; challenge.

glow *vb* incandesce, radiate, shine; blush, burn, flush, redden. • *n* blaze, brightness, brilliance, burning, incandescence, luminosity, reddening; ardor, bloom, enthusiasm, fervency, fervor, flush, impetuosity, vehemence, warmth.

glower *vb* frown, glare, lower, scowl, stare. • *n* frown, glare, scowl.

glum *adj* churlish, crabbed, crestfallen, cross-grained, crusty, depressed, frowning, gloomy, glowering, moody, morose, sour, spleenish, spleeny, sulky, sullen, surly.

glut *vb* block up, cloy, cram, gorge, satiate, stuff. • *n* excess, saturation, surfeit, surplus.

glutinous *adj* adhesive, clammy, cohesive, gluey, gummy, sticky, tenacious, viscid, viscous.

glutton *n* gobbler, gorger, gourmand, gormandizer, greedy-guts, lurcher, pig.

gnarled *adj* contorted, cross-grained, gnarly, knotted, knotty, snaggy, twisted.

go *vb* advance, move, pass, proceed, progress repair; act, operate; be about, extravagate, fare, journey, roam, rove, travel, walk, wend; depart, disappear, cease; elapse, extend, lead, reach, run; avail, concur, contribute, tend, serve; eventuate, fare, turn out; afford, bet, risk, wager. • *n* action, business, case, chance, circumstance, doings, turn; custom, fad,

fashion, mode, vogue; energy, endurance, power, stamina, verve, vivacity.

goad *vb* annoy, badger, harass, irritate, sting, worry; arouse, impel, incite, instigate, prod, spur, stimulate, urge. • *n* incentive, incitement, pressure, stimulation.

goal *n* bound, home, limit, mark, mete, post; end, object; aim, design, destination.

gobble *vb* bolt, devour, gorge, gulp, swallow.

goblin *n* apparition, elf, bogey, demon, gnome, hobgoblin, phantom, specter, sprite.

god *n* almighty, creator, deity, divinity, idol, Jehovah, omnipotence, providence.

godless *adj* atheistic, impious, irreligious, profane, ungodly, wicked.

godlike *adj* celestial, divine, heavenly, supernal.

godly *adj* devout, holy, pious, religious, righteous, saint-like, saintly.

godsend *n* fortune, gift, luck, present, windfall.

golden *adj* aureate, brilliant, bright, gilded, resplendent, shining, splendid; excellent, precious; auspicious, favorable, opportune, propitious; blessed, delightful, glorious, halcyon, happy.

good *adj* advantageous, beneficial, favorable, profitable, serviceable, useful; adequate, appropriate, becoming, convenient, fit, proper, satisfactory, suitable, well-adapted; decorous, dutiful, honest, just, pious, reliable, religious, righteous, true, upright, virtuous, well-behaved, worthy; admirable, capable, excellent, genuine, healthy, precious, sincere, sound, sterling, valid, valuable; benevolent, favorable, friendly, gracious, humane, kind, merciful, obliging, well-disposed; fair, honorable, immaculate, unblemished, unimpeachable, unimpeached, unsullied, untarnished; cheerful, companionable, lively, genial, social; able, competent, dextrous, expert, qualified, ready, skillful, thorough, well-qualified; credit-worthy; agreeable, cheering, gratifying, pleasant. • *n* advantage, benefit, boon, favor, gain, profit, utility; interest, prosperity, welfare, weal; excellence, righteousness, virtue, worth.

good breeding *n* affability, civility, courtesy, good manners, polish, politeness, urbanity.

goodbye *n* adieu, farewell, parting.

goodly *adj* beautiful, comely, good-looking, graceful; agreeable, considerate, desirable, happy, pleasant.

good-natured *adj* amiable, benevolent, friendly, kind, kind-hearted, kindly.

goodness *n* excellence, quality, value, worth; honesty, integrity, morality, principle, probity, righteousness, uprightness, virtue; benevolence, beneficence, benignity, good-will, humaneness, humanity, kindness.

goods *npl* belongings, chattels, effects, furniture, movables; commodities, merchandise, stock, wares.

goodwill *n* benevolence, kindness, good nature; ardor, earnestness, heartiness, willingness, zeal; custom, patronage.

gore *vb* horn, pierce, stab, wound.

gorge[1] *vb* bolt, devour, eat, feed, swallow; cram, fill, glut, gormandize, sate, satiate, stuff, surfeit. • *n* craw, crop, gullet, throat.

gorge[2] *n* canyon, defile, fissure, notch, ravine.

gorgeous *adj* bright, brilliant, dazzling, fine, glittering, grand, magnificent, resplendent, rich, shining, showy, splendid, superb.

Gorgon *n* bugaboo, fright, hobgoblin, hydra, ogre, spectre.

gory *adj* bloody, ensanguined, sanguinary.

gospel *n* creed, doctrine, message, news, revelation, tidings.

gossip *vb* chat, cackle, clack, gabble, prate, prattle, tattle. • *n* babbler, busybody, chatterer, gossipmonger, newsmonger, quidnunc, tale-bearer, tattler, tell-tale; cackle, chat, chit-chat, prate, prattle, tattle.

gourmet *n* connoisseur, epicure, epicurean.

govern *vb* administer, conduct, direct, manage, regulate, reign, rule, superintend, supervise; guide, pilot, steer; bridle, check, command, control, curb, restrain, rule, sway.

government *n* autonomy, command, conduct, control, direction, discipline, dominion, guidance, management, regulation, restraint, rule, rulership, sway; administration, cabinet, commonwealth, polity, sovereignty, state.

governor *n* commander, comptroller, director, head, headmaster, manager, overseer, ruler, superintendent, supervisor; chief magistrate, executive; guardian, instructor, tutor.

grab *vb* capture, clutch, seize, snatch.

grace *vb* adorn, beautify, deck, decorate, embellish; dignify, honor. • *n* benignity, condescension, favor, good-will, kindness, love; devotion, efficacy, holiness, love, piety, religion, sanctity, virtue; forgiveness, mercy, pardon, reprieve; accomplishment, attractiveness, charm, elegance, polish, propriety, refinement; beauty, comeliness, ease, gracefulness, symmetry; blessing, petition, thanks.

graceful *adj* beautiful, becoming, comely, easy, elegant; flowing, natural, rounded, unlabored; appropriate; felicitous, happy, tactful.

graceless *adj* abandoned, corrupt, depraved, dissolute, hardened, incorrigible, irreclaimable, lost, obdurate, profligate, reprobate, repugnant, shameless.

gracious *adj* beneficent, benevolent, benign, benignant, compassionate, condescending, favorable, friendly, gentle, good-natured, kind, kindly, lenient, merciful, mild, tender; affable, civil, courteous, easy, familiar, polite.

grade *vb* arrange, classify, group, order, rank, sort. • *n* brand, degree, intensity, stage, step, rank; gradient, incline, slope.

gradual *adj* approximate, continuous, gentle, progressive, regular, slow, successive.

graduate *vb* adapt, adjust, proportion, regulate. • *n* alumna, alumnus, laureate, postgraduate.

graft *vb* ingraft, inoculate, insert, transplant. • *n* bud, scion, shoot, slip, sprout; corruption, favoritism, influence, nepotism.

grain *n* kernel, ovule, seed; cereals, corn, grist; atom, bit, glimmer, jot, particle, scintilla, scrap, shadow, spark, tittle, trace, whit; disposition, fiber, humor, temper, texture; color, dye, hue, shade, stain, texture, tincture, tinge.

granary *n* corn-house, garner, grange, storehouse.

grand *adj* august, dignified, elevated, eminent, exalted, great, illustrious, lordly, majestic, princely, stately, sublime; fine, glorious, gorgeous, magnificent, pompous, lofty, noble, splendid, superb; chief, leading, main, pre-eminent, principal, superior.

grandee *n* lord, noble, nobleman.

grandeur *n* elevation, greatness, immensity, impressiveness, loftiness, vastness; augustness, dignity, eminence, glory, magnificence, majesty, nobility, pomp, splendor, state, stateliness.

grandiloquent *adj* bombastic, declamatory, high-minded, high-sounding, inflated, pompous, rhetorical, stilted, swelling, tumid, turgid.

grant *vb* accord, admit, allow, sanction; cede, concede, give, impart, indulge; bestow, confer, deign, invest, vouchsafe; convey, transfer, yield. • *n* admission, allowance, benefaction, bestowal, boon, bounty, concession, donation, endowment, gift, indulgence, largesse, present; conveyance, cession.

graphic *adj* descriptive, diagrammatic, figural, figurative, forcible, lively, pictorial, picturesque, striking, telling, vivid, well-delineated, well-drawn.

grapple *vb* catch, clutch, grasp, grip, hold, hug, seize, tackle, wrestle.

grasp *vb* catch, clasp, clinch, clutch, grapple, grip, seize; comprehend, understand. • *n* clasp, grip, hold; comprehension, power, reach, scope, understanding.

grasping *adj* acquisitive, avaricious, covetous, exacting, greedy, rapacious, sordid, tight-fisted.

grate *vb* abrade, rub, scrape, triturate; comminute, rasp; creak, fret, grind, jar, vex. • *n* bars, grating, latticework, screen; basket, fire bed.

grateful *adj* appreciative, beholden, indebted, obliged, sensible, thankful; pleasant, welcome.

gratification *n* gratifying, indulgence, indulging, pleasing, satisfaction, satisfying; delight, enjoyment, fruition, pleasure, reward.

gratify *vb* delight, gladden, please; humor, fulfill, grant, indulge, requite, satisfy.

gratifying *adj* agreeable, delightful, grateful, pleasing, welcome.

grating *adj* disagreeable, displeasing, harsh, irritating, offensive. • *n* grate, partition.

gratis *adv* freely, gratuitously.

gratitude *n* goodwill, gratitude, indebtedness, thankfulness.

gratuitous *adj* free, spontaneous, unrewarded, voluntary; assumed, baseless, groundless, unfounded, unwarranted, wanton.

gratuity *n* benefaction, bounty, charity, donation, endowment, gift, grant, largesse, present.

grave[1] *n* crypt, mausoleum, ossuary, pit, sepulcher, sepulture, tomb, vault.

grave[2] *adj* cogent, heavy, important, momentous, ponderous, pressing, serious, weighty; dignified, sage, sedate, serious, slow, solemn, staid, thoughtful; dull, grim, plain, quiet, sober, somber, subdued; cruel, hard, harsh, severe; despicable, dire, dismal, gross, heinous, infamous, outrageous, scandalous, shameful, shocking; heavy, hollow, low, low-pitched, sepulchral.

grave[3] *vb* engrave, impress, imprint, infix; carve, chisel, cut, sculpt.

gravel *vb* bewilder, embarrass, nonplus, perplex, pose, puzzle, stagger. • *n* ballast, grit, sand, shingle.

graveyard *n* burial ground, cemetery, churchyard, god's acre, mortuary, necropolis.

gravity *n* heaviness, weight; demureness, sedateness, seriousness, sobriety, thoughtfulness; importance, moment, momentousness, weightiness.

graze *vb* brush, glance, scrape, scratch; abrade, shave, skim; browse, crop, feed, pasture. • *n* abrasion, bruise, scrape, scratch.

great *adj* ample, big, bulky, Cyclopean, enormous, gigantic, Herculean, huge, immense, large, pregnant, vast; decided, excessive, high, much, pronounced; countless, numerous; chief, considerable, grand, important, leading, main, pre-eminent, principal, superior, weighty; celebrated, distinguished, eminent, exalted, excellent, famed, famous, far-famed, illustrious, noted, prominent, renowned; august, dignified, elevated, grand, lofty, majestic, noble, sublime; chivalrous, generous, high-minded, magnanimous; fine, magnificent, rich, sumptuous.

greatness *n* bulk, dimensions, largeness, magnitude, size; distinction, elevation, eminence, fame, importance, renown; augustness, dignity, grandeur, majesty, loftiness, nobility, nobleness, sublimity; chivalry, generosity, magnanimity, spirit.

greed, greediness *n* gluttony, hunger, omnivorousness, ravenousness, voracity; avidity, covetousness, desire, eagerness, longing; avarice, cupidity, graspingness, grasping, rapacity, selfishness.

greedy *adj* devouring, edacious, gluttonous, insatiable, insatiate, rapacious, ravenous, voracious; desirous, eager; avaricious, grasping, selfish.

green *adj* aquamarine, emerald, olive,

verdant, verdure, viridescent, viridian; blooming, flourishing, fresh, undecayed; fresh, new, recent; immature, unfledged, unripe; callow, crude, inexpert, ignorant, inexperienced, raw, unskillful, untrained, verdant, young; unseasoned; conservationist, ecological, environmentalist. • *n* common, grass plot, lawn, sward, turf, verdure.

greenhorn *n* beginner, novice, tyro.

greet *vb* accost, address, complement, hail, receive, salute, welcome.

greeting *n* compliment, salutation, salute, welcome.

grief *n* affliction, agony, anguish, bitterness, distress, dole, heartbreak, misery, regret, sadness, sorrow, suffering, tribulation, mourning, woe; grievance, trial; disaster, failure, mishap.

grievance *n* burden, complaint, hardship, injury, oppression, wrong; affliction, distress, grief, sorrow, trial, woe.

grieve *vb* afflict, aggrieve, agonize, discomfort, distress, hurt, oppress, pain, sadden, wound; bewail, deplore, mourn, lament, regret, sorrow, suffer.

grievous *adj* afflicting, afflictive, burdensome, deplorable, distressing, heavy, lamentable, oppressive, painful, sad, sorrowful; baleful, baneful, calamitous, destructive, detrimental, hurtful, injurious, mischievous, noxious, troublesome; aggravated, atrocious, dreadful, flagitious, flagrant, gross, heinous, iniquitous, intense, intolerable, severe, outrageous, wicked.

grill *vb* broil, griddle, roast, toast; sweat; cross-examine, interrogate, question; torment, torture. • *n* grating, gridiron; cross-examination, cross-questioning.

grim *adj* cruel, ferocious, fierce, harsh, relentless, ruthless, savage, stern, unyielding; appalling, dire, dreadful, fearful, frightful, grisly, hideous, horrid, horrible, terrific.

grimace *vb, n* frown, scowl, smirk, sneer.

grime *n* dirt, filth, foulness, smut.

grimy *adj* begrimed, defiled, dirty, filthy, foul, soiled, sullied, unclean.

grind *vb* bruise, crunch, crush, grate, grit, pulverize, rub, triturate; sharpen, whet; afflict, harass, oppress, persecute, plague, trouble. • *n* chore, drudgery, labor, toil.

grip *vb* clasp, clutch, grasp, hold, seize. • *n* clasp, clutch, control, domination, grasp, hold.

grisly *adj* appalling, frightful, dreadful, ghastly, grim, gray, hideous, horrible, horrid, terrible, terrific.

grit *vb* clench, grate, grind. • *n* bran, gravel, pebbles, sand; courage, decision, determination, firmness, perseverance, pluck, resolution, spirit.

groan *vb* complain, lament, moan, whine; creak. • *n* cry, moan, whine; complaint; grouse, grumble.

groom *vb* clean, dress, tidy; brush, tend; coach, educate, nurture, train. • *n* equerry, hostler, manservant, ostler, servant, stable-hand, valet, waiter.

groove *n* channel, cut, furrow, rabbet, rebate, recess, rut, scoring; routine.

gross *vb* accumulate, earn, make. • *adj* big, bulky, burly, fat, great, large; dense, dull, stupid, thick; beastly, broad, carnal, coarse, crass, earthy, impure, indelicate, licentious, low, obscene, unbecoming, unrefined, unseemly, vulgar, rough, sensual; aggravated, brutal, enormous, flagrant, glaring, grievous, manifest, obvious, palpable, plain, outrageous, shameful; aggregate, entire, total, whole. • *n* aggregate, bulk, total, whole.

grossness *n* bigness, bulkiness, greatness; density, thickness; coarseness, ill-breeding, rudeness, vulgarity; bestiality, brutality, carnality, coarseness, impurity, indelicacy, licentiousness, sensuality.

grotesque *adj* bizarre, extravagant, fanciful, fantastic, incongruous, odd, strange, unnatural, whimsical, wild; absurd, antic, burlesque, ludicrous, ridiculous.

ground *vb* fell, place; base, establish, fix, found, set; instruct, train. • *n* area, clod, distance, earth, loam, mold, sod, soil, turf; country, domain, land, region, territory; acres, estate, field, property; base, basis, foundation, groundwork, support; account, consideration, excuse, gist, motive, opinion, reason.

groundless *adj* baseless, causeless, false, gratuitous, idle, unauthorized, unfounded, unjustifiable, unsolicited, unsought, unwarranted.

grounds *npl* deposit, dregs, grouts, lees, precipitate, sediment, settlings; accounts, arguments, considerations, reasons, support; campus, gardens, lawns, premises, yard.

group *vb* arrange, assemble, dispose, order. • *n* aggregation, assemblage, assembly, body, combination, class, clump, cluster, collection, order.

grove n copse, glade, spinney, thicket, wood, woodland.

grovel vb cower, crawl, creep, cringe, fawn, flatter, sneak.

groveling adj creeping, crouching, squat; abject, base, beggarly, cringing, fawning, low, mean, servile, slavish, sneaking, undignified, unworthy, vile.

grow vb enlarge, expand, extend, increase, swell; arise, burgeon, develop, germinate, shoot, sprout, vegetate; advance, extend, improve, progress, thrive, wax; cultivate, produce, raise.

growl vb complain, croak, find fault, gnarl, groan, grumble, lament, murmur, snarl. • n croak, grown, snarl; complaint.

growth n augmentation, development, expansion, extension, growing, increase; burgeoning, excrescence, formation, germination, pollution, shooting, sprouting, vegetation; cultivation, produce, product, production; advance, advancement, development, improvement, progress; adulthood, maturity.

grub vb clear, dig, eradicate, root. • n caterpillar, larvae, maggot; drudge, plodder.

grudge vb begrudge, envy, repine; complain, grieve, murmur. • n aversion, dislike, enmity, grievance, hate, hatred, illwill, malevolence, malice, pique, rancor, resentment, spite, venom.

gruff adj bluff, blunt, brusque, churlish, discourteous, grumpy, harsh, impolite, rough, rude, rugged, surly, uncivil, ungracious.

grumble vb croak, complain, murmur, repine; gnarl, growl, snarl; roar, rumble. • n growl, murmur, complaint, roar, rumble.

grumpy adj crabbed, cross, glum, moody, morose, sour, sullen, surly.

guarantee vb assure, insure, pledge, secure, warrant. • n assurance, pledge, security, surety, warrant, warranty.

guard vb defend, keep, patrol, protect, safeguard, save, secure, shelter, shield, watch. • n aegis, bulwark, custody, defense, palladium, protection, rampart, safeguard, security, shield; keeper, guardian, patrol, sentinel, sentry, warden, watch, watchman; conduct, convoy, escort; attention, care, caution, circumspection, heed, watchfulness.

guarded adj careful, cautious, circumspect, reserved, reticent, wary, watchful.

guardian n custodian, defender, guard, keeper, preserver, protector, trustee, warden.

guerdon n recompense, remuneration, requital, reward.

guess vb conjecture, divine, mistrust, surmise, suspect; fathom, find out, penetrate, solve; believe, fancy, hazard, imagine, reckon, suppose, think. • n conjecture, divination, notion, supposition, surmise.

guest n caller, company, visitant.

guidance n conduct, control, direction, escort, government, lead, leadership, pilotage, steering.

guide vb conduct, escort, lead, pilot; control, direct, govern, manage, preside, regulate, rule, steer, superintend, supervise. • n cicerone, conductor, director, monitor, pilot; adviser, counselor, instructor, mentor; clew, directory, index, key, thread; guidebook, itinerary, landmark.

guild n association, brotherhood, company, corporation, fellowship, fraternity, society, union.

guile n art, artfulness, artifice, craft, cunning, deceit, deception, duplicity, fraud, knavery, ruse, subtlety, treachery, trickery, wiles, wiliness.

guileless adj artless, candid, frank, honest, ingenuous, innocent, open, pure, simpleminded, sincere, straightforward, truthful, undesigning, unsophisticated.

guilt n blame, criminality, culpability, guiltless; ill-desert, iniquity, offensiveness, wickedness, wrong; crime, offence, sin.

guiltless adj blameless, immaculate, innocent, pure, sinless, spotless, unpolluted, unspotted, unsullied, untarnished.

guilty adj criminal, culpable, evil, sinful, wicked, wrong.

guise n appearance, aspect, costume, dress, fashion, figure, form, garb, manner, mode, shape; air, behavior, demeanor, mien; cover, custom, disguise, habit, pretence, pretext, practice.

gulf n abyss, chasm, opening; bay, inlet; whirlpool.

gull vb beguile, cheat, circumvent, cozen, deceive, dupe, hoax, overreach, swindle, trick. • n cheat, deception, hoax, imposition, fraud, trick; cat's paw, dupe.

gullibility n credulity, naiveness, naivety, overtrustfulness, simplicity, unsophistication.

gullible adj confiding, credulous, naive, overtrustful, simple, unsophisticated, unsuspicious.

gumption *n* ability, astuteness, cleverness, capacity, common sense, discernment, penetration, power, sagacity, shrewdness, skill; courage, guts, spirit.

gun *n* blunderbuss, cannon, carbine, firearm, musket, pistol, revolver, rifle, shotgun.

gurgle *vb* babble, bubble, murmur, purl, ripple. • *n* babbling, murmur, ripple.

gush *vb* burst, flood, flow, pour, rush, spout, stream; emotionalize, sentimentalize. • *n* flow, jet, onrush, rush, spurt, surge; effusion, effusiveness, loquacity, loquaciousness, talkativeness.

gushing *adj* flowing, issuing, rushing; demonstrative, effusive, sentimental.

gust *vb* blast, blow, puff. • *n* blast, blow, squall; burst, fit, outburst, paroxysm.

gusto *n* enjoyment, gust, liking, pleasure, relish, zest.

gusty *adj* blustering, blustery, puffy, squally, stormy, tempestuous, unsteady, windy.

gut *vb* destroy, disembowel, embowel, eviscerate, paunch. • *n* bowels, entrails, intestines, inwards, viscera.

gutter *n* channel, conduit, kennel, pipe, tube.

guttural *adj* deep, gruff, hoarse, thick, throaty.

guy *vb* caricature, mimic, ridicule. • *n* boy, man, person; dowdy, eccentric, fright, scarecrow.

guzzle *vb* carouse, drink, gorge, gormandize, quaff, swill, tipple, tope.

gyrate *vb* revolve, rotate, spin, whirl.

H

habiliment *n* apparel, attire, clothes, costume, dress, garb, garment, habit, raiment, robes, uniform, vesture, vestment.

habit *vb* accouter, array, attire, clothe, dress, equip, robe. • *n* condition, constitution, temperament; addiction, custom, habitude, manner, practice, rule, usage, way, wont; apparel, costume, dress, garb, habiliment.

habitation *n* abode, domicile, dwelling, headquarters, home, house, lodging, quarters, residence.

habitual *adj* accustomed, common, confirmed, customary, everyday, familiar, inveterate, ordinary, regular, routine, settled, usual, wonted.

habituate *vb* accustom, familiarize, harden, inure, train, use.

habitude *n* custom, practice, usage, wont.

hack[1] *vb* chop, cut, hew, mangle, mutilate, notch; cough, rasp. • *n* cut, cleft, incision, notch; cough, rasp.

hack[2] *vb* ride. • *adj* hired, mercenary; banal, hackneyed, pedestrian, uninspired, unoriginal. • *n* horse, nag, pony; hireling, mercenary; journalist, scribbler, writer.

hackneyed *adj* banal, common, commonplace, overworked, pedestrian, stale, threadbare, trite.

hag *n* beldame, crone, fury, harridan, jezebel, she-monster, shrew, termagant, virago, vixen, witch.

haggard *adj* intractable, refractory, unruly, untamed, wild, wayward; careworn, emaciated, gaunt, ghastly, lank, lean, meager, raw, spare, thin, wasted, worn.

haggle *vb* argue, bargain, cavil, chaffer, dispute, higgle, stickle; annoy, badger, bait, fret, harass, tease, worry.

hail[1] *vb* acclaim, greet, salute, welcome; accost, address, call, hallo, signal. • *n* greeting, salute.

hail[2] *vb* assail, bombard, rain, shower, storm, volley. • *n* bombardment, rain, shower, storm, volley.

halcyon *adj* calm, golden, happy, palmy, placid, peaceful, quiet, serene, still, tranquil, unruffled, undisturbed.

hale *adj* hardy, healthy, hearty, robust, sound, strong, vigorous, well.

halfwit *n* blockhead, dunce, moron, simpleton.

halfwitted *adj* doltish, dull, dull-witted, feeble-minded, foolish, sappy, shallow, silly, simple, soft, stolid, stupid, thick.

hall *n* chamber, corridor, entrance, entry, hallway, lobby, passage, vestibule; manor, manor-house; auditorium, lecture-room.

halloo *vb* call, cry, shout. • *n* call, cry, hallo, holla, hollo, shout.

hallow *vb* consecrate, dedicate, devote, revere, sanctify, solemnize; enshrine, honor, respect, reverence, venerate.

hallowed *adj* blessed, holy, honored, revered, sacred.

hallucination *n* blunder, error, fallacy, mistake; aberration, delusion, illusion, phantasm, phantasy, self-deception, vision.

halo *n* aura, aureole, glory, nimbus.

halt[1] *vb* cease, desist, hold, rest, stand, stop. • *n* end, impasse, pause, standstill, stop.

halt[2] *vb* hesitate, pause, stammer, waver; falter, hobble, limp. • *adj* crippled, disabled, lame. • *n* hobble, limp.

hammer *vb* beat, forge, form, shape; excogitate, contrive, invent.

hammer and tongs *adv* earnestly, energetically, resolutely, strenuously, vigorously, zealously.

hamper *vb* bind, clog, confine, curb, embarrass, encumber, entangle, fetter, hinder, impede, obstruct, prevent, restrain, restrict, shackle, trammel. • *n* basket, box, crate, picnic basket; embarrassment, encumbrance, fetter, handicap, impediment, obstruction, restraint, trammel.

hand *vb* deliver, give, present, transmit; conduct, guide, lead. • *n* direction, part, side; ability, dexterity, faculty, skill, talent; course, inning, management, turn; agency, intervention, participation, share; control, possession, power; artificer, artisan, craftsman, employee, laborer, operative, workman; index, indicator, pointer; chirography, handwriting.

handbook *n* guidebook, manual.

handcuff *vb* bind, fetter, manacle, shackle. • *n* fetter, manacle, shackle.

handful *n* fistful, maniple, smattering.

handicap *vb* encumber, hamper, hinder, restrict. • *n* disadvantage, encumbrance, hampering, hindrance, restriction.

handicraft *n* hand manufacture, handwork, workmanship.

handle *vb* feel, finger, manhandle, paw, touch; direct, manage, manipulate, use, wield; discourse, discuss, treat. • *n* haft, helve, hilt, stock.

handsome *adj* admirable, comely, fine-looking, stately, well-formed, well-proportioned; appropriate, suitable, becoming, easy, graceful; generous, gracious, liberal, magnanimous, noble; ample, large, plentiful, sufficient.

handy *adj* adroit, clever, dextrous, expert, ready, skillful, skilled; close, convenient, near.

hang *vb* attach, swing; execute, truss; decline, drop, droop, incline; adorn, drape; dangle, depend, impend, suspend; rely; cling, loiter, rest, stick; float, hover, pay.

hangdog *adj* ashamed, base, blackguard, low, villainous, scurvy, sneaking.

hanger-on *n* dependant, minion, parasite, vassal.

hanker *vb* covet, crave, desire, hunger, long, lust, want, yearn.

hap *n* accident, chance, fate, fortune, lot.

haphazard *adj* aimless, chance, random.

hapless *adj* ill-fated, ill-starred, luckless, miserable, unfortunate, unhappy, unlucky, wretched.

happen *vb* befall, betide, chance, come, occur.

happily *adv* fortunately, luckily; agreeably, delightfully, prosperously, successfully.

happiness *n* brightness, cheerfulness, delight, gaiety, joy, light-heartedness, merriment, pleasure; beatitude, blessedness, bliss, felicity, enjoyment, welfare, well-being.

happy *adj* blessed, blest, blissful, cheerful, contented, joyful, joyous, light-hearted, merry; charmed, delighted, glad, gladdened, gratified, pleased; fortunate, lucky, prosperous, successful; able, adroit, apt, dextrous, expert, ready, skillful; befitting, felicitous, opportune, pertinent, seasonable, well-timed; auspicious, bright, favorable, propitious.

harangue *vb* address, declaim, spout. • *n* address, bombast, declamation, oration, rant, screed, speech, tirade.

harass *vb* exhaust, fag, fatigue, jade, tire, weary; annoy, badger, distress, gall, heckle, disturb, harry, molest, pester, plague, tantalize, tease, torment, trouble, vex, worry.

harbor *vb* protect, lodge, shelter; cherish, entertain, foster, indulge. • *n* asylum, cover, refuge, resting place, retreat, sanctuary, shelter; anchorage, destination, haven, port.

hard *adj* adamantine, compact, firm, flinty, impenetrable, marble, rigid, solid, resistant, stony, stubborn, unyielding; difficult, intricate, knotty, perplexing, puzzling; arduous, exacting, fatiguing, laborious, toilsome, wearying; austere, callous, cruel, exacting, hard-hearted, incorrigible, inflexible, insensible, insensitive, obdurate, oppressive, reprobate, rigorous, severe, unfeeling, unkind, unsusceptible, unsympathetic, unyielding, untender; calamitous, disagreeable, distressing, grievous, painful, unpleasant; acid, alcoholic, harsh, rough, sour; excessive, intemperate. • *adv* close, near; diligently, earnestly, energetically, incessantly, laboriously; distressfully, painfully, rigorously, severely; forcibly, vehemently, violently.

harden *vb* accustom, discipline, form, habituate, inure, season, train; brace, fortify, indurate, nerve, steel, stiffen, strengthen.

hardened *adj* annealed, case-hardened, tempered, indurated; abandoned, accustomed, benumbed, callous, confirmed, deadened, depraved, habituated, impenitent, incorrigible, inured, insensible, irreclaimable, lost, obdurate, reprobate, seared, seasoned, steeled, trained, unfeeling.

hard-headed *adj* astute, collected, cool, intelligent, sagacious, shrewd, well-balanced, wise.

hardhearted *adj* cruel, fell, implacable, inexorable, merciless, pitiless, relentless, ruthless, unfeeling, uncompassionate, unmerciful, unpitying, unrelenting.

hardihood *n* audacity, boldness, bravery, courage, decision, firmness, fortitude, intrepidity, manhood, msettle, pluck, resolution, stoutness; assurance, audacity, brass, effrontery, impudence.

hardly *adv* barely, scarcely; cruelly, harshly, rigorously, roughly, severely, unkindly.

hardship *n* fatigue, toil, weariness; affliction, burden, calamity, grievance, hardness, injury, misfortune, privation, suffering, trial, trouble.

hardy *adj* enduring, firm, hale, healthy, hearty, inured, lusty, rigorous, robust, rugged, sound, stout, strong, sturdy, tough; bold, brave, courageous, daring, heroic, intrepid, manly, resolute, stout-hearted, valiant.

harebrained *adj* careless, changeable, flighty, giddy, harum-scarum, headlong, heedless, rash, reckless, unsteady, volatile, wild.

hark *interj* attend, hear, hearken, listen.

harlequin *n* antic, buffoon, clown, droll, fool, jester, punch, fool.

harm *vb* damage, hurt, injure, scathe; abuse, desecrate, ill-use, ill-treat, maltreat, molest. • *n* damage, detriment, disadvantage, hurt, injury, mischief, misfortune, prejudice, wrong.

harmful *adj* baneful, detrimental, disadvantageous, hurtful, injurious, mischievous, noxious, pernicious, prejudicial.

harmless *adj* innocent, innocuous, innoxious; inoffensive, safe, unoffending.

harmonious *adj* concordant, consonant, harmonic; dulcet, euphonious, mellifluous, melodious, musical, smooth, tuneful; comfortable, congruent, consistent, correspondent, orderly, symmetrical; agreeable, amicable, brotherly, cordial, fraternal, friendly, neighborly.

harmonize *vb* adapt, attune, reconcile, unite; accord, agree, blend, chime, comport, conform, correspond, square, sympathize, tally, tune.

harmony *n* euphony, melodiousness, melody; accord, accordance, agreement, chime, concord, concordance, consonance, order, unison; adaptation, congruence, congruity, consistency, correspondence, fairness, smoothness, suitableness; amity, friendship, peace.

harness *vb* hitch, tackle. • *n* equipment, gear, tackle, tackling; accouterments, armor, array, mail, mounting.

harp *vb* dwell, iterate, reiterate, renew, repeat.

harping *n* dwelling, iteration, reiteration, repetition.

harrow *vb* harass, lacerate, rend, tear, torment, torture, wound.

harry *vb* devastate, pillage, plunder, raid, ravage, rob; annoy, chafe, disturb, fret, gall, harass, harrow, incommode, pester, plague, molest, tease, torment, trouble, vex, worry.

harsh *adj* acid, acrid, astringent, biting, caustic, corrosive, crabbed, rough, sharp, sour, tart; cacophonous, discordant, grating, jarring, metallic, raucous, strident, unmelodious; abusive, austere, crabbed, crabby, cruel, disagreeable, hard, ill-natured, ill-tempered, morose, rigorous, severe, stern, unfeeling; beurish, bluff, blunt, brutal, gruff, rude, uncivil, ungracious.

harshness *n* roughness; acerbity, asperity, austerity, churlishness, crabbedness, hardness, ill-nature, ill-temper, moroseness, rigor, severity, sternness, unkindness; bluffness, bluntness, churlishness, gruffness, incivility, ungraciousness, rudeness.

harum-scarum *adj* hare-brained, precipitate, rash, reckless, volatile, wild.

harvest *vb* gather, glean, reap. • *n* crops, produce, yield; consequence, effect, issue, outcome, produce, result.

haste *n* alacrity, celerity, dispatch, expedition, nimbleness, promptitude, quickness, rapidity, speed, urgency, velocity; flurry, hurry, hustle, impetuosity, precipitateness, precipitation, press, rashness, rush, vehemence.

hasten *vb* haste, hurry; accelerate, dispatch, expedite, precipitate, press, push, quicken, speed, urge.

hasty *adj* brisk, fast, fleet, quick, rapid, speedy, swift; cursory, hurried, passing, slight, superficial; ill-advised, rash, reckless; headlong, helter-skelter, pell-mell, precipitate; abrupt, choleric, excitable, fiery, fretful, hot-headed, irascible, irritable, passionate, peevish, peppery, pettish, petulant, testy, touchy, waspish.

hatch *vb* brew, concoct, contrive, excogitate, design, devise, plan, plot, project, scheme; breed, incubate.

hate *vb* abhor, abominate, detest, dislike, execrate, loathe, nauseate. • *n* abomination, animosity, antipathy, detestation, dislike, enmity, execration, hatred, hostility, loathing.

hateful *adj* malevolent, malicious, malign, malignant, rancorous, spiteful; abhorrent, abominable, accursed, damnable, detestable, execrable, horrid, odious, shocking; disgusting, foul, loathsome, nauseous, obnoxious, offensive, repellent, repugnant, repulsive, revolting, vile.

hatred *n* animosity, enmity, hate, hostility, ill-will, malevolence, malice, malignity, odium, rancor; abhorrence, abomination, antipathy, aversion, detestation, disgust, execration, horror, loathing, repugnance, revulsion.

haughtiness *n* arrogance, contempt, contemptuousness, disdain, hauteur, insolence, loftiness, pride, self-importance, snobbishness, stateliness, superciliousness.

haughty *adj* arrogant, assuming, contemptuous, disdainful, imperious, insolent, lofty, lordly, overbearing, overweening, proud, scornful, snobbish, supercilious.

haul *vb* drag, draw, lug, pull, tow, trail, tug. • *n* heaving, pull, tug; booty, harvest, takings, yield.

haunt *vb* frequent, resort; follow, importune; hover, inhabit, obsess. • *n* den, resort, retreat.

hauteur *n* arrogance, contempt, contemptuousness, disdain, haughtiness, insolence, loftiness, pride, self-importance, stateliness, superciliousness.

have *vb* cherish, exercise, experience, keep, hold, occupy, own, possess; acquire, gain, get, obtain, receive; accept, take.

haven *n* asylum, refuge, retreat, shelter; anchorage, harbor, port.

havoc *n* carnage, damage, desolation, destruction, devastation, ravage, ruin, slaughter, waste, wreck.

hawk-eyed *adj* eagle-eyed, sharp-sighted.

hazard *vb* adventure, risk, venture; endanger, imperil, jeopardize. • *n* accident, casualty, chance, contingency, event, fortuity, stake; danger, jeopardy, peril, risk, venture.

hazardous *adj* dangerous, insecure, perilous, precarious, risky, uncertain, unsafe.

haze *n* fog, har, mist, smog; cloud, dimness, fume, miasma, obscurity, pall.

hazy *adj* foggy, misty; cloudy, dim, nebulous, obscure; confused, indefinite, indistinct, uncertain, vague.

head *vb* command, control, direct, govern, guide, lead, rule; aim, point, tend; beat, excel, outdo, precede, surpass. • *adj* chief, first, grand, highest, leading, main, principal; adverse, contrary. • *n* acme, summit, top; beginning, commencement, origin, rise, source; chief, chieftain, commander, director, leader, master, principal, superintendent, superior; intellect, mind, thought, understanding; branch, category, class, department, division, section, subject, topic; brain, crown, headpiece, intellect, mind, thought, understanding; cape, headland, point, promontory.

headiness *n* hurry, precipitation, rashness; obstinacy, stubbornness.

headless *adj* acephalous, beheaded; leaderless, undirected; headstrong, heady, imprudent, obstinate, rash, senseless, stubborn.

headlong *adj* dangerous, hasty, heady, impulsive, inconsiderate, perilous, precipitate, rash, reckless, ruinous, thoughtless; perpendicular, precipitous, sheer, steep. • *adv* hastily, headfirst, helter-skelter, hurriedly, precipitately, rashly, thoughtlessly.

headstone *n* cornerstone, gravestone.

headstrong *adj* cantankerous, cross-grained, dogged, forward, headless, heady, intractable, obstinate, self-willed, stubborn, ungovernable, unruly, violent, wayward.

heady *adj* hasty, headlong, impetuous, impulsive, inconsiderate, precipitate, rash, reckless, rushing, stubborn, thoughtless; exciting, inebriating, inflaming, intoxicating, spirituous, strong.

heal *vb* amend, cure, remedy, repair, restore; compose, harmonize, reconcile, settle, soothe.

healing *adj* curative, palliative, remedial,

restoring, restorative; assuaging, assuasive, comforting, composing, gentle, lenitive, mild, soothing.

health *n* healthfulness, robustness, salubrity, sanity, soundness, strength, tone, vigor.

healthy *adj* active, hale, hearty, lusty, sound, vigorous, well; bracing, healthful, health-giving, hygienic, invigorating, nourishing, salubrious, salutary, wholesome.

heap *vb* accumulate, augment, amass, collect, overfill, pile up, store. • *n* accumulation, collection, cumulus, huddle, lot, mass, mound, pile, stack.

hear *vb* eavesdrop, hearken, heed, listen, overhear; ascertain, discover, gather, learn, understand; examine, judge.

heart *n* bosom, breast; center, core, essence, interior, kernel, marrow, meaning, pith; affection, benevolence, character, disposition, feeling, inclination, love, mind, passion, purpose, will; affections, ardor, emotion, feeling, love; boldness, courage, fortitude, resolution, spirit.

heartache *n* affliction, anguish, bitterness, distress, dole, grief, heartbreak, sorrow, woe.

heartbroken *adj* broken-hearted, cheerless, comfortless, desolate, disconsolate, forlorn, inconsolable, miserable, woebegone, wretched.

hearten *vb* animate, assure, cheer, comfort, console, embolden, encourage, enhearten, incite, inspire, inspirit, reassure, stimulate.

heartfelt *adj* cordial, deep, deep-felt, hearty, profound, sincere, warm.

hearth *n* fireplace, fireside, forge, hearthstone.

heartily *adv* abundantly, completely, cordially, earnestly, freely, largely, sincerely, vigorously.

heartless *adj* brutal, cold, cruel, hard, harsh, merciless, pitiless, unfeeling, unsympathetic; spiritless, timid, timorous, uncourageous.

heart-rending *adj* affecting, afflicting, anguishing, crushing, distressing.

hearty *adj* cordial, deep, earnest, fervent, heartfelt, profound, sincere, true, unfeigned, warm; active, animated, energetic, fit, vigorous, zealous; convivial, hale, healthy, robust, sound, strong, warm; abundant, full, heavy; nourishing, nutritious, rich.

heat *vb* excite, flush, inflame; animate, rouse, stimulate, stir. • *n* calorie, caloricity, torridity, warmth; excitement, fever, flush, impetuosity, passion, vehemence, violence; ardor, earnestness, fervency, fervor, glow, intensity, zeal; exasperation, fierceness, frenzy, rage.

heath *n* field, moor, wasteland, plain.

heathen *adj* animist, animistic; pagan, paganical, paganish, paganistic, unconverted; agnostic, atheist, atheistic, gentile, idolatrous, infidel, irreligious; barbarous, cruel, inhuman, savage. • *n* atheist, gentile, idolater, idolatress, infidel, pagan, unbeliever; barbarian, philistine, savage.

heave *vb* elevate, hoist, lift, raise; breathe, exhale; cast, fling, hurl, send, throw, toss; dilate, expand, pant, rise, swell; retch, throw up; strive, struggle.

heaven *n* empyrean, firmament, sky, welkin; bliss, ecstasy, elysium, felicity, happiness, paradise, rapture, transport.

heavenly *adj* celestial, empyreal, ethereal; angelic, beatific, beatified, cherubic, divine, elysian, glorious, god-like, sainted, saintly, seraphic; blissful, delightful, divine, ecstatic, enrapturing, enravishing, exquisite, golden, rapturous, ravishing, exquisite, transporting.

heaviness *n* gravity, heft, ponderousness, weight; grievousness, oppressiveness, severity; dullness, languor, lassitude, sluggishness, stupidity; dejection, depression, despondency, gloom, melancholy, sadness, seriousness.

heavy *adj* grave, hard, onerous, ponderous, weighty; afflictive, burdensome, crushing, cumbersome, grievous, oppressive, severe, serious; dilatory, dull, inactive, inanimate, indolent, inert, lifeless, listless, sleepy, slow, sluggish, stupid, torpid; chapfallen, crestfallen, crushed, depressed, dejected, despondent, disconsolate, downhearted, gloomy, low-spirited, melancholy, sad, sobered, sorrowful; difficult, laborious; tedious, tiresome, wearisome, weary; burdened, encumbered, loaded; clammy, clayey, cloggy, ill-raised, miry, muddy, soggy; boisterous, deep, energetic, loud, roaring, severe, stormy, strong, tempestuous, violent; cloudy, dark, dense, gloomy, lowering, overcast.

hebetate *adj* blunt; dull, obtuse, sluggish, stupid, stupefied.

hectic *adj* animated, excited, fevered, feverish, flushed, heated, hot.

hector vb bluster, boast, bully, menace, threaten; annoy, fret, harass, harry, irritate, provoke, tease, vex, worry. • n blusterer, bully, swaggerer.

hedge vb block, encumber, hinder, obstruct, surround; enclose, fence, fortify, guard, protect; disappear, dodge, evade, hide, skulk, temporize. • n barrier, hedgerow, fence, limit.

heed vb attend, consider, mark, mind, note, notice, observe, regard. • n attention, care, carefulness, caution, circumspection, consideration, heedfulness, mindfulness, notice, observation, regard, wariness, vigilance, watchfulness.

heedful adj attentive, careful, cautious, circumspect, mindful, observant, observing, provident, regardful, watchful, wary.

heedless adj careless, inattentive, neglectful, negligent, precipitate, rash, reckless, thoughtless, unmindful, unminding, unobserving, unobservant.

heft n handle, haft, helve; bulk, weight.

hegemony n ascendancy, authority, headship, leadership, predominance, preponderance, rule.

height n altitude, elevation, tallness; acme, apex, climax, eminence, head, meridian, pinnacle, summit, top, vertex, zenith; eminence, hill, mountain; dignity, exaltation, grandeur, loftiness, perfection.

heighten vb elevate, raise; ennoble, exalt, magnify, make greater; augment, enhance, improve, increase, strengthen; aggravate, intensify.

heinous adj aggravated, atrocious, crying, enormous, excessive, flagitious, flagrant, hateful, infamous, monstrous, nefarious, odious, villainous.

heir n child, inheritor, offspring, product.

helical adj screw-shaped, spiral, winding.

hellish adj abominable, accursed, atrocious, curst, damnable, damned, demoniacal, detestable, devilish, diabolical, execrable, fiendish, infernal, monstrous, nefarious, satanic.

helm n rudder, steering-gear, tiller, wheel; command, control, direction, rein, rule.

help vb relieve, save, succor; abet, aid, assist, back, cooperate, second, serve, support, sustain, wait; alleviate, ameliorate, better, cure, heal, improve, remedy, restore; control, hinder, prevent, repress, resist, withstand; avoid, forbear, control. • n aid, assistance, succor, support; relief, remedy; assistant, helper, servant.

helper adj aider, abettor, ally, assistant, auxiliary, coadjutor, colleague, helpmate, partner, supporter.

helpful adj advantageous, assistant, auxiliary, beneficial, contributory, convenient, favorable, kind, profitable, serviceable, useful.

helpless adj disabled, feeble, imbecile, impotent, infirm, powerless, prostrate, resourceless, weak; abandoned, defenseless, exposed, unprotected; desperate, irremediable, remediless.

helpmate n companion, consort, husband, partner, wife; aider, assistant, associate, helper.

helter-skelter adj disorderly, headlong, irregular, pell-mell, precipitate. • adv confusedly, hastily, headlong, higgledy-piggledy, pell-mell, precipitately, wildly.

hem vb border, edge, skirt; beset, confine, enclose, environ, surround, sew; hesitate. • n border, edge, trim.

henchman n attendant, follower, retainer, servant, supporter.

herald vb announce, proclaim, publish. • n announcer, crier, publisher; harbinger, precursor, proclaimer.

heraldry n blazonry, emblazonry.

herbage n greenery, herb, pasture, plants, vegetation.

herculean adj able-bodied, athletic, brawny, mighty, muscular, powerful, puissant, sinewy, stalwart, strong, sturdy, vigorous; dangerous, difficult, hard, laborious, perilous, toilsome, troublesome; colossal, Cyclopean, gigantic, great, large, strapping.

herd vb drive, gather, lead, tend; assemble, associate, flock. • n drover, herder, herdsman, shepherd; crowd, multitude, populace, rabble; assemblage, assembly, collection, drove, flock, pack.

hereditary adj ancestral, inheritable, inherited, patrimonial, transmitted.

heresy n dissent, error, heterodoxy, impiety, recusancy, unorthodoxy.

heretic n dissenter, dissident, nonconformist, recusant, schismatic, sectarian, sectary, separatist, unbeliever.

heretical adj heterodox, impious, schismatic, schismatical, sectarian, unorthodox.

heritage n estate, inheritance, legacy, patrimony, portion.

hermetic adj airtight, impervious; cabbalistic, emblematic, emblematical, magical, mysterious, mystic, mystical, occult, secret, symbolic, symbolical.

hermit *n* anchoress, anchoret, anchorite, ascetic, eremite, monk, recluse, solitaire, solitary.

heroic *adj* bold, brave, courageous, daring, dauntless, fearless, gallant, illustrious, intrepid, magnanimous, noble, valiant; desperate, extravagant, extreme, violent.

heroism *n* boldness, bravery, courage, daring, endurance, fearlessness, fortitude, gallantry, intrepidity, prowess, valor.

hesitate *vb* boggle, delay, demur, doubt, pause, scruple, shilly-shally, stickle, vacillate, waver; falter, stammer, stutter.

hesitation *n* halting, misgiving, reluctance; delay, doubt, indecision, suspense, uncertainty, vacillation; faltering, stammering, stuttering.

heterodox *adj* heretical, recusant, schismatic, unorthodox, unsound; apocryphal, uncanonical.

heterogeneous *adj* contrasted, contrary, different, dissimilar, diverse, incongruous, indiscriminate, miscellaneous, mixed, opposed, unhomogeneous, unlike.

hew *vb* chop, cut, fell, hack; fashion, form, shape, smooth.

hiatus *n* blank, break, chasm, gap, interval, lacuna, opening, rift.

hidden *adj* blind, clandestine, cloaked, close, concealed, covered, covert, enshrouded, latent, masked, occult, private, secluded, secret, suppressed, undiscovered, veiled; abstruse, cabbalistic, cryptic, dark, esoteric, hermetic, inward, mysterious, mystic, mystical, obscure, oracular, recondite.

hide *vb* bury, conceal, cover, secrete, suppress, withhold; cloak, disguise, eclipse, hoard, mask, screen, shelter, veil.

hideous *adj* abominable, appalling, awful, dreadful, frightful, ghastly, ghoulish, grim, grisly, horrible, horrid, repulsive, revolting, shocking, terrible, terrifying.

hie *vb* hasten, speed.

hieratic *adj* consecrated, devoted, priestly, sacred, sacerdotal.

hieroglyph *n* picture-writing, rebus, sign, symbol.

hieroglyphic *adj* emblematic, emblematical, figurative, obscure, symbolic, symbolical.

higgle *vb* hawk, peddle; bargain, chaffer, haggle, negotiate.

higgledy-piggledy *adj* chaotic, confused, disorderly, jumbled. • *adv* confusedly, in disorder, helter-skelter, pell-mell.

high *adj* elevated, high-reaching, lofty, soaring, tall, towering; distinguished, eminent, pre-eminent, prominent, superior; admirable, dignified, exalted, great, noble; arrogant, haughty, lordly, proud, supercilious; boisterous, strong, tumultuous, turbulent, violent; costly, dear, pricey; acute, high-pitched, high-toned, piercing, sharp, shrill; tainted, malodorous. • *adv* powerfully, profoundly; eminently, loftily; luxuriously, richly.

high-flown *adj* elevated, presumptuous, proud, lofty, swollen; extravagant, high-colored, lofty, overdrawn, overstrained; bombastic, inflated, pompous, pretentious, strained, swollen, turgid.

high-handed *adj* arbitrary, despotic, dictatorial, domineering, oppressive, overbearing, self-willed, violent, willful.

highly strung *adj* ardent, excitable, irascible, nervous, quick, tense; high-spirited, sensitive.

high-minded *adj* arrogant, haughty, lofty, proud; elevated, high-toned; generous, honorable, magnanimous, noble, spiritual.

highwayman *n* bandit, brigand, footpad, freebooter, marauder, outlaw, robber.

hilarious *adj* boisterous, cheerful, comical, convivial, riotous, uproarious, jovial, joyful, merry, mirthful, noisy.

hilarity *n* cheerfulness, conviviality, exhilarated, gaiety, glee, jollity, joviality, joyousness, merriment, mirth.

hill *n* ascent, ben, elevation, eminence, hillock, knoll, mount, mountain, rise, tor.

hind *adj* back, hinder, hindmost, posterior, rear, rearward.

hinder *vb* bar, check, clog, delay, embarrass, encumber, impede, interrupt, obstruct, oppose, prevent, restrain, retard, stop, thwart.

hindrance *n* check, deterrent, encumbrance, hitch, impediment, interruption, obstacle, obstruction, restraint, stop, stoppage.

hinge *vb* depend, hang, rest, turn.

hint *vb* allude, glance, imply, insinuate, intimate, mention, refer, suggest. • *n* allusion, clue, implication, indication, innuendo, insinuation, intimation, mention, reminder, suggestion, taste, trace.

hire *vb* buy, rent, secure; charter, employ,

engage, lease, let. • *n* allowance, bribe, compensation, pay, remuneration, rent, reward, salary, stipend, wages.

hireling *n* employee, mercenary, myrmidon.

hirsute *adj* bristled, bristly, hairy, shaggy; boorish, course, ill-bred, loutish, rough, rude, rustic, uncouth, unmannerly.

hiss *vb* shrill, sibilate, whistle, whir, whiz; condemn, damn, ridicule. • *n* fizzle, hissing, sibilant, sibilation, sizzle.

historian *n* annalist, autobiographer, biographer, chronicler, narrator, recorder.

history *n* account, autobiography, annals, biography, chronicle, genealogy, memoirs, narration, narrative, recital, record, relation, story.

hit *vb* discomfit, hurt, knock, strike; accomplish, achieve, attain, gain, reach, secure, succeed, win; accord, fit, suit; beat, clash, collide, contact, smite. • *n* blow, collision, strike, stroke; chance, fortune, hazard, success, venture.

hitch *vb* catch, impede, stick, stop; attach, connect, fasten, harness, join, tether, tie, unite, yoke. • *n* catch, check, hindrance, impediment, interruption, obstacle; knot, noose.

hoar *adj* ancient, gray, hoary, old, white.

hoard *vb* accumulate, amass, collect, deposit, garner, hive, husband, save, store, treasure. • *n* accumulation, collection, deposit, fund, mass, reserve, savings, stockpile, store.

hoarse *adj* discordant, grating, gruff, guttural, harsh, husky, low, raucous, rough.

hoary *adj* gray, hoar, silvery, white; ancient, old, venerable.

hoax *vb* deceive, dupe, fool, gammon, gull, hoodwink, swindle, trick. • *n* canard, cheat, deception, fraud, humbug, imposition, imposture, joke, trick, swindle.

hobble *vb* falter, halt, hop, limp; fasten, fetter, hopple, shackle, tie. • *n* halt, limp; clog, fetter, shackle; embarrassment, difficulty, perplexity, pickle, strait.

hobgoblin *n* apparition, bogey, bugbear, goblin, imp, specter, spirit, sprite.

hobnail *n* bumpkin, churl, clodhopper, clown, lout, rustic.

hocus-pocus *n* cheater, impostor, juggler, sharper, swindler, trickster; artifice, cheat, deceit, deception, delusion, hoax, imposition, juggle, trick.

hodgepodge *n* farrago, hash, hotchpotch, jumble, medley, miscellany, mixture, ragout, stew.

hog *n* beast, glutton, pig; grunter, porker, swine.

hoggish *adj* brutish, filthy, gluttonish, piggish, swinish; grasping, greedy, mean, selfish, sordid.

hoist *vb* elevate, heave, lift, raise, rear. • *n* elevator, lift.

hold *vb* clasp, clinch, clutch, grasp, grip, seize; have, keep, occupy, possess, retain; bind, confine, control, detain, imprison, restrain, restrict; connect, fasten, fix, lock; arrest, check, stay, stop, suspend, withhold; continue, keep up, maintain, manage, prosecute, support, sustain; cherish, embrace, entertain; account, believe, consider, count, deem, entertain, esteem, judge, reckon, regard, think; accommodate, admit, carry, contain, receive, stow; assemble, conduct, convene; endure, last, persist, remain; adhere, cleave, cling, cohere, stick. • *n* anchor, bite, clasp, control, embrace, foothold, grasp, grip, possession, retention, seizure; prop, stay, support; claim, footing, vantage point; castle, fort, fortification, fortress, stronghold, tower; locker, storage, storehouse.

hole *n* aperture, opening, perforation; abyss, bore, cave, cavern, cavity, chasm, depression, excavation, eye, hollow, pit, pore, void; burrow, cover, lair, retreat; den, hovel, kennel.

holiday *n* anniversary, celebration, feast, festival, festivity, fete, gala, recess, vacation.

holiness *n* blessedness, consecration, devotion, devoutness, godliness, piety, purity, religiousness, righteousness, sacredness, saintliness, sanctity, sinlessness.

hollow *vb* dig, excavate, groove, scoop. • *adj* cavernous, concave, depressed, empty, sunken, vacant, void; deceitful, faithless, false, false-hearted, hollow-hearted, hypocritical, insincere, pharisaical, treacherous, unfeeling; deep, low, muffled, reverberating, rumbling, sepulchral. • *n* basin, bowl, depression; cave, cavern, cavity, concavity, dent, dimple, dint, depression, excavation, hole, pit; canal, channel, cup, dimple, dig, groove, pocket, sag.

holocaust *n* carnage, destruction, devastation, genocide, massacre.

holy *adj* blessed, consecrated, dedicated, devoted, hallowed, sacred, sanctified; devout, godly, pious, pure, religious, righteous, saintlike, saintly, sinless, spiritual.

homage *n* allegiance, devotion, fealty, fidelity, loyalty; court, deference, duty, honor, obeisance, respect, reverence, service; adoration, devotion, worship.

home *adj* domestic, family; close, direct, effective, penetrating, pointed. • *n* abode, dwelling, seat, quarters, residence.

homely *adj* domestic, familiar, house-like; coarse, commonplace, homespun, inelegant, plain, simple, unattractive, uncomely, unpolished, unpretentious.

homespun *adj* coarse, homely, inelegant, plain, rude, rustic, unpolished.

homicide *n* manslaughter, murder.

homily *n* address, discourse, lecture, sermon.

homogeneous *adj* akin, alike, cognate, kindred, similar, uniform.

honest *adj* equitable, fair, faithful, honorable, open, straight, straightforward; conscientious, equitable, reliable, sound, square, true, trustworthy, trusty, uncorrupted, upright, virtuous; above-board, faithful, genuine, thorough, unadulterated; creditable, decent, proper, reputable, respectable, suitable; chaste, decent; candid, direct, frank, ingenuous, sincere, unreserved.

honesty *n* equity, fairness, faithfulness, fidelity, honor, integrity, justice, probity, trustiness, trustworthiness, uprightness; truth, truthfulness, veracity; genuineness, thoroughness; candor, frankness, ingenuousness, openness, sincerity, straightforwardness, unreserve.

honor *vb* dignify, exalt, glorify, grace; respect, revere, reverence, venerate; adore, hallow, worship; celebrate, commemorate, keep, observe. • *n* civility, deference, esteem, homage, respect, reverence, veneration; dignity, distinction, elevation, nobleness; consideration, credit, fame, glory, reputation; high-mindedness, honesty, integrity, magnanimity, probity, uprightness; chastity, purity, virtue; boast, credit, ornament, pride.

honorable *adj* elevated, famous, great, illustrious, noble; admirable, conscientious, fair, honest, just, magnanimous, true, trustworthy, upright, virtuous, worshipful; creditable, esteemed, estimable, equitable, proper, respected, reputable, right.

honorary *adj* formal, nominal, titular, unofficial, unpaid.

honors *npl* dignities, distinctions, privilege, titles; adornments, beauties, decorations, glories; civilities.

hood *n* capuche, coif, cover, cowl, head.

hoodwink *vb* blind, blindfold; cloak, conceal, cover, hide; cheat, circumvent, cozen, deceive, delete, dupe, fool, gull, impose, overreach, trick.

hook *vb* catch, ensnare, entrap, hasp, snare; bend, curve. • *n* catch, clasp, fastener, hasp; snare, trap; cutter, grass-hook, reaper, reaping-hook, sickle.

hooked *adj* aquiline, bent, crooked, curved, hamate, unciform.

hoop *vb* clasp, encircle, enclose, surround. • *n* band, circlet, girdle, ring; crinoline, farthingale.

hoot *vb* boo, cry, jeer, shout, yell; condemn, decry, denounce, execrate, hiss. • *n* boo, cry, jeer, shout, yell.

hop *vb* bound, caper, frisk, jump, leap, skip, spring; dance, trip; halt, hobble, limp. • *n* bound, caper, dance, jump, leap, skip, spring.

hope *vb* anticipate, await, desire, expect, long; believe, rely, trust. • *n* confidence, belief, faith, reliance, sanguineness, sanguinity, trust; anticipation, desire, expectancy, expectation.

hopeful *adj* anticipatory, confident, expectant, fond, optimistic, sanguine; cheerful, encouraging, promising.

hopeless *adj* abject, crushed, depressed, despondent, despairing, desperate, disconsolate, downcast, forlorn, pessimistic, woebegone; abandoned, helpless, incurable, irremediable, remediless; impossible, impracticable, unachievable, unattainable.

horde *n* clan, crew, gang, troop; crowd, multitude, pack, throng.

horn *vb* gore, pierce. • *n* trumpet, wind instrument; beaker, drinking cup, cornucopia; spike, spur; cusp, prong, wing.

horrid *adj* alarming, awful, bristling, dire, dreadful, fearful, frightful, harrowing, hideous, horrible, horrific, horrifying, rough, terrible, terrific; abominable, disagreeable, disgusting, odious, offensive, repulsive, revolting, shocking, unpleasant, vile.

horrify *vb* affright, alarm, frighten, shock, terrify, terrorise.

horror *n* alarm, awe, consternation, dismay, dread, fear, fright, panic; abhorrence, abomination, antipathy, aversion, detestation, disgust, hatred, loathing, repugnance, revulsion; shuddering.

horse *n* charger, cob, colt, courser, filly,

gelding, mare, nag, pad, palfrey, pony, stallion, steed; cavalry, horseman; buck, clotheshorse, frame, sawhorse, stand, support.

horseman *n* cavalier, equestrian, rider; cavalryman, chasseur, dragoon, horse-soldier.

hospitable *adj* attentive, bountiful, kind; bountiful, cordial, generous, liberal, open, receptive, sociable, unconstrained, unreserved.

host[1] *n* entertainer, innkeeper, landlord, master of ceremonies, presenter, proprietor, owner, receptionist.

host[2] *n* array, army, legion; assemblage, assembly, horde, multitude, throng.

host[3] *n* altar bread, bread, consecrated bread, loaf, wafer.

hostile *adj* inimical, unfriendly, warlike; adverse, antagonistic, contrary, opposed, opposite, repugnant.

hostilities *npl* conflict, fighting, war, warfare.

hostility *n* animosity, antagonism, enmity, hatred, ill-will, unfriendliness; contrariness, opposition, repugnance, variance.

hot *adj* burning, fiery, scalding; boiling, flaming, heated, incandescent, parching, roasting, torrid; heated, oppressive, sweltering, warm; angry, choleric, excitable, furious, hasty, impatient, impetuous, irascible, lustful, passionate, touchy, urgent, violent; animated, ardent, eager, fervent, fervid, glowing, passionate, vehement; acrid, biting, highly flavored, highly seasoned, peppery, piquant, pungent, sharp, stinging.

hotchpotch *n* farrago, jumble, hodgepodge, medley, miscellany, stew.

hotel *n* inn, public house, tavern.

hot-headed *adj* furious, headlong, headstrong, hot-brained, impetuous, inconsiderate, passionate, precipitate, rash, reckless, vehement, violent.

hound *vb* drive, incite, spur, urge; bate, chase, goad, harass, harry, hunt, pursue.

house *vb* harbor, lodge, protect, shelter. • *n* abode, domicile, dwelling, habitation, home, mansion, residence; building, edifice; family, household; kindred, race, lineage, tribe; company, concern, firm, partnership; hotel, inn, public house, tavern.

housing *n* accommodation, dwellings, houses; casing, container, covering, protection, shelter.

hovel *n* cabin, cot, den, hole, hut, shed.

hover *vb* flutter; hang; vacillate, waver.

however *adv* but, however, nevertheless, notwithstanding, still, though, yet.

howl *vb* bawl, cry, lament, ululate, weep, yell, yowl. • *n* cry, yell, ululation.

hoyden *n* romp, tomboy.

hoydenish *adj* bad-mannered, boisterous, bold, ill-behaved, ill-taught, inelegant, romping, rough, rude, rustic, tomboyish, uncouth, ungenteel, unladylike, unruly.

hubbub *n* clamor, confusion, din, disorder, disturbance, hullabaloo, racket, riot, outcry, tumult, uproar.

huckster *n* hawker, peddler, retailer.

huddle *vb* cluster, crowd, gather; crouch, curl up, nestle, snuggle. • *n* confusion, crowd, disorder, disturbance, jumble, tumult.

hue *n* cast, color, complexion, dye, shade, tinge, tint, tone.

huff *vb* blow, breathe, exhale, pant, puff. • *n* anger, fume, miff, passion, pet, quarrel, rage, temper, tiff.

hug *vb* clasp, cling, cuddle, embrace, grasp, grip, squeeze; cherish, nurse, retain. • *n* clasp, cuddle, embrace, grasp, squeeze.

huge *adj* bulky, colossal, Cyclopean, elephantine, enormous, gigantic, herculean, immense, stupendous, vast,

huggermugger *adj* clandestine, secret, sly; base, contemptible, mean, unfair; confused, disorderly, slovenly.

hull *vb* husk, peel, shell. • *n* covering, husk, rind, shell.

hullabaloo *n* clamor, confusion, din, disturbance, hubbub, outcry, racket, vociferation, uproar.

hum *vb* buzz, drone, murmur; croon, sing.

humane *adj* accommodating, benevolent, benign, charitable, clement, compassionate, gentle, good-hearted, kind, kindhearted, lenient, merciful, obliging, tender, sympathetic; cultivating, elevating, humanizing, refining, rational, spiritual.

humanity *n* benevolence, benignity, charity, fellow-feeling, humaneness, kindheartedness, kindness, philanthropy, sympathy, tenderness; humankind, mankind, mortality.

humanize *vb* civilize, cultivate, educate, enlighten, improve, polish, reclaim, refine, soften.

humble *vb* abase, abash, break, crush, debase, degrade, disgrace, humiliate, lower, mortify, reduce, sink, subdue. • *adj* meek, modest, lowly, simple, submissive, unambitious, unassuming, unobtrusive, unostentatious, unpretending; low, obscure, mean, plain, poor, small, undistinguished, unpretentious.

humbug vb cheat, cozen, deceive, hoax, swindle, trick. • n cheat, dodge, gammon, hoax, imposition, imposture, deception, fraud, trick; cant, charlatanism, charlatanry, hypocrisy, mummery, quackery; charlatan, impostor, fake, quack.

humdrum adj boring, dronish, dreary, dry, dull, monotonous, prosy, stupid, tedious, tiresome, wearisome.

humid adj damp, dank, moist, wet.

humiliate vb abase, abash, debase, degrade, depress, humble, mortify, shame.

humiliation n abasement, affront, condescension, crushing, degradation, disgrace, dishonoring, humbling, indignity, mortification, self-abasement, submissiveness, resignation.

humility n diffidence, humbleness, lowliness, meekness, modesty, self-abasement, submissiveness.

humor vb favor, gratify, indulge. • n bent, bias, disposition, predilection, temper, vein; mood, state; caprice, crotchet, fancy, freak, vagary, whim, whimsy, wrinkle; drollery, facetiousness, fun, jocoseness, jocularity, pleasantry, wit; fluid, moisture, vapor.

humorist n comic, comedian, droll, jester, joker, wag, wit.

humorous adj comic, comical, droll, facetious, funny, humorous, jocose, jocular, laughable, ludicrous, merry, playful, pleasant, sportive, whimsical, witty.

hunch vb arch, jostle, nudge, punch, push, shove. • n bunch, hump, knob, protuberance; nudge, punch, push, shove; feeling, idea, intuition, premonition.

hungry adj covetous, craving, desirous, greedy; famished, starved, starving; barren, poor, unfertile, unproductive.

hunk n chunk, hunch, lump, slice.

hunt vb chase, drive, follow, hound, pursue, stalk, trap, trail; poach, shoot; search, seek. • n chase, field-sport, hunting, pursuit.

hurl vb cast, dart, fling, pitch, project, send, sling, throw, toss.

hurly-burly n bustle, commotion, confusion, disturbance, hurl, hurly, uproar, tumult, turmoil.

hurricane n cyclone, gale, storm, tempest, tornado, typhoon.

hurried adj cursory, hasty, slight, superficial.

hurry vb drive, precipitate; dispatch, expedite, hasten, quicken, speed; haste, scurry. • n agitation, bustle, confusion, flurry, flutter, perturbation, precipitation; celerity, haste, dispatch, expedition, promptitude, promptness, quickness.

hurt vb damage, disable, disadvantage, harm, impair, injure, mar; bruise, pain, wound; afflict, grieve, offend; ache, smart, throb. • n damage, detriment, disadvantage, harm, injury, mischief; ache, bruise, pain, suffering, wound.

hurtful adj baleful, baneful, deleterious, destructive, detrimental, disadvantageous, harmful, injurious, mischievous, noxious, pernicious, prejudicial, unwholesome.

husband vb economize, hoard, save, store.

husbandry n agriculture, cultivation, farming, geoponics, tillage; economy, frugality, thrift.

hush vb quiet, repress, silence, still, suppress; appease, assuage, calm, console, quiet, still. • n quiet, quietness, silence, stillness.

hypocrite n deceiver, dissembler, impostor, pretender.

hypocritical adj deceiving, dissembling, false, insincere, spurious, two-faced.

hypothesis n assumption, proposition, supposition, theory.

hypothetical adj assumed, imaginary, supposed, theoretical.

hysterical adj frantic, frenzied, overwrought, uncontrollable; comical, uproarious.

I

ice vb chill, congeal, freeze. • n crystal; frosting, sugar.

icy adj glacial; chilling, cold, frosty; coldhearted, distant, frigid, indifferent, unemotional.

idea n archetype, essence, exemplar, ideal, model, pattern, plan, model; fantasy, fiction, image, imagination; apprehension, conceit, conception, fancy, illusion, impression, thought; belief, judgement, notion, opinion, sentiment, supposition.

ideal adj intellectual, mental; chimerical, fancied, fanciful, fantastic, illusory, imaginary, unreal, visionary, shadowy; complete, consummate, excellent, perfect; impractical, unattainable, utopian. • *n* criterion, example, model, standard.

identical *adj* equivalent, same, selfsame, tantamount.

identity *n* existence, individuality, personality, sameness.

ideology *n* belief, creed, dogma, philosophy, principle.

idiocy *n* fatuity, feebleness, foolishness, imbecility, insanity.

idiosyncrasy *n* caprice, eccentricity, fad, peculiarity, singularity.

idiot *n* blockhead, booby, dunce, fool, ignoramus, imbecile, simpleton.

idiotic *adj* fatuous, foolish, imbecile, irrational, senseless, sottish, stupid.

idle *adj* inactive, unemployed, unoccupied, vacant; indolent, inert, lazy, slothful, sluggish; abortive, bootless, fruitless, futile, groundless, ineffectual, unavailing, useless, vain; foolish, frivolous, trashy, trifling, trivial, unimportant, unprofitable. • *vb* dally, dawdle, laze, loiter, potter, waste; drift, shirk, slack.

idler *n* dawdler, doodle, drone, laggard, lazybones, loafer, lounger, slacker, slowcoach, sluggard, trifler.

idol *n* deity, god, icon, image, pagan, simulacrum, symbol; delusion, falsity, pretender, sham; beloved, darling, favorite, pet.

idolater *n* heathen, pagan; admirer, adorer, worshipper.

idolize *vb* canonize, deify; adore, honor, love, reverence, venerate.

idyll *n* eclogue, pastoral.

if *conj* admitting, allowing, granting, provided, supposing, though, whether. • *n* condition, hesitation, uncertainty.

igneous *adj* combustible, combustive, conflagrative, fiery, molten.

ignite *vb* burn, inflame, kindle, light, torch.

ignoble *adj* base-born, low, low-born, mean, peasant, plebeian, rustic, vulgar; contemptible, degraded, insignificant, mean, worthless; disgraceful, dishonorable, infamous, low, unworthy.

ignominious *adj* discreditable, disgraceful, dishonorable, disreputable, infamous, opprobrious, scandalous, shameful; base, contemptible, despicable.

ignominy *n* abasement, contempt, discredit, disgrace, dishonor disrepute, infamy,

obloquy, odium, opprobrium, scandal, shame.

ignoramus *n* blockhead, duffer, dunce, fool, greenhorn, novice, numskull, simpleton.

ignorance *n* benightedness, darkness, illiteracy, nescience, rusticity; blindness, unawareness.

ignorant *adj* blind, illiterate, nescient, unaware, unconversant, uneducated, unenlightened, uninformed, uninstructed, unlearned, unread, untaught, untutored, unwitting.

ignore *vb* disregard, neglect, overlook, reject, skip.

ill *adj* bad, evil, faulty, harmful, iniquitous, naughty, unfavorable, unfortunate, unjust, wicked; ailing, diseased, disordered, indisposed, sick, unwell, wrong; crabbed, cross, hateful, malicious, malevolent, peevish, surly, unkind, ill-bred; ill-favored, ugly, unprepossessing. • *adv* badly, poorly, unfortunately. • *n* badness, depravity, evil, mischief, misfortune, wickedness; affliction, ailment, calamity, harm, misery, pain, trouble.

ill-advised *adj* foolish, ill-judged, imprudent, injudicious, unwise.

ill-bred *adj* discourteous, ill-behaved, ill-mannered, impolite, rude, uncivil, uncourteous, uncourtly, uncouth.

illegal *adj* contraband, forbidden, illegitimate, illicit, prohibited, unauthorized, unlawful, unlicensed.

illegible *adj* indecipherable, obscure, undecipherable, unreadable.

illegitimate *adj* bastard, misbegotten, natural.

ill-fated *adj* ill-starred, luckless, unfortunate, unlucky.

ill-favored *adj* homely, ugly, offensive, plain, unpleasant.

ill humor *n* fretfulness, ill-temper, peevishness, petulance, testiness.

illiberal *adj* close, close-fisted, covetous, mean, miserly, narrow, niggardly, parsimonious, penurious, selfish, sordid, stingy, ungenerous; bigoted, narrow-minded, uncharitable, ungentlemanly, vulgar.

illicit *adj* illegal, illegitimate, unauthorized, unlawful, unlegalized, unlicensed; criminal, guilty, forbidden, improper, wrong.

illimitable *adj* boundless, endless, immeasurable, immense, infinite, unbounded, unlimited, vast.

illiterate *adj* ignorant, uneducated,

uninstructed, unlearned, unlettered, untaught, untutored.

ill-judged *adj* foolish, ill-advised, imprudent, injudicious, unwise.

ill-mannered *adj* discourteous, ill-behaved, ill-bred, impolite, rude, uncivil, uncourteous, uncourtly, uncouth, unpolished.

ill-natured *adj* disobliging, hateful, malevolent, unamiable, unfriendly, unkind; acrimonious, bitter, churlish, crabbed, cross, cross-grained, crusty, ill-tempered, morose, perverse, petulant, sour, spiteful, sulky, sullen, wayward.

illness *n* ailing, ailment, complaint, disease, disorder, distemper, indisposition, malady, sickness.

illogical *adj* absurd, fallacious, inconsistent, inconclusive, inconsequent, incorrect, invalid, unreasonable, unsound.

ill-proportioned *adj* awkward, ill-made, ill-shaped, misshapen, misproportioned, shapeless.

ill-starred *adj* ill-fated, luckless, unfortunate, unhappy, unlucky.

ill temper *n* bad temper, crabbedness, crossness, grouchiness, ill nature, moroseness, sulkiness, sullenness.

ill-tempered *adj* acrimonious, bad-tempered, crabbed, cross, grouchy, ill-natured, morose, sour, sulky, surly.

ill-timed *adj* inapposite, inopportune, irrelevant, unseasonable, untimely.

ill-treat *vb* abuse, ill-use, injure, maltreat, mishandle, misuse.

illude *vb* cheat, deceive, delude, disappoint, mock, swindle, trick.

illuminate *vb* illume, illumine, light; adorn, brighten, decorate, depict, edify, enlighten, inform, inspire, instruct, make wise.

illusion *n* chimera, deception, delusion, error, fallacy, false appearance, fantasy, hallucination, mockery, phantasm.

illusive, illusory *adj* barmecide, deceitful, deceptive, delusive, fallacious, imaginary, make-believe, mock, sham, unsatisfying, unreal, unsubstantial, visionary, tantalizing.

illustrate *vb* clarify, demonstrate, elucidate, enlighten, exemplify, explain; adorn, depict, draw.

illustration *n* demonstration, elucidation, enlightenment, exemplification, explanation, interpretation; adornment, decoration, picture.

illustrative *adj* elucidative, elucidatory, exemplifying.

illustrious *adj* bright, brilliant, glorious, radiant, splendid; celebrated, conspicuous, distinguished, eminent, famed, famous, noble, noted, remarkable, renowned, signal.

ill will *n* animosity, dislike, enmity, envy, grudge, hate, hatred, hostility, ill nature, malevolence, malice, malignity, rancor, spleen, spite, uncharitableness, unkindness, venom.

image *n* idol, statue; copy, effigy, figure, form, imago, likeness, picture, resemblance, representation, shape, similitude, simulacrum, statue, symbol; conception, counterpart, embodiment, idea, reflection.

imagery *n* dream, phantasm, phantom, vision

imaginable *adj* assumable, cogitable, conceivable, conjecturable, plausible, possible, supposable, thinkable.

imaginary *adj* chimerical, dreamy, fancied, fanciful, fantastic, fictitious, ideal, illusive, illusory, invented, quixotic, shadowy, unreal, utopian, visionary, wild; assumed, conceivable, hypothetical, supposed.

imagination *n* chimera, conception, fancy, fantasy, invention, unreality; position; contrivance, device, plot, scheme.

imaginative *adj* creative, dreamy, fanciful, inventive, poetical, plastic, visionary.

imagine *vb* conceive, dream, fancy, imagine, picture, pretend; contrive, create, devise, frame, invent, mold, project; assume, suppose, hypothesize; apprehend, assume, believe, deem, guess, opine, suppose, think.

imbecile *adj* cretinous, driveling, fatuous, feeble, feeble-minded, foolish, helpless, idiotic, imbecilic, inane, infirm, witless. • *n* dotard, driveler.

imbecility *n* debility, feebleness, helplessness, infirmity, weakness; foolishness, idiocy, silliness, stupidity, weak-mindedness.

imbibe *vb* absorb, assimilate, drink, suck, swallow; acquire, gain, gather, get, receive.

imbroglio *n* complexity, complication, embarrassment, entanglement, misunderstanding.

imbrue *vb* drench, embrue, gain, moisten, soak, stain, steep, wet.

imbue *vb* color, dye, stain, tincture, tinge, tint; bathe, impregnate, infuse, inoculate, permeate, pervade, provide, saturate, steep.

imitate *vb* copy, counterfeit, duplicate, echo, emulate, follow, forge, mirror, reproduce, simulate; ape, impersonate, mimic, mock, personate; burlesque, parody, travesty.

imitation *adj* artificial, fake, man-made, mock, reproduction, synthetic. • *n* aping, copying, imitation, mimicking, parroting; copy, duplicate, likeness, resemblance; mimicry, mocking; burlesque, parody, travesty.

imitative *adj* copying, emulative, imitating, mimetic, simulative; apeish, aping, mimicking.

imitator *n* copier, copycat, copyist, echo, impersonator, mimic, mimicker, parrot.

immaculate *adj* clean, pure, spotless, stainless, unblemished, uncontaminated, undefiled, unpolluted, unspotted, unsullied, untainted, untarnished; faultless, guiltless, holy, innocent, pure, saintly, sinless, stainless.

immanent *adj* congenital, inborn, indwelling, inherent, innate, internal, intrinsic, subjective.

immaterial *adj* bodiless, ethereal, extramundane, impalpable, incorporeal, mental, metaphysical, spiritual, unbodied, unfleshly, unsubstantial; inconsequential, insignificant, nonessential, unessential, unimportant.

immature *adj* crude, green, imperfect, raw, rudimental, rudimentary, unfinished, unformed, unprepared, unripe, unripened, youthful; hasty, premature, unseasonable, untimely.

immaturity *n* crudeness, crudity, greenness, imperfection, rawness, unpreparedness, unripeness.

immeasurable *adj* bottomless, boundless, illimitable, immense, infinite, limitless, measureless, unbounded, vast.

immediate *adj* close, contiguous, near, next, proximate; intuitive, primary, unmediated; direct, instant, instantaneous, present, pressing, prompt.

immediately *adv* closely, proximately; directly, forthwith, instantly, presently, presto, pronto.

immemorial *adj* ancient, hoary, olden.

immense *adj* boundless, illimitable, infinite, interminable, measureless, unbounded, unlimited; colossal, elephantine, enormous, gigantic, huge, large, monstrous, mountainous, prodigious, stupendous, titanic, tremendous, vast.

immensity *n* boundlessness, endlessness, limitlessness, infiniteness, infinitude, infinity; amplitude, enormity, greatness, hugeness, magnitude, vastness.

immerse *vb* baptize, bathe, dip, douse, duck, overwhelm, plunge, sink, souse, submerge; absorb, engage, engross, involve.

immersion *n* dipping, immersing, plunging; absorption, engagement; disappearance; baptism.

imminent *adj* close, impending, near, overhanging, threatening; alarming, dangerous, perilous.

immobile *adj* fixed, immovable, inflexible, motionless, quiescent, stable, static, stationary, steadfast; dull, expressionless, impassive, rigid, stiff, stolid.

immobility *n* fixedness, fixity, immovability, immovableness, motionlessness, stability, steadfastness, unmovableness; dullness, expressionlessness, inflexibility, rigidity, stiffness, stolidity.

immoderate *adj* excessive, exorbitant, extravagant, extreme, inordinate, intemperate, unreasonable.

immodest *adj* coarse, gross, indecorous, indelicate, lewd, shameless; bold, brazen, forward, impudent, indecent; broad, filthy, impure, unclean, obscene, smutty, unchaste.

immodesty *n* coarseness, grossness, indecorum, indelicacy, shamelessness; impurity, lewdness, obscenity, smuttiness, unchastity; boldness, brass, forwardness, impatience.

immolate *vb* kill, sacrifice.

immoral *adj* antisocial, corrupt, loose, sinful, unethical, vicious, wicked, wrong; bad, depraved, dissolute, profligate, unprincipled; abandoned, indecent, licentious.

immorality *n* corruption, corruptness, criminality, demoralization, depravity, impurity, profligacy, sin, sinfulness, vice, wickedness; wrong.

immortal *adj* deathless, ever-living, imperishable, incorruptible, indestructible, indissoluble, never-dying, undying, unfading; ceaseless, continuing, eternal, endless, everlasting, never-ending, perpetual, sempiternal; abiding, enduring, lasting, permanent. • *n* god, goddess; genius, hero.

immortality *n* deathlessness, incorruptibility, incorruptibleness, indestructibility; perpetuity.

immortalize *vb* apotheosize, enshrine, glorify, perpetuate.

immovable *adj* firm, fixed, immobile, stable, stationary; impassive, steadfast, unalterable, unchangeable, unshaken, unyielding.

immunity *n* exemption, exoneration, freedom, release; charter, franchise, liberty, license, prerogative, privilege, right.

immure *vb* confine, entomb, imprison, incarcerate.

immutability *n* constancy, inflexibility, invariability, invariableness, permanence, stability, unalterableness, unchangeableness.

immutable *adj* constant, fixed, inflexible, invariable, permanent, stable, unalterable, unchangeable, undeviating.

imp *n* demon, devil, elf, flibbertigibbet, hobgoblin, scamp, sprite; graft, scion, shoot.

impact *vb* collide, crash, strike. • *n* brunt, impression, impulse, shock, stroke, touch; collision, contact, impinging, striking.

impair *vb* blemish, damage, deface, deteriorate, injure, mar, ruin, spoil, vitiate; decrease, diminish, lessen, reduce; enervate, enfeeble, weaken.

impale *vb* hole, pierce, puncture, spear, spike, stab, transfix.

impalpable *adj* attenuated, delicate, fine, intangible; imperceptible, inapprehensible, incorporeal, indistinct, shadowy, unsubstantial.

impart *vb* bestow, confer, give, grant; communicate, disclose, discover, divulge, relate, reveal, share, tell.

impartial *adj* candid, disinterested, dispassionate, equal, equitable, even-handed, fair, honorable, just, unbiased, unprejudiced, unwarped.

impassable *adj* blocked, closed, impenetrable, impermeable, impervious, inaccessible, pathless, unattainable, unnavigable, unreachable.

impassioned *adj* animated, ardent, burning, excited, fervent, fervid, fiery, glowing, impetuous, intense, passionate, vehement, warm, zealous.

impassive *adj* calm, passionless; apathetic, callous, indifferent, insensible, insusceptible, unfeeling, unimpressible, unsusceptible.

impassivity *n* calmness, composure, indifference, insensibility, insusceptibility, passionlessness, stolidity.

impatience *n* disquietude, restlessness, uneasiness; eagerness, haste, impetuosity, precipitation, vehemence; heat, irritableness, irritability, violence.

impatient *adj* restless, uneasy, unquiet; eager, hasty, impetuous, precipitate, vehement; abrupt, brusque, choleric, fretful, hot, intolerant, irritable, peevish, sudden, testy, violent.

impeach *vb* accuse, arraign, charge, indict; asperse, censure, denounce, disparage, discredit, impair, impute, incriminate, lessen.

impeachment *n* accusation, arraignment, indictment; aspersion, censure, disparagement, imputation, incrimination, reproach.

impeccable *adj* faultless, immaculate, incorrupt, innocent, perfect, pure, sinless, stainless, uncorrupt.

impede *vb* bar, block, check, clog, curb, delay, encumber, hinder, interrupt, obstruct, restrain, retard, stop, thwart.

impediment *n* bar, barrier, block, check, curb, difficulty, encumbrance, hindrance, obstacle, obstruction, stumbling block.

impel *vb* drive, push, send, urge; actuate, animate, compel, constrain, embolden, incite, induce, influence, instigate, move, persuade, stimulate.

impend *vb* approach, menace, near, threaten.

impending *adj* approaching, imminent, menacing, near, threatening.

impenetrable *adj* impermeable, impervious, inaccessible; cold, dull, impassive, indifferent, obtuse, senseless, stolid, unsympathetic; dense, proof.

impenitence *n* hardheartedness, impenitency, impenitentness, obduracy, stubbornness.

impenitent *adj* hardened, hard-hearted, incorrigible, irreclaimable, obdurate, recusant, relentless, seared, stubborn, uncontrite, unconverted, unrepentant.

imperative *adj* authoritative, commanding, despotic, domineering, imperious, overbearing, peremptory, urgent; binding, obligatory.

imperceptible *adj* inaudible, indiscernible, indistinguishable, invisible; fine, impalpable, inappreciable, gradual, minute.

imperfect *adj* abortive, crude, deficient, garbled, incomplete, poor; defective, faulty, impaired.

imperfection n defectiveness, deficiency, faultiness, incompleteness; blemish, defect, fault, flaw, lack, stain, taint; failing, foible, frailty, limitation, vice, weakness.

imperial adj kingly, regal, royal, sovereign; august, consummate, exalted, grand, great, kingly, magnificent, majestic, noble, regal, royal, queenly, supreme, sovereign, supreme, consummate.

imperil vb endanger, expose, hazard, jeopardize, risk.

imperious adj arrogant, authoritative, commanding, compelling, despotic, dictatorial, domineering, haughty, imperative, lordly, magisterial, overbearing, tyrannical, urgent, compelling.

imperishable adj eternal, everlasting, immortal, incorruptible, indestructible, never-ending, perennial, unfading.

impermeable adj impenetrable, impervious.

impermissible adj deniable, insufferable, objectionable, unallowable, unallowed, unlawful.

impersonate vb act, ape, enact, imitate, mimic, mock, personate; embody, incarnate, personify, typify.

impersonation n incarnation, manifestation, personification; enacting, imitation, impersonating, mimicking, personating, representation.

impertinence n irrelevance, irrelevancy, unfitness, impropriety; assurance, boldness, brass, brazenness, effrontery, face, forwardness, impudence, incivility, insolence, intrusiveness, presumption, rudeness, sauciness, pertness.

impertinent adj inapplicable, inapposite, irrelevant; bold, forward, impudent, insolent, intrusive, malapert, meddling, officious, pert, rude, saucy, unmannerly.

imperturbability n calmness, collectedness, composure, dispassion, placidity, placidness, sedateness, serenity, steadiness, tranquility.

imperturbable adj calm, collected, composed, cool, placid, sedate, serene, tranquil, unmoved, undisturbed, unexcitable, unmoved, unruffled.

impervious adj impassable, impenetrable, impermeable.

impetuosity n force, fury, haste, precipitancy, vehemence, violence.

impetuous adj ardent, boisterous, brash, breakneck, fierce, fiery, furious, hasty, headlong, hot, hot-headed, impulsive, overzealous, passionate, precipitate, vehement, violent.

impetus n energy, force, momentum, propulsion.

impiety n irreverence, profanity, ungodliness; iniquity, sacreligiousness, sin, sinfulness, ungodliness, unholiness, unrighteousness, wickedness.

impinge vb clash, dash, encroach, hit, infringe, strike, touch.

impious adj blasphemous, godless, iniquitous, irreligious, irreverent, profane, sinful, ungodly, unholy, unrighteous, wicked.

implacable adj deadly, inexorable, merciless, pitiless, rancorous, relentless, unappeasable, unforgiving, unpropitiating, unrelenting.

implant vb ingraft, infix, insert, introduce, place.

implement vb effect, execute, fullfil. • n appliance, instrument, tool, utensil.

implicate vb entangle, enfold; compromise, concern, entangle, include, involve.

implication n entanglement, involvement, involution; connotation, hint, inference, innuendo, intimation; conclusion, meaning, significance.

implicit adj implied, inferred, understood; absolute, constant, firm, steadfast, unhesitating, unquestioning, unreserved, unshaken.

implicitly adv by implication, silently, tacitly, unspokenly, virtually, wordlessly.

implore vb adjure, ask, beg, beseech, entreat, petition, pray, solicit, supplicate.

imply vb betoken, connote, denote, import, include, infer, insinuate, involve, mean, presuppose, signify.

impolicy n folly, imprudence, ill-judgement, indiscretion, inexpediency.

impolite adj bearish, boorish, discourteous, disrespectful, ill-bred, insolent, rough, rude, uncivil, uncourteous, ungentle, ungentlemanly, ungracious, unmannerly, unpolished, unrefined.

impoliteness n boorishness, discourteousness, discourtesy, disrespect, ill-breeding, incivility, insolence, rudeness, unmannerliness.

impolitic adj ill-advised, imprudent, indiscreet, inexpedient, injudicious, unwise.

import vb bring in, introduce, transport; betoken, denote, imply, mean, purport, signify. • n goods, importation, merchandise;

bearing, drift, gist, intention, interpretation, matter, meaning, purpose, sense, signification, spirit, tenor; consequence, importance, significance, weight.

importance n concern, consequence, gravity, import, moment, momentousness, significance, weight, weightiness; consequence, pomposity, self-importance.

important adj considerable, grave, material, momentous, notable, pompous, ponderous, serious, significant, urgent, valuable, weighty; esteemed, influential, prominent, substantial; consequential, pompous, self-important.

importunate adj busy, earnest, persistent, pertinacious, pressing, teasing, troublesome, urgent.

importune vb ask, beset, dun, ply, press, solicit, urge.

importunity n appeal, beseechment, entreaty, petition, plying, prayer, pressing, suit, supplication, urging; contention, insistence; urgency.

impose vb lay, place, put, set; appoint, charge, dictate, enjoin, force, inflict, obtrude, prescribe, tax; (with **on**, **upon**) abuse, cheat, circumvent, deceive, delude, dupe, exploit, hoax, trick, victimize.

imposing adj august, commanding, dignified, exalted, grand, grandiose, impressive, lofty, magnificent, majestic, noble, stately, striking.

imposition n imposing, laying, placing, putting; burden, charge, constraint, injunction, levy, oppression, tax; artifice, cheating, deception, dupery, fraud, imposture, trickery.

impossibility n hopelessness, impracticability, inability, infeasibility, unattainability; inconceivability.

impossible adj hopeless, impracticable, infeasible, unachievable, unattainable; inconceivable, self-contradictory, unthinkable.

impost n custom, duty, excise, rate, tax, toil, tribute.

impostor n charlatan, cheat, counterfeiter, deceiver, double-dealer, humbug, hypocrite, knave, mountebank, pretender, quack, rogue, trickster.

imposture n artifice, cheat, deceit, deception, delusion, dodge, fraud, hoax, imposition, ruse, stratagem, trick, wile.

impotence n disability, feebleness, frailty, helplessness, inability, incapability, incapacity, incompetence, inefficaciousness, inefficacy, inefficiency, infirmity, powerlessness, weakness.

impotent adj disabled, enfeebled, feeble, frail, helpless, incapable, incapacitated, incompetent, inefficient, infirm, nerveless, powerless, unable, weak; barren, sterile.

impound vb confine, coop, engage, imprison.

impoverish vb beggar, pauperize; deplete, exhaust, ruin.

impracticability n impossibility, impracticableness, impracticality, infeasibility, unpracticability.

impracticable adj impossible, infeasible; intractable, obstinate, recalcitrant, stubborn, thorny, unmanageable; impassable, insurmountable.

impracticality n impossibility, impracticableness, impractibility, infeasibility, unpracticability; irrationality, unpracticalness, unrealism, unreality, unreasonableness.

imprecate vb anathematize, curse, execrate, invoke, maledict.

imprecation n anathema, curse, denunciation, execration, invocation, malediction.

imprecatory adj appealing, beseeching, entreating, imploratory, imploring, imprecatory, pleading; cursing, damnatory, execrating, maledictory.

impregnable adj immovable, impenetrable, indestructible, invincible, inviolable, invulnerable, irrefrangible, secure, unconquerable, unassailable, unyielding.

impregnate vb fecundate, fertilize, fructify; dye, fill, imbrue, imbue, infuse, permeate, pervade, saturate, soak, tincture, tinge.

impress vb engrave, imprint, print, stamp; affect, move, strike; fix, inculcate; draft, enlist, levy, press, requisition. • n impression, imprint, mark, print, seal, stamp; cognizance, device, emblem, motto, symbol.

impressibility n affectibility, impressionability, pliancy, receptiveness, responsiveness, sensibility, sensitiveness, susceptibility.

impressible adj affectible, excitable, impressionable, pliant, receptive, responsive, sensitive, soft, susceptible, tender.

impression n edition, imprinting, printing, stamping; brand, dent, impress, mark, stamp; effect, influence, sensation; fancy, idea, instinct, notion, opinion, recollection.

impressive adj affecting, effective,

emphatic, exciting, forcible, moving, over-powering, powerful, solemn, speaking, splendid, stirring, striking, telling, touching.

imprint *vb* engrave, mark, print, stamp; impress, inculcate. • *n* impression, mark, print, sign, stamp.

imprison *vb* confine, jail, immure, incarcerate, shut up.

imprisonment *n* captivity, commitment, confinement, constraint, durance, duress, incarceration, restraint.

improbability *n* doubt, uncertainty, unlikelihood.

improbable *adj* doubtful, uncertain, unlikely, unplausible.

improbity *n* dishonesty, faithlessness, fraud, fraudulence, knavery, unfairness.

impromptu *adj* extempore, improvised, off-hand, spontaneous, unpremeditated, unprepared, unrehearsed. • *adv* extemporaneously, extemporarily, extempore, offhand, ad-lib.

improper *adj* immodest, inapposite, inappropriate, irregular, unadapted, unapt, unfit, unsuitable, unsuited; indecent, indecorous, indelicate, unbecoming, unseemly; erroneous, inaccurate, incorrect, wrong.

impropriety *n* inappropriateness, unfitness, unsuitability, unsuitableness; indecorousness, indecorum, unseemliness.

improve *vb* ameliorate, amend, better, correct, edify, meliorate, mend, rectify, reform; cultivate; gain, mend, progress; enhance, increase, rise.

improvement *n* ameliorating, amelioration, amendment, bettering, improving, meliorating, melioration; advancement, proficiency, progress.

improvidence *n* imprudence, thriftlessness, unthriftiness.

improvident *adj* careless, heedless, imprudent, incautious, inconsiderate, negligent, prodigal, rash, reckless, shiftless, thoughtless, thriftless, unthrifty, wasteful.

improvisation *n* ad-libbing, contrivance, extemporaneousness, extemporariness, extemporization, fabrication, invention; (*mus*) extempore, impromptu.

improvise *vb* ad-lib, contrive, extemporize, fabricate, imagine, invent.

imprudence *n* carelessness, heedlessness, improvidence, incautiousness, inconsideration, indiscretion, rashness.

imprudent *adj* careless, heedless, ill-advised, ill-judged, improvident, incautious, inconsiderate, indiscreet, rash, unadvised, unwise.

impudence *n* assurance, audacity, boldness, brashness, brass, bumptiousness, cheek, cheekiness, effrontery, face, flippancy, forwardness, front, gall, impertinence, insolence, jaw, lip, nerve, pertness, presumption, rudeness, sauciness, shamelessness.

impudent *adj* bold, bold-faced, brazen, brazen-faced, cool, flippant, forward, immodest, impertinent, insolent, insulting, pert, presumptuous, rude, saucy, shameless.

impugn *vb* assail, attack, challenge, contradict, dispute, gainsay, oppose, question, resist.

impulse *n* force, impetus, impelling, momentum, push, thrust; appetite, inclination, instinct, passion, proclivity; incentive, incitement, influence, instigation, motive, instigation.

impulsive *adj* impelling, moving, propulsive; emotional, hasty, heedless, hot, impetuous, mad-cap, passionate, quick, rash, vehement, violent.

impunity *n* exemption, immunity, liberty, license, permission, security.

impure *adj* defiled, dirty, feculent, filthy, foul, polluted, unclean; bawdy, coarse, immodest, gross, immoral, indelicate, indecent, lewd, licentious, loose, obscene, ribald, smutty, unchaste; adulterated, corrupt, mixed.

impurity *n* defilement, feculence, filth, foulness, pollution, uncleanness; admixture, coarseness, grossness, immodesty, indecency, indelicacy, lewdness, licentiousness, looseness, obscenity, ribaldry, smut, smuttiness, unchastity, vulgarity.

imputable *adj* ascribable, attributable, chargeable, owing, referable, traceable, owing.

imputation *n* attributing, charging, imputing; accusation, blame, censure, charge, reproach.

impute *vb* ascribe, attribute, charge, consider, imply, insinuate, refer.

inability *n* impotence, incapacity, incapability, incompetence, incompetency, inefficiency; disability, disqualification.

inaccessible *adj* unapproachable, unattainable.

inaccuracy *n* erroneousness, impropriety, incorrectness, inexactness; blunder, defect, error, fault, mistake.

inaccurate *adj* defective, erroneous, faulty, incorrect, inexact, mistaken, wrong.

inaccurately *adv* carelessly, cursorily, imprecisely, incorrectly, inexactly, mistakenly, unprecisely, wrongly.

inactive *adj* inactive; dormant, inert, inoperative, peaceful, quiet, quiescent; dilatory, drowsy, dull, idle, inanimate, indolent, inert, lazy, lifeless, lumpish, passive, slothful, sleepy, stagnant, supine.

inactivity *n* dilatoriness, idleness, inaction, indolence, inertness, laziness, sloth, sluggishness, supineness, torpidity, torpor.

inadequacy *n* inadequateness, insufficiency; defectiveness, imperfection, incompetence, incompetency, incompleteness, insufficiency, unfitness, unsuitableness.

inadequate *adj* disproportionate, incapable, insufficient, unequal; defective, imperfect, inapt, incompetent, incomplete.

inadmissible *adj* improper, incompetent, unacceptable, unallowable, unqualified, unreasonable.

inadvertence, inadvertency *n* carelessness, heedlessness, inattention, inconsiderateness, negligence, thoughtlessness; blunder, error, oversight, slip.

inadvertent *adj* careless, heedless, inattentive, inconsiderate, negligent, thoughtless, unobservant.

inadvertently *adv* accidently, carelessly, heedlessly, inconsiderately, negligently, thoughtlessly, unintentionally.

inalienable *adj* undeprivable, unforfeitable, untransferable.

inane *adj* empty, fatuous, vacuous, void; foolish, frivolous, idiotic, puerile, senseless, silly, stupid, trifling, vain, worthless.

inanimate *adj* breathless, dead, extinct; dead, dull, inert, lifeless, soulless, spiritless.

inanition *n* emptiness, inanity, vacuity; exhaustion, hunger, malnutrition, starvation, want.

inanity *n* emptiness, foolishness, inanition, vacuity; folly, frivolousness, puerility, vanity, worthlessness.

inapplicable *adj* inapposite, inappropriate, inapt, irrelevant, unfit, unsuitable, unsuited.

inapposite *adj* impertinent, inapplicable, irrelevant, nonpertinent; inappropriate, unfit, unsuitable.

inappreciable *adj* impalpable, imperceptible, inconsiderable, inconspicuous, indiscernible, infinitesimal, insignificant, negligible, undiscernible, unnoticed.

inappropriate *adj* inapposite, unadapted, unbecoming, unfit, unsuitable, unsullied.

inapt *adj* inapposite, unapt, unfit, unsuitable; awkward, clumsy, dull, slow, stolid, stupid.

inaptitude *n* awkwardness, inapplicability, inappropriateness, inaptness, unfitness, unsuitableness.

inarticulate *adj* blurred, indistinct, thick; dumb, mute.

inartificial *adj* artless, direct, guileless, ingenuous, naive, simple, simple-minded, sincere, single-minded.

inasmuch as *conj* considering that, seeing that, since.

inattention *n* absent-mindedness, carelessness, disregard, heedlessness, inadvertence, inapplication, inconsiderateness, neglect, remissness, slip, thoughtlessness, unmindfulness, unobservance.

inattentive *adj* absent-minded, careless, disregarding, heedless, inadvertent, inconsiderate, neglectful, remiss, thoughtless, unmindful, unobservant.

inaudible *adj* faint, indistinct, muffled; mute, noiseless, silent, still.

inaugurate *vb* induct, install, introduce, invest; begin, commence, initiate, institute, originate.

inauguration *n* beginning, commencement, initiation, institution, investiture, installation, opening, origination.

inauspicious *adj* bad, discouraging, ill-omened, ill-starred, ominous, unfavorable, unfortunate, unlucky, unpromising, unpropitious, untoward.

inborn *adj* congenital, inbred, ingrained, inherent, innate, instinctive, native, natural.

incalculable *adj* countless, enormous, immense, incalculable, inestimable, innumerable, sumless, unknown, untold.

incandescence *n* candescence, glow, gleam, luminousness, luminosity.

incandescent *adj* aglow, candent, candescent, gleaming, glowing, luminous, luminant, radiant.

incantation *n* charm, conjuration, enchantment, magic, necromancy, sorcery, spell, witchcraft, witchery.

incapability *n* disability, inability, incapacity, incompetence.

incapable *adj* feeble, impotent, incompetent, insufficient, unable, unfit, unfitted, unqualified, weak.

incapacious *adj* cramped, deficient, incommodious, narrow, scant.

incapacitate *vb* cripple, disable; disqualify, make unfit.

incapacity *n* disability, inability, incapability, incompetence; disqualification, unfitness.

incarcerate *vb* commit, confine, immure, imprison, jail, restrain, restrict.

incarnate *vb* body, embody, incorporate, personify. • *adj* bodied, embodied, incorporated, personified.

incarnation *n* embodiment, exemplification, impersonation, manifestation, personification.

incautious *adj* impolitic, imprudent, indiscreet, uncircumspect, unwary; careless, headlong, heedless, inconsiderate, negligent, rash, reckless, thoughtless.

incendiary *adj* dissentious, factious, inflammatory, seditious. • *n* agitator, firebrand, fire-raiser.

incense[1] *vb* anger, chafe, enkindle, enrage, exasperate, excite, heat, inflame, irritate, madden, provoke.

incense[2] *n* aroma, fragrance, perfume, scent; admiration, adulation, applause, laudation.

incentive *n* cause, encouragement, goad, impulse, incitement, inducement, instigation, mainspring, motive, provocation, spur, stimulus.

inception *n* beginning, commencement, inauguration, initiation, origin, rise, start.

incertitude *n* ambiguity, doubt, doubtfulness, indecision, uncertainty.

incessant *adj* ceaseless, constant, continual, continuous, eternal, everlasting, never-ending, perpetual, unceasing, unending, uninterrupted, unremitting.

inchoate *adj* beginning, commencing, inceptive, incipient, initial.

incident *n* circumstance, episode, event, fact, happening, occurrence. • *adj* happening; belonging, pertaining, appertaining, accessory, relating, natural; falling, impinging.

incidental *adj* accidental, casual, chance, concomitant, contingent, fortuitous, subordinate; adventitious, extraneous, nonessential, occasional.

incinerate *vb* burn, char, conflagrate, cremate, incremate.

incipient *adj* beginning, commencing, inchoate, inceptive, originating, starting.

incised *adj* carved, cut, engraved, gashed, graved, graven.

incision *n* cut, gash, notch, opening, penetration.

incisive *adj* cutting; acute, biting, sarcastic, satirical, sharp; acute, clear, distinct, penetrating, sharp-cut, trenchant.

incite *vb* actuate, animate, arouse, drive, encourage, excite, foment, goad, hound, impel, instigate, prod, prompt, provoke, push, rouse, spur, stimulate, urge.

incitement *n* encouragement, goad, impulse, incentive, inducement, motive, provocative, spur, stimulus.

incivility *n* discourteousness, discourtesy, disrespect, ill-breeding, ill-manners, impoliteness, impudence, inurbanity, rudeness, uncourtliness, unmannerliness.

inclemency *n* boisterousness, cruelty, harshness, rigor, roughness, severity, storminess, tempestuousness, tyranny.

inclement *adj* boisterous, harsh, rigorous, rough, severe, stormy; cruel, unmerciful.

inclination *n* inclining, leaning, slant, slope; trending, verging; aptitude, bent, bias, disposition, penchant, predilection, predisposition, proclivity, proneness, propensity, tendency, turn, twist; desire, fondness, liking, taste, partiality, predilection, wish; bow, nod, obeisance.

incline *vb* lean, slant, slope; bend, nod, verge; tend; bias, dispose, predispose, turn; bow. • *n* ascent, descent, grade, gradient, rise, slope.

inclose *see* **enclose**.

include *vb* contain, hold; comprehend, comprise, contain, cover, embody, embrace, incorporate, involve, take in.

inclusive *adj* comprehending, embracing, encircling, enclosing, including, taking in.

incognito, incognita *adj* camouflaged, concealed, disguised, unknown. • *n* camouflage, concealment, disguise.

incoherent *adj* detached, loose, nonadhesive, noncohesive; disconnected, incongruous, inconsequential, inconsistent, uncoordinated; confused, illogical, irrational, rambling, unintelligible, wild.

income *n* earnings, emolument, gains, interest, pay, perquisite, proceeds, profits, receipts, rents, return, revenue, salary, wages.

incommensurate *adj* disproportionate, inadequate, insufficient, unequal.

incommode *vb* annoy, discommode, disquiet,

disturb, embarrass, hinder, inconvenience, molest, plague, trouble, upset, vex.

incommodious *adj* awkward, cumbersome, cumbrous, inconvenient, unhandy, unmanageable, unsuitable, unwieldy; annoying, disadvantageous, harassing, irritating, vexatious.

incommunicative *adj* exclusive, unsociable, unsocial, reserved.

incomparable *adj* matchless, inimitable, peerless, surpassing, transcendent, unequaled, unparalleled, unrivalled.

incompatibility *n* contrariety, contradictoriness, discrepancy, incongruity, inconsistency, irreconcilability, unsuitability, unsuitableness

incompatible *adj* contradictory, incongruous, inconsistent, inharmonious, irreconcilable, unadapted, unsuitable.

incompetence *n* inability, incapability, incapacity, incompetency; inadequacy, insufficiency; disqualification, unfitness.

incompetent *adj* incapable, unable; inadequate, insufficient; disqualified, incapacitated, unconstitutional, unfit, unfitted.

incomplete *adj* defective, deficient, imperfect, partial; inexhaustive, unaccompanied, uncompleted, unexecuted, unfinished.

incomprehensible *adj* inconceivable, inexhaustible, unfathomable, unimaginable; inconceivable, unintelligible, unthinkable.

incomputable *adj* enormous, immense, incalculable, innumerable, prodigious.

inconceivable *adj* incomprehensible, incredible, unbelievable, unimaginable, unthinkable.

inconclusive *adj* inconsequent, inconsequential, indecisive, unconvincing. illogical, unproved, unproven.

incongruity *n* absurdity, contradiction, contradictoriness, contrariety, discordance, discordancy, discrepancy, impropriety, inappropriateness, incoherence, incompatibility, inconsistency, unfitness, unsuitableness.

incongruous *adj* absurd, contradictory, contrary, disagreeing, discrepant, inappropriate, incoherent, incompatible, inconsistent, inharmonious, unfit, unsuitable.

inconsequent *adj* desultory, disconnected, fragmentary, illogical, inconclusive, inconsistent, irrelevant, loose.

inconsiderable *adj* immaterial, insignificant, petty, slight, small, trifling, trivial, unimportant.

inconsiderate *adj* intolerant, uncharitable, unthoughtful; careless, heedless, giddy, hare-brained, hasty, headlong, imprudent, inadvertent, inattentive, indifferent, indiscreet, light-headed, negligent, rash, thoughtless.

inconsistency *n* incoherence, incompatibility, incongruity, unsuitableness; contradiction, contrariety; changeableness, inconstancy, instability, vacillation, unsteadiness.

inconsistent *adj* different, discrepant, illogical, incoherent, incompatible, incongruous, inconsequent, inconsonant, irreconcilable, unsuitable; contradictory, contrary; changeable, fickle, inconstant, unstable, unsteady, vacillating, variable.

inconsolable *adj* comfortless, crushed, disconsolate, forlorn, heartbroken, hopeless, woebegone.

inconstancy *n* changeableness, mutability, variability, variation, fluctuation, faithlessness, fickleness, capriciousness, vacillation, uncertainty, unsteadiness, volatility.

inconstant *adj* capricious, changeable, faithless, fickle, fluctuating, mercurial, mutable, unsettled, unsteady, vacillating, variable, varying, volatile, wavering; mutable, uncertain, unstable.

incontestable *adj* certain, incontrovertible, indisputable, indubitable, irrefrangible, sure, undeniable, unquestionable.

incontinence *n* excess, extravagance, indulgence, intemperance, irrepressibility, lasciviousness, lewdness, licentiousness, prodigality, profligacy, riotousness, unrestraint, wantonness, wildness.

incontinent *adj* debauched, lascivious, lewd, licentious, lustful, prodigal, unchaste, uncontrolled, unrestrained.

incontrovertible *adj* certain, incontestable, indisputable, indubitable, irrefutable, sure, undeniable, unquestionable.

inconvenience *vb* discommode; annoy, disturb, molest, trouble, vex. • *n* annoyance, disadvantage, disturbance, molestation, trouble, vexation; awkwardness, cumbersomeness, incommodiousness, unwieldiness; unfitness, unseasonableness, unsuitableness.

inconvenient *adj* annoying, awkward, cumbersome, cumbrous, disadvantageous, incommodious, inopportune, troublesome, uncomfortable, unfit, unhandy, unmanageable, unseasonable, unsuitable, untimely, unwieldy, vexatious.

incorporate *vb* affiliate, amalgamate, associate, blend, combine, consolidate, include, merge, mix, unite; embody, incarnate. • *adj* incorporeal, immaterial, spiritual, supernatural; blended, consolidated, merged, united.

incorporation *n* affiliation, alignment, amalgamation, association, blend, blending, combination, consolidation, fusion, inclusion, merger, mixture, unification, union, embodiment, incarnation, personification.

incorporeal *adj* bodiless, immaterial, impalpable, incorporate, spiritual, supernatural, unsubstantial.

incorrect *adj* erroneous, false, inaccurate, inexact, untrue, wrong; faulty, improper, mistaken, ungrammatical, unbecoming, unsound.

incorrectness *n* error, inaccuracy, inexactness, mistake.

incorrigible *adj* abandoned, graceless, hardened, irreclaimable, lost, obdurate, recreant, reprobate, shameless; helpless, hopeless, irremediable, irrecoverable, irreparable, irretrievable, irreversible, remediless.

incorruptibility *n* unpurchasableness; deathlessness, immortality, imperishableness, incorruptibleness, incorruption, indestructibility.

incorruptible *adj* honest, unbribable; imperishable, indestructible, immortal, undying, deathless, everlasting.

increase *vb* accrue, advance, augment, enlarge, extend, grow, intensify, mount, wax; multiply; enhance, greaten, heighten, raise, reinforce; aggravate, prolong. • *n* accession, accretion, accumulation, addition, augmentation, crescendo, development, enlargement, expansion, extension, growth, heightening, increment, intensification, multiplication, swelling; gain, produce, product, profit; descendants, issue, offspring, progeny.

incredible *adj* absurd, inadmissible, nonsensical, unbelievable.

incredulity *n* distrust, doubt, incredulousness, scepticism, unbelief.

incredulous *adj* distrustful, doubtful, dubious, sceptical, unbelieving.

increment *n* addition, augmentation, enlargement, increase.

incriminate *vb* accuse, blame, charge, criminate, impeach.

incubate *vb* brood, develop, hatch, sit.

inculcate *vb* enforce, implant, impress, infix, infuse, ingraft, inspire, instil.

inculpable *adj* blameless, faultless, innocent, irreprehensible, irreproachable, irreprovable, sinless, unblamable, unblameable.

inculpate *vb* accuse, blame, censure, charge, incriminate, impeach, recriminate.

inculpatory *adj* criminatory, incriminating.

incumbent *adj* binding, devolved, devolving, laid, obligatory; leaning, prone, reclining, resting. • *n* holder, occupant.

incur *vb* acquire, bring, contract.

incurable *adj* cureless, hopeless, irrecoverable, remediless; helpless, incorrigible, irremediable, irreparable, irretrievable, remediless.

incurious *adj* careless, heedless, inattentive, indifferent, uninquisitive, unobservant, uninterested.

incursion *n* descent, foray, raid, inroad, irruption.

incursive *adj* aggressive, hostile, invasive, predatory, raiding.

incurvate *vb* bend, bow, crook, curve. • *adj* (*bot*) aduncous, arcuate, bowed, crooked, curved, hooked.

indebted *adj* beholden, obliged, owing.

indecency *n* impropriety, indecorum, offensiveness, outrageousness, unseemliness; coarseness, filthiness, foulness, grossness, immodesty, impurity, obscenity, vileness.

indecent *adj* bold, improper, indecorous, offensive, outrageous, unbecoming, unseemly; coarse, dirty, filthy, gross, immodest, impure, indelicate, lewd, nasty, obscene, pornographic, salacious, shameless, smutty, unchaste.

indecipherable *adj* illegible, undecipherable, undiscoverable, inexplicable, obscure, unintelligible, unreadable.

indecision *n* changeableness, fickleness, hesitation, inconstancy, irresolution, unsteadiness, vacillation.

indecisive *adj* dubious, hesitating, inconclusive, irresolute, undecided, unsettled, vacillating, wavering.

indecorous *adj* coarse, gross, ill-bred, impolite, improper, indecent, rude, unbecoming, uncivil, unseemly.

indecorum *n* grossness, ill-breeding, ill manners, impoliteness, impropriety, incivility, indecency, indecorousness.

indeed *adv* absolutely, actually, certainly, in fact, in truth, in reality, positively, really, strictly, truly, verily, veritably. • *interj* really! you don't say so! is it possible!

indefatigable *adj* assiduous, never-tiring, persevering, persistent, sedulous, tireless, unflagging, unremitting, untiring, unwearied.

indefeasible *adj* immutable, inalienable, irreversible, irrevocable, unalterable.

indefensible *adj* censurable, defenseless, faulty, unpardonable, untenable; inexcusable, insupportable, unjustifiable, unwarrantable, wrong.

indefinite *adj* confused, doubtful, equivocal, general, imprecise, indefinable, indecisive, indeterminate, indistinct, inexact, inexplicit, lax, loose, nondescript, obscure, uncertain, undefined, undetermined, unfixed, unsettled, vague.

indelible *adj* fast, fixed, ineffaceable, ingrained, permanent.

indelicacy *n* coarseness, grossness, indecorousness, indecorum, impropriety, offensiveness, unseemliness, vulgarity; immodesty, indecency, lewdness, unchastity; foulness, obscenity.

indelicate *adj* broad, coarse, gross, indecorous, intrusive, rude, unbecoming, unseemly; foul, immodest, indecent, lewd, obscene, unchaste, vulgar.

indemnification *n* compensation, reimbursement, remuneration, security.

indemnify *vb* compensate, reimburse, remunerate, requite, secure.

indent *vb* bruise, jag, notch, pink, scallop, serrate; bind, indenture.

indentation *n* bruise, dent, depression, jag, notch.

indenture *vb* bind, indent. • *n* contract, instrument; indentation.

independence *n* freedom, liberty, self-direction; distinctness, nondependence, separation; competence, ease.

independent *adj* absolute, autonomous, free, self-directing, uncoerced, unrestrained, unrestricted, voluntary; (*Person*) self-reliant, unconstrained, unconventional.

indescribable *adj* ineffable, inexpressible, nameless, unutterable.

indestructible *adj* abiding, endless, enduring, everlasting, fadeless, imperishable, incorruptible, undecaying.

indeterminate *adj* indefinite, uncertain, undetermined, unfixed.

index *vb* alphabetize, catalog, codify, earmark, file, list, mark, tabulate. • *n* catalog, list, register, tally; indicator, lead, mark,

pointer, sign, signal, token; contents, table of contents; forefinger; exponent.

indicate *vb* betoken, denote, designate, evince, exhibit, foreshadow, manifest, mark, point out, prefigure, presage, register, show, signify, specify, tell; hint, imply, intimate, sketch, suggest.

indication *n* hint, index, manifestation, mark, note, sign, suggestion, symptom, token.

indicative *adj* significant, suggestive, symptomatic; (*gram*) affirmative, declarative.

indict *vb* (*law*) accuse, charge, present.

indictment *n* (*law*) indicting, presentment; accusation, arraignment, charge, crimination, impeachment.

indifference *n* apathy, carelessness, coldness, coolness, heedlessness, inattention, insignificance, negligence, unconcern, unconcernedness, uninterestedness; disinterestedness, impartiality, neutrality.

indifferent *adj* apathetic, cold, cool, dead, distant, dull, easy-going, frigid, heedless, inattentive, incurious, insensible, insouciant, listless, lukewarm, nonchalant, perfunctory, regardless, stoical, unconcerned, uninterested, unmindful, unmoved; equal; fair, medium, middling, moderate, ordinary, passable, tolerable; mediocre, so-so; immaterial, unimportant; disinterested, impartial, neutral, unbiased.

indigence *n* destitution, distress, necessity, need, neediness, pauperism, penury, poverty, privation, want.

indigenous *adj* aboriginal, home-grown, inborn, inherent, native.

indigent *adj* destitute, distressed, insolvent, moneyless, necessitous, needy, penniless, pinched, poor, reduced.

indigested *adj* unconcocted, undigested; crude, ill-advised, ill-considered, ill-judged; confused, disorderly, ill-arranged, unmethodical.

indigestion *n* dyspepsia, dyspepsy.

indignant *adj* angry, exasperated, incensed, irate, ireful, provoked, roused, wrathful, wroth.

indignation *n* anger, choler, displeasure, exasperation, fury, ire, rage, resentment, wrath.

indignity *n* abuse, affront, contumely, dishonor, disrespect, ignominy, insult, obloquy, opprobrium, outrage, reproach, slight.

indirect *adj* circuitous, circumlocutory,

collateral, devious, oblique, roundabout, sidelong, tortuous; deceitful, dishonest, dishonorable, unfair; mediate, remote, secondary, subordinate.

indiscernible *adj* imperceptible, indistinguishable, invisible, undiscernible, undiscoverable.

indiscipline *n* laxity, insubordination.

indiscreet *adj* foolish, hasty, headlong, heedless, imprudent, incautious, inconsiderate, injudicious, rash, reckless, unwise.

indiscretion *n* folly, imprudence, inconsiderateness, rashness; blunder, faux pas, lapse, mistake, misstep.

indiscriminate *adj* confused, heterogeneous, indistinct, mingled, miscellaneous, mixed, promiscuous, undiscriminating, undistinguishable, undistinguishing.

indispensable *adj* essential, expedient, necessary, needed, needful, requisite.

indisputable *adj* certain, incontestable, indubitable, infallible, sure, undeniable, undoubted, unmistakable, unquestionable.

indisposed *adj* ailing, ill, sick, unwell; averse, backward, disinclined, loath, reluctant, unfriendly, unwilling.

indisposition *n* ailment, illness, sickness; aversion, backwardness, dislike, disinclination, reluctance, unwillingness.

indisputable *adj* certain, incontestable, indutitable, infallible, sure, undeniable, undoubted, unmistakable, unquestionable.

indissoluble *adj* abiding, enduring, firm, imperishable, incorruptible, indestructible, lasting, stable, unbreakable.

indistinct *adj* ambiguous, doubtful, uncertain; blurred, dim, dull, faint, hazy, misty, nebulous, obscure, shadowy, vague; confused, inarticulate, indefinite, indistinguishable, undefined, undistinguishable.

indistinguishable *adj* imperceptible, indiscernible, unnoticeable, unobservable; chaotic, confused, dim, indistinct, obscure, vague.

indite *vb* compose, pen, write.

individual *adj* characteristic, distinct, identical, idiosyncratic, marked, one, particular, personal, respective, separate, single, singular, special, unique; peculiar, proper; decided, definite, independent, positive, self-guided, unconventional. • *n* being, character, party, person, personage, somebody, someone; type, unit.

individuality *n* definiteness, indentity,

personality; originality, self-direction, self-determination, singularity, uniqueness.

individualize *vb* individuate, particularize, singularize, specify.

indivisible *adj* incommensurable, indissoluble, inseparable, unbreakable, unpartiable.

indocile *adj* cantankerous, contumacious, dogged, froward, inapt, headstrong, intractable, mulish, obstinate, perverse, refractory, stubborn, ungovernable, unmanageable, unruly, unteachable.

indoctrinate *vb* brainwash, imbue, initiate, instruct, rehabilitate, teach.

indoctrination *n* grounding, initiation, instruction, rehabilitation.

indolence *n* idleness, inactivity, inertia, inertness, laziness, listlessness, sloth, slothfulness, sluggishness.

indolent *adj* easy, easy-going, inactive, inert, lazy, listless, lumpish, otiose, slothful, sluggish, supine.

indomitable *adj* invincible, unconquerable, unyielding.

indorse *see* **endorse**.

indubitable *adj* certain, evident, incontestable, incontrovertible, indisputable, sure, undeniable, unquestionable.

induce *vb* actuate, allure, bring, draw, drive, entice, impel, incite, influence, instigate, move, persuade, prevail, prompt, spur, urge; bring on, cause, effect, motivate, lead, occasion, produce.

inducement *n* allurement, draw, enticement, instigation, persuasion; cause, consideration, impulse, incentive, incitement, influence, motive, reason, spur, stimulus.

induct *vb* inaugurate, initiate, install, institute, introduce, invest.

induction *n* inauguration, initiation, institution, installation, introduction; conclusion, generalization, inference.

indue *vb* assume, endow, clothe, endue, invest, supply.

indulge *vb* gratify, license, revel, satisfy, wallow, yield to; coddle, cosset, favor, humor, pamper, pet, spoil; allow, cherish, foster, harbor, permit, suffer.

indulgence *n* gratification, humoring, pampering; favor, kindness, lenience, lenity, liberality, tenderness; (*theol*) absolution, remission.

indulgent *adj* clement, easy, favoring, forbearing, gentle, humoring, kind, lenient, mild, pampering, tender, tolerant.

indurate *vb* harden, inure, sear, strengthen.

induration *n* hardening, obduracy.

industrious *adj* assiduous, diligent, hard-working, laborious, notable, operose, sedulous; brisk, busy, persevering, persistent.

industry *n* activity, application, assiduousness, assiduity, diligence; perseverance, persistence, sedulousness, vigor; effort, labor, toil.

inebriated *adj* drunk, intoxicated, stupefied.

ineffable *adj* indescribable, inexpressible, unspeakable, unutterable.

ineffaceable *adj* indelible, indestructible, inerasable, inexpungeable, ingrained.

ineffectual *adj* abortive, bootless, fruitless, futile, inadequate, inefficacious, ineffective, inoperative, useless, unavailing, vain; feeble, inefficient, powerless, impotent, weak.

inefficacy *n* ineffectualness, inefficiency.

inefficient *adj* feeble, incapable, ineffectual, ineffective, inefficacious, weak.

inelastic *adj* flabby, flaccid, inductile, inflexible, irresilient.

inelegant *adj* abrupt, awkward, clumsy, coarse, constrained, cramped, crude, graceless, harsh, homely, homespun, rough, rude, stiff, tasteless, uncourtly, uncouth, ungainly, ungraceful, unpolished, unrefined.

ineligible *adj* disqualified, unqualified; inexpedient, objectionable, unadvisable, undesirable.

inept *adj* awkward, improper, inapposite, inappropriate, unapt, unfit, unsuitable; null, useless, void, worthless; foolish, nonsensical, pointless, senseless, silly, stupid.

ineptitude *n* inappositeness, inappropriateness, inaptitude, unfitness, unsuitability, unsuitableness; emptiness, nullity, uselessness, worthlessness; folly, foolishness, nonsense, pointlessness, senselessness, silliness, stupidity.

inequality *n* disproportion, inequitableness, injustice, unfairness; difference, disparity, dissimilarity, diversity, imparity, irregularity, roughness, unevenness; inadequacy, incompetency, insufficiency.

inequitable *adj* unfair, unjust.

inert *adj* comatose, dead, inactive, lifeless, motionless, quiescent, passive; apathetic, dronish, dull, idle, indolent, lazy, lethargic, lumpish, phlegmatic, slothful, sluggish, supine, torpid.

inertia *n* apathy, inertness, lethargy, passiveness, passivity, slothfulness, sluggishness.

inestimable *adj* incalculable, invaluable, precious, priceless, valuable.

inevitable *adj* certain, necessary, unavoidable, undoubted.

inexact *adj* imprecise, inaccurate, incorrect; careless, crude, loose.

inexcusable *adj* indefensible, irremissible, unallowable, unjustifiable, unpardonable.

inexhaustible *adj* boundless, exhaustless, indefatigable, unfailing, unlimited.

inexorable *adj* cruel, firm, hard, immovable, implacable, inflexible, merciless, pitiless, relentless, severe, steadfast, unbending, uncompassionate, unmerciful, unrelenting, unyielding.

inexpedient *adj* disadvantageous, ill-judged, impolitic, imprudent, indiscreet, injudicious, inopportune, unadvisable, unprofitable, unwise.

inexperience *n* greenness, ignorance, rawness.

inexperienced *adj* callow, green, raw, strange, unacquainted, unconversant, undisciplined, uninitiated, unpracticed, unschooled, unskilled, untrained, untried, unversed, young.

inexpert *adj* awkward, bungling, clumsy, inapt, maladroit, unhandy, unskillful, unskilled.

inexpiable *adj* implacable, inexorable, irreconcilable, unappeasable; irremissible, unatonable, unpardonable.

inexplicable *adj* enigmatic, enigmatical, incomprehensible, inscrutable, mysterious, strange, unaccountable, unintelligible.

inexpressible *adj* indescribable, ineffable, unspeakable, unutterable; boundless, infinite, surpassing.

inexpressive *adj* blank, characterless, dull, unexpressive.

inextinguishable *adj* unquenchable.

in extremis *adv* moribund.

inextricable *adj* entangled, intricate, perplexed, unsolvable.

infallibility *n* certainty, infallibleness, perfection.

infallible *adj* certain, indubitable, oracular, sure, unerring, unfailing.

infamous *adj* abominable, atrocious, base, damnable, dark, detestable, discreditable, disgraceful, dishonorable, disreputable, heinous, ignominious, nefarious, odious, opprobrious, outrageous, scandalous, shameful, shameless, vile, villainous, wicked.

infamy n abasement, discredit, disgrace, dishonor, disrepute, ignominy, obloquy, odium, opprobrium, scandal, shame; atrocity, detestableness, disgracefulness, dishonorableness, odiousness, scandalousness, shamefulness, villainy, wickedness.

infancy n beginning, commencement; babyhood, childhood, minority, nonage, pupillage.

infant n babe, baby, bairn, bantling, brat, chit, minor, nursling, papoose, suckling, tot.

infantile adj childish, infantine, newborn, tender, young; babyish, childish, weak; babylike, childlike.

infatuate vb befool, besot, captivate, delude, prepossess, stultify.

infatuation n absorption, besottedness, folly, foolishness, prepossession, stupefaction.

infeasible adj impractical, unfeasible.

infect vb affect, contaminate, corrupt, defile, poison, pollute, taint, vitiate.

infection n affection, bane, contagion, contamination, corruption, defilement, pest, poison, pollution, taint, virus, vitiation.

infectious adj catching, communicable, contagious, contaminating, corrupting, defiling, demoralizing, pestiferous, pestilential, poisoning, polluting, sympathetic, vitiating.

infecund adj barren, infertile, sterile, unfruitful, unproductive, unprolific.

infecundity n unfruitfulness.

infelicitous adj calamitous, miserable, unfortunate, unhappy, wretched; inauspicious, unfavorable, unpropitious; ill-chosen, inappropriate, unfitting.

infer vb collect, conclude, deduce, derive, draw, gather, glean, guess, presume, reason.

inference n conclusion, consequence, corollary, deduction, generalization, guess, illation, implication, induction, presumption.

inferior adj lower, nether; junior, minor, secondary, subordinate; bad, base, deficient, humble, imperfect, indifferent, mean, mediocre, paltry, poor, second-rate, shabby.

inferiority n juniority, subjection, subordination, mediocrity; deficiency, imperfection, inadequacy, shortcoming.

infernal adj abominable, accursed, atrocious, damnable, dark, demoniacal, devilish, diabolical, fiendish, fiendlike, hellish, malicious, nefarious, satanic, Stygian.

infertility n barrenness, infecundity, sterility, unfruitfulness, unproductivity.

infest vb annoy, disturb, harass, haunt, molest, plague, tease, torment, trouble, vex, worry; beset, overrun, possess, swarm, throng.

infidel n agnostic, atheist, disbeliever, heathen, heretic, sceptic, unbeliever.

infidelity n adultery, disloyalty, faithlessness, treachery, unfaithfulness; disbelief, scepticism, unbelief.

infiltrate vb absorb, pervade, soak.

infinite adj boundless, endless, illimitable, immeasurable, inexhaustible, interminable, limitless, measureless, perfect, unbounded, unlimited; enormous, immense, stupendous, vast; absolue, eternal, self-determined, self-existent, unconditioned.

infinitesimal adj infinitely small; microscopic, miniscule.

infinity n absoluteness, boundlessness, endlessness, eternity, immensity, infiniteness, infinitude, interminateness, self-determination, self-existence, vastness.

infirm adj ailing, debilitated, enfeebled, feeble, frail, weak, weakened; faltering, irresolute, vacillating, wavering; insecure, precarious, unsound, unstable.

infirmity n ailment, debility, feebleness, frailness, frailty, weakness; defect, failing, fault, foible, weakness.

infix vb fasten, fix, plant, set; implant, inculcate, infuse, ingraft, instil.

inflame vb animate, arouse, excite, enkindle, fire, heat, incite, inspirit, intensify, rouse, stimulate; aggravate, anger, chafe, embitter, enrage, exasperate, incense, infuriate, irritate, madden, nettle, provoke.

inflammability n combustibility, combustibleness, inflammableness.

inflammable adj combustible, ignitible; excitable.

inflammation n burning, conflagration; anger, animosity, excitement, heat, rage, turbulence, violence.

inflammatory adj fiery, inflaming; dissentious, incendiary, seditious.

inflate vb bloat, blow up, distend, expand, swell, sufflate; elate, puff up; enlarge, increase.

inflated adj bloated, distended, puffed-up, swollen; bombastic, declamatory, grandiloquent, high-flown, magniloquent, overblown, pompous, rhetorical, stilted, tumid, turgid.

inflation *n* enlargement, increase, overenlargement, overissue; bloatedness, distension, expansion, sufflation; bombast, conceit, conceitedness, self-conceit, self-complacency, self-importance, self-sufficiency, vaingloriousness, vainglory.

inflect *vb* bend, bow, curve, turn; (*gram*) conjugate, decline, vary.

inflection *n* bend, bending, crook, curvature, curvity, flexure; (*gram*) accidence, conjugation, declension, variation; (*mus*) modulation.

inflexibility *n* inflexibleness, rigidity, stiffness; doggedness, obstinacy, perinacity, stubbornness, firmness, perseverance, resolution, tenacity.

inflexible *adj* rigid, rigorous, stiff, unbending, cantankerous, cross-grained, dogged, headstrong, heady, inexorable, intractable, obdurate, obstinant, pertinacious, refractory, stubborn, unyielding, willful; firm, immovable, persevering, resolute, steadfast, unbending.

inflict *vb* bring, impose, lay on.

infliction *n* imposition, inflicting; judgment, punishment.

inflorescence *n* blooming, blossoming, flowering.

influence *vb* affect, bias, control, direct, lead, modify, prejudice, prepossess, sway; actuate, arouse, impel, incite, induce, instigate, move, persuade, prevail upon; *roww* • *n* ascendancy, authority, control, mastery, potency, predominance, pull, rule, sway; credit, reputation, weight; inflow, inflowing, influx; magnetism, power, spell.

influential *adj* controlling, effective, effectual, potent, powerful, strong; authoritative, momentous, substantial, weighty.

influx *n* flowing in, introduction.

infold *see* enfold.

inform *vb* animate, inspire, quicken; acquaint, advise, apprise, enlighten, instruct, notify, teach, tell, tip, warn.

informal *adj* unceremonious, unconventional, unofficial; easy, familiar, natural, simple; irregular, nonconformist, unusual.

informality *n* unceremoniousness; unconventionality; ease, familiarity, naturalness, simplicity; noncomformity, irregularity, unusualness.

informant *n* advertiser, adviser, informer, intelligencer, newsmonger, notifier, relator; accuser, complainant, informer.

information *n* advice, data, intelligence, knowledge, notice; advertisement, enlightenment, instruction, message, tip, word, warning; accusation, complaint, denunciation.

informer *n* accuser, complainant, informant, snitch.

infraction *n* breach, breaking, disobedience, encroachment, infringement, nonobservance, transgression, violation.

infrangible *adj* inseparable, inviolable, unbreakable.

infrequency *n* rareness, rarity, uncommonness, unusualness.

infrequent *adj* rare, uncommon, unfrequent, unusual; occasional, scant, scarce, sporadic.

infringe *vb* break, contravene, disobey, intrude, invade, transgress, violate.

infringement *n* breach, breaking, disobedience, infraction, nonobservance, transgression, violation.

infuriated *adj* angry, enraged, furious, incensed, maddened, raging, wild.

infuse *vb* breathe into, implant, inculcate, ingraft, insinuate, inspire, instil, introduce; macerate, steep.

infusion *n* inculcation, instillation, introduction; infusing, macerating, steeping.

ingathering *n* harvest.

ingenious *adj* able, adroit, artful, bright, clever, fertile, gifted, inventive, ready, sagacious, shrewd, witty.

ingenuity *n* ability, acuteness, aptitude, aptness, capacity, capableness, cleverness, faculty, genius, gift, ingeniousness, inventiveness, knack, readiness, skill, turn.

ingenuous *adj* artless, candid, childlike, downright, frank, generous, guileless, honest, innocent, naive, open, open-hearted, plain, simple-minded, sincere, single-minded, straightforward, transparent, truthful, unreserved.

ingenuousness *n* artlessness, candor, childlikeness, frankness, guilelessness, honesty, naivety, open-heartedness, openness, sincerity, single-mindedness, truthfulness.

inglorious *adj* humble, lowly, mean, nameless, obscure, undistinguished, unhonored, unknown, unmarked, unnoted; discreditable, disgraceful, humiliating, ignominous, scandalous, shameful.

ingloriousness *n* humbleness, lowliness, meanness, namelessness, obscurity;

abasement, discredit, disgrace, dishonor, disrepute, humiliation, infamy, ignominiousness, ignominy, obloquy, odium, opprobrium, shame.

ingraft vb graft, implant, inculcate, infix, infuse, instil.

ingrain vb dye, imbue, impregnate.

ingratiate vb insinuate.

ingratitude n thanklessness, ungratefulness, unthankfulness.

ingredient n component, constituent, element.

ingress n entrance, entré, entry, introgression.

ingulf see **engulf**.

inhabit vb abide, dwell, live, occupy, people, reside, sojourn.

inhabitable adj habitable, livable.

inhabitant n citizen, denizen, dweller, inhabiter, resident.

inhalation n breath, inhaling, inspiration; sniff, snuff.

inhale vb breathe in, draw in, inbreathe, inspire.

inharmonious adj discordant, inharmonic, out of tune, unharmonious, unmusical.

inhere vb cleave to, stick, stick fast; abide, belong, exist, lie, pertain, reside.

inherent adj essential, immanent, inborn, inbred, indwelling, ingrained, innate, inseparable, intrinsic, native, natural, proper; adhering, sticking.

inherit vb get, receive.

inheritance n heritage, legacy, patrimony; inheriting.

inheritor n heir, (law) parcener.

inhibit vb bar, check, debar, hinder, obstruct, prevent, repress, restrain, stop; forbid, interdict, prohibit.

inhibition n check, hindrance, impediment, obstacle, obstruction, restraint; disallowance, embargo, interdict, interdiction, prevention, prohibition.

inhospitable adj cool, forbidding, unfriendly, unkind; bigoted, illiberal, intolerant, narrow, prejudiced, ungenerous, unreceptive; barren, wild.

inhospitality n inhospitableness, unkindness; illiberality, narrowness.

inhuman adj barbarous, brutal, cruel, fell, ferocious, merciless, pitiless, remorseless, ruthless, savage, unfeeling; nonhuman.

inhumanity n barbarity, brutality, cruelty, ferocity, savageness; hard-heartedness, unkindness.

inhume vb bury, entomb, inter.

inimical adj antagonistic, hostile, unfriendly; adverse, contrary, harmful, hurtful, noxious, opposed, pernicious; repugnant, unfavorable.

inimitable adj incomparable, matchless, peerless, unequaled, unexampled, unmatched, unparagoned, unparalleled, unrivaled, unsurpassed.

iniquitous adj atrocious, criminal, flagitious, heinous, inequitable, nefarious, sinful, wicked, wrong, unfair, unjust, unrighteous.

iniquity n injustice, sin, sinfulness, unrighteousness, wickedness, wrong; crime, misdeed, offence.

initial adj first; beginning, commencing, incipient, initiatory, introductory, opening, original; elementary, inchoate, rudimentary.

initiate vb begin, commence, enter upon, inaugurate, introduce, open; ground, indoctrinate, instruct, prime, teach.

initiation n beginning, commencement, inauguration, opening; admission, entrance, introduction; indoctrinate, instruction.

initiative n beginning; energy, enterprise.

initiatory adj inceptive, initiative.

inject vb force in, interject, insert, introduce, intromit.

injudicious adj foolish, hasty, ill-advised, ill-judged, imprudent, incautious, inconsiderate, indiscreet, rash, unwise.

injunction n admonition, bidding, command, mandate, order, precept.

injure vb damage, disfigure, harm, hurt, impair, mar, spoil, sully, wound; abuse, aggrieve, wrong; affront, dishonor, insult.

injurious adj baneful, damaging, deadly, deleterious, destructive, detrimental, disadvantageous, evil, fatal, hurtful, mischievous, noxious, pernicious, prejudicial, ruinous; inequitable, iniquitous, unjust, wrongful; contumelious, detractory, libellous, slanderous.

injury n evil, ill, injustice, wrong; damage, detriment, harm, hurt, impairment, loss, mischief, prejudice.

injustice n inequity, unfairness; grievance, iniquity, injury, wrong.

inkhorn n inkbottle, inkstand.

inkling n hint, intimation, suggestion, whisper.

inky adj atramentous, black, murky.

inland adj domestic, hinterland, home, up-country; interior, internal.

inlet *n* arm, bay, bight, cove, creek; entrance, ingress, passage.

inmate *n* denizen, dweller, guest, intern, occupant.

inmost *adj* deepest, innermost.

inn *n* hostel, hostelry, hotel, pub, public house, tavern.

innate *adj* congenital, constitutional, inborn, inbred, indigenous, inherent, inherited, instinctive, native, natural, organic.

inner *adj* interior, internal.

innermost *adj* deepest, inmost.

innkeeper *n* host, innholder, landlady, landlord, tavernkeeper.

innocence *n* blamelessness, chastity, guilelessness, guiltlessness, purity, simplicity, sinlessness, stainlessness; harmlessness, innocuousness, innoxiousness, inoffensiveness.

innocent *adj* blameless, clean, clear, faultless, guiltless, immaculate, pure, sinless, spotless, unfallen, upright; harmless, innocuous, innoxious, inoffensive; lawful, legitimate, permitted; artless, guileless, ignorant, ingenuous, simple. • *n* babe, child, ingénue, naif, naive, unsophisticate.

innocuous *adj* harmless, innocent, inoffensive, safe.

innovate *vb* change, introduce.

innovation *n* change, introduction; departure, novelty.

innuendo *n* allusion, hint, insinuation, intimation, suggestion.

innumerable *adj* countless, numberless.

inoculate *vb* infect, vaccinate.

inoffensive *adj* harmless, innocent, innocuous, innoxious, unobjectionable, unoffending.

inoperative *adj* inactive, ineffectual, inefficacious, not in force.

inopportune *adj* ill-timed, inexpedient, infelicitous, mistimed, unfortunate, unhappy, unseasonable, untimely.

inordinate *adj* excessive, extravagant, immoderate, intemperate, irregular.

inorganic *adj* inanimate, unorganized; mineral.

inquest *n* inquiry, inquisition, investigation, quest, search.

inquietude *n* anxiety, disquiet, disquietude, disturbance, restlessness, uneasiness.

inquire, enquire *vb* ask, catechize, interpellate, interrogate, investigate, query, question, quiz.

inquiry, enquiry *n* examination, exploration, investigation, research, scrutiny, study; interrogation, query, question, quiz.

inquisition *n* examination, inquest, inquiry, investigation, search.

inquisitive *adj* curious, inquiring, scrutinizing; curious, meddlesome, peeping, peering, prying.

inroad *n* encroachment, foray, incursion, invasion, irruption, raid.

insalubrious *adj* noxious, unhealthful, unhealthy, unwholesome.

insane *adj* abnormal, crazed, crazy, delirious, demented, deranged, distracted, lunatic, mad, maniacal, unhealthy, unsound.

insanity *n* craziness, delirium, dementia, derangement, lunacy, madness, mania, mental aberration, mental alienation.

insatiable *adj* greedy, rapacious, voracious; insatiate, unappeasable.

inscribe *vb* emblaze, endorse, engrave, enroll, impress, imprint, letter, mark, write; address, dedicate.

inscrutable *adj* hidden, impenetrable, incomprehensible, inexplicable, mysterious, undiscoverable, unfathomable, unsearchable.

inscrutableness *n* impenetrability, incomprehensibility, incomprehensibleness, inexplicability, inscrutability, mysteriousness, mystery, unfathomableness, unsearchableness.

insecure *adj* risky, uncertain, unconfident, unsure; exposed, ill-protected, unprotected, unsafe; dangerous, hazardous, perilous, infirm, shaking, shaky, tottering, unstable, weak, wobbly.

insecurity *n* riskiness, uncertainty; danger, hazardousness, peril; instability, shakiness, weakness, wobbliness.

insensate *adj* dull, indifferent, insensible, torpid; brutal, foolish, senseless, unwise; inanimate, insensible, insentient, nonpercipient, unconscious, unperceiving.

insensibility *n* dullness, insentience, lethargy, torpor; apathy, indifference, insusceptibility, unfeelingness, dullness, stupidity; anesthesia, coma, stupor, unconsciousness.

insensible *adj* imperceivable, imperceptible, undiscoverable; blunted, brutish, deaf, dull, insensate, numb, obtuse, senseless, sluggish, stolid, stupid, torpid, unconscious; apathetic, callous, phlegmatic, impassive, indifferent, insensitive, insentient, unfeeling, unimpressible, unsusceptible.

insensibly *adv* imperceptibly.

insentient *adj* inert, nonsentient, senseless; inanimate, insensible, insensate, nonpercipient, unconscious, unperceiving.

inseparable *adj* close, friendly, intimate, together; indissoluble, indivisible, inseverable.

insert *vb* infix, inject, intercalate, interpolate, introduce, inweave, parenthesize, place, put, set.

inside *adj* inner, interior, internal; confidential, exclusive, internal, private, secret. • *adv* indoors, within. • *n* inner part, interior; nature.

insidious *adj* creeping, deceptive, gradual, secretive; arch, artful, crafty, crooked, cunning, deceitful, designing, diplomatic, foxy, guileful, intriguing, Machiavellian, sly, sneaky, subtle, treacherous, trickish, tricky, wily.

insight *n* discernment, intuition, penetration, perception, perspicuity, understanding.

insignia *npl* badges, marks.

insignificance *n* emptiness, nothingness, paltriness, triviality, unimportance.

insignificant *adj* contemptible, empty, immaterial, inconsequential, inconsiderable, inferior, meaningless, paltry, petty, small, sorry, trifling, trivial, unessential, unimportant.

insincere *adj* deceitful, dishonest, disingenuous, dissembling, dissimulating, double-faced, double-tongued, duplicitous, empty, faithless, false, hollow, hypocritical, pharisaical, truthless, uncandid, untrue.

insincerity *n* bad faith, deceitfulness, dishonesty, disingenuousness, dissimulation, duplicity, falseness, faithlessness, hypocrisy.

insinuate *vb* hint, inculcate, infuse, ingratiate, instil, intimate, introduce, suggest.

insipid *adj* dead, dull, flat, heavy, inanimate, jejune, lifeless, monotonous, pointless, prosaic, prosy, spiritless, stupid, tame, unentertaining, uninteresting; mawkish, savorless, stale, tasteless, vapid, zestless.

insipidity, insipidness *n* dullness, heaviness, lifelessness, prosiness, stupidity, tameness; flatness, mawkishness, staleness, tastlessness, unsavoriness, vapidness, zestlessness.

insist *vb* demand, maintain, urge.

insistence *n* importunity, solicitousness, urging, urgency.

insnare *see* **ensnare**.

insolence *n* impertinence, impudence, malapertness, pertness, rudeness, sauciness; contempt, contumacy, contumely, disrespect, frowardness, insubordination.

insolent *adj* abusive, contemptuous, contumelious, disrespectful, domineering, insulting, offensive, overbearing, rude, supercilious; cheeky, impertinent, impudent, malapert, pert, saucy; contumacious, disobedient, froward, insubordinate.

insoluble *adj* indissoluble, indissolvable, irreducible; inexplicable, insolvable.

insolvable *adj* inexplicable.

insolvent *adj* bankrupt, broken, failed, ruined.

insomnia *n* sleeplessness, wakefulness.

inspect *vb* examine, investigate, look into, pry into, scrutinize; oversee, superintend, supervise.

inspection *n* examination, investigation, scrutiny; oversight, superintendence, supervision.

inspector *n* censor, critic, examiner, visitor; boss, overseer, superintendent, supervisor.

inspiration *n* breathing, inhalation; afflatus, fire, inflatus; elevation, exaltation; enthusiasm.

inspire *vb* breathe, inhale; infuse, instil; animate, cheer, enliven, inspirit; elevate, exalt, stimulate; fill, imbue, impart, inform, quicken.

inspirit *vb* animate, arouse, cheer, comfort, embolden, encourage, enhearten, enliven, fire, hearten, incite, invigorate, quicken, rouse, stimulate.

instable *see* **unstable**.

instability *n* changeableness, fickleness, inconstancy, insecurity, mutability.

install, instal *vb* inaugurate, induct, introduce; establish, place, set up.

installation *n* inauguration, induction, instalment, investiture.

instalment *n* earnest, payment, portion.

instance *vb* adduce, cite, mention, specify. • *n* case, example, exemplification, illustration, occasion; impulse, incitement, instigation, motive, prompting, request, solicitation.

instant *adj* direct, immediate, instantaneous, prompt, quick; current, present; earnest, fast, imperative, importunate, pressing, urgent; ready cooked. • *n* flash, jiffy, moment, second, trice, twinkling; hour, time.

instantaneous *adj* abrupt, immediate, instant, quick, sudden.

instantaneously *adv* forthwith, immediately, presto, quickly, right away.

instauration *n* reconstitution, reconstruction, redintegration, re-establishment, rehabilitation, reinstatement, renewal, renovation, restoration.

instead *adv* in lieu, in place, rather.

instigate *vb* actuate, agitate, encourage, impel, incite, influence, initiate, move, persuade, prevail upon, prompt, provoke, rouse, set on, spur on, stimulate, stir up, tempt, urge.

instigation *n* encouragement, incitement, influence, instance, prompting, solicitation, urgency.

instill, instil *vb* enforce, implant, impress, inculcate, ingraft; impart, infuse, insinuate.

instillation *n* infusion, insinuation, introduction.

instinct *n* natural impulse.

instinctive *adj* automatic, inherent, innate, intuitive, involuntary, natural, spontaneous; impulsive, unreflecting.

institute[1] *n* academy, college, foundation, guild, institution, school; custom, doctrine, dogma, law, maxim, precedent, principle, rule, tenet.

institute[2] *vb* begin, commence, constitute, establish, found, initial, install, introduce, organize, originate, start.

institution *n* enactment, establishment, foundation, institute, society, investiture; custom, law, practice.

instruct *vb* discipline, educate, enlighten, exercise, guide, indoctrinate, inform, initiate, school, teach, train; apprise, bid, command, direct, enjoin, order, prescribe to.

instruction *n* breeding, discipline, education, indoctrination, information, nurture, schooling, teaching, training, tuition; advice, counsel, precept; command, direction, mandate, order.

instructor *n* educator, master, preceptor, schoolteacher, teacher, tutor.

instrument *n* appliance, apparatus, contrivance, device, implement, musical instrument, tool, utensil; agent, means, medium; charter, deed, document, indenture, writing.

instrumental *adj* ancillary, assisting, auxiliary, conducive, contributory, helpful,

helping, ministerial, ministrant, serviceable, subservient, subsidiary.

instrumentality *n* agency, intermediary; intervention, means, mediation.

insubordinate *adj* disobedient, disorderly, mutinous, refractory, riotous, seditious, turbulent, ungovernable, unruly.

insubordination *n* disobedience, insurrection, mutiny, revolt, riotousness, sedition; indiscipline, laxity.

insufferable *adj* intolerable, unbearable, unendurable, insupportable; abominable, detestable, disgusting, execrable, outrageous.

insufficiency *n* dearth, defectiveness, deficiency, lack, inadequacy, inadequateness, incapability, incompetence, paucity, shortage.

insufficient *adj* deficient, inadequate, incommensurate, incompetent, scanty; incapable, incompetent, unfitted, unqualified, unsuited, unsatisfactory.

insular *adj* contracted, illiberal, limited, narrow, petty, prejudiced, restricted; isolated, remote.

insulate *vb* detach, disconnect, disengage, disunite, isolate, separate.

insulation *n* disconnection, disengagement, isolation, separation.

insult *vb* abuse, affront, injure, offend, outrage, slander, slight. • *n* abuse, affront, cheek, contumely, indignity, insolence, offence, outrage, sauce, slight.

insulting *adj* abusive, arrogant, contumelious, impertinent, impolite, insolent, rude, vituperative.

insuperable *adj* impassable, insurmountable.

insupportable *adj* insufferable, intolerable, unbearable, unendurable.

insuppressible *adj* irrepressible, uncontrollable.

insurance *n* assurance, security.

insure *vb* assure, guarantee, indemnify, secure, underwrite.

insurgent *adj* disobedient, insubordinate, mutinous, rebellious, revolting, revolutionary, seditious. • *n* mutineer, rebel, revolter, revolutionary.

insurmountable *adj* impassable, insuperable.

insurrection *n* insurgence, mutiny, rebellion, revolt, revolution, rising, sedition, uprising.

intact *adj* scathless, unharmed, unhurt,

unimpaired, uninjured, untouched; complete, entire, integral, sound, unbroken, undiminished, whole.

intangible *adj* dim, impalpable, imperceptible, indefinite, insubstantial, intactile, shadowy, vague; aerial, phantom, spiritous.

intangibility *n* imperceptibility, insubstantiality, intangibleness, shadowiness, vagueness.

integral *adj* complete, component, entire, integrant, total, whole.

integrity *n* goodness, honesty, principle, probity, purity, rectitude, soundness, uprightness, virtue; completeness, entireness, entirety, wholeness.

integument *n* coat, covering, envelope, skin, tegument.

intellect *n* brains, cognitive faculty, intelligence, mind, rational faculty, reason, reasoning, faculty, sense, thought, understanding, wit.

intellectual *adj* cerebral, intelligent, mental, scholarly, thoughtful. • *n* academic, highbrow, pundit, savant, scholar.

intelligence *n* acumen, apprehension, brightness, discernment, imagination, insight, penetration, quickness, sagacity, shrewdness, understanding, wits; information, knowledge; advice, instruction, news, notice, notification, tidings; brains, intellect, mentality, sense, spirit.

intelligent *adj* acute, alert, apt, astute, brainy, bright, clear-headed, clear-sighted, clever, discerning, keen-eyed, keen-sighted, knowing, long-headed, quick, quick-sighted, sagacious, sensible, sharp-sighted, sharp-witted, shrewd, understanding.

intelligibility *n* clarity, comprehensibility, intelligibleness, perspicuity.

intelligible *adj* clear, comprehensible, distinct, evident, lucid, manifest, obvious, patent, perspicuous, plain, transparent, understandable.

intemperate *adj* drunken; excessive, extravagant, extreme, immoderate, inordinate, unbridled, uncontrolled, unrestrained; self-indulgent.

intend *vb* aim at, contemplate, design, determine, drive at, mean, meditate, propose, purpose, think of.

intendant *n* inspector, overseer, superintendent, supervisor.

intense *adj* ardent, earnest, fervid, passionate, vehement; close, intent, severe,

strained, stretched, strict; energetic, forcible, keen, potent, powerful, sharp, strong, vigorous, violent; acute, deep, extreme, exquisite, grievous, poignant.

intensify *vb* aggravate, concentrate, deepen, enhance, heighten, quicken, strengthen, whet.

intensity *n* closeness, intenseness, severity, strictness; excess, extremity, violence; activity, energy, force, power, strength, vigor; ardor, earnestness, vehemence.

intensive *adj* emphatic, intensifying.

intent *adj* absorbed, attentive, close, eager, earnest, engrossed, occupied, pre-occupied, zealous; bent, determined, decided, resolved, set. • *n* aim, design, drift, end, import, intention, mark, meaning, object, plan, purport, purpose, purview, scope, view.

intention *n* aim, design, drift, end, import, intent, mark, meaning, object, plan, purport, purpose, purview, scope, view.

intentional *adj* contemplated, deliberate, designed, intended, preconcerted, predetermined, premeditated, purposed, studied, voluntary, willful.

inter *vb* bury, commit to the earth, entomb, inhume, inurn.

intercalate *vb* insert, interpolate.

intercede *vb* arbitrate, interpose, mediate; entreat, plead, supplicate.

intercept *vb* cut off, interrupt, obstruct, seize.

intercession *n* interposition, intervention, mediation; entreaty, pleading, prayer, supplication.

intercessor *n* interceder, mediator.

interchange *vb* alternate, change, exchange, vary. • *n* alternation.

interchangeableness *n* interchangeability.

interchangeably *adv* alternately.

intercourse *n* commerce, communication, communion, connection, converse, correspondence, dealings, fellowship, truck; acquaintance, intimacy.

interdict *vb* debar, forbid, inhibit, prohibit, prescribe, proscribe, restrain from. • *n* ban, decree, interdiction, prohibition.

interest *vb* affect, concern, touch; absorb, attract, engage, enlist, excite, grip, hold, occupy. • *n* advantage, benefit, good, profit, weal; attention, concern, regard, sympathy; part, participation, portion, share, stake; discount, premium, profit.

interested *adj* attentive, concerned, in-

volved, occupied; biassed, patial, prejudiced; selfish, self-seeking.

interesting adj attractive, engaging, entertaining, pleasing.

interfere vb intermeddle, interpose, meddle; clash, collide, conflict.

interference n intermeddling, interposition;
clashing, collision, interfering, opposition.

interim n intermediate time, interval, mean-
time.

interior adj inmost, inner, internal, inward;
inland, remote; domestic, home. • n inner part, inland, inside.

interjacent adj intermediate, interposed,
intervening, parenthetical.

interject vb comment, inject, insert, interpose.

interjection n exclamation.

interlace vb bind, complicate, entwine, intersperse, intertwine, interweave, inweave,
knit, mix, plait, twine, twist, unite.

interlard vb difersify, interminate, intersperse, intertwine, mix, vary.

interline vb insert, write between.

interlineal adj interlinear, interlined.

interlink, interlock vb connect, interchain,
interrelate, join.

interlocution n colloquy, conference, dialogue, interchange.

interlocutor n respondent, speaker.

interloper n intruder, meddler.

intermeddle vb interfere, interpose, meddle.

intermediary n go-between, mediator.

intermediate adj interjacent, interposed,
intervening, mean, median, middle, tran-
sitional.

interment n burial, entombment, inhumation, sepulture.

interminable adj boundless, endless, illimitable, immeasurable, infinite, limitless,
unbounded, unlimited; long-drawn-out,
tedious, wearisome.

intermingle vb blend, commingle, commix,
intermix, mingle, mix.

intermission n cessation, interruption, interval, lull, pause, remission, respite, rest,
stop, stoppage, suspension.

intermit vb interrupt, intervene, stop, suspend; discontinue, give over, leave off;
abate, subside.

intermittent adj broken, capricious, discontinuous, fitful, flickering, intermitting, periodic, recurrent, remittent, spasmodic.

intermix vb blend, commingle, commix,
intermingle, mingle, mix.

internal adj inner, inside, interior, inward;
incorporeal, mental, spiritual; deeper,
emblematic, hidden, higher, metaphorical,
secret, symbolical, under; genuine, inherent, intrinsic, real, true; domestic, home,
inland, inside.

international adj cosmopolitan, universal.

internecine adj deadly, destructive, exter-
minating, exterminatory, interneciary,
internecinal, internecive, mortal.

interpellate vb interrogate, question.

interpellation n interruption; intercession,
interposition; interrogation, questioning.

interplay n interaction.

interpolate vb add, foist, insert, interpose;
(math) intercalate, introduce.

interpose vb arbitrate, intercede, intervene,
mediate; interfere, intermeddle, interrupt,
meddle, tamper; insert, interject, put in,
remark, sandwich, set between; intrude,
thurst in.

interposition n intercession, interpellation,
intervention, mediation.

interpret vb decipher, decode, define, elucidate, explain, expound, solve, unfold, unravel; construe, render, translate.

interpretation n meaning, sense, signification; elucidation, explanation, explication,
exposition; construction, rendering, rendition, translation, version.

interpreter n expositor, expounder, trans-
lator.

interrogate vb ask, catechize, examine, inquire of, interpellate, question.

interrogation n catechizing, examination,
examining, interpellation, interrogating,
questioning; inquiry, query, question.

interrogative adj interrogatory, questioning.

interrupt vb break, check, disturb, hinder,
intercept, interfere with, obstruct, pretermit, stop; break, cut, disconnect, disjoin,
dissever, dissolve, disunite, divide, separate, sever, sunder; break off, cease, discontinue, intermit, leave off, suspend.

interruption n hindrance, impediment, obstacle, obstruction, stop, stoppage; cessation, discontinuance, intermission, pause,
suspension; break, breaking, disconnect-
ing, disconnection, disjunction, dissolution, disunion, disuniting, division, separation, severing, sundering.

intersect vb cross, cut, decussate, divide,
interrupt.

intersection n crossing.

interspace n interlude, interstice, interval.

intersperse *vb* intermingle, scatter, sprinkle; diversify, interlard, mix.

interstice *n* interspace, interval, space; chink, crevice.

interstitial *adj* intermediate, intervening.

intertwine *vb* interlace, intertwine, interweave, inweave, twine.

interval *n* interim, interlude, interregnum, pause, period, recess, season, space, spell, term; interstice, skip.

intervene *vb* come between, interfere, mediate; befall, happen, occur.

intervening *adj* interjacent, intermediate; interstitial.

intervention *n* interference, interposition; agency, mediation.

interview *n* conference, consultation, parley; meeting.

interweave *vb* interlace, intertwine, inweave, weave; intermingle, intermix, mingle, mix.

intestinal *adj* domestic, interior, internal.

intestines *npl* bowels, entrails, guts, insides, inwards, viscera.

intimacy *n* close acquaintance, familiarity, fellowship, friendship; closeness, nearness.

intimate[1] *adj* close, near; familiar, friendly; bosom, chummy, close, dear, homelike, special; confidential, personal, private, secret; detailed, exhaustive, first-hand, immediate, penetrating, profound; cosy, warm. • *n* chum, confidant, companion, crony, friend.

intimate[2] *vb* allude to, express, hint, impart, indicate, insinuate, signify, suggest, tell.

intimately *adv* closely, confidentially, familiarly, nearly, thoroughly.

intimation *n* allusion, hint, innuendo, insinuation, suggestion.

intimidate *vb* abash, affright, alarm, appal, browbeat, bully, cow, daunt, dishearten, dismay, frighten, overawe, scare, subdue, terrify, terrorize.

intimidation *n* fear, intimidating, terror, terrorism.

intolerable *adj* insufferable, insupportable, unbearable, unendurable.

intolerance *n* bigotry, narrowness; impatience, rejection.

intolerant *adj* bigoted, narrow, proscriptive; dictatorial, impatient, imperious, overbearing, supercilious.

intonation *n* cadence, modulation, tone; musical recitation.

in toto *adv* entirely, wholly.

intoxicate *vb* fuddle, inebriate, muddle.

intoxicated *adj* boozy, drunk, drunken, fuddled, inebriated, maudlin, mellow, muddled, stewed, tight, tipsy.

intoxication *n* drunkenness, ebriety, inebriation, inebriety; excitement, exhilaration, infatuation.

intractability *n* cantankerousness, contrariety, inflexibility, intractableness, obduracy, obstinacy, perverseness, perversity, pig-headedness, stubbornness, willfulness.

intractable *adj* cantankerous, contrary, contumacious, cross-grained, dogged, froward, headstrong, indocile, inflexible, mulish, obdurate, obstinate, perverse, pigheaded, refractory, restive, stubborn, tough, uncontrollable, ungovernable, unmanageable, unruly, unyielding, willful.

intrench *see* **entrench**.

intrenchment *see* **entrenchment**.

intrepid *adj* bold, brave, chivalrous, courageous, daring, dauntless, doughty, fearless, gallant, heroic, unappalled, unawed, undaunted, undismayed, unterrified, valiant, valorous.

intrepidity *n* boldness, bravery, courage, daring, dauntlessness, fearlessness, gallantry, heroism, intrepidness, prowess, spirit, valor.

intricacy *n* complexity, complication, difficulty, entanglement, intricateness, involution, obscurity, perplexity.

intricate *adj* complicated, difficult, entangled, involved, mazy, obscure, perplexed.

intrigue *vb* connive, conspire, machinate, plot, scheme; beguile, bewitch, captivate, charm, fascinate. • *n* artifice, cabal, conspiracy, deception, finesse, Machiavelianism, machination, maneuvre, plot, ruse, scheme, stratagem, wile; amour, liaison, love affair.

intriguing *adj* arch, artful, crafty, crooked, cunning, deceitful, designing, diplomatic, foxy, Machiavelian, insidious, politic, sly, sneaky, subtle, tortuous, trickish, tricky, wily.

intrinsic *adj* essential, genuine, real, sterling, true; inborn, inbred, ingrained, inherent, internal, inward, native, natural.

intrinsically *adv* essentially, really, truly; inherently, naturally.

introduce *vb* bring in, conduct, import, induct, inject, insert, lead in, usher in;

present; begin, broach, commence, inaugurate, initiate, institute, start.

introduction *n* exordium, preface, prelude, proem; introducing, ushering in; presentation.

introductory *adj* precursory, prefatory, preliminary, proemial.

introspection *n* introversion, self-contemplation.

intrude *vb* encroach, impose, infringe, interfere, interlope, obtrude, trespass.

intruder *n* interloper, intermeddler, meddler, stranger.

intrusion *n* encroachment, infringement, intruding, obtrusion.

intrusive *adj* obtrusive, trespassing.

Intuition *n* apprehension, cognition, insight, instinct; clairvoyance, divination, presentiment.

intuitive *adj* instinctive, intuitional, natural; clear, distinct, full, immediate.

intumesce *vb* bubble up, dilate, expand, swell.

intumescence *n* inturgescence, swelling, tumefaction, turgescence.

inundate *vb* deluge, drown, flood, glut, overflow, overwhelm, submerge.

inundation *n* cataclysm, deluge, flood, glut, overflow, superfluity.

inure *vb* accustom, discipline, familiarize, habituate, harden, toughen, train, use.

Inutile *adj* bootless, ineffectual, inoperative, unavailing, unprofitable, useless.

invade *vb* encroach upon, infringe, violate; attack, enter in, march into.

invalid[1] *adj* baseless, fallacious, false, inoperative, nugatory, unfounded, unsound, untrue, worthless; (*law*) null, void.

invalid[2] *adj* ailing, bedridden, feeble, frail, ill, infirm, sick, sickly, valetudinary, weak, weakly. • *n* convalescent, patient, valetudinarian.

invalidate *vb* abrogate, annul, cancel, nullify, overthrow, quash, repeal, reverse, undo, unmake, vitiate.

invalidity *n* baselessness, fallaciousness, fallacy, falsity, unsoundness.

invaluable *adj* inestimable, priceless.

invariable *adj* changeless, constant, unchanging, uniform, unvarying; changeless, immutable, unalterable, unchangeable.

invariableness *n* changelessness, constancy, uniformity, unvaryingness; changelessness, immutability, unchangeableness, invariability.

invasion *n* encroachment, incursion, infringement, inroad; aggression, assault, attack, foray, raid.

invective *n* abuse, censure, contumely, denunciation, diatribe, railing, reproach, sarcasm, satire, vituperation.

inveigh *vb* blame, censure, condemn, declaim against, denounce, exclaim against, rail at, reproach, vituperate.

inveigle *vb* contrive, devise; concoct, conceive, create, design, excogitate, frame, imagine, originate; coin, fabricate, forge, spin.

invent *vb* concoct, contrive, design, devise, discover, fabricate, find out, frame, originate.

invention *n* creation, discovery, ingenuity, inventing, origination, contrivance, design, device; coinage, fabrication, fiction, forgery.

inventive *adj* creative, fertile, ingenious.

inventor *n* author, contriver, creator, originator.

inventory *n* account, catalog, list, record, roll, register, schedule.

inverse *adj* indirect, inverted, opposite, reversed.

inversion *n* inverting, reversing, transposal, transposition.

invert *vb* capsize, overturn; reverse, transpose.

invertebrate *adj* invertebral; spineless.

invest *vb* put money into; confer, endow, endue; (*mil*) beset, besiege, enclose, surround, array, clothe, dress.

investigate *vb* canvass, consider, dissect, examine, explore, follow up, inquire into, look into, overhaul, probe, question, research, scrutinize, search into, search out, sift, study.

investigation *n* examination, exploration, inquiry, inquisition, overhauling, research, scrutiny, search, sifting, study.

investiture *n* habilitation, induction, installation, ordination.

investment *n* money invested; endowment; (*mil*) beleaguerment, siege; clothes, dress, garments, habiliments, robe, vestment.

inveteracy *n* inveterateness, obstinacy.

inveterate *adj* accustomed, besetting, chronic, confirmed, deep-seated, habitual, habituated, hardened, ingrained, long-established, obstinate.

invidious *adj* disagreeable, envious, hateful, odious, offensive, unfair.

invigorate *vb* animate, brace, energize, fortify, harden, nerve, quicken, refresh, stimulate, strengthen, vivify.

invincible *adj* impregnable, indomitable, ineradicable, insuperable, insurmountable, irrepressible, unconquerable, unsubduable, unyielding.

inviolable *adj* hallowed, holy, inviolate, sacramental, sacred, sacrosanct, stainless.

inviolate *adj* unbroken, unviolated; pure, stainless, unblemished, undefiled, unhurt, uninjured, unpolluted, unprofaned, unstained; inviolable, sacred.

invisibility *n* imperceptibility, indistinctness, invisibleness, obscurity.

invisible *adj* impalpable, imperceptible, indistinguishable, intangible, unapparent, undiscernable, unperceivable, unseen.

invitation *n* bidding, call, challenge, solicitation, summons.

invite *vb* ask, bid, call, challenge, request, solicit, summon; allure, attract, draw on, entice, lead, persuade, prevail upon.

inviting *adj* alluring, attractive, bewitching, captivating, engaging, fascinating, pleasing, winning; prepossessing, promising.

invocation *n* conjuration, orison, petition, prayer, summoning, supplication.

invoice *vb* bill, list. • *n* bill, inventory, list, schedule.

invoke *vb* adjure, appeal to, beseech, beg, call upon, conjure, entreat, implore, importune, pray, pray to, solicit, summon, supplicate.

involuntary *adj* automatic, blind, instinctive, mechanical, reflex, spontaneous, unintentional; compulsory, reluctant, unwilling.

involve *vb* comprise, contain, embrace, imply, include, lead to; complicate, compromise, embarrass, entangle, implicate, incriminate, inculpate; cover, envelop, enwrap, surround, wrap; blend, conjoin, connect, join, mingle; entwine, interlace, intertwine, interweave, inweave.

invulnerability *n* invincibility, invulnerableness.

invulnerable *adj* incontrovertible, invincible, unassailable, irrefragable.

inward[1] *adj* incoming, inner, interior, internal; essential, hidden, mental, spiritual; private, secret.

inward[2], **inwards** *adv* inwardly, towards the inside, within.

inweave *vb* entwine, interlace, intertwine, interweave, weave together.

iota *n* atom, bit, glimmer, grain, jot, mite, particle, scintilla, scrap, shadow, spark, tittle, trace, whit.

irascibility *n* hastiness, hot-headedness, impatience, irascibleness, irritability, peevishness, petulance, quickness, spleen, testiness, touchiness.

irascible *adj* choleric, cranky, hasty, hot, hot-headed, impatient, irritable, nettlesome, peevish, peppery, pettish, petulant, quick, splenetic, snappish, testy, touchy, waspish.

irate *adj* angry, incensed, ireful, irritated, piqued.

ire *n* anger, choler, exasperation, fury, indignation, passion, rage, resentment, wrath.

ireful *adj* angry, furious, incensed, irate, raging, passionate.

iridescent *adj* irisated, nacreous, opalescent, pavonine, prismatic, rainbow-like.

iris *n* rainbow; (*bot*) fleur-de-lis, flower-de-luce; diaphragm of the eye.

irksome *adj* annoying, burdensome, humdrum, monotonous, tedious, tiresome, wearisome, weary, wearying.

iron *adj* ferric, ferrous.

ironic, ironical *adj* mocking, sarcastic.

irons *npl* chains, fetters, gyves, hampers, manacles, shackles.

irony *n* mockery, raillery, ridicule, sarcasm, satire.

irradiate *vb* brighten, illume, illuminate, illumine, light up, shine upon.

irrational *adj* absurd, extravagant, foolish, injudicious, preposterous, ridiculous, silly, unwise; unreasonable, unreasoning, unthinking; brute, brutish; aberrant, alienated, brainless, crazy, demented, fantastic, idiotic, imbecilic, insane, lunatic.

irrationality *n* absurdity, folly, foolishness, unreasonableness; brutishness.

irreclaimable *adj* hopeless, incurable, irrecoverable, irreparable, irretrievable, irreversible, remediless; abandoned, graceless, hardened, impenitent, incorrigible, lost, obdurate, profligate, recreant, reprobate, shameless, unrepentant.

irreconcilable *adj* implacable, inexorable, inexpiable, unappeasable; incompatible, incongruous, inconsistent.

irrecoverable *adj* hopeless, incurable, irremediable, irreparable, irretrievable, remediless.

irrefragable *adj* impregnable, incontestable, incontrovertible, indisputable, invincible, irrefutable, irresistible, unanswerable, unassailable, undeniable.

irrefutable *adj* impregnable, incontestable, incontrovertible, indisputable, invincible, irrefragable, irresistible, unanswerable, unassailable, undeniable.

irregular *adj* aberrant, abnormal, anomalistic, anomalous, crooked, devious, eccentric, erratic, exceptional, heteromorphous, raged, tortuous, unconformable, unusual; capricious, changeable, desultory, fitful, spasmodic, uncertain, unpunctual, unsettled, variable; disordered, disorderly, improper, uncanonical, unparliamentary, unsystematic; asymmetric, uneven, unsymmetrical; disorderly, dissolute, immoral, loose, wild. • *n* casual, freelance, hireling, mercenary.

irregularity *n* aberration, abnormality, anomaly, anomalousness, singularity; capriciousness, changeableness, uncertainty, variableness; asymmetry; disorderliness, dissoluteness, immorality, laxity, looseness, wildness.

irrelevance, irrelevancy *n* impertinency, inapplicability, nonpertinency.

irrelevant *adj* extraneous, foreign, illogical, impertinent, inapplicable, inapposite, inappropriate, inconsequent, unessential, unrelated.

irreligion *n* atheism, godlessness, impiety, ungodliness.

irreligious *adj* godless, ungodly, undevout; blasphemous, disrespectful, impious, irreverent, profane, ribald, wicked.

irremediable *adj* hopeless, incurable, immedicable, irrecoverable, irreparable, remediless.

irremissible *adj* binding, inexpiable, obligatory, unatonable, unpardonable.

irreparable *adj* irrecoverable, irremediable, irretrievable, remediless.

irreprehensible *adj* blameless, faultless, inculpable, innocent, irreproachable, irreprovable, unblamable.

irrepressible *adj* insuppressible, uncontrollable, unquenchable, unsmotherable.

irreproachable *adj* blameless, faultless, inculpable, innocent, irreprehensible, irreprovable, unblamable.

irresistible *adj* irrefragable, irrepressible, overpowering, overwhelming, resistless.

irresolute *adj* changeable, faltering, fickle, hesitant, hesitating, inconstant, mutable, spineless, uncertain, undecided, undetermined, unsettled, unstable, unsteady, vacillating, wavering.

irrespective *adj* independent, regardless.

irresponsible *adj* unaccountable; untrustworthy.

irretrievable *adj* incurable, irrecoverable, irremediable, irreparable, remediless.

irreverence *n* blasphemy, impiety, profaneness, profanity; disesteem, disrespect.

irreverent *adj* blasphemous, impious, irreligious, profane; disrespectful, slighting.

irreversible *adj* irrepealable, irrevocable, unalterable, unchangeable; changeless, immutable, invariable.

irrevocable *adj* irrecpealable, irreversible, unalterable, unchangeable.

irrigate *vb* moisten, wash, water, wet.

irrigation *n* watering.

irritability *n* excitability, fretfulness, irascibility, peevishness, petulance, snappishness, susceptibility, testiness.

irritable *adj* captious, choleric, excitable, fiery, fretful, hasty, hot, irascible, passionate, peppery, peevish, pettish, petulant, snappish, splenetic, susceptible, testy, touchy, waspish.

irritate *vb* anger, annoy, chafe, enrage, exacerbate, exasperate, fret, incense, jar, nag, nettle, offend, provoke, rasp, rile, ruffle, vex; gall, tease; (*med*) excite, inflame, stimulate.

irritation *n* irritating; anger, exacerbation, exasperation, excitement, indignation, ire, passion, provocation, resentment, wrath; (*med*) excitation, inflammation, stimulation; burn, itch.

irruption *n* breaking in, bursting in; foray, incursion, inroad, invasion, raid.

island *n* atoll, isle, islet, reef.

isochronal *adj* isochronous, uniform.

isolate *vb* detach, dissociate, insulate, quarantine, segregate, separate, set apart.

isolated *adj* detached, separate, single, solitary.

isolation *n* detachment, disconnection, insulation, quarantine, segregation, separation; loneliness, solitariness, solitude.

issue *vb* come out, flow out, flow forth, gush, run, rush out, spout, spring, spurt, well; arise, come, emanate, ensue, flow, follow, originate, proceed, spring; end, eventuate, result, terminate; appear, come out, deliver, depart, debouch, discharge, emerge, emit, put forth, send out; distribute, give out; publish, utter. • *n* conclusion, consequence, consummation, denouement, end, effect, event, finale, outcome, result, termination, upshot; antagonism, contest, controversy; debouchment, delivering, delivery, discharge, emergence, emigration, emission, issuance; flux, outflow, outpouring, stream; copy, edition, number; egress, exit, outlet, passage out, vent, way out; escape, sally, sortie; children, offspring, posterity, progeny.

itch *vb* tingle. • *n* itching; burning, coveting, importunate craving, teasing desire, uneasy hankering.

itching *n* itch; craving, longing, importunate craving, desire, appetite, hankering.

item *adv* also, in like manner. • *n* article, detail, entry, particular, point.

iterate *vb* reiterate, repeat.

itinerant *adj* nomadic, peripatetic, roaming, roving, travelling, unsettled, wandering.

itinerary *n* guide, guidebook; circuit, route.

J

jabber *vb* chatter, gabble, prate, prattle.

jacket *n* casing, cover, sheath; anorak, blazer coat, doublet, jerkin.

jaded *adj* dull, exhausted, fatigued, satiated, tired, weary.

jagged *adj* cleft, divided, indented, notched, serrated, ragged, uneven.

jail *n* bridewell, (*sl*) clink, dungeon, lockup, (*sl*) nick, penitentiary, prison.

jam *vb* block, crowd, crush, press. • *n* block, crowd, crush, mass, pack, press.

jangle *vb* bicker, chatter, dispute, gossip, jar, quarrel, spar, spat, squabble, tiff, wrangle. • *n* clang, clangor, clash, din, dissonance.

jar[1] *vb* clash, grate, interfere, shake; bicker, contend, jangle, quarrel, spar, spat, squabble, tiff, wrangle; agitate, jolt, jounce, shake. • *n* clash, conflict, disaccord, discord, jangle, dissonance; agitation, jolt, jostle, shake, shaking, shock, start.

jar[2] *n* can, crock, cruse, ewer, flagon.

jarring *adj* conflicting, discordant, inconsistent, inconsonant, wrangling.

jargon *n* gabble, gibberish, nonsense, rigmarole: argot, cant, lingo, slang; chaos, confusion, disarray, disorder, jumble.

jaundiced *adj* biased, envious, prejudiced.

jaunt *n* excursion, ramble, tour, trip.

jaunty *adj* airy, cheery, garish, gay, fine, fluttering, showy, sprightly, unconcerned.

jealous *adj* distrustful, envious, suspicious; anxious, apprehensive, intolerant, solicitous, zealous.

jealousy *n* envy, suspicion, watchfulness.

jeer *vb* deride, despise, flout, gibe, jape, jest, mock, scoff, sneer, spurn, rail, ridicule, taunt. • *n* abuse, derision, mockery, sneer, ridicule, taunt.

jeopardize *vb* endanger, hazard, imperil, risk, venture.

jeopardy *n* danger, hazard, peril, risk, venture.

jerk *vb, n* flip, hitch, pluck, tweak, twitch, yank.

jest *vb* banter, joke, quiz. • *n* fun, joke, pleasantry, raillery, sport.

jester *n* humorist, joker, wag; buffoon, clown, droll, fool, harlequin, punch.

jibe *see* **gibe**.

jiffy *n* instant, moment, second, twinkling, trice.

jilt *vb* break with, deceive, disappoint, discard. • *n* coquette, flirt, light-o'-love.

jingle *vb* chink, clink, jangle, rattle, tinkle. • *n* chink, clink, jangle, rattle, tinkle; chorus, ditty, melody, song.

jocose *adj* comical, droll, facetious, funny, humorous, jesting, jocular, merry, sportive, waggish, witty.

jocund *adj* airy, blithe, cheerful, debonair, frolicsome, jolly, joyful, joyous, lively, merry, playful.

jog *vb* jostle, notify, nudge, push, remind, warn; canter, run, trot. • *n* push, reminder.

join *vb* add, annex, append, attach; cement, combine, conjoin, connect, couple, dovetail, link, unite, yoke; amalgamate, assemble, associate, confederate, consolidate.

joint *vb* fit, join, unite. • *adj* combined, concerted, concurrent, conjoint. • *n* connection, junction, juncture, hinge, splice.

joke *vb* banter, jest, frolic, rally. • *n* crank, jest, quip, quirk, witticism.

jolly *adj* airy, blithe, cheerful, frolicsome, gamesome, facetious, funny, gay, jovial, joyous, merry, mirthful, jocular, jocund, playful, sportive, sprightly, waggish; bouncing, chubby, lusty, plump, portly, stout.

jolt *vb* jar, shake, shock. • *n* jar, jolting, jounce, shaking.

jostle *vb* collide, elbow, hustle, joggle, shake, shoulder, shove.

jot *n* ace, atom, bit, corpuscle, iota, grain, mite, particle, scrap, whit.

journal *n* daybook, diary, log; gazette, magazine, newspapers, periodical.

journey *vb* ramble, roam, rove, travel: fare, go, proceed. • *n* excursion, expedition, jaunt, passage, pilgrimage, tour, travel, trip, voyage.

jovial *adj* airy, convivial, festive, jolly, joyous, merry, mirthful.

joy *n* beatification, beatitude, delight, ecstasy, exultation, gladness, glee, mirth, pleasure, rapture, ravishment, transport; bliss, felicity, happiness.

joyful *adj* blithe, blithesome, buoyant, delighted, elate, elated, exultant, glad, happy, jocund, jolly, joyous, merry, rejoicing.

jubilant *adj* exultant, exulting, rejoicing, triumphant.

judge *vb* conclude, decide, decree, determine, pronounce; adjudicate, arbitrate, condemn, doom, sentence, try, umpire; account, apprehend, believe, consider, deem, esteem, guess, hold, imagine, measure, reckon, regard, suppose, think; appreciate, estimate. • *n* adjudicator, arbiter, arbitrator, bencher, justice, magistrate, moderator, referee, umpire, connoisseur, critic.

judgment, judgement *n* brains, ballast, circumspection, depth, discernment, discretion, discrimination, intelligence, judiciousness, penetration, prudence, sagacity, sense, sensibility, taste, understanding, wisdom, wit; conclusion, consideration, decision, determination, estimation, notion, opinion, thought; adjudication, arbitration, award, censure, condemnation, decree, doom, sentence.

judicious *adj* cautious, considerate, cool, critical, discriminating, discreet, enlightened, provident, politic, prudent, rational, reasonable, sagacious, sensible, sober, solid, sound, staid, wise.

jug *n* cruse, ewer, flagon, pitcher, vessel.

juicy *adj* lush, moist, sappy, succulent, watery; entertaining, exciting, interesting, lively, racy, spicy.

jumble *vb* confound, confuse, disarrange, disorder, mix, muddle. • *n* confusion, disarrangement, disorder, medley, mess, mixture, muddle.

jump *vb* bound, caper, clear, hop, leap, skip, spring, vault. • *n* bound, caper, hop, leak, skip, spring, vault; fence, hurdle, obstacle; break, gap, interruption, space; advance, boost, increase, rise; jar, jolt, shock, start, twitch.

junction *n* combination, connection, coupling, hook-up, joining, linking, seam, union; conjunction, joint, juncture.

junta *n* cabal, clique, combination, confederacy, coterie, faction, gang, league, party, set.

just *adj* equitable, lawful, legitimate, reasonable, right, rightful; candid, even-handed, fair, fair-minded, impartial; blameless, conscientious, good, honest, honorable, pure, square, straightforward, virtuous; accurate, correct, exact, normal, proper, regular, true; condign, deserved, due, merited, suitable.

justice *n* accuracy, equitableness, equity, fairness, honesty, impartiality, justness, right; judge, justiciary.

justifiable *adj* defensible, fit, proper, right, vindicable, warrantable.

justification *n* defense, exculpation, excuse, exoneration, reason, vindication, warrant.

justify *vb* approve, defend, exculpate, excuse, exonerate, maintain, vindicate, support, warrant.

justness *n* accuracy, correctness, fitness, justice, precision, propriety.

juvenile *adj* childish, immature, puerile, young, youthful. • *n* boy, child, girl, youth.

juxtaposition *n* adjacency, contiguity, contact, proximity.

K

keen[1] *adj* ardent, eager, earnest, fervid, intense, vehement, vivid; acute, sharp; cutting; acrimonious, biting, bitter, caustic, poignant, pungent, sarcastic, severe; astute, discerning, intelligent, quick, sagacious, sharp-sighted, shrewd.

keen[2] *vb* bemoan, bewail, deplore, grieve, lament, mourn, sorrow, weep. • *n* coronach, dirge, elegy, lament, lamentation, monody, plaint, requiem, threnody.

keenness *n* ardor, eagerness, fervor, vehemence, zest; acuteness, sharpness; rigour, severity, sternness; acrimony, asperity, bitterness, causticity, causticness, pungency; astuteness, sagacity, shrewdness.

keep *vb* detain, hold, retain; continue, preserve; confine, detain, reserve, restrain, withhold; attend, guard, preserve, protect;

adhere to, fulfill; celebrate, commemorate, honor, observe, perform, solemnize; maintain, support, sustain; husband, save, store; abide, dwell, lodge, stay, remain; endure, last. • *n* board, maintenance, subsistence, support; donjon, dungeon, stronghold, tower.

keeper *n* caretaker, conservator, curator, custodian, defender, gaoler, governor, guardian, jailer, superintendent, warden, warder, watchman.

keeping *n* care, charge, custody, guard, possession; feed, maintenance, support; agreement, conformity, congruity, consistency, harmony.

keepsake *n* memento, souvenir, token.

ken *n* cognizance, sight, view.

key *adj* basic, crucial, essential, important, major, principal. • *n* lock-opener, opener; clue, elucidation, explanation, guide, solution, translation; (*mus*) keynote, tonic; clamp, lever, wedge.

kick *vb* boot, punt; oppose, rebel, resist, spurn. • *n* force, intensity, power, punch, vitality; excitement, pleasure, thrill.

kidnap *vb* abduct, capture, carry off, remove, steal away.

kill *vb* assassinate, butcher, dispatch, destroy, massacre, murder, slaughter, slay.

kin *adj* akin, allied, cognate, kindred, related. • *n* affinity, consanguinity, relationship; connections, family, kindred, kinsfolk, relations, relatives, siblings.

kind[1] *adj* accommodating, amiable, beneficent, benevolent, benign, bland, bounteous, brotherly, charitable, clement, compassionate, complaisant, gentle, good, good-natured, forbearing, friendly, generous, gracious, humane, indulgent, lenient, mild, obliging, sympathetic, tender, tender-hearted.

kind[2] *n* breed, class, family, genus, race, set, species, type; brand, character, color, denomination, description, form, make, manner, nature, persuasion, sort, stamp, strain, style.

kindle *vb* fire, ignite, inflame, light; animate, awaken, bestir, exasperate, excite, foment, incite, provoke, rouse, stimulate, stir, thrill, warm.

kindliness *n* amiability, benevolence, benignity, charity, compassion, friendliness, humanity, kindness, sympathy; gentleness, mildness, softness.

kindly *adj* appropriate, congenial, kindred,

natural, proper; benevolent, considerate, friendly, gracious, humane, sympathetic, well-disposed. • *adv* agreeably, graciously, humanely, politely, thoughtfully.

kindness *n* benefaction, charity, favor; amiability, beneficence, benevolence, benignity, clemency, generosity, goodness, grace, humanity, kindliness, mildness, philanthropy, sympathy, tenderness.

kindred *adj* akin, allied, congenial, connected, related, sympathetic. • *n* affinity, consanguinity, flesh, relationship; folks, kin, kinsfolk, kinsmen, relations, relatives.

king *n* majesty, monarch, sovereign.

kingdom *n* dominion, empire, monarchy, rule, sovereignty, supremacy; region, tract; division, department, domain, province, realm.

kingly *adj* imperial, kinglike, monarchical, regal, royal, sovereign; august, glorious, grand, imperial, imposing, magnificent, majestic, noble, splendid.

kink *n* cramp, crick, curl, entanglement, knot, loop, twist; crochet, whim, wrinkle.

kinsfolk *n* kin, kindred, kinsmen, relations, relatives.

kit *n* equipment, implements, outfit, set, working.

knack *n* ability, address, adroitness, aptitude, aptness, dexterity, dextrousness, expertness, facility, quickness, readiness, skill.

knave *n* caitiff, cheat, miscreant, rascal, rogue, scamp, scapegrace, scoundrel, sharper, swindler, trickster, villain.

knavery *n* criminality, dishonesty, fraud, knavishness, rascality, scoundrelism, trickery, villainy.

knavish *adj* dishonest, fraudulent, rascally, scoundrelly, unprincipled, roguish, trickish, tricky, villainous.

knell *vb* announce, peal, ring, toll. • *n* chime, peal, ring, toll.

knife *vb* cut, slash, stab. • *n* blade, jack-knife, lance.

knit *vb* connect, interlace, join, unite, weave.

knob *n* boss, bunch, hunch, lump, protuberance, stud.

knock *vb* clap, cuff, hit, rap, rattle, slap, strike, thump; beat, blow, box. • *n* blow, slap, smack, thump; blame, criticism, rejection, setback.

knoll *n* hill, hillock, mound.

knot *vb* complicate, entangle, gnarl, kink, tic, weave. • *n* complication, entanglement; connection, tie; joint, node, knag;

bunch, rosette, tuft; band, cluster, clique, crew, gang, group, pack, set, squad.

knotty *adj* gnarled, hard, knaggy, knurled, knotted, rough, rugged; complex, difficult, harassing, intricate, involved, perplexing, troublesome.

know *vb* apprehend, comprehend, cognize, discern, perceive, recognize, see, understand; discriminate, distinguish.

knowing *adj* accomplished, competent, experienced, intelligent, proficient, qualified, skillful, well-informed; aware, conscious, percipient, sensible, thinking; cunning, expressive, significant.

knowingly *adv* consciously, intentionally, purposely, wittingly.

knowledge *n* apprehension, command, comprehension, discernment, judgment, perception, understanding, wit; acquaintance, acquirement, attainments, enlightenment, erudition, information, learning, lore, mastery, scholarship, science; cognition, cognizance, consciousness, ken, notice, prescience, recognition.

knowledgeable *adj* aware, conscious, experienced, well-informed; educated, intelligent, learned, scholarly.

knuckle *vb* cringe, crouch, stoop, submit, yield.

L

laborious *adj* assiduous, diligent, hardworking, indefatigable, industrious, painstaking, sedulous, toiling; arduous, difficult, fatiguing, hard, Herculean, irksome, onerous, tiresome, toilsome, wearisome.

labor *vb* drudge, endeavor, exert, strive, toil, travail, work. • *n* drudgery, effort, exertion, industry, pains, toil, work; childbirth, delivery, parturition.

labyrinth *n* entanglement, intricacy, maze, perplexity, windings.

labyrinthine *adj* confused, convoluted, intricate, involved, labyrinthian, labyrinthic, perplexing, winding.

lace *vb* attach, bind, fasten, intertwine, tie, twine. • *n* filigree, lattice, mesh, net, netting, network, openwork, web.

lacerate *vb* claw, cut, lancinate, mangle, rend, rip, sever, slash, tear, wound; afflict, harrow, rend, torture, wound.

lack *vb* need, want. • *n* dearth, default, defectiveness, deficiency, deficit, destitution, insufficiency, need, scantiness, scarcity, shortcoming, shortness, want.

lackadaisical *adj* languishing, sentimental, pensive.

laconic *adj* brief, compact, concise, pithy, sententious, short, succinct, terse.

lad *n* boy, schoolboy, stripling, youngster, youth.

lading *n* burden, cargo, freight, load.

ladylike *adj* courtly, genteel, refined, well-bred.

lag *vb* dawdle, delay, idle, linger, loiter, saunter, tarry.

laggard *n* idler, lingerer, loiterer, lounger, saunterer, sluggard.

lair *n* burrow, couch, den, form, resting place.

lambent *adj* flickering, gliding, gleaming, licking, touching, twinkling.

lame *vb* cripple, disable, hobble. • *adj* crippled, defective, disabled, halt, hobbling, limping; feeble, insufficient, poor, unsatisfactory, weak.

lament *vb* complain, grieve, keen, moan, mourn, sorrow, wail, weep; bemoan, bewail, deplore, regret. • *n* complaint, lamentation, moan, moaning, plaint, wailing; coronach, dirge, elegy, keen, monody, requiem, threnody.

lamentable *adj* deplorable, doleful, grievous, lamented, melancholy, woeful; contemptible, miserable, pitiful, poor, wretched.

lamentation *n* dirge, grief, lament, moan, moaning, mourning, plaint, ululation, sorrow, wailing.

lampoon *vb* calumniate, defame, lash, libel, parody, ridicule, satirize, slander. • *n* calumny, defamation, libel, parody, pasquinade, parody, satire, slander.

land *vb* arrive, debark, disembark. • *n* earth, ground, soil; country, district, province, region, reservation, territory, tract, weald.

landlord *n* owner, proprietor; host, hotelier, innkeeper.

landscape *n* prospect, scene, view.

language *n* dialect, speech, tongue, vernacular; conversation; expression, idiom, jargon, parlance, phraseology, slang, style, terminology; utterance, voice.

languid *adj* drooping, exhausted, faint, feeble, flagging, languishing, pining, weak;

dull, heartless, heavy, inactive, listless, lukewarm, slow, sluggish, spiritless, torpid.

languish *vb* decline, droop, fade, fail, faint, pine, sicken, sink, wither.

languor *n* debility, faintness, feebleness, languidness, languishment, weakness; apathy, ennui, heartlessness, heaviness, lethargy, listlessness, torpidness, torpor, weariness.

lank *adj* attenuated, emaciated, gaunt, lean, meager, scraggy, slender, skinny, slim, starveling, thin.

lap[1] *vb* drink, lick, mouth, tongue; plash, ripple, splash, wash; quaff, sip, sup, swizzle, tipple. • *n* draught, dram, drench, drink, gulp, lick, swig, swill, quaff, sip, sup, suck; plash, splash, wash.

lap[2] *vb* cover, enfold, fold, turn, twist, swaddle, wrap; distance, pass, outdistance, overlap. • *n* fold, flap, lappet, lapel, ply, plait; ambit, beat, circle, circuit, cycle, loop, orbit, revolution, round, tour, turn, walk.

lapse *vb* glide, sink, slide, slip; err, fail, fall. • *n* course, flow, gliding; declension, decline, fall; error, fault, indiscretion, misstep, shortcoming, slip.

larceny *n* pilfering, robbery, stealing, theft, thievery.

large *adj* big, broad, bulky, colossal, elephantine, enormous, heroic, great, huge, immense, vast; broad, expanded, extensive, spacious, wide; abundant, ample, copious, full, liberal, plentiful; capacious, comprehensive.

lascivious *adj* concupiscent, immodest, incontinent, goatish, lecherous, lewd, libidinous, loose, lubricious, lustful, prurient, salacious, sensual, unchaste, voluptuous, wanton.

lash[1] *vb* belay, bind, strap, tie; fasten, join, moor, pinion, secure.

lash[2] *vb* beat, castigate, chastise, flagellate, flail, flay, flog, goad, scourge, swinge, thrash, whip; assail, censure, excoriate, lampoon, satirize, trounce. • *n* scourge, strap, thong, whip; cut, slap, smack, stroke, stripe.

lass *n* damsel, girl, lassie, maiden, miss.

lassitude *n* dullness, exhaustion, fatigue, languor, languidness, prostration, tiredness, weariness.

last[1] *vb* abide, carry on, continue, dwell, endure, extend, maintain, persist, prevail, remain, stand, stay, survive.

last[2] *adj* hindermost, hindmost, latest; conclusive, final, terminal, ultimate; eventual, endmost, extreme, farthest, ultimate; greatest, highest, maximal, maximum, most, supreme, superlative, utmost; latest, newest; aforegoing, foregoing, latter, preceding; departing, farewell, final, leaving, parting, valedictory. • *n* conclusion, consummation, culmination, end, ending, finale, finis, finish, termination.

last[3] *n* cast, form, matrix, mold, shape, template.

lasting *adj* abiding, durable, enduring, fixed, perennial, permanent, perpetual, stable.

lastly *adv* conclusively, eventually, finally, ultimately.

late *adj* behindhand, delayed, overdue, slow, tardy; deceased, former; recent. • *adv* lately, recently, sometime; tardily.

latent *adj* abeyant, concealed, hidden, invisible, occult, secret, unseen, veiled.

latitude *n* amplitude, breadth, compass, extent, range, room, scope; freedom, indulgence, liberty; laxity.

latter *adj* last, latest, modern, recent.

lattice *n* espalier, grating, latticework, trellis.

laud *vb* approve, celebrate, extol, glorify, magnify, praise.

laudable *adj* commendable, meritorious, praiseworthy.

laugh *vb* cackle, chortle, chuckle, giggle, guffaw, snicker, snigger, titter. • *n* chortle, chuckle, giggle, guffaw, laughter, titter.

laughable *adj* amusing, comical, diverting, droll, farcical, funny, ludicrous, mirthful, ridiculous.

laughter *n* cackle, chortle, chuckle, glee, giggle, guffaw, laugh, laughing.

launch *vb* cast, dart, dispatch, hurl, lance, project, throw; descant, dilate, enlarge, expiate; begin, commence, inaugurate, open, start.

lavish *vb* dissipate, expend, spend, squander, waste. • *adj* excessive, extravagant, generous, immoderate, overliberal, prodigal, profuse, thriftless, unrestrained, unstinted, unthrifty, wasteful.

law *n* act, code, canon, command, commandment, covenant, decree, edict, enactment, order, precept, principle, statute, regulation, rule; jurisprudence; litigation, process, suit.

lawful *adj* constitutional, constituted, legal, legalized, legitimate; allowable, authorized, permissible, warrantable; equitable, rightful, just, proper, valid.

lawless *adj* anarchic, anarchical, chaotic, disorderly, insubordinate, rebellious, reckless, riotous, seditious, wild.

lawyer *n* advocate, attorney, barrister, counsel, counselor, pettifogger, solicitor.

lax *adj* loose, relaxed, slow; drooping, flabby, soft; neglectful, negligent, remiss; dissolute, immoral, licentious, seditious, wild.

lay[1] *vb* deposit, establish, leave, place, plant, posit, put, set, settle, spread; arrange, dispose, locate, organize, position; bear, produce; advance, lodge, offer, submit; allocate, allot, ascribe, assign, attribute, charge, impute; concoct, contrive, design, plan, plot, prepare; apply, burden, encumber, impose, saddle, tax; bet, gamble, hazard, risk, stake, wager; allay, alleviate, appease, assuage, calm, relieve, soothe, still, suppress; disclose, divulge, explain, reveal, show, unveil; acquire, grab, grasp, seize; assault, attack, beat up; discover, find, unearth; bless, confirm, consecrate, ordain. • *n* arrangement, array, form, formation; attitude, aspect, bearing, demeanor, direction, lie, pose, position, posture, set.

lay[2] *adj* amateur, inexpert, nonprofessional; civil, laic, laical, nonclerical, nonecclesiastical, nonreligious, secular, temporal, unclerical.

lay[3] *n* ballad, carol, ditty, lied, lyric, ode, poem, rhyme, round, song, verse.

layer *n* bed, course, lay, seam, stratum.

laziness *n* idleness, inactivity, indolence, slackness, sloth, fulness, sluggishness, tardiness.

lazy *adj* idle, inactive, indolent, inert, slack, slothful, slow, sluggish, supine, torpid.

lead *vb* conduct, deliver, direct, draw, escort, guide; front, head, precede; advance, excel, outstrip, pass; allure, entice, induce, persuade, prevail; conduce, contribute, serve, tend. • *adj* chief, first, foremost, main, primary, prime, principal. • *n* direction, guidance, leadership; advance; precedence, priority.

leader *n* conductor, director, guide; captain, chief, chieftain, commander, head; superior, dominator, victor.

leading *adj* governing, ruling; capital, chief, first, foremost, highest, principal, superior.

league *vb* ally, associate, band, combine, confederate, unite. • *n* alliance, association, coalition, combination, combine, confederacy, confederation, consortium, union.

leak *vb* drip, escape, exude, ooze, pass, percolate, spill. • *n* chink, crack, crevice, hole, fissure, oozing, opening; drip, leakage, leaking, percolation.

lean[1] *adj* bony, emaciated, gaunt, lank, meager, poor, skinny, thin; dull, barren, jejune, meager, tame; inadequate, pitiful, scanty, slender; bare, barren, infertile, unproductive.

lean[2] *vb* incline, slope; bear, recline, repose, rest; confide, depend, rely, trust.

leaning *n* aptitude, bent, bias, disposition, inclination, liking, predilection, proneness, propensity, tendency.

leap *vb* bound, clear, jump, spring, vault; caper, frisk, gambol, hop, skip. • *n* bound, jump, spring, vault; caper, frisk, gambol, hop, skip.

learn *vb* acquire, ascertain, attain, collect, gain, gather, hear, memorize.

learned *adj* erudite, lettered, literate, scholarly, well-read; expert, experienced, knowing, skilled, versed, well-informed.

learner *n* beginner, novice, pupil, student, tyro.

learning *n* acquirements, attainments, culture, education, information, knowledge, lore, scholarship, tuition.

least *adj* meanest, minutest, smallest, tiniest.

leave[1] *vb* abandon, decamp, go, quit, vacate, withdraw; desert, forsake, relinquish, renounce; commit, consign, refer; cease, desist from, discontinue, refrain, stop; allow, let, let alone, permit; bequeath, demise, desist, will.

leave[2] *n* allowance, liberty, permission, license, sufferance; departure, retirement, withdrawal; adieu, farewell, goodbye.

leaven *vb* ferment, lighten, raise; color, elevate, imbue, inspire, lift, permeate, tinge; infect, vitiate. • *n* barm, ferment, yeast; influence, inspiration.

leavings *npl* bits, dregs, fragments, leftovers, pieces, relics, remains, remnants, scraps.

lecherous *adj* carnal, concupiscent, incontinent, lascivious, lewd, libidinous, lubricious, lustful, wanton, salacious, unchaste.

lechery *n* concupiscence, lasciviousness,

lewdness, lubriciousness, lubricity, lust, salaciousness, salacity.

lecture vb censure, chide, reprimand, reprove, scold, sermonize; address, harangue, teach. • n censure, lecturing, lesson, reprimand, reproof, scolding; address, discourse, prelection.

ledge n projection, ridge, shelf.

lees npl dregs, precipitate, refuse, sediment, settlings.

leg n limb, prop.

legacy n bequest, gift, heirloom; heritage, inheritance, tradition.

legal adj allowable, authorized, constitutional, lawful, legalized, legitimate, proper, sanctioned.

legalize vb authorize, legitimate, legitimatize, legitimize, permit, sanction.

legend n fable, fiction, myth, narrative, romance, story, tale.

legendary adj fabulous, fictitious, mythical, romantic.

legible adj clear, decipherable, fair, distinct, plain, readable; apparent, discoverable, recognizable, manifest.

legion n army, body, cohort, column, corps, detachment, detail, division, force, maniple, phalanx, platoon; squad; army, horde, host, multitude, number, swarm, throng. • adj many, multitudinous, myriad, numerous.

legislate vb enact, ordain.

legitimacy n lawfulness, legality; genuineness.

legitimate adj authorized, lawful, legal, sanctioned; genuine, valid; correct, justifiable, logical, reasonable, warrantable, warranted.

leisure n convenience, ease, freedom, liberty, opportunity, recreation, retirement, vacation.

lend vb advance, afford, bestow, confer, furnish, give, grant, impart, loan, supply.

lengthen vb elongate, extend, produce, prolong, stretch; continue, protract.

lengthy adj diffuse, lengthened, long, long-drawn-out, prolix, prolonged, protracted.

lenience, leniency n clemency, compassion, forbearance, gentleness, lenity, mercy, mildness, tenderness.

lenient adj assuasive, lenitive, mitigating, mitigative, softening, soothing; clement, easy, forbearing, gentle, humoring, indulgent, long-suffering, merciful, mild, tender, tolerant.

lesion n derangement, disorder, hurt, injury.

less adj baser, inferior, lower, smaller; decreased, fewer, lesser, reduced, smaller, shorter; • adv barely, below, least, under; decreasingly. • prep excepting, lacking, minus, sans, short of, without.

lessen vb abate, abridge, contract, curtail, decrease, diminish, narrow, reduce, shrink; degrade, lower; dwindle, weaken.

lesson n exercise, task; instruction, precept; censure, chiding, lecture, lecturing, rebuke, reproof, scolding.

let[1] vb admit, allow, authorize, permit, suffer; charter, hire, lease, rent.

let[2] vb hinder, impede, instruct, prevent. • n hindrance, impediment, interference, obstacle, obstruction, restriction.

lethal adj deadly, destructive, fatal, mortal, murderous.

lethargic adj apathetic, comatose, drowsy, dull, heavy, inactive, inert, sleepy, stupid, stupefied, torpid.

lethargy n apathy, coma, drowsiness, dullness, hypnotism, inactiveness, inactivity, inertia, sleepiness, sluggishness, stupefaction, stupidity, stupor, torpor.

letter n epistle, missive, note.

lettered adj bookish, educated, erudite, learned, literary, versed, well-read.

levee n ceremony, entertainment, reception, party, soiree; embankment.

level vb equalize, flatten, horizontalize, smooth; demolish, destroy, raze; aim, direct, point. • adj equal, even, flat, flush, horizontal, plain, plane, smooth. • n altitude, degree, equality, evenness, plain, plane, smoothness; deck, floor, layer, stage, storey, tier.

levity n buoyancy, facetiousness, fickleness, flightiness, flippancy, frivolity, giddiness, inconstancy, levity, volatility.

levy vb collect, exact, gather, tax; call, muster, raise, summon. • n duty, tax.

lewd adj despicable, impure, lascivious, libidinous, licentious, loose, lustful, profligate, unchaste, vile, wanton, wicked.

liability n accountableness, accountability, duty, obligation, responsibility, tendency; exposedness; debt, indebtedness, obligation.

liable adj accountable, amenable, answerable, bound, responsible; exposed, likely, obnoxious, subject.

liaison n amor, intimacy, intrigue; connection, relation, union.

libel *vb* calumniate, defame, lampoon, satirize, slander, vilify. • *n* calumny, defamation, lampoon, satire, slander, vilification, vituperation.

liberal *adj* beneficent, bountiful, charitable, disinterested, free, generous, munificent, open-hearted, princely, unselfish; broadminded, catholic, chivalrous, enlarged, high-minded, honorable, magnanimous, tolerant, unbiased, unbigoted; abundant, ample, bounteous, full, large, plentiful, unstinted; humanizing, liberalizing, refined, refining.

liberality *n* beneficence, bountifulness, bounty, charity, disinterestedness, generosity, kindness, munificence; benefaction, donation, gift, gratuity, present; broadmindedness, catholicity, candor, impartiality, large-mindedness, magnanimity, toleration.

liberate *vb* deliver, discharge, disenthral, emancipate, free, manumit, ransom, release.

libertine *adj* corrupt, depraved, dissolute, licentious, profligate, rakish. • *n* debauchee, lecher, profligate, rake, roue, voluptuary.

liberty *n* emancipation, freedom, independence, liberation, self-direction, self-government; franchise, immunity, privilege; leave, license, permission.

libidinous *adj* carnal, concupiscent, debauched, impure, incontinent, lascivious, lecherous, lewd, loose, lubricious, lustful, salacious, sensual, unchaste, wanton, wicked.

license *n* authorization, leave, permission, privilege, right; certificate, charter, dispensation, imprimatur, permit, warrant; anarchy, disorder, freedom, lawlessness, laxity, liberty. *vb* allow, authorize, grant, permit, warrant; suffer, tolerate.

licentious *adj* disorderly, riotous, uncontrolled, uncurbed, ungovernable, unrestrained, unruly, wanton; debauched, dissolute, lax, libertine, loose, profligate, rakish; immoral, impure, lascivious, lecherous, lewd, libertine, libidinous, lustful, sensual, unchaste, wicked.

lick *vb* beat, flog, spank, thrash; lap, taste. • *n* blow, slap, stroke; salt-spring.

lie[1] *vb* couch, recline, remain, repose, rest; consist, pertain.

lie[2] *vb* equivocate, falsify, fib, prevaricate, romance. • *n* equivocation, falsehood,

falsification, fib, misrepresentation, prevarication, untruth; delusion, illusion.

lief *adv* freely, gladly, willingly.

life *n* activity, alertness, animation, briskness, energy, sparkle, spirit, sprightliness, verve, vigor, vivacity; behavior, conduct, deportment; being, duration, existence, lifetime; autobiography, biography, curriculum vitae, memoirs, story.

lifeless *adj* dead, deceased, defunct, extinct, inanimate; cold, dull, flat, frigid, inert, lethargic, passive, pulseless, slow, sluggish, tame, torpid.

lift *vb* elevate, exalt, hoist, raise, uplift. • *n* aid, assistance, help; elevator.

light[1] *vb* alight, land, perch, settle. • *adj* porous, sandy, spongy, well-leavened; loose, sandy, free, portable, unburdened, unencumbered; inconsiderable, moderate, negligible, slight, small, trifling, trivial, unimportant; ethereal, feathery, flimsy, gossamer, insubstantial, weightless; easy, effortless, facile; fickle, frivolous, unsettled, unsteady, volatile; airy, buoyant, carefree, light-hearted, lightsome; unaccented, unstressed, weak.

light[2] *vb* conflagrate, fire, ignite, inflame, kindle; brighten, illume, illuminate, illumine, luminate, irradiate, lighten. • *adj* bright, clear, fair, lightsome, luminous, pale, pearly, whitish. • *n* dawn, day, daybreak, sunrise; blaze, brightness, effulgence, gleam, illumination, luminosity, phosphorescence, radiance, ray; candle, lamp, lantern, lighthouse, taper, torch; comprehension, enlightenment, information, insight, instruction, knowledge; elucidation, explanation, illustration; attitude, construction, interpretation, observation, reference, regard, respect, view.

lighten[1] *vb* allay, alleviate, ease, mitigate, palliate; disburden, disencumber, relieve, unburden, unload.

lighten[2] *vb* brighten, gleam, shine; light, illume, illuminate, illumine, irradiate; enlighten, inform; emit, flash.

light-headed *adj* dizzy, giddy, vertiginous; confused, delirious, wandering; addlepated, frivolous, giddy, heedless, indiscreet, light, rattle-brained, thoughtless, volatile.

light-hearted *adj* blithe, blithesome, carefree, cheerful, frolicsome, gay, glad, gladsome, gleeful, happy, jocund, jovial, joyful, lightsome, merry.

lightness *n* flightiness, frivolity, giddiness, levity, volatility; agility, buoyancy, facility.

like[1] *vb* approve, please; cherish, enjoy, love, relish; esteem, fancy, regard; choose, desire, elect, list, prefer, select, wish. • *n* liking, partiality, preference.

like[2] *adj* alike, allied, analogous, cognate, corresponding, parallel, resembling, similar; equal, same; likely, probable. • *adv* likely, probably. • *n* counterpart, equal, match, peer, twin.

likelihood *n* probability, verisimilitude.

likely *adj* credible, liable, possible, probable; agreeable, appropriate, convenient, likable, pleasing, suitable, well-adapted, well-suited. • *adv* doubtlessly, presumably, probably.

likeness *n* appearance, form, parallel, resemblance, semblance, similarity, similitude; copy, counterpart, effigy, facsimile, image, picture, portrait, representation.

liking *n* desire, fondness, partiality, wish; appearance, bent, bias, disposition, inclination, leaning, penchant, predisposition, proneness, propensity, tendency, turn.

limb *n* arm, extremity, leg, member; bough, branch, offshoot.

limit *vb* bound, circumscribe, define; check, condition, hinder, restrain, restrict. • *n* bound, boundary, bourn, confine, frontier, march, precinct, term, termination, terminus; check, hindrance, obstruction, restraint, restriction.

limitation *n* check, constraint, restraint, restriction.

limitless *adj* boundless, endless, eternal, illimitable, immeasurable, infinite, never-ending, unbounded, undefined, unending, unlimited.

limp[1] *vb* halt, hitch, hobble, totter. • *n* hitch, hobble, shamble, shuffle, totter.

limp[2] *adj* drooping, droopy, floppy, sagging, weak; flabby, flaccid, flexible, limber, pliable, relaxed, slack, soft.

limpid *adj* bright, clear, crystal, crystalline, lucid, pellucid, pure, translucent, transparent.

line *vb* align, line up, range, rank, regiment; border, bound, edge, fringe, hem, interline, march, rim, verge; seam, stripe, streak, striate, trace; carve, chisel, crease, cut, crosshatch; define, delineate, describe. • n mark, streak, stripe; cable, cord, rope, string, thread; rank, row; ancestry, family, lineage, race, succession;

course, method; business, calling, employment, job, occupation, post, pursuit.

lineage *n* ancestry, birth, breed, descendants, descent, extraction, family, forebears, forefathers, genealogy, house, line, offspring, progeny, race.

lineament *n* feature, line, outline, trait.

linen *n* cloth, fabric, flax, lingerie.

linger *vb* dally, dawdle, delay, idle, lag, loiter, remain, saunter, stay, tarry, wait.

link *vb* bind, conjoin, connect, fasten, join, tie, unite. • *n* bond, connection, connective, copula, coupler, joint, juncture; division, member, part, piece.

liquefy *vb* dissolve, fuse, melt, thaw.

liquid *adj* fluid; clear, dulcet, flowing, mellifluous, mellifluent, melting, soft. • *n* fluid, liquor.

list[1] *vb* alphabetize, catalog, chronicle, codify, docket, enumerate, file, index, inventory, record, register, tabulate, tally; enlist, enroll; choose, desire, elect, like, please, prefer, wish. • *n* catalog, enumeration, index, inventory, invoice, register, roll, schedule, scroll, series, table, tally; border, bound, limit; border, edge, selvedge, strip, stripe; fillet, listel.

list[2] *vb* cant, heel, incline, keel, lean, pitch, tilt, tip. • *n* cant, inclination, incline, leaning, pitch, slope, tilt, tip.

listen *vb* attend, eavesdrop, hark, hear, hearken, heed, obey, observe.

listless *adj* apathetic, careless, heedless, impassive, inattentive, indifferent, indolent, languid, torpid, vacant, supine, thoughtless, vacant.

listlessness *n* apathy, carelessness, heedlessness, impassivity, inattention, indifference, indolence, languidness, languor, supineness, thoughtlessness, torpor, torpidity, vacancy.

literally *adv* actually, really; exactly, precisely, rigorously, strictly.

literary *adj* bookish, book-learned, erudite, instructed, learned, lettered, literate, scholarly, well-read.

literature *n* erudition, learning, letters, lore, writings.

lithe *adj* flexible, flexile, limber, pliable, pliant, supple.

litigation *n* contending, contest, disputing, lawsuit.

litigious *adj* contentious, disputatious, quarrelsome; controvertible, disputable.

litter *vb* derange, disarrange, disorder,

scatter, strew; bear. • n bedding, couch, palanquin, sedan, stretcher; confusion, disarray, disorder, mess, untidiness; fragments, rubbish, shreds, trash.

little adj diminutive, infinitesimal, minute, small, tiny, wee; brief, short, small; feeble, inconsiderable, insignificant, moderate, petty, scanty, slender, slight, trivial, unimportant, weak; contemptible, illiberal, mean, narrow, niggardly, paltry, selfish, stingy. • n handful, jot, modicum, pinch, pittance, trifle, whit.

live[1] vb be, exist; continue, endure, last, remain, survive; abide, dwell, reside; fare, feed, nourish, subsist, support; continue, lead, pass.

live[2] adj alive, animate, living, quick; burning, hot, ignited; bright, brilliant, glowing, lively, vivid; active, animated, earnest, glowing, wide-awake.

livelihood n living, maintenance, subsistence, support, sustenance.

liveliness n activity, animation, briskness, gaiety, spirit, sprightliness, vivacity.

lively adj active, agile, alert, brisk, energetic, nimble, quick, smart, stirring, supple, vigorous, vivacious; airy, animated, blithe, blithesome, buoyant, frolicsome, gleeful, jocund, jolly, merry, spirited, sportive, sprightly, spry; bright, brilliant, clear, fresh, glowing, strong, vivid; dynamic, forcible, glowing, impassioned, intense, keen, nervous, piquant, racy, sparkling, strenuous, vigorous.

living adj alive, breathing, existing, live, organic, quick; active, lively, quickening. • n livelihood, maintenance, subsistence, support; estate, keeping; benefice.

load vb freight, lade; burden, cumber, encumber, oppress, weigh. • n burden, freightage, pack, weight; cargo, freight, lading; clog, deadweight, encumbrance, incubus, oppression, pressure.

loafer n (sl) bum, idler, lounger, vagabond, vagrant.

loath adj averse, backward, disinclined, indisposed, reluctant, unwilling.

loathe vb abhor, abominate, detest, dislike, hate, recoil.

loathing n abhorrence, abomination, antipathy, aversion, detestation, disgust, hatred, horror, repugnance, revulsion.

loathsome adj disgusting, nauseating, nauseous, offensive, palling, repulsive, revolting, sickening; abominable, abhorrent,

detestable, execrable, hateful, odious, shocking.

local adj limited, neighboring, provincial, regional, restricted, sectional, territorial, topical.

locality n location, neighborhood, place, position, site, situation, spot.

locate vb determine, establish, fix, place, set, settle.

lock[1] vb bolt, fasten, padlock, seal; confine; clog, impede, restrain, stop; clasp, embrace, encircle, enclose, grapple, hug, join, press. • n bolt, fastening, padlock; embrace, grapple, hug.

lock[2] n curl, ringlet, tress, tuft.

lodge vb deposit, fix, settle; fix, place, plant; accommodate, cover, entertain, harbor, quarter, shelter; abide, dwell, inhabit, live, reside, rest; remain, rest, sojourn, stay, stop. • n cabin, cot, cottage, hovel, hut, shed; cave, den, haunt, lair; assemblage, assembly, association club, group, society.

lodging n abode, apartment, dwelling, habitation, quarters, residence; cover, harbor, protection, refuge, shelter.

loftiness n altitude, elevation, height; arrogance, haughtiness, pride, vanity; dignity, grandeur, sublimity.

lofty adj elevated, high, tall, towering; arrogant, haughty, proud; eminent, exalted, sublime; dignified, imposing, majestic, stately.

logical adj close, coherent, consistent, dialectical, sound, valid; discriminating, rational, reasoned.

loiter vb dally, dawdle, delay, dilly-dally, idle, lag, linger, saunter, stroll, tarry.

loneliness n isolation, retirement, seclusion, solitariness, solitude; desolation, dreariness, forlornness.

lonely adj apart, dreary, isolated, lonesome, remote, retired, secluded, separate, sequestered, solitary; alone, lone, companionless, friendless, unaccompanied; deserted, desolate, forlorn, forsaken, withdrawn.

lonesome adj cheerless, deserted, desolate, dreary, gloomy, lone, lonely.

long[1] vb anticipate, await, expect; aspire, covet, crave, desire, hanker, lust, pine, wish, yearn.

long[2] adj drawn-out, extended, extensive, far-reaching, lengthy, prolonged, protracted, stretched; diffuse, long-winded, prolix, tedious, wearisome; backward, behindhand, dilatory, lingering, slack, slow, tardy.

longing *n* aspiration, coveting, craving, desire, hankering, hunger, pining, yearning.

long-suffering *adj* enduring, forbearing, patient. • *n* clemency, endurance, forbearing.

look *vb* behold, examine, notice, see, search; consider, inspect, investigate, observe, study, contemplate, gaze, regard, scan, survey, view; anticipate, await, expect; heed, mind, watch; face, front; appear, seem. • *n* examination, gaze, glance, peep, peer, search; appearance, aspect, complexion; air, aspect, manner, mien.

loophole *n* aperture, crenellation, loop, opening; excuse, plea, pretence, pretext, subterfuge.

loose *vb* free, liberate, release, unbind, undo, unfasten, unlash, unlock, untie; ease, loosen, relax, slacken; detach, disconnect, disengage. • *adj* unbound, unconfined, unfastened, unsewn, untied; disengaged, free, unattached; relaxed; diffuse, diffusive, prolix, rambling, unconnected; ill-defined, indefinite, indeterminate, indistinct, vague; careless, heedless, negligent, lax, slack; debauched, dissolute, immoral, licentious, unchaste, wanton.

loosen *vb* liberate, relax, release, separate, slacken, unbind, unloose, untie.

looseness *n* easiness, slackness; laxity, levity; lewdness, unchastity, wantonness, wickedness; diarrhea, flux.

loot *vb* pillage, plunder, ransack, rifle, rob, sack. • *n* booty, plunder, spoil.

lop *vb* cut, truncate; crop, curtail, dock, prune; detach, dissever, sever.

loquacious *adj* garrulous, talkative, voluble, wordy; noisy, speaking, talking; babbling, blabbing, tattling, tell-tale.

loquacity *n* babbling, chattering, gabbling, garrulity, loquaciousness, talkativeness, volubility.

lord *n* earl, noble, nobleman, peer, viscount; governor, king, liege, master, monarch, prince, ruler, seigneur, seignior, sovereign, superior; husband, spouse.

lordly *adj* aristocratic, dignified, exalted, grand, lofty, majestic, noble; arrogant, despotic, domineering, haughty, imperious, insolent, masterful, overbearing, proud, tyrannical; large, liberal.

lordship *n* authority, command, control, direction, domination, dominion, empire, government, rule, sovereignty, sway; manor, domain, seigneury, seigniory.

lore *n* erudition, knowledge, learning, letters, scholarship; admonition, advice, counsel, doctrine, instruction, lesson, teaching, wisdom.

lose *vb* deprive, dispossess, forfeit, miss; dislodge, displace, mislay, misspend, squander, waste; decline, fall, succumb, yield.

loss *n* deprivation, failure, forfeiture, privation; casualty, damage, defeat, destruction, detriment, disadvantage, injury, overthrow, ruin; squandering, waste.

lost *adj* astray, missing; forfeited, missed, unredeemed; dissipated, misspent, squandered, wasted; bewildered, confused, distracted, perplexed, puzzled; absent, absent-minded, abstracted, dreamy, napping, preoccupied; abandoned, corrupt, debauched, depraved, dissolute, graceless, hardened, incorrigible, irreclaimable, licentious, profligate, reprobate, shameless, unchaste, wanton; destroyed, ruined.

lot *n* allotment, apportionment, destiny, doom, fate; accident, chance, fate, fortune, hap, haphazard, hazard; division, parcel, part, portion.

loth *adj* averse, disinclined, disliking, reluctant, unwilling.

loud *adj* high-sounding, noisy, resounding, sonorous; deafening, stentorian, strong, stunning; boisterous, clamorous, noisy, obstreperous, tumultuous, turbulent, uproarious, vociferous; emphatic, impressive, positive, vehement; flashy, gaudy, glaring, loud, ostentatious, showy, vulgar.

lounge *vb* loll, recline, sprawl; dawdle, idle, loaf, loiter.

love *vb* adore, like, worship. • *n* accord, affection, amity, courtship, delight, fondness, friendship, kindness, regard, tenderness, warmth; adoration, amour, ardour, attachment, passion; devotion, inclination, liking; benevolence, charity, goodwill.

lovely *adj* beautiful, charming, delectable, delightful, enchanting, exquisite, graceful, pleasing, sweet, winning; admirable, adorable, amiable.

loving *adj* affectionate, dear, fond, kind, tender.

low[1] *vb* bellow, moo.

low[2] *adj* basal, depressed, profound; gentle, grave, soft, subdued; cheap, humble, mean, plebeian, vulgar; abject, base, base-minded, degraded, dirty, groveling, ignoble, low-minded, menial, scurvy, servile, shabby, slavish, vile; derogatory, disgraceful, dishonorable, disreputable, unbecoming, undignified, ungentlemanly, unhandsome, unmanly; exhausted, feeble, reduced, weak; frugal, plain, poor, simple, spare; lowly, reverent, submissive; dejected, depressed, dispirited.

lower[1] *vb* depress, drop, sink, subside; debase, degrade, disgrace, humble, humiliate, reduce; abate, decrease, diminish, lessen. • *adj* baser, inferior, less, lesser, shorter, smaller; subjacent, under.

lower[2] *vb* blacken, darken, frown, glower, threaten.

lowering *adj* dark, clouded, cloudy, lurid, murky, overcast, threatening.

lowliness *n* humbleness, humility, meekness, self-abasement, submissiveness.

lowly *adj* gentle, humble, meek, mild, modest, plain, poor, simple, unassuming, unpretending, unpretentious; low-born, mean, servile.

loyal *adj* constant, devoted, faithful, patriotic, true.

loyalty *n* allegiance, constancy, devotion, faithfulness, fealty, fidelity, patriotism.

lubricious *adj* slippery, smooth; uncertain, unstable, wavering; impure, incontinent, lascivious, lecherous, lewd, libidinous, ligentious, lustful, salacious, unchaste, wanton.

lucid *adj* beaming, bright, brilliant, luminous, radiant, resplendent, shining, clear, crystalline, diaphanous, limpid, lucent, pellucid, pure, transparent; clear, distinct, evident, intelligible, obvious, perspicuous, plain; reasonable, sane, sober, sound.

luck *n* accident, casualty, chance, fate, fortune, hap, haphazard, hazard, serendipity, success.

luckless *adj* ill-fated, ill-starred, unfortunate, unhappy, unlucky, unpropitious, unprosperous, unsuccessful.

lucky *adj* blessed, favored, fortunate, happy, successful; auspicious, favorable, propitious, prosperous.

lucrative *adj* advantageous, gainful, paying, profitable, remunerative.

ludicrous *adj* absurd, burlesque, comic, comical, droll, farcical, funny, laughable, odd, ridiculous, sportive.

lugubrious *adj* complaining, doleful, gloomy, melancholy, mournful, sad, serious, somber, sorrowful.

lukewarm *adj* blood-warm, tepid, thermal; apathetic, cold, dull, indifferent, listless, unconcerned, torpid.

lull *vb* calm, compose, hush, quiet, still, tranquillize; abate, cease, decrease, diminish, subside. • *n* calm, calmness, cessation.

lumber[1] *vb* rumble, shamble, trudge.

lumber[2] *n* refuse, rubbish, trash, trumpery; wood.

luminous *adj* effulgent, incandescent, radiant, refulgent, resplendent, shining; bright, brilliant, clear; clear, lucid, lucent, perspicuous, plain.

lunacy *n* aberration, craziness, dementia, derangement, insanity, madness, mania.

lunatic *adj* crazy, demented, deranged, insane, mad, psychopathic. • *n* madman, maniac, psychopath.

lurch *vb* appropriate, filch, pilfer, purloin, steal; deceive, defeat, disappoint, evade; ambush, lurk, skulk; contrive, dodge, shift, trick; pitch, sway.

lure *vb* allure, attract, decoy, entice, inveigle, seduce, tempt. • *n* allurement, attraction, bait, decoy, enticement, temptation.

lurid *adj* dismal, ghastly, gloomy, lowering, murky, pale, wan; glaring, sensational, startling, unrestrained.

lurk *vb* hide, prowl, skulk, slink, sneak, snoop.

luscious *adj* delicious, delightful, grateful, palatable, pleasing, savory, sweet.

lush *adj* fresh, juicy, luxuriant, moist, sappy, succulent, watery.

lust *vb* covet, crave, desire, hanker, need, want, yearn. • *n* cupidity, desire, longing; carnality, concupiscence, lasciviousness, lechery, lewdness, lubricity, salaciousness, salacity, wantonness.

lustful *adj* carnal, concupiscent, hankering, lascivious, lecherous, licentious, libidinous, lubricious, salacious.

lustily *adv* strongly, vigorously.

lustiness *n* hardihood, power, robustness, stoutness, strength, sturdiness, vigor.

lustre *n* brightness, brilliance, brilliancy, splendor.

lusty *adj* healthful, lively, robust, stout, strong, sturdy, vigorous; bulky, burly, corpulent, fat, large, stout.

luxuriance *n* exuberance, profusion, superabundance.

luxuriant adj exuberant, plenteous, plentiful, profuse, superabundant.

luxuriate vb abound, delight, enjoy, flourish, indulge, revel.

luxurious adj epicurean, opulent, pampered, self-indulgent, sensual, sybaritic, voluptuous.

luxury n epicureanism, epicurism, luxuriousness, opulence, sensuality, voluptuousness; delight, enjoyment, gratification, indulgence, pleasure; dainty, delicacy, treat.

lying adj equivocating, false, mendacious, untruthful, untrue.

lyric adj dulcet, euphonious, lyrical, mellifluous, mellifluent, melodic, melodious, musical, poetic, silvery, tuneful.

lyrical adj ecstatic, enthusiastic, expressive, impassion; dulcet, lyric, mellifluous, mellifluent, melodic, melodious, musical, poetic.

M

macabre adj cadaverous, deathlike, deathly, dreadful, eerie, frightening, frightful, ghoulish, grim, grisly, gruesome, hideous, horrid, morbid, unearthly, weird.

mace n baton, staff, truncheon.

macerate vb harass, mortify, torture; digest, soak, soften, steep.

Machiavellian adj arch, artful, astute, crafty, crooked, cunning, deceitful, designing, diplomatic, insidious, intriguing, shrewd, sly, subtle, tricky, wily.

machination n artifice, cabal, conspiracy, contrivance, design, intrigue, plot, scheme, stratagem, trick.

machine n instrument, puppet, tool; machinery, organization, system; engine.

mad adj crazed, crazy, delirious, demented, deranged, distracted, insane, irrational, lunatic, maniac, maniacal; enraged, furious, rabid, raging, violent; angry, enraged, exasperated, furious, incensed, provoked, wrathful; distracted, infatuated, wild; frantic, frenzied, raving.

madden vb annoy, craze, enrage, exasperate, inflame, infuriate, irritate, provoke.

madness n aberration, craziness, dementia, derangement, insanity, lunacy, mania; delirium, frenzy, fury, rage.

magazine n depository, depot, entrepot, receptacle, repository, storehouse, warehouse; pamphlet, paper, periodical.

magic adj bewitching, charming, enchanting, fascinating, magical, miraculous, spellbinding. • n conjuring, enchantment, necromancy, sorcery, thaumaturgy, voodoo, witchcraft; char, fascination, witchery.

magician n conjurer, enchanter, juggler, magus, necromancer, shaman, sorcerer, wizard.

magisterial adj august, dignified, majestic, pompous; authoritative, despotic, domineering, imperious, dictatorial.

magnanimity n chivalry, disinterestedness, forbearance, high-mindedness, generosity, nobility.

magnificence n brilliance, éclat, grandeur, luxuriousness, luxury, majesty, pomp, splendor.

magnificent adj elegant, grand, majestic, noble, splendid, superb; brilliant, gorgeous, imposing, lavish, luxurious, pompous, showy, stately.

magnify vb amplify, augment, enlarge; bless, celebrate, elevate, exalt, extol, glorify, laud, praise; exaggerate.

magnitude n bulk, dimension, extent, mass, size, volume; consequence, greatness, importance; grandeur, loftiness, sublimity.

maid n damsel, girl, lass, lassie, maiden, virgin; maidservant, servant.

maiden adj chaste, pure, undefiled, virgin; fresh, new, unused. • n girl, maid, virgin.

maidenly adj demure, gentle, modest, maidenlike, reserved.

maim vb cripple, disable, disfigure, mangle, mar, mutilate. • n crippling, disfigurement, mutilation; harm, hurt, injury, mischief.

main[1] adj capital, cardinal, chief, leading, principal; essential, important, indispensable, necessary, requisite, vital; enormous, huge, mighty, vast; pure, sheer; absolute, direct, entire, mere. • n channel, pipe; force, might, power, strength, violence.

main[2] n high seas, ocean; continent, mainland.

maintain vb keep, preserve, support, sustain, uphold; hold, possess; defend, vindicate, justify; carry on, continue, keep up; feed, provide, supply; allege, assert, declare; affirm, aver, contend, hold, say.

maintenance n defense, justification, preservation, support, sustenance, vindication;

bread, food, livelihood, provisions, subsistence, sustenance, victuals.

majestic *adj* august, dignified, imperial, imposing, lofty, noble, pompous, princely, stately, regal, royal; grand, magnificent, splendid, sublime.

majesty *n* augustness, dignity, elevation, grandeur, loftiness, stateliness.

majority *n* bulk, greater, mass, more, most, plurality, preponderance, superiority; adulthood, manhood.

make *vb* create; fashion, figure, form, frame, mold, shape; cause, construct, effect, establish, fabricate, produce; do, execute, perform, practice; acquire, gain, get, raise, secure; cause, compel, constrain, force, occasion; compose, constitute, go, journey, move, proceed, tend, travel; conduce, contribute, effect, favor, operate; estimate, judge, reckon, suppose, think. • *n* brand, build, constitution, construction, form, shape, structure.

maker *n* creator, god; builder, constructor, fabricator, framer, manufacturer; author, composer, poet, writer.

maladministration *n* malversation, misgovernment, misrule.

maladroit *adj* awkward, bungling, clumsy, inept, inexpert, unhandy, unskillful, unskilled.

malady *n* affliction, ailment, complaint, disease, disorder, illness, indisposition, sickness.

malcontent *adj* discontented, dissatisfied, insurgent, rebellious, resentful, uneasy, unsatisfied. • *n* agitator, complainer, fault-finder, grumbler, spoilsport.

malediction *n* anathema, ban, curse, cursing, denunciation, execration, imprecation, malison.

malefactor *n* convict, criminal, culprit, delinquent, evildoer, felon, offender, outlaw.

malevolence *n* hate, hatred, ill-will, malice, malignity, rancour, spite, spitefulness, vindictiveness.

malevolent *adj* evil-minded, hateful, hostile, ill-natured, malicious, malignant, mischievous, rancorous, spiteful, venomous, vindictive.

malice *n* animosity, bitterness, enmity, grudge, hate, ill-will, malevolence, maliciousness, malignity, pique, rancor, spite, spitefulness, venom, vindictiveness.

malicious *adj* bitter, envious, evil-minded, ill-disposed, ill-natured, invidious,

malevolent, malignant, mischievous, rancorous, resentful, spiteful, vicious.

malign *vb* abuse, asperse, blacken, calumniate, defame, disparage, revile, scandalize, slander, traduce, vilify. • *adj* malevolent, malicious, malignant, ill-disposed; baneful, injurious, pernicious, unfavorable, unpropitious.

malignant *adj* bitter, envious, hostile, inimical, malevolent, malicious, malign, spiteful, rancorous, resentful, virulent; heinous, pernicious; ill-boding, unfavorable, unpropitious; dangerous, fatal.

malignity *n* animosity, hatred, ill-will, malice, malevolence, maliciousness, rancour, spite; deadliness, destructiveness, fatality, harmfulness, malignancy, perniciousness, virulence; enormity, evilness, heinousness.

malpractice *n* dereliction, malversation, misbehavior, misconduct, misdeed, misdoing, sin, transgression.

maltreat *vb* abuse, harm, hurt, ill-treat, illuse, injure.

mammoth *adj* colossal, enormous, gigantic, huge, immense, vast.

man *vb* crew, garrison, furnish; fortify, reinforce, strengthen. • *n* adult, being, body, human, individual, one, person, personage, somebody, soul; humanity, humankind, mankind; attendant, butler, dependant, liege, servant, subject, valet, vassal; employee, workman.

manacle *vb* bind, chain, fetter, handcuff, restrain, shackle, tie. • *n* bond, chain, handcuff, gyve, hand-fetter, shackle.

manage *vb* administer, conduct, direct, guide, handle, operate, order, regulate, superintend, supervise, transact, treat; control, govern, rule; handle, manipulate, train, wield; contrive, economize, husband, save.

manageable *adj* controllable, docile, easy, governable, tamable, tractable.

management *n* administration, care, charge, conduct, control, direction, disposal, economy, government, guidance, superintendence, supervision, surveillance, treatment.

manager *n* comptroller, conductor, director, executive, governor, impresario, overseer, superintendent, supervisor.

mandate *n* charge, command, commission, edict, injunction, order, precept, requirement.

manful *adj* bold, brave, courageous, daring,

heroic, honorable, intrepid, noble, stout, strong, undaunted, vigorous.

mangily *adv* basely, foully, meanly, scabbily, scurvily, vilely.

mangle[1] *vb* hack, lacerate, mutilate, rend, tear; cripple, crush, destroy, maim, mar, spoil.

mangle[2] *vb* calender, polish, press, smooth.

manhood *n* virility; bravery, courage, firmness, fortitude, hardihood, manfulness, manliness, resolution; human nature, humanity; adulthood, maturity.

mania *n* aberration, craziness, delirium, dementia, derangement, frenzy, insanity, lunacy, madness; craze, desire, enthusiasm, fad, fanaticism.

manifest *vb* declare, demonstrate, disclose, discover, display, evidence, evince, exhibit, express, reveal, show. • *adj* apparent, clear, conspicuous, distinct, evident, glaring, indubitable, obvious, open, palpable, patent, plain, unmistakable, visible.

manifestation *n* disclosure, display, exhibition, exposure, expression, revelation.

manifold *adj* complex, diverse, many, multifarious, multiplied, multitudinous, numerous, several, sundry, varied, various.

manipulate *vb* handle, operate, work.

manliness *n* boldness, bravery, courage, dignity, fearlessness, firmness, heroism, intrepidity, nobleness, resolution, valor.

manly *adj* bold, brave, courageous, daring, dignified, firm, heroic, intrepid, manful, noble, stout, strong, undaunted, vigorous; male, masculine, virile.

manner *n* fashion, form, method, mode, style, way; custom, habit, practice; degree, extent, measure; kind, kinds, sort, sorts; air, appearance, aspect, behavior, carriage, demeanor, deportment, look, mien; mannerism, peculiarity; behavior, conduct, habits, morals; civility, deportment.

mannerly *adj* ceremonious, civil, complaisant, courteous, polite, refined, respectful, urbane, well-behaved, well-bred.

manners *npl* conduct, habits, morals; air, bearing, behavior, breeding, carriage, comportment, deportment, etiquette.

manoeuvre *vb* contrive, finesse, intrigue, manage, plan, plot, scheme. • *n* evolution, exercise, movement, operation; artifice, finesse, intrigue, plan, plot, ruse, scheme, stratagem, trick.

mansion *n* abode, dwelling, dwelling house, habitation, hall, residence, seat.

mantle *vb* cloak, cover, discover, obscure; expand, spread; bubble, cream, effervesce, foam, froth, sparkle. • *n* chasuble, cloak, toga; cover, covering, hood.

manufacture *vb* build, compose, construct, create, fabricate, forge, form, make, mold, produce, shape. • *n* constructing, fabrication, making, production.

manumission *n* deliverance, emancipation, enfranchisement, freedom, liberation, release.

manumit *vb* deliver, emancipate, enfranchise, free, liberate, release.

manure *vb* enrich, fertilize. • *n* compost, dressing, fertilizer, guano, muck.

many *adj* abundant, diverse, frequent, innumerable, manifold, multifarious, multifold, multiplied, multitudinous, numerous, sundry, varied, various. • *n* crowd, multitude, people.

map *vb* chart, draw up, plan, plot, set out, sketch. • *n* chart, diagram, outline, plot, sketch.

mar *vb* blot, damage, harm, hurt, impair, injure, ruin, spoil, stain; deface, deform, disfigure, maim, mutilate.

marauder *n* bandit, brigand, desperado, filibuster, freebooter, outlaw, pillager, plunderer, ravager, robber, rover.

march *vb* go, pace, parade, step, tramp, walk. • *n* hike, tramp, walk; parade, procession; gait, step, stride; advance, evolution, progress.

marches *npl* borders, boundaries, confines, frontiers, limits, precincts.

margin *n* border, brim, brink, confine, edge, limit, rim, skirt, verge; latitude, room, space, surplus.

marine *adj* oceanic, pelagic, saltwater, sea; maritime, naval, nautical. • *n* navy, shipping; sea-dog, sea soldier, soldier; sea piece, seascape.

mariner *n* navigator, sailor, salt, seafarer, seaman, tar.

marital *adj* connubial, conjugal, matrimonial.

maritime *adj* marine, naval, nautical, oceanic, sea, seafaring, seagoing; coastal, seaside.

mark *vb* distinguish, earmark, label; betoken, brand, characterize, denote, designate, engrave, impress, imprint, indicate, print, stamp; evince, heed, note, notice, observe, regard, remark, show, spot. • *n* brand, character, characteristic, impression, impress, line, note, print, sign, stamp, symbol, token, race; evidence, indication, proof, symptom, trace, track, vestige; badge; footprint; bull's-eye, butt, object, target; consequence, distinction, eminence, fame, importance, notability, position, preeminence, reputation, significance.

marked *adj* conspicuous, distinguished, eminent, notable, noted, outstanding, prominent, remarkable.

marriage *n* espousals, nuptials, spousals, wedding; matrimony, wedlock; union; alliance, association, confederation.

marrow *n* medulla, pith; cream, essence, quintessence, substance.

marsh *n* bog, fen, mire, morass, quagmire, slough, swamp.

marshal *vb* arrange, array, dispose, gather, muster, range, order, rank; guide, herald, lead. • *n* conductor, director, master of ceremonies, regulator; harbinger, herald, pursuivant.

marshy *adj* boggy, miry, mossy, swampy, wet.

martial *adj* brave, heroic, military, soldierlike, warlike.

marvel *vb* gape, gaze, goggle, wonder. • *n* miracle, prodigy, wonder; admiration, amazement, astonishment, surprise.

marvellous *adj* amazing, astonishing, extraordinary, miraculous, prodigious, strange, stupendous, wonderful, wondrous; improbable, incredible, surprising, unbelievable.

masculine *adj* bold, hardy, manful, manlike, manly, mannish, virile; potent, powerful, robust, strong, vigorous; bold, coarse, forward.

mask *vb* cloak, conceal, cover, disguise, hide, screen, shroud, veil. • *n* blind, cloak, disguise, screen, veil; evasion, pretence, plea, pretext, ruse, shift, subterfuge, trick; masquerade; bustle, mummery.

masquerade *vb* cover, disguise, hide, mask, revel, veil. • *n* mask, mummery, revel, revelry.

Mass *n* communion, Eucharist.

mass *vb* accumulate, amass, assemble, collect, gather, rally, throng. • *adj* extensive, general, large-scale, widespread. • *n* cake, clot, lump; assemblage, collection, combination, congeries, heap; bulk, dimension, magnitude, size; accumulation, aggregate, body, sum, total, totality, whole.

massacre *vb* annihilate, butcher, exterminate,

kill, murder, slaughter, slay. • *n* annihilation, butchery, carnage, extermination, killing, murder, pogrom, slaughter.

massive *adj* big, bulky, colossal, enormous, heavy, huge, immense, ponderous, solid, substantial, vast, weighty.

master *vb* conquer, defeat, direct, govern, overcome, overpower, rule, subdue, subjugate, vanquish; acquire, learn. • *adj* cardinal, chief, especial, grand, great, main, leading, prime, principal; adept, expert, proficient. • *n* director, governor, lord, manager, overseer, superintendent, ruler; captain, commander; instructor, pedagogue, preceptor, schoolteacher, teacher, tutor; holder, owner, possessor, proprietor; chief, head, leader, principal.

masterly *adj* adroit, clever, dextrous, excellent, expert, finished, skillful, skilled; arbitrary, despotic, despotical, domineering, imperious.

mastery *n* command, dominion, mastership, power, rule, supremacy, sway; ascendancy, conquest, leadership, preeminence, superiority, upper-hand, victory; acquisition, acquirement, attainment; ability, cleverness, dexterity, proficiency, skill.

masticate *vb* chew, eat, munch.

match *vb* equal, rival; adapt, fit, harmonize, proportion, suit; marry, mate; combine, couple, join, sort; oppose, pit; correspond, suit, tally. • *n* companion, equal, mate, tally; competition, contest, game, trial; marriage, union.

matchless *adj* consummate, excellent, exquisite, incomparable, inimitable, peerless, perfect, surpassing, unequaled, unmatched, unparalleled, unrivaled.

mate *vb* marry, match, wed; compete, equal, vie; appal, confound, crush, enervate, subdue, stupefy. • *n* associate, companion, compeer, consort, crony, friend, fellow, intimate; companion, equal, match; assistant, subordinate; husband, spouse, wife.

material *adj* bodily, corporeal, nonspiritual, physical, temporal; essential, important, momentous, relevant, vital, weighty. • *n* body, element, stuff, substance.

maternal *adj* motherlike, motherly.

matrimonial *adj* conjugal, connubial, espousal, hymeneal, marital, nuptial, spousal.

matrimony *n* marriage, wedlock.

matter *vb* import, signify, weigh. • *n* body,

content, sense, substance; difficulty, distress, trouble; material, stuff; question, subject, subject matter, topic; affair, business, concern, event; consequence, import, importance, moment, significance; discharge, purulence, pus.

mature *vb* develop, perfect, ripen. • *adj* complete, fit, full-grown, perfect, ripe; completed, prepared, ready, well-considered, well-digested.

maturity *n* completeness, completion, matureness, perfection, ripeness.

mawkish *adj* disgusting, flat, insipid, nauseous, sickly, stale, tasteless, vapid; emotional, feeble, maudlin, sentimental.

maxim *n* adage, aphorism, apothegm, axiom, byword, dictum, proverb, saw, saying, truism.

maze *vb* amaze, bewilder, confound, confuse, perplex. • *n* intricacy, labyrinth, meander; bewilderment, embarrassment, intricacy, perplexity, puzzle, uncertainty.

mazy *adj* confused, confusing, intricate, labyrinthian, labyrinthic, labyrinthine, perplexing, winding.

meager *adj* emaciated, gaunt, lank, lean, poor, skinny, starved, spare, thin; barren, poor, sterile, unproductive; bald, barren, dry, dull, mean, poor, prosy, feeble, insignificant, jejune, scanty, small, tame, uninteresting, vapid.

mean[1] *vb* contemplate, design, intend, purpose; connote, denote, express, imply, import, indicate, purport, signify, symbolize.

mean[2] *adj* average, medium, middle; intermediate, intervening. • *n* measure, mediocrity, medium, moderation; average; agency, instrument, instrumentality, means, measure, method, mode, way.

mean[3] *adj* coarse, common, humble, ignoble, low, ordinary, plebeian, vulgar; abject, base, base-minded, beggarly, contemptible, degraded, dirty, dishonorable, disingenuous, groveling, low-minded, pitiful, rascally, scurvy, servile, shabby, sneaking, sorry, spiritless, unfair, vile; illiberal, mercenary, miserly, narrow, narrow-minded, niggardly, parsimonious, penurious, selfish, sordid, stingy, ungenerous, unhandsome; contemptible, despicable, diminutive, insignificant, paltry, petty, poor, small, wretched.

meaning *n* acceptation, drift, import, intention, purport, purpose, sense, signification.

means *npl* instrument, method, mode, way; appliance, expedient, measure, resource, shift, step; estate, income, property, resources, revenue, substance, wealth, wherewithal.

measure *vb* mete; adjust, gauge, proportion; appraise, appreciate, estimate, gauge, value. • *n* gauge, meter, rule, standard; degree, extent, length, limit; allotment, share, proportion; means, step; foot, meter, rhythm, tune, verse.

measureless *adj* boundless, endless, immeasurable, immense, limitless, unbounded, unlimited, vast.

meat *n* aliment, cheer, diet, fare, feed, flesh, food, nourishment, nutriment, provision, rations, regimen, subsistence, sustenance, viands, victuals.

mechanic *n* artificer, artisan, craftsman, hand, handicraftsman, machinist, operative, workman.

meddle *vb* interfere, intermeddle, interpose, intrude.

meddlesome *adj* interfering, intermeddling, intrusive, officious, prying.

mediate *vb* arbitrate, intercede, interpose, intervene, settle. • *adj* interposed, intervening, middle.

mediation *n* arbitration, intercession, interposition, intervention.

mediator *n* advocate, arbitrator, interceder, intercessor, propitiator, umpire.

medicine *n* drug, medicament, medication, physic; therapy.

mediocre *adj* average, commonplace, indifferent, mean, medium, middling, ordinary.

meditate *vb* concoct, contrive, design, devise, intend, plan, purpose, scheme; chew, contemplate, ruminate, study; cogitate, muse, ponder, think.

meditation *n* cogitation, contemplation, musing, pondering, reflection, ruminating, study, thought.

meditative *adj* contemplative, pensive, reflective, studious, thoughtful.

medium *adj* average, mean, mediocre, middle. • *n* agency, channel, intermediary, instrument, instrumentality, means, organ; conditions, environment, influences; average, means.

medley *n* confusion, farrago, hodgepodge, hotchpotch, jumble, mass, melange, miscellany, mishmash, mixture.

meed *n* award, guerdon, premium, prize, recompense, remuneration, reward.

meek *adj* gentle, humble, lowly, mild, modest, pacific, soft, submissive, unassuming, yielding.

meekness *n* gentleness, humbleness, humility, lowliness, mildness, modesty, submission, submissiveness.

meet *vb* cross, intersect, transact; confront, encounter, engage; answer, comply, fulfill, gratify, satisfy; converge, join, unite; assemble, collect, convene, congregate, forgather, muster, rally. • *adj* adapted, appropriate, befitting, convenient, fit, fitting, proper, qualified, suitable, suited.

meeting *n* encounter, interview; assemblage, assembly, audience, company, concourse, conference, congregation, convention, gathering; assignation, encounter, introduction, rendezvous; confluence, conflux, intersection, joining, junction, union; collision.

melancholy *adj* blue, dejected, depressed, despondent, desponding, disconsolate, dismal, dispirited, doleful, down, downcast, downhearted, gloomy, glum, hypochondriac, low-spirited, lugubrious, moody, mopish, sad, somber, sorrowful, unhappy; afflictive, calamitous, unfortunate, unlucky; dark, gloomy, grave, quiet. • *n* blues, dejection, depression, despondency, dismals, dumps, gloom, gloominess, hypochondria, sadness, vapors.

melee *n* affray, brawl, broil, contest, fight, fray, scuffle.

mellifluous, mellifluent *adj* dulcet, euphonic, euphonical, euphonious, mellow, silver-toned, silvery, smooth, soft, sweet.

mellow *vb* mature, ripen; improve, smooth, soften, tone; pulverize; perfect. • *adj* mature, ripe; dulcet, mellifluous, mellifluent, rich, silver-toned, silvery, smooth, soft; delicate; genial, good-humored, jolly, jovial, matured, softened; mellowy, loamy, unctuous; perfected, well-prepared; disguised, fuddled, intoxicated, tipsy.

melodious *adj* arioso, concordant, dulcet, euphonious, harmonious, mellifluous, mellifluent, musical, silvery, sweet, tuneful.

melody *n* air, descant, music, plainsong, song, theme, tune.

melt *vb* dissolve, fuse, liquefy, thaw; mollify, relax, soften, subdue; dissipate, waste; blend, pass, shade.

member *n* arm, leg, limb, organ; component, constituent, element, part, portion; branch, clause, division, head.

memento *n* memorial, remembrance, reminder, souvenir.

memoir *n* account, autobiography, biography, journal, narrative, record, register.

memorable *adj* celebrated, distinguished, extraordinary, famous, great, illustrious, important, notable, noteworthy, remarkable, signal, significant.

memorandum *n* minute, note, record.

memorial *adj* commemorative, monumental. • *n* cairn, commemoration, memento, monument, plaque, record, souvenir; memorandum, remembrance.

memory *n* recollection, remembrance, reminiscence; celebrity, fame, renown, reputation; commemoration, memorial.

menace *vb* alarm, frighten, intimidate, threaten. • *n* danger, hazard, peril, threat, warning; nuisance, pest, troublemaker.

menage *n* household, housekeeping, management.

mend *vb* darn, patch, rectify, refit, repair, restore, retouch; ameliorate, amend, better, correct, emend, improve, meliorate, reconcile, rectify, reform; advance, help; augment, increase.

mendacious *adj* deceitful, deceptive, fallacious, false, lying, untrue, untruthful.

mendacity *n* deceit, deceitfulness, deception, duplicity, falsehood, lie, untruth.

mendicant *n* beggar, pauper, tramp.

menial *adj* base, low, mean, servile, vile. • *n* attendant, bondsman, domestic, flunkey, footman, lackey, serf, servant, slave, underling, valet, waiter.

mensuration *n* measurement, measuring; survey, surveying.

mental *adj* ideal, immaterial, intellectual, psychiatric, subjective.

mention *vb* acquaint, allude, cite, communicate, declare, disclose, divulge, impart, inform, name, report, reveal, state, tell. • *n* allusion, citation, designation, notice, noting, reference.

mentor *n* adviser, counselor, guide, instructor, monitor.

mephitic *adj* baleful, baneful, fetid, foul, mephitical, noisome, noxious, poisonous, pestilential.

mercantile *adj* commercial, marketable, trading.

mercenary *adj* hired, paid, purchased, venal; avaricious, covetous, grasping, mean, niggardly, parsimonious, penurious, sordid, stingy. • *n* hireling, soldier.

merchandise n commodities, goods, wares.

merchant n dealer, retailer, shopkeeper, trader, tradesman.

merciful adj clement, compassionate, forgiving, gracious, lenient, pitiful; benignant, forbearing, gentle, humane, kind, mild, tender, tender-hearted.

merciless adj barbarous, callous, cruel, fell, hard-hearted, inexorable, pitiless, relentless, remorseless, ruthless, savage, severe, uncompassionate, unfeeling, unmerciful, unrelenting, unrepenting, unsparing.

mercurial adj active, lively, nimble, prompt, quick, sprightly; cheerful, light-hearted; changeable, fickle, flighty, inconstant, mobile, volatile.

mercy n benevolence, clemency, compassion, gentleness, kindness, lenience, leniency, lenity, mildness, pity, tenderness; blessing, favor, grace; discretion, disposal; forgiveness, pardon.

mere adj bald, bare, naked, plain, sole, simple; absolute, entire, pure, sheer, unmixed. • n lake, pond, pool.

meretricious adj deceitful, brummagem, false, gaudy, make-believe, sham, showy, spurious, tawdry.

merge vb bury, dip, immerse, involve, lose, plunge, sink, submerge.

meridian n acme, apex, climax, culmination, summit, zenith; midday, noon, noontide.

merit vb deserve, earn, incur; acquire, gain, profit, value. • n claim, right; credit, desert, excellence, goodness, worth, worthiness.

meritorious adj commendable, deserving, excellent, good, worthy.

merriment n amusement, frolic, gaiety, hilarity, jocularity, jollity, joviality, laughter, liveliness, mirth, sport, sportiveness.

merry adj agreeable, brisk, delightful, exhilarating, lively, pleasant, stirring; airy, blithe, blithesome, buxom, cheerful, comical, droll, facetious, frolicsome, gladsome, gleeful, hilarious, jocund, jolly, jovial, joyous, light-hearted, lively, mirthful, sportive, sprightly, vivacious.

mess n company, set; farrago, hodgepodge, hotchpotch, jumble, medley, mass, melange, miscellany, mishmash, mixture; confusion, muddle, perplexity, pickle, plight, predicament.

message n communication, dispatch, intimation, letter, missive, notice, telegram, wire, word.

messenger n carrier, courier, emissary, envoy, express, mercury, nuncio; forerunner, harbinger, herald, precursor.

metamorphic adj changeable, mutable, variable.

metamorphose vb change, mutate, transfigure, transform, transmute.

metamorphosis n change, mutation, transfiguration, transformation, transmutation.

metaphorical adj allegorical, figurative, symbolic, symbolical.

metaphysical adj abstract, allegorical, figurative, general, intellectual, parabolic, subjective, unreal.

mete vb dispense, distribute, divide, measure, ration, share. • n bound, boundary, butt, limit, measure, term, terminus.

meteor n aerolite, falling star, shooting star.

method n course, manner, means, mode, procedure, process, rule, way; arrangement, classification, disposition, order, plan, regularity, scheme, system.

methodical adj exact, orderly, regular, systematic, systematical.

metropolis n capital, city, conurbation.

mettle n constitution, element, material, stuff; character, disposition, spirit, temper; ardor, courage, fire, hardihood, life, nerve, pluck, sprightliness, vigor.

mettlesome adj ardent, brisk, courageous, fiery, frisky, high-spirited, lively, spirited, sprightly.

mew vb confine, coop, encase, enclose, imprison; cast, change, mold, shed.

microscopic adj infinitesimal, minute, tiny.

middle adj central, halfway, mean, medial, mid; intermediate, intervening. • n center, halfway, mean, midst.

middleman n agent, broker, factor, go-between, intermediary.

mien n air, appearance, aspect, bearing, behavior, carriage, countenance, demeanor, deportment, look, manner.

might n ability, capacity, efficacy, efficiency, force, main, power, prowess, puissance, strength.

mighty adj able, bold, courageous, potent, powerful, puissant, robust, strong, sturdy, valiant, valorous, vigorous; bulky, enormous, huge, immense, monstrous, stupendous, vast.

migratory adj nomadic, roving, shifting, strolling, unsettled, wandering, vagrant.

mild adj amiable, clement, compassionate, gentle, good-natured, indulgent, kind, lenient, meek, merciful, pacific, tender;

bland, pleasant, soft, suave; calm, kind, placid, temperate, tranquil; assuasive, compliant, demulcent, emollient, lenitive, mollifying, soothing.

mildness n amiability, clemency, gentleness, indulgence, kindness, meekness, moderation, softness, tenderness, warmth.

mildew n blight, blast, mold, must, mustiness, smut, rust.

milieu n background, environment, sphere, surroundings.

militant adj belligerent, combative, contending, fighting.

military adj martial, soldier, soldierly, warlike. • n army, militia, soldiers.

mill vb comminute, crush, grate, grind, levigate, powder, pulverize. • n factory, manufactory; grinder; crowd, throng.

mimic vb ape, counterfeit, imitate, impersonate, mime, mock, parody. • adj imitative, mock, simulated. • n imitator, impersonator, mime, mocker, parodist, parrot.

mince[1] vb chop, cut, hash, shatter. • n forcemeat, hash, mash, mincemeat.

mince[2] vb attenuate, diminish, extenuate, mitigate, palliate, soften; pose, sashay, simper, smirk.

mind[1] vb attend, heed, mark, note, notice, regard, tend, watch; obey, observe, submit; design, incline, intend, mean; recall, recollect, remember, remind; beware, look out, watch out. • n soul, spirit; brains, common sense, intellect, reason, sense, understanding; belief, consideration, contemplation, judgement, opinion, reflection, sentiment, thought; memory, recollection, remembrance; bent, desire, disposition, inclination, intention, leaning, purpose, tendency, will.

mind[2] vb balk, begrudge, grudge, object, resent.

mindful adj attentive, careful, heedful, observant, regardful, thoughtful.

mindless adj dull, heavy, insensible, senseless, sluggish, stupid, unthinking; careless, forgetful, heedless, neglectful, negligent, regardless.

mine vb dig, excavate, quarry, unearth; sap, undermine, weaken; destroy, ruin. • n colliery, deposit, lode, pit, shaft.

mingle vb blend, combine, commingle, compound, intermingle, intermix, join, mix, unite.

miniature adj bantam, diminutive, little, small, tiny.

minion n creature, dependant, favorite, hanger-on, parasite, sycophant; darling, favorite, flatterer, pet.

minister vb administer, afford, furnish, give, supply; aid, assist, contribute, help, succor. • n agent, assistant, servant, subordinate, underling; administrator, executive; ambassador, delegate, envoy, plenipotentiary; chaplain, churchman, clergyman, cleric, curate, divine, ecclesiastic, parson, pastor, preacher, priest, rector, vicar.

ministry n agency, aid, help, instrumentality, interposition, intervention, ministration, service, support; administration, cabinet, council, government.

minor adj less, smaller; inferior, junior, secondary, subordinate, younger; inconsiderable, petty, unimportant, small.

minstrel n bard, musician, singer, troubadour.

mint vb coin, stamp; fabricate, fashion, forge, invent, make, produce. • adj fresh, new, perfect, undamaged. • n die, punch, seal, stamp; fortune, (inf) heap, million, pile, wad.

minute[1] adj diminutive, fine, little, microscopic, miniature, slender, slight, small, tiny; circumstantial, critical, detailed, exact, fussy, meticulous, nice, particular, precise.

minute[2] n account, entry, item, memorandum, note, proceedings, record; instant, moment, second, trice, twinkling.

miracle n marvel, prodigy, wonder.

miraculous adj supernatural, thaumaturgic, thaumaturgical; amazing, extraordinary, incredible, marvellous, unaccountable, unbelievable, wondrous.

mirror vb copy, echo, emulate, reflect, show. • n looking-glass, reflector, speculum; archetype, exemplar, example, model, paragon, pattern, prototype.

mirth n cheerfulness, festivity, frolic, fun, gaiety, gladness, glee, hilarity, festivity, jollity, joviality, joyousness, laughter, merriment, merry-making, rejoicing, sport.

mirthful adj cheery, cheery, festive, frolicsome, hilarious, jocund, jolly, merry, jovial, joyous, lively, playful, sportive, vivacious; comic, droll, humorous, facetious, funny, jocose, jocular, ludicrous, merry, waggish, witty.

misadventure n accident, calamity, catastrophe, cross, disaster, failure, ill-luck, infelicity, mischance, misfortune, mishap, reverse.

misanthrope n cynic, egoist, egotist, man-hater, misanthropist.

misapply vb abuse, misuse, pervert.

misapprehend vb misconceive, mistake, misunderstand.

misbehaviour n ill-behavior, ill-conduct, incivility, miscarriage, misconduct, misdemeanor, naughtiness, rudeness.

miscarriage n calamity, defeat, disaster, failure, mischance, mishap; misbehavior, misconduct, ill-behavior.

miscellaneous adj confused, diverse, diversified, heterogeneous, indiscriminate, jumbled, many, mingled, mixed, promiscuous, stromatic, stromatous, various.

miscellany n collection, diversity, farrago, gallimaufry, hodgepodge, hotchpotch, jumble, medley, mishmash, melange, miscellaneous, mixture, variety.

mischance n accident, calamity, disaster, ill-fortune, ill-luck, infelicity, misadventure, misfortune, mishap.

mischief n damage, detriment, disadvantage, evil, harm, hurt, ill, injury, prejudice; ill-consequence, misfortune, trouble; devilry, wrong-doing.

mischievous adj destructive, detrimental, harmful, hurtful, injurious, noxious, pernicious; malicious, sinful, vicious, wicked; annoying, impish, naughty, troublesome, vexatious.

misconceive vb misapprehend, misjudge, mistake, misunderstand.

misconduct vb botch, bungle, misdirect, mismanage. • n bad conduct, ill-conduct, misbehavior, misdemeanor, rudeness, transgression; ill-management, mismanagement.

misconstrue vb misread, mistranslate; misapprehend, misinterpret, mistake, misunderstand.

miscreant adj corrupt, criminal, evil, rascally, unprincipled, vicious, villainous, wicked. • n caitiff, knave, ragamuffin, rascal, rogue, ruffian, scamp, scoundrel, vagabond, villain.

misdemeanor n fault, ill-behavior, misbehavior, misconduct, misdeed, offence, transgression, trespass.

miser n churl, curmudgeon, lickpenny, money-grabber, niggard, penny-pincher, pinch-fist, screw, scrimp, skinflint.

miserable adj afflicted, broken-hearted, comfortless, disconsolate, distressed, forlorn, heartbroken, unhappy, wretched; calamitous, hapless, ill-starred, pitiable, unfortunate, unlucky; poor, valueless, worthless; abject, contemptible, despicable, low, mean, worthless.

miserly adj avaricious, beggarly, close, close-fisted, covetous, grasping, mean, niggardly, parsimonious, penurious, sordid, stingy, tight-fisted.

misery n affliction, agony, anguish, calamity, desolation, distress, grief, heartache, heavy-heartedness, misfortune, sorrow, suffering, torment, torture, tribulation, unhappiness, woe, wretchedness.

misfortune n adversity, affliction, bad luck, blow, calamity, casualty, catastrophe, disaster, distress, hardship, harm, ill, infliction, misadventure, mischance, mishap, reverse, scourge, stroke, trial, trouble, visitation.

misgiving n apprehension, distrust, doubt, hesitation, suspicion, uncertainty.

mishap n accident, calamity, disaster, ill luck, misadventure, mischance, misfortune.

misinterpret vb distort, falsify, misapprehend, misconceive, misconstrue, misjudge.

mislead vb beguile, deceive, delude, misdirect, misguide.

mismanage vb botch, fumble, misconduct, mishandle, misrule.

misprize vb slight, underestimate, underrate, undervalue.

misrepresent vb belie, caricature, distort, falsify, misinterpret, misstate, pervert.

misrule n anarchy, confusion, disorder, maladministration, misgovernment, mismanagement.

miss[1] vb blunder, err, fail, fall short, forgo, lack, lose, miscarry, mistake, omit, overlook, trip; avoid, escape, evade, skip, slip; feel the loss of, need, want, wish. • n blunder, error, failure, fault, mistake, omission, oversight, slip, trip; loss, want.

miss[2] n damsel, girl, lass, maid, maiden.

misshapen adj deformed, ill-formed, ill-shaped, ill-proportioned, misformed, ugly, ungainly.

missile n projectile, weapon.

mission n commission, legation; business, charge, duty, errand, office, trust; delegation, deputation, embassy.

missive n communication, epistle, letter, message, note.

mist vb cloud, drizzle, mizzle, smog. • n

cloud, fog, haze; bewilderment, obscurity, perplexity.

mistake vb misapprehend, miscalculate, misconceive, misjudge, misunderstand; confound, take; blunder, err. • n misapprehension, miscalculation, misconception, mistaking, misunderstanding; blunder, error, fault, inaccuracy, oversight, slip, trip.

mistaken adj erroneous, inaccurate, incorrect, misinformed, wrong.

mistrust vb distrust, doubt, suspect; apprehend, fear, surmise, suspect. • n doubt, distrust, misgiving, suspicion.

misty adj cloudy, clouded, dark, dim, foggy, obscure, overcast.

misunderstand vb misapprehend, misconceive, misconstrue, mistake.

misunderstanding n error, misapprehension, misconception, mistake; difference, difficulty, disagreement, discord, dissension, quarrel.

misuse vb desecrate, misapply, misemploy, pervert, profane; abuse, ill-treat, maltreat, ill-use; fritter, squander, waste. • n abuse, perversion, profanation, prostitution; ill-treatment, ill-use, ill-usage, misusage; misapplication, solecism.

mitigate vb abate, alleviate, assuage, diminish, extenuate, lessen, moderate, palliate, relieve; allay, appease, calm, mollify, pacify, quell, quiet, reduce, soften, soothe; moderate, temper.

mitigation n abatement, allaying, alleviation, assuagement, diminution, moderation, palliation, relief.

mix vb alloy, amalgamate, blend, commingle, combine, compound, incorporate, interfuse, interlard, mingle, unite; associate, join. • n alloy, amalgam, blend, combination, compound, mixture.

mixture n admixture, association, intermixture, union; compound, farrago, hash, hodgepodge, hotchpotch, jumble, medley, melange, mishmash; diversity, miscellany, variety.

moan vb bemoan, bewail, deplore, grieve, groan, lament, mourn, sigh, weep. • n groan, lament, lamentation, sigh, wail.

mob vb crowd, jostle, surround, swarm, pack, throng. • n assemblage, crowd, rabble, multitude, throng, tumult; dregs, canaille, populace, rabble, riffraff, scum.

mobile adj changeable, fickle, expressive, inconstant, sensitive, variable, volatile.

mock vb ape, counterfeit, imitate, mimic, take off; deride, flout, gibe, insult, jeer, ridicule, taunt; balk, cheat, deceive, defeat, disappoint, dupe, elude, illude, mislead. • adj assumed, clap-trap, counterfeit, fake, false, feigned, make-believe, pretended, spurious. • n fake, imitation, phoney, sham; gibe, insult, jeer, scoff, taunt.

mockery n contumely, counterfeit, deception, derision, imitation, jeering, mimicry, ridicule, scoffing, scorn, sham, travesty.

mode n fashion, manner, method, style, way; accident, affection, degree, graduation, modification, quality, variety.

model vb design, fashion, form, mold, plan, shape. • adj admirable, archetypal, estimable, exemplary, ideal, meritorious, paradigmatic, perfect, praiseworthy, worthy. • n archetype, design, mold, original, pattern, protoplast, prototype, type; dummy, example, form; copy, facsimile, image, imitation, representation.

moderate vb abate, allay, appease, assuage, blunt, dull, lessen, soothe, mitigate, mollify, pacify, quell, quiet, reduce, repress, soften, still, subdue; diminish, qualify, slacken, temper; control, govern, regulate. • adj abstinent, frugal, sparing, temperate; limited, mediocre; abstemious, sober; calm, cool, judicious, reasonable, steady; gentle, mild, temperate, tolerable.

moderation n abstemiousness, forbearance, frugality, restraint, sobriety, temperance; calmness, composure, coolness, deliberateness, equanimity, mildness, sedateness.

modern adj fresh, late, latest, new, novel, present, recent, up-to-date.

modest adj bashful, coy, diffident, humble, meek, reserved, retiring, shy, unassuming, unobtrusive, unostentatious, unpretending, unpretentious; chaste, proper, pure, virtuous; becoming, decent, moderate.

modesty n bashfulness, coyness, diffidence, humility, meekness, propriety, prudishness, reserve, shyness, unobtrusiveness; chastity, purity, virtue; decency, moderation.

modification n alteration, change, qualification, reformation, variation; form, manner, mode, state.

modify vb alter, change, qualify, reform, shape, vary; lower, moderate, qualify, soften.

modish adj fashionable, stylish; ceremonious, conventional, courtly, genteel.

modulate *vb* attune, harmonize; tune; inflict, vary; adapt, adjust, proportion.

moiety *n* half; part, portion, share.

moil *vb* drudge, labor, toil; bespatter, daub, defile, soil, splash, spot, stain; fatigue, weary, tire.

moist *adj* damp, dank, humid, marshy, muggy, swampy, wet.

moisture *n* dampness, dankness, humidity, wetness.

mold[1] *vb* carve, cast, fashion, form, make, model, shape. • *n* cast, character, fashion, form, matrix, pattern, shape; material, matter, substance.

mold[2] *n* blight, mildew, moldiness, must, mustiness, rot; fungus, lichen, mushroom, puffball, rust, smut, toadstool; earth, loam, soil.

molder *vb* crumble, decay, perish, waste.

moldy *adj* decaying, fusty, mildewed, musty.

mole *n* breakwater, dike, dyke, jetty, mound, pier, quay.

molecule *n* atom, monad, particle.

molest *vb* annoy, badger, bore, bother, chafe, discommode, disquiet, disturb, harass, harry, fret, gull, hector, incommode, inconvenience, irritate, oppress, pester, plague, tease, torment, trouble, vex, worry.

mollify *vb* soften; appease, calm, compose, pacify, quiet, soothe, tranquillize; abate, allay, assuage, blunt, dull, ease, lessen, mitigate, moderate, relieve, temper; qualify, tone down.

moment *n* flash, instant, jiffy, second, trice, twinkling, wink; avail, consequence, consideration, force, gravity, importance, significance, signification, value, weight; drive, force, impetus, momentum.

momentous *adj* grave, important, serious, significant, vital, weighty.

momentum *n* impetus, moment.

monarch *n* autocrat, despot; chief, dictator, emperor, king, potentate, prince, queen, ruler, sovereign.

monastery *n* abbey, cloister, convent, lamasery, nunnery, priory.

monastic *adj* coenobitic, coenobitical, conventual, monkish, secluded.

money *n* banknotes, cash, coin, currency, riches, specie, wealth.

moneyed, monied *adj* affluent, opulent, rich, well-off, well-to-do.

monitor *vb* check, observe, oversee, supervise, watch. • *n* admonisher, admonitor, adviser, counselor, instructor, mentor, overseer.

monomania *n* delusion, hallucination, illusion, insanity, self-deception.

monopolize *vb* control, dominate, engross, forestall.

monotonous *adj* boring, dull, tedious, tiresome, undiversified, uniform, unvaried, unvarying, wearisome.

monotony *n* boredom, dullness, sameness, tedium, tiresomeness, uniformity, wearisomeness.

monster *adj* enormous, gigantic, huge, immense, mammoth, monstrous. • *n* enormity, marvel, prodigy, wonder; brute, demon, fiend, miscreant, ruffian, villain, wretch.

monstrous *adj* abnormal, preternatural, prodigious, unnatural; colossal, enormous, extraordinary, huge, immense, stupendous, vast; marvellous, strange, wonderful; bad, base, dreadful, flagrant, frightful, hateful, hideous, horrible, shocking, terrible.

monument *n* memorial, record, remembrance, testimonial; cairn, cenotaph, gravestone, mausoleum, memorial, pillar, tomb, tombstone.

mood *n* disposition, humor, temper, vein.

moody *adj* capricious, humorsome, variable; angry, crabbed, crusty, fretful, ill-tempered, irascible, irritable, passionate, pettish, peevish, petulant, snappish, snarling, sour, testy; cross-grained, dogged, frowning, glowering, glum, intractable, morose, perverse, spleeny, stubborn, sulky, sullen, wayward; abstracted, gloomy, melancholy, pensive, sad, saturnine.

moonshine *n* balderdash, fiction, flummery, fudge, fustian, nonsense, pretence, stuff, trash, twaddle, vanity.

moor[1] *vb* anchor, berth, fasten, fix, secure, tie.

moor[2] *n* bog, common, heath, moorland, morass, moss, wasteland.

moot *vb* agitate, argue, debate, discuss, dispute. • *adj* arguable, debatable, doubtful, unsettled.

mopish *adj* dejected, depressed, desponding, downcast, down-hearted, gloomy, glum, sad.

moral *adj* ethical, good, honest, honorable, just, upright, virtuous;
abstract, ideal, intellectual, mental. • *n* intent, meaning, significance.

morals *npl* ethics, morality; behavior, conduct, habits, manners.

morass *n* bog, fen, marsh, quagmire, slough, swamp.

morbid *adj* ailing, corrupted, diseased, sick, sickly, tainted, unhealthy, unsound, vitiated; depressed, downcast, gloomy, pessimistic, sensitive.

mordacious *adj* acrid, biting, cutting, mordant, pungent, sharp, stinging; caustic, poignant, satirical, sarcastic, scathing, severe.

mordant *adj* biting, caustic, keen, mordacious, nipping, sarcastic.

moreover *adv, conj* also, besides, further, furthermore, likewise, too.

morning *n* aurora, daybreak, dawn, morn, morningtide, sunrise.

morose *adj* austere, churlish, crabbed, crusty, dejected, desponding, downcast, downhearted, gloomy, glum, melancholy, moody, sad, severe, sour, sullen, surly.

morsel *n* bite, mouthful, titbit; bit, fragment, part, piece, scrap.

mortal *adj* deadly, destructive, fatal, final, human, lethal, perishable, vital. • *n* being, earthling, human, man, person, woman.

mortality *n* corruption, death, destruction, fatality.

mortification *n* chagrin, disappointment, discontent, dissatisfaction, displeasure, humiliation, trouble, shame, vexation; humility, penance, self-abasement, self-denial; gangrene, necrosis.

mortify *vb* annoy, chagrin, depress, disappoint, displease, disquiet, dissatisfy, harass, humble, plague, vex, worry; abase, abash, confound, humiliate, restrain, shame, subdue; corrupt, fester, gangrene, putrefy.

mortuary *n* burial place, cemetery, churchyard, graveyard, necropolis; charnel house, morgue.

mostly *adv* chiefly, customarily, especially, generally, mainly, particularly, principally.

mote *n* atom, corpuscle, flaw, mite, particle, speck, spot.

motherly *adj* affectionate, kind, maternal, paternal, tender.

motion *vb* beckon, direct, gesture, signal. • *n* action, change, drift, flux, movement, passage, stir, transit; air, gait, port; gesture, impulse, prompting, suggestion; proposal, proposition.

motionless *adj* fixed, immobile, quiescent, stable, stagnant, standing, stationary, still, torpid, unmoved.

motive *adj* activating, driving, moving, operative. • *n* cause, consideration, ground, impulse, incentive, incitement, inducement, influence, occasion, prompting, purpose, reason, spur, stimulus.

motley *adj* colored, dappled, mottled, speckled, spotted, variegated; composite, diversified, heterogeneous, mingled, mixed.

mottled *adj* dappled, motley, piebald, speckled, spotted, variegated.

mound *n* bank, barrow, hill, hillock, knoll, tumulus; bulwark, defense, rampart.

mount[1] *n* hill, mountain, peak.

mount[2] *vb* arise, ascend, climb, rise, soar, tower; escalate, scale; embellish, ornament; bestride, get upon. • *n* charger, horse, ride, steed.

mountain *n* alp, height, hill, mount, peak; abundance, heap, mound, stack.

mountebank *n* charlatan, cheat, impostor, pretender, quack.

mourn *vb* bemoan, bewail, deplore, grieve, lament, sorrow, wail.

mournful *adj* afflicting, afflictive, calamitous, deplorable, distressed, grievous, lamentable, sad, woeful; doleful, heavy, heavyhearted, lugubrious, melancholy, sorrowful, tearful.

mouth *vb* clamor, declaim, rant, roar, vociferate. • *n* chaps, jaws; aperture, opening, orifice; entrance, inlet; oracle, mouthpiece, speaker, spokesman.

movables *npl* chattels, effects, furniture, goods, property, wares.

move *vb* dislodge, drive, impel, propel, push, shift, start, stir; actuate, incite, instigate, rouse; determine, incline, induce, influence, persuade, prompt; affect, impress, touch, trouble; agitate, awaken, excite, incense, irritate; propose, recommend, suggest; go, march, proceed, walk; act, live; flit, remove. • *n* action, motion, movement.

movement *n* change, move, motion, passage; emotion; crusade, drive.

moving *adj* impelling, influencing, instigating, persuading, persuasive; affecting, impressive, pathetic, touching.

mucous *adj* glutinous, gummy, mucilaginous, ropy, slimy, viscid.

mud *n* dirt, mire, muck, slime.

muddle *vb* confuse, disarrange, disorder; fuddle, inebriate, stupefy; muff, mull, spoil. • *n* confusion, disorder, mess, plight, predicament.

muddy vb dirty, foul, smear, soil; confuse, obscure. • adj dirty, foul, impure, slimy, soiled, turbid; bothered, confused, dull, heavy, stupid; incoherent, obscure, vague.

muffle vb cover, envelop, shroud, wrap; conceal, disguise, involve; deaden, soften, stifle, suppress.

mulish adj cross-grained, headstrong, intractable, obstinate, stubborn.

multifarious adj different, divers, diverse, diversified, manifold, multiform, multitudinous, various.

multiloquence n garrulity, loquacity, loquaciousness, talkativeness.

multiply vb augment, extend, increase, spread.

multitude n numerousness; host, legion; army, assemblage, assembly, collection, concourse, congregation, crowd, horde, mob, swarm, throng; commonality, herd, mass, mob, pack, populace, rabble.

mundane adj earthly, secular, sublunary, temporal, terrene, terrestrial, worldly.

munificence n benefice, bounteousness, bountifulness, bounty, generosity, liberality.

munificent adj beneficent, bounteous, bountiful, free, generous, liberal, princely.

murder vb assassinate, butcher, destroy, dispatch, kill, massacre, slaughter, slay; abuse, mar, spoil. • n assassination, butchery, destruction, homicide, killing, manslaughter, massacre.

murderer n assassin, butcher, cut-throat, killer, manslaughterer, slaughterer, slayer.

murderous adj barbarous, bloodthirsty, bloody, cruel, fell, sanguinary, savage.

murky adj cheerless, cloudy, dark, dim, dusky, gloomy, hazy, lowering, lurid, obscure, overcast.

murmur vb croak, grumble, mumble, mutter; hum, whisper. • n complaint, grumble, mutter, plaint, whimper; hum, undertone, whisper.

muscular adj sinewy; athletic, brawny, powerful, lusty, stalwart, stout, strong, sturdy, vigorous.

muse vb brood, cogitate, consider, contemplate, deliberate, dream, meditate, ponder, reflect, ruminate, speculate, think. • n abstraction, musing, reverie.

music n harmony, melody, symphony.

musical adj dulcet, harmonious, melodious, sweet, sweet-sounding, symphonious, tuneful.

musing adj absent-minded, meditative, preoccupied. • n absent-mindedness, abstraction, contemplation, daydreaming, meditation, muse, reflection, reverie, rumination.

muster vb assemble, collect, congregate, convene, convoke, gather, marshal, meet, rally, summon. • n assemblage, assembly, collection, congregation, convention, convocation, gathering, meeting, rally.

musty adj fetid, foul, fusty, moldy, rank, sour, spoiled; hackneyed, old, stale, threadbare, trite; ill-favored, insipid, vapid; dull, heavy, rusty, spiritless.

mutable adj alterable, changeable; changeful, fickle, inconstant, irresolute, mutational, unsettled, unstable, unsteady, vacillating, variable, wavering.

mutation n alteration, change, variation.

mute vb dampen, lower, moderate, muffle, soften. • adj dumb, voiceless; silent, speechless, still, taciturn.

mutilate vb cripple, damage, disable, disfigure, hamstring, injure, maim, mangle, mar.

mutinous adj contumacious, insubordinate, rebellious, refractory, riotous, tumultuous, turbulent, unruly; insurgent, seditious.

mutiny vb rebel, revolt, rise, resist. • n insubordination, insurrection, rebellion, revolt, revolution, riot, rising, sedition, uprising.

mutter vb grumble, muffle, mumble, murmur.

mutual adj alternate, common, correlative, interchangeable, interchanged, reciprocal, requited.

myopic adj near-sighted, purblind, short-sighted.

myriad adj innumerable, manifold, multitudinous, uncounted. • n host, million(s), multitude, score(s), sea, swarm, thousand(s).

mysterious adj abstruse, cabbalistic, concealed, cryptic, dark, dim, enigmatic, enigmatical, hidden, incomprehensible, inexplicable, inscrutable, mystic, mystical, obscure, occult, puzzling, recondite, secret, sphinx-like, unaccountable, unfathomable, unintelligible, unknown.

mystery n enigma, puzzle, riddle, secret; art, business, calling, trade.

mystical adj abstruse, cabbalistic, dark, enigmatical, esoteric, hidden, inscrutable, mysterious, obscure, occult, recondite, transcendental; allegorical, emblematic, emblematical, symbolic, symbolical.

mystify vb befog, bewilder, confound, confuse, dumbfound, embarrass, obfuscate, perplex, pose, puzzle.

myth n fable, legend, tradition; allegory, fiction, invention, parable, story; falsehood, fancy, figment, lie, untruth.

mythical adj allegorical, fabled, fabulous, fanciful, fictitious, imaginary, legendary, mythological.

N

nab vb catch, clutch, grasp, seize.

nag[1] vb carp, fuss, hector, henpeck, pester, torment, worry. • n nagger, scold, shrew, tartar.

nag[2] n bronco, crock, hack, horse, pony, scrag.

naive adj artless, candid, ingenuous, natural, plain, simple, unaffected, unsophisticated.

naked adj bare, nude, uncovered; denuded, unclad, unclothed, undressed; defenseless, exposed, open, unarmed, unguarded, unprotected; evident, manifest, plain, stark, unconcealed, undisguised; mere, sheer, simple; bare, destitute, rough, rude, unfurnished, unprovided; uncolored, unexaggerated, unvarnished.

name vb call, christen, denounce, dub, entitle, phrase, style, term; mention; denominate, designate, indicate, nominate, specify. • n appellation, cognomen, denomination, designation, epithet, nickname, surname, sobriquet, title; character, credit, reputation, repute; celebrity, distinction, eminence, fame, honor, note, praise, renown.

narcotic adj stupefacient, stupefactive, stupefying. • n anesthetic, anodyne, dope, opiate, sedative, stupefacient, tranquillizer.

narrate vb chronicle, describe, detail, enumerate, recite, recount, rehearse, relate, tell.

narration n account, description, chronicle, history, narrative, recital, rehearsal, relation, story, tale.

narrow vb confine, contract, cramp, limit, restrict, straiten. • adj circumscribed, confined, contracted, cramped, incapacious, limited, pinched, scanty, straitened;

bigoted, hidebound, illiberal, ungenerous; close, near.

nastiness n defilement, dirtiness, filth, filthiness, foulness, impurity, pollution, squalor, uncleanness; indecency, grossness, obscenity, pornography, ribaldry, smut, smuttiness.

nasty adj defiled, dirty, filthy, foul, impure, loathsome, polluted, squalid, unclean; gross, indecent, indelicate, lewd, loose, obscene, smutty, vile; disagreeable, disgusting, nauseous, odious, offensive, repulsive, sickening; aggravating, annoying, pesky, pestering, troublesome.

nation n commonwealth, realm, state; community, people, population, race, stock, tribe.

native adj aboriginal, autochthonal, autochthonous, domestic, home, indigenous, vernacular; genuine, intrinsic, natural, original, real; congenital, inborn, inbred, inherent, innate, natal. • n aborigine, autochthon, inhabitant, national, resident.

natty adj dandyish, fine, foppish, jaunty, neat, nice, spruce, tidy.

natural adj indigenous, innate, native, original; characteristic, essential; legitimate, normal, regular; artless, authentic, genuine, ingenuous, unreal, simple, spontaneous, unaffected; bastard, illegitimate.

nature n universe, world; character, constitution, essence; kind, quality, species, sort; disposition, grain, humor, mood, temper; being, intellect, intelligence, mind.

naughty adj bad, corrupt, mischievous, perverse, worthless.

nausea n queasiness, seasickness; loathing, qualm; aversion, disgust, repugnance.

nauseous adj abhorrent, disgusting, distasteful, loathsome, offensive, repulsive, revolting, sickening.

naval adj marine, maritime, nautical.

navigate vb cruise, direct, guide, pilot, plan, sail, steer.

navy n fleet, shipping, vessels.

near vb approach, draw close. • adj adjacent, approximate, close, contiguous, neighbouring, nigh; approaching, forthcoming, imminent, impending; dear, familiar, friendly, intimate; direct, immediate, short, straight; accurate, literal; narrow, parsimonious.

nearly adv almost, approximately, well-nigh; closely, intimately, pressingly; meanly, parsimoniously, penuriously, stingily.

neat *adj* clean, cleanly, orderly, tidy, trim, unsoiled; nice, smart, spruce; chaste, pure, simple; excellent, pure, unadulterated; adroit, clever, exact, finished; dainty, nice.

nebulous *adj* cloudy, hazy, misty.

necessary *adj* inevitable, unavoidable; essential, expedient, indispensable, needful, requisite; compelling, compulsory, involuntary. • *n* essential, necessity, requirement, requisite.

necessitate *vb* compel, constrain, demand, force, impel, oblige.

necessitous *adj* destitute, distressed, indigent, moneyless, needy, penniless, pinched, poor, poverty-stricken; narrow, pinching.

necessity *n* inevitability, inevitableness, unavoidability, unavoidableness; compulsion, destiny, fatality, fate; emergency, urgency; exigency, indigence, indispensability, indispensableness, need, needfulness, poverty, want; essentiality, essentialness, requirement, requisite.

necromancy *n* conjuration, divination, enchantment, magic, sorcery, witchcraft, wizardry.

necropolis *n* burial ground, cemetery, churchyard, crematorium, graveyard, mortuary.

need *vb* demand, lack, require, want. • *n* emergency, exigency, extremity, necessity, strait, urgency, want; destitution, distress, indigence, neediness, penury, poverty, privation.

needful *adj* distressful, necessitous, necessary; essential, indispensable, requisite.

needless *adj* superfluous, unnecessary, useless.

needy *adj* destitute, indigent, necessitous, poor.

nefarious *adj* abominable, atrocious, detestable, dreadful, execrable, flagitious, heinous, horrible, infamous, iniquitous, scandalous, vile, wicked.

negation *n* denial, disavowal, disclaimer, rejection, renunciation.

neglect *vb* condemn, despise, disregard, forget, ignore, omit, overlook, slight. • *n* carelessness, default, failure, heedlessness, inattention, omission, remissness; disregard, disrespect, slight; indifference, negligence.

negligence *n* carelessness, disregard, heedlessness, inadvertency, inattention, indifference, neglect, remissness, slackness, thoughtlessness; defect, fault, inadvertence, omission, shortcoming.

negligent *adj* careless, heedless, inattentive, indifferent, neglectful, regardless, thoughtless.

negotiate *vb* arrange, bargain, deal, debate, sell, settle, transact, treat.

neighborhood *n* district, environs, locality, vicinage, vicinity; adjacency, nearness, propinquity, proximity.

neighbourly *adj* attentive, civil, friendly, kind, obliging, social.

neophyte *n* beginner, catechumen, convert, novice, pupil, tyro.

nerve *vb* brace, energize, fortify, invigorate, strengthen. • *n* force, might, power, strength, vigor; coolness, courage, endurance, firmness, fortitude, hardihood, manhood, pluck, resolution, self-command, steadiness.

nervous *adj* forcible, powerful, robust, strong, vigorous; irritable, fearful, shaky, timid, timorous, weak, weakly.

nestle *vb* cuddle, harbor, lodge, nuzzle, snug, snuggle.

nettle *vb* chafe, exasperate, fret, harass, incense, irritate, provoke, ruffle, sting, tease, vex.

neutral *adj* impartial, indifferent; colorless, mediocre.

neutralize *vb* cancel, counterbalance, counterpoise, invalidate, offset.

nevertheless *adv* however, nonetheless, notwithstanding, yet.

new *adj* fresh, latest, modern, novel, recent, unused; additional, another, further; reinvigorated, renovated, repaired.

news *n* advice, information, intelligence, report, tidings, word.

nice *adj* accurate, correct, critical, definite, delicate, exact, exquisite, precise, rigorous, strict; dainty, difficult, exacting, fastidious, finical, punctilious, squeamish; discerning, discriminating, particular, precise, scrupulous; neat, tidy, trim; fine, minute, refined, subtle; delicate, delicious, luscious, palatable, savory, soft, tender; agreeable, delightful, good, pleasant.

nicety *n* accuracy, exactness, niceness, precision, truth, daintiness, fastidiousness, squeamishness; discrimination, subtlety.

niggard *n* churl, curmudgeon, miser, screw, scrimp, skinflint.

niggardly *adj* avaricious, close, close-fisted,

illiberal, mean, mercenary, miserly, parsimonious, penurious, skinflint, sordid, stingy.

nigh *adj* adjacent, adjoining, contiguous, near; present, proximate. • *adv* almost, near, nearly.

nimble *adj* active, agile, alert, brisk, lively, prompt, quick, speedy, sprightly, spry, swift, tripping.

nobility *n* aristocracy, dignity, elevation, eminence, grandeur, greatness, loftiness, magnanimity, nobleness, peerage, superiority, worthiness.

noble *adj* dignified, elevated, eminent, exalted, generous, great, honorable, illustrious, magnanimous, superior, worthy; choice, excellent; aristocratic, gentle, high-born, patrician; grand, lofty, lordly, magnificent, splendid, stately. • *n* aristocrat, grandee, lord, nobleman, peer.

noctambulist *n* sleepwalker, somnambulist.

noise *vb* bruit, gossip, repeat, report, rumor. • *n* ado, blare, clamor, clatter, cry, din, fuss, hubbub, hullabaloo, outcry, pandemonium, racket, row, sound, tumult, uproar, vociferation.

noiseless *adj* inaudible, quiet, silent, soundless.

noisome *adj* bad, baneful, deleterious, disgusting, fetid, foul, hurtful, injurious, mischievous, nocuous, noxious, offensive, pernicious, pestiferous, pestilential, poisonous, unhealthy, unwholesome.

noisy *adj* blatant, blustering, boisterous, brawling, clamorous, loud, uproarious, riotous, tumultuous, vociferous.

nomadic *adj* migratory, pastoral, vagrant, wandering.

nominal *adj* formal, inconsiderable, minimal, ostensible, pretended, professed, so-called, titular.

nominate *vb* appoint, choose, designate, name, present, propose.

nonchalant *adj* apathetic, careless, cool, indifferent, unconcerned.

nondescript *adj* amorphous, characterless, commonplace, dull, indescribable, odd, ordinary, unclassifiable, uninteresting, unremarkable.

nonentity *n* cipher, futility, inexistence, inexistency, insignificance, nobody, nonexistence, nothingness.

nonplus *vb* astonish, bewilder, confound, confuse, discomfit, disconcert, embarrass, floor, gravel, perplex, pose, puzzle.

nonsensical *adj* absurd, foolish, irrational, senseless, silly, stupid.

norm *n* model, pattern, rule, standard.

normal *adj* analogical, legitimate, natural, ordinary, regular, usual; erect, perpendicular, vertical.

notable *adj* distinguished, extraordinary, memorable, noted, remarkable, signal; conspicuous, evident, noticeable, observable, plain, prominent, striking; notorious, rare, well-known. • *n* celebrity, dignitary, notability, worthy.

note *vb* heed, mark, notice, observe, regard, remark; record, register; denote, designate. • *n* memorandum, minute, record; annotation, comment, remark, scholium; indication, mark, sign, symbol, token; account, bill, catalog, reckoning; billet, epistle, letter; consideration, heed, notice, observation; celebrity, consequence, credit, distinction, eminence, fame, notability, notedness, renown, reputation, respectability; banknote, bill, promissory note; song, strain, tune, voice.

noted *adj* celebrated, conspicuous, distinguished, eminent, famed, famous, illustrious, notable, notorious, remarkable, renowned, well-known.

nothing *n* inexistence, nonentity, nonexistence, nothingness, nullity; bagatelle, trifle.

notice *vb* mark, note, observe, perceive, regard, see; comment on, mention, remark; attend to, heed. • *n* cognizance, heed, note, observation, regard; advice, announcement, information, intelligence, mention, news, notification; communication, intimation, premonition, warning; attention, civility, consideration, respect; comments, remarks.

notify *vb* advertise, announce, declare, publish, promulgate; acquaint, apprise, inform.

notion *n* concept, conception, idea; apprehension, belief, conceit, conviction, expectation, estimation, impression, judgement, opinion, sentiment, view.

notoriety *n* celebrity, fame, figure, name, note, publicity, reputation, repute, vogue.

notorious *adj* apparent, egregious, evident, notable, obvious, open, overt, manifest, patent, well-known; celebrated, conspicuous, distinguished, famed, famous, flagrant, infamous, noted, remarkable, renowned.

notwithstanding *conj* despite, however, nevertheless, yet. • *prep* despite.

nourish *vb* feed, nurse, nurture; maintain, supply, support; breed, educate, instruct, train; cherish, encourage, foment, foster, promote, succor.

nourishment *n* aliment, diet, food, nutriment, nutrition, sustenance.

novel *adj* fresh, modern, new, rare, recent, strange, uncommon, unusual. • *n* fiction, romance, story, tale.

novice *n* convert, proselyte; initiate, neophyte, novitiate, probationer; apprentice, beginner, learner, tyro.

noxious *adj* baneful, deadly, deleterious, destructive, detrimental, hurtful, injurious, insalubrious, mischievous, noisome, pernicious, pestilent, poisonous, unfavorable, unwholesome.

nude *adj* bare, denuded, exposed, naked, uncovered, unclothed, undressed.

nugatory *adj* frivolous, insignificant, trifling, trivial, vain, worthless; bootless, ineffectual, inefficacious, inoperative, null, unavailing, useless.

nuisance *n* annoyance, bore, bother, infliction, offence, pest, plague, trouble.

null *adj* ineffectual, invalid, nugatory, useless, void; characterless, colorless.

nullify *vb* abolish, abrogate, annul, cancel, invalidate, negate, quash, repeal, revoke.

numb *vb* benumb, deaden, stupefy. • *adj* benumbed, deadened, dulled, insensible, paralysed.

number *vb* calculate, compute, count, enumerate, numerate, reckon, tell; account, reckon. • *n* digit, figure, numeral; horde, multitude, numerousness, throng; aggregate, collection, sum, total.

numerous *adj* abundant, many, numberless.

nuncio *n* ambassador, legate, messenger.

nunnery *n* abbey, cloister, convent, monastery.

nuptial *adj* bridal, conjugal, connubial, hymeneal, matrimonial.

nuptials *npl* espousal, marriage, wedding.

nurse *vb* nourish, nurture; rear, suckle; cherish, encourage, feed, foment, foster, pamper, promote, succour; economize, manage; caress, dandle, fondle. • *n* auxiliary, orderly, sister; amah, *au pair*, babysitter, nanny, nursemaid, nurseryma id.

nurture *vb* feed, nourish, nurse, tend; breed, discipline, educate, instruct, rear, school,

train. • *n* diet, food, nourishment; breeding, discipline, education, instruction, schooling, training, tuition; attention, nourishing, nursing.

nutriment *n* aliment, food, nourishment, nutrition, pabulum, subsistence, sustenance.

nutrition *n* diet, food, nourishment, nutriment.

nutritious *adj* invigorating, nourishing, strengthening, supporting, sustaining.

nymph *n* damsel, dryad, lass, girl, maid, maiden, naiad.

O

oaf *n* blockhead, dolt, dunce, fool, idiot, simpleton.

oath *n* blasphemy, curse, expletive, imprecation, malediction; affirmation, pledge, promise, vow.

obduracy *n* contumacy, doggedness, obstinacy, stubbornness, tenacity; depravity, impenitence.

obdurate *adj* hard, harsh, rough, rugged; callous, cantankerous, dogged, firm, hardened, inflexible, insensible, obstinate, pigheaded, unfeeling, stubborn, unbending, unyielding; depraved, graceless, lost, reprobate, shameless, impenitent, incorrigible, irreclaimable.

obedience *n* acquiescence, agreement, compliance, duty, respect, reverence, submission, submissiveness, subservience.

obedient *adj* acquiescent, compliant, deferential, duteous, dutiful, observant, regardful, respectful, submissive, subservient, yielding.

obeisance *n* bow, courtesy, curtsy, homage, reverence, salutation.

obelisk *n* column, pillar.

obese *adj* corpulent, fat, fleshy, gross, plump, podgy, portly, stout.

obesity *n* corpulence, corpulency, embonpoint, fatness, fleshiness, obeseness, plumpness.

obey *vb* comply, conform, heed, keep, mind, observe, submit, yield.

obfuscate *vb* cloud, darken, obscure; bewilder, confuse, muddle.

object[1] *vb* cavil, contravene, demur, deprecate, disapprove of, except to, impeach, oppose, protest, refuse.

object[2] *n* particular, phenomenon, precept, reality, thing; aim, butt, destination, end, mark, recipient, target; design, drift, goal, intention, motive, purpose, use, view.

objection *n* censure, difficulty, doubt, exception, protest, remonstrance, scruple.

objurgate *vb* chide, reprehend, reprove.

oblation *n* gift, offering, sacrifice.

obligation *n* accountability, accountableness, responsibility; agreement, bond, contract, covenant, engagement, stipulation; debt, indebtedness, liability.

obligatory *adj* binding, coercive, compulsory, enforced, necessary, unavoidable.

oblige *vb* bind, coerce, compel, constrain, force, necessitate, require; accommodate, benefit, convenience, favor, gratify, please; obligate, bind.

obliging *adj* accommodating, civil, complaisant, considerate, kind, friendly, polite.

oblique *adj* aslant, inclined, sidelong, slanting; indirect, obscure.

obliterate *vb* cancel, delete, destroy, efface, eradicate, erase, expunge.

oblivious *adj* careless, forgetful, heedless, inattentive, mindless, negligent, neglectful.

obloquy *n* aspersion, backbiting, blame, calumny, censure, contumely, defamation, detraction, disgrace, odium, reproach, reviling, slander, traducing.

obnoxious *adj* blameworthy, censurable, faulty, reprehensible; hateful, objectionable, obscene, odious, offensive, repellent, repugnant, repulsive, unpleasant, unpleasing.

obscene *adj* broad, coarse, filthy, gross, immodest, impure, indecent, indelicate, ribald, unchaste, lewd, licentious, loose, offensive, pornographic, shameless, smutty; disgusting, dirty, foul.

obscure *vb* becloud, befog, blur, cloud, darken, eclipse, dim, obfuscate, obnubilate, shade; conceal, cover, equivocate, hide. • *adj* dark, darksome, dim, dusky, gloomy, lurid, murky, rayless, shadowy, sombre, unenlightened, unilluminated; abstruse, blind, cabbalistic, difficult, doubtful, enigmatic, high, incomprehensible, indefinite, indistinct, intricate, involved, mysterious, mystic, recondite, undefined, unintelligible, vague; remote, secluded; humble, inglorious, nameless, renownless, undistinguished, unhonored, unknown, unnoted, unnoticed.

obsequious *adj* cringing, deferential, fawning, flattering, servile, slavish, supple, subservient, sycophantic, truckling.

observant *adj* attentive, heedful, mindful, perceptive, quick, regardful, vigilant, watchful.

observation *n* attention, cognition, notice, observance; annotation, note, remark; experience, knowledge.

observe *vb* eye, mark, note, notice, remark, watch; behold, detect, discover, perceive, see; express, mention, remark, say, utter; comply, conform, follow, fulfill, obey; celebrate, keep, regard, solemnize.

obsolete *adj* ancient, antiquated, antique, archaic, disused, neglected, old, old-fashioned, obsolescent, out-of-date, past, passé, unfashionable.

obstacle *n* barrier, check, difficulty, hindrance, impediment, interference, interruption, obstruction, snag, stumbling block.

obstinacy *n* contumacy, doggedness, headiness, firmness, inflexibility, intractability, obduracy, persistence, perseverance, perversity, resoluteness, stubbornness, tenacity, willfulness.

obstinate *adj* cross-grained, contumacious, dogged, firm, headstrong, inflexible, immovable, intractable, mulish, obdurate, opinionated, persistent, pertinacious, perverse, resolute, self-willed, stubborn, tenacious, unyielding, willful.

obstreperous *adj* boisterous, clamorous, loud, noisy, riotous, tumultuous, turbulent, unruly, uproarious, vociferous.

obstruct *vb* bar, barricade, block, blockade, block up, choke, clog, close, glut, jam, obturate, stop; hinder, impede, oppose, prevent; arrest, check, curb, delay, embrace, interrupt, retard, slow.

obstruction *n* bar, barrier, block, blocking, check, difficulty, hindrance, impediment, obstacle, stoppage; check, clog, embarrassment, interruption, obturation.

obtain *vb* achieve, acquire, attain, bring, contrive, earn, elicit, gain, get, induce, procure, secure; hold, prevail, stand, subsist.

obtrude *vb* encroach, infringe, interfere, intrude, trespass.

obtrusive *adj* forward, interfering, intrusive, meddling, officious.

obtuse *adj* blunt; blockish, doltish, dull, dull-witted, heavy, stockish, stolid, stupid, slow, unintellectual, unintelligent.

obviate *vb* anticipate, avert, counteract, preclude, prevent, remove.

obvious *adj* exposed, liable, open, subject; apparent, clear, distinct, evident, manifest, palatable, patent, perceptible, plain, self-evident, unmistakable, visible.

occasion *vb* breed, cause, create, originate, produce; induce, influence, move, persuade. • *n* casualty, event, incident, occurrence; conjuncture, convenience, juncture, opening, opportunity; condition, necessity, need, exigency, requirement, want; cause, ground, reason; inducement, influence; circumstance, exigency.

occasional *adj* accidental, casual, incidental, infrequent, irregular, uncommon; causative, causing.

occasionally *adv* casually, sometimes.

occult *adj* abstruse, cabbalistic, hidden, latent, secret, invisible, mysterious, mystic, mystical, recondite, shrouded, undetected, undiscovered, unknown, unrevealed, veiled. • *n* magic, sorcery, witchcraft.

occupation *n* holding, occupancy, possession, tenure, use; avocation, business, calling, craft, employment, engagement, job, post, profession, trade, vocation.

occupy *vb* capture, hold, keep, possess; cover, fill, garrison, inhabit, take up, tenant; engage, employ, use.

occur *vb* appear, arise, offer; befall, chance, eventuate, happen, result, supervene.

occurrence *n* accident, adventure, affair, casualty, event, happening, incident, proceeding, transaction.

odd *adj* additional, redundant, remaining; casual, incidental; inappropriate, queer, unsuitable; comical, droll, erratic, extravagant, extraordinary, fantastic, grotesque, irregular, peculiar, quaint, singular, strange, uncommon, uncouth, unique, unusual, whimsical.

odds *npl* difference, disparity, inequality; advantage, superiority, supremacy.

odious *adj* abominable, detestable, execrable, hateful, shocking; hated, obnoxious, unpopular; disagreeable, forbidding, loathsome, offensive.

odium *n* abhorrence, detestation, dislike, enmity, hate, hatred; odiousness, repulsiveness; obloquy, opprobrium, reproach, shame.

odor *n* aroma, fragrance, perfume, redolence, scent, smell.

odorous *adj* aromatic, balmy, fragrant, perfumed, redolent, scented, sweet-scented, sweet-smelling.

offal *n* carrion, dregs, garbage, refuse, rubbish, waste.

offence *n* aggression, attack, assault; anger, displeasure, indignation, pique, resentment, umbrage, wrath; affront, harm, injury, injustice, insult, outrage, wrong; crime, delinquency, fault, misdeed, misdemeanor, sin, transgression, trespass.

offend *vb* affront, annoy, chafe, displease, fret, gall, irritate, mortify, nettle, provoke, vex; molest, pain, shock, wound; fall, sin, stumble, transgress.

offender *n* convict, criminal, culprit, delinquent, felon, malefactor, sinner, transgressor, trespasser.

offensive *adj* aggressive, attacking, invading; disgusting, loathsome, nauseating, nauseous, repulsive, sickening; abominable, detestable, disagreeable, displeasing, execrable, hateful, obnoxious, repugnant, revolting, shocking, unpalatable, unpleasant; abusive, disagreeable, impertinent, insolent, insulting, irritating, opprobrious, rude, saucy, unpleasant. • *n* attack, onslaught.

offer *vb* present, proffer, tender; exhibit; furnish, propose, propound, show; volunteer; dare, essay, endeavor, venture. • *n* overture, proffering, proposal, proposition, tender, overture; attempt, bid, endeavor, essay.

offhand *adj* abrupt, brusque, casual, curt, extempore, impromptu, informal, unpremeditated, unstudied. • *adv* carelessly, casually, clumsily, haphazardly, informally, slapdash; ad-lib, extemporaneously, extemporarily, extempore, impromptu.

office *n* duty, function, service, work; berth, place, position, post, situation; business, capacity, charge, employment, trust; bureau, room.

officiate *vb* act, perform, preside, serve.

officious *adj* busy, dictatorial, forward, impertinent, interfering, intermeddling, meddlesome, meddling, obtrusive, pushing, pushy.

offset *vb* balance, counteract, counterbalance, counterpoise. • *n* branch, offshoot, scion, shoot, slip, sprout, twig; counterbalance, counterpoise, set-off, equivalent.

offspring *n* brood, children, descendants, issue, litter, posterity, progeny; cadet, child, scion.

often *adv* frequently, generally, oftentimes, repeatedly.

ogre *n* bugbear, demon, devil, goblin, hobgoblin, monster, specter.

old *adj* aged, ancient, antiquated, antique, archaic, elderly, obsolete, olden, old-fashioned, superannuated; decayed, done, senile, worn-out; original, primitive, pristine; former, preceding, pre-existing.

oleaginous *adj* adipose, fat, fatty, greasy, oily, sebaceous, unctuous.

omen *n* augury, auspice, foreboding, portent, presage, prognosis, sign, warning.

ominous *adj* inauspicious, monitory, portentous, premonitory, threatening, unpropitious.

omission *n* default, failure, forgetfulness, neglect, oversight.

omit *vb* disregard, drop, eliminate, exclude, miss, neglect, overlook, skip.

omnipotent *adj* almighty, all-powerful.

omniscient *adj* all-knowing, all-seeing, all-wise.

oneness *n* individuality, singleness, unity.

onerous *adj* burdensome, difficult, hard, heavy, laborious, oppressive, responsible, weighty.

one-sided *adj* partial, prejudiced, unfair, unilateral, unjust.

only *adj* alone, single, sole, solitary. • *adv* barely, merely, simply.

onset *n* assault, attack, charge, onslaught, storm, storming.

onus *n* burden, liability, load, responsibility.

ooze *vb* distil, drip, drop, shed; drain, exude, filter, leak, percolate, stain, transude. • *n* mire, mud, slime.

opaque *adj* dark, dim, hazy, muddy; abstruse, cryptic, enigmatic, enigmatical, obscure, unclear.

open *vb* expand, spread; begin, commence, initiate; disclose, exhibit, reveal, show; unbar, unclose, uncover, unlock, unseal, untie. • *adj* expanded, extended, unclosed, spread wide; aboveboard, artless, candid, cordial, fair, frank, guileless, hearty, honest, sincere, openhearted, single-minded, undesigning, undisguised, undissembling, unreserved; bounteous, bountiful, free, generous, liberal, munificent; ajar, uncovered; exposed, undefended, unprotected; clear, unobstructed; accessible, public, unenclosed, unrestricted; mild, moderate; apparent, debatable, evident, obvious, patent, plain, undetermined.

opening *adj* commencing, first, inaugural, initiatory, introductory. • *n* aperture, breach, chasm, cleft, fissure, flaw, gap, gulf, hole, interspace, loophole, orifice, perforation, rent, rift; beginning, commencement, dawn; chance, opportunity, vacancy.

openly *adv* candidly, frankly, honestly, plainly, publicly.

openness *n* candor, frankness, honesty, ingenuousness, plainness, unreservedness.

operate *vb* act, function, work; cause, effect, occasion, produce; manipulate, use, run.

operation *n* manipulation, performance, procedure, proceeding, process; action, affair, maneuvre, motion, movement.

operative *adj* active, effective, effectual, efficient, serviceable, vigorous; important, indicative, influential, significant. • *n* artisan, employee, laborer, mechanic, worker, workman.

opiate *adj* narcotic, sedative, soporiferous, soporific. • *n* anodyne, drug, narcotic, sedative, tranquillizer.

opine *vb* apprehend, believe, conceive, fancy, judge, suppose, presume, surmise, think.

opinion *n* conception, idea, impression, judgment, notion, sentiment, view; belief, persuasion, tenet; esteem, estimation, judgment.

opinionated *adj* biased, bigoted, cocksure, conceited, dictatorial, dogmatic, opinionative, prejudiced, stubborn.

opponent *adj* adverse, antagonistic, contrary, opposing, opposite, repugnant. • *n* adversary, antagonist, competitor, contestant, counteragent, enemy, foe, opposite, opposer, party, rival.

opportune *adj* appropriate, auspicious, convenient, favorable, felicitous, fit, fitting, fortunate, lucky, propitious, seasonable, suitable, timely, well-timed.

opportunity *n* chance, convenience, moment, occasion.

oppose *vb* combat, contravene, counteract, dispute, obstruct, oppugn, resist, thwart, withstand; check, prevent; confront, counterpoise.

opposite *adj* facing, fronting; conflicting, contradictory, contrary, different, diverse, incompatible, inconsistent, irreconcilable; adverse, antagonistic, hostile, inimical, opposed, opposing, repugnant. • *n* contradiction, contrary, converse, reverse.

opposition *n* antagonism, antinomy, contrariety, inconsistency, repugnance; counteraction, counterinfluence, hostility, resistance; hindrance, obstacle, obstruction, oppression, prevention.

oppress *vb* burden, crush, depress, harass, load, maltreat, overburden, overpower, overwhelm, persecute, subdue, suppress, tyrannize, wrong.

oppression *n* abuse, calamity, cruelty, hardship, injury, injustice, misery, persecution, severity, suffering, tyranny; depression, dullness, heaviness, lassitude.

oppressive *adj* close, muggy, stifling, suffocating, sultry.

opprobrious *adj* abusive, condemnatory, contemptuous, damnatory, insolent, insulting, offensive, reproachable, scandalous, scurrilous, vituperative; despised, dishonorable, disreputable, hateful, infamous, shameful.

opprobrium *n* contumely, scurrility; calumny, disgrace, ignominy, infamy, obloquy, odium, reproach.

oppugn *vb* assail, argue, attack, combat, contravene, oppose, resist, thwart, withstand.

option *n* choice, discretion, election, preference, selection.

optional *adj* discretionary, elective, nonobligatory, voluntary.

opulence *n* affluence, fortune, independence, luxury, riches, wealth.

opulent *adj* affluent, flush, luxurious, moneyed, plentiful, rich, sumptuous, wealthy.

oracular *adj* ominous, portentous, prophetic; authoritative, dogmatic, magisterial, positive; aged, grave, wise; ambiguous, blind, dark, equivocal, obscure.

oral *adj* nuncupative, spoken, verbal, vocal.

oration *n* address, declamation, discourse, harangue, speech.

orb *n* ball, globe, sphere; circle, circuit, orbit, ring; disk, wheel.

orbit *vb* circle, encircle, revolve around. • *n* course, path, revolution, track.

ordain *vb* appoint, call, consecrate, elect, experiment, constitute, establish, institute, regulate; decree, enjoin, enact, order, prescribe.

order *vb* adjust, arrange, methodize, regulate, systematize; carry on, conduct, manage; bid, command, direct, instruct, require. • *n* arrangement, disposition, method, regularity, symmetry, system; law, regulation, rule; discipline, peace, quiet; command, commission, direction, injunction, instruction, mandate, prescription; class, degree, grade, kind, rank; family, tribe; brotherhood, community, fraternity, society; sequence, succession.

orderly *adj* methodical, regular, systematic; peaceable, quiet, well-behaved; neat, shipshape, tidy.

ordinance *n* appointment, command, decree, edict, enactment, law, order, prescript, regulation, rule, statute; ceremony, observance, sacrament, rite, ritual.

ordinary *adj* accustomed, customary, established, everyday, normal, regular, settled, wonted, everyday, regular; common, frequent, habitual, usual; average, commonplace, indifferent, inferior, mean, mediocre, second-rate, undistinguished; homely, plain.

organization *n* business, construction, constitution, organism, structure, system.

organize *vb* adjust, constitute, construct, form, make, shape; arrange, coordinate, correlate, establish, systematize.

orgy *n* carousal, debauch, debauchery, revel, saturnalia.

orifice *n* aperture, hole, mouth, perforation, pore, vent.

origin *n* beginning, birth, commencement, cradle, derivation, foundation, fountain, fountainhead, original, rise, root, source, spring, starting point; cause, occasion; heritage, lineage, parentage.

original *adj* aboriginal, first, primary, primeval, primitive, primordial, pristine; fresh, inventive, novel; eccentric, odd, peculiar. • *n* cause, commencement, origin, source, spring; archetype, exemplar, model, pattern, prototype, protoplast, type.

originate *vb* arise, begin, emanate, flow, proceed, rise, spring; create, discover, form, invent, produce.

originator *n* author, creator, former, inventor, maker, parent.

orison *n* petition, prayer, solicitation, supplication.

ornament *vb* adorn, beautify, bedeck, bedizen, decorate, deck, emblazon, garnish, grace. • *n* adornment, bedizenment, decoration, design, embellishment, garnish, ornamentation.

ornate *adj* beautiful, bedecked, decorated, elaborate, elegant, embellished, florid, flowery, ornamental, ornamented.

orthodox *adj* conventional, correct, sound, true.

oscillate vb fluctuate, sway, swing, vacillate, vary, vibrate.

ostensible adj apparent, assigned, avowed, declared, exhibited, manifest, presented, visible; plausible, professed, specious.

ostentation n dash, display, flourish, pageantry, parade, pomp, pomposity, pompousness, show, vaunting; appearance, semblance, showiness.

ostentatious adj boastful, dashing, flaunting, pompous, pretentious, showy, vain, vainglorious; gaudy.

ostracize vb banish, boycott, exclude, excommunicate, exile, expatriate, expel, evict.

oust vb dislodge, dispossess, eject, evict, expel.

outbreak n ebullition, eruption, explosion, outburst; affray, broil, conflict, commotion, fray, riot, row; flare-up, manifestation.

outcast n exile, expatriate; castaway, pariah, reprobate, vagabond.

outcome n conclusion, consequence, event, issue, result, upshot.

outcry n cry, scream, screech, yell; bruit, clamor, noise, tumult, vociferation.

outdo vb beat, exceed, excel, outgo, outstrip, outvie, surpass.

outlandish adj alien, exotic, foreign, strange; barbarous, bizarre, uncouth.

outlaw vb ban, banish, condemn, exclude, forbid, make illegal, prohibit. • n bandit, brigand, crook, freebooter, highwayman, lawbreaker, marauder, robber, thief.

outlay n disbursement, expenditure, outgoings.

outline vb delineate, draft, draw, plan, silhouette, sketch. • n contor, profile; delineation, draft, drawing, plan, rough draft, silhouette, sketch.

outlive vb last, live longer, survive.

outlook n future, prospect, sight, view; lookout, watch-tower.

outrage vb abuse, injure, insult, maltreat, offend, shock, injure. • n abuse, affront, indignity, insult, offence.

outrageous adj abusive, frantic, furious, frenzied, mad, raging, turbulent, violent, wild; atrocious, enormous, flagrant, heinous, monstrous, nefarious, villainous; enormous, excessive, extravagant, unwarrantable.

outré adj excessive, exorbitant, extravagant, immoderate, inordinate, overstrained, unconventional.

outrun vb beat, exceed, outdistance, outgo, outstrip, outspeed, surpass.

outset n beginning, commencement, entrance, opening, start, starting point.

outshine vb eclipse, outstrip, overshadow, surpass.

outspoken adj abrupt, blunt, candid, frank, plain, plainspoken, unceremonious, unreserved.

outstanding adj due, owing, uncollected, ungathered, unpaid, unsettled; conspicuous, eminent, prominent, striking.

outward adj exterior, external, outer, outside.

outwit vb cheat, circumvent, deceive, defraud, diddle, dupe, gull, outmaneuvre, overreach, swindle, victimize.

overawe vb affright, awe, browbeat, cow, daunt, frighten, intimidate, scare, terrify.

overbalance vb capsize, overset, overturn, tumble, upset; outweigh, preponderate.

overbearing adj oppressive, overpowering; arrogant, dictatorial, dogmatic, domineering, haughty, imperious, overweening, proud, supercilious.

overcast vb cloud, darken, overcloud, overshadow, shade, shadow. • adj cloudy, darkened, hazy, murky, obscure.

overcharge vb burden, oppress, overburden, overload, surcharge; crowd, overfill; exaggerate, overstate, overstrain.

overcome vb beat, choke, conquer, crush, defeat, discomfit, overbear, overmaster, overpower, overthrow, overturn, overwhelm, prevail, rout, subdue, subjugate, surmount, vanquish.

overflow vb brim over, fall over, pour over, pour out, shower, spill; deluge, inundate, submerge. • n deluge, inundation, profusion, superabundance.

overhaul vb overtake; check, examine, inspect, repair, survey. • n check, examination, inspection.

overlay vb cover, spread over; overlie, overpress, smother; crush, overpower, overwhelm; cloud, hide, obscure, overcast. • n appliqué, covering, decoration, veneer.

overlook vb inspect, oversee, superintend, supervise; disregard, miss, neglect, slight; condone, excuse, forgive, pardon, pass over.

overpower vb beat, conquer, crush, defeat, discomfit, overbear, overcome, overmaster, overturn, overwhelm, subdue, subjugate, vanquish.

overreach vb exceed, outstrip, overshoot, pass, surpass; cheat, circumvent, deceive, defraud.

override vb outride, outweigh, pass, quash, supersede, surpass.

overrule vb control, govern, sway; annul, cancel, nullify, recall, reject, repeal, repudiate, rescind, revoke, reject, set aside, supersede, suppress.

oversight n care, charge, control, direction, inspection, management, superintendence, supervision, surveillance; blunder, error, fault, inadvertence, inattention, lapse, miss, mistake, neglect, omission, slip, trip.

overt adj apparent, glaring, open, manifest, notorious, patent, public, unconcealed.

overthrow vb overturn, upset, subvert; demolish, destroy; level; beat, conquer, crush, defeat, discomfit, foil, master, overcome, overpower, overwhelm, rout, subjugate, vanquish, worst. • n downfall, fall, prostration, subversion; destruction, demolition, ruin; defeat, discomfiture, dispersion, rout.

overturn vb invert, overthrow, reverse, subvert, upset.

overture n invitation, offer, proposal, proposition.

overweening adj arrogant, conceited, consequential, egotistical, haughty, opinionated, proud, supercilious, vain, vainglorious.

overwhelm vb drown, engulf, inundate, overflow, submerge, swallow up, swamp; conquer, crush, defeat, overbear, overcome, overpower, subdue, vanquish.

overwrought adj overdone, overelaborate; agitated, excited, overexcited, overworked, stirred.

own[1] vb have, hold, possess; avow, confess; acknowledge, admit, allow, concede.

own[2] adj particular, personal, private.

owner n freeholder, holder, landlord, possessor, proprietor.

P

pace vb go, hasten, hurry, move, step, walk. • n amble, gait, step, walk.

pacific adj appeasing, conciliatory, ironic, mollifying, placating, peacemaking, propitiatory; calm, gentle, peaceable, peaceful, quiet, smooth, tranquil, unruffled.

pacify vb appease, conciliate, harmonize, tranquillize; allay, appease, assuage, calm, compose, hush, lay, lull, moderate, mollify, placate, propitiate, quell, quiet, smooth, soften, soothe, still.

pack vb compact, compress, crowd, fill; bundle, burden, load, stow. • n bale, budget, bundle, package, packet, parcel; burden, load; assemblage, assembly, assortment, collection, set; band, bevy, clan, company, crew, gang, knot, lot, party, squad.

pact n agreement, alliance, bargain, bond, compact, concordat, contract, convention, covenant, league, stipulation.

pagan adj heathen, heathenish, idolatrous, irreligious, paganist, paganistic. • n gentile, heathen, idolater.

pageantry n display, flourish, magnificence, parade, pomp, show, splendor, state.

pain vb agonize, bite, distress, hurt, rack, sting, torment, torture; afflict, aggrieve, annoy, bore, chafe, displease, disquiet, fret, grieve, harass, incommode, plague, tease, trouble, vex, worry; rankle, smart, shoot, sting, twinge. • n ache, agony, anguish, discomfort, distress, gripe, hurt, pang, smart, soreness, sting, suffering, throe, torment, torture, twinge; affliction, anguish, anxiety, bitterness, care, chagrin, disquiet, dolor, grief, heartache, misery, punishment, solicitude, sorrow, trouble, uneasiness, unhappiness, vexation, woe, wretchedness.

painful adj agonizing, distressful, excruciating, racking, sharp, tormenting, torturing; afflicting, afflictive, annoying, baleful, disagreeable, displeasing, disquieting, distressing, dolorous, grievous, provoking, troublesome, unpleasant, vexatious; arduous, careful, difficult, hard, severe, sore, toilsome.

pains npl care, effort, labor, task, toilsomeness, trouble; childbirth, labor, travail.

painstaking adj assiduous, careful, conscientious, diligent, hardworking, industrious, laborious, persevering, plodding, sedulous, strenuous.

paint vb delineate, depict, describe, draw, figure, pencil, portray, represent, sketch; adorn, beautify, deck, embellish, ornament. • n coloring, dye, pigment, stain; cosmetics, greasepaint, make-up.

pair vb couple, marry, mate, match. • n brace, couple, double, duo, match, twosome.

pal *n* buddy, chum, companion, comrade, crony, friend, mate, mucker.

palatable *adj* acceptable, agreeable, appetizing, delicate, delicious, enjoyable, flavorful, flavorsome, gustative, gustatory, luscious, nice, pleasant, pleasing, savory, relishable, tasteful, tasty, toothsome.

palaver *vb* chat, chatter, converse, patter, prattle, say, speak, talk; confer, parley; blandish, cajole, flatter, wheedle. • *n* chat, chatter, conversation, discussion, language, prattle, speech, talk; confab, confabulation, conference, conclave, parley, powwow; balderdash, cajolery, flummery, gibberish.

pale *vb* blanch, lose color, whiten. • *adj* ashen, ashy, blanched, bloodless, pallid, sickly, wan, white; blank, dim, obscure, spectral. • *n* picket, stake; circuit, enclosure; district, region, territory; boundary, confine, fence, limit.

pall[1] *n* cloak, cover, curtain, mantle, pallium, shield, shroud, veil.

pall[2] *vb* cloy, glut, gorge, satiate, surfeit; deject, depress, discourage, dishearten; dispirit; cloak, cover, drape, invest, overspread, shroud.

palliate *vb* cloak, conceal, cover, excuse, extenuate, hide, gloss, lessen; abate, allay, alleviate, assuage, blunt, diminish, dull, ease, mitigate, moderate, mollify, quell, quiet, relieve, soften, soothe, still.

pallid *adj* ashen, ashy, cadaverous, colorless, pale, sallow, wan, whitish.

palm[1] *vb* foist, impose, obtrude, pass off; handle, touch.

palm[2] *n* bays, crown, laurels, prize, trophy, victory.

palmy *adj* flourishing, fortunate, glorious, golden, halcyon, happy, joyous, prosperous, thriving, victorious.

palpable *adj* corporeal, material, tactile, tangible; evident, glaring, gross, intelligible, manifest, obvious, patent, plain, unmistakable.

palpitate *vb* flutter, pulsate, throb; quiver, shiver, tremble.

palter *vb* dodge, equivocate, evade, haggle, prevaricate, quibble, shift, shuffle, trifle.

paltry *adj* diminutive, feeble, inconsiderable, insignificant, little, miserable, petty, slender, slight, small, sorry, trifling, trivial, unimportant, wretched.

pamper *vb* baby, coddle, fondle, gratify, humor, spoil.

panacea *n* catholicon, cure-all, medicine, remedy.

panegyric *adj* commendatory, encomiastic, encomiastical, eulogistic, eulogistical, laudatory, panegyrical. • *n* eulogy, laudation, praise, paean, tribute.

pang *n* agony, anguish, distress, gripe, pain, throe, twinge.

panic *vb* affright, alarm, scare, startle, terrify; become terrified, overreact. • *n* alarm, consternation, fear, fright, jitters, terror.

pant *vb* blow, gasp, puff; heave, palpitate, pulsate, throb; languish; desire, hunger, long, sigh, thirst, yearn. • *n* blow, gasp, puff.

parable *n* allegory, fable, story.

paraclete *n* advocate, comforter, consoler, intercessor, mediator.

parade *vb* display, flaunt, show, vaunt. • *n* ceremony, display, flaunting, ostentation, pomp, show; array, pageant, review, spectacle; mall, promenade.

paradox *n* absurdity, contradiction, mystery.

paragon *n* flower, ideal, masterpiece, model, nonpareil, pattern, standard.

paragraph *n* clause, item, notice, passage, section, sentence, subdivision.

parallel *vb* be alike, compare, conform, correlate, match. • *adj* abreast, concurrent; allied, analogous, correspondent, equal, like, resembling, similar. • *n* conformity, likeness, resemblance, similarity; analogue, correlative, counterpart.

paramount *adj* chief, dominant, eminent, pre-eminent, principal, superior, supreme.

paraphernalia *n* accoutrements, appendages, appurtenances, baggage, belongings, effects, equipage, equipment, ornaments, trappings.

parasite *n* bloodsucker, fawner, flatterer, flunky, hanger-on, leech, spaniel, sycophant, toady, wheedler.

parcel *vb* allot, apportion, dispense, distribute, divide. • *n* budget, bundle, package; batch, collection, group, lot, set; division, part, patch, pierce, plot, portion, tract.

parched *adj* arid, dry, scorched, shriveled, thirsty.

pardon *vb* condone, forgive, overlook, remit; absolve, acquit, clear, discharge, excuse, release. • *n* absolution, amnesty, condonation, discharge, excuse, forgiveness, grace, mercy, overlook, release.

parentage *n* ancestry, birth, descent,

extraction, family, lineage, origin, parenthood, pedigree, stock.

pariah *n* outcast, wretch.

parish *n* community, congregation, parishioners; district, subdivision.

parity *n* analogy, correspondence, equality, equivalence, likeness, sameness, similarity.

parody *vb* burlesque, caricature, imitate, lampoon, mock, ridicule, satirize, travesty. • *n* burlesque, caricature, imitation, ridicule, satire, travesty.

paroxysm *n* attack, convulsion, exacerbation, fit, outburst, seizure, spasm, throe.

parsimonious *adj* avaricious, close, close-fisted, covetous, frugal, grasping, grudging, illiberal, mean, mercenary, miserly, near, niggardly, penurious, shabby, sordid, sparing, stingy, tightfisted.

parson *n* churchman, clergyman, divine, ecclesiastic, incumbent, minister, pastor, priest, rector.

part *vb* break, dismember, dissever, divide, sever, subdivide, sunder; detach, disconnect, disjoin, dissociate, disunite, separate; allot, apportion, distribute, divide, mete, share; secrete. • *n* crumb, division, fraction, fragment, moiety, parcel, piece, portion, remnant, scrap, section, segment, subdivision; component, constituent, element, ingredient, member, organ; lot, share; concern, interest, participation; allotment, apportionment, dividend; business, charge, duty, function, office, work; faction, party, side; character, cue, lines, role; clause, paragraph, passage.

partake *vb* engage, participate, share; consume, eat, take; evince, evoke, show, suggest.

partial *adj* component, fractional, imperfect, incomplete, limited; biased, influential, interested, one-sided, prejudiced, prepossessed, unfair, unjust, warped; fond, indulgent.

participate *vb* engage in, partake, perform, share.

particle *n* atom, bit, corpuscle, crumb, drop, glimmer, grain, granule, iota, jot, mite, molecule, morsel, mote, scrap, shred, snip, spark, speck, whit.

particular *adj* especial, special, specific; distinct, individual, respective, separate, single; characteristic, distinctive, peculiar; individual, intimate, own, personal, private; notable, noteworthy; circumstantial, definite, detailed, exact, minute, narrow, precise; careful, close, conscientious, critical, fastidious, nice, scrupulous, strict; marked, odd, singular, strange, uncommon. • *n* case, circumstance, count, detail, feature, instance, item, particularity, point, regard, respect.

parting *adj* breaking, dividing, separating; final, last, valedictory; declining, departing. • *n* breaking, disruption, rupture, severing; detachment, division, separation; death, departure, farewell, leave-taking.

partisan *adj* biased, factional, interested, partial, prejudiced. • *n* adherent, backer, champion, disciple, follower, supporter, votary; baton, halberd, pike, quarterstaff, truncheon, staff.

partition *vb* apportion, distribute, divide, portion, separate, share. • *n* division, separation; barrier, division, screen, wall; allotment, apportionment, distribution.

partner *n* associate, colleague, copartner, partaker, participant, participator; accomplice, ally, coadjutor, confederate; companion, consort, spouse.

partnership *n* association, company, copartnership, firm, house, society; connection, interest, participation, union.

parts *npl* abilities, accomplishments, endowments, faculties, genius, gifts, intellect, intelligence, mind, qualities, powers, talents; districts, regions.

party *n* alliance, association, cabal, circle, clique, combination, confederacy, coterie, faction, group, junta, league, ring, set; body, company, detachment, squad, troop; assembly, gathering; partaker, participant, participator, sharer; defendant, litigant, plaintiff; individual, one, person, somebody; cause, division, interest, side.

pass[1] *vb* devolve, fall, go, move, proceed; change, elapse, flit, glide, lapse, slip; cease, die, fade, expire, vanish; happen, occur; convey, deliver, send, transmit, transfer; disregard, ignore, neglect; exceed, excel, surpass; approve, ratify, sanction; answer, do, succeed, suffice, suit; express, pronounce, utter; beguile, wile.

pass[2] *n* avenue, ford, road, route, way; defile, gorge, passage, ravine; authorization, license, passport, permission, ticket; condition, conjecture, plight, situation, state; lunge, push, thrust, tilt; transfer, trick.

passable *adj* admissible, allowable, mediocre, middling, moderate, ordinary, so-so, tolerable; acceptable, current, receivable; navigable, traversable.

passage n going, passing, progress, transit; evacuation, journey, migration, transit, voyage; avenue, channel, course, pass, path, road, route, thoroughfare, vennel, way; access, currency, entry, reception; act, deed, event, feat, incidence, occurrence, passion; corridor, gallery, gate, hall; clause, paragraph, sentence, text; course, death, decease, departure, expiration, lapse; affair, brush, change, collision, combat, conflict, contest, encounter, exchange, joust, skirmish, tilt.

passenger n fare, itinerant, tourist, traveler, voyager, wayfarer.

passionate adj animated, ardent, burning, earnest, enthusiastic, excited, fervent, fiery, furious, glowing, hot-blooded, impassioned, impetuous, impulsive, intense, vehement, warm, zealous; hot-headed, irascible, quick-tempered, tempestuous, violent.

passive adj inactive, inert, quiescent, receptive; apathetic, enduring, long-suffering, nonresistant, patient, stoical, submissive, suffering, unresisting.

past adj accomplished, elapsed, ended, gone, spent; ancient, bygone, former, obsolete, outworn. • adv above, extra, beyond, over. • prep above, after, beyond, exceeding. • n antiquity, heretofore, history, olden times, yesterday.

pastime n amusement, diversion, entertainment, hobby, play, recreation, sport.

pastor n clergyman, churchman, divine, ecclesiastic, minister, parson, priest, vicar.

pat[1] vb dab, hit, rap, tap; caress, chuck, fondle, pet. • n dab, hit, pad, rap, tap; caress.

pat[2] adj appropriate, apt, fit, pertinent, suitable. • adv aptly, conveniently, fitly, opportunely, seasonably.

patch vb mend, repair. • n repair; parcel, plot, tract.

patent adj expanded, open, spreading; apparent, clear, conspicuous, evident, glaring, indisputable, manifest, notorious, obvious, public, open, palpable, plain, unconcealed, unmistakable. • n copyright, privilege, right.

paternity n derivation, descent, fatherhood, origin.

path n access, avenue, course, footway, passage, pathway, road, route, track, trail, way.

pathetic adj affecting, melting, moving, pitiable, plaintive, sad, tender, touching.

patience n endurance, fortitude, long-sufferance, resignation, submission, sufferance; calmness, composure, quietness; forbearance, indulgence, leniency; assiduity, constancy, diligence, indefatigability, indefatigableness, perseverance, persistence.

patient adj meek, passive, resigned, submissive, uncomplaining, unrepining; calm, composed, contented, quiet; indulgent, lenient, long-suffering; assiduous, constant, diligent, indefatigable, persevering, persistent. • n case, invalid, subject, sufferer.

patrician adj aristocratic, blue-blooded, highborn, noble, senatorial, well-born. • n aristocrat, blue blood, nobleman.

patron n advocate, defender, favorer, guardian, helper, protector, supporter.

patronize vb aid, assist, befriend, countenance, defend, favor, maintain, support; condescend, disparage, scorn.

pattern vb copy, follow, imitate. • n archetype, exemplar, last, model, original, paradigm, plan, prototype; example, guide, sample, specimen; mirror, paragon; design, figure, shape, style, type.

paucity n deficiency, exiguity, insufficiency, lack, poverty, rarity, shortage.

paunch n abdomen, belly, gut, stomach.

pauperism n beggary, destitution, indigence, mendicancy, mendicity, need, poverty, penury, want.

pause vb breathe, cease, delay, desist, rest, stay, stop, wait; delay, forbear, intermit, stay, stop, tarry, wait; deliberate, demur, hesitate, waver. • n break, caesura, cessation, halt, intermission, interruption, interval, remission, rest, stop, stoppage, stopping, suspension; hesitation, suspense, uncertainty; paragraph.

pawn[1] n cat's-paw, dupe, plaything, puppet, stooge, tool, toy.

pawn[2] vb bet, gage, hazard, lay, pledge, risk, stake, wager. • n assurance, bond, guarantee, pledge, security.

pay vb defray, discharge, discount, foot, honor, liquidate, meet, quit, settle; compensate, recompense, reimburse, requite, reward; punish, revenge; give, offer, render. • n allowance, commission, compensation, emolument, hire, recompense, reimbursement, remuneration, requital, reward, salary, wages.

peace n calm, calmness, quiet, quietness, repose, stillness; accord, amity, friendliness, harmony; composure, equanimity, imperturbability, placidity, quietude, tranquillity; agreement, armistice.

peaceable *adj* pacific, peaceful; amiable, amicable, friendly, gentle, inoffensive, mild; placid, quiet, serene, still, tranquil, undisturbed, unmoved.

peaceful *adj* quiet, undisturbed; amicable, concordant, friendly, gentle, harmonious, mild, pacific, peaceable; calm, composed, placid, serene, still.

peak *vb* climax, culminate, top; dwindle, thin. • *n* acme, apex, crest, crown, pinnacle, summit, top, zenith.

peaked *adj* piked, pointed, thin.

peasant *n* boor, countryman, clown, hind, laborer, rustic, swain.

peculate *vb* appropriate, defraud, embezzle, misappropriate, pilfer, purloin, rob, steal.

peculiar *adj* appropriate, idiosyncratic, individual, proper; characteristic, eccentric, exceptional, extraordinary, odd, queer, rare, singular, strange, striking, uncommon, unusual; individual, especial, particular, select, special, specific.

peculiarity *n* appropriateness, distinctiveness, individuality, specialty; characteristic, idiosyncrasy, oddity, peculiarity, singularity.

pedantic *adj* conceited, fussy, officious, ostentatious, over-learned, particular, pedagogical, pompous, pragmatical, precise, pretentious, priggish, stilted.

pedlar *n* chapman, costermonger, hawker, packman, vendor.

pedigree *adj* purebred, thoroughbred. • *n* ancestry, breed, descent, extraction, family, genealogy, house, line, lineage, race, stock, strain.

peer[1] *vb* gaze, look, peek, peep, pry, squinny, squint; appear, emerge.

peer[2] *n* associate, co-equal, companion, compeer, equal, equivalent, fellow, like, mate, match; aristocrat, baron, count, duke, earl, grandee, lord, marquis, noble, nobleman, viscount.

peerless *adj* excellent, incomparable, matchless, outstanding, superlative, unequaled, unique, unmatched, unsurpassed.

peevish *adj* acrimonious, captious, churlish, complaining, crabbed, cross, crusty, discontented, fretful, ill-natured, ill-tempered, irascible, irritable, pettish, petulant, querulous, snappish, snarling, splenetic,

spleeny, testy, waspish; forward, headstrong, obstinate, self-willed, stubborn; childish, silly, thoughtless, trifling.

pellucid *adj* bright, clear, crystalline, diaphanous, limpid, lucid, transparent.

pelt[1] *vb* assail, batter, beat, belabor, bombard, pepper, stone, strike; cast, hurl, throw; hurry, rush, speed, tear.

pelt[2] *n* coat, hide, skin.

pen[1] *vb* compose, draft, indite, inscribe, write.

pen[2] *vb* confine, coop, encage, enclose, impound, imprison, incarcerate. • *n* cage, coop, corral, crib, hutch, enclosure, paddock, pound, stall, sty.

penalty *n* chastisement, fine, forfeiture, mulct, punishment, retribution.

penance *n* humiliation, maceration, mortification, penalty, punishment.

penchant *n* bent, bias, disposition, fondness, inclination, leaning, liking, predilection, predisposition, proclivity, proneness, propensity, taste, tendency, turn.

penetrate *vb* bore, burrow, cut, enter, invade, penetrate, percolate, perforate, pervade, pierce, soak, stab; affect, sensitize, touch; comprehend, discern, perceive, understand.

penetrating *adj* penetrative, permeating, piercing, sharp, subtle; acute, clearsighted, discerning, intelligent, keen, quick, sagacious, sharp-witted, shrewd.

penetration *n* acuteness, discernment, insight, sagacity.

penitence *n* compunction, contrition, qualms, regret, remorse, repentance, sorrow.

penitent *adj* compunctious, consciencestricken, contrite, regretful, remorseful, repentant, sorrowing, sorrowful. • *n* penance-doer, penitentiary, repentant.

penniless *adj* destitute, distressed, impecunious, indigent, moneyless, pinched, poor, necessitous, needy, pensive, povertystricken, reduced.

pensive *adj* contemplative, dreamy, meditative, reflective, sober, thoughtful; grave, melancholic, melancholy, mournful, sad, serious, solemn.

penurious *adj* inadequate, ill-provided, insufficient, meager, niggardly, poor, scanty, stinted; avaricious, close, close-fisted, covetous, illiberal, grasping, grudging, mean, mercenary, miserly, near, niggardly, parsimonious, sordid, stingy, tightfisted.

penury n beggary, destitution, indigence, need, poverty, privation, want.

people vb colonize, inhabit, populate. • n clan, country, family, nation, race, state, tribe; folk, humankind, persons, population, public; commons, community, democracy, populace, proletariat; mob, multitude, rabble.

perceive vb behold, descry, detect, discern, discover, discriminate, distinguish, note, notice, observe, recognize, remark, see, spot; appreciate, comprehend, know, understand.

perceptible adj apparent, appreciable, cognizable, discernible, noticeable, perceivable, understandable, visible.

perception n apprehension, cognition, discernment, perceiving, recognition, seeing; comprehension, conception, consciousness, perceptiveness, perceptivity, understanding, feeling.

perchance adv haply, maybe, mayhap, peradventure, perhaps, possibly, probably.

percolate vb drain, drip, exude, filter, filtrate, ooze, penetrate, stain, transude.

percussion n collision, clash, concussion, crash, encounter, shock.

perdition n damnation, demolition, destruction, downfall, hell, overthrow, ruin, wreck.

peremptory adj absolute, authoritative, categorical, commanding, decisive, express, imperative, imperious, positive; determined, resolute, resolved; arbitrary, dogmatic, incontrovertible.

perennial adj ceaseless, constant, continual, deathless, enduring, immortal, imperishable, lasting, never-failing, permanent, perpetual, unceasing, undying, unfailing, uninterrupted.

perfect vb accomplish, complete, consummate, elaborate, finish. • adj completed, finished; complete, entire, full, unqualified, utter, whole; capital, consummate, excellent, exquisite, faultless, ideal; accomplished, disciplined, expert, skilled; blameless, faultless, holy, immaculate, pure, spotless, unblemished.

perfection n completeness, completion, consummation, correctness, excellence, faultlessness, finish, maturity, perfection, perfectness, wholeness; beauty, quality.

perfidious adj deceitful, dishonest, disloyal, double-faced, faithless, false, false-hearted, traitorous, treacherous, unfaithful, untrustworthy, venal.

perfidy n defection, disloyalty, faithlessness,

infidelity, perfidiousness, traitorousness, treachery, treason.

perforate vb bore, drill, penetrate, pierce, pink, prick, punch, riddle, trepan.

perform vb accomplish, achieve, compass, consummate, do, effect, transact; complete, discharge, execute, fulfill, meet, observe, satisfy; act, play, represent.

performance n accomplishment, achievement, completion, consummation, discharge, doing, execution, fulfillment; act, action, deed, exploit, feat, work; composition, production; acting, entertainment, exhibition, play, representation, hold; execution, playing.

perfume n aroma, balminess, bouquet, fragrance, incense, odor, redolence, scent, smell, sweetness.

perfunctory adj careless, formal, heedless, indifferent, mechanical, negligent, reckless, slight, slovenly, thoughtless, unmindful.

perhaps adv haply, peradventure, perchance, possibly.

peril vb endanger, imperil, jeopardize, risk. • n danger, hazard, insecurity, jeopardy, pitfall, risk, snare, uncertainty.

perilous adj dangerous, hazardous, risky, unsafe.

period n aeon, age, cycle, date, eon, epoch, season, span, spell, stage, term, time; continuance, duration; bound, conclusion, determination, end, limit, term, termination; clause, phrase, proposition, sentence.

periodical adj cyclical, incidental, intermittent, recurrent, recurring, regular, seasonal, systematic. • n magazine, paper, review, serial, weekly.

periphery n boundary, circumference, outside, perimeter, superficies, surface.

perish vb decay, molder, shrivel, waste, wither; decease, die, expire, vanish.

perishable adj decaying, decomposable, destructible; dying, frail, mortal, temporary.

perjured adj false, forsworn, perfidious, traitorous, treacherous, untrue.

permanent adj abiding, constant, continuing, durable, enduring, fixed, immutable, invariable, lasting, perpetual, persistent, stable, standing, steadfast, unchangeable, unchanging, unfading, unmovable.

permissible adj admissible, allowable, free, lawful, legal, legitimate, proper, sufferable, unprohibited.

permission n allowance, authorization, consent, dispensation, leave, liberty, license, permit, sufferance, toleration, warrant.

permit vb agree, allow, endure, let, suffer, tolerate; admit, authorize, consent, empower, license, warrant. • n leave, liberty, license, passport, permission, sanction, warrant.

pernicious adj baleful, baneful, damaging, deadly, deleterious, destructive, detrimental, disadvantageous, fatal, harmful, hurtful, injurious, malign, mischievous, noisome, noxious, prejudicial, ruinous; evilhearted, malevolent, malicious, malignant, mischief-making, wicked.

perpetrate vb commit, do, execute, perform.

perpetual adj ceaseless, continual, constant, endless, enduring, eternal, ever-enduring, everlasting, incessant, interminable, never-ceasing, never-ending, perennial, permanent, sempiternal, unceasing, unending, unfailing, uninterrupted.

perplex vb complicate, encumber, entangle, involve, snarl, tangle; beset, bewilder, confound, confuse, corner, distract, embarrass, fog, mystify, nonplus, pother, puzzle, set; annoy, bother, disturb, harass, molest, pester, plague, tease, trouble, vex, worry.

persecute vb afflict, distress, harass, molest, oppress, worry; annoy, beset, importune, pester, solicit, tease.

perseverance n constancy, continuance, doggedness, indefatigableness, persistence, persistency, pertinacity, resolution, steadfastness, steadiness, tenacity.

persevere vb continue, determine, endure, maintain, persist, remain, resolve, stick.

persist vb continue, endure, last, remain; insist, persevere.

persistent adj constant, continuing, enduring, fixed, immovable, persevering, persisting, steady, tenacious; contumacious, dogged, indefatigable, obdurate, obstinate, pertinacious, perverse, pigheaded, stubborn.

personable adj comely, good-looking, graceful, seemly, well-turned-out.

personal adj individual, peculiar, private, special; bodily, corporal, corporeal, exterior, material, physical.

personate vb act, impersonate, personify, play, represent; disguise, mast; counterfeit, feign, simulate.

perspective n panorama, prospect, view, vista; proportion, relation.

perspicacious adj keen-sighted, quick-sighted, sharp-sighted; acute, clever, discerning, keen, penetrating, sagacious, sharp-witted, shrewd.

perspicacity n acumen, acuteness, astuteness, discernment, insight, penetration, perspicaciousness, sagacity, sharpness, shrewdness.

perspicuity n clearness, distinctness, explicitness, intelligibility, lucidity, lucidness, perspicuousness, plainness, transparency.

perspicuous adj clear, distinct, explicit, intelligible, lucid, obvious, plain, transparent, unequivocal.

perspire vb exhale, glow, sweat, swelter.

persuade vb allure, actuate, entice, impel, incite, induce, influence, lead, move, prevail upon, urge; advise, counsel, convince, satisfy; inculcate, teach.

persuasion n exhortation, incitement, inducement, influence; belief, conviction, opinion; creed, doctrine, dogma, tenet; kind, sort, variety.

persuasive adj cogent, convincing, inducing, inducible, logical, persuading, plausible, sound, valid, weighty.

pert adj brisk, dapper, lively, nimble, smart, sprightly, perky; bold, flippant, forward, free, impertinent, impudent, malapert, presuming, smart, saucy.

pertain vb appertain, befit, behove, belong, concern, refer, regard, relate.

pertinacious adj constant, determined, firm, obdurate, persevering, resolute, staunch, steadfast, steady; dogged, headstrong, inflexible, mulish, intractable, obstinate, perverse, stubborn, unyielding, wayward, willful.

pertinent adj adapted, applicable, apposite, appropriate, apropos, apt, fit, germane, pat, proper, relevant, suitable; appurtenant, belonging, concerning, pertaining, regarding.

perturb vb agitate, disquiet, distress, disturb, excite, trouble, unsettle, upset, vex, worry; confuse.

pervade vb affect, animate, diffuse, extend, fill, imbue, impregnate, infiltrate, penetrate, permeate.

perverse adj bad, disturbed, oblique, perverted; contrary, dogged, headstrong, mulish, obstinate, pertinacious, perversive, stubborn, ungovernable, intractable, unyielding, wayward, willful; cantankerous, churlish, crabbed, cross, cross-grained, crusty, cussed, morose, peevish, petulant, snappish, snarling, spiteful, spleeny, surly, testy, touchy, wicked, wrong-headed; inconvenient, troublesome, untoward, vexatious.

perversion n abasement, corruption, debasement, impairment, injury, prostitution, vitiation.

perverted adj corrupt, debased, distorted, evil, impaired, misguiding, vitiated, wicked.

pessimistic adj cynical, dark, dejected, depressed, despondent, downhearted, gloomy, glum, melancholy, melancholic, morose, sad.

pest n disease, epidemic, infection, pestilence, plague; annoyance, bane, curse, infliction, nuisance, scourge, trouble.

pestilent adj contagious, infectious, malignant, pestilential; deadly, evil, injurious, malign, mischievous, noxious, poisonous; annoying, corrupt, pernicious, troublesome, vexatious.

petition vb ask, beg, crave, entreat, pray, solicit, sue, supplicate. • n address, appeal, application, entreaty, prayer, request, solicitation, supplication, suit.

petrify vb calcify, fossilize, lapidify; benumb, deaden; amaze, appal, astonish, astound, confound, dumbfound, paralyse, stun, stupefy.

petty adj diminutive, frivolous, inconsiderable, inferior, insignificant, little, mean, slight, small, trifling, trivial, unimportant.

petulant adj acrimonious, captious, cavilling, censorious, choleric, crabbed, cross, crusty, forward, fretful, hasty, ill-humored, ill-tempered, irascible, irritable, peevish, perverse, pettish, querulous, snappish, snarling, testy, touchy, waspish.

phantom n apparition, ghost, illusion, phantasm, specter, vision, wraith.

pharisaism n cant, formalism, hypocrisy, phariseeism, piety, sanctimoniousness, self-righteousness.

phenomenal adj marvellous, miraculous, prodigious, wondrous.

philanthropy n alms-giving, altruism, benevolence, charity, grace, humanitarianism, humanity, kindness.

philosophical, philosophic adj rational, reasonable, sound, wise; calm, collected, composed, cool, imperturbable, sedate, serene, stoical, tranquil, unruffled.

phlegmatic adj apathetic, calm, cold, cold-blooded, dull, frigid, heavy, impassive, indifferent, inert, sluggish, stoical, tame, unfeeling.

phobia n aversion, detestation, dislike, distaste, dread, fear, hatred.

phrase vb call, christen, denominate, designate, describe, dub, entitle, name, style. • n diction, expression, phraseology, style.

phraseology n diction, expression, language, phrasing, style.

physical adj material, natural; bodily, corporeal, external, substantial, tangible, sensible.

physiognomy n configuration, countenance, face, look, visage.

picaroon n adventurer, cheat, rogue; buccaneer, corsair, freebooter, marauder, pirate, plunderer, sea-rover.

pick vb peck, pierce, strike; cut, detach, gather, pluck; choose, cull, select; acquire, collect, get; pilfer, steal. • n pickaxe, pike, spike, toothpick.

picture vb delineate, draw, imagine, paint, represent. • n drawing, engraving, painting, print; copy, counterpart, delineation, embodiment, illustration, image, likeness, portraiture, portrayal, semblance, representation, resemblance, similitude; description.

picturesque adj beautiful, charming, colorful, graphic, scenic, striking, vivid.

piece vb mend, patch, repair; augment, complete, enlarge, increase; cement, join, unite. • n amount, bit, chunk, cut, fragment, hunk, part, quantity, scrap, shred, slice; portion; article, item, object; composition, lucubration, work, writing.

pied adj irregular, motley, mottled, particolored, piebald, spotted, variegated.

pierce vb gore, impale, pink, prick, stab, transfix; bore, drill, excite, penetrate, perforate, puncture; affect, move, rouse, strike, thrill, touch.

piety n devotion, devoutness, holiness, godliness, grace, religion, sanctity.

pile[1] vb accumulate, amass; collect, gather, heap, load. • n accumulation, collection, heap, mass, stack; fortune, wad; building, edifice, erection, fabric, pyramid, skyscraper, structure, tower; reactor, nuclear reactor.

pile[2] n beam, column, pier, pillar, pole, post.

pile[3] n down, feel, finish, fur, fluff, fuzz, grain, nap, pappus, shag, surface, texture.

pilfer vb filch, purloin, rob, steal, thieve.

pilgrim n journeyer, sojourner, traveler, wanderer, wayfarer; crusader, devotee, palmer.

pilgrimage n crusade, excursion, expedition, journey, tour, trip.

pillage vb despoil, loot, plunder, rifle, sack, spoil, strip. • n depredation, destruction, devastation, plundering, rapine, spoliation; despoilation, plunder, rifling, sack, spoils.

pillar n column, pier, pilaster, post, shaft, stanchion; maintainer, prop, support, supporter, upholder.

pilot vb conduct, control, direct, guide, navigate, steer. • adj experimental, model, trial. • n helmsman, navigator, steersman; airman, aviator, conductor, director, flier, guide.

pinch vb compress, contract, cramp, gripe, nip, squeeze; afflict, distress, famish, oppress, straiten, stint; frost, nip; apprehend, arrest; economize, spare, stint. • n gripe, nip; pang, throe; crisis, difficulty, emergency, exigency, oppression, pressure, push, strait, stress.

pine vb decay, decline, droop, fade, flag, languish, waste, wilt, wither; desire, long, yearn.

pinion vb bind, chain, fasten, fetter, maim, restrain, shackle. • n pennon, wing; feather, quill, pen, plume, wing; fetter.

pinnacle n minaret, turret; acme, apex, height, peak, summit, top, zenith.

pious adj filial; devout, godly, holy, religious, reverential, righteous, saintly.

piquant adj biting, highly flavored, piercing, prickling, pungent, sharp, stinging; interesting, lively, racy, sparkling, stimulating; cutting, keen, pointed, severe, strong, tart.

pique vb goad, incite, instigate, spur, stimulate, urge; affront, chafe, displease, fret, incense, irritate, nettle, offend, provoke, sting, vex, wound. • n annoyance, displeasure, irritation, offence, resentment, vexation.

pirate vb copy, crib, plagiarize, reproduce, steal. • n buccaneer, corsair, freebooter, marauder, picaroon, privateer, seadog, sea-robber, sea-rover, sea wolf.

pit vb match, oppose; dent, gouge, hole, mark, nick, notch, scar. • n cavity, hole, hollow; crater, dent, depression, dint, excavation, well; abyss, chasm, gulf; pitfall, snare, trap: auditorium, orchestra.

pitch vb fall, lurch, plunge, reel; light, settle, rest; cast, dart, fling, heave, hurl, lance, launch, send, toss, throw; erect, establish, fix, locate, place, plant, set, settle, station. • n degree, extent, height, intensity, measure, modulation, rage, rate; declivity, descent, inclination, slope; cast, jerk, plunge, throw, toss; place, position, spot; field, ground; line, patter.

piteous adj affecting, distressing, doleful, grievous, mournful, pathetic, rueful, sorrowful, woeful; deplorable, lamentable, miserable, pitiable, wretched; compassionate, tender.

pith n chief, core, essence, heart, gist, kernel, marrow, part, quintessence, soul, substance; importance, moment, weight; cogency, force, energy, strength, vigor.

pithy adj cogent, energetic, forcible, powerful; compact, concise, brief, laconic, meaty, pointed, short, sententious, substantial, terse; corky, porous.

pitiable adj deplorable, lamentable, miserable, pathetic, piteous, pitiable, woeful, wretched; abject, base, contemptible, despicable, disreputable, insignificant, low, paltry, mean, rascally, sorry, vile, worthless.

pitiably adv deplorably, distressingly, grievously, lamentably, miserably, pathetically, piteously, woefully, wretchedly.

pitiful adj compassionate, kind, lenient, merciful, mild, sympathetic, tender, tenderhearted; deplorable, lamentable, miserable, pathetic, piteous, pitiable, wretched; abject, base, contemptible, despicable, disreputable, insignificant, mean, paltry, rascally, sorry, vile, worthless.

pitiless adj cruel, hardhearted, implacable, inexorable, merciless, unmerciful, relentless, remorseless, unfeeling, unpitying, unrelenting, unsympathetic.

pittance n allowance, allotment, alms, charity, dole, gift; driblet, drop, insufficiency, mite, modicum, trifle.

pity vb commiserate, condole, sympathize. • n clemency, commiseration, compassion, condolence, fellow-feeling, grace, humanity, leniency, mercy, quarter, sympathy, tenderheartedness.

pivot vb depend, hinge, turn. • n axis, axle, center, focus, hinge, joint.

place vb arrange, bestow, commit, deposit, dispose, fix, install, lay, locate, lodge, orient, orientate, pitch, plant, pose, put, seat, set, settle, situate, stand, station, rest; allocate, arrange, class, classify, identify, order, organize, recognize; appoint, assign, commission, establish, induct, nominate. • *n* area, courtyard, square; bounds, district, division, locale, locality, location, part, position, premises, quarter, region, scene, site, situation, spot, station, tract, whereabouts; calling, charge, employment, function, occupation, office, pitch, post; calling, condition, grade, precedence, rank, sphere, stakes, standing; abode, building, dwelling, habitation, mansion, residence, seat; city, town, village; fort, fortress, stronghold; paragraph, part, passage, portion; ground, occasion, opportunity, reason, room; lieu, stead.

placid *adj* calm, collected, composed, cool, equable, gentle, peaceful, quiet, serene, tranquil, undisturbed, unexcitable, unmoved, unruffled, halcyon, mild, serene.

plague *vb* afflict, annoy, badger, bore, bother, pester, chafe, disquiet, distress, disturb, embarrass, harass, fret, gall, harry, hector, incommode, irritate, molest, perplex, tantalize, tease, torment, trouble, vex, worry. • *n* disease, pestilence, pest; affliction, annoyance, curse, molestation, nuisance, thorn, torment, trouble, vexation, worry.

plain *adj* dull, even, flat, level, plane, smooth, uniform; clear, open, unencumbered, uninterrupted; apparent, certain, conspicuous, evident, distinct, glaring, manifest, notable, notorious, obvious, overt, palpable, patent, prominent, pronounced, staring, transparent, unmistakable, visible; explicit, intelligible, perspicuous, unambiguous, unequivocal; homely, ugly; aboveboard, blunt, crude, candid, direct, downright, frank, honest, ingenuous, open, openhearted, sincere, single-minded, straightforward, undesigning, unreserved, unsophisticated; artless, common, natural, simple, unaffected, unlearned; absolute, mere, unmistakable; clear, direct, easy; audible, articulate, definite; frugal, homely; unadorned, unfigured, unornamented, unvariegated. • *n* expanse, flats, grassland, pampas, plateau, prairie, steppe, stretch.

plaint *n* complaint, cry, lament, lamentation, moan, wail.

plaintiff *n* accuser, prosecutor.

plaintive *adj* dirge-like, doleful, grievous, melancholy, mournful, piteous, rueful, sad, sorrowful, woeful.

plan *vb* arrange, calculate, concert, delineate, devise, diagram, figure, premeditate, project, represent, study; concoct, conspire, contrive, design, digest, hatch, invent, maneuvre, machinate, plot, prepare, scheme. • *n* chart, delineation, diagram, draught, drawing, layout, map, plot, sketch; arrangement, conception, contrivance, design, device, idea, method, program, project, proposal, proposition, scheme, system; cabal, conspiracy, intrigue, machination; custom, process, way.

plane *vb* even, flatten, level, smooth; float, fly, glide, skate, skim, soar. • *adj* even, flat, horizontal, level, smooth. • *n* degree, evenness, level, levelness, smoothness; airplane, aircraft; groover, jointer, rabbet, rebate, scraper.

plant *vb* bed, sow; breed, engender; direct, point, set; colonize, furnish, inhabit, settle; establish, introduce; deposit, establish, fix, found, hide. • *n* herb, organism, vegetable; establishment, equipment, factory, works.

plaster *vb* bedaub, coat, cover, smear, spread. • *n* cement, gypsum, mortar, stucco.

plastic *adj* ductile, flexible, formative, moldable, pliable, pliant, soft.

platitude *n* dullness, flatness, insipidity, mawkishness; banality, commonplace, truism; balderdash, chatter, flummery, fudge, jargon, moonshine, nonsense, palaver, stuff, trash, twaddle, verbiage.

plaudit *n* acclaim, acclamation, applause, approbation, clapping, commendation, encomium, praise.

plausible *adj* believable, credible, probable, reasonable; bland, fair-spoken, glib, smooth, suave.

play *vb* caper, disport, frisk, frolic, gambol, revel, romp, skip, sport; dally, flirt, idle, toy, trifle, wanton; flutter, hover, wave; act, impersonate, perform, personate, represent; bet, gamble, stake, wager. • *n* amusement, exercise, frolic, gambols, game, jest, pastime, prank, romp, sport; gambling, gaming; act, comedy, drama, farce, performance, tragedy; action, motion, movement; elbowroom, freedom, latitude, movement, opportunity, range, scope, sweep, swing, use.

playful *adj* frisky, frolicsome, gamesome, jolly, kittenish, merry, mirthful, rollicking, sportive; amusing, arch, humorous, lively, mischievous, roguish, skittish, sprightly, vivacious.

plead *vb* answer, appeal, argue, reason; argue, defend, discuss, reason, rejoin; beg, beseech, entreat, implore, petition, sue, supplicate.

pleasant *adj* acceptable, agreeable, delectable, delightful, enjoyable, grateful, gratifying, nice, pleasing, pleasurable, prepossessing, seemly, welcome; cheerful, enlivening, good-humored, gracious, likable, lively, merry, sportive, sprightly, vivacious; amusing, facetious, humorous, jocose, jocular, sportive, witty.

please *vb* charm, delight, elate, gladden, gratify, pleasure, rejoice; content, oblige, satisfy; choose, like, prefer.

pleasure *n* cheer, comfort, delight, delectation, elation, enjoyment, exhilaration, joy, gladness, gratifying, gusto, relish, satisfaction, solace; amusement, diversion, entertainment, indulgence, refreshment, treat; gratification, luxury, sensuality, voluptuousness; choice, desire, preference, purpose, will, wish; favor, kindness.

plebeian *adj* base, common, ignoble, low, lowborn, mean, obscure, popular, vulgar. • *n* commoner, peasant, proletarian.

pledge *vb* hypothecate, mortgage, pawn, plight; affiance, bind, contract, engage, plight, promise. • *n* collateral, deposit, gage, pawn; earnest, guarantee, security; hostage, security.

plenipotentiary *n* ambassador, envoy, legate, minister.

plenitude *n* abundance, completeness, fullness, plenteousness, plentifulness, plenty, plethora, profusion, repletion.

plentiful *adj* abundant, ample, copious, full, enough, exuberant, fruitful, luxuriant, plenteous, productive, sufficient.

plenty *n* abundance, adequacy, affluence, amplitude, copiousness, enough, exuberance, fertility, fruitfulness, fullness, overflow, plenteousness, plentifulness, plethora, profusion, sufficiency, supply.

pleonastic *adj* circumlocutory, diffuse, redundant, superfluous, tautological, verbose, wordy.

plethora *n* fullness, plenitude, repletion; excess, redundance, redundancy, superabundance, superfluity, surfeit.

pliable *adj* flexible, limber, lithe, lithesome, pliable, pliant, supple; adaptable, compliant, docile, ductile, facile, manageable, obsequious, tractable, yielding.

plight[1] *n* case, category, complication, condition, dilemma, imbroglio, mess, muddle, pass, predicament, scrape, situation, state, strait.

plight[2] *vb* avow, contract, covenant, engage, honor, pledge, promise, propose, swear, vow. • *n* avowal, contract, covenant, oath, pledge, promise, troth, vow, word; affiancing, betrothal, engagement.

plod *vb* drudge, lumber, moil, persevere, persist, toil, trudge.

plot[1] *vb* connive, conspire, intrigue, machinate, scheme; brew, concoct, contrive, devise, frame, hatch, compass, plan, project; chart, map. • *n* blueprint, chart, diagram, draft, outline, plan, scenario, skeleton; cabal, combination, complicity, connivance, conspiracy, intrigue, plan, project, scheme, stratagem; script, story, subject, theme, thread, topic.

plot[2] *n* field, lot, parcel, patch, piece, plat, section, tract.

pluck[1] *vb* cull, gather, pick; jerk, pull, snatch, tear, tug, twitch.

pluck[2] *n* backbone, bravery, courage, daring, determination, energy, force, grit, hardihood, heroism, indomitability, indomitableness, manhood, mettle, nerve, resolution, spirit, valor.

plump[1] *adj* bonny, bouncing, buxom, chubby, corpulent, fat, fleshy, full-figured, obese, portly, rotund, round, sleek, stout, well-rounded; distended, full, swollen, tumid.

plump[2] *vb* dive, drop, plank, plop, plunge, plunk, put; choose, favor, support • *adj* blunt, complete, direct, downright, full, unqualified, unreserved.

plunder *vb* desolate, despoil, devastate, fleece, forage, harry, loot, maraud, pillage, raid, ransack, ravage, rifle, rob, sack, spoil, spoliate, plunge. • *n* freebooting, devastation, harrying, marauding, rapine, robbery, sack; booty, pillage, prey, spoil.

ply[1] *vb* apply, employ, exert, manipulate, wield; exercise, practice; assail, belabor, beset, press; importune, solicit, urge; offer, present.

ply[2] *vb* fold, layer, plait, twist; bent, bias, direction, turn.

pocket *vb* appropriate, steal; bear, endure, suffer, tolerate. • *n* cavity, cul-de-sac, hollow, pouch, receptacle.

poignant *adj* bitter, intense, penetrating, pierce, severe, sharp; acrid, biting, mordacious, piquant, prickling, pungent, sharp, stinging; caustic, irritating, keen, mordant, pointed, satirical, severe.

point *vb* acuminate, sharpen; aim, direct, level; designate indicate, show; punctuate. • *n* apex, needle, nib, pin, prong, spike, stylus, tip; cape, headland, projection, promontory; eve, instant, moment, period, verge; place, site, spot, stage, station; condition, degree, grade, state; aim, design, end, intent, limit, object, purpose; nicety, pique, punctilio, trifle; position, proposition, question, text, theme, thesis; aspect, matter, respect; characteristic, peculiarity, trait; character, mark, stop; dot, jot, speck; epigram, quip, quirk, sally, witticism; poignancy, sting.

point-blank *adj* categorical, direct, downright, explicit, express, plain, straight • *adv* categorically, directly, flush, full, plainly, right, straight.

pointless *adj* blunt, obtuse; aimless, dull, flat, fruitless, futile, meaningless, vague, vapid, stupid.

poise *vb* balance, float, hang, hover, support, suspend. • *n* aplomb, balance, composure, dignity, equanimity, equilibrium, equipoise, serenity.

poison *vb* adulterate, contaminate, corrupt, defile, embitter, envenom, impair, infect, intoxicate, pollute, taint, vitiate. • *adj* deadly, lethal, poisonous, toxic. • *n* bane, canker, contagion, pest, taint, toxin, venom, virulence, virus.

poisonous *adj* baneful, corruptive, deadly, fatal, noxious, pestiferous, pestilential, toxic, venomous.

poke *vb* jab, jog, punch, push, shove, thrust; interfere, meddle, pry, snoop. • *n* jab, jog, punch, push, shove, thrust; bag, pocket, pouch, sack.

pole[1] *n* caber, mast, post, rod, spar, staff, stick; bar, beam, pile, shaft; oar, paddle, scull.

pole[2] *n* axis, axle, hub, pivot, spindle.

poles *npl* antipodes, antipoles, counterpoles, opposites.

policy *n* administration, government, management, rule; plan, plank, platform, role; art, address, cunning, discretion, prudence, shrewdness, skill, stratagem, strategy, tactics; acumen, astuteness, wisdom, wit.

polish *vb* brighten, buff, burnish, furbish, glaze, gloss, scour, shine, smooth; civilize,

refine. • *n* brightness, brilliance, brilliancy, luster, splendor; accomplishment, elegance, finish, grace, refinement.

polished *adj* bright, burnished, glossed, glossy, lustrous, shining, smooth; accomplished, cultivated, elegant, finished, graceful, polite, refined.

polite *adj* attentive, accomplished, affable, chivalrous, civil, complaisant, courtly, courteous, cultivated, elegant, gallant, genteel, gentle, gentlemanly, gracious, mannerly, obliging, polished, refined, suave, urbane, well, well-bred, well-mannered.

politic *adj* civic, civil, political; astute, discreet, judicious, long-headed, noncommittal, provident, prudent, prudential, sagacious, wary, wise; artful, crafty, cunning, diplomatic, expedient, foxy, ingenious, intriguing, Machiavellian, shrewd, skilful, sly, subtle, strategic, timeserving, unscrupulous, wily; well-adapted, well-devised.

political *adj* civic, civil, national, politic, public.

pollute *vb* defile, foul, soil, taint; contaminate, corrupt, debase, demoralize, deprave, impair, infect, pervert, poison, stain, tarnish, vitiate; desecrate, profane; abuse, debauch, defile, deflower, dishonor, ravish, violate.

pollution *n* abomination, contamination, corruption, defilement, foulness, impurity, pollutedness, taint, uncleanness, vitiation.

poltroon *n* coward, crave, dastard, milksop, recreant, skulk, sneak.

pomp *n* display, flourish, grandeur, magnificence, ostentation, pageant, pageantry, parade, pompousness, pride, show, splendor, state, style.

pompous *adj* august, boastful, bombastic, dignified, gorgeous, grand, inflated, lofty, magisterial, ostentatious, pretentious, showy, splendid, stately, sumptuous, superb, vainglorious.

ponder *vb* cogitate, consider, contemplate, deliberate, examine, meditate, muse, reflect, study, weigh.

ponderous *adj* bulky, heavy, massive, weighty; dull, labored, slow-moving; important, momentous; forcible, mighty.

poniard *n* dagger, dirk, stiletto.

poor *adj* indigent, necessitous, needy, pinched, straitened; destitute, distressed, embarrassed, impecunious, impoverished, insolvent, moneyless, penniless, poverty-stricken, reduced, seedy, unprosperous;

emaciated, gaunt, spare, lank, lean, shrunk, skinny, spare, thin; barren, fruitless, sterile, unfertile, unfruitful, unproductive, unprolific; flimsy, inadequate, insignificant, insufficient, paltry, slender, slight, small, trifling, trivial, unimportant, valueless, worthless; decrepit, delicate, feeble, frail, infirm, unsound, weak; inferior, shabby, valueless, worthless; bad, beggarly, contemptible, despicable, humble, inferior, low, mean, pitiful, sorry; bald, cold, dry, dull, feeble, frigid, jejune, languid, meager, prosaic, prosing, spiritless, tame, vapid, weak; ill-fated, ill-starred, inauspicious, indifferent, luckless, miserable, pitiable, unfavorable, unfortunate, unhappy, unlucky, wretched; deficient, imperfect, inadequate, insufficient, mediocre, scant, scanty; faulty, unsatisfactory; feeble.

populace n citizens, crowd, inhabitants, masses, people, public, throng.

popular adj plebeian, public; comprehensible, easy, familiar, plain; acceptable, accepted, accredited, admired, approved, favored, liked, pleasing, praised, received; common, current, prevailing, prevalent; cheap, inexpensive.

pore[1] n hole, opening, orifice, spiracle.

pore[2] vb brood, consider, dwell, examine, gaze, read, study.

porous adj honeycombed, light, loose, open, penetrable, perforated, permeable, pervious, sandy.

porridge n broth, gruel, mush, pap, pottage, soup.

port[1] n anchorage, harbor, haven, shelter; door, entrance, gate, passageway; embrasure, porthole.

port[2] n air, appearance, bearing, behavior, carriage, demeanor, deportment, mien, presence.

portable adj convenient, handy, light, manageable, movable, portative, transmissible.

portend vb augur, betoken, bode, forebode, foreshadow, foretoken, indicate, presage, procrastinate, signify, threaten.

portent n augury, omen, presage, prognosis, sign, warning; marvel, phenomenon, wonder.

portion vb allot, distribute, divide, parcel; endow, supply. • n bit, fragment, morsel, part, piece, scrap, section; allotment, contingent, dividend, division, lot, measure, quantity, quota, ration, share; inheritance.

portly adj dignified, grand, imposing,

magisterial, majestic, stately; bulky, burly, corpulent, fleshy, large, plump, round, stout.

portray vb act, draw, depict, delineate, describe, paint, picture, represent, pose, position, sketch.

pose vb arrange, place, set; bewilder, confound, dumbfound, embarrass, mystify, nonplus, perplex, place, puzzle, set, stagger; affect, attitudinize. • n attitude, posture; affectation, air, facade, mannerism, pretence, role.

position vb arrange, array, fix, locate, place, put, set, site, stand. • n locality, place, post, site, situation, spot, station; relation; attitude, bearing, posture; affirmation, assertion, doctrine, predication, principle, proposition, thesis; caste, dignity, honor, rank, standing, status; circumstance, condition, phase, place, state; berth, billet, incumbency, place, post, situation.

positive adj categorical, clear, defined, definite, determinate, explicit, express, expressed, precise, unequivocal, unmistakable, unqualified; absolute, actual, real, substantial, true, veritable; assured, certain, confident, convinced, sure; decisive, incontrovertible, indisputable, indubitable, inescapable; imperative, unconditional, undeniable; decided, dogmatic, emphatic, obstinate, overbearing, overconfident, peremptory, stubborn, tenacious.

possess vb control, have, hold, keep, obsess, obtain, occupy, own, seize.

possession n monopoly, ownership, proprietorship; control, occupation, occupancy, retention, tenancy, tenure; bedevilment, lunacy, madness, obsession; (pl) assets, effects, estate, property, wealth.

possessor n owner, proprietor.

possible adj conceivable, contingent, imaginable, potential; accessible, feasible, likely, practical, practicable, workable.

possibly adv haply, maybe, mayhap, peradventure, perchance, perhaps.

post[1] vb advertise, announce, inform, placard, publish; brand, defame, disgrace, vilify; enter, slate, record, register. • n column, picket, pier, pillar, stake, support.

post[2] vb establish, fix, place, put, set, station. • n billet, employment, office, place, position, quarter, seat, situation, station.

post[3] vb drop, dispatch, mail. • n carrier, courier, express, mercury, messenger, postman; dispatch, haste, hurry, speed.

posterior *adj* after, ensuing, following, later, latter, postprandial, subsequent. • *n* back, buttocks, hind, hinder, rump.

posterity *n* descendants, offspring, progeny, seed; breed, brood, children, family, heirs, issue.

postpone *vb* adjourn, defer, delay, procrastinate, prorogue, retard.

postscript *n* addition, afterthought, appendix, supplement.

postulate *vb* assume, presuppose; beseech, entreat, solicit, supplicate. • *n* assumption, axiom, conjecture, hypothesis, proposition, speculation, supposition, theory.

posture *vb* attitudinize, pose. • *n* attitude, pose, position, condition, disposition, mood, phase, state.

pot *n* kettle, pan, saucepan, skillet; can, cup, mug, tankard; crock, jar, jug.

potency *n* efficacy, energy, force, intensity, might, power, strength, vigor; authority, control, influence, sway.

potent *adj* efficacious, forceful, forcible, intense, powerful, strong, virile; able, authoritative, capable, efficient, mighty, puissant, strong; cogent, influential.

potentate *n* emperor, king, monarch, prince, sovereign, ruler.

potential *adj* able, capable, inherent, latent, possible. • *n* ability, capability, dynamic, possibility, potentiality, power.

pother *vb* beset, bewilder, confound, confuse, embarrass, harass, perplex, pose, puzzle, tease. • *n* bustle, commotion, confusion, disturbance, flutter, fuss, huddle, hurly-burly, rumpus, tumult, turbulence, turmoil.

pound[1] *vb* beat, strike, thump; bray, bruise, comminute, crush, levigate, pulverize, triturate; confound, coop, enclose, impound.

pound[2] *n* enclosure, fold, pen.

pour *vb* cascade, emerge, flood, flow, gush, issue, rain, shower, stream.

pouting *adj* bad-tempered, cross, ill-humored, moody, morose, sulky, sullen.

poverty *n* destitution, difficulties, distress, impecuniosity, impecuniousness, indigence, necessity, need, neediness, penury, privation, straits, want; beggary, mendicancy, pauperism, pennilessness; dearth, jejuneness, lack, scantiness, sparingness, meagerness; exiguity, paucity, poorness, smallness; humbleness, inferiority, lowliness; barrenness, sterility, unfruitfulness, unproductiveness.

power *n* ability, ableness, capability, cogency, competency, efficacy, faculty, might, potency, validity, talent; energy, force, strength, virtue; capacity, susceptibility; endowment, faculty, gift, talent; ascendancy, authoritativeness, authority, carte blanche, command, control, domination, dominion, government, influence, omnipotence, predominance, prerogative, pressure, proxy, puissance, rule, sovereignty, sway, warrant; governor, monarch, potentate, ruler, sovereign; army, host, troop.

powerful *adj* mighty, potent, puissant; able-bodied, herculean, muscular, nervous, robust, sinewy, strong, sturdy, vigorous, vivid; able, commanding, dominating, forceful, forcible, overpowering; cogent, effective, effectual, efficacious, efficient, energetic, influential, operative, valid.

practicable *adj* achievable, attainable, bearable, feasible, performable, possible, workable; operative, passable, penetrable.

practical *adj* hardheaded, matter-of-fact, pragmatic, pragmatical; able, experienced, practiced, proficient, qualified, trained, skilled, thoroughbred, versed; effective, useful, virtual, workable.

practice *n* custom, habit, manner, method, repetition; procedure, usage, use; application, drill, exercise, pursuit; action, acts, behavior, conduct, dealing, proceeding.

practise *vb* apply, do, exercise, follow, observe, perform, perpetrate, pursue.

practiced *adj* able, accomplished, experienced, instructed, practical, proficient, qualified, skilled, thoroughbred, trained, versed.

pragmatic *adj* impertinent, intermeddling, interfering, intrusive, meddlesome, meddling, obtrusive, officious, over-busy; earthy, hard-headed, matter-of-fact, practical, pragmatical, realistic, sensible, stolid.

praise *vb* approbate, acclaim, applaud, approve, commend; celebrate, compliment, eulogize, extol, flatter, laud; adore, bless, exalt, glorify, magnify, worship. • *n* acclaim, approbation, approval, commendation; encomium, eulogy, glorification, laud, laudation, panegyric; exaltation, extolling, glorification, homage, tribute, worship; celebrity, distinction, fame, glory, honor, renown; desert, merit, praiseworthiness.

praiseworthy *adj* commendable, creditable, good, laudable, meritorious.

prank n antic, caper, escapade, frolic, gambol, trick.

prate vb babble, chatter, gabble, jabber, palaver, prattle, tattle. • n chatter, gabble, nonsense, palaver, prattle, twaddle.

pray vb ask, beg, beseech, conjure, entreat, implore, importune, invoke, petition, request, solicit, supplicate.

prayer n beseeching, entreaty, imploration, petition, request, solicitation, suit, supplication; adoration, devotion(s), litany, invocation, orison, praise, suffrage.

preach vb declare, deliver, proclaim, pronounce, publish; inculcate, press, teach, urge; exhort, lecture, moralize, sermonize.

preamble n foreword, introduction, preface, prelude, prologue.

precarious adj critical, doubtful, dubious, equivocal, hazardous, insecure, perilous, unassured, riskful, risky, uncertain, unsettled, unstable, unsteady.

precaution n care, caution, circumspection, foresight, forethought, providence, prudence, safeguard, wariness; anticipation, premonition, provision.

precautionary adj preservative, preventative, provident.

precede vb antedate, forerun, head, herald, introduce, lead, utter.

precedence n advantage, antecedence, lead, pre-eminence, preference, priority, superiority, supremacy.

precedent n antecedent, authority, custom, example, instance, model, pattern, procedure, standard, usage.

precept n behest, bidding, canon, charge, command, commandment, decree, dictate, edict, injunction, instruction, law, mandate, ordinance, ordination, order, regulation; direction, doctrine, maxim, principle, teaching, rubric, rule.

preceptor n instructor, lecturer, master, pedagogue, professor, schoolteacher, teacher, tutor.

precinct n border, bound, boundary, confine, environs, frontier, enclosure, limit, list, march, neighborhood, purlieus, term, terminus; area, district.

precious adj costly, inestimable, invaluable, priceless, prized, valuable; adored, beloved, cherished, darling, dear, idolized, treasured; fastidious, overnice, over-refined, precise.

precipice n bluff, cliff, crag, steep.

precipitate vb advance, accelerate, dispatch, expedite, forward, further, hasten, hurry, plunge, press, quicken, speed. • adj hasty, hurried, headlong, impetuous, indiscreet, overhasty, rash, reckless; abrupt, sudden, violent.

precipitous adj abrupt, cliffy, craggy, perpendicular, uphill, sheer, steep.

precise adj accurate, correct, definite, distinct, exact, explicit, express, nice, pointed, severe, strict, unequivocal, well-defined; careful, scrupulous; ceremonious, finical, formal, prim, punctilious, rigid, starched, stiff.

precision n accuracy, correctness, definiteness, distinctness, exactitude, exactness, nicety, preciseness.

preclude vb bar, check, debar, hinder, inhibit, obviate, prevent, prohibit, restrain, stop.

precocious adj advanced, forward, overforward, premature.

preconcert vb concoct, prearrange, predetermine, premeditate, prepare.

precursor n antecedent, cause, forerunner, predecessor; harbinger, herald, messenger, pioneer; omen, presage, sign.

precursory adj antecedent, anterior, forerunning, precedent, preceding, previous, prior; initiatory, introductory, precursive, prefatory, preliminary, prelusive, prelusory, premonitory, preparatory, prognosticative.

predatory adj greedy, pillaging, plundering, predacious, rapacious, ravaging, ravenous, voracious.

predestination n doom, fate, foredoom, foreordainment, foreordination, necessity, predetermination, preordination.

predicament n attitude, case, condition, plight, position, posture, situation, state; corner, dilemma, emergency, exigency, fix, hole, impasse, mess, pass, pinch, push, quandary, scrape.

predict vb augur, betoken, bode, divine, forebode, forecast, foredoom, foresee, forespeak, foretell, foretoken, forewarn, portend, prognosticate, prophesy, read, signify, soothsay.

predilection n bent, bias, desire, fondness, inclination, leaning, liking, love, partiality, predisposition, preference, prejudice, prepossession.

predisposition n aptitude, bent, bias, disposition, inclination, leaning, proclivity, proneness, propensity, willingness.

predominant *adj* ascendant, controlling, dominant, overruling, prevailing, prevalent, reigning, ruling, sovereign, supreme.

predominate *vb* dominate, preponderate, prevail, rule.

pre-eminent *adj* chief, conspicuous, consummate, controlling, distinguished, excellent, excelling, paramount, peerless, predominant, renowned, superior, supreme, surpassing, transcendent, unequalled.

preface *vb* begin, introduce, induct, launch, open, precede. • *n* exordium, foreword, induction, introduction, preamble, preliminary, prelude, prelusion, premise, proem, prologue, prolusion.

prefatory *adj* antecedent, initiative, introductory, precursive, precursory, preliminary, prelusive, prelusory, preparatory, proemial.

prefer *vb* address, offer, present, proffer, tender; advance, elevate, promote, raise; adopt, choose, elect, fancy, pick, select, wish.

preference *n* advancement, choice, election, estimation, precedence, priority, selection.

preferment *n* advancement, benefice, dignity, elevation, exaltation, promotion.

pregnant *adj* big, enceinte, parturient; fraught, full, important, replete, significant, weighty; fecund, fertile, fruitful, generative, potential, procreant, procreative, productive, prolific.

prejudice *vb* bias, incline, influence, turn, warp; damage, diminish, hurt, impair, injure. • *n* bias, intolerance, partiality, preconception, predilection, prejudgement, prepossession, unfairness; damage, detriment, disadvantage, harm, hurt, impairment, injury, loss, mischief.

prejudiced *adj* biased, bigoted, influenced, one-sided, partial, partisan, unfair.

preliminary *adj* antecedent, initiatory, introductory, precedent, precursive, precursory, prefatory, prelusive, prelusory, preparatory, previous, prior, proemial. • *n* beginning, initiation, introduction, opening, preamble, preface, prelude, start.

prelude *n* introduction, opening, overture, prelusion, preparation, voluntary; exordium, preamble, preface, preliminary, proem.

premature *adj* hasty, ill-considered, precipitate, unmatured, unprepared, unripe, unseasonable, untimely.

premeditation *n* deliberation, design, forethought, intention, prearrangement, predetermination, purpose.

premise *vb* introduce, preamble, preface, prefix. • *n* affirmation, antecedent, argument, assertion, assumption, basis, foundation, ground, hypothesis, position, premiss, presupposition, proposition, support, thesis, theorem.

premium *n* bonus, bounty, encouragement, fee, gift, guerdon, meed, payment, prize, recompense, remuneration, reward; appreciation, enhancement.

premonition *n* caution, foreboding, foreshadowing, forewarning, indication, omen, portent, presage, presentiment, sign, warning.

preoccupied *adj* absent, absentminded, abstracted, dreaming, engrossed, inadvertent, inattentive, lost, musing, unobservant.

prepare *vb* adapt, adjust, fit, qualify; arrange, concoct, fabricate, make, order, plan, procure, provide.

preponderant *adj* outweighing, overbalancing, preponderating.

prepossessing *adj* alluring, amiable, attractive, bewitching, captivating, charming, engaging, fascinating, inviting, taking, winning.

preposterous *adj* absurd, excessive, exorbitant, extravagant, foolish, improper, irrational, monstrous, nonsensical, perverted, ridiculous, unfit, unreasonable, wrong.

prerogative *n* advantage, birthright, claim, franchise, immunity, liberty, privilege, right.

presage *vb* divine, forebode; augur, betoken, bode, foreshadow, foretell, foretoken, indicate, portend, predict, prognosticate, prophesy, signify, soothsay. • *n* augury, auspice, boding, foreboding, foreshowing, indication, omen, portent, prognostication, sign, token; foreknowledge, precognition, prediction, premonition, presentiment, prophecy.

prescribe *vb* advocate, appoint, command, decree, dictate, direct, enjoin, establish, institute, ordain, order.

presence *n* attendance, company, inhabitance, inhabitancy, nearness, neighborhood, occupancy, propinquity, proximity, residence, ubiquity, vicinity; air, appearance, carriage, demeanor, mien, personality.

present[1] *adj* near; actual, current, existing, happening, immediate, instant, living; available, quick, ready; attentive, favorable. • *n* now, time being, today.

present[2] *n* benefaction, boon, donation, favor, gift, grant, gratuity, largesse, offering.

present[3] *vb* introduce, nominate; exhibit, offer; bestow, confer, give, grant; deliver, hand; advance, express, prefer, proffer, tender.

presentiment *n* anticipation, apprehension, foreboding, forecast, foretaste, forethought, prescience.

presently *adv* anon, directly, forthwith, immediately, shortly, soon.

preservation *n* cherishing, conservation, curing, maintenance, protection, support; safety, salvation, security; integrity, keeping, soundness.

preserve *vb* defend, guard, keep, protect, rescue, save, secure, shield; maintain, uphold, sustain, support; conserve, economize, husband, retain. • *n* comfit, compote, confection, confiture, conserve, jam, jelly, marmalade, sweetmeat; enclosure, warren.

preside *vb* control, direct, govern, manage, officiate.

press *vb* compress, crowd, crush, squeeze; flatten, iron, smooth; clasp, embrace, hug; force, compel, constrain; emphasize, enforce, enjoin, inculcate, stress, urge; hasten, hurry, push, rush; crowd, throng; entreat, importune, solicit. • *n* crowd, crush, multitude, throng; hurry, pressure, urgency; case, closet, cupboard, repository.

pressing *adj* constraining, critical, distressing, imperative, importunate, persistent, serious, urgent, vital.

pressure *n* compressing, crushing, squeezing; influence, force; compulsion, exigency, hurry, persuasion, press, stress, urgency; affliction, calamity, difficulty, distress, embarrassment, grievance, oppression, straits; impression, stamp.

prestidigitation *n* conjuring, juggling, legerdemain, sleight-of-hand.

prestige *n* credit, distinction, importance, influence, reputation, weight.

presume *vb* anticipate, apprehend, assume, believe, conjecture, deduce, expect, infer, surmise, suppose, think; consider, presuppose; dare, undertake, venture.

presumption *n* anticipation, assumption, belief, concession, conclusion, condition, conjecture, deduction, guess, hypothesis, inference, opinion, supposition, understanding; arrogance, assurance, audacity, boldness, brass, effrontery, forwardness, haughtiness, presumptuousness; probability.

presumptuous *adj* arrogant, assuming, audacious, bold, brash, forward, irreverent, insolent, intrusive, presuming; foolhardy, overconfident, rash.

pretence *n* affectation, cloak, color, disguise, mask, semblance, show, simulation, veil, window-dressing; excuse, evasion, fabrication, feigning, makeshift, pretext, sham, subterfuge; claim, pretension.

pretend *vb* affect, counterfeit, deem, dissemble, fake, falsify, feign, sham, simulate; act, imagine, lie, profess; aspire, claim.

pretension *n* assertion, assumption, claim, demand, pretence; affectation, airs, conceit, ostentation, pertness, pretentiousness, priggishness, vanity.

pretentious *adj* affected, assuming, conceited, conspicuous, ostentatious, presuming, priggish, showy, tawdry, unnatural, vain.

preternatural *adj* abnormal, anomalous, extraordinary, inexplicable, irregular, miraculous, mysterious, odd, peculiar, strange, unnatural.

pretext *n* affectation, appearance, blind, cloak, color, guise, mask, pretence, semblance, show, simulation, veil; excuse, justification, plea, vindication.

pretty *adj* attractive, beautiful, bonny, comely, elegant, fair, handsome, neat, pleasing, trim; affected, foppish. • *adv* fairly, moderately, quite, rather, somewhat.

prevail *vb* overcome, succeed, triumph, win; obtain, predominate, preponderate, reign, rule.

prevailing *adj* controlling, dominant, effectual, efficacious, general, influential, operative, overruling, persuading, predominant, preponderant, prevalent, ruling, successful.

prevalent *adj* ascendant, compelling, efficacious, governing, predominant, prevailing, successful, superior; extensive, general, rife, widespread.

prevaricate *vb* cavil, deviate, dodge, equivocate, evade, palter, pettifog, quibble, shift, shuffle, tergiversate.

prevent *vb* bar, check, debar, deter, forestall,

help, hinder, impede, inhibit, intercept, interrupt, obstruct, obviate, preclude, prohibit, restrain, save, stop, thwart.

prevention n anticipation, determent, deterrence, deterrent, frustration, hindrance, interception, interruption, obstruction, preclusion, prohibition, restriction, stoppage.

previous adj antecedent, anterior, earlier, foregoing, foregone, former, precedent, preceding, prior.

prey vb devour, eat, feed on, live off; exploit, intimidate, terrorize; burden, distress, haunt, oppress, trouble, worry. • n booty, loot, pillage, plunder, prize, rapine, spoil; food, game, kill, quarry, victim; depredation, ravage.

price vb assess, estimate, evaluate, rate, value. • n amount, cost, expense, outlay, value; appraisal, charge, estimation, excellence, figure, rate, quotation, valuation, value, worth; compensation, guerdon, recompense, return, reward.

priceless adj dear, expensive, precious, inestimable, invaluable, valuable; amusing, comic, droll, funny, humorous, killing, rich.

prick vb perforate, pierce, puncture, stick; drive, goad, impel, incite, spur, urge; cut, hurt, mark, pain, sting, wound; hasten, post, ride. • n mark, perforation, point, puncture; prickle, sting, wound.

pride vb boast, brag, crow, preen, revel in. • n conceit, egotism, self-complacency, self-esteem, self-exaltation, self-importance, self-sufficiency, vanity; arrogance, assumption, disdain, haughtiness, hauteur, insolence, loftiness, lordliness, pomposity, presumption, superciliousness, vainglory; decorum, dignity, elevation, self-respect; decoration, glory, ornament, show, splendor.

priest n churchman, clergyman, divine, ecclesiastic, minister, pastor, presbyter.

prim adj demure, formal, nice, precise, prudish, starch, starched, stiff, straitlaced.

primary adj aboriginal, earliest, first, initial, original, prime, primitive, primeval, primordial, pristine; chief, main, principal; basic, elementary, fundamental, preparatory: radical.

prime[1] adj aboriginal, basic, first, initial, original, primal, primary, primeval, primitive, primordial, pristine; chief, foremost,

highest, leading, main, paramount, principal; blooming, early; capital, cardinal, dominant, predominant; excellent, first-class, first-rate, optimal, optimum, quintessential, superlative; beginning, opening. • n beginning, dawn, morning, opening; spring, springtime, youth; bloom, cream, flower, height, heyday, optimum, perfection, quintessence, zenith.

prime[2] vb charge, load, prepare, undercoat; coach, groom, train, tutor.

primeval adj original, primitive, primordial, pristine.

primitive adj aboriginal, first, fundamental, original, primal, primary, prime, primitive, primordial, pristine; ancient, antiquated, crude, old-fashioned, quaint, simple, uncivilized, unsophisticated.

prince n monarch, potentate, ruler, sovereign; dauphin, heir apparent, infant; chief, leader, potentate.

princely adj imperial, regal, royal; august, generous, grand, liberal, magnanimous, magnificent, majestic, munificent, noble, pompous, splendid, superb, titled; dignified, elevated, high-minded, lofty, noble, stately.

principal adj capital, cardinal, chief, essential, first, foremost, highest, leading, main, pre-eminent, prime. • n chief, head, leader; head teacher, master.

principally adv chiefly, essentially, especially, mainly, particularly.

principle n cause, fountain, fountainhead, groundwork, mainspring, nature, origin, source, spring; basis, constituent, element, essence, substratum; assumption, axiom, law, maxim, postulation; doctrine, dogma, impulse, maxim, opinion, precept, rule, tenet, theory; conviction, ground, motive, reason; equity, goodness, honesty, honor, incorruptibility, integrity, justice, probity, rectitude, righteousness, trustiness, truth, uprightness, virtue, worth; faculty, power.

prink vb adorn, deck, decorate; preen, primp, spruce.

print vb engrave, impress, imprint, mark, stamp; issue, publish. • n book, periodical, publication; copy, engraving, photograph, picture; characters, font, fount, lettering, type, typeface.

prior adj antecedent, anterior, earlier, foregoing, precedent, preceding, precursory, previous, superior.

priority n antecedence, anteriority, precedence, pre-eminence, pre-existence, superiority.

priory n abbey, cloister, convent, monastery, nunnery.

prison n confinement, dungeon, gaol, jail, keep, lockup, penitentiary, reformatory; can, clink, cooler, jug.

pristine adj ancient, earliest, first, former, old, original, primary, primeval, primitive, primordial.

privacy n concealment, secrecy; retirement, retreat, seclusion, solitude.

private adj retired, secluded, sequestrated, solitary; individual, own, particular, peculiar, personal, special, unofficial; confidential, privy; clandestine, concealed, hidden, secret. • n GI, soldier, tommy.

privation n bereavement, deprivation, dispossession, loss; destitution, distress, indigence, necessity, need, want; absence, negation; degradation.

privilege n advantage, charter, claim, exemption, favor, franchise, immunity, leave, liberty, license, permission, prerogative, right.

privy adj individual, particular, peculiar, personal, private, special; clandestine, secret; retired, sequestrated.

prize[1] vb appreciate, cherish, esteem, treasure, value.

prize[2] adj best, champion, first-rate, outstanding, winning. • n guerdon, honors, meed, premium, reward; cup, decoration, medal, laurels, palm, trophy; booty, capture, lot, plunder, spoil; advantage, gain, privilege.

probability n chance, prospect, likelihood, presumption; appearance, credibility, credibleness, likeliness, verisimilitude.

probable adj apparent, credible, likely, presumable, reasonable.

probably adv apparently, likely, maybe, perchance, perhaps, presumably, possibly, seemingly.

probation n essay, examination, ordeal, proof, test, trial; novitiate.

probe vb examine, explore, fathom, investigate, measure, prove, scrutinize, search, sift, sound, test, verify. • n examination, exploration, inquiry, investigation, scrutiny, study.

probity n candor, conscientiousness, equity, fairness, faith, goodness, honesty, honor, incorruptibility, integrity, justice, loyalty, morality, principle, rectitude, righteousness, sincerity, soundness, trustworthiness, truth, truthfulness, uprightness, veracity, virtue, worth.

problem adj difficult, intractable, uncontrollable, unruly. • n dilemma, dispute, doubt, enigma, exercise, proposition, puzzle, riddle, theorem.

problematic adj debatable, disputable, doubtful, dubious, enigmatic, problematical, puzzling, questionable, suspicious, uncertain, unsettled.

procedure n conduct, course, custom, management, method, operation, policy, practice, process; act, action, deed, measure, performance, proceeding, step, transaction.

proceed vb advance, continue, go, pass, progress; accrue, arise, come, emanate, ensue, flow, follow, issue, originate, result, spring.

proceeds npl balance, earnings, effects, gain, income, net, produce, products, profits, receipts, returns, yield.

process vb advance, deal with, fulfill, handle, progress; alter, convert, refine, transform. • n advance, course, progress, train; action, conduct, management, measure, mode, operation, performance, practice, procedure, proceeding, step, transaction, way; action, case, suit, trial; outgrowth, projection, protuberance.

procession n cavalcade, cortege, file, march, parade, retinue, train.

proclaim vb advertise, announce, blazon, broach, broadcast, circulate, cry, declare, herald, promulgate, publish, trumpet; ban, outlaw, proscribe.

proclamation n advertisement, announcement, blazon, declaration, promulgation, publication; ban, decree, edict, manifesto, ordinance.

proclivity n bearing, bent, bias, determination, direction, disposition, drift, inclination, leaning, predisposition, proneness, propensity, tendency, turn; aptitude, facility, readiness.

procrastinate vb adjourn, defer, delay, postpone, prolong, protract, retard; neglect, omit; lag, loiter.

procrastination n delay, dilatoriness, postponement, protraction, slowness, tardiness.

procreate vb beget, breed, engender, generate, produce, propagate.

procurable adj acquirable, compassable, obtainable.

procurator n agent, attorney, deputy, proctor, proxy, representative, solicitor.

procure vb acquire, gain, get, obtain; cause, compass, contrive, effect.

procurer n bawd, pander, pimp.

prodigal adj abundant, dissipated, excessive, extravagant, generous, improvident, lavish, profuse, reckless, squandering, thriftless, unthrifty, wasteful. • n spendthrift, squanderer, waster, wastrel.

prodigality n excess, extravagance, lavishness, profusion, squandering, unthriftiness, waste, wastefulness.

prodigious adj amazing, astonishing, astounding, extraordinary, marvellous, miraculous, portentous, remarkable, startling, strange, surprising, uncommon, wonderful, wondrous; enormous, huge, immense, monstrous, vast.

prodigy n marvel, miracle, phenomenon, portent, sign, wonder; curiosity, monster, monstrosity.

produce vb exhibit, show; bear, beget, breed, conceive, engender, furnish, generate, hatch, procreate, yield; accomplish, achieve, cause, create, effect, make, occasion, originate; accrue, afford, give, impart, make, render; extend, lengthen, prolong, protract; fabricate, fashion, manufacture. • n crop, fruit, greengrocery, harvest, product, vegetables, yield.

producer n creator, inventor, maker, originator; agriculturalist, farmer, greengrocer, husbandman, raiser.

product n crops, fruits, harvest, outcome, proceeds, produce, production, returns, yield; consequence, effect, fruit, issue, performance, production, result, work.

production n fruit, produce, product; construction, creation, erection, fabrication, making, performance; completion, fruition; birth, breeding, development, growth, propagation; opus, publication, work; continuation, extension, lengthening, prolongation.

productive adj copious, fertile, fruitful, luxuriant, plenteous, prolific, teeming; causative, constructive, creative, efficient, life-giving, producing.

proem n exordium, foreword, introduction, preface, prelims, prelude, prolegomena.

profane vb defile, desecrate, pollute, violate; abuse, debase. • adj blasphemous, godless, heathen, idolatrous, impious, impure, pagan, secular, temporal, unconsecrated, unhallowed, unholy, unsanctified, worldly, unspiritual; impure, polluted, unholy.

profanity n blasphemy, impiety, irreverence, profaneness, sacrilege.

profess vb acknowledge, affirm, allege, aver, avouch, avow, confess, declare, own, proclaim, state; affect, feign, pretend.

profession n acknowledgement, assertion, avowal, claim, declaration; avocation, evasion, pretence, pretension, protestation, representation; business, calling, employment, engagement, occupation, office, trade, vocation.

proffer vb offer, propose, propound, suggest, tender, volunteer. • n offer, proposal, suggestion, tender.

proficiency n advancement, forwardness, improvement; accomplishment, aptitude, competency, dexterity, mastery, skill.

proficient adj able, accomplished, adept, competent, conversant, dextrous, expert, finished, masterly, practiced, skilled, skillful, thoroughbred, trained, qualified, well-versed. • n adept, expert, master, master-hand.

profit vb advance, benefit, gain, improve. • n aid, clearance, earnings, emolument, fruit, gain, lucre, produce, return; advancement, advantage, benefit, interest, perquisite, service, use, utility, weal.

profitable adj advantageous, beneficial, desirable, gainful, productive, useful; lucrative, remuncrative.

profitless adj bootless, fruitless, unprofitable, useless, valueless, worthless.

profligate adj abandoned, corrupt, corrupted, degenerate, depraved, dissipated, dissolute, graceless, immoral, shameless, vicious, vitiated, wicked. • n debauchee, libertine, rake, reprobate, roué.

profound adj abysmal, deep, fathomless; heavy, undisturbed; erudite, learned, penetrating, sagacious, skilled; deeply felt, far-reaching, heartfelt, intense, lively, strong, touching, vivid; low, submissive; abstruse, mysterious, obscure, occult, subtle, recondite; complete, thorough.

profundity n deepness, depth, profoundness.

profuse adj abundant, bountiful, copious, excessive, extravagant, exuberant, generous, improvident, lavish, overabundant, plentiful, prodigal, wasteful.

profusion *n* abundance, bounty, copiousness, excess, exuberance, extravagance, lavishness, prodigality, profuseness, superabundance, waste.

progenitor *n* ancestor, forebear, forefather.

progeny *n* breed, children, descendants, family, issue, lineage, offshoot, offspring, posterity, race, scion, stock, young.

prognostic *adj* foreshadowing, foreshowing, foretokening. • *n* augury, foreboding, indication, omen, presage, prognostication, sign, symptom, token; foretelling, prediction, prophecy.

prognosticate *vb* foretell, predict, prophesy; augur, betoken, forebode, foreshadow, foreshow, foretoken, indicate, portend, presage.

prognostication *n* foreknowledge, foreshowing, foretelling, prediction, presage; augury, foreboding, foretoken, indication, portent, prophecy.

progress *vb* advance, continue, proceed; better, gain, improve, increase. • *n* advance, advancement, progression; course, headway, ongoing, passage; betterment, development, growth, improvement, increase, reform; circuit, procession.

prohibit *vb* debar, hamper, hinder, preclude, prevent; ban, disallow, forbid, inhibit, interdict.

prohibition *n* ban, bar, disallowance, embargo, forbiddance, inhibition, interdict, interdiction, obstruction, prevention, proscription, taboo, veto.

prohibitive *adj* forbidding, prohibiting, refraining, restrictive.

project *vb* cast, eject, fling, hurl, propel, shoot, throw; brew, concoct, contrive, design, devise, intend, plan, plot, purpose, scheme; delineate, draw, exhibit; bulge, extend, jut, protrude. • *n* contrivance, design, device, intention, plan, proposal, purpose, scheme.

projectile *n* bullet, missile, shell.

projection *n* delivery, ejection, emission, propulsion, throwing; contriving, designing, planning, scheming; bulge, extension, outshoot, process, prominence, protuberance, salience, saliency, salient, spur; delineation, map, plan.

proletarian *adj* mean, plebeian, vile, vulgar. • *n* commoner, plebeian.

proletariat *n* commonality, hoi polloi, masses, mob, plebs, working class.

prolific *adj* abundant, fertile, fruitful, generative, productive, teeming.

prolix *adj* boring, circumlocutory, discursive, diffuse, lengthy, long, long-winded, loose, prolonged, protracted, prosaic, rambling, tedious, tiresome, verbose, wordy.

prologue *n* foreword, introduction, preamble, preface, preliminary, prelude, proem.

prolong *vb* continue, extend, lengthen, protract, sustain; defer, postpone.

promenade *vb* saunter, walk. • *n* dance, stroll, walk; boulevard, esplanade, parade, walkway.

prominent *adj* convex, embossed, jutting, projecting, protuberant, raised, relieved; celebrated, conspicuous, distinguished, eminent, famous, foremost, influential, leading, main, noticeable, outstanding; conspicuous, distinctive, important, manifest, marked, principal, salient.

promiscuous *adj* confused, heterogeneous, indiscriminate, intermingled, mingled, miscellaneous, mixed; abandoned, dissipated, dissolute, immoral, licentious, loose, unchaste, wanton.

promise *vb* covenant, engage, pledge, subscribe, swear, underwrite, vow; assure, attest, guarantee, warrant; agree, bargain, engage, stipulate, undertake. • *n* agreement, assurance, contract, engagement, oath, parole, pledge, profession, undertaking, vow, word.

promising *adj* auspicious, encouraging, hopeful, likely, propitious.

promote *vb* advance, aid, assist, cultivate, encourage, further, help, promote; dignify, elevate, exalt, graduate, honor, pass, prefer, raise.

promotion *n* advancement, encouragement, furtherance; elevation, exaltation, preferment.

prompt *vb* actuate, dispose, impel, incite, incline, induce, instigate, stimulate, urge; remind; dictate, hint, influence, suggest. • *adj* active, alert, apt, quick, ready; forward, hasty; disposed, inclined, prone; early, exact, immediate, instant, precise, punctual, seasonable, timely. • *adv* apace, directly, forthwith, immediately, promptly. • *n* cue, hint, prompter, reminder, stimulus.

promptly *adv* apace, directly, expeditiously, forthwith, immediately, instantly, pronto, punctually, quickly, speedily, straightway, straightaway, summarily, swiftly.

promptness n activity, alertness, alacrity, promptitude, readiness, quickness.

promulgate vb advertise, announce, broadcast, bruit, circulate, declare, notify, proclaim, publish, spread, trumpet.

prone adj flat, horizontal, prostrate, recumbent; declivitous, inclined, inclining, sloping; apt, bent, disposed, inclined, predisposed, tending; eager, prompt, ready.

pronounce vb articulate, enunciate, frame, say, speak, utter; affirm, announce, assert, declare, deliver, state.

proof adj firm, fixed, impenetrable, stable, steadfast. • n essay, examination, ordeal, test, trial; attestation, certification, conclusion, conclusiveness, confirmation, corroboration, demonstration, evidence, ratification, substantiation, testimony, verification.

prop vb bolster, brace, buttress, maintain, shore, stay, support, sustain, truss, uphold. • n support, stay; buttress, fulcrum, pin, shore, strut.

propaganda n inculcation, indoctrination, promotion.

propagate vb continue, increase, multiply; circulate, diffuse, disseminate, extend, promote, promulgate, publish, spread, transmit; beget, breed, engender, generate, originate, procreate.

propel vb drive, force, impel, push, urge; cast, fling, hurl, project, throw.

propensity n aptitude, bent, bias, disposition, inclination, ply, proclivity, proneness, tendency.

proper adj individual, inherent, natural, original, particular, peculiar, special, specific; adapted, appropriate, becoming, befitting, convenient, decent, decorous, demure, fit, fitting, legitimate, meet, pertinent, respectable, right, seemly, suitable; accurate, correct, exact, fair, fastidious, formal, just, precise; actual, real.

property n attribute, characteristic, disposition, mark, peculiarity, quality, trait, virtue; appurtenance, assets, belongings, chattels, circumstances, effects, estate, goods, possessions, resources, wealth; ownership, possession, proprietorship, tenure; claim, copyright, interest, participation, right, title.

prophecy n augury, divination, forecast, foretelling, portent, prediction, premonition, presage, prognostication; exhortation, instruction, preaching.

prophesy vb augur, divine, foretell, predict, prognosticate.

propinquity n adjacency, contiguity, nearness, neighborhood, proximity, vicinity; affinity, connection, consanguinity, kindred, relationship.

propitiate vb appease, atone, conciliate, intercede, mediate, pacify, reconcile, satisfy.

propitious adj benevolent, benign, friendly, gracious, kind, merciful; auspicious, encouraging, favorable, fortunate, happy, lucky, opportune, promising, prosperous, thriving, timely, well-disposed.

proportion vb adjust, graduate, regulate; form, shape. • n arrangement, relation; adjustment, commensuration, dimension, distribution, symmetry; extent, lot, part, portion, quota, ratio, share.

proposal n design, motion, offer, overture, proffer, proposition, recommendation, scheme, statement, suggestion, tender.

propose vb move, offer, pose, present, propound, proffer, put, recommend, state, submit, suggest, tender; design, intend, mean, purpose.

proposition vb accost, proffer, solicit. • n offer, overture, project, proposal, suggestion, tender, undertaking; affirmation, assertion, axiom, declaration, dictum, doctrine, position, postulation, predication, statement, theorem, thesis.

proprietor n lord, master, owner, possessor, proprietary.

propriety n accuracy, adaptation, appropriation, aptness, becomingness, consonance, correctness, fitness, justness, reasonableness, rightness, seemliness, suitableness; conventionality, decency, decorum, demureness, fastidiousness, formality, modesty, properness, respectability.

prorogation n adjournment, continuance, postponement.

prosaic adj commonplace, dull, flat, humdrum, matter-of-fact, pedestrian, plain, prolix, prosing, sober, stupid, tame, tedious, tiresome, unentertaining, unimaginative, uninspired, uninteresting, unromantic, vapid.

proscribe vb banish, doom, exile, expel, ostracize, outlaw; exclude, forbid, interdict, prohibit; censure, condemn, curse, denounce, reject.

prosecute vb conduct, continue, exercise, follow, persist, pursue; arraign, indict, sue, summon.

prospect *vb* explore, search, seek, survey. • *n* display, field, landscape, outlook, perspective, scene, show, sight, spectacle, survey, view, vision, vista; picture, scenery; anticipation, calculation, contemplation, expectance, expectancy, expectation, foreseeing, foresight, hope, presumption, promise, trust; likelihood, probability.

prospectus *n* announcement, conspectus, description, design, outline, plan, program, sketch, syllabus.

prosper *vb* aid, favor, forward, help; advance, flourish, grow rich, thrive, succeed; batten, increase.

prosperity *n* affluence, blessings, happiness, felicity, good luck, success, thrift, weal, welfare, well-being; boom, heyday.

prosperous *adj* blooming, flourishing, fortunate, golden, halcyon, rich, successful, thriving; auspicious, booming, bright, favorable, good, golden, lucky, promising, propitious, providential, rosy.

prostrate *vb* demolish, destroy, fell, level, overthrow, overturn, ruin; depress, exhaust, overcome, reduce. • *adj* fallen, prostrated, prone, recumbent, supine; helpless, powerless.

prostration *n* demolition, destruction, overthrow; dejection, depression, exhaustion.

prosy *adj* prosaic, unpoetic, unpoetical; dull, flat, jejune, stupid, tedious, tiresome, unentertaining, unimaginative, uninteresting.

protect *vb* cover, defend, guard, shield; fortify, harbor, house, preserve, save, screen, secure, shelter; champion, countenance, foster, patronize.

protector *n* champion, custodian, defender, guardian, patron, warden.

protest *vb* affirm, assert, asseverate, attest, aver, avow, declare, profess, testify; demur, expostulate, object, remonstrate, repudiate. • *n* complaint, declaration, disapproval, objection, protestation.

prototype *n* archetype, copy, exemplar, example, ideal, model, original, paradigm, precedent, protoplast, type.

protract *vb* continue, extend, lengthen, prolong; defer, delay, postpone.

protrude *vb* beetle, bulge, extend, jut, project.

protuberance *n* bulge, bump, elevation, excrescence, hump, lump, process, projection, prominence, roundness, swelling, tumor.

proud *adj* assuming, conceited, contended, egotistical, overweening, self-conscious, self-satisfied, vain; arrogant, boastful, haughty, high-spirited, highly strung, imperious, lofty, lordly, presumptuous, supercilious, uppish, vainglorious.

prove *vb* ascertain, conform, demonstrate, establish, evidence, evince, justify, manifest, show, substantiate, sustain, verify; assay, check, examine, experiment, test, try.

proverb *n* adage, aphorism, apothegm, byword, dictum, maxim, precept, saw, saying.

proverbial *adj* acknowledged, current, notorious, unquestioned.

provide *vb* arrange, collect, plan, prepare, procure; gather, keep, store; afford, contribute, feed, furnish, produce, stock, supply, yield; cater, purvey; agree, bargain, condition, contract, covenant, engage, stipulate.

provided, providing *conj* granted, if, supposing.

provident *adj* careful, cautious, considerate, discreet, farseeing, forecasting, forehanded, foreseeing, prudent; economical, frugal, thrifty.

province *n* district, domain, region, section, territory, tract; colony, dependency; business, calling, capacity, charge, department, duty, employment, function, office, part, post, sphere; department, division, jurisdiction.

provincial *adj* annexed, appendant, outlying; bucolic, countrified, rude, rural, rustic, unpolished, unrefined; insular, local, narrow. • *n* peasant, rustic, yokel.

provision *n* anticipation, providing; arrangement, care, preparation, readiness; equipment, fund, grist, hoard, reserve, resources, stock, store, supplies, supply; clause, condition, prerequisite, proviso, reservation, stipulation.

provisions *npl* eatables, fare, food, provender, supplies, viands, victuals.

proviso *n* clause, condition, provision, stipulation.

provocation *n* incentive, incitement, provocativeness, stimulant, stimulus; affront, indignity, insult, offence; angering, vexation.

provoke *vb* animate, arouse, awaken, excite,

impel, incite, induce, inflame, instigate, kindle, move, rouse, stimulate; affront, aggravate, anger, annoy, chafe, enrage, exacerbate, exasperate, incense, infuriate, irritate, nettle, offend, pique, vex; cause, elicit, evoke, instigate, occasion, produce, promote.

provoking adj aggravating, annoying, exasperating, irritating, offensive, tormenting, vexatious, vexing.

prowess n bravery, courage, daring, fearlessness, gallantry, heroism, intrepidity, valor; aptitude, dexterity, expertness, facility.

proximity n adjacency, contiguity, nearness, neighborhood, propinquity, vicinage, vicinity.

proxy n agent, attorney, commissioner, delegate, deputy, lieutenant, representative, substitute.

prudence n carefulness, caution, circumspection, common sense, considerateness, discretion, forecast, foresight, judgment, judiciousness, policy, providence, sense, tact, wariness, wisdom.

prudent adj cautious, careful, circumspect, considerate, discreet, foreseeing, heedful, judicious, politic, provident, prudential, wary, wise.

prudish adj coy, demure, modest, precise, prim, reserved, strait-laced.

prune vb abbreviate, clip, cut, dock, lop, thin, trim; dress, preen.

prurient adj covetous, craving, desiring, hankering, itching, lascivious, libidinous, longing, lustful.

pry vb examine, ferret, inspect, investigate, peep, peer, question, scrutinize, search; force, lever, prise.

public adj civil, common, countrywide, general, national, political, state; known, notorious, open, popular, published, well-known. • n citizens, community, country, everyone, general public, masses, nation, people, population; audience, buyers, following, supporters.

publication n advertisement, announcement, disclosure, divulgement, divulgence, proclamation, promulgation, report; edition, issue, issuance, printing.

publicity n daylight, currency, limelight, notoriety, spotlight; outlet, vent.

publish vb advertise, air, bruit, announce, blaze, blazon, broach, communicate, declare, diffuse, disclose, disseminate,

impart, placard, post, proclaim, promulgate, reveal, tell, utter, vent, ventilate.

pucker vb cockle, contract, corrugate, crease, crinkle, furrow, gather, pinch, purse, shirr, wrinkle. • n crease, crinkle, fold, furrow, wrinkle.

puerile adj boyish, childish, infantile, juvenile, youthful; foolish, frivolous, idle, nonsensical, petty, senseless, silly, simple, trifling, trivial, weak.

puffy adj distended, swelled, swollen, tumid, turgid; bombastic, extravagant, inflated, pompous.

pugnacious adj belligerent, bellicose, contentious, fighting, irascible, irritable, petulant, quarrelsome.

puissant adj forcible, mighty, potent, powerful, strong.

pull vb drag, draw, haul, row, tow, tug; cull, extract, gather, pick, pluck; detach, rend, tear, wrest. • n pluck, shake, tug, twitch, wrench; contest, struggle; attraction, gravity, magnetism; graft, influence, power.

pulsate vb beat, palpitate, pant, throb, thump, vibrate.

pulverize vb bruise, comminute, grind, levigate, triturate.

pun vb assonate, alliterate, play on words. • n assonance, alliteration, clinch, conceit, double-meaning, paranomasia, play on words, quip, rhyme, witticism, wordplay.

punctilious adj careful, ceremonious, conscientious, exact, formal, nice, particular, precise, punctual, scrupulous, strict.

punctual adj exact, nice, precise, punctilious; early, prompt, ready, regular, seasonable, timely.

puncture vb bore, penetrate, perforate, pierce, prick. • n bite, hole, sting, wound.

pungent adj acid, acrid, biting, burning, caustic, hot, mordant, penetrating, peppery, piercing, piquant, prickling, racy, salty, seasoned, sharp, smart, sour, spicy, stimulating, stinging; acute, acrimonious, cutting, distressing, irritating, keen, painful, peevish, poignant, pointed, satirical, severe, tart, trenchant, waspish.

punish vb beat, castigate, chasten, chastise, correct, discipline, flog, lash, scourge, torture, whip.

punishment n castigation, chastening, chastisement, correction, discipline, infliction, retribution, scourging, trial; judgment, nemesis, penalty.

puny adj feeble, inferior, weak; dwarf,

dwarfish, insignificant, diminutive, little, petty, pygmy, small, stunted, tiny, underdeveloped, undersized.

pupil *n* beginner, catechumen, disciple, learner, neophyte, novice, scholar, student, tyro.

pupillage *n* minority, nonage, tutelage, wardship.

puppet *n* doll, image, manikin, marionette; cat's-paw, pawn, tool.

purchase *vb* buy, gain, get, obtain, pay for, procure; achieve, attain, earn, win. • *n* acquisition, buy, gain, possession, property; advantage, foothold, grasp, hold, influence, support.

pure *adj* clean, clear, fair, immaculate, spotless, stainless, unadulterated, unalloyed, unblemished, uncorrupted, undefiled, unpolluted, unspotted, unstained, unsullied, untainted, untarnished; chaste, continent, guileless, guiltless, holy, honest, incorrupt, innocent, modest, sincere, true, uncorrupt, upright, virgin, virtuous; genuine, perfect, real, simple, true, unadorned; absolute, essential, mere, sheer, thorough; classic, classical.

purge *vb* cleanse, clear, purify; clarify, defecate, evacuate; deterge, scour; absolve, pardon, shrive. • *n* elimination, eradication, expulsion, removal, suppression; cathartic, emetic, enema, laxative, physic.

purify *vb* clean, cleanse, clear, depurate, expurgate, purge, refine, wash; clarify, fine.

puritanical *adj* ascetic, narrow-minded, overscrupulous, prim, prudish, rigid, severe, strait-laced, strict.

purity *n* clearness, fineness; cleanness, correctness, faultlessness, immaculacy, immaculateness; guilelessness, guiltlessness, holiness, honesty, innocence, integrity, piety, simplicity, truth, uprightness, virtue; excellence, genuineness; homogeneity, simpleness; chasteness, chastity, continence, modesty, pudency, virginity.

purlieus *npl* borders, bounds, confines, environs, limits, neighborhood, outskirts, precincts, suburbs, vicinage, vicinity.

purloin *vb* abstract, crib, filch, pilfer, rob, steal, thieve.

purport *vb* allege, assert, claim, maintain, pretend, profess; denote, express, imply, indicate, mean, signify, suggest. • *n* bearing, current, design, drift, gist, import, intent, meaning, scope, sense, significance, signification, spirit, tendency, tenor.

purpose *vb* contemplate, design, intend, mean, meditate; determine, resolve. • *n* aim, design, drift, end, intent, intention, object, resolution, resolve, view; plan, project; meaning, purport, sense; consequence, effect.

pursue *vb* chase, dog, follow, hound, hunt, shadow, track; conduct, continue, cultivate, maintain, practice, prosecute; seek, strive; accompany, attend.

pursuit *n* chase, hunt, race; conduct, cultivation, practice, prosecution, pursuance; avocation, calling, business, employment, fad, hobby, occupation, vocation.

pursy *adj* corpulent, fat, fleshy, plump, podgy, pudgy, short, thick; short-breathed, short-winded; opulent, rich.

purview *n* body, compass, extent, limit, reach, scope, sphere, view.

push *vb* elbow, crowd, hustle, impel, jostle, shoulder, shove, thrust; advance, drive, hurry, propel, urge; importune, persuade, tease. • *n* pressure, thrust; determination, perseverance; emergency, exigency, extremity, pinch, strait, test, trial; assault, attack, charge, endeavor, onset.

pusillanimous *adj* chicken, chicken-hearted, cowardly, dastardly, faint-hearted, feeble, lily-livered, mean-spirited, spiritless, timid, recreant, timorous, weak.

pustule *n* abscess, blain, blister, blotch, boil, fester, gathering, pimple, sore, ulcer.

put *vb* bring, collocate, deposit, impose, lay, locate, place, set; enjoin, impose, inflict, levy; offer, present, propose, state; compel, constrain, force, oblige; entice, incite, induce, urge; express, utter.

putative *adj* deemed, reckoned, reported, reputed, supposed.

putrefy *vb* corrupt, decay, decompose, fester, rot, stink.

putrid *adj* corrupt, decayed, decomposed, fetid, rank, rotten, stinking.

puzzle *vb* bewilder, confound, confuse, embarrass, gravel, mystify, nonplus, perplex, pose, stagger; complicate, entangle. • *n* conundrum, enigma, labyrinth, maze, paradox, poser, problem, riddle; bewilderment, complication, confusion, difficulty, dilemma, embarrassment, mystification, perplexity, point, quandary, question.

pygmy *adj* diminutive, dwarf, dwarfish, Lilliputian, little, midget, stunted, tiny. • *n* dwarf, Lilliputian, midget.

Q

quack[1] *vb, n* cackle, cry, squeak.

quack[2] *adj* fake, false, sham. • *n* charlatan, empiric, humbug, impostor, mountebank, pretender.

quadruple *adj* fourfold, quadruplicate.

quagmire *n* bog, fen, marsh, morass, slough, swamp; difficulty, impasse, muddle, predicament.

quail *vb* blench, cower, droop, faint, flinch, shrink, tremble.

quaint *adj* antiquated, antique, archaic, curious, droll, extraordinary, fanciful, odd, old-fashioned, queer, singular, uncommon, unique, unusual; affected, fantastic, far-fetched, whimsical; artful, ingenious.

quake *vb* quiver, shake, shiver, shudder; move, vibrate. • *n* earthquake, shake, shudder.

qualification *n* ability, accomplishment, capability, competency, eligibility, fitness, suitability; condition, exception, limitation, modification, proviso, restriction, stipulation; abatement, allowance, diminution, mitigation.

qualified *adj* accomplished, certificated, certified, competent, fitted, equipped, licensed, trained; adapted, circumscribed, conditional, limited, modified, restricted.

qualify *vb* adapt, capacitate, empower, entitle, equip, fit; limit, modify, narrow, restrain, restrict; abate, assuage, ease, mitigate, moderate, reduce, soften; diminish, modulate, temper, regulate, vary.

quality *n* affection, attribute, characteristic, color, distinction, feature, flavor, mark, nature, peculiarity, property, singularity, timbre, tinge, trait; character, condition, disposition, humor, mood, temper; brand, caliber, capacity, class, description, excellence, grade, kind, rank, sort, stamp, standing, station, status, virtue; aristocracy, gentility, gentry, noblesse, nobility.

qualm *n* agony, pang, throe; nausea, queasiness, sickness; compunction, remorse, uneasiness, twinge.

quandary *n* bewilderment, difficulty, dilemma, doubt, embarrassment, perplexity, pickle, plight, predicament, problem, puzzle, strait, uncertainty.

quantity *n* content, extent, greatness, measure, number, portion, share, size; aggregate, batch, amount, bulk, lot, mass, quantum, store, sum, volume; duration, length.

quarrel *vb* altercate, bicker, brawl, carp, cavil, clash, contend, differ, dispute, fight, jangle, jar, scold, scuffle, spar, spat, squabble, strive, wrangle. • *n* altercation, affray, bickering, brawl, breach, breeze, broil, clash, contention, contest, controversy, difference, disagreement, discord, dispute, dissension, disturbance, feud, fight, fray, imbroglio, jar, miff, misunderstanding, quarreling, row, rupture, spat, squabble, strife, tiff, tumult, variance, wrangle.

quarrelsome *adj* argumentative, choleric, combative, contentious, cross, discordant, disputatious, dissentious, fiery, irascible, irritable, petulant, pugnacious, ugly, wranglesome.

quarter *vb* billet, lodge, post, station; allot, furnish, share. • *n* abode, billet, dwelling, habitation, lodgings, posts, quarters, stations; direction, district, locality, location, lodge, position, region, territory; clemency, mercy, mildness.

quash *vb* abate, abolish, annul, cancel, invalidate, nullify, overthrow; crush, extinguish, repress, stop, subdue, suppress.

queasy *adj* nauseated, pukish, seasick, sick, squeamish.

queer *vb* botch, harm, impair, mar, spoil. • *adj* curious, droll, extraordinary, fantastic, odd, peculiar, quaint, singular, strange, uncommon, unusual, whimsical; gay, homosexual.

quell *vb* conquer, crush, overcome, overpower, subdue; bridle, check, curb, extinguish, lay, quench, rein in, repress, restrain, stifle; allay, calm, compose, hush, lull, pacify, quiet, quieten, still, tranquilize; alleviate, appease, blunt, deaden, dull, mitigate, mollify, soften, soothe.

quench *vb* extinguish, put out; check, destroy, repress, satiate, stifle, still, suppress; allay, cool, dampen, extinguish, slake.

querulous *adj* bewailing, complaining, cross, discontented, dissatisfied, fretful, fretting, irritable, mourning, murmuring, peevish, petulant, plaintive, touchy, whining.

query *vb* ask, enquire, inquire, question; dispute, doubt. • *n* enquiry, inquiry, interrogatory, issue, problem, question.

quest *n* expedition, journey, search, voyage;

pursuit, suit; examination, enquiry, inquiry; demand, desire, invitation, prayer, request, solicitation.

question vb ask, catechize, enquire, examine, inquire, interrogate, quiz, sound out; doubt, query; challenge, dispute. • n examination, enquiry, inquiry, interpellation, interrogation; enquiry, inquiry, interrogatory, query; debate, discussion, disquisition, examination, investigation, issue, trial; controversy, dispute, doubt; motion, mystery, point, poser, problem, proposition, puzzle, topic.

questionable adj ambiguous, controversial, controvertible, debatable, doubtful, disputable, equivocal, problematic, problematical, suspicious, uncertain, undecided.

quibble vb cavil, equivocate, evade, prevaricate, shuffle. • n equivocation, evasion, pretence, prevarication, quirk, shift, shuffle, sophism, subtlety, subterfuge.

quick adj active, agile, alert, animated, brisk, lively, nimble, prompt, ready, smart, sprightly; expeditious, fast, fleet, flying, hurried, rapid, speedy, swift; adroit, apt, clever, dextrous, expert, skillful; choleric, hasty, impetuous, irascible, irritable, passionate, peppery, petulant, precipitate, sharp, unceremonious, testy, touchy, waspish; alive, animate, live, living.

quicken vb animate, energize, resuscitate, revivify, vivify; cheer, enliven, invigorate, reinvigorate, revive, whet; accelerate, dispatch, expedite, hasten, hurry, speed; actuate, excite, incite, kindle, refresh, sharpen, stimulate; accelerate, live, take effect.

quickly adv apace, fast, immediately, nimbly, quick, rapidly, readily, soon, speedily, swiftly.

quickness n celerity, dispatch, expedition, haste, rapidity, speed, swiftness, velocity; agility, alertness, activity, briskness, liveliness, nimbleness, promptness, readiness, smartness; adroitness, aptitude, aptness, dexterity, facility, knack; acumen, acuteness, keenness, penetration, perspicacity, sagacity, sharpness, shrewdness.

quiescent adj at rest, hushed, motionless, quiet, resting, still; calm, mute, placid, quiet, serene, still, tranquil, unagitated, undisturbed, unruffled.

quiet adj hushed, motionless, quiescent, still, unmoved; calm, contented, gentle, mild, meek, modest, peaceable, peaceful,

placid, silent, smooth, tranquil, undemonstrative, unobtrusive, unruffled; patient; retired, secluded. • n calmness, peace, repose, rest, silence, stillness.

quieten vb arrest, discontinue, intermit, interrupt, still, stop, suspend; allay, appease, calm, compose, lull, pacify, sober, soothe, tranquillize; hush, silence; alleviate, assuage, blunt, dull, mitigate, moderate, mollify, soften.

quip n crank, flout, gibe, jeer, mock, quirk, repartee, retort, sarcasm, sally, scoff, sneer, taunt, witticism.

quit vb absolve, acquit, deliver, free, release; clear, deliver, discharge from, free, liberate, relieve; acquit, behave, conduct; carry through, perform; discharge, pay, repay, requite; relinquish, renounce, resign, stop, surrender; depart from, leave, withdraw from; abandon, desert, forsake, forswear. • adj absolved, acquitted, clear, discharged, free, released.

quite adv completely, entirely, exactly, perfectly, positively, precisely, totally, wholly.

quiver vb flicker, flutter, oscillate, palpitate, quake, play, shake, shiver, shudder, tremble, twitch, vibrate. • n shake, shiver, shudder, trembling.

quixotic adj absurd, chimerical, fanciful, fantastic, fantastical, freakish, imaginary, mad, romantic, utopian, visionary, wild.

quiz vb examine, question, test; peer at; banter, hoax, puzzle, ridicule. • n enigma, hoax, jest, joke, puzzle; jester, joker, hoax.

quota n allocation, allotment, apportionment, contingent, portion, proportion, quantity, share.

quotation n citation, clipping, cutting, extract, excerpt, reference, selection; estimate, rate, tender.

quote vb adduce, cite, excerpt, extract, illustrate, instance, name, repeat, take; estimate, tender.

R

rabble n commonality, horde, mob, populace, riffraff, rout, scum, trash.

rabid adj frantic, furious, mad, raging, wild; bigoted, fanatical, intolerant, irrational, narrow-minded, rampant.

race[1] n ancestry, breed, family, generation, house, kindred, line, lineage, pedigree, stock, strain; clan, folk, nation, people, tribe; breed, children, descendants, issue, offspring, progeny, stock.

race[2] *vb* career, compete, contest, course, hasten, hurry, run, speed. • *n* career, chase, competition, contest, course, dash, heat, match, pursuit, run, sprint; flavor, quality, smack, strength, taste.

rack *vb* agonize, distress, excruciate, rend, torment, torture, wring; exhaust, force, harass, oppress, strain, stretch, wrest. • *n* agony, anguish, pang, torment, torture; crib, manger; neck, crag; dampness, mist, moisture, vapor.

racket *n* clamor, clatter, din, dissipation, disturbance, fracas, frolic, hubbub, noise, outcry, tumult, uproar; game, graft, scheme, understanding

racy *adj* flavorsome, palatable, piquant, pungent, rich, spicy, strong; forcible, lively, pungent, smart, spirited, stimulating, vigorous, vivacious.

radiance *n* brightness, brilliance, brilliancy, effluence, efflux, emission, glare, glitter, light, luster, refulgence, resplendence, shine, splendor.

radiant *adj* beaming, brilliant, effulgent, glittering, glorious, luminous, lustrous, resplendent, shining, sparkling, splendid; ecstatic, happy, pleased.

radiate *vb* beam, gleam, glitter, shine; emanate, emit; diffuse, spread.

radical *adj* constitutional, deep-seated, essential, fundamental, ingrained, inherent, innate, native, natural, organic, original, uncompromising; original, primitive, simple, uncompounded, underived; complete, entire, extreme, fanatic, insurgent, perfect, rebellious, thorough, total. • *n* etymon, radix, root; fanatic, revolutionary.

rage *vb* bluster, boil, chafe, foam, fret, fume, ravage, rave. • *n* excitement, frenzy, fury, madness, passion, rampage, raving, vehemence, wrath; craze, fashion, mania, mode, style, vogue.

ragged *adj* rent, tattered, torn; contemptible, mean, poor, shabby; jagged, rough, rugged, shaggy, uneven; discordant, dissonant, inharmonious, unmusical.

raid *vb* assault, forage, invade, pillage, plunder. • *n* attack, foray, invasion, inroad, plunder.

rail *vb* abuse, censure, inveigh, scoff, scold, sneer, upbraid.

raillery *n* banter, chaff, irony, joke, pleasantry, ridicule, satire.

raiment *n* array, apparel, attire, clothes, clothing, costume, dress, garb, garments, habiliment, habit, vestments, vesture.

rain *vb* drizzle, drop, fall, pour, shower, sprinkle, teem; bestow, lavish. • *n* cloudburst, downpour, drizzle, mist, shower, sprinkling.

raise *vb* boost, construct, erect, heave, hoist, lift, uplift, upraise, rear; advance, elevate, ennoble, exalt, promote; aggravate, amplify, augment, enhance, heighten, increase, invigorate; arouse, awake, cause, effect, excite, originate, produce, rouse, stir up, occasion, start; assemble, collect, get, levy, obtain; breed, cultivate, grow, propagate, rear; ferment, leaven, work.

rake[1] *vb* collect, comb, gather, scratch; ransack, scour.

rake[2] *n* debauchee, libertine, profligate, roué.

rakish *adj* debauched, dissipated, dissolute, lewd, licentious; cavalier, jaunty.

ramble *vb* digress, maunder, range, roam, rove, saunter, straggle, stray, stroll, wander. • *n* excursion, rambling, roving, tour, trip, stroll, wandering.

rambling *adj* discursive, irregular; straggling, strolling, wandering.

ramification *n* arborescence, branching, divarication, forking, radiation; branch, division, offshoot, subdivision; consequence, upshot.

ramify *vb* branch, divaricate, extend, separate.

rampant *adj* excessive, exuberant, luxuriant, rank, wanton; boisterous, dominant, headstrong, impetuous, predominant, raging, uncontrollable, unbridled, ungovernable, vehement, violent.

rampart *n* bulwark, circumvallation, defense, fence, fortification, guard, security, wall.

rancid *adj* bad, fetid, foul, fusty, musty, offensive, rank, sour, stinking, tainted.

rancorous *adj* bitter, implacable, malevolent, malicious, malign, malignant, resentful, spiteful, vindictive, virulent.

rancour *n* animosity, antipathy, bitterness, enmity, gall, grudge, hate, hatred, ill-will, malevolence, malice, malignity, spite, venom, vindictiveness.

random *adj* accidental, casual, chance, fortuitous, haphazard, irregular, stray, wandering.

range *vb* course, cruise, extend, ramble,

roam, rove, straggle, stray, stroll, wander; bend, lie, run; arrange, class, dispose, rank. • *n* file, line, row, rank, tier; class, kind, order, sort; excursion, expedition, ramble, roving, wandering; amplitude, bound, command, compass, distance, extent, latitude, reach, scope, sweep, view; register.

rank[1] *vb* arrange, class, classify, range. • *n* file, line, order, range, row, tier; class, division, group, order, series; birth, blood, caste, degree, estate, grade, position, quality, sphere, stakes, standing; dignity, distinction, eminence, nobility.

rank[2] *adj* dense, exuberant, luxuriant, overabundant, overgrown, vigorous, wild; excessive, extreme, extravagant, flagrant, gross, rampant, sheer, unmitigated, utter, violent; fetid, foul, fusty, musty, offensive, rancid; fertile, productive, rich; coarse, disgusting.

ransack *vb* pillage, plunder, ravage, rifle, sack, strip; explore, overhaul, rummage, search thoroughly.

ransom *vb* deliver, emancipate, free, liberate, redeem, rescue, unfetter. • *n* money, payment pay-off, price; deliverance, liberation, redemption, release.

rant *vb* declaim, mouth, spout, vociferate. • *n* bombast, cant, exaggeration, fustian.

rapacious *adj* predacious, preying, raptorial; avaricious, grasping, greedy, ravenous, voracious.

rapid *adj* fast, fleet, quick, swift; brisk, expeditious, hasty, hurried, quick, speedy.

rapine *n* depredation, pillage, plunder, robbery, spoliation.

rapt *adj* absorbed, charmed, delighted, ecstatic, engrossed, enraptured, entranced, fascinated, inspired, spellbound.

rapture *vb* enrapture, ravish, transport. • *n* delight, exultation, enthusiasm, rhapsody; beatification, beatitude, bliss, ecstasy, felicity, happiness, joy, spell, transport.

rare[1] *adj* sparse, subtle, thin; extraordinary, infrequent, scarce, singular, strange, uncommon, unique, unusual; choice, excellent, exquisite, fine, incomparable, inimitable.

rare[2] *adj* bloody, underdone.

rarity *n* attenuation, ethereality, etherealness, rarefaction, rareness, tenuity, tenuousness, thinness; infrequency, scarcity, singularity, sparseness, uncommonness, unwontedness.

rascal *n* blackguard, caitiff, knave, miscreant, rogue, reprobate, scallywag, scapegrace, scamp, scoundrel, vagabond, villain.

rash[1] *adj* adventurous, audacious, careless, foolhardy, hasty, headlong, headstrong, heedless, incautious, inconsiderate, indiscreet, injudicious, impetuous, impulsive, incautious, precipitate, quick, rapid, reckless, temerarious, thoughtless, unguarded, unwary, venturesome.

rash[2] *n* breaking-out, efflorescence, eruption; epidemic, flood, outbreak, plague, spate.

rashness *n* carelessness, foolhardiness, hastiness, heedlessness, inconsideration, indiscretion, precipitation, recklessness, temerity, venturesomeness.

rate[1] *vb* appraise, compute, estimate, value. • *n* cost, price; class, degree, estimate, rank, value, valuation, worth; proportion, ration; assessment, charge, impost, tax.

rate[2] *vb* abuse, berate, censure, chide, criticize, find fault, reprimand, reprove, scold.

ratify *vb* confirm, corroborate, endorse, establish, seal, settle, substantiate; approve, bind, consent, sanction.

ration *vb* apportion, deal, distribute, dole, restrict. • *n* allowance, portion, quota, share.

rational *adj* intellectual, reasoning; equitable, fair, fit, just, moderate, natural, normal, proper, reasonable, right; discreet, enlightened, intelligent, judicious, sagacious, sensible, sound, wise.

raucous *adj* harsh, hoarse, husky, rough.

ravage *vb* consume, desolate, despoil, destroy, devastate, harry, overrun, pillage, plunder, ransack, ruin, sack, spoil, strip, waste. • *n* desolation, despoilment, destruction, devastation, havoc, pillage, plunder, rapine, ruin, spoil, waste.

ravenous *adj* devouring, ferocious, gluttonous, greedy, insatiable, omnivorous, ravening, rapacious, voracious.

ravine *n* canyon, cleft, defile, gap, gorge, gulch, gully, pass.

raving *adj* delirious, deranged, distracted, frantic, frenzied, furious, infuriated, mad, phrenetic, raging. • *n* delirium, frenzy, fury, madness, rage.

ravish *vb* abuse, debauch, defile, deflower, force, outrage, violate; captivate, charm, delight, enchant, enrapture, entrance, overjoy, transport; abduct, kidnap, seize, snatch, strip.

raw *adj* fresh, inexperienced, unpracticed, unprepared, unseasoned, untried, unskilled; crude, green, immature, unfinished, unripe; bare, chafed, excoriated, galled, sensitive, sore; bleak, chilly, cold, cutting, damp, piercing, windswept; uncooked.

ray *n* beam, emanation, gleam, moonbeam, radiance, shaft, streak, sunbeam.

raze *vb* demolish, destroy, dismantle, extirpate, fell, level, overthrow, ruin, subvert; efface, erase, obliterate.

reach *vb* extend, stretch; grasp, hit, strike, touch; arrive at, attain, gain, get, obtain, win. • *n* capability, capacity, grasp.

readily *adv* easily, promptly, quickly; cheerfully, willingly.

readiness *n* alacrity, alertness, expedition, quickness, promptitude, promptness; aptitude, aptness, dexterity, easiness, expertness, facility, quickness, skill; preparation, preparedness, ripeness; cheerfulness, disposition, eagerness, ease, willingness.

ready *vb* arrange, equip, organize, prepare. • *adj* alert, expeditious, prompt, quick, punctual, speedy; adroit, apt, clever, dextrous, expert, facile, handy, keen, nimble, prepared, prompt, ripe, quick, sharp, skillful, smart; cheerful, disposed, eager, free, inclined, willing; accommodating, available, convenient, near, handy; easy, facile, fluent, offhand, opportune, short, spontaneous.

real *adj* absolute, actual, certain, literal, positive, practical, substantial, substantive, veritable; authentic, genuine, true; essential, internal, intrinsic.

realize *vb* accomplish, achieve, discharge, effect, effectuate, perfect, perform; apprehend, comprehend, experience, recognize, understand; externalize, substantiate; acquire, earn, gain, get, net, obtain, produce, sell.

reality *n* actuality, certainty, fact, truth, verity.

really *adv* absolutely, actually, certainly, indeed, positively, truly, verily, veritably.

reap *vb* acquire, crop, gain, gather, get, harvest, obtain, receive.

rear[1] *adj* aft, back, following, hind, last. • *n* background, reverse, setting; heel, posterior, rear end, rump, stern, tail; path, trail, train, wake.

rear[2] *vb* construct, elevate, erect, hoist, lift, raise; cherish, educate, foster, instruct, nourish, nurse, nurture, train; breed, grow; rouse, stir up.

reason *vb* argue, conclude, debate, deduce, draw from, infer, intellectualize, syllogize, think, trace. • *n* faculty, intellect, intelligence, judgement, mind, principle, sanity, sense, thinking, understanding; account, argument, basis, cause, consideration, excuse, explanation, gist, ground, motive, occasion, pretence, proof; aim, design, end, object, purpose; argument, reasoning; common sense, reasonableness, wisdom; equity, fairness, justice, right; exposition, rationale, theory.

reasonable *adj* equitable, fair, fit, honest, just, proper, rational, right, suitable; enlightened, intelligent, judicious, sagacious, sensible, wise; considerable, fair, moderate, tolerable; credible, intellectual, plausible, well-founded; sane, sober, sound; cheap, inexpensive, low-priced.

rebate *vb* abate, bate, blunt, deduct, diminish, lessen, reduce; cut, pare, rabbet. • *n* decrease, decrement, diminution, lessening; allowance, deduction, discount, reduction.

rebel *vb* mutiny, resist, revolt, strike. • *adj* insubordinate, insurgent, mutinous, rebellious. • *n* insurgent, mutineer, traitor.

rebellion *n* anarchy, insubordination, insurrection, mutiny, resistance, revolt, revolution, uprising.

rebellious *adj* contumacious, defiant, disloyal, disobedient, insubordinate, intractable, obstinate, mutinous, rebel, refractory, seditious.

rebuff *vb* check, chide, oppose, refuse, reject, repel, reprimand, resist, snub. • *n* check, defeat, discouragement, opposition, rejection, resistance, snub.

rebuke *vb* blame, censure, chide, lecture, upbraid, reprehend, reprimand, reprove, scold, silence. • *n* blame, censure, chiding, expostulation, remonstrance, reprimand, reprehension, reproach, reproof, reproval; affliction, chastisement, punishment.

recall *vb* abjure, abnegate, annul, cancel, countermand, deny, nullify, overrule, recant, repeal, repudiate, rescind, retract, revoke, swallow, withdraw; commemorate, recollect, remember, retrace, review, revive. • *n* abjuration, abnegation, annulment, cancellation, nullification, recantation, repeal, repudiation, rescindment, retraction, revocation, withdrawal; memory, recollection, remembrance, reminiscence.

recant *vb* abjure, annul, disavow, disown, recall, renounce, repudiate, retract, revoke, unsay.

recapitulate *vb* epitomize, recite, rehearse, reiterate, repeat, restate, review, summarize.

recede *vb* desist, ebb, retire, regress, retreat, retrograde, return, withdraw.

receive *vb* accept, acquire, derive, gain, get, obtain, take; admit, shelter, take in; entertain, greet, welcome; allow, permit, tolerate; adopt, approve, believe, credit, embrace, follow, learn, understand; accommodate, carry, contain, hold, include, retain; bear, encounter, endure, experience, meet, suffer, sustain.

recent *adj* fresh, new, novel; latter, modern, young; deceased, foregoing, late, preceding, retiring.

reception *n* acceptance, receipt, receiving; entertainment, greeting, welcome; levee, soiree, party; admission, credence; belief, credence, recognition.

recess *n* alcove, corner, depth, hollow, niche, nook, privacy, retreat, seclusion; break, holiday, intermission, interval, respite, vacation; recession, retirement, retreat, withdrawal.

reciprocal *adj* alternate, commutable, complementary, correlative, correspondent, mutual.

recital *n* rehearsal, repetition, recitation; account, description, detail, explanation, narration, relation, statement, telling.

recite *vb* declaim, deliver, rehearse, repeat; describe, mention, narrate, recount, relate, tell; count, detail, enumerate, number, recapitulate.

reckless *adj* breakneck, careless, desperate, devil-may-care, flighty, foolhardy, giddy, harebrained, headlong, heedless, inattentive, improvident, imprudent, inconsiderate, indifferent, indiscreet, mindless, negligent, rash, regardless, remiss, thoughtless, temerarious, uncircumspect, unconcerned, unsteady, volatile, wild.

reckon *vb* calculate, cast, compute, consider, count, enumerate, guess, number; account, class, esteem, estimate, regard, repute, value.

reckoning *n* calculation, computation, consideration, counting; account, bill, charge,

estimate, register, score; arrangement, settlement.

reclaim *vb* amend, correct, reform; recover, redeem, regenerate, regain, reinstate, restore; civilize, tame.

recline *vb* couch, lean, lie, lounge, repose, rest.

recluse *adj* anchoritic, anchoritical, cloistered, eremitic, eremitical, hermitic, hermitical, reclusive, solitary. • *n* anchorite, ascetic, eremite, hermit, monk, solitary.

reclusive *adj* recluse, retired, secluded, sequestered, sequestrated, solitary.

recognition *n* identification, memory, recollection, remembrance; acknowledgement, appreciation, avowal, comprehension, confession, notice; allowance, concession.

recognize *vb* apprehend, identify, perceive, remember; acknowledge, admit, avow, confess, own; allow, concede, grant; greet, salute.

recoil *vb* react, rebound, reverberate; retire, retreat, withdraw; blench, fail, falter, quail, shrink. • *n* backstroke, boomerang, elasticity, kick, reaction, rebound, repercussion, resilience, revulsion, ricochet, shrinking.

recollect *vb* recall, remember, reminisce.

recollection *n* memory, remembrance, reminiscence.

recommend *vb* approve, commend, endorse, praise, sanction; commit; advise, counsel, prescribe, suggest.

recommendation *n* advocacy, approbation, approval, commendation, counsel, credential, praise, testimonial.

recompense *vb* compensate, remunerate, repay, requite, reward, satisfy; indemnify, redress, reimburse. • *n* amends, compensation, indemnification, indemnity, remuneration, repayment, reward, satisfaction; requital, retribution.

reconcilable *adj* appeasable, forgiving, placable; companionable, congruous, consistent.

reconcile *vb* appease, conciliate, pacify, placate, propitiate, reunite; content, harmonize, regulate; adjust, compose, heal, settle.

recondite *adj* concealed, dark, hidden, mystic, mystical, obscure, occult, secret, transcendental.

record *vb* chronicle, enter, note, register.

• *n* account, annals, archive, chronicle, diary, docket, enrolment, entry, file, list, minute, memoir, memorandum, memorial, note, proceedings, register, registry, report, roll, score; mark, memorial, relic, trace, track, trail, vestige; memory, remembrance; achievement, career, history.

recount *vb* describe, detail, enumerate, mention, narrate, particularize, portray, recite, relate, rehearse, report, tell.

recover *vb* recapture, reclaim, regain; rally, recruit, repair, retrieve; cure, heal, restore, revive; redeem, rescue, salvage, save; convalesce, recuperate.

recreant *adj* base, cowardly, craven, dastardly, faint-hearted, mean-spirited, pusillanimous, yielding; apostate, backsliding, faithless, false, perfidious, treacherous, unfaithful, untrue. • *n* coward, dastard; apostate, backslider, renegade.

recreation *n* amusement, cheer, diversion, entertainment, fun, game, leisure, pastime, play, relaxation, sport.

recreational *adj* amusing, diverting, entertaining, refreshing, relaxing, relieving.

recruit *vb* repair, replenish; recover, refresh, regain, reinvigorate, renew, renovate, restore, retrieve, revive, strengthen, supply. • *n* auxiliary, beginner, helper, learner, novice, tyro.

rectify *vb* adjust, amend, better, correct, emend, improve, mend, redress, reform, regulate, straighten.

rectitude *n* conscientiousness, equity, goodness, honesty, integrity, justice, principle, probity, right, righteousness, straightforwardness, uprightness, virtue.

recumbent *adj* leaning, lying, prone, prostrate, reclining; idle, inactive, listless, reposing.

recur *vb* reappear, resort, return, revert.

recusancy *n* dissent, heresy, heterodoxy, nonconformity.

redeem *vb* reform, regain, repurchase, retrieve; free, liberate, ransom, rescue, save; deliver, reclaim, recover, reinstate; atone, compensate for, recompense; discharge, fulfill, keep, perform, satisfy.

redemption *n* buying, compensation, recovery, repurchase, retrieval; deliverance, liberation, ransom, release, rescue, salvation; discharge, fulfillment, performance.

redolent *adj* aromatic, balmy, fragrant, odoriferous, odorous, scented, sweet, sweet-smelling.

redoubtable *adj* awful, doughty, dreadful, formidable, terrible, valiant.

redound *vb* accrue, conduce, contribute, result, tend.

redress *vb* amend, correct, order, rectify, remedy, repair; compensate, ease, relieve. • *n* abatement, amends, atonement, compensation, correction, cure, indemnification, rectification, repair, righting, remedy, relief, reparation, satisfaction.

reduce *vb* bring; form, make, model, mold, remodel, render, resolve, shape; abate, abbreviate, abridge, attenuate, contract, curtail, decimate, decrease, diminish, lessen, minimize, shorten, thin; abase, debase, degrade, depress, dwarf, impair, lower, weaken; capture, conquer, master, overpower, overthrow, subject, subdue, subjugate, vanquish; impoverish, ruin; resolve, solve.

redundant *adj* copious, excessive, exuberant, fulsome, inordinate, lavish, needless, overflowing, overmuch, plentiful, prodigal, superabundant, replete, superfluous, unnecessary, useless; diffuse, periphrastic, pleonastic, tautological, verbose, wordy.

reel[1] *n* capstan, winch, windlass; bobbin, spool.

reel[2] *vb* falter, flounder, heave, lurch, pitch, plunge, rear, rock, roll, stagger, sway, toss, totter, tumble, wallow, welter, vacillate; spin, swing, turn, twirl, wheel, whirl. • *n* gyre, pirouette, spin, turn, twirl, wheel, whirl.

re-establish *vb* re-found, rehabilitate, reinstall, reinstate, renew, renovate, replace, restore.

refer *vb* commit, consign, direct, leave, relegate, send, submit; ascribe, assign, attribute, impute; appertain, belong, concern, pertain, point, relate, respect, touch; appeal, apply, consult; advert, allude, cite, quote.

referee *vb* arbitrate, judge, umpire. • *n* arbiter, arbitrator, judge, umpire.

reference *n* concern, connection, regard, respect; allusion, ascription, citation, hint, intimation, mark, reference, relegation.

refine *vb* clarify, cleanse, defecate, fine, purify; cultivate, humanize, improve, polish, rarefy, spiritualize.

refined *adj* courtly, cultured, genteel, polished, polite; discerning, discriminating, fastidious, sensitive; filtered, processed, purified.

refinement n clarification, filtration, purification, sublimation; betterment, improvement; delicacy, cultivation, culture, elegance, elevation, finish, gentility, good breeding, polish, politeness, purity, spirituality, style.

reflect vb copy, imitate, mirror, reproduce; cogitate, consider, contemplate, deliberate, meditate, muse, ponder, ruminate, study, think.

reflection n echo, shadow; cogitation, consideration, contemplation, deliberation, idea, meditation, musing, opinion, remark, rumination, thinking, thought; aspersion, blame, censure, criticism, disparagement, reproach, slur.

reflective adj reflecting, reflexive; cogitating, deliberating, musing, pondering, reasoning, thoughtful.

reform vb amend, ameliorate, better, correct, improve, mend, meliorate, rectify, reclaim, redeem, regenerate, repair, restore; reconstruct, remodel, reshape. • n amendment, correction, progress, reconstruction, rectification, reformation.

reformation n amendment, emendation, improvement, reform; adoption, conversion, redemption; refashioning, regeneration, reproduction, reconstruction.

refractory adj cantankerous, contumacious, cross-grained, disobedient, dogged, headstrong, heady, incoercible, intractable, mulish, obstinate, perverse, recalcitrant, self-willed, stiff, stubborn, sullen, ungovernable, unmanageable, unruly, unyielding.

refrain[1] vb abstain, cease, desist, forbear, stop, withhold.

refrain[2] n chorus, song, undersong.

refresh vb air, brace, cheer, cool, enliven, exhilarate, freshen, invigorate, reanimate, recreate, recruit, reinvigorate, revive, regale, slake.

refreshing adj comfortable, cooling, grateful, invigorating, pleasant, reanimating, restful, reviving.

refuge n asylum, covert, harbor, haven, protection, retreat, safety, sanction, security, shelter.

refulgent adj bright, brilliant, effulgent, lustrous, radiant, resplendent, shining.

refund vb reimburse, repay, restore, return. • n reimbursement, repayment.

refuse[1] n chaff, discard, draff, dross, dregs, garbage, junk, leavings, lees, litter, lumber, offal, recrement, remains, rubbish, scoria, scum, sediment, slag, sweepings, trash, waste.

refuse[2] vb decline, deny, withhold; disallow, disavow, exclude, rebuff, reject, renege, renounce, repel, repudiate, repulse, revoke, veto.

refute vb confute, defeat, disprove, overcome, overthrow, rebut, repel, silence.

regain vb recapture, recover, re-obtain, repossess, retrieve.

regal adj imposing, imperial, kingly, noble, royal, sovereign.

regale vb delight, entertain, gratify, refresh; banquet, feast.

regard vb behold, gaze, look, notice, mark, observe, remark, see, view, watch; attend to, consider, heed, mind, respect; esteem, honor, revere, reverence, value; account, believe, estimate, deem, hold, imagine, reckon, suppose, think, treat, use. • n aspect, gaze, look, view; attention, attentiveness, care, concern, consideration, heed, notice, observance; account, reference, relation, respect; admiration, affection, attachment, deference, esteem, estimation, favor, honor, interest, liking, love, respect, reverence, sympathy, value; account, eminence, note, reputation, repute; condition, matter, point.

regardful adj attentive, careful, considerate, deferential, heedful, mindful, observing, thoughtful, watchful.

regarding prep concerning, respecting, touching.

regardless adj careless, disregarding, heedless, inattentive, indifferent, mindless, neglectful, negligent, unconcerned, unmindful, unobservant. • adv however, irrespectively, nevertheless, nonetheless, notwithstanding.

regenerate vb reproduce; renovate, revive; change, convert, renew, sanctify. • adj born-again, converted, reformed, regenerated.

regime n administration, government, rule.

region n climate, clime, country, district, division, latitude, locale, locality, province, quarter, scene, territory, tract; area, neighborhood, part, place, portion, spot, space, sphere, terrain, vicinity.

register vb delineate, portray, record, show. • n annals, archive, catalog, chronicle, list, record, roll, schedule; clerk, registrar, registry; compass, range.

regret *vb* bewail, deplore, grieve, lament, repine, sorrow; bemoan, repent, mourn, rue. • *n* concern, disappointment, grief, lamentation, rue, sorrow, trouble; compunction, contrition, penitence, remorse, repentance, repining, self-condemnation, self-reproach.

regular *adj* conventional, natural, normal, ordinary, typical; correct, customary, cyclic, established, fixed, habitual, periodic, periodical, recurring, reasonable, rhythmic, seasonal, stated, usual; steady, constant, uniform, even; just, methodical, orderly, punctual, systematic, unvarying; complete, genuine, indubitable, out-and-out, perfect, thorough; balanced, consistent, symmetrical.

regulate *vb* adjust, arrange, dispose, methodize, order, organize, settle, standardize, time, systematize; conduct, control, direct, govern, guide, manage, rule.

regulation *adj* customary, mandatory, official, required, standard. • *n* adjustment, arrangement, control, disposal, disposition, law, management, order, ordering, precept, rule, settlement.

rehabilitate *vb* reinstate, re-establish, restore; reconstruct, reconstitute, reintegrate, reinvigorate, renew, renovate.

rehearsal *n* drill, practice, recital, recitation, repetition; account, history, mention, narration, narrative, recounting, relation, statement, story, telling.

rehearse *vb* recite, repeat; delineate, depict, describe, detail, enumerate, narrate, portray, recapitulate, recount, relate, tell.

reign *vb* administer, command, govern, influence, predominate, prevail, rule. • *n* control, dominion, empire, influence, power, royalty, sovereignty, power, rule, sway.

reimburse *vb* refund, repay, restore; compensate, indemnify, requite, satisfy.

rein *vb* bridle, check, control, curb, guide, harness, hold, restrain, restrict. • *n* bridle, check, curb, harness, restraint, restriction.

reinforce *vb* augment, fortify, strengthen.

reinstate *vb* re-establish, rehabilitate, reinstall, replace, restore.

reject *vb* cashier, discard, dismiss, eject, exclude, pluck; decline, deny, disallow, despise, disapprove, disbelieve, rebuff, refuse, renounce, repel, repudiate, scout, slight, spurn, veto. • *n* cast-off, discard, failure, refusal, repudiation.

rejoice *vb* cheer, delight, enliven, enrapture, exhilarate, gladden, gratify, please, transport; crow, exult, delight, gloat, glory, jubilate, triumph, vaunt.

rejoin *vb* answer, rebut, respond, retort.

relate *vb* describe, detail, mention, narrate, recite, recount, rehearse, report, tell; apply, connect, correlate.

relation *n* account, chronicle, description, detail, explanation, history, mention, narration, narrative, recital, rehearsal, report, statement, story, tale; affinity, application, bearing, connection, correlation, dependency, pertinence, relationship; concern, reference, regard, respect; alliance, nearness, propinquity, rapport; blood, consanguinity, cousinship, kin, kindred, kinship, relationship; kinsman, kinswoman, relative.

relax *vb* loose, loosen, slacken, unbrace, unstrain; debilitate, enervate, enfeeble, prostrate, unbrace, unstring, weaken; abate, diminish, lessen, mitigate, reduce, remit; amuse, divert, ease, entertain, recreate, unbend.

release *vb* deliver, discharge, disengage, exempt, extricate, free, liberate, loose, unloose; acquit, discharge, quit, relinquish, remit. • *n* deliverance, discharge, freedom, liberation; absolution, dispensation, excuse, exemption, exoneration; acquaintance, clearance.

relentless *adj* cruel, hard, impenitent, implacable, inexorable, merciless, obdurate, pitiless, rancorous, remorseless, ruthless, unappeasable, uncompassionate, unfeeling, unforgiving, unmerciful, unpitying, unrelenting, unyielding, vindictive.

relevant *adj* applicable, appropriate, apposite, apt, apropos, fit, germane, pertinent, proper, relative, suitable.

reliable *adj* authentic, certain, constant, dependable, sure, trustworthy, trusty, unfailing.

reliance *n* assurance, confidence, credence, dependence, hope, trust.

relic *n* keepsake, memento, memorial, remembrance, souvenir, token, trophy; trace, vestige.

relics *npl* fragments, leavings, remainder, remains, remnants, ruins, scraps; body, cadaver, corpse, remains.

relict *n* dowager, widow.

relief *n* aid, alleviation, amelioration, assistance, assuagement, comfort, deliverance, ease, easement, help, mitigation, reinforcement, respite, rest, succor, softening, support; indemnification, redress, remedy; embossment, projection, prominence, protrusion; clearness, distinction, perspective, vividness.

relieve *vb* aid, comfort, help, spell, succor, support, sustain; abate, allay, alleviate, assuage, cure, diminish, ease, lessen, lighten, mitigate, remedy, remove, soothe; indemnify, redress, right, repair; disengage, free, release, remedy, rescue.

religious *adj* devotional, devout, god-fearing, godly, holy, pious, prayerful, spiritual; conscientious, exact, rigid, scrupulous, strict; canonical, divine, theological.

relinquish *vb* abandon, desert, forsake, forswear, leave, quit, renounce, resign, vacate; abdicate, cede, forbear, forgo, give up, surrender, yield.

relish *vb* appreciate, enjoy, like, prefer; season, flavor, taste. • *n* appetite, appreciation, enjoyment, fondness, gratification, gusto, inclination, liking, partiality, predilection, taste, zest; cast, flavor, manner, quality, savor, seasoning, sort, tang, tinge, touch; appetizer, condiment.

reluctance *n* aversion, backwardness, disinclination, dislike, loathing, repugnance, unwillingness.

reluctant *adj* averse, backward, disinclined, hesitant, indisposed, loath, unwilling.

rely *vb* confide, count, depend, hope, lean, reckon, repose, trust.

remain *vb* abide, continue, endure, last; exceed, persist, survive; abide, continue, dwell, halt, inhabit, rest, sojourn, stay, stop, tarry, wait.

remainder *n* balance, excess, leavings, remains, remnant, residue, rest, surplus.

remark *vb* heed, notice, observe, regard; comment, express, mention, observe, say, state, utter. • *n* consideration, heed, notice, observation, regard; annotation, comment, gloss, note, stricture; assertion, averment, comment, declaration, saying, statement, utterance.

remarkable *adj* conspicuous, distinguished, eminent, extraordinary, famous, notable, noteworthy, noticeable, pre-eminent, rare, singular, strange, striking, uncommon, unusual, wonderful.

remedy *vb* cure, heal, help, palliate, relieve; amend, correct, rectify, redress, repair, restore, retrieve. • *n* antidote, antitoxin,

corrective, counteractive, cure, help, medicine, nostrum, panacea, restorative, specific; redress, reparation, restitution, restoration; aid, assistance, relief.

remembrance *n* recollection, reminiscence, retrospection; keepsake, memento, memorial, memory, reminder, souvenir, token; consideration, regard, thought.

reminiscence *n* memory, recollection, remembrance, retrospective.

remiss *adj* backward, behindhand, dilatory, indolent, languid, lax, lazy, slack, slow, tardy; careless, dilatory, heedless, idle, inattentive, neglectful, negligent, shiftless, slothful, thoughtless.

remission *n* abatement, decrease, diminution, lessening, mitigation, moderation, reduction, relaxation; cancellation, discharge, release, relinquishment; intermission, interruption, pause, rest, stop, stoppage, suspense, suspension; absolution, acquittal, excuse, exoneration, forgiveness, indulgence, pardon.

remit *vb* replace, restore, return; abate, bate, diminish, relax; release; absolve, condone, excuse, forgive, overlook, pardon; relinquish, resign, surrender; consign, forward, refer, send, transmit. • *n* authorization, brief, instructions, orders.

remnant *n* remainder, remains, residue, rest, trace; fragment, piece, scrap.

remorse *n* compunction, contrition, penitence, qualm, regret, repentance, reproach, self-reproach, sorrow.

remorseless *adj* cruel, barbarous, hard, harsh, implacable, inexorable, merciless, pitiless, relentless, ruthless, savage, uncompassionate, unmerciful, unrelenting.

remote *adj* distant, far, out-of-the-way; alien, far-fetched, foreign, inappropriate, unconnected, unrelated; abstracted, separated; inconsiderable, slight; isolated, removed, secluded, sequestrated.

removal *n* abstraction, departure, dislodgement, displacement, relegation, remove, shift, transference; elimination, extraction, withdrawal; abatement, destruction; discharge, dismissal, ejection, expulsion.

remove *vb* carry, dislodge, displace, shift, transfer, transport; abstract, extract, withdraw; abate, banish, destroy, suppress; cashier, depose, discharge, dismiss, eject, expel, oust, retire; depart, move.

remunerate *vb* compensate, indemnify, pay,

recompense, reimburse, repay, requite, reward, satisfy.

remuneration *n* compensation, earnings, indemnity, pay, payment, recompense, reimbursement, reparation, repayment, reward, salary, wages.

remunerative *adj* gainful, lucrative, paying, profitable; compensatory, recompensing, remuneratory, reparative, requiting, rewarding.

rend *vb* break, burst, cleave, crack, destroy, dismember, dissever, disrupt, divide, fracture, lacerate, rive, rupture, sever, shiver, snap, split, sunder, tear.

render *vb* restore, return, surrender; assign, deliver, give, present; afford, contribute, furnish, supply, yield; construe, interpret, translate.

rendition *n* restitution, return, surrender; delineation, exhibition, interpretation, rendering, representation, reproduction; translation, version.

renegade *adj* apostate, backsliding, disloyal, false, outlawed, rebellious, recreant, unfaithful. • *n* apostate, backslider, recreant, turncoat; deserter, outlaw, rebel, revolter, traitor; vagabond, wretch.

renew *vb* rebuild, recreate, re-establish, refit, refresh, rejuvenate, renovate, repair, replenish, restore, resuscitate, revive; continue, recommence, repeat; iterate, reiterate; regenerate, transform.

renounce *vb* abjure, abnegate, decline, deny, disclaim, disown, forswear, neglect, recant, repudiate, reject, slight; abandon, abdicate, drop, forgo, forsake, desert, leave, quit, relinquish, resign.

renovate *vb* reconstitute, re-establish, refresh, refurbish, renew, restore, revamp; reanimate, recreate, regenerate, reproduce, resuscitate, revive, revivify.

renown *n* celebrity, distinction, eminence, fame, figure, glory, honor, greatness, name, note, notability, notoriety, reputation, repute.

renowned *adj* celebrated, distinguished, eminent, famed, famous, honored, illustrious, remarkable, wonderful.

rent[1] *n* breach, break, crack, cleft, crevice, fissure, flaw, fracture, gap, laceration, opening, rift, rupture, separation, split, tear; schism.

rent[2] *vb* hire, lease, let. • *n* income, rental, revenue.

repair[1] *vb* mend, patch, piece, refit, retouch,

tinker, vamp; correct, recruit, restore, retrieve. • *n* mending, refitting, renewal, reparation, restoration.

repair[2] *vb* betake oneself, go, move, resort, turn.

repairable *adj* curable, recoverable, reparable, restorable, retrievable.

reparable *adj* curable, recoverable, repairable, restorable, retrievable.

reparation *n* renewal, repair, restoration; amends, atonement, compensation, correction, indemnification, recompense, redress, requital, restitution, satisfaction.

repay *vb* refund, reimburse, restore, return; compensate, recompense, remunerate, reward, satisfy; avenge, retaliate, revenge.

repeal *vb* abolish, annul, cancel, recall, rescind, reverse, revoke. • *n* abolition, abrogation, annulment, cancellation, rescission, reversal, revocation.

repeat *vb* double, duplicate, iterate; cite, narrate, quote, recapitulate, recite, rehearse; echo, renew, reproduce. • *n* duplicate, duplication, echo, iteration, recapitulation, reiteration, repetition.

repel *vb* beat, disperse, repulse, scatter; check, confront, oppose, parry, rebuff, resist, withstand; decline, refuse, reject; disgust, revolt, sicken.

repellent *adj* abhorrent, disgusting, forbidding, repelling, repugnant, repulsive, revolting, uninviting.

repent *vb* atone, regret, relent, rue, sorrow.

repentance *n* compunction, contriteness, contrition, penitence, regret, remorse, self-accusation, self-condemnation, self-reproach.

repentant *adj* contrite, penitent, regretful, remorseful, rueful, sorrowful, sorry.

repercussion *n* rebound, recoil, reverberation; backlash, consequence, result.

repetition *n* harping, iteration, recapitulation, reiteration; diffuseness, redundancy, tautology, verbosity; narration, recital, rehearsal, relation, retailing; recurrence, renewal.

repine *vb* croak, complain, fret, grumble, long, mope, murmur.

replace *vb* re-establish, reinstate, reset; refund, repay, restore; succeed, supersede, supplant.

replenish *vb* fill, refill, renew, re-supply; enrich, furnish, provide, store, supply.

replete *adj* abounding, charged, exuberant, fraught, full, glutted, gorged, satiated, well-stocked.

repletion n abundance, exuberance, fullness, glut, profusion, satiation, satiety, surfeit.

replica n autograph, copy, duplicate, facsimile, reproduction.

reply vb answer, echo, rejoin, respond. • n acknowledgement, answer, rejoinder, repartee, replication, response, retort.

report vb announce, annunciate, communicate, declare; advertise, broadcast, bruit, describe, detail, herald, mention, narrate, noise, promulgate, publish, recite, relate, rumor, state, tell; minute, record. • n account, announcement, communication, declaration, statement; advice, description, detail, narration, narrative, news, recital, story, tale, talk, tidings; gossip, hearsay, rumor; clap, detonation, discharge, explosion, noise, repercussion, sound; fame, reputation, repute; account, bulletin, minute, note, record, statement.

repose[1] vb compose, recline, rest, settle; couch, lie, recline, sleep, slumber; confide, lean. • n quiet, recumbence, recumbency, rest, sleep, slumber; breathing time, inactivity, leisure, respite, relaxation; calm, ease, peace, peacefulness, quietness, quietude, stillness, tranquillity.

repose[2] vb place, put, stake; deposit, lodge, reposit, store.

repository n conservatory, depository, depot, magazine, museum, receptacle, repertory, storehouse, storeroom, thesaurus, treasury, vault.

reprehend vb accuse, blame, censure, chide, rebuke, reprimand, reproach, reprove, upbraid.

reprehensible adj blameable, blameworthy, censurable, condemnable, culpable, reprovable.

reprehension n admonition, blame, censure, condemnation, rebuke, reprimand, reproof.

represent vb exhibit, express, show; delineate, depict, describe, draw, portray, sketch; act, impersonate, mimic, personate, personify; exemplify, illustrate, image, reproduce, symbolize, typify.

representation n delineation, exhibition, show; impersonation, personation, simulation; account, description, narration, narrative, relation, statement; image, likeness, model, portraiture, resemblance, semblance; sight, spectacle; expostulation, remonstrance.

representative adj figurative, illustrative, symbolic, typical; delegated, deputed, representing. • n agent, commissioner, delegate, deputy, emissary, envoy, legate, lieutenant, messenger, proxy, substitute.

repress vb choke, crush, dull, overcome, overpower, silence, smother, subdue, suppress, quell; bridle, chasten, chastise, check, control, curb, restrain; appease, calm, quiet.

reprimand vb admonish, blame, censure, chide, rebuke, reprehend, reproach, reprove, upbraid. • n admonition, blame, censure, rebuke, reprehension, reproach, reprobation, reproof, reproval.

reprint vb republish. • n reimpression, republication; copy.

reproach vb blame, censure, rebuke, reprehend, reprimand, reprove, upbraid; abuse, accuse, asperse, condemn, defame, discredit, disparage, revile, traduce, vilify. • n abuse, blame, censure, condemnation, contempt, contumely, disapprobation, disapproval, expostulation, insolence, invective, railing, rebuke, remonstrance, reprobation, reproof, reviling, scorn, scurrility, upbraiding, vilification; abasement, discredit, disgrace, dishonor, disrepute, indignity, ignominy, infamy, insult, obloquy, odium, offence, opprobrium, scandal, shame, slur, stigma.

reproachful adj abusive, censorious, condemnatory, contemptuous, contumelious, damnatory, insolent, insulting, offensive, opprobrious, railing, reproving, sacrifice, scolding, scornful, scurrilous, upbraiding, vituperative; base, discreditable, disgraceful, dishonorable, disreputable, infamous, scandalous, shameful, vile.

reprobate vb censure, condemn, disapprove, discard, reject, reprehend; disallow; abandon, disown. • adj abandoned, base, castaway, corrupt, depraved, graceless, hardened, irredeemable, lost, profligate, shameless, vile, vitiated, wicked. • n caitiff, castaway, miscreant, outcast, rascal, scamp, scoundrel, sinner, villain.

reproduce vb copy, duplicate, emulate, imitate, print, repeat, represent; breed, generate, procreate, propagate.

reproof n admonition, animadversion, blame, castigation, censure, chiding, condemnation, correction, criticism, lecture, monition, objurgation, rating, rebuke, reprehension, reprimand, reproach, reproval, upbraiding.

reprove *vb* admonish, blame, castigate, censure, chide, condemn, correct, criticize, inculpate, lecture, objurgate, rate, rebuke, reprimand, reproach, scold, upbraid.

reptilian *adj* abject, crawling, creeping, groveling, low, mean, treacherous, vile, vulgar.

repudiate *vb* abjure, deny, disavow, discard, disclaim, disown, nullify, reject, renounce.

repugnance *n* contrariety, contrariness, incompatibility, inconsistency, irreconcilability, irreconcilableness, unsuitability, unsuitableness; contest, opposition, resistance, struggle; antipathy, aversion, detestation, dislike, hatred, hostility, reluctance, repulsion, unwillingness.

repugnant *adj* incompatible, inconsistent, irreconcilable; adverse, antagonistic, contrary, hostile, inimical, opposed, opposing, unfavorable; detestable, distasteful, offensive, repellent, repulsive.

repulse *vb* check, defeat, refuse, reject, repel. • *n* repelling, repulsion; denial, refusal; disappointment, failure.

repulsion *n* abhorrence, antagonism, anticipation, aversion, discard, disgust, dislike, hatred, hostility, loathing, rebuff, rejection, repugnance, repulse, spurning.

repulsive *adj* abhorrent, cold, disagreeable, disgusting, forbidding, frigid, harsh, hateful, loathsome, nauseating, nauseous, odious, offensive, repellent, repugnant, reserved, revolting, sickening, ugly, unpleasant.

reputable *adj* creditable, estimable, excellent, good, honorable, respectable, worthy.

reputation *n* account, character, fame, mark, name, repute; celebrity, credit, distinction, eclat, esteem, estimation, glory, honor, prestige, regard, renown, report, respect; notoriety.

repute *vb* account, consider, deem, esteem, estimate, hold, judge, reckon, regard, think.

request *vb* ask, beg, beseech, call, claim, demand, desire, entreat, pray, solicit, supplicate. • *n* asking, entreaty, importunity, invitation, petition, prayer, requisition, solicitation, suit, supplication.

require *vb* beg, beseech, bid, claim, crave, demand, dun, importune, invite, pray, requisition, request, sue, summon; need, want; direct, enjoin, exact, order, prescribe.

requirement *n* claim, demand, exigency, market, need, needfulness, requisite, requisition, request, urgency, want; behest, bidding, charge, command, decree, exaction, injunction, mandate, order, precept.

requisite *adj* essential, imperative, indispensable, necessary, needful, needed, required. • *n* essential, necessity, need, requirement.

requite *vb* compensate, pay, remunerate, reciprocate, recompense, repay, reward, satisfy; avenge, punish, retaliate, satisfy.

rescind *vb* abolish, abrogate, annul, cancel, countermand, quash, recall, repeal, reverse, revoke, vacate, void.

rescue *vb* deliver, extricate, free, liberate, preserve, ransom, recapture, recover, redeem, release, retake, save. • *n* deliverance, extrication, liberation, redemption, release, salvation.

research *vb* analyze, examine, explore, inquire, investigate, probe, study. • *n* analysis, examination, exploration, inquiry, investigation, scrutiny, study.

resemblance *n* affinity, agreement, analogy, likeness, semblance, similarity, similitude; counterpart, facsimile, image, representation.

resemble *vb* compare, liken; copy, counterfeit, imitate.

resentful *adj* angry, bitter, choleric, huffy, hurt, irascible, irritable, malignant, revengeful, sore, touchy.

resentment *n* acrimony, anger, annoyance, bitterness, choler, displeasure, dudgeon, fury, gall, grudge, heartburning, huff, indignation, ire, irritation, pique, rage, soreness, spleen, sulks, umbrage, vexation, wrath.

reservation *n* reserve, suppression; appropriation, booking, exception, restriction, saving; proviso; salvo; custody, park, reserve, sanctuary.

reserve *vb* hold, husband, keep, retain, store. • *adj* alternate, auxiliary, spare, substitute. • *n* reservation; aloofness, backwardness, closeness, coldness, concealment, constraint, suppression, reservedness, retention, restraint, reticence, uncommunicativeness, unresponsiveness; coyness, demureness, modesty, shyness, taciturnity; park, reservation, sanctuary.

reserved *adj* coy, demure, modest, shy, taciturn; aloof, backward, cautious, cold, distant, incommunicative, restrained, reticent, self-controlled, unsociable, unsocial;

bespoken, booked, excepted, held, kept, retained, set apart, taken, withheld.

reside *vb* abide, domicile, domiciliate, dwell, inhabit, live, lodge, remain, room, sojourn, stay.

residence *n* inhabitance, inhabitancy, sojourn, stay, stop, tarrying; abode, domicile, dwelling, habitation, home, house, lodging, mansion.

residue *n* leavings, remainder, remains, remnant, residuum, rest; excess, overplus, surplus.

resign *vb* abandon, abdicate, abjure, cede, commit, disclaim, forego, forsake, leave, quit, relinquish, renounce, surrender, yield.

resignation *n* abandonment, abdication, relinquishment, renunciation, retirement, surrender; acquiescence, compliance, endurance, forbearance, fortitude, long-sufferance, patience, submission, sufferance.

resist *vb* assail, attack, baffle, block, check, confront, counteract, disappoint, frustrate, hinder, impede, impugn, neutralize, obstruct, oppose, rebel, rebuff, stand against, stem, stop, strive, thwart, withstand.

resolute *adj* bold, constant, decided, determined, earnest, firm, fixed, game, hardy, inflexible, persevering, pertinacious, relentless, resolved, staunch, steadfast, steady, stout, stouthearted, sturdy, tenacious, unalterable, unbending, undaunted, unflinching, unshaken, unwavering, unyielding.

resolution *n* boldness, disentanglement, explication, unraveling; backbone, constancy, courage, decision, determination, earnestness, energy, firmness, fortitude, grit, hardihood, inflexibility, intention, manliness, pluck, perseverance, purpose, relentlessness, resolve, resoluteness, stamina, steadfastness, steadiness, tenacity.

resolve *vb* analyze, disperse, scatter, separate, reduce; change, dissolve, liquefy, melt, reduce, transform; decipher, disentangle, elucidate, explain, interpret, unfold, solve, unravel; conclude, decide, determine, fix, intend, purpose, will. • *n* conclusion, decision, determination, intention, will; declaration, resolution.

resonant *adj* booming, clangorous, resounding, reverberating, ringing, roaring, sonorous, thundering, vibrant.

resort *vb* frequent, haunt; assemble, congregate, convene, go, repair. • *n*

application, expedient, recourse; haunt, refuge, rendezvous, retreat, spa; assembling, confluence, concourse, meeting; recourse, reference.

resound *vb* echo, re-echo, reverberate, ring; celebrate, extol, praise, sound.

resource *n* dependence, resort; appliance, contrivance, device, expedient, instrumentality, means, resort.

resources *npl* capital, funds, income, money, property, reserve, supplies, wealth.

respect *vb* admire, esteem, honor, prize, regard, revere, reverence, spare, value, venerate; consider, heed, notice, observe. • *n* attention, civility, courtesy, consideration, deference, estimation, homage, honor, notice, politeness, recognition, regard, reverence, veneration; consideration, favor, goodwill, kind; aspect, bearing, connection, feature, matter, particular, point, reference, regard, relation.

respects *npl* compliments, greetings, regards.

respectable *adj* considerable, estimable, honorable, presentable, proper, upright, worthy; adequate, moderate; tolerable.

respectful *adj* ceremonious, civil, complaisant, courteous, decorous, deferential, dutiful, formal, polite.

respire *vb* breathe, exhale, live.

respite *vb* delay, relieve, reprieve. • *n* break, cessation, delay, intermission, interval, pause, recess, rest, stay, stop; forbearance, postponement, reprieve.

resplendent *adj* beaming, bright, brilliant, effulgent, lucid, glittering, glorious, gorgeous, luminous, lustrous, radiant, shining, splendid.

respond *vb* answer, reply, rejoin; accord, correspond, suit.

response *n* answer, replication, rejoinder, reply, retort.

responsible *adj* accountable, amenable, answerable, liable, trustworthy.

rest[1] *vb* cease, desist, halt, hold, pause, repose, stop; breathe, relax, unbend; repose, sleep, slumber; lean, lie, lounge, perch, recline, ride; acquiesce, confide, trust; confide, rely, trust; calm, comfort, ease. • *n* fixity, immobility, inactivity, motionlessness, quiescence, quiet, repose; hush, peace, peacefulness, quietness, relief, security, stillness, tranquillity; cessation, intermission, interval, lull, pause, relaxation, respite, stop, stay; siesta, sleep, slumber;

death; brace, stay, support; axis, fulcrum, pivot.

rest[2] *vb* be left, remain. • *n* balance, remainder, remnant, residuum; overplus, surplus.

restaurant *n* bistro, café, cafeteria, chophouse, eatery, eating house, pizzeria, trattoria.

restitution *n* restoration, return; amends, compensation, indemnification, recompense, rehabilitation, remuneration, reparation, repayment, requital, satisfaction.

restive *adj* mulish, obstinate, stopping, stubborn, unwilling; impatient, recalcitrant, restless, uneasy, unquiet.

restless *adj* disquieted, disturbed, restive, sleepless, uneasy, unquiet, unresting; changeable, inconstant, irresolute, unsteady, vacillating; active, astatic, roving, transient, unsettled, unstable, wandering; agitated, fidgety, fretful, turbulent.

restoration *n* recall, recovery, re-establishment, reinstatement, reparation, replacement, restitution, return; reconsideration, redemption, reintegration, renewal, renovation, repair, resuscitation, revival; convalescence, cure, recruitment, recuperation.

restorative *adj* curative, invigorating, recuperative, remedial, restoring, stimulating. • *n* corrective, curative, cure, healing, medicine, remedy, reparative, stimulant.

restore *vb* refund, repay, return; caulk, cobble, emend, heal, mend, patch, reintegrate, re-establish, rehabilitate, reinstate, renew, repair, replace, retrieve; cure, heal, recover, revive; resuscitate.

restrain *vb* bridle, check, coerce, confine, constrain, curb, debar, govern, hamper, hinder, hold, keep, muzzle, picket, prevent, repress, restrict, rule, subdue, tie, withhold; abridge, circumscribe, narrow.

restraint *n* bridle, check, coercion, control, compulsion, constraint, curb, discipline, repression, suppression; arrest, deterrence, hindrance, inhibition, limitation, prevention, prohibition, restriction, stay, stop; confinement, detention, imprisonment, shackles; constraint, stiffness, reserve, unnaturalness.

restrict *vb* bound, circumscribe, confine, limit, qualify, restrain, straiten.

restriction *n* confinement, limitation; constraint, restraint; reservation, reserve.

result *vb* accrue, arise, come, ensue, flow,

follow, issue, originate, proceed, spring, rise; end, eventuate, terminate. • *n* conclusion, consequence, deduction, inference, outcome; corollary, effect, end, event, eventuality, fruit, harvest, issue, product, sequel, termination; decision, determination, finding, resolution, resolve, solution, verdict.

resume *vb* continue, recommence, renew, restart, summarize.

résumé *n* abstract, curriculum vitae, epitome, recapitulation, summary, synopsis.

resuscitate *vb* quicken, reanimate, renew, resurrect, restore, revive, revivify.

retain *vb* detain, hold, husband, keep, preserve, recall, recollect, remember, reserve, save, withhold; engage, maintain.

retainer *n* adherent, attendant, dependant, follower, hanger-on, servant.

retaliate *vb* avenge, match, repay, requite, retort, return, turn.

retaliation *n* boomerang, counterstroke, punishment, repayment, requital, retribution, revenge.

retard *vb* check, clog, hinder, impede, obstruct, slacken; adjourn, defer, delay, postpone, procrastinate.

reticent *adj* close, reserved, secretive, silent, taciturn, uncommunicative.

retinue *n* bodyguard, cortege, entourage, escort, followers, household, ménage, suite, tail, train.

retire *vb* discharge, shelve, superannuate, withdraw; depart, leave, resign, retreat.

retired *adj* abstracted, removed, withdrawn; apart, private, secret, sequestrated, solitary.

retirement *n* isolation, loneliness, privacy, retreat, seclusion, solitude, withdrawal.

retiring *adj* coy, demure, diffident, modest, reserved, retreating, shy, withdrawing.

retort *vb* answer, rejoin, reply, respond. • *n* answer, rejoinder, repartee, reply, response; crucible, jar, vessel, vial.

retract *vb* reverse, withdraw; abjure, cancel, disavow, recall, recant, revoke, unsay.

retreat *vb* recoil, retire, withdraw; recede. • *n* departure, recession, recoil, retirement, withdrawal; privacy, seclusion, solitude; asylum, cove, den, habitat, haunt, niche, recess, refuge, resort, shelter.

retrench *vb* clip, curtail, cut, delete, dock, lop, mutilate, pare, prune; abridge, decrease, diminish, lessen; confine, limit; economize, encroach.

retribution n compensation, desert, judgement, nemesis, penalty, recompense, repayment, requital, retaliation, return, revenge, reward, vengeance.

retrieve vb recall, recover, recoup, recruit, re-establish, regain, repair, restore.

retrograde vb decline, degenerate, recede, retire, retrocede. • adj backward, inverse, retrogressive, unprogressive.

retrospect n recollection, re-examination, reminiscence, re-survey, review, survey.

return vb reappear, recoil, recur, revert; answer, reply, respond; recriminate, retort; convey, give, communicate, reciprocate, recompense, refund, remit, repay, report, requite, send, tell, transmit; elect. • n payment, reimbursement, remittance, repayment; recompense, recovery, recurrence, renewal, repayment, requital, restitution, restoration, reward; advantage, benefit, interest, profit, rent, yield.

reunion n assemblage, assembly, gathering, meeting, re-assembly; rapprochement, reconciliation.

reveal vb announce, communicate, confess, declare, disclose, discover, display, divulge, expose, impart, open, publish, tell, uncover, unmask, unseal, unveil.

revel vb carouse, disport, riot, roister, tipple; delight, indulge, luxuriate, wanton. • n carousal, feast, festival, saturnalia, spree.

revelry n bacchanal, carousal, carouse, debauch, festivity, jollification, jollity, orgy, revel, riot, rout, saturnalia, wassail.

revenge vb avenge, repay, requite, retaliate, vindicate. • n malevolence, rancor, reprisal, requital, retaliation, retribution, vengeance, vindictiveness.

revengeful adj implacable, malevolent, malicious, malignant, resentful, rancorous, spiteful, vengeful, vindictive.

revenue n fruits, income, produce, proceeds, receipts, return, reward, wealth.

reverberate vb echo, re-echo, resound, return.

revere vb adore, esteem, hallow, honor, reverence, venerate, worship.

reverence vb adore, esteem, hallow, honor, revere, venerate, worship. • n adoration, awe, deference, homage, honor, respect, veneration, worship.

reverential adj deferential, humble, respectful, reverent, submissive.

reverse vb invert, transpose; overset, overthrow, overturn, quash, subvert, undo, unmake; annul, countermand, repeal, rescind, retract, revoke; back, back up, retreat. • adj back, converse, contrary, opposite, verso. • n back, calamity, check, comedown, contrary, counterpart, defeat, opposite, tail; change, vicissitude; adversity, affliction, hardship, misadventure, mischance, misfortune, mishap, trial.

revert vb repel, reverse; backslide, lapse, recur, relapse, return.

review vb inspect, overlook, reconsider, re-examine, retrace, revise, survey; analyze, criticize, discuss, edit, judge, scrutinize, study. • n reconsideration, re-examination, re-survey, retrospect, survey; analysis, digest, synopsis; commentary, critique, criticism, notice, review, scrutiny, study.

revile vb abuse, asperse, backbite, calumniate, defame, execrate, malign, reproach, slander, traduce, upbraid, vilify.

revise vb reconsider, re-examine, review; alter, amend, correct, edit, overhaul, polish.

revive vb reanimate, reinspire, reinspirit, reinvigorate, resuscitate, revitalize, revivify; animate, cheer, comfort, invigorate, quicken, reawaken, recover, refresh, renew, renovate, rouse, strengthen; reawake, recall.

revocation n abjuration, recall, recantation, repeal, retraction, reversal.

revoke vb abolish, abrogate, annul, cancel, countermand, invalidate, quash, recall, recant, repeal, repudiate, rescind, retract.

revolt vb desert, mutiny, rebel, rise; disgust, nauseate, repel, sicken. • n defection, desertion, faithlessness, inconstancy; disobedience, insurrection, mutiny, outbreak, rebellion, sedition, strike, uprising.

revolting adj abhorrent, abominable, disgusting, hateful, monstrous, nauseating, nauseous, objectionable, obnoxious, offensive, repulsive, shocking, sickening; insurgent, mutinous, rebellious.

revolution n coup, disobedience, insurrection, mutiny, outbreak, rebellion, sedition, strike, uprising; change, innovation, reformation, transformation, upheaval; circle, circuit, cycle, lap, orbit, rotation, spin, turn.

revolve vb circle, circulate, rotate, swing, turn, wheel; devolve, return; consider, mediate, ponder, ruminate, study.

revulsion n abstraction, shrinking, withdrawal; change, reaction, reversal, transition; abhorrence, disgust, loathing, repugnance.

reward *vb* compensate, gratify, indemnify, pay, punish, recompense, remember, remunerate, requite. • *n* compensation, gratification, guerdon, indemnification, pay, recompense, remuneration, requital; bounty, bonus, fee, gratuity, honorarium, meed, perquisite, premium, remembrance, tip; punishment, retribution.

rhythm *n* cadence, lilt, pulsation, swing; measure, meter, number.

ribald *adj* base, blue, coarse, filthy, gross, indecent, lewd, loose, low, mean, obscene, vile.

rich *adj* affluent, flush, moneyed, opulent, prosperous, wealthy; costly, estimable, gorgeous, luxurious, precious, splendid, sumptuous, superb, valuable; delicious, luscious, savory; abundant, ample, copious, enough, full, plentiful, plenteous, sufficient; fertile, fruitful, luxuriant, productive, prolific; bright, dark, deep, exuberant, vivid; harmonious, mellow, melodious, soft, sweet; comical, funny, humorous, laughable.

riches *npl* abundance, affluence, fortune, money, opulence, plenty, richness, wealth, wealthiness.

rickety *adj* broken, imperfect, shaky, shattered, tottering, tumbledown, unsteady, weak.

rid *vb* deliver, free, release; clear, disburden, disencumber, scour, sweep; disinherit, dispatch, dissolve, divorce, finish, sever.

riddance *n* deliverance, disencumberment, extrication, escape, freedom, release, relief.

riddle[1] *vb* explain, solve, unriddle. • *n* conundrum, enigma, mystery, puzzle, rebus.

riddle[2] *vb* sieve, sift, perforate, permeate, spread. • *n* colander, sieve, strainer.

ridge *n* chine, hogback, ledge, saddle, spine, rib, watershed, weal, wrinkle.

ridicule *vb* banter, burlesque, chaff, deride, disparage, jeer, mock, lampoon, rally, satirize, scout, taunt. • *n* badinage, banter, burlesque, chaff, derision, game, gibe, irony, jeer, mockery, persiflage, quip, raillery, sarcasm, satire, sneer, squib, wit.

ridiculous *adj* absurd, amusing, comical, droll, eccentric, fantastic, farcical, funny, laughable, ludicrous, nonsensical, odd, outlandish, preposterous, queer, risible, waggish.

rife *adj* abundant, common, current, general, numerous, plentiful, prevailing, prevalent, replete.

riffraff *n* horde, mob, populace, rabble, scum, trash.

rifle *vb* despoil, fleece, pillage, plunder, ransack, rob, strip.

rift *vb* cleave, rive, split. • *n* breach, break, chink, cleft, crack, cranny, crevice, fissure, fracture, gap, opening, reft, rent.

rig *vb* accouter, clothe, dress. • *n* costume, dress, garb; equipment, team.

right *vb* adjust, correct, regulate, settle, straighten, vindicate. • *adj* direct, rectilinear, straight; erect, perpendicular, plumb, upright; equitable, even-handed, fair, just, justifiable, honest, lawful, legal, legitimate, rightful, square, unswerving; appropriate, becoming, correct, conventional, fit, fitting, meet, orderly, proper, reasonable, seemly, suitable, well-done; actual, genuine, real, true, unquestionable; dexter, dextral, right-handed. • *adv* equitably, fairly, justly, lawfully, rightfully, rightly; correctly, fitly, properly, suitably, truly; actually, exactly, just, really, truly, well. • *n* authority, claim, liberty, permission, power, privilege, title; equity, good, honor, justice, lawfulness, legality, propriety, reason, righteousness, truth.

righteous *adj* devout, godly, good, holy, honest, incorrupt, just, pious, religious, saintly, uncorrupt, upright, virtuous; equitable, fair, right, rightful.

righteousness *n* equity, faithfulness, godliness, goodness, holiness, honesty, integrity, justice, piety, purity, right, rightfulness, sanctity, uprightness, virtue.

rightful *adj* lawful, legitimate, true; appropriate, correct, deserved, due, equitable, fair, fitting, honest, just, legal, merited, proper, reasonable, suitable.

rigid *adj* firm, hard, inflexible, permanent, stiff, stiffened, unbending, unpliant, unyielding; bristling, erect, precipitous, steep; austere, conventional, correct, exact, formal, harsh, meticulous, precise, rigorous, severe, sharp, stern, strict, unmitigated; cruel.

rigmarole *n* balderdash, flummery, gibberish, gobbledegook, jargon, nonsense, palaver, trash, twaddle, verbiage.

rigor *n* hardness, inflexibility, rigidity, rigidness, stiffness; asperity, austerity, harshness, severity, sternness; evenness, strictness; inclemency.

rile *vb* anger, annoy, irritate, upset, vex.

rim *n* brim, brink, border, confine, curb, edge, flange, girdle, margin, ring, skirt.

ring[1] *vb* circle, encircle, enclose, girdle, surround. • *n* circle, circlet, girdle, hoop, round, whorl; cabal, clique, combination, confederacy, coterie, gang, junta, league, set.

ring[2] *vb* chime, clang, jingle, knell, peal, resound, reverberate, sound, tingle, toll; call, phone, telephone. • *n* chime, knell, peal, tinkle, toll; call, phone call, telephone call.

riot *vb* carouse, luxuriate, revel. • *n* affray, altercation, brawl, broil, commotion, disturbance, fray, outbreak, pandemonium, quarrel, squabble, tumult, uproar; dissipation, excess, luxury, merrymaking, revelry.

riotous *adj* boisterous, luxurious, merry, reveling, unrestrained, wanton; disorderly, insubordinate, lawless, mutinous, rebellious, refractory, seditious, tumultuous, turbulent, ungovernable, unruly, violent.

ripe *adj* advanced, grown, mature, mellow, seasoned, soft; fit, prepared, ready; accomplished, complete, consummate, finished, perfect, perfected.

ripen *vb* burgeon, develop, mature, prepare.

rise *vb* arise, ascend, clamber, climb, levitate, mount; excel, succeed; enlarge, heighten, increase, swell, thrive; revive; grow, kindle, wax; begin, flow, head, originate, proceed, spring, start; mutiny, rebel, revolt; happen, occur. • *n* ascension, ascent, rising; elevation, grade, hill, slope; beginning, emergence, flow, origin, source, spring; advance, augmentation, expansion, increase.

risible *adj* amusing, comical, droll, farcical, funny, laughable, ludicrous, ridiculous.

risk *vb* bet, endanger, hazard, jeopardize, peril, speculate, stake, venture, wager. • *n* chance, danger, hazard, jeopardy, peril, venture.

rite *n* ceremonial, ceremony, form, formulary, ministration, observance, ordinance, ritual, rubric, sacrament, solemnity.

ritual *adj* ceremonial, conventional, formal, habitual, routine, stereotyped. • *n* ceremonial, ceremony, liturgy, observance, rite, sacrament, service; convention, form, formality, habit, practice, protocol.

rival *vb* emulate, match, oppose. • *adj* competing, contending, emulating, emulous, opposing. • *n* antagonist, competitor, emulator, opponent.

rive *vb* cleave, rend, split.

river *n* affluent, current, reach, stream, tributary.

road *n* course, highway, lane, passage, path, pathway, roadway, route, street, thoroughfare, track, trail, turnpike, way.

roam *vb* jaunt, prowl, ramble, range, rove, straggle, stray, stroll, wander.

roar *vb* bawl, bellow, cry, howl, vociferate, yell; boom, peal, rattle, resound, thunder. • *n* bellow, roaring; rage, resonance, storm, thunder; cry, outcry, shout; laugh, laughter, shout.

rob *vb* despoil, fleece, pilfer, pillage, plunder, rook, strip; appropriate, deprive, embezzle, plagiarize.

robber *n* bandit, brigand, desperado, depredator, despoiler, footpad, freebooter, highwayman, marauder, pillager, pirate, plunderer, rifler, thief.

robbery *n* depredation, despoliation, embezzlement, freebooting, larceny, peculation, piracy, plagiarism, plundering, spoliation, theft.

robe *vb* array, clothe, dress, invest. • *n* attire, costume, dress, garment, gown, habit, vestment; bathrobe, dressing gown, housecoat.

robust *adj* able-bodied, athletic, brawny, energetic, firm, forceful, hale, hardy, hearty, iron, lusty, muscular, powerful, seasoned, self-assertive, sinewy, sound, stalwart, stout, strong, sturdy, vigorous.

rock[1] *n* boulder, cliff, crag, reef, stone; asylum, defense, foundation, protection, refuge, strength, support; gneiss, granite, marble, slate, etc.

rock[2] *vb* calm, cradle, lull, quiet, soothe, still, tranquillize; reel, shake, sway, teeter, totter, wobble.

rogue *n* beggar, vagabond, vagrant; caitiff, cheat, knave, rascal, scamp, scapegrace, scoundrel, sharper, swindler, trickster, villain.

roguish *adj* dishonest, fraudulent, knavish, rascally, scoundrelly, trickish, tricky; arch, sportive, mischievous, puckish, waggish, wanton.

role *n* character, function, impersonation, part, task.

roll *vb* gyrate, revolve, rotate, turn, wheel; curl, muffle, swathe, wind; bind, involve, enfold, envelop; flatten, level, smooth, spread; bowl, drive, trundle, wheel; gybe, lean, lurch, stagger, sway, yaw; billow, swell, undulate; wallow, welter; flow, glide, run. • *n* document, scroll, volume; annals, chronicle, history, record, rota; catalog, inventory, list, register, schedule; booming, resonance, reverberation, thunder; cylinder, roller.

rollicking adj frisky, frolicking, frolicsome, jolly, jovial, lively, swaggering.

romance vb exaggerate, fantasize. • n fantasy, fiction, legend, novel, story, tale; exaggeration, falsehood, lie; ballad, idyll, song.

romantic adj extravagant, fanciful, fantastic, ideal, imaginative, sentimental, wild; chimerical, fabulous, fantastic, fictitious, imaginary, improbable, legendary, picturesque, quixotic, sentimental. • n dreamer, idealist, sentimentalist, visionary.

romp vb caper, gambol, frisk, sport. • n caper, frolic, gambol.

room n accommodation, capacity, compass, elbowroom, expanse, extent, field, latitude, leeway, play, scope, space, swing; place, stead; apartment, chamber, lodging; chance, occasion, opportunity.

roomy adj ample, broad, capacious, comfortable, commodious, expansive, extensive, large, spacious, wide.

root[1] vb anchor, embed, fasten, implant, place, settle; confirm, establish. • n base, bottom, foundation; cause, occasion, motive, origin, reason, source; etymon, radical, radix, stem.

root[2] vb destroy, eradicate, extirpate, exterminate, remove, unearth, uproot; burrow, dig, forage, grub, rummage; applaud, cheer, encourage.

rooted adj chronic, confirmed, deep, established, fixed, radical.

roseate adj blooming, blushing, rose-colored, rosy, rubicund; hopeful.

rostrum n platform, stage, stand, tribune.

rosy adj auspicious, blooming, blushing, favorable, flushed, hopeful, roseate, ruddy, sanguine.

rot vb corrupt, decay, decompose, degenerate, putrefy, spoil, taint. • n corruption, decay, decomposition, putrefaction.

rotary adj circular, rotating, revolving, rotatory, turning, whirling.

rotten adj carious, corrupt, decomposed, fetid, putrefied, putrescent, putrid, rank, stinking; defective, unsound; corrupt, deceitful, immoral, treacherous, unsound, untrustworthy.

rotund adj buxom, chubby, full, globular, obese, plump, round, stout; fluent, grandiloquent.

roué n debauchee, libertine, profligate, rake.

rough vb coarsen, roughen; manhandle, mishandle, molest. • adj bumpy, craggy, irregular, jagged, rugged, scabrous, scraggy, scratchy, stubby, uneven; approximate, cross-grained, crude, formless, incomplete, knotty, rough-hewn, shapeless, sketchy, uncut, unfashioned, unfinished, unhewn, unpolished, unwrought, vague; bristly, bushy, coarse, disordered, hairy, hirsute, ragged, shaggy, unkempt; austere, bearish, bluff, blunt, brusque, burly, churlish, discourteous, gruff, harsh, impolite, indelicate, rude, surly, uncivil, uncourteous, ungracious, unpolished, unrefined; harsh, severe, sharp, violent; astringent, crabbed, hard, sour, tart; discordant, grating, inharmonious, jarring, raucous, scabrous, unmusical; boisterous, foul, inclement, severe, stormy, tempestuous, tumultuous, turbulent, untamed, violent, wild; acrimonious, brutal, cruel, disorderly, riotous, rowdy, severe, uncivil, unfeeling, ungentle. • n bully, rowdy, roughneck, ruffian; draft, outline, sketch, suggestion; unevenness.

round vb curve; circuit, encircle, encompass, surround. • adj bulbous, circular, cylindrical, globular, orbed, orbicular, rotund, spherical; complete, considerable, entire, full, great, large, unbroken, whole; chubby, corpulent, plump, stout, swelling; continuous, flowing, harmonious, smooth; brisk, quick; blunt, candid, fair, frank, honest, open, plain, upright. • adv around, circularly, circuitously. • prep about, around. • n bout, cycle, game, lap, revolution, rotation, succession, turn; canon, catch, dance; ball, circle, circumference, cylinder, globe, sphere; circuit, compass, perambulation, routine, tour, watch.

roundabout adj circuitous, circumlocutory, indirect, tortuous; ample, broad, extensive; encircling, encompassing.

rouse vb arouse, awaken, raise, shake, wake, waken; animate, bestir, brace, enkindle, excite, inspire, kindle, rally, stimulate, stir, whet; startle, surprise.

rout vb beat, conquer, defeat, discomfit, overcome, overpower, overthrow, vanquish; chase away, defeat, disperse, scatter. • n defeat, discomfiture, flight, ruin; concourse, multitude, rabble; brawl, disturbance, noise, roar, uproar.

route vb direct, forward, send, steer. • n

course, circuit, direction, itinerary, journey, march, road, passage, path, way.

routine adj conventional, familiar, habitual, ordinary, standard, typical, usual; boring, dull, humdrum, predictable, tiresome. • n beat, custom, groove, method, order, path, practice, procedure, round, rut.

rove vb prowl, ramble, range, roam, stray, struggle, stroll, wander.

row[1] n file, line, queue, range, rank, series, string, tier; alley, street, terrace.

row[2] vb argue, dispute, fight, quarrel, squabble. • n affray, altercation, brawl, broil, commotion, dispute, disturbance, noise, outbreak, quarrel, riot, squabble, tumult, uproar.

royal adj august, courtly, dignified, generous, grand, imperial, kingly, kinglike, magnanimous, magnificent, majestic, monarchical, noble, princely, regal, sovereign, splendid, superb.

rub vb abrade, chafe, grate, graze, scrape; burnish, clean, massage, polish, scour, wipe; apply, put, smear, spread. • n caress, massage, polish, scouring, shine, wipe; catch, difficulty, drawback, impediment, obstacle, problem.

rubbish n debris, detritus, fragments, refuse, ruins, waste; dregs, dross, garbage, litter, lumber, scoria, scum, sweepings, trash, trumpery.

rubicund adj blushing, erubescent, florid, flushed, red, reddish, ruddy.

rude adj coarse, crude, ill-formed, rough, rugged, shapeless, uneven, unfashioned, unformed, unwrought; artless, barbarous, boorish, clownish, ignorant, illiterate, loutish, raw, savage, uncivilized, uncouth, uncultivated, undisciplined, unpolished, ungraceful, unskillful, unskilled, untaught, untrained, untutored, vulgar; awkward, barbarous, bluff, blunt, boorish, brusque, brutal, churlish, gruff, ill-bred, impertinent, impolite, impudent, insolent, insulting, ribald, saucy, uncivil, uncourteous, unrefined; boisterous, fierce, harsh, severe, tumultuous, turbulent, violent; artless, inelegant, rustic, unpolished; hearty, robust.

rudimentary adj elementary, embryonic, fundamental, initial, primary, rudimental, undeveloped.

rue vb deplore, grieve, lament, regret, repent.

rueful adj dismal, doleful, lamentable,

lugubrious, melancholic, melancholy, mournful, penitent, regretful, sad, sorrowful, woeful.

ruffian n bully, caitiff, cutthroat, hoodlum, miscreant, monster, murderer, rascal, robber, roisterer, rowdy, scoundrel, villain, wretch.

ruffle vb damage, derange, disarrange, dishevel, disorder, ripple, roughen, rumple; agitate, confuse, discompose, disquiet, disturb, excite, harass, irritate, molest, plague, perturb, torment, trouble, vex, worry; cockle, flounce, pucker, wrinkle. • n edging, frill, ruff; agitation, bustle, commotion, confusion, contention, disturbance, excitement, fight, fluster, flutter, flurry, perturbation, tumult.

rugged adj austere, bristly, coarse, crabbed, cragged, craggy, hard, hardy, irregular, ragged, robust, rough, rude, scraggy, severe, seamed, shaggy, uneven, unkempt, wrinkled; boisterous, inclement, stormy, tempestuous, tumultuous, turbulent, violent; grating, harsh, inharmonious, unmusical, scabrous.

ruin vb crush, damn, defeat, demolish, desolate, destroy, devastate, overthrow, overturn, overwhelm, seduce, shatter, smash, subvert, wreck; beggar, impoverish. • n damnation, decay, defeat, demolition, desolation, destruction, devastation, discomfiture, downfall, fall, loss, perdition, prostration, rack, ruination, shipwreck, subversion, undoing, wrack, wreck; bane, mischief, pest.

ruination n demolition, destruction, overthrow, ruin, subversion.

ruinous adj decayed, demolished, dilapidated; baneful, calamitous, damnatory, destructive, disastrous, mischievous, noisome, noxious, pernicious, subversive, wasteful.

rule vb bridle, command, conduct, control, direct, domineer, govern, judge, lead, manage, reign, restrain; advise, guide, persuade; adjudicate, decide, determine, establish, settle; obtain, prevail, predominate. • n authority, command, control, direction, domination, dominion, empire, government, jurisdiction, lordship, mastery, mastership, regency, reign, sway; behavior, conduct; habit, method, order, regularity, routine, system; aphorism, canon, convention, criterion, formula, guide, law, maxim, model, precedent,

precept, standard, system, test, touchstone; decision, order, prescription, regulation, ruling.

ruler *n* chief, governor, king, lord, master,
monarch, potentate, regent, sovereign; director, head, manager, president; control-
ler, guide, rule; straight-edge.

ruminate *vb* brood, chew, cogitate, consider,
contemplate, meditate, muse, ponder, reflect, think.

rumour *vb* bruit, circulate, report, tell. • *n*
bruit, gossip, hearsay, report, talk; news,
report, story, tidings; celebrity, fame, reputation, repute.

rumple *vb* crease, crush, corrugate, crumple, disarrange, dishevel, pucker, ruffle,
wrinkle. • *n* crease, corrugation, crumple,
fold, pucker, wrinkle.

run *vb* bolt, career, course, gallop, haste,
hasten, hie, hurry, lope, post, race,
scamper, scour, scud, scuttle, speed, trip;
flow, glide, go, move, proceed, stream;
fuse, liquefy, melt; advance, pass, proceed,
vanish; extend, lie, spread, stretch; circulate, pass, press; average, incline, tend;
flee; pierce, stab; drive, force, propel, push,
thrust, turn; cast, form, mold, shape; follow, perform, pursue, take; discharge,
emit; direct, maintain, manage. • *n* race,
running; course, current, flow, motion,
passage, progress, way, wont; continuance,
currency, popularity; excursion, gallop,
journey, trip, trot; demand, pressure;
brook, burn, flow, rill, rivulet, runlet, runnel, streamlet.

rupture *vb* break, burst, fracture, sever, split.
• *n* breach, break, burst, disruption, fracture, split; contention, faction, feud, hostility, quarrel, schism.

rural *adj* agrarian, bucolic, country, pastoral, rustic, sylvan.

ruse *n* artifice, deception, deceit, fraud,
hoax, imposture, maneuvre, sham, stratagem, trick, wile.

rush *vb* attack, career, charge, dash, drive,
gush, hurtle, precipitate, surge, sweep,
tear. • *n* dash, onrush, onset, plunge, pre-
cipitance, precipitancy, rout, stampede,
tear.

rust *vb* corrode, decay, degenerate. • *n*
blight, corrosion, crust, mildew, must,
mold, mustiness.

rustic *adj* country, rural; awkward, boorish,
clownish, countrified, loutish, outlandish,
rough, rude, uncouth, unpolished,

untaught; coarse, countrified, homely,
plain, simple, unadorned; artless, honest,
unsophisticated. • *n* boor, bumpkin,
clown, countryman, peasant, swain, yokel.

ruthless *adj* barbarous, cruel, fell, ferocious,
hardhearted, inexorable, inhuman, merciless, pitiless, relentless, remorseless,
savage, truculent, uncompassionate, unmerciful, unpitying, unrelenting, unsparing.

S

sable *adj* black, dark, dusky, ebony, somber.

sabulous *adj* gritty, sabulose, sandy.

sack[1] *n* bag, pouch.

sack[2] *vb* despoil, devastate, pillage, plunder, ravage, spoil. • *n* desolation, despoliation, destruction, devastation, havoc,
ravage, sacking, spoliation, waste; booty,
plunder, spoil.

sacred *adj* consecrated, dedicated, devoted,
divine, hallowed, holy; inviolable, inviolate;
sainted, venerable.

sacrifice *vb* forgo, immolate, surrender. • *n*
immolation, oblation, offering; destruction, devotion, loss, surrender.

sacrilege *n* desecration, profanation, violation.

sacrilegious *adj* desecrating, impious, irreverent, profane.

sad *adj* grave, pensive, sedate, serious, sober, somber, staid.

saddle *vb* burden, charge, clog, encumber,
load.

sadly *adv* grievously, miserable, mournfully,
sorrowfully; afflictively, badly, calamitously;
darkly; gravely, seriously, soberly.

sadness *n* dejection, depression, despondency, melancholy, mournful, sorrow, sor-
rowfulness; dolefulness, gloominess, grief,
mournfulness, sorrow; gravity, sedateness,
seriousness.

safe *adj* undamaged, unharmed, unhurt,
unscathed; guarded, protected, secure,
snug, unexposed; certain, dependable, reliable, sure, trustworthy; good, harmless,
sound, whole. • *n* chest, coffer, strongbox.

safeguard *vb* guard, protect. • *n* defense,
protection, security; convoy, escort, guard,
safe-conduct; pass, passport.

sagacious *adj* acute, apt, astute, clear-
sighted, discerning, intelligent, judicious,

keen, penetrating, perspicacious, rational, sage, sharp-witted, wise, shrewd.

sagacity *n* acuteness, astuteness, discernment, ingenuity, insight, penetration, perspicacity, quickness, readiness, sense, sharpness, shrewdness, wisdom.

sage *adj* acute, discerning, intelligent, prudent, sagacious, sapient, sensible, shrewd, wise; judicious, well-judged; grave, serious, solemn. • *n* philosopher, pundit, savant.

sailor *n* mariner, navigator, salt, seafarer, seaman, tar.

saintly *adj* devout, godly, holy, pious, religious.

sake *n* end, cause, purpose, reason; account, consideration, interest, regard, respect, score.

saleable *adj* marketable, merchantable, vendible.

salacious *adj* carnal, concupiscent, incontinent, lascivious, lecherous, lewd, libidinous, loose, lustful, prurient, unchaste, wanton.

salary *n* allowance, hire, pay, stipend, wages.

salient *adj* bounding, jumping, leaping; beating, springing, throbbing; jutting, projecting, prominent; conspicuous, remarkable, striking.

saline *adj* briny, salty.

sally *vb* issue, rush. • *n* digression, excursion, sortie, run, trip; escapade, frolic; crank, fancy, jest, joke, quip, quirk, sprightly, witticism.

salt *adj* saline, salted, salty; bitter, pungent, sharp. • *n* flavor, savor, seasoning, smack, relish, taste; humor, piquancy, poignancy, sarcasm, smartness, wit, zest; mariner, sailor, seaman, tar.

salubrious *adj* beneficial, benign, healthful, healthy, salutary, sanitary, wholesome.

salutary *adj* healthy, healthful, helpful, safe, salubrious, wholesome; advantageous, beneficial, good, profitable, serviceable, useful.

salute *vb* accost, address, congratulate, greet, hail, welcome. • *n* address, greeting, salutation.

salvation *n* deliverance, escape, preservation, redemption, rescue, saving.

same *adj* ditto, identical, selfsame; corresponding, like, similar.

sample *vb* savor, sip, smack, sup, taste; test, try; demonstrate, exemplify, illustrate, instance. • *adj* exemplary, illustrative, rep-

resentative. • *n* demonstration, exemplification, illustration, instance, piece, specimen; example, model, pattern.

sanctify *vb* consecrate, hallow, purify; justify, ratify, sanction.

sanctimonious *adj* affected, devout, holy, hypocritical, pharisaical, pious, self-righteous.

sanction *vb* authorize, countenance, encourage, support; confirm, ratify. • *n* approval, authority, authorization, confirmation, countenance, endorsement, ratification, support, warranty; ban, boycott, embargo, penalty.

sanctity *n* devotion, godliness, goodness, grace, holiness, piety, purity, religiousness, saintliness.

sanctuary *n* altar, church, shrine, temple; asylum, protection, refuge, retreat, shelter.

sane *adj* healthy, lucid, rational, reasonable, sober, sound.

sang-froid *n* calmness, composure, coolness, imperturbability, indifference, nonchalance, phlegm, unconcern.

sanguinary *adj* bloody, gory, murderous; barbarous, bloodthirsty, cruel, fell, pitiless, savage, ruthless.

sanguine *adj* crimson, florid, red; animated, ardent, cheerful, lively, warm; buoyant, confident, enthusiastic, hopeful, optimistic; full-blooded.

sanitary *adj* clean, curative, healing, healthy, hygienic, remedial, therapeutic, wholesome.

sanity *n* normality, rationality, reason, saneness, soundness.

sapient *adj* acute, discerning, intelligent, knowing, sagacious, sage, sensible, shrewd, wise.

sarcastic *adj* acrimonious, biting, cutting, mordacious, mordant, sardonic, satirical, sharp, severe, sneering, taunting.

sardonic *adj* bitter, derisive, ironical, malevolent, malicious, malignant, sarcastic.

satanic *adj* devilish, diabolical, evil, false, fiendish, hellish, infernal, malicious.

satellite *adj* dependent, subordinate, tributary, vassal. • *n* attendant, dependant, follower, hanger-on, retainer, vassal.

satiate *vb* fill, sate, satisfy, suffice; cloy, glut, gorge, overfeed, overfill, pall, surfeit.

satire *n* burlesque, diatribe, invective, fling, irony, lampoon, pasquinade, philippic, ridicule, sarcasm, skit, squib.

satirical *adj* abusive, biting, bitter, censorious, cutting, invective, ironical, keen, mordacious, poignant, reproachful, sarcastic, severe, sharp, taunting.

satirize *vb* abuse, censure, lampoon, ridicule.

satisfaction *n* comfort, complacency, contentment, ease, enjoyment, gratification, pleasure, satiety; amends, appeasement, atonement, compensation, indemnification, recompense, redress, remuneration, reparation, requital, reward.

satisfactory *adj* adequate, conclusive, convincing, decisive, sufficient; gratifying, pleasing.

satisfy *vb* appease, content, fill, gratify, please, sate, satiate, suffice; indemnify, compensate, liquidate, pay, recompense, remunerate, requite; discharge, settle; assure, convince, persuade; answer, fulfill, meet.

saturate *vb* drench, fill, fit, imbue, soak, steep, wet.

saturnine *adj* dark, dull, gloomy, grave, heavy, leaden, morose, phlegmatic, sad, sedate, somber; melancholic, mournful, serious, unhappy; mischievous, naughty, troublesome, vexatious, wicked.

sauce *n* cheekiness, impudence, insolence; appetizer, compound, condiment, relish, seasoning.

saucy *adj* bold, cavalier, disrespectful, flippant, forward, immodest, impertinent, impudent, insolent, pert, rude.

saunter *vb* amble, dawdle, delay, dilly-dally, lag, linger, loiter, lounge, stroll, tarry. • *n* amble, stroll, walk.

savage *vb* attack, lacerate, mangle, maul. • *adj* rough, uncultivated, wild; rude, uncivilized, unpolished, untaught; bloodthirsty, feral, ferine, ferocious, fierce, rapacious, untamed, vicious; beastly, bestial, brutal, brutish, inhuman; atrocious, barbarous, barbaric, bloody, brutal, cruel, fell, fiendish, hardhearted, heathenish, merciless, murderous, pitiless, relentless, ruthless, sanguinary, truculent; native, rough, rugged. • *n* barbarian, brute, heathen, vandal.

save *vb* keep, liberate, preserve, rescue; salvage, recover, redeem; economize, gather, hoard, husband, reserve, store; hinder, obviate, prevent, spare. • *prep* but, deducting, except.

savior *n* defender, deliverer, guardian, protector, preserver, rescuer, saver.

savor *vb* affect, appreciate, enjoy, like, partake, relish; flavor, season. • *n* flavor, gusto, relish, smack, taste; fragrance, odor, smell, scent.

savory *adj* agreeable, delicious, flavorful, luscious, nice, palatable, piquant, relishing.

saw *n* adage, aphorism, apothegm, axiom, byword, dictum, maxim, precept, proverb, sententious saying.

say *vb* declare, express, pronounce, speak, tell, utter; affirm, allege, argue; recite, rehearse, repeat; assume, presume, suppose. • *n* affirmation, declaration, speech, statement; decision, voice, vote.

saying *n* declaration, expression, observation, remark, speech, statement; adage, aphorism, byword, dictum, maxim, proverb, saw.

scale[1] *n* basin, dish, pan; balance.

scale[2] *n* flake, lamina, lamella, layer, plate.

scale[3] *vb* ascend, climb, escalate, mount. • *n* graduation.

scamp *n* cheat, knave, rascal, rogue, scapegrace, scoundrel, swindler, trickster, villain.

scamper *vb* haste, hasten, hie, run, scud, speed, trip.

scan *vb* examine, investigate, scrutinize, search, sift.

scandal *vb* asperse, defame, libel, traduce. • *n* aspersion, calumny, defamation, obloquy, reproach; discredit, disgrace, dishonor, disrepute, ignominy, infamy, odium, opprobrium, offence, shame.

scandalize *vb* offend; asperse, backbite, calumniate, decry, defame, disgust, lampoon, libel, reproach, revile, satirize, slander, traduce, vilify.

scandalous *adj* defamatory, libellous, opprobrious, slanderous; atrocious, disgraceful, disreputable, infamous, inglorious, ignominious, odious, shameful.

scanty *adj* insufficient, meager, narrow, scant, small; hardly, scarce, short, slender; niggardly, parsimonious, penurious, scrimpy, skimpy, sparing.

scar[1] *vb* hurt, mark, wound. • *n* cicatrice, cicatrix, seam; blemish, defect, disfigurement, flaw, injury, mark.

scar[2] *n* bluff, cliff, crag, precipice.

scarce *adj* deficient, wanting; infrequent, rare, uncommon. • *adv* barely, hardly, scantily.

scarcely *adv* barely, hardly, scantily.

scarcity *n* dearth, deficiency, insufficiency, lack, want; infrequency, rareness, rarity, uncommonness.

scare *vb* affright, alarm, appal, daunt, fright, frighten, intimidate, shock, startle, terrify. • *n* alarm, fright, panic, shock, terror.

scathe *vb* blast, damage, destroy, injure, harm, haste. • *n* damage, harm, injury, mischief, waste.

scatter *vb* broadcast, sprinkle, strew; diffuse, disperse, disseminate, dissipate, distribute, separate, spread; disappoint, dispel, frustrate, overthrow.

scene *n* display, exhibition, pageant, representation, show, sight, spectacle, view; place, situation, spot; arena, stage.

scent *vb* breathe in, inhale, nose, smell, sniff; detect, smell out, sniff out; aromatize, perfume. • *n* aroma, balminess, fragrance, odor, perfume, smell, redolence.

sceptic *n* doubter, freethinker, questioner, unbeliever.

sceptical *adj* doubtful, doubting, dubious, hesitating, incredulous, questioning, unbelieving.

scepticism *n* doubt, dubiety, freethinking, incredulity, unbelief.

schedule *vb* line up, list, plan, program, tabulate. • *n* document, scroll; catalog, inventory, list, plan, record, register, roll, table, timetable.

scheme *vb* contrive, design, frame, imagine, plan, plot, project. • *n* plan, system, theory; cabal, conspiracy, contrivance, design, device, intrigue, machination, plan, plot, project, stratagem; arrangement, draught, diagram, outline.

schism *n* division, separation, split; discord, disunion, division, faction, separation.

scholar *n* disciple, learner, pupil, student; don, fellow, intellectual, pedant, savant.

scholarship *n* accomplishments, acquirements, attainments, erudition, knowledge, learning; bursary, exhibition, foundation, grant, maintenance.

scholastic *adj* academic, bookish, lettered, literary; formal, pedantic.

school *vb* drill, educate, exercise, indoctrinate, instruct, teach, train; admonish, control, chide, discipline, govern, reprove, tutor. • *adj* academic, collegiate, institutional, scholastic, schoolish. • *n* academy, college, gymnasium, institute, institution, kindergarten, lyceum, manège, polytechnic, seminary, university; adherents, camarilla, circle, clique, coterie, disciples, followers; body, order, organization, party, sect.

schooling *n* discipline, education, instruction, nurture, teaching, training, tuition.

scintillate *vb* coruscate, flash, gleam, glisten, glitter, sparkle, twinkle.

scoff *vb* deride, flout, jeer, mock, ridicule, taunt; gibe, sneer. • *n* flout, gibe, jeer, sneer, mockery, taunt; derision, ridicule.

scold *vb* berate, blame, censure, chide, rate, reprimand, reprove; brawl, rail, rate, reprimand, upbraid, vituperate. • *n* shrew, termagant, virago, vixen.

scope *n* aim, design, drift, end, intent, intention, mark, object, purpose, tendency, view; amplitude, field, latitude, liberty, margin, opportunity, purview, range, room, space, sphere, vent; extent, length, span, stretch, sweep.

scorch *vb* blister, burn, char, parch, roast, sear, shrivel, singe.

score *vb* cut, furrow, mark, notch, scratch; charge, note, record; impute, note; enter, register. • *n* incision, mark, notch; account, bill, charge, debt, reckoning; consideration, ground, motive, reason.

scorn *vb* condemn, despise, disregard, disdain, scout, slight, spurn. • *n* contempt, derision, disdain, mockery, slight, sneer; scoff.

scornful *adj* contemptuous, defiant, disdainful, contemptuous, regardless.

scot-free *adj* untaxed; clear, unhurt, uninjured, safe.

scoundrel *n* cheat, knave, miscreant, rascal, reprobate, rogue, scamp, swindler, trickster, villain.

scour[1] *vb* brighten, buff, burnish, clean, cleanse, polish, purge, scrape, scrub, rub, wash, whiten; rake; efface, obliterate, overrun.

scour[2] *vb* career, course, range, scamper, scud, scuttle; comb, hunt, rake, ransack, rifle, rummage, search.

scourge *vb* lash, whip; afflict, chasten, chastise, correct, chide, punish; harass, torment. • *n* cord, cowhide, lash, strap, thong, whip; affliction, bane, curse, infliction, nuisance, pest, plague, punishment.

scout *vb* contemn, deride, disdain, despise, ridicule, scoff, scorn, sneer, spurn; investigate, probe, search. • *n* escort, lookout, precursor, vanguard.

scowl *vb* frown, glower, lower. • *n* frown, glower, lower.

scraggy *adj* broken, craggy, rough, rugged, scabrous, scragged, uneven; attenuated, bony, emaciated, gaunt, lank, lean, meager, scrawny, skinny, thin.

scrap[1] *vb* discard, junk, trash. • *n* bit, fragment, modicum, particle, piece, snippet; bite, crumb, morsel, mouthful; debris, junk, litter, rubbish, rubble, trash, waste.

scrap[2] *vb* altercate, bicker, dispute, clash, fight, hassle, quarrel, row, spat, squabble, tiff, tussle, wrangle. • *n* affray, altercation, bickering, clash, dispute, fight, fray, hassle, melee, quarrel, row, run-in, set-to, spat, squabble, tiff, tussle, wrangle.

scrape *vb* bark, grind, rasp, scuff; accumulate, acquire, collect, gather, save; erase, remove. • *n* difficulty, distress, embarrassment, perplexity, predicament.

scream *vb* screech, shriek, squall, ululate. • *n* cry, outcry, screech, shriek, shrill, ululation.

screen *vb* cloak, conceal, cover, defend, fence, hide, mask, protect, shelter, shroud. • *n* blind, curtain, lattice, partition; defense, guard, protection, shield; cloak, cover, veil, disguise; riddle, sieve.

screw *vb* force, press, pressurize, squeeze, tighten, twist, wrench; oppress, rack; distort. • *n* extortioner, extortionist, miser, scrimp, skinflint; prison guard; sexual intercourse.

scrimmage *n* brawl, melee, riot, scuffle, skirmish.

scrimp *vb* contract, curtail, limit, pinch, reduce, scant, shorten, straiten.

scrimpy *adj* contracted, deficient, narrow, scanty.

scroll *n* inventory, list, parchment, roll, schedule.

scrub[1] *adj* contemptible, inferior, mean, niggardly, scrubby, shabby, small, stunted. • *n* brushwood, underbrush, underwood.

scrub[2] *vb* clean, cleanse, rub, scour, scrape, wash.

scruple *vb* boggle, demur, falter, hesitate, object, pause, stickle, waver. • *n* delicacy, hesitancy, hesitation, nicety, perplexity, qualm.

scrupulous *adj* conscientious, fastidious, nice, precise, punctilious, rigorous, strict; careful, cautious, circumspect, exact, vigilant.

scrutinize *vb* canvass, dissect, examine, explore, investigate, overhaul, probe, search, sift, study.

scrutiny *n* examination, exploration, inquisition, inspection, investigation, search, searching, sifting.

scud *vb* flee, fly, haste, hasten, hie, post, run, scamper, speed, trip.

scuffle *vb* contend, fight, strive, struggle. • *n* altercation, brawl, broil, contest, encounter, fight, fray, quarrel, squabble, struggle, wrangle.

sculpt *vb* carve, chisel, cut, sculpture; engrave, grave.

scurrilous *adj* abusive, blackguardly, contumelious, foul, foul-mouthed, indecent, infamous, insolent, insulting, offensive, opprobrious, reproachful, ribald, vituperative; coarse, gross, low, mean, obscene, vile, vulgar.

scurry *vb* bustle, dash, hasten, hurry, scamper, scud, scutter. • *n* burst, bustle, dash, flurry, haste, hurry, scamper, scud, spurt.

scurvy *adj* scabbed, scabby, scurfy; abject, bad, base, contemptible, despicable, low, mean, pitiful, sorry, vile, vulgar, worthless; malicious, mischievous, offensive.

scuttle[1] *vb* hurry, hustle, run, rush, scamper, scramble, scud, scurry. • *n* dash, drive, flurry, haste, hurry, hustle, race, rush, scamper, scramble, scud, scurry.

scuttle[2] *vb* capsize, founder, go down, sink, overturn, upset. • *n* hatch, hatchway.

seal *vb* close, fasten, secure; attest, authenticate, confirm, establish, ratify, sanction; confine, enclose, imprison. • *n* fastening, stamp, wafer, wax; assurance, attestation, authentication, confirmation, pledge, ratification.

seamy *adj* disreputable, nasty, seedy, sordid, unpleasant.

sear *vb* blight, brand, cauterize, dry, scorch, wither. • *adj* dried up, dry, sere, withered.

search *vb* examine, explore, ferret, inspect, investigate, overhaul, probe, ransack, scrutinize, sift; delve, hunt, forage, inquire, look, rummage. • *n* examination, exploration, hunt, inquiry, inspection, investigation, pursuit, quest, research, seeking, scrutiny.

searching *adj* close, keen, penetrating, trying; examining, exploring, inquiring, investigating, probing, seeking.

seared *adj* callous, graceless, hardened, impenitent, incorrigible, obdurate, shameless, unrepentant.

season *vb* acclimatize, accustom, form,

habituate, harden, inure, mature, qualify, temper, train; flavor, spice. • *n* interval, period, spell, term, time, while.

seasonable *adj* appropriate, convenient, fit, opportune, suitable, timely.

seasoning *n* condiment, flavoring, relish, salt, sauce.

seat *vb* establish, fix, locate, place, set, station. • *n* place, site, situation, station; abode, capital, dwelling, house, mansion, residence; bottom, fundament; bench, chair, pew, settle, stall, stool.

secede *vb* apostatize, resign, retire, withdraw.

secluded *adj* close, covert, embowered, isolated, private, removed, retired, screened, sequestrated, withdrawn.

seclusion *n* obscurity, privacy, retirement, secrecy, separation, solitude, withdrawal.

second[1] *n* instant, jiffy, minute, moment, trice.

second[2] *vb* abet, advance, aid, assist, back, encourage, forward, further, help, promote, support, sustain; approve, favor. • *adj* inferior, second-rate, secondary; following, next, subsequent; additional, extra, other; double, duplicate. • *n* another, other; assistant, backer, supporter.

secondary *adj* collateral, inferior, minor, subsidiary, subordinate. • *n* delegate, deputy, proxy.

secrecy *n* clandestineness, concealment, furtiveness, stealth, surreptitiousness.

secret *adj* close, concealed, covered, covert, cryptic, hid, hidden, mysterious, privy, shrouded, veiled, unknown, unrevealed, unseen; cabbalistic, clandestine, furtive, privy, sly, stealthy, surreptitious, underhand; confidential, private, retired, secluded, unseen; abstruse, latent, mysterious, obscure, occult, recondite, unknown. • *n* confidence, enigma, key, mystery.

secretary *n* clerk, scribe, writer; escritoire, writing-desk.

secrete[1] *vb* bury, cache, conceal, disguise, hide, shroud, stash; screen, separate.

secrete[2] *vb* discharge, emit, excrete, exude, release, secern.

secretive *adj* cautious, close, reserved, reticent, taciturn, uncommunicative, wary.

sect *n* denomination, faction, schism, school.

section *n* cutting, division, fraction, part, piece, portion, segment, slice.

secular *adj* civil, laic, laical, lay, profane, temporal, worldly.

secure *vb* guard, protect, safeguard; assure, ensure, guarantee, insure; fasten; acquire, gain, get, obtain, procure. • *adj* assured, certain, confident, sure; insured, protected, safe; fast, firm, fixed, immovable, stable; careless, easy, undisturbed, unsuspecting; heedless, inattentive, incautious, negligent, overconfident.

security *n* bulwark, defense, guard, palladium, protection, safeguard, safety, shelter; bond, collateral, deposit, guarantee, pawn, pledge, stake, surety, warranty; carelessness, heedlessness, overconfidence, negligence; assurance, assuredness, certainty, confidence, ease.

sedate *adj* calm, collected, composed, contemplative, cool, demure, grave, placid, philosophical, quiet, serene, serious, sober, still, thoughtful, tranquil, undisturbed, unemotional, unruffled.

sedative *adj* allaying, anodyne, assuasive, balmy, calming, composing, demulcent, lenient, lenitive, soothing, tranquillizing. • *n* anesthetic, anodyne, hypnotic, narcotic, opiate.

sedentary *adj* inactive, motionless, sluggish, torpid.

sediment *n* dregs, grounds, lees, precipitate, residue, residuum, settlings.

sedition *n* insurgence, insurrection, mutiny, rebellion, revolt, riot, rising, treason, tumult, uprising, uproar.

seditious *adj* factious, incendiary, insurgent, mutinous, rebellious, refractory, riotous, tumultuous, turbulent.

seduce *vb* allure, attract, betray, corrupt, debauch, deceive, decoy, deprave, ensnare, entice, inveigle, lead, mislead.

seductive *adj* alluring, attractive, enticing, tempting.

sedulous *adj* active, assiduous, busy, diligent, industrious, laborious, notable, painstaking, persevering, unremitting, untiring.

see *vb* behold, contemplate, descry, glimpse, sight, spot, survey; comprehend, conceive, distinguish, espy, know, notice, observe, perceive, recognize, remark, understand; beware, consider, envisage, regard, visualize; experience, feel, suffer; examine, inspire, notice, observe; discern, look; call on, visit.

seed *n* semen, sperm; embryo, grain, kernel, matured ovule; germ, original; children, descendants, offspring, progeny; birth, generation, race.

seedy *adj* faded, old, shabby, worn; destitute, distressed, indigent, needy, penniless, pinched, poor.

seek *vb* hunt, look, search; court, follow, prosecute, pursue, solicit; attempt, endeavor, strive, try.

seem *vb* appear, assume, look, pretend.

seeming *adj* apparent, appearing, ostensible, specious. • *n* appearance, color, guise, look, semblance.

seemly *adj* appropriate, becoming, befitting, congruous, convenient, decent, decorous, expedient, fit, fitting, meet, proper, right, suitable; beautiful, comely, fair, good-looking, graceful, handsome, pretty, well-favored.

seer *n* augur, diviner, foreteller, predictor, prophet, soothsayer.

segment *n* bit, division, part, piece, portion, section, sector.

segregate *vb* detach, disconnect, disperse, insulate, part, separate.

segregation *n* apartheid, discrimination, insulation, separation.

seize *vb* capture, catch, clutch, grab, grapple, grasp, grip, snatch; confiscate, impress, impound; apprehend, comprehend; arrest, take.

seldom *adv* infrequently, occasionally, rarely.

select *vb* choose, cull, pick, prefer. • *adj* choice, chosen, excellent, exquisite, good, picked, rare, selected.

selection *n* choice, election, pick, preference.

self-conscious *adj* awkward, diffident, embarrassed, insecure, nervous.

self-control *n* restraint, willpower.

self-important *adj* assuming, consequential, proud, haughty, lordly, overbearing, overweening.

selfish *adj* egoistic, egotistical, greedy, illiberal, mean, narrow, self-seeking, ungenerous.

self-possessed *adj* calm, collected, composed, cool, placid, sedate, undisturbed, unexcited, unruffled.

self-willed *adj* contumacious, dogged, headstrong, obstinate, pig-headed, stubborn, uncompliant, willful.

sell *vb* barter, exchange, hawk, market, peddle, trade, vend.

semblance *n* likeness, resemblance, similarity; air, appearance, aspect, bearing, exterior, figure, form, mien, seeming, show; image, representation, similitude.

seminal *adj* important, original; germinal, radical, rudimental, rudimentary, unformed.

seminary *n* academy, college, gymnasium, high school, institute, school, university.

send *vb* cast, drive, emit, fling, hurl, impel, lance, launch, project, propel, throw, toss; delegate, depute, dispatch; forward, transmit; bestow, confer, give, grant.

senile *adj* aged, doddering, superannuated; doting, imbecile.

senior *adj* elder, older; higher.

seniority *n* eldership, precedence, priority, superiority.

sensation *n* feeling, sense, perception; excitement, impression, thrill.

sensational *adj* exciting, melodramatic, startling, thrilling.

sense *vb* appraise, appreciate, estimate, notice, observe, perceive, suspect, understand. • *n* brains, intellect, intelligence, mind, reason, understanding; appreciation, apprehension, discernment, feeling, perception, recognition, tact; connotation, idea, implication, judgment, notion, opinion, sentiment, view; import, interpretation, meaning, purport, significance; sagacity, soundness, substance, wisdom.

senseless *adj* apathetic, inert, insensate, unfeeling; absurd, foolish, ill-judged, nonsensical, silly, unmeaning, unreasonable, unwise; doltish, foolish, simple, stupid, witless, weak-minded.

sensible *adj* apprehensible, perceptible; aware, cognizant, conscious, convinced, persuaded, satisfied; discreet, intelligent, judicious, rational, reasonable, sagacious, sage, sober, sound, wise; observant, understanding; impressionable, sensitive.

sensitive *adj* perceptive, sentient; affected, impressible, impressionable, responsive, susceptible; delicate, tender, touchy.

sensual *adj* animal, bodily, carnal, voluptuous; gross, lascivious, lewd, licentious, unchaste.

sentence *vb* condemn, doom, judge. • *n* decision, determination, judgment, opinion, verdict; doctrine, dogma, opinion, tenet; condemnation, conviction, doom; period, proposition.

sententious *adj* compendious, compact, concise, didactic, laconic, pithy, pointed, succinct, terse.

sentiment *n* judgment, notion, opinion;

maxim, saying; emotion, tenderness; disposition, feeling, thought.

sentimental *adj* impressible, impressionable, over-emotional, romantic, tender.

sentinel *n* guard, guardsman, patrol, picket, sentry, watchman.

separate *vb* detach, disconnect, disjoin, disunite, dissever, divide, divorce, part, sever, sunder; eliminate, remove, withdraw; cleave, open. • *adj* detached, disconnected, disjoined, disjointed, dissociated, disunited, divided, parted, severed; discrete, distinct, divorced, unconnected; alone, segregated, withdrawn.

separation *n* disjunction, disjuncture, dissociation; disconnection, disseverance, disseveration, disunion, division, divorce; analysis, decomposition.

sepulchral *adj* deep, dismal, funereal, gloomy, grave, hollow, lugubrious, melancholy, mournful, sad, sombre, woeful.

sepulchre *n* burial place, charnel house, grave, ossuary, sepulture, tomb.

sequel *n* close, conclusion, denouement, end, termination; consequence, event, issue, result, upshot.

sequence *n* following, graduation, progression, succession; arrangement, series, train.

sequestrated *adj* hidden, private, retired, secluded, unfrequented, withdrawn; seized.

seraphic *adj* angelic, celestial, heavenly, sublime; holy, pure, refined.

serene *adj* calm, collected, placid, peaceful, quiet, tranquil, sedate, undisturbed, unperturbed, unruffled; bright, calm, clear, fair, unclouded.

serenity *n* calm, calmness, collectedness, composure, coolness, imperturbability, peace, peacefulness, quiescence, sedateness, tranquillity; brightness, calmness, clearness, fairness, peace, quietness, stillness.

serf *n* bondman, servant, slave, thrall, villein.

serfdom *n* bondage, enslavement, enthralment, servitude, slavery, subjection, thraldom.

series *n* chain, concatenation, course, line, order, progression, sequence, succession, train.

serious *adj* earnest, grave, demure, pious, resolute, sedate, sober, solemn, staid, thoughtful; dangerous, great, important, momentous, weighty.

sermon *n* discourse, exhortation, homily, lecture.

serpentine *adj* anfractuous, convoluted, crooked, meandering, sinuous, spiral, tortuous, twisted, undulating, winding.

servant *n* attendant, dependant, factotum, helper, henchman, retainer, servitor, subaltern, subordinate, underling; domestic, drudge, flunky, lackey, menial, scullion, slave.

serve *vb* aid, assist, attend, help, minister, oblige, succour; advance, benefit, forward, promote; content, satisfy, supply; handle, officiate, manage, manipulate, work.

service *vb* check, maintain, overhaul, repair. • *n* labor, ministration, work; attendance, business, duty, employ, employment, office; advantage, benefit, good, gain, profit; avail, purpose, use, utility; ceremony, function, observance, rite, worship.

serviceable *adj* advantageous, available, beneficial, convenient, functional, handy, helpful, operative, profitable, useful.

servile *adj* dependent, menial; abject, base, beggarly, cringing, fawning, groveling, low, mean, obsequious, slavish, sneaking, sycophantic, truckling.

servility *n* bondage, dependence, slavery; abjection, abjectness, baseness, fawning, meanness, obsequiousness, slavishness, sycophancy.

servitor *n* attendant, dependant, footman, lackey, retainer, servant, squire, valet, waiter.

servitude *n* bondage, enslavement, enthralment, serfdom, service, slavery, thraldom.

set[1] *vb* lay, locate, mount, place, put, stand, station; appoint, determine, establish, fix, settle; risk, stake, wager; adapt, adjust, regulate; adorn, stud, variegate; arrange, dispose, pose, post; appoint, assign, predetermine, prescribe; estimate, prize, rate, value; embarrass, perplex, pose; contrive, produce; decline, sink; congeal, concern, consolidate, harden, solidify; flow, incline, run, tend; (*with* **about**) begin, commence; (*with* **apart**) appropriate, consecrate, dedicate, devote, reserve, set aside; (*with* **aside**) abrogate, annul, omit, reject; reserve, set apart; (*with* **before**) display, exhibit; (*with* **down**) chronicle, jot down, record, register, state, write down; (*with* **forth**) display, exhibit, explain, expound, manifest, promulgate, publish, put forward, represent, show; (*with* **forward**) advance, further, promote; (*with* **free**) acquit, clear, emancipate, liberate, release; (*with* **off**) adorn, decorate, embellish; define, portion off; (*with* **on**) actuate, encourage, impel, influence, incite, instigate, prompt, spur, urge; attack, assault, set upon; (*with* **out**) display, issue, publish, proclaim, prove, recommend, show; (*with* **right**) correct, put in order; (*with* **to rights**) adjust, regulate; (*with* **up**) elevate, erect, exalt, raise; establish, found, institute; (*with* **upon**) assail, assault, attack, fly at, rush upon. • *adj* appointed, established, formal, ordained, prescribed, regular, settled; determined, fixed, firm, obstinate, positive, stiff, unyielding; immovable, predetermined; located, placed, put. • *n* attitude, position, posture; scene, scenery, setting.

set[2] *n* assortment, collection, suit; class, circle, clique, cluster, company, coterie, division, gang, group, knot, party, school, sect.

setback *n* blow, hitch, hold-up, rebuff; defeat, disappointment, reverse.

set-off *n* adornment, decoration, embellishment, ornament; counterbalance, counterclaim, equivalent.

settle *vb* adjust, arrange, compose, regulate; account, balance, close up, conclude, discharge, liquidate, pay, pay up, reckon, satisfy, square; allay, calm, compose, pacify, quiet, repose, rest, still, tranquillize; confirm, decide, determine, make clear; establish, fix, set; fall, gravitate, sink, subside; abide, colonize, domicile, dwell, establish, inhabit, people, place, plant, reside; (*with* **on**) determine on, fix on, fix upon; establish. • *n* bench, seat, stool.

settled *adj* established, fixed, stable; decided, deep-rooted, steady, unchanging; adjusted, arranged; methodical, orderly, quiet; common, customary, everyday, ordinary, usual, wonted.

set-to *n* combat, conflict, contest, fight.

sever *vb* divide, part, rend, separate, sunder; detach, disconnect, disjoin, disunite.

several *adj* individual, single, particular; distinct, exclusive, independent, separate; different, divers, diverse, manifold, many, sundry, various.

severance *n* partition, separation.

severe *adj* austere, bitter, dour, hard, harsh, inexorable, morose, painful, relentless, rigid, rigorous, rough, sharp, stern, stiff, strait-laced, unmitigated, unrelenting,

unsparing; accurate, exact, methodical, strict; chaste, plain, restrained, simple, unadorned; biting, caustic, cruel, cutting, harsh, keen, sarcastic, satirical, trenchant; acute, afflictive, distressing, excruciating, extreme, intense, stringent, violent; critical, exact.

severity *n* austerity, gravity, harshness, rigor, seriousness, sternness, strictness; accuracy, exactness, niceness; chasteness, plainness, simplicity; acrimony, causticity, keenness, sharpness; afflictiveness, extremity, keenness, stringency, violence; cruelty.

sew *vb* baste, bind, hem, stitch, tack.

sex *n* gender, femininity, masculinity, sexuality; coitus, copulation, fornication, lovemaking.

shabby *adj* faded, mean, poor, ragged, seedy, threadbare, worn, worn-out; beggarly, mean, paltry, penurious, stingy, ungentlemanly, unhandsome.

shackle *vb* chain, fetter, gyve, hamper, manacle; bind, clog, confine, cumber, embarrass, encumber, impede, obstruct, restrict, trammel. • *n* chain, fetter, gyve, hamper, manacle.

shade *vb* cloud, darken, dim, eclipse, obfuscate, obscure; cover, ensconce, hide, protect, screen, shelter. • *n* darkness, dusk, duskiness, gloom, obscurity, shadow; cover, protection, shelter; awning, blind, curtain, screen, shutter, veil; degree, difference, kind, variety; cast, color, complexion, dye, hue, tinge, tint, tone; apparition, ghost, manes, phantom, shadow, specter, spirit.

shadow *vb* becloud, cloud, darken, obscure, shade; adumbrate, foreshadow, symbolize, typify; conceal, cover, hide, protect, screen, shroud. • *n* penumbra, shade, umbra, umbrage; darkness, gloom, obscurity; cover, protection, security, shelter; adumbration, foreshadowing, image, prefiguration, representation; apparition, ghost, phantom, shade, spirit; image, portrait, reflection, silhouette.

shadowy *adj* shady, umbrageous; dark, dim, gloomy, murky, obscure; ghostly, imaginary, impalpable, insubstantial, intangible, spectral, unreal, unsubstantial, visionary.

shady *adj* shadowy, umbrageous; crooked.

shaft *n* arrow, missile, weapon; handle, helve; pole, tongue; axis, spindle; pinnacle, spire; stalk, stem, trunk.

shaggy *adj* rough, rugged.

shake *vb* quake, quaver, quiver, shiver, shudder, totter, tremble; agitate, convulse, jar, jolt, stagger; daunt, frighten, intimidate; endanger, move, weaken; oscillate, vibrate, wave; move, put away, remove, throw off. • *n* agitation, concussion, flutter, jar, jolt, quaking, shaking, shivering, shock, trembling, tremor.

shaky *adj* jiggly, quaky, shaking, tottering, trembling.

shallow *adj* flimsy, foolish, frivolous, puerile, trashy, trifling, trivial; empty, ignorant, silly, slight, simple, superficial, unintelligent.

sham *vb* ape, feign, imitate, pretend; cheat, deceive, delude, dupe, impose, trick. • *adj* assumed, counterfeit, false, feigned, mock, make-believe, pretended, spurious. • *n* delusion, feint, fraud, humbug, imposition, imposture, pretence, trick.

shamble *vb* hobble, shuffle.

shambles *npl* abattoir, slaughterhouse; confusion, disorder, mess.

shame *vb* debase, degrade, discredit, disgrace, dishonor, stain, sully, taint, tarnish; abash, confound, confuse, discompose, disconcert, humble, humiliate; deride, flout, jeer, mock, ridicule, sneer. • *n* contempt, degradation, derision, discredit, disgrace, dishonor, disrepute, ignominy, infamy, obloquy, odium, opprobrium; abashment, chagrin, confusion, embarrassment, humiliation, mortification; reproach, scandal; decency, decorousness, decorum, modesty, propriety, seemliness.

shamefaced *adj* bashful, diffident, overmodest.

shameful *adj* atrocious, base, disgraceful, dishonorable, disreputable, heinous, ignominious, infamous, nefarious, opprobrious, outrageous, scandalous, vile, villainous, wicked; degrading, indecent, unbecoming.

shameless *adj* assuming, audacious, bold-faced, brazen, brazen-faced, cool, immodest, impudent, indecent, indelicate, insolent, unabashed, unblushing; abandoned, corrupt, depraved, dissolute, graceless, hardened, incorrigible, irreclaimable, lost, obdurate, profligate, reprobate, sinful, unprincipled, vicious.

shape *vb* create, form, make, produce; fashion, model, mold; adjust, direct, frame, regulate; conceive, conjure up, figure, image, imagine. • *n* appearance, aspect, fashion, figure, form, guise, make; build, cast, cut, model, mold, pattern; apparition, image.

shapeless *adj* amorphous, formless; grotesque, irregular, rude, uncouth, unsymmetrical.

shapely *adj* comely, symmetrical, trim, well-formed.

share *vb* apportion, distribute, divide, parcel out, portion, split; partake, participate; experience, receive. • *n* part, portion, quantum; allotment, allowance, contingent, deal, dividend, division, interest, lot, proportion, quantity, quota.

sharer *n* communicant, partaker, participator.

sharp *adj* acute, cutting, keen, keen-edged, knife-edged, razor-edged, trenchant; acuminate, needle-shaped, peaked, pointed, ridged; apt, astute, canny, clear-sighted, clever, cunning, discerning, discriminating, ingenious, inventive, keen-witted, penetrating, perspicacious, quick, ready, sagacious, sharp-witted, shrewd, smart, subtle, witty; acid, acrid, biting, bitter, burning, high-flavored, high-seasoned, hot, mordacious, piquant, poignant, pungent, sour, stinging; acrimonious, biting, caustic, cutting, harsh, mordant, sarcastic, severe, tart, trenchant; cruel, hard, rigid; afflicting, distressing, excruciating, intense, painful, piercing, shooting, sore, violent; nipping, pinching; ardent, eager, fervid, fierce, fiery, impetuous, strong; high, screeching, shrill; attentive, vigilant; severe; close, exacting, shrewd, cold, crisp, freezing, icy wintry. • *adv* abruptly, sharply, suddenly; exactly, precisely, punctually.

sharp-cut *adj* clear, distinct, well-defined.

sharpen *vb* edge, intensify, point.

sharper *n* cheat, deceiver, defrauder, knave, rogue, shark, swindler, trickster.

sharply *adv* rigorously, roughly, severely; acutely, keenly; vehemently, violently; accurately, exactly, minutely, trenchantly, wittily; abruptly, steeply.

sharpness *n* acuteness, keenness, trenchancy; acuity, spinosity; acumen, cleverness, discernment, ingenuity, quickness, sagacity, shrewdness, smartness, wit; acidity, acridity, piquancy, pungency, sting, tartness; causticness, incisiveness, pungency, sarcasm, satire, severity; afflictiveness, intensity, painfulness, poignancy; ardor, fierceness, violence; discordance, dissonance, highness, screechiness, squeakiness, shrillness.

sharp-sighted *adj* clear-sighted, keen, keen-eyed, keen-sighted.

sharp-witted *adj* acute, clear-sighted, cunning, discerning, ingenious, intelligent, keen, keen-sighted, long-headed, quick, sagacious, sharp, shrewd.

shatter *vb* break, burst, crack, rend, shiver, smash, splinter, split; break up, derange, disorder, overthrow.

shave *vb* crop, cut off, mow, pare; slice; graze, skim, touch.

shaver *n* boy, child, youngster; bargainer, extortioner, sharper.

shear *vb* clip, cut, fleece, strip; divest; break off.

sheath *n* case, casing, covering, envelope, scabbard, sheathing.

sheathe *vb* case, cover, encase, enclose.

shed[1] *n* cabin, cot, hovel, hut, outhouse, shack, shelter.

shed[2] *vb* effuse, let fall, pour out, spill; diffuse, emit, give out, scatter, spread; cast, let fall, put off, slough, throw off.

sheen *n* brightness, gloss, glossiness, shine, splendor.

sheep *n* ewe, lamb, ram.

sheepish *adj* bashful, diffident, overmodest, shamefaced, timid, timorous.

sheer[1] *adj* perpendicular, precipitous, steep, vertical; clear, downright, mere, pure, simple, unadulterated, unmingled, unmixed, unqualified, utter; clear; fine, transparent.
• *adv* outright; perpendicularly, steeply.

sheer[2] *vb* decline, deviate, move aside, swerve. • *n* bow, curve.

shelf *n* bracket, console, ledge, mantelpiece.

shell *vb* exfoliate, fall off, peel off; bombard.
• *n* carapace, case, covering, shard; bomb, grenade, sharpnel; framework.

shelter *vb* cover, defend, ensconce, harbor, hide, house, protect, screen, shield, shroud. • *n* asylum, cover, covert, harbor, haven, hideaway, refuge, retreat, sanctuary; defense, protection, safety, screen, security, shield; guardian, protector.

shelve *vb* dismiss, put aside; incline, slope.

shepherd *vb* escort, guide, marshal, usher; direct, drive, drove, herd, lead; guard, tend, watch over. • *n* drover, grazier, herder, herdsman; chaplain, churchman, clergyman, cleric, divine, ecclesiastic, minister,

padre, parson, pastor; chaperon, duenna, escort, guide, squire, usher.

shield *vb* cover, defend, guard, protect, shelter; repel, ward off; avert, forbid, forfend.
• *n* aegis, buckler, escutcheon, scutcheon, targe; bulwark, cover, defense, guard, palladium, protection, rampart, safeguard, security, shelter.

shift *vb* alter, change, fluctuate, move, vary; chop, dodge, swerve, veer; contrive, devise, manage, plan, scheme, shuffle. • *n* change, substitution, turn; contrivance, expedient, means, resort, resource; artifice, craft, device, dodge, evasion, fraud, mask, ruse, stratagem, subterfuge, trick, wile; chemise, smock.

shiftless *adj* improvident, imprudent, negligent, slack, thriftless, unresourceful.

shifty *adj* tricky, undependable, wily.

shillyshally *vb* hesitate, waver. • *n* hesitation, irresolute, wavering.

shimmer *vb* flash, glimmer, glisten, shine.
• *n* blink, glimmer, glitter, twinkle.

shin *vb* climb, swarm. • *n* shinbone, tibia.

shindy *n* disturbance, riot, roughhouse, row, spree, uproar.

shine *vb* beam, blaze, coruscate, flare, give light, glare, gleam, glimmer, glisten, glitter, glow, lighten, radiate, sparkle; excel.
• *n* brightness, brilliancy, glaze, gloss, polish, sheen.

shining *adj* beaming, bright, brilliant, effulgent, gleaming, glowing, glistening, glittering, luminous, lustrous, radiant, resplendent, splendid; conspicuous, distinguished, illustrious.

shiny *adj* bright, clear, luminous, sunshiny, unclouded; brilliant, burnished, glassy, glossy, polished.

ship *n* boat, craft, steamer, vessel.

shipshape *adj* neat, orderly, tidy, trim, well-arranged.

shipwreck *vb* cast away, maroon, strand, wreck. • *n* demolition, destruction, miscarriage, overthrow, perdition, ruin, subversion, wreck.

shirk *vb* avoid, dodge, evade, malinger, quit, slack; cheat, shark, trick.

shiver[1] *vb* break, shatter, splinter. • *n* bit, fragment, piece, slice, sliver, splinter.

shiver[2] *vb* quake, quiver, shake, shudder, tremble. • *n* shaking, shivering, shuddering, tremor.

shivery[1] *adj* brittle, crumbly, frangible, friable, shatterable, splintery.

shivery[2] *adj* quaking, quavering, quivering, shaky, trembly, tremulous; chilly, shivering.

shoal[1] *vb* crowd, throng. • *n* crowd, horde, multitude, swarm, throng.

shoal[2] *n* sandbank, shallows; danger.

shock *vb* appall, horrify; disgust, disquiet, disturb, nauseate, offend, outrage, revolt, scandalize, sicken; astound, stagger, stun; collide with, jar, jolt, shake, strike against; encounter, meet. • *n* agitation, blow, offence, stroke, trauma; assault, brunt, conflict; clash, collision, concussion, impact, percussion.

shocking *adj* abominable, detestable, disgraceful, disgusting, execrable, foul, hateful, loathsome, obnoxious, odious, offensive, repugnant, repulsive, revolting; appalling, awful, dire, dreadful, fearful, frightful, ghastly, hideous, horrible, horrid, horrific, monstrous, terrible.

shoot *vb* catapult, expel, hurl, let fly, propel; discharge, fire, let off; dart, fly, pass, pelt; extend, jut, project, protrude, protuberate, push, put forth, send forth, stretch; bud, germinate, sprout; (*with* **up**) grow increase, spring up, run up, start up. • *n* branch, offshoot, scion, sprout, twig.

shop *n* emporium, market, mart, store; workshop.

shore[1] *n* beach, brim, coast, seabord, seaside, strand, waterside.

shore[2] *vb* brace, buttress, prop, stay, support. • *n* beam, brace, buttress, prop, stay, support.

shorn *adj* cut-off; deprived.

short *adj* brief, curtailed; direct, near, straight; compendious, concise, condensed, laconic, pithy, terse, sententious, succinct, summary; abrupt, curt, petulant, pointed, sharp, snappish, uncivil; defective, deficient, inadequate, insufficient, niggardly, scanty, scrimpy; contracted, desitute, lacking, limited, minus, wanting; dwarfish, squat, undersized; brittle, crisp, crumbling, friable. • *adv* abruptly, at once, forthwith, suddenly.

shortcoming *n* defect, deficiency, delinquency, error, failing, failure, fault, imperfection, inadequacy, remissness, slip, weakness.

shorten *vb* abbreviate, abridge, curtail, cut short; abridge, contract, diminish, lessen, retrench, reduce; cut off, dock, lop, trim; confine, hinder, restrain, restrict.

shortening *n* abbreviation, abridgment, contraction, curtailment, diminution, retrenchment, reduction.

shorthand *n* brachygraphy, stenography, tachygraphy.

short-lived *adj* emphemeral, transient, transitory.

shortly *adv* quickly, soon; briefly, concisely, succinctly, tersely.

short-sighted *adj* myopic, nearsighted, purblind; imprudent, indiscreet.

shot[1] *n* discharge; ball, bullet, missile, projectile; marksman, shooter.

shot[2] *adj* chatoyant, iridescent, irisated, moiré, watered; intermingled, interspersed, interwoven.

shoulder *vb* bear, bolster, carry, hump, maintain, pack, support, sustain, tote; crowd, elbow, jostle, press forward, push, thrust. • *n* projection, protuberance.

shoulder blade *n* blade bone, omoplate, scapula, shoulder bone.

shout *vb* bawl, cheer, clamor, exclaim, halloo, roar, vociferate, whoop, yell. • *n* cheer, clamor, exclamation, halloo, hoot, huzza, outcry, roar, vociferation, whoop, yell.

shove *vb* jostle, press against, propel, push, push aside; (*with* **off**) push away, thrust away.

show *vb* blazon, display, exhibit, flaunt, parade, present; indicate, mark, point out; disclose, discover, divulge, explain, make clear, make known, proclaim, publish, reveal, unfold; demonstrate, evidence, manifest, prove, verify; conduct, guide, usher; direct, inform, instruct, teach; expound, elucidate, interpret; (*with* **off**) display, exhibit, make a show, set off; (*with* **up**) expose. • *n* array, exhibition, representation, sight, spectacle; blazonry, bravery, ceremony, dash, demonstration, display, flourish, ostentation, pageant, pageantry, parade, pomp, splendour, splurge; likeness, resemblance, semblance; affectation, appearance, color, illusion, mask, plausibility, pose, pretence, pretext, simulation, speciousness; entertainment, production.

showy *adj* bedizened, dressy, fine, flashy, flaunting, garish, gaudy, glaring, gorgeous, loud, ornate, smart, swanky, splendid; grand, magnificent, ostentatious, pompous, pretentious, stately, sumptuous.

shred *vb* tear. • *n* bit, fragment, piece, rag, scrap, strip, tatter.

shrew n brawler, fury, scold, spitfire, termagant, virago, vixen.

shrewd adj arch, artful, astute, crafty, cunning, Machiavellian, sly, subtle, wily; acute, astute, canny, discerning, discriminating, ingenious, keen, knowing, penetrating, sagacious, sharp, sharp-sighted.

shrewdness n address, archness, art, artfulness, astuteness, craft, cunning, policy, skill, slyness, subtlety; acumen, acuteness, discernment, ingenuity, keenness, penetration, perspicacity, sagacity, sharpness, wit.

shrewish adj brawling, clamorous, froward, peevish, petulant, scolding, vixenish.

shriek vb scream, screech, squeal, yell, yelp. • n cry, scream, screech, yell.

shrill adj acute, high, high-toned, high-pitched, piercing, piping, sharp.

shrine n reliquary, sacred tomb; altar, hallowed place, sacred place.

shrink vb contract, decrease, dwindle, shrivel, wither; balk, blench, draw back, flinch, give way, quail, recoil, retire, swerve, wince, withdraw.

shrivel vb dry, dry up, parch; contract, decrease, dwindle, shrink, wither, wrinkle.

shroud vb bury, cloak, conceal, cover, hide, mask, muffle, protect, screen, shelter, veil. • n covering, garment; grave clothes, winding sheet.

shrub n bush, dwarf tree, low tree.

shrubby adj bushy.

shudder vb quake, quiver, shake, shiver, tremble. • n shaking, shuddering, trembling, tremor.

shuffle vb confuse, disorder, intermix, jumble, mix, shift; cavil, dodge, equivocate, evade, prevaricate, quibble, vacillate; struggle. • n artifice, cavil, evasion, fraud, pretence, pretext, prevarication, quibble, ruse, shuffling, sophism, subterfuge, trick.

shun vb avoid, elude, eschew, escape, evade, get clear of.

shut vb close, close up, stop; confine, coop up, enclose, imprison, lock up, shut up; (with **in**) confine, enclose; (with **off**) bar, exclude, intercept; (with **up**) close up, shut; confine, enclose, fasten in, imprison, lock in, lock up.

shy vb cast, chuck, fling, hurl, jerk, pitch, sling, throw, toss; boggle, sheer, start aside. • adj bashful, coy, diffident, reserved, retiring, sheepish, shrinking, timid; cautious, chary, distrustful, heedful, wary. • n start; fling, throw.

sibilant adj buzzing, hissing, sibilous.

sick adj ailing, ill, indisposed, laid-up, unwell, weak; nauseated, queasy; disgusted, revolted, tired, weary; diseased, distempered, disordered, feeble, morbid, unhealthy, unsound, weak; languishing, longing, pining.

sicken vb ail, disease, fall sick, make sick; nauseate; disgust, weary; decay, droop, languish, pine.

sickening adj nauseating, nauseous, palling, sickish; disgusting, distasteful, loathsome, offensive, repulsive, revolting.

sickly adj ailing, diseased, faint, feeble, infirm, languid, languishing, morbid, unhealthy, valetudinary, weak, weakly.

sickness n ail, ailment, complaint, disease, disorder, distemper, illness, indisposition, invalidism, malady, morbidity; nausea, qualmishness, queasiness.

side vb border, bound, edge, flank, frontier, march, rim, skirt, verge; avert, turn aside; (with **with**) befriend, favor, flock to, join with, second, support. • adj flanking, later, skirting; indirect, oblique; extra, odd, off, spare. • n border, edge, flank, margin, verge; cause, faction, interest, party, sect.

sideboard n buffet, dresser.

side by side abreast, alongside, by the side.

sidelong adj lateral, oblique. • adv laterally, obliquely; on the side.

sidewalk n footpath, footway, pavement.

sideways, sidewise adv laterally. • adv athwart, crossways, crosswise, laterally, obliquely, sidelong, sidewards.

siesta n doze, nap.

sift vb part, separate; bolt, screen, winnow; analyze, canvass, discuss, examine, fathom, follow up, inquire into, investigate, probe, scrutinize, sound, try.

sigh vb complain, grieve, lament, mourn. • n long breath, sough, suspiration.

sight vb get sight of, perceive, see. • n cognizance, ken, perception, view; beholding, eyesight, seeing, vision; exhibition, prospect, representation, scene, show, spectacle, wonder; consideration, estimation, knowledge; examination, inspection.

sightless adj blind, eyeless, unseeing.

sightly adj beautiful, comely, handsome.

sign vb indicate, signal, signify; countersign, endorse, subscribe. • n emblem, index, indication, manifestation, mark, note, proof, signal, signification, symbol, symptom, token; beacon; augury, auspice, foreboding, miracle, omen, portent, presage, prodigy, prognostic, wonder; type; countersign, password.

signal vb flag, glance, hail, nod, nudge, salute, sign, signalize, sound, speak, touch, wave, wink. • adj conspicuous, eminent, extraordinary, memorable, notable, noteworthy, remarkable. • n cue, indication, mark, sign, token.

signalize vb celebrate, distinguish, make memorable.

signature n mark, sign, stamp; autograph, hand.

significance n implication, import, meaning, purport, sense; consequence, importance, moment, portent, weight; emphasis, energy, expressiveness, force, impressiveness.

significant adj betokening, expressive, indicative, significative, signifying; important, material, momentous, portentous, weighty; forcible, emphatic, expressive, telling.

signification n expression; acceptation, import, meaning, purport, sense.

signify vb betoken, communication, express, indicate, intimate; denote, imply, import, mean, purport, suggest; announce, declare, give notice of, impart, make known, manifest, proclaim, utter; augur, foreshadow, indicate, portend, represent; matter, weigh.

silence vb hush, muzzle, still; allay, calm, quiet. • interj be silent, be still, hush, soft, tush, tut, whist. • n calm, hush, lull, noiselessness, peace, quiet, quietude, soundlessness, stillness; dumbness, mumness, muteness, reticence, speechlessness, taciturnity.

silent adj calm, hushed, noiseless, quiet, soundless, still; dumb, inarticulate, mum, mute, nonvocal, speechless, tacit; reticent, taciturn, uncommunicative.

silken adj flossy, silky, soft.

silkiness n smoothness, softness.

silly adj brainless, childish, foolish, inept, senseless, shallow, simple, stupid, weak-minded, witless; absurd, extravagant, frivolous, imprudent, indiscreet, nonsensical, preposterous, trifling, unwise. • n ass, duffer, goose, idiot, simpleton.

silt n alluvium, deposit, deposition, residue, settlement, settlings, sediment.

silver adj argent, silvery; bright, silvery, white; clear, mellifluous, soft.

similar adj analogous, duplicate, like, resembling, twin; homogeneous, uniform.

similarity n agreement, analogy, correspondence, likeness, parallelism, parity, resemblance, sameness, semblance, similitude.

simile n comparison, metaphor, similitude.

similitude n image, likeness, resemblance; comparison, metaphor, simile.

simmer vb boil, bubble, seethe, stew.

simper vb smile, smirk.

simple adj bare, elementary, homogeneous, incomplex, mere, single, unalloyed, unblended, uncombined, uncompounded, unmingled, unmixed; chaste, plain, homespun, inornate, natural, neat, unadorned, unaffected, unembellished, unpretentious, unstudied, unvarnished; artless, downright, frank, guileless, inartificial, ingenuous, naive, open, simple-hearted, simple-minded, sincere, single-minded, straightforward, true, unconstrained, undesigning, unsophisticated; credulous, fatuous, foolish, shallow, silly, unwise, weak; clear, intelligible, understandable, uninvolved, unmistakable.

simple-hearted adj artless, frank, ingenuous, open, simple, single-hearted.

simpleton n fool, greenhorn, nincompoop, ninny.

simplicity n chasteness, homeliness, naturalness, neatness, plainness; artlessness, frankness, naivety, openness, simplesse, sincerity; clearness; gullibility, folly, silliness, weakness.

simply adv artlessly, plainly, sincerely, unaffectedly; barely, merely, of itself, solely; absolutely, alone.

simulate vb act, affect, ape, assume, counterfeit, dissemble, feign, mimic, pretend, sham.

simulation n counterfeiting, feigning, personation, pretence.

simultaneous adj coeval, coincident, concomitant, concurrent, contemporaneous, synchronous.

sin vb do wrong, err, transgress, trespass. • n delinquency, depravity, guilt, iniquity, misdeed, offence, transgression, unrighteousness, wickedness, wrong.

since conj as, because, considering, seeing that. • adv ago, before this; from that time. • prep after, from the time of, subsequently to.

sincere adj pure, unmixed; genuine, honest, inartificial, real, true, unaffected, unfeigned, unvarnished; artless, candid, direct, frank, guileless, hearty, honest, ingenuous, open, plain, single, straightforward, truthful, undissembling, upright, whole-hearted.

sincerity n artlessness, candor, earnestness, frankness, genuineness, guilelessness, honesty, ingenuousness, probity, truth, truthfulness, unaffectedness, veracity.

sinew n ligament, tendon; brawn, muscle, nerve, strength.

sinewy adj able-bodied, brawny, firm, Herculean, muscular, nervous, powerful, robust, stalwart, strapping, strong, sturdy, vigorous, wiry.

sinful adj bad, criminal, depraved, immoral, iniquitous, mischievous, peccant, transgressive, unholy, unrighteous, wicked, wrong.

sinfulness n corruption, criminality, depravity, iniquity, irreligion, ungodliness, unholiness, unrighteousness, wickedness.

sing vb cantillate, carol, chant, hum, hymn, intone, lilt, troll, warble, yodel.

singe vb burn, scorch, sear.

singer n cantor, caroler, chanter, gleeman, prima donna, minstrel, psalmodist, songster, vocalist.

single vb (with **out**) choose, pick, select, single. • adj alone, isolated, one only, sole, solitary; individual, particular, separate; celibate, unmarried, unwedded; pure, simple, uncompounded, unmixed; honest, ingenuous, sincere, unbiased, uncorrupt, upright.

single-handed adj alone, by one's self, unaided, unassisted.

single-minded adj artless, candid, guileless, ingenuous, sincere.

singleness n individuality, unity; purity, simplicity; ingenuousness, integrity, sincerity, uprightness.

singular adj eminent, exceptional, extraordinary, rare, remarkable, strange, uncommon, unusual, unwonted; particular, unexampled, unparalleled, unprecedented; unaccountable; bizarre, curious, eccentric, fantastic, odd, peculiar, queer; individual, single; not complex, single, uncompounded, unique.

singularity n aberration, abnormality, irregularity, oddness, rareness, rarity, strangeness, uncommonness; characteristic, idiosyncrasy, individuality, particularity, peculiarity; eccentricity, oddity.

sinister adj baleful, injurious, untoward; boding ill, inauspicious, ominous, unlucky; left, on the left hand.

sink vb droop, drop, fall, founder, go down, submerge, subside; enter, penetrate; collapse, fail; decay, decline, decrease, dwindle, give way, languish, lose strength; engulf, immerse, merge, submerge, submerse; dig, excavate, scoop out; abase, bring down, crush, debase, degrade, depress, diminish, lessen, lower, overbear; destroy, overthrow, overwhelm, reduce, ruin, swamp, waste. • n basin, cloaca, drain.

sinless adj faultless, guiltless, immaculate, impeccable, innocent, spotless, unblemished, undefiled, unspotted, unsullied, untarnished.

sinner n criminal, delinquent, evildoer, offender, reprobate, wrongdoer.

sinuosity n crook, curvature, flexure, sinus, tortuosity, winding.

sinuous adj bending, crooked, curved, curvilinear, flexuous, serpentine, sinuate, sinuated, tortuous, undulating, wavy, winding.

sip vb drink, suck up, sup; absorb, drink in. • n small draught, taste.

sire vb father, reproduce; author, breed, conceive, create, generate, originate, produce, propagate. • n father, male parent, progenitor; man, male person; sir, sirrah; author, begetter, creator, father, generator, originator.

siren adj alluring, bewitching, fascinating, seducing, tempting. • n mermaid; charmer, Circe, seducer, seductress, tempter, temptress.

sit vb be, remain, repose, rest, stay; bear on, lie, rest; abide, dwell, settle; perch; brood, incubate; become, be suited, fit.

site vb locate, place, position, situate, station. • n ground, locality, location, place, position, seat, situation, spot, station, whereabouts.

sitting n meeting, session.

situation n ground, locality, location, place, position, seat, site, spot, whereabouts; case, category, circumstances, condition, juncture, plight, predicament, state; employment, office, place, post, station.

size n amplitude, bigness, bulk, dimensions, expanse, greatness, largeness, magnitude, mass, volume.

skeleton n framework; draft, outline, sketch.

sketch *vb* design, draft, draw out; delineate, depict, paint, portray, represent. • *n* delineation, design, draft, drawing, outline, plan, skeleton.

sketchy *adj* crude, incomplete, unfinished.

skilful *adj* able, accomplished, adept, adroit, apt, clever, competent, conversant, cunning, deft, dexterous, dextrous, expert, handy, ingenious, masterly, practiced, proficient, qualified, quick, ready, skilled, trained, versed, well-versed.

skill *n* ability, address, adroitness, aptitude, aptness, art, cleverness, deftness, dexterity, expertise, expertness, facility, ingenuity, knack, quickness, readiness, skilfulness; discernment, discrimination, knowledge, understanding, wit.

skim *vb* brush, glance, graze, kiss, scrape, scratch, sweep, touch lightly; coast, flow, fly, glide, sail, scud, whisk; dip into, glance at, scan, skip, thumb over, touch upon.

skin *vb* pare, peel; decorticate, excoriate, flay. • *n* cuticle, cutis, derm, epidermis, hide, integument, pellicle, pelt; hull, husk, peel, rind.

skinflint *n* churl, curmudgeon, lickpenny, miser, niggard, scrimp.

skinny *adj* emaciated, lank, lean, poor, shriveled, shrunk, thin.

skip *vb* bound, caper, frisk, gambol, hop, jump, leap, spring; disregard, intermit, miss, neglect, omit, pass over, skim. • *n* bound, caper, frisk, gambol, hop, jump, leap, spring.

skirmish *vb* battle, brush, collide, combat, contest, fight, scuffle, tussle. • *n* affair, affray, battle, brush, collision, combat, conflict, contest, encounter, fight, scuffle, tussle.

skirt *vb* border, bound, edge, fringe, hem, march, rim; circumnavigate, circumvent, flank, go along. • *n* border, boundary, edge, margin, rim, verge; flap, kilt, overskirt, petticoat.

skittish *adj* changeable, fickle, inconstant; hasty, volatile, wanton; shy, timid, timorous.

skulk *vb* hide, lurk, slink, sneak.

skulker *n* lurker, sneak; shirk, slacker, malingerer.

skull *n* brain pan, cranium.

sky *n* empyrean, firmament, heaven, heavens, welkin.

sky-blue *adj* azure, cerulean, sapphire, sky-colored.

skylarking *n* carousing, frolicking, sporting.

slab *adj* slimy, thick, viscous. • *n* beam, board, layer, panel, plank, slat, table, tablet; mire, mud, puddle, slime.

slabber *vb* drivel, slaver, slobber; drop, let fall, shed, spill.

slack *vb* ease off, let up; abate, ease up, relax, slacken; malinger, shirk; choke, damp, extinguish, smother, stifle. • *adj* backward, careless, inattentive, lax, negligent, remiss; abated, dilatory, diminished, lingering, slow, tardy; loose, relaxed; dull, idle, inactive, quiet, sluggish. • *n* excess, leeway, looseness, play; coal dust, culm, residue.

slacken *vb* abate, diminish, lessen, lower, mitigate, moderate, neglect, remit, relieve, retard, slack; loosen, relax; flag, slow down; bridle, check, control, curb, repress, restrain.

slackness *n* looseness; inattention, negligence, remissness; slowness, tardiness.

slander *vb* asperse, backbite, belie, brand, calumniate, decry, defame, libel, malign, reproach, scandalize, traduce, vilify; detract from, disparage. • *n* aspersion, backbiting, calumny, defamation, detraction, libel, obloquy, scandal, vilification.

slanderous *adj* calumnious, defamatory, false, libellous, malicious, maligning.

slang *n* argo, cant, jargon, lingo.

slant *vb* incline, lean, lie obliquely, list, slope. • *n* inclination, slope, steep, tilt.

slap *vb* dab, clap, pat, smack, spank, strike. • *adv* instantly, quickly, plumply. • *n* blow, clap.

slapdash *adv* haphazardly, hurriedly, precipitately.

slash *vb* cut, gash, slit. • *n* cut, gash, slit.

slashed *adj* cut, slit; (*bot*) jagged, laciniate, multifid.

slattern *adj* slatternly, slovenly, sluttish. • *n* drab, slut, sloven, trollop.

slatternly *adj* dirty, slattern, slovenly, sluttish, unclean, untidy. • *adv* carelessly, negligently, sluttishly.

slaughter *vb* butcher, kill, massacre, murder, slay. • *n* bloodshed, butchery, carnage, havoc, killing, massacre, murder, slaying.

slaughterer *n* assassin, butcher, cutthroat, destroyer, killer, murderer, slayer.

slave *vb* drudge, moil, toil. • *n* bondmaid, bondservant, bondslave, bondman, captive, dependant, henchman, helot, peon, serf, thrall, vassal, villein; drudge, menial.

slavery n bondage, bond-service, captivity, enslavement, enthralment, serfdom, servitude, thraldom, vassalage, villeinage; drudgery, mean labour.

slavish adj abject, beggarly, base, cringing, fawning, groveling, low, mean, obsequious, servile, sycophantic; drudging, laborious, menial, servile.

slay vb assassinate, butcher, dispatch, kill, massacre, murder, slaughter; destroy, ruin.

slayer n assassin, destroyer, killer, murderer, slaughterer.

sledge n drag, sled; cutter, pung, sleigh.

sleek adj glossy, satin, silken, silky, smooth.

sleekly adv evenly, glossily, nicely, smoothly.

sleep vb catnap, doze, drowse, nap, slumber. • n dormancy, hypnosis, lethargy, repose, rest, slumber.

sleeping adj dormant, inactive, quiescent.

sleepwalker n night-walker, noctambulist, somnambulist.

sleepwalking n somnambulism.

sleepy adj comatose, dozy, drowsy, heavy, lethargic, nodding, somnolent; narcotic, opiate, slumberous, somniferous, somnific, soporiferous, soporific; dull, heavy, inactive, lazy, slow, sluggish, torpid.

sleight n adroitness, dexterity, maneuvring.

sleight of hand n conjuring, hocus-pocus, jugglery, legerdemain, prestdigitation.

slender adj lank, lithe, narrow, skinny, slim, spindly, thin; feeble, fine, flimsy, fragile, slight, tenuous, weak; inconsiderable, moderate, small, trivial; exiguous, inadequate, insufficient, lean, meager, pitiful, scanty; abstemious, light, simple, spare, sparing.

slice vb cut, divide, part, section; cut off, sever. • n chop, collop, piece.

slick adj glassy, glossy, polished, sleek, smooth; alert, clever, cunning, shrewd, slippery, unctuous. vb burnish, gloss, lacquer, polish, shine, sleek, varnish; grease, lubricate, oil.

slide vb glide, move smoothly, slip. • n glide, glissade, skid, slip.

sliding adj gliding, slippery, uncertain. • n backsliding, falling, fault, lapse, transgression.

slight vb cold-shoulder, disdain, disregard, neglect, snub; overlook; scamp, skimp, slur. • adj inconsiderable, insignificant, little, paltry, petty, small, trifling, trivial, unimportant, unsubstantial; delicate, feeble, frail, gentle, weak; careless, cursory, desultory, hasty, hurried, negligent, scanty, superficial; flimsy, perishable; slender, slim. • n discourtesy, disregard, disrespect, inattention, indignity, neglect.

slightingly adv contemptuously, disrespectfully, scornfully, slightly.

slightly adv inconsiderably, little, somewhat; feebly, slenderly, weakly; cursorily, hastily, negligently, superficially.

slim vb bant, diet, lose weight, reduce, slenderize. • adj gaunt, lank, lithe, narrow, skinny, slender, spare; inconsiderable, paltry, poor, slight, trifling, trivial, unsubstantial, weak; insufficient, meager.

slime n mire, mud, ooze, sludge.

slimy adj miry, muddy, oozy; clammy, gelatinous, glutinous, gummy, lubricious, mucilaginous, mucous, ropy, slabby, viscid, viscous.

sling vb cast, fling, hurl, throw; hang up, suspend.

slink vb skulk, slip away, sneak, steal away.

slip vb glide, slide; err, mistake, trip; lose, omit; disengage, throw off; escape, let go, loose, loosen, release. • n glide, slide, slipping; blunder, lapse, misstep, mistake, oversight, peccadillo, trip; backsliding, error, fault, impropriety, indiscretion, transgression; desertion, escape; cord, leash, strap, string; case, covering, wrapper.

slippery adj glib, slithery, smooth; changeable, insecure, mutable, perilous, shaky, uncertain, unsafe, unstable, unsteady; cunning, dishonest, elusive, faithless, false, knavish, perfidious, shifty, treacherous.

slipshod adj careless, shuffling, slovenly, untidy.

slit vb cut; divide, rend, slash, split, sunder. • n cut, gash.

slobber vb drivel, drool, slabber, slaver; daub, obscure, smear, stain.

slobbery adj dank, floody, moist, muddy, sloppy, wet.

slope vb incline, slant, tilt. • n acclivity, cant, declivity, glacis, grade, gradient, incline, inclination, obliquity, pitch, ramp.

sloping adj aslant, beveled, declivitous, inclining, oblique, shelving, slanting.

sloppy adj muddy, plashy, slabby, slobbery, splashy, wet.

sloth n dilatoriness, slowness, tardiness; idleness, inaction, inactivity, indolence, inertness, laziness, lumpishness, slothfulness, sluggishness, supineness, torpor.

slothful *adj* dronish, idle, inactive, indolent, inert, lazy, lumpish, slack, sluggish, supine, torpid.

slouch *vb* droop, loll, slump; shamble, shuffle. • *n* malingerer, shirker, slacker; shamble, shuffle, stoop.

slouching *adj* awkward, clownish, loutish, lubberly, uncouth, ungainly.

slough[1] *n* bog, fen, marsh, morass, quagmire; dejection, depression, despondence, despondency.

slough[2] *vb* cast, desquamate, excuviate, moult, shed, throw off; cast off, discard, divest, jettison, reject. • *n* cast, desquamation.

sloven *n* slattern, slob, slouch, slut.

slovenly *adj* unclean, untidy; blowsy, disorderly, dowdy, frowsy, loose, slatternly, tacky, unkempt, untidy; careless, heedless, lazy, negligent, perfunctory.

slow *vb* abate, brake, check, decelerate, diminish, lessen, mitigate, moderate, modulate, reduce, weaken; delay, detain, retard; ease, ease up, relax, slack, slacken, slack off. • *adj* deliberate, gradual; dead, dull, heavy, inactive, inert, sluggish, stupid; behindhand, late, tardy, unready; delaying, dilatory, lingering, slack.

sludge *n* mire, mud; slosh, slush.

sluggard *n* dawdler, drone, idler, laggard, lounger, slug.

sluggish *adj* dronish, drowsy, idle, inactive, indolent, inert, languid, lazy, listless, lumpish, phlegmatic, slothful, torpid; slow; dull, stupid, supine, tame.

sluice *vb* drain, drench, flood, flush, irrigate. • *n* floodgate, opening, vent.

slumber *vb* catnap, doze, nap, repose, rest, sleep. • *n* catnap, doze, nap, repose, rest, siesta, sleep.

slumberous *adj* drowsy, sleepy, somniferous, somnific, soporific.

slump *vb* droop, drop, fall, flop, founder, sag, sink, sink down; decline, depreciate, deteriorate, ebb, fail, fall away, lose ground, recede, slide, slip, subside, wane. • *n* droop, drop, fall, flop, lowering, sag, sinkage; decline, depreciation, deterioration, downturn, downtrend, subsidence, ebb, falling off, wane; crash, recession, smash.

slur *vb* asperse, calumniate, disparage, depreciate, reproach, traduce; conceal, disregard, gloss over, obscure, pass over, slight. • *n* mark, stain; brand, disgrace, reproach, stain, stigma; innuendo.

slush *n* slosh, sludge.

slushy *vb* plashy, sloppy, sloshy, sludgy.

slut *n* drab, slattern, sloven, trollop.

sluttish *adj* careless, dirty, disorderly, unclean, untidy.

sly *adj* artful, crafty, cunning, insidious, subtle, wily; astute, cautious, shrewd; arch, knowing, clandestine, secret, stealthy, underhand.

smack[1] *vb* smell, taste. • *n* flavor, savor, tang, taste, tincture; dash, infusion, little, space, soupçon, sprinkling, tinge, touch; smattering.

smack[2] *vb* slap, strike; crack, slash, snap; buss, kiss. • *n* crack, slap, slash, snap; buss, kiss.

small *adj* diminutive, Lilliputian, little, miniature, petite, pygmy, tiny, wee; infinitesimal, microscopic, minute; inappreciable, inconsiderable, insignificant, petty, trifling, trivial, unimportant; moderate, paltry, scanty, slender; faint, feeble, puny, slight, weak; illiberal, mean, narrow, narrow-minded, paltry, selfish, sorded, ungenerous, unworthy.

small talk *n* chat, conversation, gossip.

smart[1] *vb* hurt, pain, sting; suffer. • *adj* keen, painful, poignant, pricking, pungent, severe, sharp, stinging.

smart[2] *adj* active, agile, brisk, fresh, lively, nimble, quick, spirited, sprightly, spry; effective, efficient, energetic, forcible, vigorous; adroit, alert, clever, dexterous, dextrous, expert, intelligent, stirring; acute, apt, pertinent, ready, witty; chic, dapper, fine, natty, showy, spruce, trim.

smartness *n* acuteness, keenness, poignancy, pungency, severity, sharpness; efficiency, energy, force, vigor; activity, agility, briskness, liveliness, nimbleness, sprightliness, spryness, vivacity; alertness, cleverness, dexterity, expertise, expertness, intelligence, quickness; acuteness, aptness, pertinency, wit, wittiness; chic, nattiness, spruceness, trimness.

smash *vb* break, crush, dash, mash, shatter. • *n* crash, debacle, destruction, ruin; bankruptcy, failure.

smattering *n* dabbling, smatter, sprinkling.

smear *vb* bedaub, begrime, besmear, daub, plaster, smudge; contaminate, pollute, smirch, smut, soil, stain, sully, tarnish. • *n* blot, blotch, daub, patch, smirch, smudge, spot, stain; calumny, defamation, libel, slander.

smell *vb* scent, sniff, stench, stink. • *n* aroma, bouquet, fragrance, fume, odor, perfume, redolence, scent, stench, stink; sniff, snuff.

smelt *vb* fuse, melt.

smile *vb* grin, laugh, simper, smirk. • *n* grin, simper, smirk.

smite *vb* beat, box, collide, cuff, knock, strike, wallop, whack; destroy, kill, slay; afflict, chasten, punish; blast, destroy.

smitten *adj* attracted, captivated, charmed, enamored, fascinated, taken; destroyed, killed, slain; smit, struck; afflicted, chastened, punished.

smock *n* chemise, shift, slip; blouse, gaberdine.

smoke *vb* emit, exhale, reek, steam; fumigate, smudge; discover, find out, smell out. • *n* effluvium, exhalation, fume, mist, reek, smother, steam, vapor; fumigation, smudge.

smoky *adj* fuliginous, fumid, fumy, smudgy; begrimed, blackened, dark, reeky, sooty, tanned.

smooth *vb* flatten, level, plane; ease, lubricate; extenuate, palliate, soften; allay, alleviate, assuage, calm, mitigate, mollify. • *adj* even, flat, level, plane, polished, unruffled, unwrinkled; glabrous, glossy, satiny, silky, sleek, soft, velvet; euphonious, flowing, liquid, mellifluent; fluent, glib, voluble; bland, flattering, ingratiating, insinuating, mild, oily, smooth-tongued, soothing, suave, unctuous.

smoothly *adv* evenly; easily, readily, unobstructedly; blandly, flatteringly, gently, mildly, pleasantly, softly, soothingly.

smooth-tongued *adj* adulatory, cozening, flattering, plausible, smooth, smooth-spoken.

smother *vb* choke, stifle, suffocate; conceal, deaden, extinguish, hide, keep down, repress, suppress; smoke, smoulder.

smudge *vb* besmear, blacken, blur, smear, smut, smutch, soil, spot, stain. • *n* blur, blot, smear, smut, spot, stain.

smug *adj* complacent, self-satisfied; neat, nice, spruce, trim.

smuggler *n* contrabandist, runner.

smut *vb* blacken, smouch, smudge, soil, stain, sully, taint, tarnish. • *n* dirt, smudge, smutch, soot; nastiness, obscenity, ribaldry, smuttiness; pornography.

smutty *adj* coarse, gross, immodest, impure, indecent, indelicate, loose, nasty; dirty, foul, nasty, soiled, stained.

snack *n* bite, light meal, nibble.

snag *vb* catch, enmesh, entangle, hook, snare, sniggle, tangle. • *n* knarl, knob, knot, projection, protuberance, snub; catch, difficulty, drawback, hitch, rub, shortcoming, weakness; obstacle.

snaky *adj* serpentine, snaking, winding; artful, cunning, deceitful, insinuating, sly, subtle.

snap *vb* break, fracture; bite, catch at, seize, snatch at, snip; crack; crackle, crepitate, decrepitate, pop. • *adj* casual, cursory, hasty, offhand, sudden, superficial. • *n* bite, catch, nip, seizure; catch, clasp, fastening, lock; crack, fillip, flick, flip, smack; briskness, energy, verve, vim.

snappish *adj* acrimonious, captious, churlish, crabbed, cross, crusty, froward, irascible, ill-tempered, peevish, perverse, pettish, petulant, snarling, splenetic, surly, tart, testy, touchy, waspish.

snare *vb* catch, ensnare, entangle, entrap. • *n* catch, gin, net, noose, springe, toil, trap, wile.

snarl[1] *vb* girn, gnarl, growl, grumble, murmur. • *n* growl, grumble.

snarl[2] *vb* complicate, disorder, entangle, knot; confuse, embarrass, ensnare. • *n* complication, disorder, entanglement, tangle; difficulty, embarrassment, intricacy.

snatch *vb* catch, clutch, grasp, grip, pluck, pull, seize, snip, twich, wrest, wring. • *n* bit, fragment, part, portion; catch, effort.

sneak *vb* lurk, skulk, slink, steal; crouch, truckle. • *adj* clandestine, concealed, covert, hidden, secret, sly, underhand. • *n* informer, telltale; lurker, shirk.

sneaky *adj* furtive, skulking, slinking; abject, crouching, groveling, mean; clandestine, concealed, covert, hidden, secret, sly, underhand.

sneer *vb* flout, gibe, jeer, mock, rail, scoff; (*with* at) deride, despise, disdain, laugh at, mock, rail at, scoff, spurn. • *n* flouting, gibe, jeer, scoff.

snicker *vb* giggle, laugh, snigger, titter.

sniff *vb* breathe, inhale, snuff; scent, smell.

snip *vb* clip, cut, nip; snap, snatch. • *n* bit, fragment, particle, piece, shred; share, snack.

snivel *vb* blubber, cry, fret, sniffle, snuffle, weep, whimper, whine.

snivelly *adj* snotty; pitiful, whining.

snob *n* climber, toady.

snooze *vb* catnap, doze, drowse, nap, sleep, slumber. • *n* catnap, nap, sleep, slumber.

snout *n* muzzle, nose; nozzle.

snowy *adj* immaculate, pure, spotless, unblemished, unstained, unsullied, white.

snub[1] *vb* abash, cold-shoulder, cut, discomfit, humble, humiliate, mortify, slight, take down. • *n* check, rebuke, slight.

snub[2] *vb* check, clip, cut short, dock, nip, prune, stunt. • *adj* pug, retroussé, snubbed, squashed, squat, stubby, turned-up.

snuff[1] *vb* breathe, inhale, sniff; scent, smell; snort.

snuff[2] *vb* (*with* **out**) annihilate, destroy, efface, extinguish, obliterate.

snuffle *vb* sniffle; snort, snuff.

snug *adj* close, concealed; comfortable, compact, convenient, neat, trim.

snuggle *vb* cuddle, nestle, nuzzle.

so *adv* thus, with equal reason; in such a manner; in this way, likewise; as it is, as it was, such; for this reason, therefore; be it so, thus be it. • *conj* in case that, on condition that, provided that.

soak *vb* drench, moisten, permeate, saturate, wet; absorb, imbibe; imbue, macerate, steep.

soar *vb* ascend, fly aloft, glide, mount, rise, tower.

sob *vb* cry, sigh convulsively, weep.

sober *vb* (*with* **up**) calm down, collect oneself, compose oneself, control oneself, cool off, master, moderate, simmer down. • *adj* abstemious, abstinent, temperate, unintoxicated; rational, reasonable, sane, sound; calm, collected, composed, cool, dispassionate, moderate, rational, reasonable, regular, restrained, steady, temperate, unimpassioned, unruffled, well-regulated; demure, grave, quiet, sedate, serious, solemn, sombre, staid; dark, drab, dull-looking, quiet, sad, subdued.

sobriety *n* abstemiousness, abstinence, soberness, temperance; calmness, coolness, gravity, sedateness, sober-mindedness, staidness, thoughtfulness; gravity, seriousness, solemnity.

sobriquet *n* appellation, nickname, nom de plume, pseudonym.

sociability *n* companionableness, comradeship, good fellowship, sociality.

sociable *adj* accessible, affable, communicative, companionable, conversable, friendly, genial, neighborly, social.

social *adj* civic, civil; accessible, affable, communicative, companionable, familiar, friendly, hospitable, neighborly, sociable; convivial, festive, gregarious. • *n* conversazione, gathering, get-together, party, reception, soiree.

society *n* association, companionship, company, converse, fellowship; the community, populace, the public, the world; élite, *monde*; body, brotherhood, copartnership, corporation, club, fraternity, partnersnip, sodality, union.

sodden *adj* drenched, saturated, soaked, steeped, wet; boiled, decocted, seethed, stewed.

sofa *n* couch, davenport, divan, ottoman, settee.

soft *adj* impressible, malleable, plastic, pliable, yielding; downy, fleecy, velvety, mushy, pulpy, squashy; compliant, facile, irresolute, submissive, undecided, weak; bland, mild, gentle, kind, lenient, soft-hearted, tender; delicate; easy, even, quiet, smooth-going, steady; effeminate, luxurious, unmanly; dulcet, fluty, mellifluous, melodious, smooth. • *interj* hold, stop.

soften *vb* intenerate, mellow, melt, tenderize; abate, allay, alleviate, appease, assuage, attemper, balm, blunt, calm, dull, ease, lessen, make easy, mitigate, moderate, mollify, milden, qualify, quell, quiet, relent, relieve, soothe, still, temper; extenuate, modify, palliate, qualify; enervate, weaken.

soil[1] *n* earth, ground loam, mold; country, land.

soil[2] *vb* bedaub, begrime, bemire, besmear, bespatter, contaminate, daub, defile, dirty, foul, pollute, smirch, stain, sully, taint, tarnish. • *n* blemish, defilement, dirt, filth, foulness; blot, spot, stain, taint, tarnish.

sojourn *vb* abide, dwell, live, lodge, remain, reside, rest, stay, stop, tarry, visit. • *n* residence, stay.

solace *vb* cheer, comfort, console, soothe; allay, assuage, mitigate, relieve, soften. • *n* alleviation, cheer, comfort, consolation, relief.

soldier *n* fighting man, man-at-arms, warrior; GI, private.

soldierly *adj* martial, military, warlike; brave, courageous, gallant, heroic, honorable, intrepid, valiant.

sole *adj* alone, individual, one, only, single, solitary, unique.

solecism n barbarism, blunder, error, faux pas, impropriety, incongruity, mistake, slip.

solemn adj ceremonial, formal, ritual; devotional, devout, religious, reverential, sacred; earnest, grave, serious, sober; august, awe-inspiring, awful, grand, imposing, impressive, majestic, stately, venerable.

solemnity n celebration, ceremony, observance, office, rite; awfulness, sacredness, sanctity; gravity, impressiveness, seriousness.

solemnize vb celebrate, commemorate, honor, keep, observe.

solicit vb appeal to, ask, beg, beseech, conjure, crave, entreat, implore, importune, petition, pray, press, request, supplicate, urge; arouse, awaken, entice, excite, invite, summon; canvass, seek.

solicitation n address, appeal, asking, entreaty, imploration, importunity, insistence, petition, request, suit, supplication, urgency; bidding, call, invitation, summons.

solicitor n attorney, law agent, lawyer; asker, canvasser, drummer, petitioner, solicitant.

solicitous adj anxious, apprehensive, careful, concerned, disturbed, eager, troubled, uneasy.

solicitude n anxiety, care, carefulness, concern, perplexity, trouble.

solid adj congealed, firm, hard, impenetrable, rock like; compact, dense, impermeable, massed; cubic; sound, stable, stout, strong, substantial; just, real, true, valid, weighty; dependable, faithful, reliable, safe, staunch, steadfast, trustworthy, well established.

solidarity n communion of interests, community, consolidation, fellowship, joint interest, mutual responsibility.

solidify vb compact, congeal, consolidate, harden, petrify.

solidity n compactness, consistency, density, firmness, hardness, solidness; fullness; massiveness, stability, strength; dependability, gravity, justice, reliability, soundness, steadiness, validity, weight; cubic content, volume.

soliloquy n monologue.

solitariness n isolation, privacy, reclusion, retirement, seclusion; loneliness, solitude.

solitary adj alone, companionless, lone, lonely, only, separate, unaccompanied; individual, single, sole; desert, deserted, desolate, isolated, lonely, remote, retired, secluded, unfrequented.

solitude n isolation, loneliness, privacy, recluseness, retiredness, retirement, seclusion, solitariness; desert, waste, wilderness.

solution n answer, clue, disentanglement, elucidation, explication, explanation, key, resolution, unraveling, unriddling; disintegration, dissolution, liquefaction, melting, resolution, separation; breach, disconnection, discontinuance, disjunction, disruption.

solve vb clear, clear up, disentangle, elucidate, explain, expound, interpret, make plain, resolve, unfold.

solvent n diluent, dissolvent, menstruum.

somatic adj bodily, corporeal.

sombre adj cloudy, dark, dismal, dull, dusky, gloomy, murky, overcast, rayless, shady, sombrous, sunless; doleful, funereal, grave, lugubrious, melancholy, mournful, sad, sober.

some adj a, an, any, one; about, near; certain, little, moderate, part, several.

somebody n one, someone, something; celebrity, VIP.

somehow adv in some way.

something n part, portion, thing; somebody; affair, event, matter.

sometime adj former, late. • adv formerly, once; now and then, at one time or other, sometimes.

sometimes adv at intervals, at times, now and then, occasionally; at a past period, formerly, once.

somewhat adv in some degree, more or less, rather, something. • n something, a little, more or less, part.

somewhere adv here and there, in one place or another, in some place.

somnambulism n sleepwalking, somnambulation.

somnambulist n night-walker, noctambulist, sleepwalker, somnambulator, somnambule.

somniferous adj narcotic, opiate, slumberous, somnific, soporific, soporiferous.

somnolence n doziness, drowsiness, sleepiness, somnolency.

somnolent adj dozy, drowsy, sleepy.

son n cadet, heir, junior, scion.

song n aria, ballad, canticle, canzonet, carol, ditty, glee, lay, lullaby, snatch; descant, melody; anthem, hymn, poem, psalm, strain; poesy, poetry, verse.

sonorous *adj* full-toned, resonant, resounding, ringing, sounding; high-sounding, loud.

soon *adv* anon, before long, by and by, in a short time, presently, shortly; betimes, early, forthwith, promptly, quick; gladly, lief, readily, willingly.

soot *n* carbon, crock, dust.

soothe *vb* cajole, flatter, humor; appease, assuage, balm, calm, compose, lull, mollify, pacify, quiet, soften, still, tranquillize; allay, alleviate, blunt, check, deaden, dull, ease, lessen, mitigate, moderate, palliate, qualify, relieve, repress, soften, subdue, temper.

soothsayer *n* augur, diviner, foreteller, necromancer, predictor, prophet, seer, sorcerer, vaticinator.

sooty *adj* black, dark, dusky, fuliginous, murky, sable.

sophism *n* casuistry, fallacy, paralogism, paralogy, quibble, specious argument.

sophist *n* quibbler.

sophistical *adj* casuistical, fallacious, illogical, quibbling, subtle, unsound.

soporific *adj* dormitive, hypnotic, narcotic, opiate, sleepy, slumberous, somnific, somniferous, soporiferous, soporous.

soppy *adj* drenched, saturated, soaked, sopped; emotional, mawkish, sentimental.

soprano *n* (*mus*) descant, discant, treble.

sorcerer *n* charmer, conjurer, diviner, enchanter, juggler, magician, necromancers, seer, shaman, soothsayer, thaumaturgist, wizard.

sorcery *n* black art, charm, divination, enchantment, necromancy, occultism, shamanism, spell, thaumaturgy, voodoo, witchcraft.

sordid *adj* base, degraded, low, mean, vile; avaricious, close-fisted, covetous, illiberal, miserly, niggardly, penurious, stingy, ungenerous.

sore *adj* irritated, painful, raw, tender, ulcerated; aggrieved, galled, grieved, hurt, irritable, vexed; afflictive, distressing, severe, sharp, violent. • *n* abscess, boil, fester, gathering, imposthume, pustule, ulcer; affliction, grief, pain, sorrow, trouble.

sorely *adv* greatly, grievously, severely, violently.

sorrily *adv* despicably, meanly, pitiably, poorly, wretchedly.

sorrow *vb* bemoan, bewail, grieve, lament, mourn, weep. • *n* affliction, dolor, grief, heartache, mourning, sadness, trouble, woe.

sorrowful *adj* afflicted, dejected, depressed, grieved, grieving, heartsore, sad; baleful, distressing, grievous, lamentable, melancholy, mournful, painful; disconsolate, dismal, doleful, dolorous, drear, dreary, lugubrious, melancholy, piteous, rueful, woebegone, woeful.

sorry *adj* afflicted, dejected, grieved, pained, poor, sorrowful; distressing, pitiful; chagrined, mortified, pained, regretful, remorseful, sad, vexed; abject, base, beggarly, contemptible, despicable, low, mean, paltry, insignificant, miserable, shabby, worthless, wretched.

sort *vb* arrange, assort, class, classify, distribute, order; conjoin, join, put together; choose, elect, pick out, select; associate, consort, fraternize; accord, agree with, fit, suit. • *n* character, class, denomination, description, kind, nature, order, race, rank, species, type; manner, way.

sortie *n* attack, foray, raid, sally.

so-so *adj* indifferent, mediocre, middling, ordinary, passable, tolerable.

sot *n* blockhead, dolt, dullard, dunce, fool, simpleton; drunkard, tippler, toper.

sottish *adj* doltish, dull, foolish, senseless, simple, stupid; befuddled, besotted, drunken, insensate, senseless, tipsy.

sotto voce *adv* in a low voice, in an undertone, softly.

sough *n* murmur, sigh; breath, breeze, waft.

soul *n* mind, psyche, spirit; being, person; embodiment, essence, personification, spirit, vital principle; ardor, energy, fervor, inspiration, vitality.

soulless *adj* dead, expressionless, lifeless, unfeeling.

sound[1] *adj* entire, intact, unbroken, unhurt, unimpaired, uninjured, unmutilated, whole; hale, hardy, healthy, hearty, vigorous; good, perfect, undecayed; sane, well-balanced; correct, orthodox, right, solid, valid, well-founded; legal; deep, fast, profound, unbroken, undisturbed; forcible, lusty, severe, stout.

sound[2] *n* channel, narrows, strait.

sound[3] *vb* resound; appear, seem; play on; express, pronounce, utter; announce, celebrate, proclaim, publish, spread. • *n* noise, note, tone, voice, whisper.

sound[4] vb fathom, gauge, measure, test; examine, probe, search, test, try.

sounding adj audible, resonant, resounding, ringing, sonorous; imposing, significant.

soundless adj dumb, noiseless, silent; abysmal, bottomless, deep, profound, unfathomable, unsounded.

soundly adv satisfactorily, thoroughly, well; healthily, heartily, forcibly, lustily, severely, smartly, stoutly; correctly, rightly, truly; firmly, strongly; deeply, fast, profoundly.

soundness n entireness, entirety, integrity, wholeness; healthiness, vigor, saneness, sanity, correctness, orthodoxy, rectitude, reliability, truth, validity; firmness, solidity, strength, validity.

soup n broth, consommé, purée.

sour vb acidulate; embitter, envenom. • adj acetose, acetous, acid, astringent, pricked, sharp, tart, vinegary; acrimonious, crabbed, cross, crusty, fretful, glum, illhumored, ill-natured, ill-tempered, peevish, pettish, petulant, snarling, surly; bitter, disagreeable, unpleasant; austere, dismal, gloomy, morose, sad, sullen; bad, coagulated, curdled, musty, rancid, turned.

source n beginning, fountain, fountainhead, head, origin, rise, root, spring, well; cause, original.

sourness n acidity, sharpness, tartness; acrimony, asperity, churlishness, crabbedness, crossness, discontent, harshness, moroseness, peevishness.

souse vb pickle; dip, douse, immerse, plunge, submerge.

souvenir n keepsake, memento, remembrance, reminder.

sovereign adj imperial, monarchical, princely, regal, royal, supreme; chief, commanding, excellent, highest, paramount, predominant, principal, supreme, utmost; efficacious, effectual. • n autocrat, monarch, suzerain; emperor, empress, king, lord, potentate, prince, princess, queen, ruler.

sovereignty n authority, dominion, empire, power, rule, supremacy, sway.

sow vb scatter, spread, strew; disperse, disseminate, propagate, spread abroad; plant; besprinkle, scatter.

space n expanse, expansion, extension, extent, proportions, spread; accommodation, capacity, room, place; distance, interspace, interval.

spacious adj extended, extensive, vast, wide; ample, broad, capacious, commodious, large, roomy, wide.

span vb compass, cross, encompass, measure, overlay. • n brief period, spell; pair, team, yoke.

spank vb slap, strike.

spar[1] n beam, boom, pole, sprit, yard.

spar[2] vb box, fight; argue, bicker, contend, dispute, quarrel, spat, squabble, wrangle.

spare vb lay aside, lay by, reserve, save, set apart, set aside; dispense with, do without, part with; forbear, omit, refrain, withhold; exempt, forgive, keep from; afford, allow, give, grant; save; economize, pinch. • adj frugal, scanty, sparing, stinted; chary, parsimonious; emaciated, gaunt, lank, lean, meager, poor, thin, scraggy, skinny, raw-boned; additional, extra, supernumerary.

sparing adj little, scanty, scarce; abstemious, meager, spare; chary, economical, frugal, parsimonious, saving; compassionate, forgiving, lenient, merciful.

spark vb scintillate, sparkle; begin, fire, incite, instigate, kindle, light, set off, start, touch off, trigger. • n scintilla, scintillation, sparkle; beginning, element, germ, seed.

sparkle vb coruscate, flash, gleam, glisten, glister, glitter, radiate, scintillate, shine, twinkle; bubble, effervesce, foam, froth. • n glint, scintillation, spark; luminosity, luster.

sparkling adj brilliant, flashing, glistening, glittering, glittery, twinkling; bubbling, effervescing, eloquent, foaming, frothing, mantling; brilliant, glowing, lively, nervous, piquant, racy, spirited, sprightly, witty.

sparse adj dispersed, infrequent, scanty, scattered, sporadic, thin.

spartan adj bold, brave, chivalric, courageous, daring, dauntless, doughty, fearless, hardy, heroic, intrepid, lion-hearted, undaunted, valiant, valorous; austere, exacting, hard, severe, tough, unsparing; enduring, long-suffering, self-controlled, stoic.

spasm n contraction, cramp, crick, twitch; fit, paroxysm, seizure, throe.

spasmodic adj erratic, fitful, intermittent, irregular, sporadic; convulsive, paroxysmal, spasmodical, violent.

spat vb argue, bicker, dispute, jangle, quarrel, spar, squabble, wrangle.

spatter vb bespatter, besprinkle, plash, splash, sprinkle; spit, sputter.

spawn *vb* bring forth, generate, produce. • *n* eggs, roe; fruit, offspring, product.

speak *vb* articulate, deliver, enunciate, express, pronounce, utter; announce, confer, declare, disclose, mention, say, tell; celebrate, make known, proclaim, speak abroad; accost, address, greet, hail; exhibit; argue, converse, dispute, talk; declaim, discourse, hold forth, harangue, orate, plead, spout, treat.

speaker *n* discourse, elocutionist, orator, prolocutor, spokesman; chairman, presiding officer.

speaking *adj* rhetorical, talking; eloquent, expressive; lifelike. • *n* discourse, talk, utterance; declamation, elocution, oratory.

spear *n* dart, gaff, harpoon, javelin, lance, pike; shoot, spire.

special *adj* specific, specifical; especial, individual, particular, peculiar, unique; exceptional, extraordinary, marked, particular, uncommon; appropriate, express.

specialty, speciality *n* particularity; feature, forte, pet subject.

species *n* assemblage, class, collection, group; description, kind, sort, variety; (*law*) fashion, figure, form, shape.

specific *adj* characteristic, especial, particular, peculiar; definite, limited, precise, specified.

specification *n* characterization, designation; details, particularization.

specify *vb* define, designate, detail, indicate, individualize, name, show, particularize.

specimen *n* copy, example, model, pattern, sample.

specious *adj* manifest, obvious, open, showy; flimsy, illusory, ostensible, plausible, sophistical.

speck *n* blemish, blot, flaw, speckle, spot, stain; atom, bit, corpuscle, mite, mote, particle, scintilla.

spectacle *n* display, exhibition, pageant, parade, representation, review, scene, show, sight; curiosity, marvel, phenomenon, wonder.

spectacles *npl* glasses, goggles, shades.

spectator *n* beholder, bystander, observer, onlooker, witness.

specter, spectre *n* apparition, banshee, ghost, goblin, hobgoblin, phantom, shade, shadow, spirit, sprite, wraith.

spectral *adj* eerie, ghostlike, ghostly, phantomlike, shadowy, spooky, weird, wraithlike.

spectrum *n* appearance, image, representation.

speculate *vb* cogitate, conjecture, contemplate, imagine, meditate, muse, ponder, reflect, ruminate, theorize, think; bet, gamble, hazard, risk, trade, venture.

speculation *n* contemplation, intellectualization; conjecture, hypothesis, scheme, supposition, reasoning, reflection, theory, view.

speculative *adj* contemplative, philosophical, speculatory, unpractical; ideal, imaginary, theoretical; hazardous, risky, unsecured.

speculator *n* speculatist, theorist, theorizer; adventurer, dealer, gambler, trader.

speech *n* articulation, language, words; dialect, idiom, locution, tongue; conversation, oral communication, parlance, talk, verbal intercourse; mention, observation, remark, saying; address, declaration, discourse, harangue, oration, palaver.

speechless *adj* dumb, gagged, inarticulate, mute, silent; dazed, dumbfounded, flabbergasted, shocked.

speed *vb* hasten, hurry, rush, scurry; flourish, prosper, succeed, thrive; accelerate, expedite, hasten, hurry, quicken, press forward, urge on; carry through, dispatch, execute; advance, aid, assist, help; favor. • *n* acceleration, celerity, dispatch, expedition, fleetness, haste, hurry, quickness, rapidity, swiftness, velocity; good fortune, good luck, prosperity, success; impetuosity.

speedy *adj* fast, fleet, flying, hasty, hurried, hurrying, nimble, quick, rapid, swift; expeditious, prompt, quick; approaching, early, near.

spell[1] *n* charm, exorcism, hoodoo, incantation, jinx, witchery; allure, bewitchment, captivation, enchantment, entrancement, fascination.

spell[2] *vb* decipher, interpret, read, unfold, unravel, unriddle.

spell[3] *n* fit, interval, period, round, season, stint, term, turn.

spellbound *adj* bewitched, charmed, enchanted, entranced, enthralled, fascinated.

spend *vb* disburse, dispose of, expend, lay out, part with; consume, dissipate, exhaust, lavish, squander, use up, wear, waste; apply, bestow, devote, employ, pass.

spendthrift *n* prodigal, spender, squanderer, waster.

spent *adj* exhausted, fatigued, played out, used up, wearied, worn out.

spew *vb* cast up, puke, throw up, vomit; cast forth, eject.

spheral *adj* complete, perfect, symmetrical.

sphere *n* ball, globe, orb, spheroid; ambit, beat, bound, circle, circuit, compass, department, function, office, orbit, province, range, walk; order, rank, standing; country, domain, quarter, realm, region.

spherical *adj* bulbous, globated, globous, globular, orbicular, rotund, round, spheroid; planetary.

spice *n* flavor, flavoring, relish, savor, taste; admixture, dash, grain, infusion, particle, smack, soupçon, sprinkling, tincture.

spicily *adv* pungently, wittily.

spicy *adj* aromatic, balmy, fragrant; keen, piquant, pointed, pungent, sharp; indelicate, off-color, racy, risqué, sensational, suggestive.

spill *vb* effuse, pour out, shed. • *n* accident, fall, tumble.

spin *vb* twist; draw out, extend; lengthen, prolong, protract, spend; pirouette, turn, twirl, whirl. • *n* drive, joyride, ride; autorotation, gyration, loop, revolution, rotation, turning, wheeling; pirouette, reel, turn, wheel, whirl.

spindle *n* axis, shaft.

spine *n* barb, prickle, thorn; backbone; ridge.

spinose *adj* briery, spinous, spiny, thorny.

spiny *adj* briery, prickly, spinose, spinous, thorny; difficult, perplexed, troublesome.

spiracle *n* aperture, blowhole, orifice, pore, vent.

spiral *adj* cochlear, cochleated, curled, helical, screw-shaped, spiry, winding. • *n* helix, winding, worm.

spire *n* curl, spiral, twist, wreath; steeple; blade, shoot, spear, stalk; apex, summit.

spirit *vb* animate, encourage, excite, inspirit; carry off, kidnap. • *n* immaterial substance, life, vital essence; person, soul; angel, apparition, demon, elf, fairy, genius, ghost, phantom, shade, specter, sprite; disposition, frame of mind, humor, mood, temper; spirits; ardor, cheerfulness, courage, earnestness, energy, enterprise, enthusiasm, fire, force, mettle, resolution, vigour, vim, vivacity, zeal; animation, cheerfulness, enterprise, esprit, glow, liveliness, piquancy, spice, spunk, vivacity, warmth; drift, gist,

intent, meaning, purport, sense, significance, tenor; character, characteristic, complexion, essence, nature, quality, quintessence; alcohol, liquor; (*with* **the**) Comforter, Holy Ghost, Paraclete.

spirited *adj* active, alert, animated, ardent, bold, brisk, courageous, earnest, frisky, high-mettled, high-spirited, high-strung, lively, mettlesome, sprightly, vivacious.

spiritless *adj* breathless, dead, extinct, lifeless; dejected, depressed, discouraged, dispirited, low-spirited; apathetic, cold, dull, feeble, languid, phlegmatic, sluggish, soulless, torpid, unenterprising; dull, frigid, heavy, insipid, prosaic, prosy, stupid, tame, uninteresting.

spiritual *adj* ethereal, ghostly, immaterial incorporeal, psychical, supersensible; ideal, moral, unwordly, divine, holy, pure, sacred; ecclesiastical.

spiritualize *vb* elevate, etherealize, purify, refine.

spirituous *adj* alcoholic, ardent, spiritous.

spit[1] *vb* impale, thrust through, transfix.

spit[2] *vb* eject, throw out; drivel, drool, expectorate, salivate, slobber, spawl, splutter. • *n* saliva, spawl, spittle, sputum.

spite *vb* injure, mortify, thwart; annoy, offend, vex. • *n* grudge, hate, hatred, ill-nature, ill-will, malevolence, malice, maliciousness, malignity, pique, rancor, spleen, venom, vindictiveness.

spiteful *adj* evil-minded, hateful, ill-disposed, ill-natured, malevolent, malicious, malign, malignant, rancorous.

spittoon *n* cuspidor.

splash *vb* dabble, dash, plash, spatter, splurge, swash, swish. • *n* blot, daub, spot.

splay *adj* broad, spreading out, turned out, wide.

spleen *n* anger, animosity, chagrin, gall, grudge, hatred, ill-humor, irascibility, malevolence, malice, malignity, peevishness, pique, rancor, spite.

spleeny *adj* angry, fretful, ill-tempered, irritable, peevish, spleenish, splenetic.

splendid *adj* beaming, bright, brilliant, effulgent, glowing, lustrous, radiant, refulgent, resplendent, shining; dazzling, gorgeous, imposing, kingly, magnificent, pompous, showy, sumptuous, superb; celebrated, conspicuous, distinguished, eminent, excellent, famous, glorious, illustrious, noble, pre-eminent, remarkable, signal; grand, heroic, lofty, noble, sublime.

splendor n brightness, brilliance, brilliancy, luster, radiance, refulgence; display, éclat, gorgeousness, grandeur, magnificence, parade, pomp, show, showiness, stateliness; celebrity, eminence, fame, glory, grandeur, renown; grandeur, loftiness, nobleness, sublimity.

splenetic adj choleric, cross, fretful, irascible, irritable, peevish, pettish, petulant, snappish, testy, touchy, waspish; churlish, crabbed, morose, sour, sulky, sullen; gloomy, jaundiced.

splice vb braid, connect, join, knit, mortise.

splinter vb rend, shiver, sliver, split. • n fragment, piece.

split vb cleave, rive; break, burst, rend, splinter; divide, part, separate, sunder. • n crack, fissure, rent; breach, division, separation.

splotch n blot, daub, smear, spot, stain.

splutter vb sputter, stammer, stutter.

spoil vb despoil, fleece, loot, pilfer, plunder, ravage, rob, steal, strip, waste; corrupt, damage, destroy, disfigure, harm, impair, injure, mar, ruin, vitiate; decay, decompose. • n booty, loot, pillage, plunder, prey; rapine, robbery, spoliation, waste.

spoiler n pillager, plunderer, robber; corrupter, destroyer.

spokesman n mouthpiece, prolocutor, speaker.

spoliate vb despoil, destroy, loot, pillage, plunder, rob, spoil.

spoliation n depradation, deprivation, despoliation, destruction, robbery; destruction, devastation, pillage, plundering, rapine, ravagement.

sponge vb cleanse, wipe; efface, expunge, obliterate, rub out, wipe out.

sponger n hanger-on, parasite.

spongy adj absorbent, porous, spongeous; rainy, showery, wet; drenched, marshy, saturated, soaked, wet.

sponsor vb back, capitalize, endorse, finance, guarantee, patronize, promote, support, stake, subsidize, take up, underwrite. • n angel, backer, guarantor, patron, promoter, supporter, surety, underwriter; godfather, godmother, godparent.

spontaneity n improvisation, impulsiveness, spontaneousness.

spontaneous adj free, gratuitous, impulsive, improvised, instinctive, self-acting, self-moving, unbidden, uncompelled, unconstrained, voluntary, willing.

sporadic adj dispersed, infrequent, isolated, rare, scattered, separate, spasmodic.

sport vb caper, disport, frisk, gambol, have fun, make merry, play, romp, skip; trifle; display, exhibit. • n amusement, diversion, entertainment, frolic, fun, gambol, game, jollity, joviality, merriment, merrymaking, mirth, pastime, pleasantry, prank, recreation; jest, joke; derision, jeer, mockery, ridicule; monstrosity.

sportive adj frisky, frolicsome, gamesome, hilarious, lively, merry, playful, prankish, rollicking, sprightly, tricksy; comic, facetious, funny, humorous, jocose, jocular, lively, ludicrous, mirthful, vivacious, waggish.

spot vb besprinkle, dapple, dot, speck, stud, variegate; blemish, disgrace, soil, splotch, stain, sully, tarnish; detect, discern, espy, make out, observe, see, sight. • n blot, dapple, fleck, freckle, maculation, mark, mottle, patch, pip, speck, speckle; blemish, blotch, flaw, pock, splotch, stain, taint; locality, place, site.

spotless adj perfect, undefaced, unspotted; blameless, immaculate, innocent, irreproachable, pure, stainless, unblemished, unstained, untainted, untarnished.

spotted adj bespeckled, bespotted, dotted, flecked, freckled, maculated, ocellated, speckled, spotty.

spousal adj bridal, conjugal, connubial, hymeneal, marital, matrimonial, nuptial, wedded.

spouse n companion, consort, husband, mate, partner, wife.

spout vb gush, jet, pour out, spirit, spurt, squirt; declaim, mouth, speak, utter. • n conduit, tube; beak, nose, nozzle, waterspout.

sprain vb overstrain, rick, strain, twist, wrench, wrick.

spray[1] vb atomize, besprinkle, douche, gush, jet, shower, splash, splatter, spout, sprinkle, squirt. • n aerosol, atomizer, douche, foam, froth, shower, sprinkler, spume.

spray[2] n bough, branch, shoot, sprig, twig.

spread vb dilate, expand, extend, mantle, stretch; diffuse, disperse, distribute, radiate, scatter, sprinkle, strew; broadcast, circulate, disseminate, divulge, make known, make public, promulgate, propagate, publish; open, unfold, unfurl; cover, extend over, overspread. • n compass, extent, range, reach, scope, stretch; expansion, extension; circulation, dissemination, propagation; cloth, cover; banquet, feast, meal.

spree *n* bacchanal, carousal, debauch, frolic, jollification, orgy, revel, revelry, saturnalia.

sprig *n* shoot, spray, twig; lad, youth.

sprightliness *n* animation, activity, briskness, cheerfulness, frolicsomeness, gaiety, life, liveliness, nimbleness, vigor, vivacity.

sprightly *adj* airy, animated, blithe, blithesome, brisk, buoyant, cheerful, debonair, frolicsome, joyous, lively, mercurial, vigorous, vivacious.

spring *vb* bound, hop, jump, leap, prance, vault; arise, emerge, grow, issue, proceed, put forth, shoot forth, stem; derive, descend, emanate, flow, originate, rise, start; fly back, rebound, recoil; bend, warp; grow, thrive, wax. • *adj* hopping, jumping, resilient, springy. • *n* bound, hop, jump, leap, vault; elasticity, flexibility, resilience, resiliency, springiness; fount, fountain, fountainhead, geyser, springhead, well; cause, origin, original, principle, source; seed time, springtime.

springe *n* gin, net, noose, snare, trap.

springiness *n* elasticity, resilience, spring; sponginess, wetness.

springy *adj* bouncing, bounding, elastic, rebounding, recoiling, resilient.

sprinkle *vb* scatter, strew; bedew, besprinkle, dust, powder, sand, spatter; wash, cleanse, purify, shower.

sprinkling *n* affusion, baptism, bedewing, spattering, splattering, spraying, wetting; dash, scattering, seasoning, smack, soupçon, suggestion, tinge, touch, trace, vestige.

sprite *n* apparition, elf, fairy, ghost, goblin, hobgoblin, phantom, pixie, shade, spectre, spirit.

sprout *vb* burgeon, burst forth, germinate, grow, pullulate, push, put forth, ramify, shoot, shoot forth. • *n* shoot, sprig.

spruce *vb* preen, prink; adorn, deck, dress, smarten, trim. • *adj* dandyish, dapper, fine, foppish, jaunty, natty, neat, nice, smart, tidy, trig, trim.

spry *adj* active, agile, alert, brisk, lively, nimble, prompt, quick, ready, smart, sprightly, stirring, supple.

spume *n* foam, froth, scum, spray.

spumy *adj* foamy, frothy, spumous.

spur *vb* gallop, hasten, press on, prick; animate, arouse, drive, goad, impel, incite, induce, instigate, rouse, stimulate, urge forward. • *n* goad, point, prick, rowel; fillip, impulse, incentive, incitement, inducement, instigation, motive, provocation, stimulus, whip; gnarl, knob, knot, point, projection, snag.

spurious *adj* bogus, counterfeit, deceitful, false, feigned, fictitious, make-believe, meretricious, mock, pretended, sham, supposititious, unauthentic.

spurn *vb* drive away, kick; contemn, despise, disregard, flout, scorn, slight; disdain, reject, repudiate.

spurt *vb* gush, jet, spirt, spout, spring out, stream out, well. • *n* gush, jet, spout, squirt; burst, dash, ruch.

sputter *vb* spawl, spit, splutter, stammer.

spy *vb* behold, discern, espy, see; detect, discover, search out; explore, inspect, scrutinize, search; shadow, trail, watch. • *n* agent, detective, double agent, mole, scout, undercover agent.

squabble *vb* brawl, fight, quarrel, scuffle, struggle, wrangle; altercate, bicker, contend, dispute, jangle. • *n* brawl, dispute, fight, quarrel, rumpus, scrimmage.

squad *n* band, bevy, crew, gang, knot, lot, relay, set.

squalid *adj* dirty, filthy, foul, mucky, slovenly, unclean, unkempt.

squalidness *n* filthiness, foulness, squalidity, squalor.

squall *vb* bawl, cry, cry out, scream, yell. • *n* bawl, cry, outcry, scream, yell; blast, flurry, gale, gust, hurricane, storm, tempest.

squally *adj* blustering, blustery, gusty, stormy, tempestuous, windy.

squander *vb* dissipate, expend, lavish, lose, misuse, scatter, spend, throw away, waste.

squanderer *n* lavisher, prodigal, spendthrift, waster.

square *vb* make square, quadrate; accommodate, adapt, fit, mold, regulate, shape, suit; adjust, balance, close, make even, settle; accord, chime in, cohere, comport, fall in, fit, harmonize, quadrate, suit. • *adj* four-square, quadrilateral, quadrate; equal, equitable, exact, fair, honest, just, upright; adjusted, balanced, even, settled; true, suitable. • *n* four-sided figure, quadrate, rectangle, tetragon; open area, parade, piazza, plaza.

squash *vb* crush, mash.

squashy *adj* pulpy, soft.

squat *vb* cower, crouch; occupy, plant, settle. • *adj* cowering, crouching; dumpy, pudgy, short, stocky, stubby, thickset.

squeal *vb* creak, cry, howl, scream, screech, shriek, squawk, yell; betray, inform on. • *n* creak, cry, howl, scream, screech, shriek, squawk, yell.

squeamish *adj* nauseated, qualmish, queasy, sickish; dainty, delicate, fastidious, finical, hypercritical, nice, over-nice, particular, priggish.

squeeze *vb* clutch, compress, constrict, grip, nip, pinch, press; drive, force; crush, harass, oppress; crowd, force through; press; (*with* **out**) extract. • *n* congestion, crowd, crush, throng; compression.

squelch *vb* crush, quash, quell; silence, squash, suppress.

squib *n* firework, fuse; lampoon, pasquinade, satire.

squint *vb* look askance, look obliquely, peer. • *adj* askew, aslant, crooked, oblique, skew, skewed, twisted.

squire *vb* accompany, attend, escort, wait on.

squirm *vb* twist, wriggle, writhe.

squirt *vb* eject, jet, splash, spurt.

stab *vb* broach, gore, jab, pierce, pink, spear, stick, transfix, transpierce; wound. • *n* cut, jab, prick, thrust; blow, dagger-stroke, injury, wound.

stability *n* durability, firmness, fixedness, immovability, permanence, stableness, steadiness; constancy, firmness, reliability.

stable *adj* established, fixed, immovable, immutable, invariable, permanent, unalterable, unchangeable; constant, firm, staunch, steadfast, steady, unwavering; abiding, durable, enduring, fast, lasting, permanent, perpetual, secure, sure.

staff *n* baton, cane, pole, rod, stick, wand; bat, bludgeon, club, cudgel, mace; prop, stay, support; employees, personnel, team, workers, work force.

stage *vb* dramatize, perform, present, produce, put on. • *n* dais, platform, rostrum, scaffold, staging, stand; arena, field; boards, playhouse, theater; degree, point, step; diligence, omnibus, stagecoach.

stagey *adj* bombastic, declamatory, dramatic, melodramatic, ranting, theatrical.

stagger *vb* reel, sway, totter; alternate, fluctuate, overlap, vacillate, vary; falter, hesitate, waver; amaze, astonish, astound,

confound, dumbfound, nonplus, pose, shock, surprise.

stagnant *adj* close, motionless, quiet, standing; dormant, dull, heavy, inactive, inert, sluggish, torpid.

stagnate *vb* decay, deteriorate, languish, rot, stand still, vegetate.

staid *adj* calm, composed, demure, grave, sedate, serious, settled, sober, solemn, steady, unadventurous.

stain *vb* blemish, blot, blotch, discolor, maculate, smirch, soil, splotch, spot, sully, tarnish; color, dye, tinge; contaminate, corrupt, debase, defile, deprave, disgrace, dishonor, pollute, taint. • n blemish, blot, defect, discoloration, flaw, imperfection, spot, tarnish; contamination, disgrace, dishonor, infamy, pollution, reproach, shame, taint, tarnish.

stainless *adj* spotless, unspotted, untarnished; blameless, faultless, innocent, guiltless, pure, spotless, uncorrupted, unsullied.

stairs *npl* flight of steps, staircase, stairway.

stake[1] *vb* brace, mark, prop, secure, support. • *n* pale, palisade, peg, picket, post, stick.

stake[2] *vb* finance, pledge, wager; hazard, imperil, jeopardize, peril, risk, venture. • *n* bet, pledge, wager; adventure, hazard, risk, venture.

stale *adj* flat, fusty, insipid, mawkish, moldy, musty, sour, tasteless, vapid; decayed, effete, faded, old, time-worn, worn-out; common, commonplace, hackneyed, stereotyped, threadbare, trite.

stalk[1] *n* culm, pedicel, peduncle, petiole, shaft, spire, stem, stock.

stalk[2] *vb* march, pace, stride, strut, swagger; follow, hunt, shadow, track, walk stealthily.

stall[1] *n* stable; cell, compartment, recess; booth, kiosk, shop, stand.

stall[2] *vb* block, delay, equivocate, filibuster, hinder, postpone, procrastinate, temporize; arrest, check, conk out, die, fail, halt, stick, stop.

stalwart *adj* able-bodied, athletic, brawny, lusty, muscular, powerful, robust, sinewy, stout, strapping, strong, sturdy, vigorous; bold, brave, daring, gallant, indomitable, intrepid, redoubtable, resolute, valiant, valorous. • *n* backer, member, partisan, supporter.

stamina *n* energy, force, lustiness, power, stoutness, strength, sturdiness, vigor.

stammer vb falter, hesitate, stutter. • n faltering, hesitation, stutter.

stamp vb brand, impress, imprint, mark, print. • n brand, impress, impression, print; cast, character, complexion, cut, description, fashion, form, kind, make, mold, sort, type.

stampede vb charge, flee, panic. • n charge, flight, rout, running away, rush.

stanch see **staunch**[1].

stanchion n prop, shore, stay, support.

stand vb be erect, remain upright; abide, be fixed, continue, endure, hold good, remain; halt, pause, stop; be firm, be resolute, stand ground, stay; be valid, have force; depend, have support, rest; bear, brook, endure, suffer, sustain, weather; abide, admit, await, submit, tolerate, yield; fix, place, put, set upright; (with **against**) oppose, resist, withstand; (with **by**) be near, be present; aid, assist, defend, help, side with, support; defend, make good, justify, maintain, support, vindicate; (naut) attend, be ready; (with **fast**) be fixed, be immovable; (with **for**) mean, represent, signify; aid, defend, help, maintain, side with, support; (with **off**) keep aloof, keep off; not to comply; (with **out**) be prominent, jut, project, protrude; not comply, not yield, persist; (with **up for**) defend, justify, support, sustain, uphold; (with **with**) agree. • n place, position, post, standing place, station; halt, stay, stop; dais, platform, rostrum; booth, stall; opposition, resistance.

standard[1] n banner, colors, ensign, flag, gonfalon, pennon, streamer.

standard[2] adj average, conventional, customary, normal, ordinary, regular, usual; accepted, approved, authoritative, orthodox, received; formulary, prescriptive, regulation. • n canon, criterion, model, norm, rule, test, type; gauge, measure, model, scale; support, upright.

standing adj established, fixed, immovable, settled; durable, lasting, permanent; motionless, stagnant. • n position, stand, station; continuance, duration, existence; footing, ground, hold; condition, estimation, rank, reputation, status.

standpoint n point of view, viewpoint.

standstill n cessation, interruption, stand, stop; deadlock.

stanza n measure, staff, stave, strophe, verse.

staple adj basic, chief, essential, fundamental, main, primary, principal. • n fiber, filament, pile, thread; body, bulk, mass, substance.

star vb act, appear, feature, headline, lead, perform, play; emphasize, highlight, stress, underline. • adj leading, main, paramount, principal; celebrated, illustrious, well-known. • n heavenly body, luminary; asterisk, pentacle, pentagram; destiny, doom, fate, fortune, lot; diva, headliner, hero, heroine, lead, leading lady, leading man, prima ballerina, prima donna, principal, protagonist.

starchy adj ceremonious, exact, formal, precise, prim, punctilious, rigid, starched, stiff.

stare vb gape, gaze, look intently, watch.

stark adj rigid, stiff; absolute, bare, downright, entire, gross, mere, pure, sheer, simple. • adv absolutely, completely, entirely, fully, wholly.

starry adj astral, sidereal, star-spangled, stellar; bright, brilliant, lustrous, shining, sparkling, twinkling.

start vb begin, commence, inaugurate, initiate, institute; discover, invent; flinch, jump, shrink, startle, wince; alarm, disturb, fright, rouse, scare; depart, set off, take off; arise, call forth, evoke, raise; dislocate, move suddenly, spring. • n beginning, commencement, inauguration, outset; fit, jump, spasm, twitch; impulse, sally.

startle vb flinch, shrink, start, wince; affright, alarm, fright, frighten, scare, shock, amaze, astonish, astound.

startling adj abrupt, alarming, astonishing, shocking, sudden, surprising, unexpected, unforeseen, unheard of.

starvation n famine, famishment.

starve vb famish, perish; be in need, lack, want; kill, subdue.

starveling adj attenuated, emaciated, gaunt, hungry, lank, lean, meager, scraggy, skinny, thin. • n beggar, mendicant, pauper.

state vb affirm, assert, aver, declare, explain, expound, express, narrate, propound, recite, say, set forth, specify, voice. • adj civic, national, public. • n case, circumstances, condition, pass, phase, plight, position, posture, predicament, situation, status; condition, guise, mode, quality, rank; dignity, glory, grandeur, magnificence, pageantry, parade, pomp, splendor; body politic, civil community, commonwealth, nation, realm.

statecraft *n* diplomacy, political subtlety, state management, statesmanship.

stated *adj* established, fixed, regular, settled; detailed, set forth, specified.

stately *adj* august, dignified, elevated, grand, imperial, imposing, lofty, magnificent, majestic, noble, princely, royal; ceremonious, formal, magisterial, pompous, solemn.

statement *n* account, allegation, announcement, communiqué, declaration, description, exposition, mention, narration, narrative, recital, relation, report, specification; assertion, predication, proposition, pronouncement, thesis.

statesman *n* politician.

station *vb* establish, fix, locate, place, post, set. • *n* location, place, position, lost, seat, situation; business, employment, function, occupation, office; character, condition, degree, dignity, footing, rank, standing, state, status; depot, stop, terminal.

stationary *adj* fixed, motionless, permanent, quiescent, stable, standing, still.

statuary *n* carving, sculpture, statues.

statue *n* figurine, image, statuette.

stature *n* height, physique, size, tallness; altitude, consequence, elevation, eminence, prominence.

status *n* caste, condition, footing, position, rank, standing, station.

statute *n* act, decree, edict, enactment, law, ordinance, regulation.

staunch[1], **stanch** *vb* arrest, block, check, dam, plug, stem, stop.

staunch[2] *adj* firm, sound, stout, strong; constant, faithful, firm, hearty, loyal, resolute, stable, steadfast, steady, strong, trustworthy, trusty, unwavering, zealous.

stave *vb* break, burst; (*with* **off**) adjourn, defer, delay, postpone, procrastinate, put off, waive.

stay *vb* abide, dwell, lodge, rest, sojourn, tarry; continue, halt, remain, stand still, stop; attend, delay, linger, wait; arrest, check, curb, hold, keep in, prevent, rein in, restrain, withhold; delay, detain, hinder, obstruct; hold up, prop, shore up, support, sustain, uphold. • *n* delay, repose, rest, sojourn; halt, stand, stop; bar, check, curb, hindrance, impediment, interruption, obstacle, obstruction, restraint, stumbling block; buttress, dependence, prop, staff, support, supporter.

stead *n* place, room.

steadfast *adj* established, fast, firm, fixed, stable; constant, faithful, implicit, persevering, pertinacious, resolute, resolved, staunch, steady, unhesitating, unreserved, unshaken, unwavering, wholehearted.

steadiness *n* constancy, firmness, perseverance, persistence, resolution, steadfastness; fixedness, stability.

steady *vb* balance, counterbalance, secure, stabilize, support. • *adj* firm, fixed, stable; constant, equable, regular, undeviating, uniform, unremitting; persevering, resolute, staunch, steadfast, unchangeable, unwavering.

steal *vb* burglarize, burgle, crib, embezzle, filch, peculate, pilfer, plagiarize, poach, purloin, shoplift, thieve; creep, sneak, pass stealthily.

stealing *n* burglary, larceny, peculation, shoplifting, robbery, theft, thievery.

stealth *n* secrecy, slyness, stealthiness.

stealthy *adj* clandestine, furtive, private, secret, skulking, sly, sneaking, surreptitious, underhand.

steam *vb* emit vapor, fume; evaporate, vaporize; coddle, cook, poach; navigate, sail; be hot, sweat. • *n* vapour; effluvium, exhalation, fume, mist, reek, smoke.

steamboat *n* steamer, steamship.

steamy *adj* misty, moist, vaporous; erotic, voluptuous.

steed *n* charger, horse, mount.

steel *vb* case-harden, edge; brace, fortify, harden, make firm, nerve, strengthen.

steep[1] *adj* abrupt, declivitous, precipitous, sheer, sloping, sudden. • *n* declivity, precipice.

steep[2] *vb* digest, drench, imbrue, imbue, macerate, saturate, soak.

steeple *n* belfry, spire, tower, turret.

steer *vb* direct, conduct, govern, guide, pilot, point.

steersman *n* conductor, guide, helmsman, pilot.

stellar *adj* astral, starry, star-spangled, stellary.

stem[1] *vb* (*with* **from**) bud, descend, generate, originate, spring, sprout. • *n* axis, stipe, trunk; pedicel, peduncle, petiole, stalk; branch, descendant, offspring, progeny, scion, shoot; ancestry, descent, family, generation, line, lineage, pedigree, race, stock; (*naut*) beak, bow, cutwater, forepart, prow; helm, lookout; etymon, radical, radix, origin, root.

stem[2] *vb* breast, oppose, resist, withstand; check, dam, oppose, staunch, stay, stop.

stench *n* bad smell, fetor, offensive odor, stink.

stenography *n* brachygraphy, shorthand, tachygraphy.

stentorian *adj* loud-voiced, powerful, sonorous, thundering, trumpet-like.

step *vb* pace, stride, tramp, tread, walk. • *n* footstep, pace, stride; stair, tread; degree, gradation, grade, interval; advance, advancement, progression; act, action, deed, procedure, proceeding; footprint, trace, track, vestige; footfall, gait, pace, walk; expedient, means, measure, method; round, rundle, rung.

steppe *n* pampa, prairie, savannah.

sterile *adj* barren, infecund, unfruitful, unproductive, unprolific; bare, dry, empty, poor; (*bot*) acarpous, male, staminate.

sterility *n* barrenness, fruitlessness, infecundity, unfruitfulness, unproductiveness.

sterling *adj* genuine, positive, pure, real, sound, standard, substantial, true.

stern[1] *adj* austere, dour, forbidding, grim, severe; bitter, cruel, hard, harsh, inflexible, relentless, rigid, rigorous, severe, strict, unrelenting; immovable, incorruptible, steadfast, uncompromising.

stern[2] *n* behind, breach, hind part, posterior, rear, tail; (*naut*) counter, poop, rudderpost, tailpost; butt, buttocks, fundament, rump.

sternness *n* austerity, rigidity, severity; asperity, cruelty, harshness, inflexibility, relentlessness, rigor.

sternum *n* (*anat*) breastbone, sternon.

stertorous *adj* hoarsely breathing, snoring.

stew *vb* boil, seethe, simmer, stive. • *n* ragout; confusion, difficulty, mess, scrape.

steward *n* chamberlain, majordomo, seneschal; manciple, purveyor.

stick[1] *vb* gore, penetrate, pierce, puncture, spear, stab, transfix; infix, insert, thrust; attach, cement, glue, paste; fix in, set; adhere, cleave, cling, hold; abide, persist, remain, stay, stop; doubt, hesitate, scruple, stickle, waver; (*with* **by**) adhere to, be faithful, support. • *n* prick, stab, thrust.

stick[2] *n* birch, rod, switch; bat, bludgeon, club, cudgel, shillelah; cane, staff, walking stick; cue, pole, spar, stake.

stickiness *n* adhesiveness, glutinousness, tenacity, viscosity, viscousness.

stickle *vb* altercate, contend, contest, struggle; doubt, hesitate, scruple, stick, waver.

sticky *adj* adhesive, clinging, gluey, glutinous, gummy, mucilaginous, tenacious, viscid, viscous.

stiff *adj* inflexible, rigid, stark, unbending, unyielding; firm, tenacious, thick; obstinate, pertinacious, strong, stubborn; absolute, austere, dogmatic, inexorable, peremptory, positive, rigorous, severe, straitlaced, strict, stringent, uncompromising; ceremonious, chilling, constrained, formal, frigid, prim, punctilious, stately, starchy, stilted; abrupt, cramped, crude, graceless, harsh, inelegant.

stiff-necked *adj* contumacious, cross-grained, dogged, headstrong, intractable, mulish, obdurate, obstinate, stubborn, unruly.

stiffness *n* hardness, inflexibility, rigidity, rigidness, rigour, starkness; compactness, consistence, denseness, density, thickness; contumaciousness, inflexibility, obstinacy, pertinacity, stubbornness; austerity, harshness, rigorousness, severity, sternness, strictness; constraint, formality, frigidity, precision, primness, tenseness.

stifle *vb* choke, smother, suffocate; check, deaden, destroy, extinguish, quench, repress, stop, suppress; conceal, gag, hush, muffle, muzzle, silence, smother, still.

stigma *n* blot, blur, brand, disgrace, dishonor, reproach, shame, spot, stain, taint, tarnish.

stigmatize *vb* brand, defame, discredit, disgrace, dishonor, post, reproach, slur, villify.

stiletto *n* dagger, dirk, poniard, stylet; bodkin, piercer.

still[1] *vb* hush, muffle, silence, stifle; allay, appease, calm, compose, lull, pacify, quiet, smooth, tranquillize; calm, check, immobilize, restrain, stop, subdue, suppress. • *adj* hushed, mum, mute, noiseless, silent; calm, placid, quiet, serene, stilly, tranquil, unruffled; inert, motionless, quiescent, stagnant, stationary. • *n* hush, lull, peace, quiet, quietness, quietude, silence, stillness, tranquillity; picture, photograph, shot.

still[2] *n* distillery, still-house; distillatory, retort, stillatory.

still[3] *adv, conj* till now, to this time, yet; however, nevertheless, notwithstanding; always, continually, ever, habitually, uniformly; after that, again, in continuance.

stilted *adj* bombastic, fustian, grandiloquent, grandiose, high-flown, high-sounding, inflated, magniloquent, pompous, pretentious, stilty, swelling, tumid, turgid.

stimulant *adj* exciting, stimulating, stimulative. • *n* bracer, cordial, pick-me-up, tonic; fillip, incentive, provocative, spur, stimulus.

stimulate *vb* animate, arouse, awaken, brace, encourage, energize, excite, fire, foment, goad, impel, incite, inflame, inspirit, instigate, kindle, prick, prompt, provoke, rally, rouse, set on, spur, stir up, urge, whet, work up.

stimulus *n* encouragement, fillip, goad, incentive, incitement, motivation, motive, provocation, spur, stimulant.

sting *vb* hurt, nettle, prick, wound; afflict, cut, pain.

stinging *adj* acute, painful, piercing; biting, nipping, pungent, tingling.

stingy *adj* avaricious, close, close-fisted, covetous, grudging, mean, miserly, narrow-hearted, niggardly, parsimonious, penurious.

stink *vb* emit a stench, reek, smell bad. • *n* bad smell, fetor, offensive odor, stench.

stint *vb* bound, confine, limit, restrain; begrudge, pinch, scrimp, skimp, straiten; cease, desist, stop. • *n* bound, limit, restraint; lot, period, project, quota, share, shift, stretch, task, time, turn.

stipend *n* allowance, compensation, emolument, fee, hire, honorarium, pay, remuneration, salary, wages.

stipulate *vb* agree, bargain, condition, contract, covenant, engage, provide, settle terms.

stipulation *n* agreement, bargain, concordat, condition, contract, convention, covenant, engagement, indenture, obligation, pact.

stir *vb* budge, change place, go, move; agitate, bestir, disturb, prod; argue, discuss, moot, raise, start; animate, arouse, awaken, excite, goad, incite, instigate, prompt, provoke, quicken, rouse, spur, stimulate; appear, happen, turn up; get up, rise; (*with* **up**) animate, awaken, incite, instigate, move, provoke, quicken, rouse, stimulate. • *n* activity, ado, agitation, bustle, confusion, excitement, fidget, flurry, fuss, hurry, movement; commotion, disorder, disturbance, tumult, uproar.

stirring *adj* active, brisk, diligent, industrious, lively, smart; animating, arousing, awakening, exciting, quickening, stimulating.

stitch *vb* backstitch, baste, bind, embroider, fell, hem, seam, sew, tack, whip.

stive *vb* stow, stuff; boil, seethe, stew; make close, hot or sultry.

stock *vb* fill, furnish, store, supply; accumulate, garner, hoard, lay in, reposit, reserve, save, treasure up. • *adj* permanent, standard, standing. • *n* assets, capital, commodities, fund, principal, shares; accumulation, hoard, inventory, merchandise, provision, range, reserve, store, supply; ancestry, breed, descent, family, house, line, lineage, parentage, pedigree, race; cravat, neckcloth; butt, haft, hand; block, log, pillar, post, stake; stalk, stem, trunk.

stockholder *n* shareholder.

stocking *n* hose, sock.

stock market *n* stock exchange; cattle market.

stocks *npl* funds, public funds, public securities; shares.

stockstill *adj* dead-still, immobile, motionless, stationary, still, unmoving.

stocky *adj* chubby, chunky, dumpy, plump, short, stout, stubby, thickset.

stoic, stoical *adj* apathetic, cold-blooded, impassive, imperturbable, passionless, patient, philosophic, philosophical, phlegmatic, unimpassioned.

stoicism *n* apathy, coldness, coolness, impassivity, indifference, insensibility, nonchalance, phlegm.

stolen *adj* filched, pilfered, purloined; clandestine, furtive, secret, sly, stealthy, surreptitious.

stolid *adj* blockish, doltish, dull, foolish, heavy, obtuse, slow, stockish, stupid.

stolidity *n* doltishness, dullness, foolishness, obtuseness, stolidness, stupidity.

stomach *vb* abide, bear, brook, endure, put up with, stand, submit to, suffer, swallow, tolerate. • *n* abdomen, belly, gut, paunch, pot, tummy; appetite, desire, inclination, keenness, liking, relish, taste.

stone *vb* cover, face, slate, tile; lapidate, pelt. • *n* boulder, cobble, gravel, pebble, rock; gem, jewel, precious stone; cenotaph, gravestone, monument, tombstone; nut, pit; adamant, agate, flint, gneiss, granite, marble, slate, etc.

stony *adj* gritty, hard, lapidose, lithic, petrous, rocky; adamantine, flinty, hard, inflexible, obdurate; cruel, hard-hearted, inexorable, pitiless, stony-hearted, unfeeling, unrelenting.

stoop *vb* bend forward, bend down, bow, lean, sag, slouch, slump; abase, cower, cringe, give in, submit, succumb, surrender; condescend, deign, descend, vouchsafe; fall, sink. • *n* bend, inclination, sag, slouch, slump; descent, swoop.

stop *vb* block, blockade, close, close up, obstruct, occlude; arrest, check, halt, hold, pause, stall, stay; bar, delay, embargo, hinder, impede, intercept, interrupt, obstruct, preclude, prevent, repress, restrain, staunch, suppress, thwart; break off, cease, desist, discontinue, forbear, give over, leave off, refrain from; intermit, quiet, quicten, terminate; lodge, tarry. • *n* halt, intermission, pause, respite, rest, stoppage, suspension, truce; block, cessation, check, hindrance, interruption, obstruction, repression; bar, impediment, obstacle; full stop, point.

stopcock *n* cock, faucet, tap.

stoppage *n* arrest, block, check, closure, hindrance, interruption, obstruction, prevention.

stopper *n* cork, plug, stopple.

store *vb* accumulate, amass, cache, deposit, garner, hoard, husband, lay by, lay in, lay up, put by, reserve, save, store up, stow away, treasure up; furnish, provide, replenish, stock, supply. • *n* accumulation, cache, deposit, fund, hoard, provision, reserve, stock, supply, treasure, treasury; abundance, plenty; storehouse; emporium, market, shop.

storehouse *n* depository, depot, godown, magazine, repository, store, warehouse.

storm *vb* assail, assault, attack; blow violently; fume, rage, rampage, rant, rave, tear. • *n* blizzard, gale, hurricane, squall, tempest, tornado, typhoon, whirlwind; agitation, clamor, commotion, disturbance, insurrection, outbreak, sedition, tumult, turmoil; adversity, affliction, calamity, distress; assault, attack, brunt, onset, onslaught; violence.

storminess *n* inclemency, roughness, tempestuousness.

stormy *adj* blustering, boisterous, gusty, squally, tempestuous, windy; passionate, riotous, rough, turbulent, violent, wild; agitated, furious.

story *n* annals, chronicle, history, record; account, narration, narrative, recital, record, rehearsal, relation, report, statement, tale; fable, fiction, novel, romance; anecdote, incident, legend, tale; canard, fabrication, falsehood, fib, figure, invention, lie, untruth.

storyteller *n* bard, chronicler, narrator, raconteur.

stout *adj* able-bodied, athletic, brawny, lusty, robust, sinewy, stalwart, strong, sturdy, vigorous; courageous, hardy, indomitable, stouthearted; contumacious, obstinate, proud, resolute, stubborn; compact, firm, solid, staunch; bouncing, bulky, burly, chubby, corpulent, fat, heavy, jolly, large, obese, plump, portly, stocky, strapping, thickset.

stouthearted *adj* fearless, heroic, redoubtable; bold, brave, courageous, dauntless, doughty, firm, gallant, hardy, indomitable, intrepid, resolute, valiant, valorous.

stow *vb* load, pack, put away, store, stuff.

straddle *vb* bestride.

straggle *vb* rove, wander; deviate, digress, ramble, range, roam, stray, stroll.

straggling *adj* rambling, roving, straying, strolling, wandering; scattered.

straight *adj* direct, near, rectilinear, right, short, undeviating, unswerving; erect, perpendicular, plumb, right, upright, vertical; equitable, fair, honest, honorable, just, square, straightforward. • *adv* at once, directly, forthwith, immediately, straightaway, straightway, without delay.

straightaway, straightway *adv* at once, directly, forthwith, immediately, speedily, straight, suddenly, without delay.

straighten *vb* arrange, make straight, neaten, order, tidy.

straight-laced *see* **strait-laced**.

strain[1] *vb* draw tightly, make tense, stretch, tighten; injure, sprain, wrench; exert, overexert, overtax, rack; embrace, fold, hug, press, squeeze; compel, constrain, force; dilute, distill, drain, filter, filtrate, ooze, percolate, purify, separate; fatigue, overtask, overwork, task, tax, tire. • *n* stress, tenseness, tension, tensity; effort, exertion, force, overexertion; burden, task, tax; sprain, wrench; lay, melody, movement, snatch, song, stave, tune.

strain[2] *n* manner, style, tone, vein; disposition, tendency, trait, turn; descent, extraction, family, lineage, pedigree, race, stock.

strait *adj* close, confined, constrained, constricted, contracted, narrow; rigid, rigorous, severe, strict; difficult, distressful, grievous, straitened. • *n* channel, narrows, pass, sound.

straits *npl* crisis, difficulty, dilemma, distress, embarrassment, emergency, exigency, extremity, hardship, pass, perplexity, pinch, plight, predicament.

straiten *vb* confine, constrain, constrict, contract, limit; narrow; intensify, stretch; distress, embarrass, perplex, pinch, press.

straitened *adj* distressed, embarrassed limited, perplexed, pinched.

strait-laced, straight-laced *adj* austere, formal, prim, rigid, rigorous, stern, stiff, strict, uncompromising.

straitness *n* narrowness, rigor, severity, strictness; difficulty, distress, trouble; insufficiency, narrowness, scarcity, want.

strand[1] *vb* abandon, beach, be wrecked, cast away, go aground, ground, maroon, run aground, wreck. • *n* beach, coast, shore.

strand[2] *n* braid, cord, fiber, filament, line, rope, string, tress.

stranded *adj* aground, ashore, cast away, lost, shipwrecked, wrecked.

strange *adj* alien, exotic, far-fetched, foreign, outlandish, remote; new, novel; curious, exceptional, extraordinary, irregular, odd, particular, peculiar, rare, singular, surprising, uncommon, unusual; abnormal, anomalous, extraordinary, inconceivable, incredible, inexplicable, marvellous, mysterious, preternatural, unaccountable, unbelievable, unheard of, unique, unnatural, wonderful; bizarre, droll, grotesque, quaint, queer; inexperienced, unacquainted, unfamiliar, unknown; bashful, distant, distrustful, reserved, shy, uncommunicative.

strangeness *n* foreignness; bashfulness, coldness, distance, reserve, shyness, uncommunicativeness; eccentricity, grotesqueness, oddness, singularity, uncommonness, uncouthness.

stranger *n* alien, foreigner, newcomer, immigrant, outsider; guest, visitor.

strangle *vb* choke, contract, smother, squeeze, stifle, suffocate, throttle, tighten; keep back, quiet, repress, still, suppress.

strap *vb* beat, thrash, whip; bind, fasten, sharpen, strop. • *n* thong; band, ligature, strip, tie; razor-strap, strop.

strapping *adj* big, burly, large, lusty, stalwart, stout, strong, tall.

stratagem *n* artifice, cunning, device, dodge, finesse, intrigue, machination, maneuvre, plan, plot, ruse, scheme, trick, wile.

strategic, strategical *adj* calculated, deliberate, diplomatic, maneuvering, planned, politic, tactical; critical, decisive, key, vital.

strategy *n* generalship, maneuvering, plan, policy, stratagem, strategetics, tactics.

stratum *n* band, bed, layer.

straw *n* culm, stalk, stem; button, farthing, fig, penny, pin, rush, snap.

stray *vb* deviate, digress, err, meander, ramble, range, roam, rove, straggle, stroll, swerve, transgress, wander. • *adj* abandoned, lost, strayed, wandering; accidental, erratic, random, scattered.

streak *vb* band, bar, striate, stripe, vein; dart, dash, flash, hurtle, run, speed, sprint, stream, tear. • *n* band, bar, belt, layer, line, strip, stripe, thread, trace, vein; cast, grain, tone, touch, vein; beam, bolt, dart, dash, flare, flash, ray, stream.

streaky *adj* streaked, striped, veined.

stream *vb* course, flow, glide, pour, run, spout; emit, pour out, shed; emanate, go forth, issue, radiate; extend, float, stretch out, wave. • *n* brook, burn, race, rill, rivulet, run, runlet, runnel, trickle; course, current, flow, flux, race, rush, tide, torrent, wake, wash; beam, gleam, patch, radiation, ray, streak.

streamer *n* banner, colors, ensign, flag, pennon, standard.

street *n* avenue, highway, road, way.

strength *n* force, might, main, nerve, potency, power, vigor; hardness, solidity, toughness; impregnability, proof; brawn, grit, healthy, lustiness, muscle, robustness, sinew, stamina, thews, vigorousness; animation, courage, determination, firmness, fortitude, resolution, spirit; cogency, efficacy, soundness, validity; emphasis, energy; security, stay, support; brightness, brilliance, clearness, intensity, vitality, vividness; body, excellence, virtue; impetuosity, vehemence, violence; boldness.

strengthen *vb* buttress, recruit, reinforce; fortify; brace, energize, harden, nerve, steel, stimulate; freshen, invigorate, vitalize; animate, encourage; clench, clinch, confirm, corroborate, establish, fix, justify, sustain, support.

strenuous *adj* active, ardent, eager, earnest, energetic, resolute, vigorous, zealous;

bold, determined, doughty, intrepid, resolute, spirited, strong, valiant.

stress *vb* accent, accentuate, emphasize, highlight, point up, underline, underscore; bear, bear upon, press, pressurize; pull, rack, strain, stretch, tense, tug. • *n* accent, accentuation, emphasis; effort, force, pull, strain, tension, tug; boisterousness, severity, violence; pressure, urgency.

stretch *vb* brace, screw, strain, tense, tighten; elongate, extend, lengthen, protract, pull; display, distend, expand, spread, unfold, widen; sprain, strain; distort, exaggerate, misrepresent. • *n* compass, extension, extent, range, reach, scope; effort, exertion, strain, struggle; course, direction.

strict *adj* close, strained, tense, tight; accurate, careful, close, exact, literal, particular, precise, scrupulous; austere, inflexible, harsh, orthodox, puritanical, rigid, rigorous, severe, stern, strait-laced, stringent, uncompromising, unyielding.

stricture *n* animadversion, censure, denunciation, criticism, compression, constriction, contraction.

strife *n* battle, combat, conflict, contention, contest, discord, quarrel, struggle, warfare.

strike *vb* bang, beat, belabor, box, buffet, cudgel, cuff, hit, knock, lash, pound, punch, rap, slap, slug, smite, thump, whip; impress, imprint, stamp; afflict, chastise, deal, give, inflict, punish; affect, astonish, electrify, stun; clash, collide, dash, touch; surrender, yield; mutiny, rebel, rise.

stringent *adj* binding, contracting, rigid, rigorous, severe, strict.

strip[1] *n* piece, ribbon, shred, slip.

strip[2] *vb* denude, hull, skin, uncover; bereave, deprive, deforest, desolate, despoil, devastate, disarm, dismantle, disrobe, divest, expose, fleece, loot, shave; plunder, pillage, ransack, rob, sack, spoil; disrobe, uncover, undress.

strive *vb* aim, attempt, endeavor, exert, labor, strain, struggle, toil; contend, contest, fight, tussle, wrestle; compete, cope.

stroke[1] *n* blow, glance, hit, impact, knock, lash, pat, percussion, rap, shot, switch, thump; attack, paralysis, stroke; affliction, damage, hardship, hurt, injury, misfortune, reverse, visitation; dash, feat, masterstroke, touch.

stroke[2] *vb* caress, feel, palpate, pet, knead, massage, nuzzle, rub, touch.

stroll *vb* loiter, lounge, ramble, range, rove, saunter, straggle, stray, wander. • *n* excursion, promenade, ramble, rambling, roving, tour, trip, walk, wandering.

strong *adj* energetic, forcible, powerful, robust, sturdy; able, enduring; cogent, firm, valid.

structure *vb* arrange, constitute, construct, make, organize. • *n* arrangement, conformation, configuration, constitution, construction, form, formation, make, organization; anatomy, composition, texture; building, edifice, fabric, framework, pile.

struggle *vb* aim, endeavor, exert, labor, strive, toil, try; battle, contend, contest, fight, wrestle; agonize, flounder, writhe. • *n* effort, endeavor, exertion, labor, pains; battle, conflict, contention, contest, fight, strife; agony, contortions, distress.

stubborn *adj* contumacious, dogged, headstrong, heady, inflexible, intractable, mulish, obdurate, obstinate, perverse, positive, refractory, ungovernable, unmanageable, unruly, unyielding, willful; constant, enduring, firm, hardy, persevering, persistent, steady, stoical, uncomplaining, unremitting; firm, hard, inflexible, stiff, strong, tough, unpliant, studied.

studious *adj* contemplative, meditative, reflective, thoughtful; assiduous, attentive, desirous, diligent, eager, lettered, scholarly, zealous.

study *vb* cogitate, lucubrate, meditate, muse, ponder, reflect, think; analyze, contemplate, examine, investigate, ponder, probe, scrutinize, search, sift, weigh. • *n* exercise, inquiry, investigation, reading, research, stumble; cogitation, consideration, contemplation, examination, meditation, reflection, thought; stun; model, object, representation, sketch; den, library, office, studio.

stunning *adj* deafening, stentorian; dumbfounding, stupefying.

stunted *adj* checked, diminutive, dwarfed, dwarfish, lilliputian, little, nipped, small, undersized.

stupendous *adj* amazing, astonishing, astounding, marvellous, overwhelming, surprising, wonderful; enormous, huge, immense, monstrous, prodigious, towering, tremendous, vast.

stupid *adj* brainless, crass, doltish, dull, foolish, idiotic, inane, inept, obtuse, pointless, prosaic, senseless, simple, slow, sluggish, stolid, tedious, tiresome, witless.

stupor *n* coma, confusion, daze, lethargy, narcosis, numbness, stupefaction, torpor.

sturdy *adj* bold, determined, dogged, firm, hardy, obstinate, persevering, pertinacious, resolute, stiff, stubborn, sturdy; athletic, brawny, forcible, lusty, muscular, powerful, robust, stalwart, stout, strong, thickset, vigorous, well-set.

style *vb* address, call, characterize, denominate, designate, dub, entitle, name, term. • *n* dedication, expression, phraseology, turn; cast, character, fashion, form, genre, make, manner, method, mode, model, shape, vogue, way; appellation, denomination, designation, name, title; chic, elegance, smartness; pen, pin, point, stylus.

stylish *adj* chic, courtly, elegant, fashionable, genteel, modish, polished, smart.

suave *adj* affable, agreeable, amiable, bland, courteous, debonair, delightful, glib, gracious, mild, pleasant, smooth, sweet, oily, unctuous, urbane.

subdue *vb* beat, bend, break, bow, conquer, control, crush, defeat, discomfit, foil, master, overbear, overcome, overpower, overwhelm, quell, rout, subject, subjugate, surmount, vanquish, worst; allay, choke, curb, mellow, moderate, mollify, reduce, repress, restrain, soften, suppress, temper.

subject *vb* control, master, overcome, reduce, subdue, subjugate, tame; enslave, enthral; abandon, refer, submit, surrender. • *adj* beneath, subjacent, underneath; dependent, enslaved, inferior, servile, subjected, subordinate, subservient; conditional, obedient, submissive; disposed, exposed to, liable, obnoxious, prone. • *n* dependent, henchman, liegeman, slave, subordinate; matter, point, subject matter, theme, thesis, topic; nominative, premise; case, object, patient, recipient; ego, mind, self, thinking.

subjoin *vb* add, affix, annex, append, join, suffix.

subjugate *vb* conquer, enslave, enthral, master, overcome, overpower, overthrow, subdue, subject, vanquish.

sublimate *vb* alter, change, repress.

sublime *adj* aloft, elevated, high, sacred; eminent, exalted, grand, great, lofty, mighty; august, glorious, magnificent, majestic, noble, stately, solemn, sublunary; elated, elevated, eloquent, exhilarated, raised.

submission *n* capitulation, cession, relinquishment, surrender, yielding; acquiescence, compliance, obedience, resignation; deference, homage, humility, lowliness, obeisance, passiveness, prostration, self-abasement, submissiveness.

submissive *adj* amenable, compliant, docile, pliant, tame, tractable, yielding; acquiescent, long-suffering, obedient, passive, patient, resigned, unassertive, uncomplaining, unrepining; deferential, humble, lowly, meek, obsequious, prostrate, self-abasing.

submit *vb* cede, defer, endure, resign, subject, surrender, yield; commit, propose, refer; offer; acquiesce, bend, capitulate, comply, stoop, succumb.

subordinate *adj* ancillary, dependent, inferior, junior, minor, secondary, subject, subservient, subsidiary. • *n* assistant, dependant, inferior, subject, underling.

subscribe *vb* accede, approve, agree, assent, consent, yield; contribute, donate, give, offer, promise.

subscription *n* aid, assistance, contribution, donation, gift, offering.

subsequent *adj* after, attendant, ensuing, later, latter, following, posterior, sequent, succeeding.

subservient *adj* inferior, obsequious, servile, subject, subordinate; accessory, aiding, auxiliary, conducive, contributory, helpful, instrumental, serviceable, useful.

subside *vb* settle, sink; abate, decline, decrease, diminish, drop, ebb, fall, intermit, lapse, lessen, lower, lull, wane.

subsidence *n* settling, sinking; abatement, decline, decrease, descent, ebb, diminution, lessening.

subsidiary *adj* adjutant, aiding, assistant, auxiliary, cooperative, corroborative, helping, subordinate, subservient.

subsidize *vb* aid, finance, fund, sponsor, support, underwrite.

subsidy *n* aid, bounty, grant, subvention, support, underwriting.

subsist *vb* be, breathe, consist, exist, inhere, live, prevail; abide, continue, endure, persist, remain; feed, maintain, ration, support.

subsistence *n* aliment, food, livelihood, living, maintenance, meat, nourishment, nutriment, provision, rations, support, sustenance, victuals.

substance *n* actuality, element, groundwork, hypostasis, reality, substratum; burden, content, core, drift, essence, gist, heart, import, meaning, pith, sense, significance, solidity, soul, sum, weight; estate, income, means, property, resources, wealth.

substantial *adj* actual, considerable, essential, existent, hypostatic, pithy, potential, real, subsistent, virtual; concrete, durable, positive, solid, tangible, true; corporeal, bodily, material; bulky, firm, goodly, heavy, large, massive, notable, significant, sizable, solid, sound, stable, stout, strong, well-made; cogent, just, efficient, influential, valid, weighty.

substantially *adv* adequately, essentially, firmly, materially, positively, really, truly.

substantiate *vb* actualize, confirm, corroborate, establish, prove, ratify, verify.

subterfuge *n* artifice, evasion, excuse, expedient, mask, pretence, pretext, quirk, shift, shuffle, sophistry, trick.

subtle *adj* arch, artful, astute, crafty, crooked, cunning, designing, diplomatic, intriguing, insinuating, sly, tricky, wily; clever, ingenious; acute, deep, discerning, discriminating, keen, profound, sagacious, shrewd; airy, delicate, ethereal, light, nice, rare, refined, slender, subtle, thin, volatile.

subtlety *n* artfulness, artifice, astuteness, craft, craftiness, cunning, guile, subtleness; acumen, acuteness, cleverness, discernment, intelligence, keenness, sagacity, sharpness, shrewdness; attenuation, delicacy, fitness, nicety, rareness, refinement.

subtract *vb* deduct, detract, diminish, remove, take, withdraw.

suburbs *npl* environs, confines, neighborhood, outskirts, precincts, purlieus, vicinage.

subversive *adj* destructive, overthrowing, pervasive, ruining, upsetting. • *n* collaborator, dissident, insurrectionist, saboteur, terrorist, traitor.

subvert *vb* invert, overset, overthrow, overturn, reverse, upset; demolish, destroy, extinguish, raze, ruin; confound, corrupt, injure, pervert.

succeed *vb* ensue, follow, inherit, replace; flourish, gain, hit, prevail, prosper, thrive, win.

success *n* attainment, issue, result; fortune, happiness, hit, luck, prosperity, triumph.

successful *adj* auspicious, booming, felicitous, fortunate, happy, lucky, prosperous, victorious, winning.

succession *n* chain, concatenation, cycle, consecution, following, procession, progression, rotation, round, sequence, series, suite; descent, entail, inheritance, lineage, race, reversion.

succinct *adj* brief, compact, compendious, concise, condensed, curt, laconic, pithy, short, summary, terse.

succor *vb* aid, assist, help, relieve; cherish, comfort, encourage, foster, nurse. • *n* aid, assistance, help, relief, support.

succulent *adj* juicy, luscious, lush, nutritive, sappy.

succumb *vb* capitulate, die, submit, surrender, yield.

sudden *adj* abrupt, hasty, hurried, immediate, instantaneous, rash, unanticipated, unexpected, unforeseen, unusual; brief, momentary, quick, rapid.

sue *vb* charge, court, indict, prosecute, solicit, summon, woo; appeal, beg, demand, entreat, implore, petition, plead, pray, supplicate.

suffer *vb* feel, undergo; bear, endure, sustain, tolerate; admit, allow, indulge, let, permit.

sufferable *adj* allowable, bearable, endurable, permissible, tolerable.

sufferance *n* endurance, inconvenience, misery, pain, suffering; long-suffering, moderation, patience, submission; allowance, permission, toleration.

suffice *vb* avail, content, satisfy, serve.

sufficient *adj* adequate, ample, commensurate, competent, enough, full, plenteous, satisfactory; able, equal, fit, qualified, responsible.

suffocate *vb* asphyxiate, choke, smother, stifle, strangle.

suffrage *n* ballot, franchise, voice, vote; approval, attestation, consent, testimonial, witness.

suggest *vb* advise, allude, hint, indicate, insinuate, intimate, move, present, prompt, propose, propound, recommend.

suggestion *n* allusion, hint, indication, insinuation, intimation, presentation, prompting, proposal, recommendation, reminder.

suit *vb* accommodate, adapt, adjust, fashion, fit, level, match; accord, become, befit, gratify, harmonize, please, satisfy, tally.

• n appeal, entreaty, invocation, petition, prayer, request, solicitation, supplication; courtship, wooing; action, case, cause, process, prosecution, trial; clothing, costume, habit.

suitable adj adapted, accordant, agreeable, answerable, apposite, applicable, appropriate, apt, becoming, befitting, conformable, congruous, convenient, consonant, correspondent, decent, due, eligible, expedient, fit, fitting, just, meet, pertinent, proper, relevant, seemly, worthy.

suite n attendants, bodyguard, convoy, cortege, court, escort, followers, staff, retainers, retinue, train; collection, series, set, suit; apartment, rooms.

sulky adj aloof, churlish, cross, cross-grained, dogged, grouchy, ill-humored, ill-tempered, moody, morose, perverse, sour, spleenish, spleeny, splenetic, sullen, surly, vexatious, wayward.

sullen adj cross, crusty, glum, grumpy, ill-tempered, moody, morose, sore, sour, sulky; cheerless, cloudy, dark, depressing, dismal, foreboding, funereal, gloomy, lowering, melancholy, mournful, somber; dull, heavy, slow, sluggish; intractable, obstinate, perverse, refractory, stubborn, vexatious; baleful, evil, inauspicious, malign, malignant, sinister, unlucky, unpropitious.

sully vb blemish, blot, contaminate, deface, defame, dirty, disgrace, dishonor, foul, smirch, soil, slur, spot, stain, tarnish.

sultry adj close, damp, hot, humid, muggy, oppressive, stifling, stuffy, sweltering.

sum vb add, calculate, compute, reckon; collect, comprehend, condense, epitomize, summarize. • n aggregate, amount, total, totality, whole; compendium, substance, summary; acme, completion, height, summit.

summary adj brief, compendious, concise, curt, laconic, pithy, short, succinct, terse; brief, quick, rapid. • n abridgement, abstract, brief, compendium, digest, epitome, precis, résumé, syllabus, synopsis.

summit n acme, apex, cap, climax, crest, crown, pinnacle, top, vertex, zenith.

summon vb arouse, bid, call, cite, invite, invoke, rouse; convene, convoke; charge, indict, prosecute, subpoena, sue.

sumptuous adj costly, dear, expensive, gorgeous, grand, lavish, luxurious, magnificent, munificent, pompous, prodigal, rich, showy, splendid, stately, superb.

sunburnt adj bronzed, brown, ruddy, tanned.

sunder vb break, disconnect, disjoin, dissociate, dissever, disunited, divide, part, separate, sever.

sundry adj different, divers, several, some, various.

sunny adj bright, brilliant, clear, fine, luminous, radiant, shining, unclouded, warm; cheerful, genial, happy, joyful, mild, optimistic, pleasant, smiling.

superannuated adj aged, anile, antiquated, decrepit, disqualified, doting, effete, imbecile, passé, retired, rusty, time-worn, unfit.

superb adj august, beautiful, elegant, exquisite, grand, gorgeous, imposing, magnificent, majestic, noble, pompous, rich, showy, splendid, stately, sumptuous.

supercilious adj arrogant, condescending, contemptuous, dictatorial, domineering, haughty, high, imperious, insolent, intolerant, lofty, lordly, magisterial, overbearing, overweening, proud, scornful, vainglorious.

superficial adj external, flimsy, shallow, untrustworthy.

superfluity n excess, exuberance, redundancy, superabundance, surfeit.

superfluous adj excessive, redundant, unnecessary.

superintend vb administer, conduct, control, direct, inspect, manage, overlook, oversee, supervise.

superintendence n care, charge, control, direction, guidance, government, inspection, management, oversight, supervision, surveillance.

superior adj better, greater, high, higher, finer, paramount, supreme, ultra, upper; chief, foremost, principal; distinguished, matchless, noble, pre-eminent, preferable, sovereign, surpassing, unrivaled, unsurpassed; predominant, prevalent. • n boss, chief, director, head, higher-up, leader, manager, principal, senior, supervisor.

superiority n advantage, ascendency, lead, odds, predominance, pre-eminence, prevalence, transcendence; excellence, nobility, worthiness.

superlative adj consummate, greatest, incomparable, peerless, pre-eminent, supreme, surpassing, transcendent.

supernatural adj abnormal, marvellous, metaphysical, miraculous, otherworldly, preternatural, unearthly.

supernumerary *adj* excessive, odd, redundant, superfluous.

supersede *vb* annul, neutralize, obviate, overrule, suspend; displace, remove, replace, succeed, supplant.

supervise *vb* administer, conduct, control, direct, inspect, manage, overlook, oversee, superintend.

supine *adj* apathetic, careless, drowsy, dull, idle, indifferent, indolent, inert, languid, lethargic, listless, lumpish, lazy, negligent, otiose, prostrate, recumbent, sleepy, slothful, sluggish, spineless, torpid.

supplant *vb* overpower, overthrow, undermine; displace, remove, replace, supersede.

supple *adj* elastic, flexible, limber, lithe, pliable, pliant; compliant, humble, submissive, yielding; adulatory, cringing, fawning, flattering, groveling, obsequious, oily, parasitical, servile, slavish, sycophantic.

supplement *vb* add, augment, extend, reinforce, supply. • *n* addendum, addition, appendix, codicil, complement, continuation, postscript.

suppliant *adj* begging, beseeching, entreating, imploring, precative, precatory, praying, suing, supplicating. • *n* applicant, petitioner, solicitor, suitor, supplicant.

supplicate *vb* beg, beseech, crave, entreat, implore, importune, petition, pray, solicit.

supplication *n* invocation, orison, petition, prayer; entreaty, petition, prayer, request, solicitation.

supply *vb* endue, equip, furnish, minister, outfit, provide, replenish, stock, store; afford, accommodate, contribute, furnish, give, grant, yield. • *n* hoard, provision, reserve, stock, store.

support *vb* brace, cradle, pillow, prop, sustain, uphold; bear, endure, undergo, suffer, tolerate; cherish, keep, maintain, nourish, nurture; act, assume, carry, perform, play, represent; accredit, confirm, corroborate, substantiate, verify; abet, advocate, aid, approve, assist, back, befriend, champion, countenance, encourage, favor, float, hold, patronize, relieve, reinforce, succor, vindicate. • *n* bolster, brace, buttress, foothold, guy, hold, prop, purchase, shore, stay, substructure, supporter, underpinning; groundwork, mainstay, staff; base, basis, bed, foundation; keeping, living, livelihood, maintenance, subsistence,

sustenance; confirmation, evidence; aid, assistance, backing, behalf, championship, comfort, countenance, encouragement, favor, help, patronage, succor.

suppose *vb* apprehend, believe, conceive, conclude, consider, conjecture, deem, imagine, judge, presume, presuppose, think; assume, hypothesize, imply, posit, predicate, think; fancy, opine, speculate, surmise, suspect, theorize, wean.

supposition *n* conjecture, guess, guesswork, presumption, surmise; assumption, hypothesis, postulation, theory, thesis; doubt, uncertainty.

suppress *vb* choke, crush, destroy, overwhelm, overpower, overthrow, quash, quell, quench, smother, stifle, subdue, withhold; arrest, inhibit, obstruct, repress, restrain, stop; conceal, extinguish, keep, retain, secret, silence, stifle, strangle.

supremacy *n* ascendancy, domination, headship, lordship, mastery, predominance, pre-eminence, primacy, sovereignty.

supreme *adj* chief, dominant, first, greatest, highest, leading, paramount, predominant, pre-eminent, principal, sovereign.

sure *adj* assured, certain, confident, positive; accurate, dependable, effective, honest, infallible, precise, reliable, trustworthy, undeniable, undoubted, unmistakable, well-proven; guaranteed, inevitable, irrevocable; fast, firm, safe, secure, stable, steady.

surely *adv* assuredly, certainly, infallibly, sure, undoubtedly; firmly, safely, securely, steadily.

surety *n* bail, bond, certainty, guarantee, pledge, safety, security.

surfeit *vb* cram, gorge, overfeed, sate, satiate; cloy, nauseate, pall. • *n* excess, fullness, glut, oppression, plethora, satiation, satiety, superabundance, superfluity.

surge *vb* billow, rise, rush, sweep, swell, swirl, tower. • *n* billow, breaker, roller, wave, white horse.

surly *adj* churlish, crabbed, cross, crusty, discourteous, fretful, gruff, grumpy, harsh, ill-natured, ill-tempered, morose, peevish, perverse, pettish, petulant, rough, rude, snappish, snarling, sour, sullen, testy, touchy, uncivil, ungracious, waspish; dark, tempestuous.

surmise *vb* believe, conclude, conjecture, consider, divine, fancy, guess, imagine, presume, suppose, think, suspect. • *n* conclusion, conjecture, doubt, guess, notion, possibility, supposition, suspicion, thought.

surmount *vb* clear, climb, crown, overtop, scale, top, vault; conquer, master, overcome, overpower, subdue, vanquish; exceed, overpass, pass, surpass, transcend.

surpass *vb* beat, cap, eclipse, exceed, excel, outdo, outmatch, outnumber, outrun, outstrip, override, overshadow, overtop, outshine, surmount, transcend.

surplus *adj* additional, leftover, remaining, spare, superfluous, supernumerary, supplementary. • *n* balance, excess, overplus, remainder, residue, superabundance, surfeit.

surprise *vb* amaze, astonish, astound, bewilder, confuse, disconcert, dumbfound, startle, stun. • *n* amazement, astonishment, blow, shock, wonder.

surprising *adj* amazing, astonishing, astounding, extraordinary, marvellous, unexpected, remarkable, startling, strange, unexpected, wonderful.

surrender *vb* cede, sacrifice, yield; abdicate, abandon, forgo, relinquish, renounce, resign, waive; capitulate, comply, succumb. • *n* abandonment, capitulation, cession, delivery, relinquishment, renunciation, resignation, yielding.

surreptitious *adj* clandestine, fraudulent, furtive, secret, sly, stealthy, unauthorized, underhand.

surround *vb* beset, circumscribe, compass, embrace, encircle, encompass, environ, girdle, hem, invest, loop.

surveillance *n* care, charge, control, direction, inspection, management, oversight, superintendence, supervision, surveyorship, vigilance, watch.

survey *vb* contemplate, observe, overlook, reconnoiter, review, scan, scout, view; examine, inspect, scrutinize; oversee, supervise; estimate, measure, plan, plot, prospect. • *n* prospect, retrospect, sight, view; examination, inspection, reconnaissance, review; estimating, measuring, planning, plotting, prospecting, work-study.

survive *vb* endure, last, outlast, outlive.

susceptible *adj* capable, excitable, impressible, impressionable, inclined, predisposed, receptive, sensitive.

suspect *vb* believe, conclude, conjecture, fancy, guess, imagine, judge, suppose,

surmise, think; distrust, doubt, mistrust. • *adj* doubtful, dubious, suspicious.

suspend *vb* append, hang, sling, swing; adjourn, arrest, defer, delay, discontinue, hinder, intermit, interrupt, postpone, stay, withhold; debar, dismiss, rusticate.

suspicion *n* assumption, conjecture, dash, guess, hint, inkling, suggestion, supposition, surmise, trace; apprehension, distrust, doubt, fear, jealousy, misgiving, mistrust.

suspicious *adj* distrustful, jealous, mistrustful, suspect, suspecting; doubtful, questionable.

sustain *vb* bear, bolster, fortify, prop, strengthen, support, uphold; maintain, nourish, perpetuate, preserve; aid, assist, comfort, relieve; brave, endure, suffer, undergo; approve, confirm, ratify, sanction, validate; confirm, establish, justify, prove.

sustenance *n* maintenance, subsistence, support; aliment, bread, food, nourishment, nutriment, nutrition, provisions, supplies, victuals.

swagger *vb* bluster, boast, brag, bully, flourish, hector, ruffle, strut, swell, vapor. • *n* airs, arrogance, bluster, boastfulness, braggadocio, ruffling, strut.

swain *n* clown, countryman, hind, peasant, rustic; adorer, gallant, inamorata, lover, suitor, wooer.

swallow *vb* bolt, devour, drink, eat, englut, engorge, gobble, gorge, gulp, imbibe, ingurgitate, swamp; absorb, appropriate, arrogate, devour, engulf, submerge; consume, employ, occupy; brook, digest, endure, pocket, stomach; recant, renounce, retract. • *n* gullet, esophagus, throat; inclination, liking, palate, relish, taste; deglutition, draught, gulp, ingurgitation, mouthful, taste.

swamp *vb* engulf, overwhelm, sink; capsize, embarrass, overset, ruin, upset, wreck. • *n* bog, fen, marsh, morass, quagmire, slough.

sward *n* grass, lawn, sod, turf.

swarm *vb* abound, crowd, teem, throng. • *n* cloud, concourse, crowd, drove, flock, hive, horde, host, mass, multitude, press, shoal, throng.

swarthy *adj* black, brown, dark, darkskinned, dusky, tawny.

sway *vb* balance, brandish, move, poise, rock, roll, swing, wave, wield; bend, bias, influence, persuade, turn, urge; control,

dominate, direct, govern, guide, manage, rule; hoist, raise; incline, lean, lurch, yaw.
• *n* ascendency, authority, command, control, domination, dominion, empire, government, mastership, mastery, omnipotence, predominance, power, rule, sovereignty; bias, direction, influence, weight; preponderance, preponderation; oscillation, sweep, swing, wag, wave.

swear *vb* affirm, attest, avow, declare, depose, promise, say, state, testify, vow; blaspheme, curse.

sweep *vb* clean, brush; graze, touch; rake, scour, traverse. • *n* amplitude, compass, drive, movement, range, reach, scope; destruction, devastation, havoc, ravage; curvature, curve.

sweeping *adj* broad, comprehensive, exaggerated, extensive, extravagant, general, unqualified, wholesale.

sweet *adj* candied, cloying, honeyed, luscious, nectareous, nectarous, sugary, saccharine; balmy, fragrant, odorous, redolent, spicy; harmonious, dulcet, mellifluous, mellow, melodious, musical, pleasant, soft, tuneful, silver-toned, silvery; beautiful, fair, lovely, agreeable, charming, delightful, grateful, gratifying; affectionate, amiable, attractive, engaging, gentle, mild, lovable, winning; benignant, serene; clean, fresh, pure, sound. • *n* fragrance, perfume, redolence; blessing, delight, enjoyment, gratification, joy, pleasure; candy, treat.

swell *vb* belly, bloat, bulge, dilate, distend, expand, inflate, intumesce, puff, swell, tumefy; augment, enlarge, increase; heave, rise, surge; strut, swagger. • *n* swelling; augmentation, excrescence, protuberance; ascent, elevation, hill, rise; force, intensity, power; billows, surge, undulation, waves; beau, blade, buck, coxcomb, dandy, exquisite, fop, popinjay.

swerve *vb* deflect, depart, deviate, stray, turn, wander; bend, incline, yield; climb, swarm, wind.

swift *adj* expeditious, fast, fleet, flying, quick, rapid, speedy; alert, eager, forward, prompt, ready, zealous; instant, sudden.

swiftness *n* celerity, expedition, fleetness, quickness, rapidity, speed, velocity.

swindle *vb* cheat, con, cozen, deceive, defraud, diddle, dupe, embezzle, forge, gull, hoax, overreach, steal, trick, victimize. • *n* cheat, con, deceit, deception, fraud, hoax, imposition, knavery, roguery, trickery.

swindler *n* blackleg, cheat, defaulter, embezzler, faker, fraud, impostor, jockey, knave, peculator, rogue, sharper, trickster.

swing *vb* oscillate, sway, vibrate, wave; dangle, depend, hang; brandish, flourish, whirl; administer, manage. • *n* fluctuation, oscillation, sway, undulation, vibration; elbow-room, freedom, margin, play, range, scope, sweep; bias, tendency.

swoop *vb* descend, pounce, rush, seize, stoop, sweep. • *n* clutch, pounce, seizure; stoop, descent.

sword *n* brand, broadsword, claymore, cutlass, epee, falchion, foil, hanger, rapier, saber, scimitar.

sybarite *n* epicure, voluptuary.

sycophancy *n* adulation, cringing, fawning, flattery, grovelling, obsequiousness, servility.

sycophant *n* cringer, fawner, flunky, hanger-on, lickspittle, parasite, spaniel, toady, wheedler.

syllabus *n* abridgement, abstract, breviary, brief, compendium, digest, epitome, outline, summary, synopsis.

symbol *n* badge, emblem, exponent, figure, mark, picture, representation, representative, sign, token, type.

symbolic, symbolical *adj* emblematic, figurative, hieroglyphic, representative, significant, typical.

symmetry *n* balance, congruity, evenness, harmony, order, parallelism, proportion, regularity, shapeliness.

sympathetic *adj* affectionate, commiserating, compassionate, condoling, kind, pitiful, tender.

sympathy *n* accord, affinity, agreement, communion, concert, concord, congeniality, correlation, correspondence, harmony, reciprocity, union; commiseration, compassion, condolence, fellow-feeling, kindliness, pity, tenderness, thoughtfulness.

symptom *n* diagnostic, indication, mark, note, prognostic, sign, token.

symptomatic *adj* characteristic, indicative, symbolic, suggestive.

synonymous *adj* equipollent, equivalent, identical, interchangeable, similar, tantamount.

synopsis *n* abridgement, abstract, compendium, digest, epitome, outline, precis, résumé, summary, syllabus.

system *n* method, order, plan.

systematic *adj* methodic, methodical, orderly, regular.

T

tabernacle *n* pavilion, tent; cathedral, chapel, church, minster, synagogue, temple.

table *vb* enter, move, propose, submit, suggest. • *n* plate, slab, tablet; board, counter, desk, stand; catalog, chart, compendium, index, list, schedule, syllabus, synopsis, tabulation; diet, fare, food, victuals.

tableau *n* picture, scene, representation.

taboo *vb* forbid, interdict, prohibit, proscribe. • *adj* banned, forbidden, inviolable, outlawed, prohibited, proscribed. • *n* ban, interdict, prohibition, proscription.

tacit *adj* implicit, implied, inferred, silent, understood, unexpressed; unspoken.

taciturn *adj* close, dumb, laconic, mum, reserved, reticent, silent, tight-lipped, uncommunicative.

tack *vb* add, affix, append, attach, fasten, tag; gybe, yaw, zigzag. • *n* nail, pin, staple; bearing, course, direction, heading, path, plan, procedure.

tackle *vb* attach, grapple, seize; attempt, try, undertake. • *n* apparatus, cordage, equipment, furniture, gear, harness, implements, rigging, tackling, tools, weapons.

tact *n* address, adroitness, cleverness, dexterity, diplomacy, discernment, finesse, insight, knack, perception, skill, understanding.

tail *vb* dog, follow, shadow, stalk, track. • *adj* abridged, curtailed, limited, reduced. • *n* appendage, conclusion, end, extremity, stub; flap, skirt; queue, retinue, train.

taint *vb* imbue, impregnate; contaminate, corrupt, defile, inflect, mildew, pollute, poison, spoil, touch; blot, stain, sully, tarnish. • *n* stain, tincture, tinge, touch; contamination, corruption, defilement, depravation, infection, pollution; blemish, defect, fault, flaw, spot.

take *vb* accept, obtain, procure, receive; clasp, clutch, grasp, grip, gripe, seize, snatch; filch, misappropriate, pilfer, purloin, steal; abstract, apprehend, appropriate, arrest, bag, capture, ensnare, entrap; attack, befall, smite; capture, carry off, conquer, gain, win; allure, attract, bewitch, captivate, charm, delight, enchant, engage, fascinate, interest, please; consider, hold,

interrupt, suppose, regard, understand; choose, elect, espouse, select; employ, expend, use; claim, demand, necessitate, require; bear, endure, experience, feel, perceive, tolerate; deduce, derive, detect, discover, draw; carry, conduct, convey, lead, transfer; clear, surmount; drink, eat, imbibe, inhale, swallow. • *n* proceeds, profits, return, revenue, takings, yield.

tale *n* account, fable, legend, narration, novel, parable, recital, rehearsal, relation, romance, story, yarn; catalog, count, enumeration, numbering, reckoning, tally.

talent *n* ableness, ability, aptitude, capacity, cleverness, endowment, faculty, forte, genius, gift, knack, parts, power, turn.

talk *vb* chatter, communicate, confer, confess, converse, declaim, discuss, gossip, pontificate, speak. • *n* chatter, communication, conversation, diction, gossip, jargon, language, rumor, speech, utterance.

talkative *adj* chatty, communicative, garrulous, loquacious, voluble.

tally *vb* accord, agree, conform, coincide, correspond, harmonize, match, square, suit. • *n* match, mate; check, counterpart, muster, roll call; account, reckoning.

tame *vb* domesticate, reclaim, train; conquer, master, overcome, repress, subdue, subjugate. • *adj* docile, domestic, domesticated, gentle, mild, reclaimed; broken, crushed, meek, subdued, unresisting, submissive; barren, commonplace, dull, feeble, flat, insipid, jejune, languid, lean, poor, prosaic, prosy, spiritless, tedious, uninteresting, vapid.

tamper *vb* alter, conquer, dabble, damage, interfere, meddle; intrigue, seduce, suborn.

tang *n* aftertaste, flavor, relish, savor, smack, taste; keenness, nip, sting.

tangible *adj* corporeal, material, palpable, tactile, touchable; actual, certain, embodied, evident, obvious, open, perceptible, plain, positive, real, sensible, solid, stable, substantial.

tangle *vb* complicate, entangle, intertwine, interweave, mat, perplex, snarl; catch, ensnare, entrap, involve, catch; embarrass, embroil, perplex. • *n* complication, disorder, intricacy, jumble, perplexity, snarl; dilemma, embarrassment, quandary, perplexity.

tantalize *vb* balk, disappoint, frustrate, irritate, provoke, tease, torment, vex.

tantamount *adj* equal, equivalent, synonymous.

tantrum *n* fit, ill-humor, outburst, paroxysm, temper, whim.

tap[1] *vb* knock, pat, rap, strike, tip, touch. • *n* pat, tip, rap, touch.

tap[2] *vb* broach, draw off, extract, pierce; draw on, exploit, mine, use, utilize; bug, eavesdrop, listen in. • *n* faucet, plug, spigot, spout, stopcock, valve; bug, listening device, transmitter.

tardiness *n* delay, dilatoriness, lateness, procrastination, slackness, slowness.

tardy *adj* slow, sluggish, snail-like; backward, behindhand, dilatory, late, loitering, overdue, slack.

tarn *n* bog, fen, marsh, morass, swamp.

tarnish *vb* blemish, deface, defame, dim, discolor, dull, slur, smear, soil, stain, sully. • *n* blemish, blot, soiling, spot, stain.

tarry *vb* delay, dally, linger, loiter, remain, stay, stop, wait; defer; abide, lodge, rest, sojourn.

tart *adj* acid, acidulous, acrid, astringent, piquant, pungent, sharp, sour; acrimonious, caustic, crabbed, curt, harsh, ill-humored, ill-tempered, keen, petulant, sarcastic, severe, snappish, testy.

task *vb* burden, overwork, strain, tax. • *n* drudgery, labor, toil, work; business, charge, chore, duty, employment, enterprise, job, mission, stint, undertaking; assignment, exercise, lesson.

taste *vb* experience, feel, perceive, undergo; relish, savor, sip. • *n* flavor, gusto, relish, savor, smack, piquancy; admixture, bit, dash, fragment, hint, infusion, morsel, mouthful, sample, shade, sprinkling, suggestion, tincture; appetite, desire, fondness, liking, partiality, predilection; acumen, cultivation, culture, delicacy, discernment, discrimination, elegance, fine-feeling, grace, judgement, polish, refinement; manner, style.

tasteful *adj* appetizing, delicious, flavorsome, palatable, savory, tasty, toothsome; aesthetic, artistic, attractive, elegant.

tasteless *adj* flat, insipid, savorless, stale, watery; dull, mawkish, uninteresting, vapid.

tattle *vb* babble, chat, chatter, jabber, prate, prattle; blab, gossip, inform. • *n* gabble, gossip, prate, prattle, tittle-tattle, twaddle.

taunt *vb* censure, chaff, deride, flout, jeer, mock, scoff, sneer, revile, reproach, ridicule, twit, upbraid. • *n* censure, derision, gibe, insult, jeer, quip, quirk, reproach, ridicule, scoff.

taut *adj* strained, stretched, tense, tight.

tautology *n* iteration, pleonasm, redundancy, reiteration, repetition, verbosity, wordiness.

tavern *n* bar, chophouse, hostelry, inn, pub, public house.

tawdry *adj* flashy, gaudy, garish, glittering, loud, meretricious, ostentatious, showy.

tax *vb* burden, demand, exact, load, overtax, require, strain, task; accuse, charge. • *n* assessment, custom, duty, excise, impost, levy, rate, taxation, toll, tribute; burden, charge, demand, requisition, strain; accusation, censure.

teach *vb* catechize, coach, discipline, drill, edify, educate, enlighten, inform, indoctrinate, initiate, instruct, ground, prime, school, train, tutor; communicate, disseminate, explain, expound, impart, implant, inculcate, infuse, instil, interpret, preach, propagate; admonish, advise, counsel, direct, guide, signify, show.

teacher *n* coach, educator, inculcator, informant, instructor, master, pedagogue, preceptor, schoolteacher, trainer, tutor; adviser, counselor, guide, mentor; pastor, preacher.

tear *vb* burst, slit, rive, rend, rip; claw, lacerate, mangle, shatter, rend, wound; sever, sunder; fume, rage, rant, rave. • *n* fissure, laceration, rent, rip, wrench.

tease *vb* annoy, badger, beg, bother, chafe, chagrin, disturb, harass, harry, hector, importune, irritate, molest, pester, plague, provoke, tantalize, torment, trouble, vex, worry.

tedious *adj* dull, fatiguing, irksome, monotonous, tiresome, trying, uninteresting, wearisome; dilatory, slow, sluggish, tardy.

teem *vb* abound, bear, produce, swarm; discharge, empty, overflow.

teeming *adj* abounding, fraught, full, overflowing, pregnant, prolific, replete, swarming.

tell *vb* compute, count, enumerate, number, reckon; describe, narrate, recount, rehearse, relate, report; acknowledge, announce, betray, confess, declare, disclose, divulge, inform, own, reveal; acquaint, communicate, instruct, teach; discern, discover, distinguish; express, mention, publish, speak, state, utter.

temper *vb* modify, qualify; appease, assuage, calm, mitigate, mollify, moderate, pacify, restrain, soften, soothe; accommodate, adapt, adjust, fit, suit. • *n* character, constitution, nature, organization, quality, structure, temperament, type; disposition, frame, grain, humor, mood, spirits, tone, vein; calmness, composure, equanimity, moderation, tranquillity; anger, ill-temper, irritation, spleen, passion.

temperament *n* character, constitution, disposition, habit, idiosyncrasy, nature, organization, temper.

temperate *adj* abstemious, ascetic, austere, chaste, continent, frugal, moderate, self-controlled, self-denying, sparing; calm, cool, dispassionate, mild, sober, sedate.

tempest *n* cyclone, gale, hurricane, squall, storm, tornado; commotion, disturbance, excitement, perturbation, tumult, turmoil.

temporal *adj* civil, lay, mundane, political, profane, secular, terrestrial, worldly; brief, ephemeral, evanescent, fleeting, momentary, short-lived, temporal, transient, transitory.

temporary *adj* brief, ephemeral, evanescent, fleeting, impermanent, momentary, short-lived, transient, transitory.

tempt *vb* prove, test, try; allure, decoy, entice, induce, inveigle, persuade, seduce; dispose, incite, incline, instigate, lead, prompt, provoke.

tempting *adj* alluring, attractive, enticing, inviting, seductive.

tenable *adj* defensible, maintainable, rational, reasonable, sound.

tenacious *adj* retentive, unforgetful; adhesive, clinging, cohesive, firm, glutinous, gummy, resisting, retentive, sticky, strong, tough, unyielding, viscous; dogged, fast, obstinate, opinionated, opinionative, pertinacious, persistent, resolute, stubborn, unwavering.

tenacity *n* retentiveness, tenaciousness; adhesiveness, cohesiveness, glutinosity, glutinousness, gumminess, toughness, stickiness, strength, viscidity; doggedness, firmness, obstinacy, perseverance, persistency, pertinacity, resolution, stubbornness.

tend[1] *vb* accompany, attend, graze, guard, keep, protect, shepherd, watch.

tend[2] *vb* aim, exert, gravitate, head, incline, influence, lead, lean, point, trend, verge; conduce, contribute.

tendency *n* aim, aptitude, bearing, bent, bias, course, determination, disposition, direction, drift, gravitation, inclination, leaning, liability, predisposition, proclivity, proneness, propensity, scope, set, susceptibility, turn, twist, warp.

tender[1] *vb* bid, offer, present, proffer, propose, suggest, volunteer. • *n* bid, offer, proffer, proposal; currency, money.

tender[2] *adj* callow, delicate, effeminate, feeble, feminine, fragile, immature, infantile, soft, weak, young; affectionate, compassionate, gentle, humane, kind, lenient, loving, merciful, mild, pitiful, sensitive, sympathetic, tender-hearted; affecting, disagreeable, painful, pathetic, touching, unpleasant.

tenebrous *adj* cloudy, dark, darksome, dusky, gloomy, murky, obscure, shadowy, shady, somber, tenebrious.

tenement *n* abode, apartment, domicile, dwelling, flat, house.

tenet *n* belief, creed, position, dogma, doctrine, notion, opinion, position, principle, view.

tenor *n* cast, character, cut, fashion, form, manner, mood, nature, stamp, tendency, trend, tone; drift, gist, import, intent, meaning, purport, sense, significance, spirit.

tense *vb* flex, strain, tauten, tighten. • *adj* rigid, stiff, strained, stretched, taut, tight; excited, highly strung, intent, nervous, rapt.

tentative *adj* essaying, experimental, provisional, testing, toying.

tenure *n* holding, occupancy, occupation, possession, tenancy, tenement, use.

term *vb* call, christen, denominate, designate, dub, entitle, name, phrase, style. • *n* bound, boundary, bourn, confine, limit, mete, terminus; duration, period, season, semester, span, spell, termination, time; denomination, expression, locution, name, phrase, word.

termagant *n* beldam, hag, scold, shrew, spitfire, virago, vixen.

terminal *adj* bounding, limiting; final, terminating, ultimate. • *n* end, extremity, termination; bound, limit; airport, depot, station, terminus.

terminate *vb* bound, limit; end, finish, close, complete, conclude; eventuate, issue, prove.

termination *n* ending, suffix; bound, extend, limit; end, completion, conclusion, consequence, effect, issue, outcome, result.

terms *npl* conditions, provisions, stipulations.

terrestrial *adj* earthly, mundane, subastral, subcelestial, sublunar, sublunary, tellurian, worldly. • *n* earthling, human.

terrible *adj* appalling, dire, dreadful, fearful, formidable, frightful, gruesome, hideous, horrible, horrid, shocking, terrific, tremendous; alarming, awe-inspiring, awful, dread; great, excessive, extreme, severe.

terrific *adj* marvellous, sensational, superb; immense, intense; alarming, dreadful, formidable, frightful, terrible, tremendous.

terrify *vb* affright, alarm, appal, daunt, dismay, fright, frighten, horrify, scare, shock, startle, terrorize.

territory *n* country, district, domain, dominion, division, land, place, province, quarter, region, section, tract.

terror *n* affright, alarm, anxiety, awe, consternation, dismay, dread, fear, fright, horror, intimidation, panic, terrorism.

terse *adj* brief, compact, concise, laconic, neat, pithy, polished, sententious, short, smooth, succinct.

test *vb* assay; examine, prove, try. • *n* attempt, essay, examination, experiment, ordeal, proof, trial; criterion, standard, touchstone; example, exhibition; discrimination, distinction, judgment.

testify *vb* affirm, assert, asseverate, attest, avow, certify, corroborate, declare, depose, evidence, state, swear.

testimonial *n* certificate, credential, recommendation, voucher; monument, record.

testimony *n* affirmation, attestation, confession, confirmation, corroboration, declaration, deposition, profession; evidence, proof, witness.

testy *adj* captious, choleric, cross, fretful, hasty, irascible, irritable, quick, peevish, peppery, pettish, petulant, snappish, splenetic, touchy, waspish.

tetchy *adj* crabbed, cross, fretful, irritable, peevish, sullen, touchy.

tether *vb* chain, fasten, picket, stake, tie. • *n* chain, fastening, rope.

text *n* copy, subject, theme, thesis, topic, treatise.

texture *n* fabric, web, weft; character, coarseness, composition, constitution, fiber, fineness, grain, make-up, nap, organization, structure, tissue.

thankful *adj* appreciative, beholden, grateful, indebted, obliged.

thankfulness *n* appreciation, gratefulness, gratitude.

thankless *adj* profitless, ungracious, ungrateful, unthankful.

thaw *vb* dissolve, liquefy, melt, soften, unbend.

theater *n* opera house, playhouse; arena, scene, seat, stage.

theatrical *adj* dramatic, dramaturgic, dramaturgical, histrionic, scenic, spectacular; affected, ceremonious, meretricious, ostentatious, pompous, showy, stagy, stilted, unnatural.

theft *n* depredation, embezzlement, fraud, larceny, peculation, pilfering, purloining, robbery, spoliation, stealing, swindling, thieving.

theme *n* composition, essay, motif, subject, text, thesis, topic, treatise.

theoretical *adj* abstract, conjectural, doctrinaire, ideal, hypothetical, pure, speculative, unapplied.

theory *n* assumption, conjecture, hypothesis, idea, plan, postulation, principle, scheme, speculation, surmise, system; doctrine, philosophy, science; explanation, exposition, philosophy, rationale.

therefore *adv* accordingly, afterward, consequently, hence, so, subsequently, then, thence, whence.

thesaurus *n* dictionary, encyclopedia, repository, storehouse, treasure.

thick *adj* bulky, chunky, dumpy, plump, solid, squab, squat, stubby, thickset; clotted, coagulated, crass, dense, dull, gross, heavy, viscous; blurred, cloudy, dirty, foggy, hazy, indistinguishable, misty, obscure, vaporous; muddy, roiled, turbid; abundant, frequent, multitudinous, numerous; close, compact, crowded, set, thickset; confused, guttural, hoarse, inarticulate, indistinct; dim, dull, weak; familiar, friendly, intimate, neighborly, well-acquainted. • *adv* fast, frequently, quick; closely, densely, thickly. • *n* center, middle, midst.

thicket *n* clump, coppice, copse, covert, forest, grove, jungle, shrubbery, underbrush, undergrowth, wood, woodland.

thief *n* depredator, filcher, pilferer, lifter, marauder, purloiner, robber, shark, stealer; burglar, corsair, defaulter, defrauder, embezzler, footpad, highwayman, housebreaker, kidnapper, pickpocket, pirate, poacher, privateer, sharper, swindler, peculator.

thieve *vb* cheat, embezzle, peculate, pilfer, plunder, purloin, rob, steal, swindle.

thin *vb* attenuate, dilute, diminish, prune, reduce, refine, weaken. • *adj* attenuated, bony, emaciated, fine, fleshless, flimsy, gaunt, haggard, lank, lanky, lean, meager, peaked, pinched, poor, scanty, scraggy, scrawny, slender, slight, slim, small, sparse, spindly.

thing *n* being, body, contrivance, creature, entity, object, something, substance; act, action, affair, arrangement, circumstance, concern, deed, event, matter, occurrence, transaction.

think *vb* cogitate, contemplate, dream, meditate, muse, ponder, reflect, ruminate, speculate; consider, deliberate, reason, undertake; apprehend, believe, conceive, conclude, deem, determine, fancy, hold, imagine, judge, opine, presume, reckon, suppose, surmise; design, intend, mean, purpose; account, count, deem, esteem, hold, regard; compass, design, plan, plot. • *n* assessment, contemplation, deliberation, meditation, opinion, reasoning, reflection.

thirst *n* appetite, craving, desire, hunger, longing, yearning; aridity, drought, dryness.

thirsty *adj* arid, dry, parched; eager, greedy, hungry, longing, yearning.

thorn *n* prickle, spine; annoyance, bane, care, evil, infliction, nettle, nuisance, plague, torment, trouble, scourge.

thorny *adj* briary, briery, prickly, spinose, spinous, spiny; acuminate, barbed, pointed, prickling, sharp, spiky; annoying, difficult, harassing, perplexing, rugged, troublesome, trying, vexatious.

thorough, thoroughgoing *adj* absolute, arrant, complete, downright, entire, exhaustive, finished, perfect, radical, sweeping, total unmitigated, utter; accurate, correct, reliable, trustworthy.

though *conj* admitting, allowing, although, granted, granting, if, notwithstanding, still. • *adv* however, nevertheless, still, yet.

thought *n* absorption, cogitation, engrossment, meditation, musing, reflection, reverie, rumination; contemplation, intellect, ratiocination, thinking, thoughtfulness; application, conception, consideration, deliberation, idea, pondering, speculation, study; consciousness, imagination, intellect, perception, understanding; conceit, fancy, notion; conclusion, judgment, motion, opinion, sentiment, supposition, view; anxiety, attention, care, concern, provision, regard, solicitude, thoughtfulness; design, expectation, intention, purpose.

thoughtful *adj* absorbed, contemplative, deliberative, dreamy, engrossed, introspective, pensive, philosophic, reflecting, reflective, sedate, speculative; attentive, careful, cautious, circumspect, considerate, discreet, heedful, friendly, kindhearted, kindly, mindful, neighborly, provident, prudent, regardful, watchful, wary; quiet, serious, sober, studious.

thoughtless *adj* careless, casual, flighty, heedless, improvident, inattentive, inconsiderate, neglectful, negligent, precipitate, rash, reckless, regardless, remiss, trifling, unmindful, unthinking; blank, blockish, dull, insensate, stupid, vacant, vacuous.

thraldom *n* bondage, enslavement, enthralment, serfdom, servitude, slavery, subjection, thrall, vassalage.

thrash *vb* beat, bruise, conquer, defeat, drub, flog, lash, maul, pommel, punish, thwack, trounce, wallop, whip.

thread *vb* course, direction, drift, tenor; reeve, trace. • *n* cord, fiber, filament, hair, line, twist; pile, staple.

threadbare *adj* napless, old, seedy, worn; common, commonplace, hackneyed, stale, trite, worn-out.

threat *n* commination, defiance, denunciation, fulmination, intimidation, menace, thunder, thunderbolt.

threaten *vb* denounce, endanger, fulminate, intimidate, menace, thunder; augur, forebode, foreshadow, indicate, portend, presage, prognosticate, warn.

threshold *n* doorsill, sill; door, entrance, gate; beginning, commencement, opening, outset, start.

thrift *n* economy, frugality, parsimony, saving, thriftiness; gain, luck, profit, prosperity, success.

thriftless *adj* extravagant, improvident, lavish, profuse, prodigal, shiftless, unthrifty, wasteful.

thrifty *adj* careful, economical, frugal, provident, saving, sparing; flourishing, prosperous, thriving, vigorous.

thrill *vb* affect, agitate, electrify, inspire, move, penetrate, pierce, rouse, stir, touch.

• *n* excitement, sensation, shock, tingling, tremor.

thrilling *adj* affecting, exciting, gripping, moving, sensational, touching.

thrive *vb* advance, batten, bloom, boom, flourish, prosper, succeed.

throng *vb* congregate, crowd, fill, flock, pack, press, swarm. • *n* assemblage, concourse, congregation, crowd, horde, host, mob, multitude, swarm.

throttle *vb* choke, silence, strangle, suffocate.

throw *vb* cast, chuck, dart, fling, hurl, lance, launch, overturn, pitch, pitchfork, send, sling, toss, whirl. • *n* cast, fling, hurl, launch, pitch, sling, toss, whirl; chance, gamble, try, venture.

thrust *vb* clap, dig, drive, force, impel, jam, plunge, poke, propel, push, ram, run, shove, stick. • *n* dig, jab, lunge, pass, plunge, poke, propulsion, push, shove, stab, tilt.

thump *vb* bang, batter, beat, belabor, knock, punch, strike, thrash, thwack, whack. • *n* blow, knock, punch, strike, stroke.

thwart *vb* baffle, balk, contravene, counteract, cross, defeat, disconcert, frustrate, hinder, impede, oppose, obstruct, oppugn; cross, intersect, traverse.

tickle *vb* amuse, delight, divert, enliven, gladden, gratify, please, rejoice, titillate.

ticklish *adj* dangerous, precarious, risky, tottering, uncertain, unstable, unsteady; critical, delicate, difficult, nice.

tide *n* course, current, ebb, flow, stream.

tidings *npl* advice, greetings, information, intelligence, news, report, word.

tidy *vb* clean, neaten, order, straighten. • *adj* clean, neat, orderly, shipshape, spruce, trig, trim.

tie *vb* bind, confine, fasten, knot, lock, manacle, secure, shackle, fetter, yoke; complicate, entangle, interlace, knit; connect, hold, join, link, unite; constrain, oblige, restrain, restrict. • *n* band, fastening, knot, ligament, ligature; allegiance, bond, obligation; bow, cravat, necktie.

tier *n* line, rank, row, series.

tiff *n* fit, fume, passion, pet, miff, rage.

tight *adj* close, compact, fast, firm; taut, tense, stretched; impassable, narrow, strait.

till *vb* cultivate, plough, harrow.

tillage *n* agriculture, cultivation, culture, farming, geoponics, husbandry.

tilt *vb* cant, incline, slant, slope, tip; forge, hammer; point, thrust; joust, rush. • *n* awning, canopy, tent; lunge, pass, thrust; cant, inclination, slant, slope, tip.

time *vb* clock, control, count, measure, regulate, schedule. • *n* duration, interim, interval, season, span, spell, tenure, term, while; aeon, age, date, epoch, eon, era; term; cycle, dynasty, reign; confinement, delivery, parturition; measure, rhythm.

timely *adj* acceptable, appropriate, apropos, early, opportune, prompt, punctual, seasonable, well-timed.

timid *adj* afraid, cowardly, faint-hearted, fearful, irresolute, meticulous, nervous, pusillanimous, skittish, timorous, unadventurous; bashful, coy, diffident, modest, shame-faced, shrinking.

tincture *vb* color, dye, shade, stain, tinge, tint; flavor, season; imbue, impregnate, impress, infuse. • *n* grain, hue, shade, stain, tinge, tint, tone; flavor, smack, spice, taste; admixture, dash, infusion, seasoning, sprinkling, touch.

tinge *vb* color, dye, stain, tincture, tint; imbue, impregnate, impress, infuse. • *n* cast, color, dye, hue, shade, stain, tincture, tint; flavor, smack, spice, quality, taste.

tint *n* cast, color, complexion, dye, hue, shade, tinge, tone.

tiny *adj* diminutive, dwarfish, Lilliputian, little, microscopic, miniature, minute, puny, pygmy, small, wee.

tip[1] *n* apex, cap, end, extremity, peak, pinnacle, point, top, vertex.

tip[2] *vb* incline, overturn, tilt; dispose of, dump. • *n* donation, fee, gift, gratuity, perquisite, reward; inclination, slant; hint, pointer, suggestion; strike, tap.

tirade *n* abuse, denunciation, diatribe, harangue, outburst.

tire *vb* exhaust, fag, fatigue, harass, jade, weary; bore, bother, irk.

tiresome *adj* annoying, arduous, boring, dull, exhausting, fatiguing, fagging, humdrum, irksome, laborious, monotonous, tedious, wearisome, vexatious.

tissue *n* cloth, fabric; membrane, network, structure, texture, web; accumulation, chain, collection, combination, conglomeration, mass, series, set.

titanic *adj* colossal, Cyclopean, enormous, gigantic, herculean, huge, immense, mighty, monstrous, prodigious, stupendous, vast.

title *vb* call, designate, name, style, term. • *n* caption, legend, head, heading; appellation, application, cognomen, completion, denomination, designation, epithet, name; claim, due, ownership, part, possession, prerogative, privilege, right.

tittle *n* atom, bit, grain, iota, jot, mite, particle, scrap, speck, whit.

tittle-tattle *vb, n* babble, cackle, chatter, discourse, gabble, gossip, prattle.

toast *vb* brown, dry, heat; honor, pledge, propose, salute. • *n* compliment, drink, pledge, salutation, salute; favorite, pet.

toil *vb* drudge, labor, strive, work. • *n* drudgery, effort, exertion, exhaustion, grinding, labor, pains, travail, work; gin, net, noose, snare, spring, trap.

toilsome *adj* arduous, difficult, fatiguing, hard, laborious, onerous, painful, severe, tedious, wearisome.

token *adj* nominal, superficial, symbolic. • *n* badge, evidence, index, indication, manifestation, mark, note, sign, symbol, trace, trait; keepsake, memento, memorial, reminder, souvenir.

tolerable *adj* bearable, endurable, sufferable, supportable; fair, indifferent, middling, ordinary, passable, so-so.

tolerance *n* endurance, receptivity, sufferance, toleration.

tolerate *vb* admit, allow, indulge, let, permit, receive; abide, brook, endure, suffer.

toll[1] *n* assessment, charge, customs, demand, dues, duty, fee, impost, levy, rate, tax, tribute; cost, damage, loss.

toll[2] *vb* chime, knell, peal, ring, sound. • *n* chime, knell, peal, ring, ringing, tolling.

tomb *n* catacomb, charnel house, crypt, grave, mausoleum, sepulcher, vault.

tone *vb* blend, harmonize, match, suit. • *n* note, sound; accent, cadence, emphasis, inflection, intonation, modulation; key, mood, strain, temper; elasticity, energy, force, health, strength, tension, vigor; cast, color, manner, hue, shade, style, tint; drift, tenor.

tongue *n* accent, dialect, language, utterance, vernacular; discourse, parlance, speech, talk; nation, race.

too *adv* additionally, also, further, likewise, moreover, overmuch.

toothsome *adj* agreeable, dainty, delicious, luscious, nice, palatable, savory.

top *vb* cap, head, tip; ride, surmount; outgo, surpass. • *adj* apical, best, chief, culminating, finest, first, foremost, highest, leading, prime, principal, topmost, uppermost. • *n* acme, apex, crest, crown, head, meridian, pinnacle, summit, surface, vertex, zenith.

topic *n* business, question, subject, text, theme, thesis; division, head, subdivision; commonplace, dictum, maxim, precept, proposition, principle, rule; arrangement, scheme.

topple *vb* fall, overturn, tumble, upset.

torment *vb* annoy, agonize, distress, excruciate, pain, rack, torture; badger, fret, harass, harry, irritate, nettle, plague, provoke, tantalize, tease, trouble, vex, worry. • *n* agony, anguish, pang, rack, torture.

tornado *n* blizzard, cyclone, gale, hurricane, storm, tempest, typhoon, whirlwind.

torpid *adj* benumbed, lethargic, motionless, numb; apathetic, dormant, dull, inactive, indolent, inert, listless, sleepy, slothful, sluggish, stupid.

torpor *n* coma, insensibility, lethargy, numbness, torpidity; inaction, inactivity, inertness, sluggishness, stupidity.

torrid *adj* arid, burnt, dried, parched; burning, fiery, hot, parching, scorching, sultry, tropical, violent.

tortuous *adj* crooked, curved, curvilineal, curvilinear, serpentine, sinuate, sinuated, sinuous, twisted, winding; ambiguous, circuitous, crooked, deceitful, indirect, perverse, roundabout.

torture *vb* agonize, distress, excruciate, pain, rack, torment. • *n* agony, anguish, distress, pain, pang, rack, torment.

toss *vb* cast, fling, hurl, pitch, throw; agitate, rock, shake; disquiet, harass, try; roll, writhe. • *n* cast, fling, pitch, throw.

total *vb* add, amount to, reach, reckon. • *adj* complete, entire, full, whole; integral, undivided. • *n* aggregate, all, gross, lump, mass, sum, totality, whole.

totter *vb* falter, reel, stagger, vacillate; lean, oscillate, reel, rock, shake, sway, tremble, waver; fail, fall, flag.

touch *vb* feel, graze, handle, hit, pat, strike, tap; concern, interest, regard; affect, impress, move, stir; grasp, reach, stretch; melt, mollify, soften; afflict, distress, hurt, injure, molest, sting, wound. • *n* hint, smack, suggestion, suspicion, taste, trace; blow, contract, hit, pat, tap.

touchiness *n* fretfulness, irritability, irascibility, peevishness, pettishness, petulance, snappishness, spleen, testiness.

touching adj affecting, heart-rending, impressive, melting, moving, pathetic, pitiable, tender; abutting, adjacent, bordering, tangent.

touchy adj choleric, cross, fretful, hot-tempered, irascible, irritable, peevish, petulant, quick-tempered, snappish, splenetic, tetchy, testy, waspish.

tough adj adhesive, cohesive, flexible, tenacious; coriaceous, leathery; clammy, ropy, sticky, viscous; inflexible, intractable, rigid, stiff; callous, hard, obdurate, stubborn; difficult, formidable, hard, troublesome. • n brute, bully, hooligan, ruffian, thug.

tour vb journey, perambulate, travel, visit. • n circuit, course, excursion, expedition, journey, perambulation, pilgrimage, round.

tow vb drag, draw, haul, pull, tug. • n drag, lift, pull.

tower vb mount, rise, soar, transcend. • n belfry, bell tower, column, minaret, spire, steeple, turret; castle, citadel, fortress, stronghold; pillar, refuge, rock, support.

towering adj elevated, lofty; excessive, extreme, prodigious, violent.

toy vb dally, play, sport, trifle, wanton. • n bauble, doll, gewgaw, gimmick, knick-knack, plaything, puppet, trinket; bagatelle, bubble, trifle; play, sport.

trace vb follow, track, train; copy, deduce, delineate, derive, describe, draw, sketch. • n evidence, footmark, footprint, footstep, impression, mark, remains, sign, token, track, trail, vestige, wake; memorial, record; bit, dash, flavor, hint, suspicion, streak, tinge.

track vb chase, draw, follow, pursue, scent, track, trail. • n footmark, footprint, footstep, spoor, trace, vestige; course, pathway, rails, road, runway, trace, trail, wake, way.

trackless adj pathless, solitary, unfrequented, unused.

tract[1] n area, district, quarter, region, territory; parcel, patch, part, piece, plot, portion.

tract[2] n disquisition, dissertation, essay, homily, pamphlet, sermon, thesis, tractate, treatise.

tractable adj amenable, docile, governable, manageable, submissive, willing, yielding; adaptable, ductile, malleable, plastic, tractile.

trade vb bargain, barter, chaffer, deal, exchange, interchange, sell, traffic. • n bargaining, barter, business, commerce, dealing, traffic; avocation, calling, craft, employment, occupation, office, profession, pursuit, vocation.

traditional adj accustomed, apocryphal, customary, established, historic, legendary, old, oral, transmitted, uncertain, unverified, unwritten.

traduce vb abuse, asperse, blemish, brand, calumniate, decry, defame, depreciate, disparage, revile, malign, slander, vilify.

traducer n calumniator, defamer, detractor, slanderer, vilifier.

traffic vb bargain, barter, chaffer, deal, exchange, trade. • n barter, business, chaffer, commerce, exchange, intercourse, trade, transportation, truck.

tragedy n drama, play; adversity, calamity, catastrophe, disaster, misfortune.

tragic adj dramatic; calamitous, catastrophic, disastrous, dreadful, fatal, grievous, heart-breaking, mournful, sad, shocking, sorrowful.

trail vb follow, hunt, trace, track; drag, draw, float, flow, haul, pull. • n footmark, footprint, footstep, mark, trace, track.

train vb drag, draw, haul, trail, tug; allure, entice; discipline, drill, educate, exercise, instruct, school, teach; accustom, break in, familiarize, habituate, inure, prepare, rehearse, use. • n trail, wake; entourage, cortege, followers, retinue, staff, suite; chain, consecution, sequel, series, set, succession; course, method, order, process; allure, artifice, device, enticement, lure, persuasion, stratagem, trap.

trait n line, mark, stroke, touch; characteristic, feature, lineage, particularity, peculiarity, quality.

traitor n apostate, betrayer, deceiver, Judas, miscreant, quisling, renegade, turncoat; conspirator, deserter, insurgent, mutineer, rebel, revolutionary.

traitorous adj faithless, false, perfidious, recreant, treacherous; insidious, treasonable.

trammel vb clog, confine, cramp, cumber, hamper, hinder, fetter, restrain, restrict, shackle, tie. • n bond, chain, fetter, hindrance, impediment, net, restraint, shackle.

tramp vb hike, march, plod, trudge, walk. • n excursion, journey, march, walk; landloper, loafer, stroller, tramper, vagabond, vagrant.

trample *vb* crush, tread; scorn, spurn.

trance *n* dream, ecstasy, hypnosis, rapture; catalepsy, coma.

tranquil *adj* calm, hushed, peaceful, placid, quiet, serene, still, undisturbed, unmoved, unperturbed, unruffled, untroubled.

tranquillity *n* calmness, peace, peacefulness, placidity, placidness, quiet, quietness, serenity, stillness, tranquilness.

tranquillize *vb* allay, appease, assuage, calm, compose, hush, lay, lull, moderate, pacify, quell, quiet, silence, soothe, still.

transact *vb* conduct, dispatch, enact, execute, do, manage, negotiate, perform, treat.

transaction *n* act, action, conduct, doing, management, negotiation, performance; affair, business, deal, dealing, incident, event, job, matter, occurrence, procedure, proceeding.

transcend *vb* exceed, overlap, overstep, pass, transgress; excel, outstrip, outrival, outvie, overtop, surmount, surpass.

transcendent *adj* consummate, inimitable, peerless, pre-eminent, supereminent, surpassing, unequalled, unparaleled, unrivaled, unsurpassed; metempiric, metempirical, noumenal, super-sensible.

transcript *n* duplicate, engrossment, rescript.

transfer *vb* convey, dispatch, move, remove, send, translate, transmit, transplant, transport; abalienate, alienate, assign, cede, confer, convey, consign, deed, devise, displace, forward, grant, pass, relegate. • *n* abalienation, alienation, assignment, bequest, carriage, cession, change, conveyance, copy, demise, devisal, gift, grant, move, relegation, removal, shift, shipment, transference, transferring, transit, transmission, transportation.

transfigure *vb* change, convert, dignify, idealize, metamorphose, transform.

transform *vb* alter, change, metamorphose, transfigure; convert, resolve, translate, transmogrify, transmute.

transgress *vb* exceed, transcend, overpass, overstep; break, contravene, disobey, infringe, violate; err, intrude, offend, sin, slip, trespass.

transgression *n* breach, disobedience, encroachment, infraction, infringement, transgression, violation; crime, delinquency, error, fault, iniquity, misdeed, misdemeanor, misdoing, offence, sin, slip, trespass, wrongdoing.

transient *adj* diurnal, ephemeral, evanescent, fleeting, fugitive, impertinent, meteoric, mortal, passing, perishable, shortlived, temporary, transitory, volatile; hasty, imperfect, momentary, short.

transitory *adj* brief, ephemeral, evanescent, fleeting, flitting, fugacious, momentary, passing, short, temporary, transient.

translate *vb* remove, transfer, transport; construe, decipher, decode, interpret, render, turn.

translucent *adj* diaphanous, hyaline, pellucid, semi-opaque, semi-transparent.

transmit *vb* forward, remit, send; communicate, conduct, radiate; bear, carry, convey.

transparent *adj* bright, clear, diaphanous, limpid, lucid; crystalline, hyaline, pellucid, serene, translucent, transpicuous, unclouded; open, porous, transpicuous; evident, obvious, manifest, patent.

transpire *vb* befall, chance, happen, occur; evaporate, exhale.

transport *vb* bear, carry, cart, conduct, convey, fetch, remove, ship, take, transfer, truck; banish, expel; beatify, delight, enrapture, enravish, entrance, ravish. • *n* carriage, conveyance, movement, transportation, transporting; beatification, beatitude, bliss, ecstasy, felicity, happiness, rapture, ravishment; frenzy, passion, vehemence, warmth.

transude *vb* exude, filter, ooze, percolate, strain.

trap *vb* catch, ensnare, entrap, noose, snare, springe; ambush, deceive, dupe, trick; enmesh, tangle, trepan. • *n* gin, snare, springe, toil; ambush, artifice, pitfall, stratagem, trepan.

trappings *npl* adornments, decorations, dress, embellishments, frippery, gear, livery, ornaments, paraphernalia, rigging; accoutrements, caparisons, equipment, gear.

trash *n* dregs, dross, garbage, refuse, rubbish, trumpery, waste; balderdash, nonsense, twaddle.

travel *vb* journey, peregrinate, ramble, roam, rove, tour, voyage, walk, wander; go, move, pass. • *n* excursion, expedition, journey, peregrination, ramble, tour, trip, voyage, walk.

traveler *n* excursionist, explorer, globe-trotter, itinerant, passenger, pilgrim, rover, sightseer, tourist, trekker, tripper, voyager, wanderer, wayfarer.

traverse vb contravene, counteract, defeat, frustrate, obstruct, oppose, thwart; ford, pass, play, range.

travesty vb imitate, parody, take off. • n burlesque, caricature, imitation, parody, take-off.

treacherous adj deceitful, disloyal, faithless, false, false-hearted, insidious, perfidious, recreant, sly, traitorous, treasonable, unfaithful, unreliable, unsafe, untrustworthy.

treachery n betrayal, deceitfulness, disloyalty, double-dealing, faithlessness, foul play, infidelity, insidiousness, perfidiousness, treason, perfidy.

treason n betrayal, disloyalty, lèse-majesté, lese-majesty, perfidy, sedition, traitorousness, treachery.

treasonable adj disloyal, traitorous, treacherous.

treasure vb accumulate, collect, garner, hoard, husband, save, store; cherish, idolize, prize, value, worship. • n cash, funds, jewels, money, riches, savings, valuables, wealth; abundance, reserve, stock, store.

treasurer n banker, bursar, purser, receiver, trustee.

treat vb entertain, feast, gratify, refresh; attend, doctor, dose, handle, manage, serve; bargain, covenant, negotiate, parley. • n banquet, entertainment, feast; delight, enjoyment, entertainment, gratification, luxury, pleasure, refreshment.

treatise n commentary, discourse, dissertation, disquisition, monograph, tractate.

treatment n usage, use; dealing, handling, management, manipulation; doctoring, therapy.

treaty n agreement, alliance, bargain, compact, concordat, convention, covenant, entente, league, pact.

tremble vb quake, quaver, quiver, shake, shiver, shudder, vibrate, wobble. • n quake, quiver, shake, shiver, shudder, tremor, vibration, wobble.

tremendous adj colossal, enormous, huge, immense; excellent, marvellous, wonderful; alarming, appalling, awful, dreadful, fearful, frightful, horrid, horrible, terrible.

tremor n agitation, quaking, quivering, shaking, trembling, trepidation, tremulousness, vibration.

tremulous adj afraid, fearful, quavering, quivering, shaking, shaky, shivering, timid, trembling, vibrating.

trench vb carve, cut; ditch, channel, entrench, furrow. • n channel, ditch, drain, furrow, gutter, moat, pit, sewer, trough; dugout, entrenchment, fortification.

trenchant adj cutting, keen, sharp; acute, biting, caustic, crisp, incisive, pointed, piquant, pungent, sarcastic, sententious, severe, unsparing, vigorous.

trend vb drift, gravitate, incline, lean, run, stretch, sweep, tend, turn. • n bent, course, direction, drift, inclination, set, leaning, tendency, trending.

trepidation n agitation, quaking, quivering, shaking, trembling, tremor; dismay, excitement, fear, perturbation, tremulousness.

trespass vb encroach, infringe, intrude, trench, offend, sin, transgress. • n encroachment, infringement, injury, intrusion, invasion; crime, delinquency, error, fault, sin, misdeed, misdemeanor, offence, transgression; trespasser.

trial adj experimental, exploratory, testing. • n examination, experiment, test; experience, knowledge; aim, attempt, effort, endeavor, essay, exertion, struggle; assay, criterion, ordeal, prohibition, proof, test, touchstone; affliction, burden, chagrin, dolor, distress, grief, hardship, heartache, inclination, misery, mortification, pain, sorrow, suffering, tribulation, trouble, unhappiness, vexation, woe, wretchedness; action, case, cause, hearing, suit.

tribe n clan, family, lineage, race, sept, stock; class, distinction, division, order.

tribulation n adversity, affliction, distress, grief, misery, pain, sorrow, suffering, trial, trouble, unhappiness, woe, wretchedness.

tribunal n bench, judgement seat; assizes, bar, court, judicature, session.

tribute n subsidy, tax; custom, duty, excise, impost, tax, toll; contribution, grant, offering.

trice n flash, instant, jiffy, moment, second, twinkling.

trick vb cheat, circumvent, cozen, deceive, defraud, delude, diddle, dupe, fob, gull, hoax, overreach. • n artifice, blind, deceit, deception, dodge, fake, feint, fraud, game, hoax, imposture, maneuvre, shift, ruse, swindle, stratagem, wile; antic, caper, craft, deftness, gambol, sleight; habit, mannerism, peculiarity, practice.

trickle vb distil, dribble, drip, drop, ooze, percolate, seep. • n dribble, drip, percolation, seepage.

tricky adj artful, cunning, deceitful, deceptive, subtle, trickish.

trifle vb dally, dawdle, fool, fribble, palter, play, potter, toy. • n bagatelle, bauble, bean, fig, nothing, triviality; iota, jot, modicum, particle, trace.

trifling adj empty, frippery, frivolous, inconsiderable, insignificant, nugatory, petty, piddling, shallow, slight, small, trivial, unimportant, worthless.

trill vb shake, quaver, warble. • n quaver, shake, tremolo, warbling.

trim vb adjust, arrange, prepare; balance, equalize, fill; adorn, array, bedeck, decorate, dress, embellish, garnish, ornament; clip, curtail, cut, lop, mow, poll, prune, shave, shear; berate, chastise, chide, rebuke, reprimand, reprove, trounce; fluctuate, hedge, shift, shuffle, vacillate. • adj compact, neat, nice, shapely, snug, tidy, well-adjusted, well-ordered; chic, elegant, finical, smart, spruce. • n dress, embellishment, gear, ornaments, trappings, trimmings; case, condition, order, plight, state.

trinket n bagatelle, bauble, bijoux, gewgaw, gimcrack, knick-knack, toy, trifle.

trinkets npl bijouterie, jewelry, jewels, ornaments.

trip vb caper, dance, frisk, hop, skip; misstep, stumble; bungle, blunder, err, fail, mistake; overthrow, supplant, upset; catch, convict, detect. • n hop, skip; lurch, misstep, stumble; blunder, bungle, error, failure, fault, lapse, miss, mistake, oversight, slip; circuit, excursion, expedition, jaunt, journey, ramble, route, stroll, tour.

trite adj banal, beaten, common, commonplace, hackneyed, old, ordinary, stale, stereotyped, threadbare, usual, worn.

triturate vb beat, bray, bruise, grind, pound, rub, thrash; comminute, levigate, pulverize.

triumph vb exult, rejoice; prevail, succeed, win; flourish, prosper, thrive; boast, brag, crow, gloat, swagger, vaunt. • n celebration, exultation, joy, jubilation, jubilee, ovation; accomplishment, achievement, conquest, success, victory.

triumphant adj boastful, conquering, elated, exultant, exulting, jubilant, rejoicing, successful, victorious.

trivial adj frivolous, gimcrack, immaterial, inconsiderable, insignificant, light, little, nugatory, paltry, petty, small, slight, slim, trifling, trumpery, unimportant.

trollop n prostitute, slattern, slut, whore.

troop vb crowd, flock, muster, throng. • n company, crowd, flock, herd, multitude, number, throng; band, body, party, squad, troupe.

trophy n laurels, medal, palm, prize.

troth n candor, sincerity, truth, veracity, verity; allegiance, belief, faith, fidelity, word; betrothal.

trouble vb agitate, confuse, derange, disarrange, disorder, disturb; afflict, ail, annoy, badger, concern, disquiet, distress, fret, grieve, harass, molest, perplex, perturb, pester, plague, torment, vex, worry. • n adversity, affliction, calamity, distress, dolor, grief, hardship, misfortune, misery, pain, sorrow, suffering, tribulation, woe; ado, annoyance, anxiety, bother, care, discomfort, embarrassment, fuss, inconvenience, irritation, pains, perplexity, plague, torment, vexation, worry; commotion, disturbance, row; bewilderment, disquietude, embarrassment, perplexity, uneasiness.

troublesome adj annoying, distressing, disturbing, galling, grievous, harassing, painful, perplexing, vexatious, worrisome; burdensome, irksome, tiresome, wearisome; importunate, intrusive, teasing; arduous, difficult, hard, inconvenient, trying, unwieldy.

troublous adj agitated, disquieted, disturbed, perturbed, tumultuous, turbulent.

trough n hutch, manger; channel, depression, hollow, furrow.

truant vb be absent, desert, dodge, malinger, shirk, skive. • n absentee, deserter, idler, laggard, loiterer, lounger, malingerer, quitter, runaway, shirker, vagabond.

truce n armistice, breathing space, cessation, delay, intermission, lull, pause, recess, reprieve, respite, rest.

truck vb barter, deal, exchange, trade, traffic. • n lorry, van, wagon.

truckle vb roll, trundle; cringe, crouch, fawn, knuckle, stoop, submit, yield.

truculent adj barbarous, bloodthirsty, ferocious, fierce, savage; cruel, malevolent, relentless; destructive, deadly, fatal, ruthless.

true adj actual, unaffected, authentic, genuine, legitimate, pure, real, rightful, sincere, sound, truthful, veritable; substantial, veracious; constant, faithful, loyal, staunch, steady; equitable, honest, honorable, just, upright, trusty, trustworthy, virtuous;

accurate, correct, even, exact, right, straight, undeviating. • *adv* good, well.

truism *n* axiom, commonplace, platitude.

trumpery *adj* pinchbeck, rubbishy, trashy, trifling, worthless. • *n* deceit, deception, falsehood, humbug, imposture; frippery, rubbish, stuff, trash, trifles.

truncheon *n* club, cudgel, nightstick, partisan, staff; baton, wand.

trunk *n* body, bole, butt, shaft, stalk, stem, stock, torso; box, chest, coffer.

trundle *vb* bowl, revolve, roll, spin, truckle, wheel.

truss *vb* bind, bundle, close, cram, hang, pack. • *n* bundle, package, packet; apparatus, bandage, support.

trust *vb* confide, depend, expect, hope, rely; believe, credit; commit, entrust. • *n* belief, confidence, credence, faith; credit, tick; charge, deposit; commission, duty, errand; assurance, conviction, expectation, hope, reliance, security.

trustful *adj* confiding, trusting, unquestioning, unsuspecting; faithful, trustworthy, trusty.

trustworthy *adj* confidential, constant, credible, dependable, faithful, firm, honest, incorrupt, upright, reliable, responsible, straightforward, staunch, true, trusty, uncorrupt, upright.

truth *n* fact, reality, veracity; actuality, authenticity, realism; canon, law, oracle, principle; right, truthfulness, veracity; candor, fidelity, frankness, honesty, honor, ingenuousness, integrity, probity, sincerity, virtue; constancy, devotion, faith, fealty, loyalty, steadfastness; accuracy, correctness, exactitude, exactness, nicety, precision, regularity, trueness.

truthful *adj* correct, reliable, true, trustworthy, veracious; artless, candid, frank, guileless, honest, ingenuous, open, sincere, straightforward, trusty.

truthless *adj* canting, disingenuous, dishonest, false, faithless, hollow, hypocritical, insincere, pharisaical, treacherous, unfair, untrustworthy.

try *vb* examine, prove, test; attempt, essay; adjudicate, adjudge, examine, hear; purify, refine; sample, sift, smell, taste; aim, attempt, endeavor, seek, strain, strive. • *n* attempt, effort, endeavor, experiment, trial.

trying *adj* difficult, fatiguing, hard, irksome, tiresome, wearisome; afflicting, afflictive,

calamitous, deplorable, dire, distressing, grievous, hard, painful, sad, severe.

tryst *n* appointment, assignation, rendezvous.

tube *n* bore, bronchus, cylinder, duct, hollow, hose, pipe, pipette, worm.

tuft *n* brush, bunch, crest, feather, knot, plume, topknot, tussock; clump, cluster, group.

tug *vb* drag, draw, haul, pull, tow, wrench; labour, strive, struggle. • *n* drag, haul, pull, tow, wrench.

tuition *n* education, instruction, schooling, teaching, training.

tumble *vb* heave, pitch, roll, toss, wallow; fall, sprawl, stumble, topple, trip; derange, disarrange, dishevel, disorder, disturb, rumple, tousle. • *n* collapse, drop, fall, plunge, spill, stumble, trip.

tumbler *n* acrobat, juggler; glass.

tumid *adj* bloated, distended, enlarged, puffed-up, swelled, swollen, turgid; bombastic, declamatory, fustian, grandiloquent, grandiose, high-flown, inflated, pompous, puffy, rhetorical, stilted, swelling.

tumor *n* boil, carbuncle, swelling, tumefaction.

tumult *n* ado, affray, agitation, altercation, bluster, brawl, disturbance, ferment, flurry, feud, fracas, fray, fuss, hubbub, huddle, hurly-burly, melee, noise, perturbation, pother, quarrel, racket, riot, row, squabble, stir, turbulence, turmoil, uproar.

tumultuous *adj* blustery, breezy, bustling, confused, disorderly, disturbed, riotous, turbulent, unruly.

tune *vb* accord, attune, harmonize, modulate; adapt, adjust, attune. • *n* air, aria, melody, strain, tone; agreement, concord, harmony; accord, order.

tuneful *adj* dulcet, harmonious, melodious, musical.

turbid *adj* foul, impure, muddy, thick, unsettled.

turbulence *n* agitation, commotion, confusion, disorder, disturbance, excitement, tumult, tumultuousness, turmoil, unruliness, uproar; insubordination, insurrection, mutiny, rebellion, riot, sedition.

turbulent *adj* agitated, disturbed, restless, tumultuous, wild; blatant, blustering, boisterous, brawling, disorderly, obstreperous, tumultuous, uproarious, vociferous; factious, insubordinate, insurgent, mutinous, raging, rebellious, refractory, revolutionary, riotous, seditious, stormy, violent.

turf *n* grass, greensward, sod, sward; horse racing, racecourse, race-ground.

turgid *adj* bloated, distended, protuberant, puffed-up, swelled, swollen, tumid; bombastic, declamatory, diffuse, digressive, fustian, high-flown, inflated, grandiloquent, grandiose, ostentatious, pompous, puffy, rhetorical, stilted.

turmoil *n* activity, agitation, bustle, commotion, confusion, disorder, disturbance, ferment, flurry, huddle, hubbub, hurly-burly, noise, trouble, tumult, turbulence, uproar.

turn *vb* revolve, rotate; bend, cast, defect, inflict, round, spin, sway, swivel, twirl, twist, wheel; crank, grind, wind; deflect, divert, transfer, warp; form, mold, shape; adapt, fit, maneuvre, suit; alter, change, conform, metamorphose, transform, transmute, vary; convert, persuade, prejudice; construe, render, translate; depend, hang, hinge, pivot; eventuate, issue, result, terminate; acidify, curdle, ferment. • *n* cycle, gyration, revolution, rotation, round; bending, deflection, deviation, diversion, doubling, flection, flexion, flexure, reel, retroversion, slew, spin, sweep, swing, swirl, swivel, turning, twist, twirl, whirl, winding; alteration, change, variation, vicissitude; bend, circuit, drive, ramble, run, round, stroll; bout, hand, innings, opportunity, shift, spell; act, action, deed, office; convenience, occasion, purpose; cast, fashion, form, guise, manner, mold, phase, shape; aptitude, bent, bias, disposition, faculty, genius, gift, inclination, leaning, proclivity, proneness, propensity, talent, tendency.

turncoat *n* apostate, backslider, deserter, recreant, renegade, traitor, wretch.

turpitude *n* baseness, degradation, depravity, vileness, wickedness.

turret *n* cupola, minaret, pinnacle.

tussle *vb* conflict, contend, contest, scuffle, struggle, wrestle. • *n* conflict, contest, fight, scuffle, struggle.

tutelage *n* care, charge, dependence, guardianship, protection, teaching, tutorage, tutorship, wardship.

tutor *vb* coach, educate, instruct, teach; discipline, train. • *n* coach, governess, governor, instructor, master, preceptor, schoolteacher, teacher.

twaddle *vb* chatter, gabble, maunder, prate,

prattle. • *n* balderdash, chatter, flummery, gabble, gibberish, gobbledegook, gossip, jargon, moonshine, nonsense, platitude, prate, prattle, rigmarole, stuff, tattle.

tweak *vb, n* jerk, pinch, pull, twinge, twitch.

twig[1] *n* bough, branch, offshoot, shoot, slip, spray, sprig, stick, switch.

twig[2] *vb* catch on, comprehend, discover, grasp, realize, recognize, see, understand.

twin *vb* couple, link, match, pair. • *adj* double, doubled, duplicate, geminate, identical, matched, matching, second, twain. • *n* corollary, double, duplicate, fellow, likeness, match.

twine *vb* embrace, encircle, entwine, interlace, surround, wreathe; bend, meander, wind; coil, twist. • *n* convolution, coil, twist; embrace, twining, winding; cord, string.

twinge *vb* pinch, tweak, twitch. • *n* pinch, tweak, twitch; gripe, pang, spasm.

twinkle *vb* blink, twink, wink; flash, glimmer, scintillate, sparkle. • *n* blink, flash, gleam, glimmer, scintillation, sparkle; flash, instant, jiffy, moment, second, tick, trice, twinkling.

twinkling *n* flashing, sparkling, twinkle; flash, instant, jiffy, moment, second, tick, trice.

twirl *vb* revolve, rotate, spin, turn, twist, twirl. • *n* convolution, revolution, turn, twist, whirling.

twist *vb* purl, rotate, spin, twine; complicate, contort, convolute, distort, pervert, screw, wring; coil, writhe; encircle, wind, wreathe. • *n* coil, curl, spin, twine; braid, roll; change, complication, development, variation; bend, convolution, turn; defect, distortion, flaw, imperfection; jerk, pull, sprain, wrench; aberration, characteristic, eccentricity, oddity, peculiarity, quirk.

twit[1] *vb* banter, blame, censure, reproach, taunt, tease, upbraid.

twit[2] *n* blockhead, fool, idiot, nincompoop, nitwit.

twitch *vb* jerk, pluck, pull, snatch. • *n* jerk, pull; contraction, pull, quiver, spasm, twitching.

type *n* emblem, mark, stamp; adumbration, image, representation, representative, shadow, sign, symbol, token; archetype, exemplar, model, original, pattern, prototype, protoplast, standard; character, form, kind, nature, sort; figure, letter, text, typography.

typical *adj* emblematic, exemplary, figurative, ideal, indicative, model, representative, symbolic, true.

typify *vb* betoken, denote, embody, exemplify, figure, image, indicate, represent, signify.

tyrannical *adj* absolute, arbitrary, autocratic, cruel, despotic, dictatorial, domineering, high, imperious, irresponsible, severe, tyrannical, unjust; galling, grinding, inhuman, oppressive, overbearing, severe.

tyranny *n* absolutism, autocracy, despotism, dictatorship, harshness, oppression.

tyrant *n* autocrat, despot, dictator, oppressor.

tyro *n* beginner, learner, neophyte, novice; dabbler, smatterer.

U

ubiquitous *adj* omnipresent, present, universal.

udder *n* nipple, pap, teat.

ugly *adj* crooked, homely, ill-favored, plain, ordinary, unlovely, unprepossessing, unshapely, unsightly; forbidding, frightful, gruesome, hideous, horrible, horrid, loathsome, monstrous, shocking, terrible, repellent, repulsive; bad-tempered, cantankerous, churlish, cross, quarrelsome, spiteful, surly, spiteful, vicious.

ulcer *n* boil, fester, gathering, pustule, sore.

ulterior *adj* beyond, distant, farther; hidden, personal, secret, selfish, undisclosed.

ultimate *adj* conclusive, decisive, eventual, extreme, farthest, final, last. • *n* acme, consummation, culmination, height, peak, pink, quintessence, summit.

ultra *adj* advanced, beyond, extreme, radical.

umbrage *n* shadow, shade; anger, displeasure, dissatisfaction, dudgeon, injury, offence, pique, resentment.

umpire *vb* adjudicate, arbitrate, judge, referee. • *n* adjudicator, arbiter, arbitrator, judge, referee.

unabashed *adj* bold, brazen, confident, unblushing, undaunted, undismayed.

unable *adj* impotent, incapable, incompetent, powerless, weak.

unacceptable *adj* disagreeable, distasteful, offensive, unpleasant, unsatisfactory, unwelcome.

unaccommodating *adj* disobliging, non-compliant, uncivil, ungracious.

unaccomplished *adj* incomplete, unachieved, undone, unperformed, unexecuted, unfinished; ill-educated, uncultivated, unpolished.

unaccountable *adj* inexplicable, incomprehensible, inscrutable, mysterious, unintelligible; irresponsible, unanswerable.

unaccustomed *adj* uninitiated, unskilled, unused; foreign, new, strange, unfamiliar, unusual.

unaffected *adj* artless, honest, naive, natural, plain, simple, sincere, real, unfeigned; chaste, pure, unadorned; insensible, unchanged, unimpressed, unmoved, unstirred, untouched.

unanimity *n* accord, agreement, concert, concord, harmony, union, unity.

unanimous *adj* agreeing, concordant, harmonious, like-minded, solid, united.

unassuming *adj* humble, modest, reserved, unobtrusive, unpretending, unpretentious.

unattainable *adj* inaccessible, unobtainable.

unavailing *adj* abortive, fruitless, futile, ineffectual, ineffective, inept, nugatory, unsuccessful, useless, vain.

unbalanced *adj* unsound, unsteady; unadjusted, unsettled.

unbearable *adj* insufferable, insupportable, unendurable.

unbecoming *adj* inappropriate, indecent, indecorous, improper, unbefitting, unbeseeming, unseemly, unsuitable.

unbelief *n* disbelief, dissent, distrust, incredulity, incredulousness, miscreance, miscreancy, nonconformity; doubt, freethinking, infidelity, scepticism.

unbeliever *n* agnostic, deist, disbeliever, doubter, heathen, infidel, sceptic.

unbending *adj* inflexible, rigid, stiff, unpliant, unyielding; firm, obstinate, resolute, stubborn.

unbiased *adj* disinterested, impartial, indifferent, neutral, uninfluenced, unprejudiced, unwarped.

unbind *vb* loose, undo, unfasten, unloose, untie; free, unchain, unfetter.

unblemished *adj* faultless, guiltless, immaculate, impeccable, innocent, intact, perfect, pure, sinless, spotless, stainless, undefiled, unspotted, unsullied, untarnished.

unblushing *adj* boldfaced, impudent, shameless.

unbounded *adj* absolute, boundless, endless, immeasurable, immense, infinite, interminable, measureless, unlimited, vast; immoderate, uncontrolled, unrestrained, unrestricted.

unbridled *adj* dissolute, intractable, lax, licensed, licentious, loose, uncontrolled, ungovernable, unrestrained, violent, wanton.

unbroken *adj* complete, entire, even, full, intact, unimpaired; constant, continuous, fast, profound, sound, successive, undisturbed; inviolate, unbetrayed, unviolated.

unbuckle *vb* loose, unfasten, unloose.

uncanny *adj* inopportune, unsafe; eerie, eery, ghostly, unearthly, unnatural, weird.

unceremonious *adj* abrupt, bluff, blunt, brusque, course, curt, gruff, plain, rough, rude, ungracious; casual, familiar, informal, offhand, unconstrained.

uncertain *adj* ambiguous, doubtful, dubious, equivocal, indefinite, indeterminate, indistinct, questionable, unsettled; insecure, precarious, problematical; capricious, changeable, desultory, fitful, fluctuating, irregular, mutable, shaky, slippery, unreliable, variable.

unchaste *adj* dissolute, incontinent, indecent, immoral, lascivious, lecherous, libidinous, lewd, loose, obscene, wanton.

unchecked *adj* uncurbed, unhampered, unhindered, unobstructed, unrestrained, untrammeled.

uncivil *adj* bearish, blunt, boorish, brusque, discourteous, disobliging, disrespectful, gruff, ill-bred, ill-mannered, impolite, irreverent, rough, rude, uncomplaisant, uncourteous, uncouth, ungentle, ungracious, unmannered, unseemly.

unclean *adj* abominable, beastly, dirty, filthy, foul, grimy, grubby, miry, muddy, nasty, offensive, purulent, repulsive, soiled, sullied; improper, indecent, indecorous, obscene, polluted, risqué, sinful, smutty, unholy, uncleanly.

uncomfortable *adj* disagreeable, displeasing, disquieted, distressing, disturbed, uneasy, unpleasant, restless; cheerless, close, oppressive; dismal, miserable, unhappy.

uncommon *adj* choice, exceptional, extraordinary, infrequent, noteworthy, odd, original, queer, rare, remarkable, scarce, singular, strange, unexampled, unfamiliar, unusual, unwonted.

uncommunicative *adj* close, inconversable, reserved, reticent, taciturn, unsociable, unsocial.

uncomplaining *adj* long-suffering, meek, patient, resigned, tolerant.

uncompromising *adj* inflexible, narrow, obstinate, orthodox, rigid, stiff, strict, unyielding.

unconcerned *adj* apathetic, careless, indifferent.

unconditional *adj* absolute, categorical, complete, entire, free, full, positive, unlimited, unqualified, unreserved, unrestricted.

uncongenial *adj* antagonistic, discordant, displeasing, ill-assorted, incompatible, inharmonious, mismatched, unsuited, unsympathetic.

uncouth *adj* awkward, boorish, clownish, clumsy, gawky, inelegant, loutish, lubberly, rough, rude, rustic, uncourtly, ungainly, unpolished, unrefined, unseemly; odd, outlandish, strange, unfamiliar, unusual.

uncover *vb* denude, divest, lay bare, strip; disclose, discover, expose, reveal, unmask, unveil; bare, doff; open, unclose, unseal.

unctuous *adj* adipose, greasy, oily, fat, fatty, oleaginous, pinguid, sebaceous; bland, lubricious, smooth, slippery; bland, fawning, glib, obsequious, plausible, servile, suave, sycophantic; fervid, gushing.

uncultivated *adj* fallow, uncultured, unreclaimed, untilled; homely, ignorant, illiterate, rude, uncivilized, uncultured, uneducated, unfit, unlettered, unpolished, unread, unready, unrefined, untaught; rough, savage, sylvan, uncouth, wild.

undaunted *adj* bold, brave, courageous, dauntless, fearless, intrepid, plucky, resolute, undismayed.

undefiled *adj* clean, immaculate, pure, spotless, stainless, unblemished, unspotted, unsullied, untarnished; honest, innocent, inviolate, pure, uncorrupted, unpolluted, unstained.

undemonstrative *adj* calm, composed, demure, impassive, modest, placid, quiet, reserved, sedate, sober, staid, tranquil.

undeniable *adj* certain, conclusive, evident, incontestable, incontrovertible, indisputable, indubitable, obvious, unquestionable.

under *prep* below, beneath, inferior to, lower than, subordinate to, underneath. • *adv* below, beneath, down, lower.

underestimate *vb* belittle, underrate, undervalue.

undergo *vb* bear, endure, experience, suffer, sustain.

underhand *adj* clandestine, deceitful, disingenuous, fraudulent, hidden, secret, sly, stealthy, underhanded, unfair. • *adv* clandestinely, privately, secretly, slyly, stealthily, surreptitiously; fraudulently, unfairly.

underling *n* agent, inferior, servant, subordinate.

undermine *vb* excavate, mine, sap; demoralize, foil, frustrate, thwart, weaken.

understand *vb* apprehend, catch, comprehend, conceive, discern, grasp, know, penetrate, perceive, see, seize, twig; assume, interpret, take; imply, mean.

understanding *adj* compassionate, considerate, forgiving, kind, kindly, patient, sympathetic, tolerant. • *n* brains, comprehension, discernment, faculty, intellect, intelligence, judgement, knowledge, mind, reason, sense.

undertake *vb* assume, attempt, begin, embark on, engage in, enter upon, take in hand; agree, bargain, contract, covenant, engage, guarantee, promise, stipulate.

undertaking *n* adventure, affair, attempt, business, effort, endeavor, engagement, enterprise, essay, move, project, task, venture.

undesigned *adj* spontaneous, unintended, unintentional, unplanned, unpremeditated.

undigested *adj* crude, ill-advised, ill-considered, ill-judged; confused, disorderly, ill-arranged, unmethodical.

undivided *adj* complete, entire, whole; one, united.

undo *vb* annul, cancel, frustrate, invalidate, neutralize, nullify, offset, reverse; disengage, loose, unfasten, unmake, unravel, untie; crush, destroy, overturn, ruin.

undoubted *adj* incontrovertible, indisputable, indubitable, undisputed, unquestionable, unquestioned.

undress *vb* denude, dismantle, disrobe, unclothe, unrobe, peel, strip. • *n* disarray, nakedness, nudity; mufti, negligee.

undue *adj* illegal, illegitimate, improper, unlawful, excessive, disproportionate, disproportioned, immoderate, unsuitable; unfit.

undulation *n* billowing, fluctuation, pulsation, ripple, wave.

undying *adj* deathless, endless, immortal, imperishable.

unearthly *adj* preternatural, supernatural, uncanny, weird.

uneasy *adj* disquieted, disturbed, fidgety, impatient, perturbed, restless, restive, unquiet, worried; awkward, stiff, ungainly, ungraceful; constraining, cramping, disagreeable, uncomfortable.

unending *adj* endless, eternal, everlasting, interminable, never-ending, perpetual, unceasing.

unequal *adj* disproportionate, disproportioned, ill-matched, inferior, irregular, insufficient, not alike, uneven.

unequaled *adj* exceeding, incomparable, inimitable, matchless, new, nonpareil, novel, paramount, peerless, pre-eminent, superlative, surpassing, transcendent, unheard of, unique, unparalleled, unrivaled.

unequivocal *adj* absolute, certain, clear, evident, incontestable, indubitable, positive; explicit, unambiguous, unmistakable.

uneven *adj* hilly, jagged, lumpy, ragged, rough, rugged, stony; motley, unequal, variable, variegated.

uneventful *adj* commonplace, dull, eventless, humdrum, quiet, monotonous, smooth, uninteresting.

unexceptionable *adj* excellent, faultless, good, irreproachable.

unexpected *adj* abrupt, sudden, unforeseen.

unfair *adj* dishonest, dishonorable, faithless, false, hypocritical, inequitable, insincere, oblique, one-sided, partial, unequal, unjust, wrongful.

unfaithful *adj* adulterous, derelict, deceitful, dishonest, disloyal, false, faithless, fickle, perfidious, treacherous, unreliable; negligent; changeable, inconstant, untrue.

unfamiliar *adj* bizarre, foreign, new, novel, outlandish, queer, singular, strange, uncommon, unusual.

unfashionable *adj* antiquated, destitute, disused, obsolete, old-fashioned, unconventional.

unfavorable *adj* adverse, contrary, disadvantageous, discouraging, ill, inauspicious, inimical, inopportune, indisposed, malign, sinister, unfriendly, unlucky, unpropitious, untimely; foul, inclement.

unfeeling *adj* apathetic, callous, heartless, insensible, numb, obdurate, torpid, unconscious, unimpressionable; adamantine, cold-blooded, cruel, hard, merciless, pitiless, stony, unkind, unsympathetic.

unfit vb disable, disqualify, incapacitate.
• adj improper, inappropriate, incompetent, inconsistent, unsuitable; ill-equipped, inadequate, incapable, unqualified, useless; debilitated, feeble, flabby, unhealthy, unsound.

unflagging adj constant, indefatigable, never-ending, persevering, steady, unfaltering, unremitting, untiring, unwearied.

unflinching adj firm, resolute, steady, unshrinking.

unfold vb display, expand, open, separate, unfurl, unroll; declare, disclose, reveal, tell; decipher, develop, disentangle, evolve, explain, illustrate, interpret, resolve, unravel.

unfortunate adj hapless, ill-fated, ill-starred, infelicitous, luckless, unhappy, unlucky, unprosperous, unsuccessful, wretched; calamitous, deplorable, disastrous; inappropriate, inexpedient.

unfrequented adj abandoned, deserted, forsaken, lone, solitary, uninhabited, unoccupied.

unfruitful adj barren, fruitless, sterile; infecund, unprolific; unprofitable, unproductive.

ungainly adj awkward, boorish, clownish, clumsy, gawky, inelegant, loutish, lubberly, lumbering, slouching, stiff, uncourtly, uncouth, ungraceful.

ungentlemanly adj ill-bred, impolite, rude, uncivil, ungentle, ungracious, unmannerly.

unhappy adj afflicted, disastrous, dismal, distressed, drear, evil, inauspicious, miserable, painful, unfortunate, wretched.

unhealthy adj ailing, diseased, feeble, indisposed, infirm, poorly, sickly, toxic, unsanitary, unsound, toxic, venomous.

uniform adj alike, constant, even, equable, equal, smooth, steady, regular, unbroken, unchanged, undeviating, unvaried, unvarying. • n costume, dress, livery, outfit, regalia, suit.

uniformity n constancy, continuity, permanence, regularity, sameness, stability; accordance, agreement, conformity, consistency, unanimity.

unimportant adj immaterial, inappreciable, inconsequent, inconsequential, inconsiderable, indifferent, insignificant, mediocre, minor, paltry, petty, small, slight, trifling, trivial.

unintentional adj accidental, casual, fortuitous, inadvertent, involuntary, spontaneous, undesigned, unmeant, unplanned, unpremeditated, unthinking.

uninterrupted adj continuous, endless, incessant, perpetual, unceasing.

union n coalescence, coalition, combination, conjunction, coupling, fusion, incorporation, joining, junction, unification, uniting; agreement, concert, concord, concurrence, harmony, unanimity, unity; alliance, association, club, confederacy, federation, guild, league.

unique adj choice, exceptional, matchless, only, peculiar, rare, single, sole, singular, uncommon, unexampled, unmatched.

unison n accord, accordance, agreement, concord, harmony.

unite vb amalgamate, attach, blend, centralize, coalesce, confederate, consolidate, embody, fuse, incorporate, merge, weld; associate, conjoin, connect, couple, link, marry; combine, join; harmonize, reconcile; agree, concert, concur, cooperate, fraternize.

universal adj all-reaching, catholic, cosmic, encyclopedic, general, ubiquitous, unlimited; all, complete, entire, total, whole.

unjust adj inequitable, injurious, partial, unequal, unfair, unwarranted, wrong, wrongful; flagitious, heinous, influenced, iniquitous, nefarious, unrighteous, wicked; biased, prejudiced, uncandid.

unjustifiable adj indefensible, unjust, unreasonable, unwarrantable; inexcusable, unpardonable.

unknown adj unappreciated, unascertained; undiscovered, unexplored, uninvestigated; concealed, dark, enigmatic, hidden, mysterious, mystic; anonymous, incognito, inglorious, nameless, obscure, renownless, undistinguished, unheralded, unnoted.

unladylike adj ill-bred, impolite, rude, uncivil, ungentle, ungracious, unmannerly.

unlamented adj unmourned, unregretted.

unlimited adj boundless, infinite, interminable, limitless, measureless, unbounded; absolute, full, unconfined, unconstrained, unrestricted; indefinite, undefined.

unlucky adj baleful, disastrous, ill-fated, ill-starred, luckless, unfortunate, unprosperous, unsuccessful; ill-omened, inauspicious; miserable, unhappy.

unmanageable adj awkward, cumbersome, inconvenient, unwieldy; intractable, unruly, unworkable, vicious; difficult, impractical.

unmatched *adj* matchless, unequaled, unparalleled, unrivaled.

unmitigated *adj* absolute, complete, consummate, perfect, sheer, stark, thorough, unqualified, utter.

unnatural *adj* aberrant, abnormal, anomalous, foreign, irregular, prodigious, uncommon; brutal, cold, heartless, inhuman, unfeeling, unusual; affected, artificial, constrained, forced, insincere, self-conscious, stilted, strained; factitious.

unpleasant *adj* disagreeable, displeasing, distasteful, obnoxious, offensive, repulsive, unlovely, ungrateful, unacceptable, unpalatable, unwelcome.

unpremeditated *adj* extempore, impromptu, offhand, spontaneous, undesigned, unintentional, unstudied.

unprincipled *adj* bad, crooked, dishonest, fraudulent, immoral, iniquitous, knavish, lawless, profligate, rascally, roguish, thievish, trickish, tricky, unscrupulous, vicious, villainous, wicked.

unqualified *adj* disqualified, incompetent, ineligible, unadapted, unfit; absolute, certain, consummate, decided, direct, downright, full, outright, unconditional, unmeasured, unrestricted, unmitigated; exaggerated, sweeping.

unreal *adj* chimerical, dreamlike, fanciful, flimsy, ghostly, illusory, insubstantial, nebulous, shadowy, spectral, visionary, unsubstantial.

unreasonable *adj* absurd, excessive, exorbitant, foolish, ill-judged, illogical, immoderate, impractical, injudicious, irrational, nonsensical, preposterous, senseless, silly, stupid, unfair, unreasoning, unwarrantable, unwise.

unreliable *adj* fallible, fickle, irresponsible, treacherous, uncertain, undependable, unstable, unsure, untrustworthy.

unremitting *adj* assiduous, constant, continual, diligent, incessant, indefatigable, persevering, sedulous, unabating, unceasing.

unrepentant *adj* abandoned, callous, graceless, hardened, impenitent, incorrigible, irreclaimable, lost, obdurate, profligate, recreant, seared, shameless.

unrequited *adj* unanswered, unreturned, unrewarded.

unreserved *adj* absolute, entire, full, unlimited; above-board, artless, candid, communicative, fair, frank, guileless, honest, ingenuous, open, sincere, single-minded, undesigning, undissembling; demonstrative, emotional, open-hearted.

unresisting *adj* compliant, long-suffering, non-resistant, obedient, passive, patient, submissive, yielding.

unresponsive *adj* irresponsive, unsympathetic.

unrestrained *adj* unbridled, unchecked, uncurbed, unfettered, unhindered, unobstructed, unreserved; broad, dissolute, incontinent, inordinate, lax, lewd, licentious, loose, wanton; lawless, wild.

unrestricted *adj* free, unbridled, unconditional, unconfined, uncurbed, unfettered, unlimited, unqualified, unrestrained; clear, open, public, unobstructed.

unrevealed *adj* hidden, occult, secret, undiscovered, unknown.

unrewarded *adj* unpaid, unrecompensed.

unriddle *vb* explain, expound, solve, unfold, unravel.

unrighteous *adj* evil, sinful, ungodly, unholy, vicious, wicked, wrong; heinous, inequitable, iniquitous, nefarious, unfair, unjust.

unripe *adj* crude, green, hard, immature, premature, sour; incomplete, unfinished.

unrivaled *adj* incomparable, inimitable, matchless, peerless, unequaled, unexampled, unique, unparalleled.

unrobe *vb* disrobe, undress.

unroll *vb* develop, discover, evolve, open, unfold; display, lay open.

unromantic *adj* literal, matter-of-fact, prosaic.

unroot *vb* eradicate, extirpate, root out, uproot.

unruffled *adj* calm, peaceful, placid, quiet, serene, smooth, still, tranquil; collected, composed, cool, imperturbable, peaceful, philosophical, placid, tranquil, undisturbed, unexcited, unmoved.

unruly *adj* disobedient, disorderly, fractious, headstrong, insubordinate, intractable, mutinous, obstreperous, rebellious, refractory, riotous, seditious, turbulent, ungovernable, unmanageable, wanton, wild; lawless, obstinate, rebellious, stubborn, vicious.

unsafe *adj* dangerous, hazardous, insecure, perilous, precarious, risky, treacherous, uncertain, unprotected.

unsaid *adj* tacit, unmentioned, unspoken, unuttered.

unsanctified *adj* profane, unhallowed, unholy.

unsatisfactory *adj* insufficient; disappointing; faulty, feeble, imperfect, poor, weak.

unsatisfied *adj* insatiate, unsated, unsatiated, unstaunched; discontented, displeased, dissatisfied, malcontent; undischarged, unpaid, unperformed, unrendered.

unsavory *adj* flat, insipid, mawkish, savorless, tasteless, unflavored, unpalatable, vapid; disagreeable, disgusting, distasteful, nasty, nauseating, nauseous, offensive, rank, revolting, sickening, uninviting, unpleasing.

unsay *vb* recall, recant, retract, take back.

unscathed *adj* unharmed, uninjured.

unschooled *adj* ignorant, uneducated, uninstructed; undisciplined, untrained.

unscrupulous *adj* dishonest, reckless, ruthless, unconscientious, unprincipled, unrestrained.

unsealed *adj* open, unclosed.

unsearchable *adj* hidden, incomprehensible, inscrutable, mysterious.

unseasonable *adj* ill-timed, inappropriate, infelicitous, inopportune, untimely; late, too late; inexpedient, undesireable, unfit, ungrateful, unsuitable, unwelcome; premature, too early.

unseasonably *adv* malapropos, unsuitably, untimely.

unseasoned *adj* inexperienced, unaccustomed, unqualified, untrained; immoderate, inordinate, irregular; green; fresh, unsalted.

unseeing *adj* blind, sightless.

unseemly *adj* improper, indecent, inappropriate, indecorous, unbecoming, uncomcly, unfit, unmeet, unsuitable.

unseen *adj* undiscerned, undiscovered, unobserved, unperceived; imperceptible, indiscoverable, invisible, latent.

unselfish *adj* altruistic, devoted, disinterested, generous, high-minded, impersonal, liberal, magnanimous, self-denying, self-forgetful, selfless, self-sacrificing.

unserviceable *adj* ill-conditioned, unsound, useless; profitless, unprofitable.

unsettle *vb* confuse, derange, disarrange, disconcert, disorder, disturb, trouble, unbalance, unfix, unhinge, upset.

unsettled *adj* changeable, fickle, inconstant, restless, transient, unstable, unsteady, vacillating, wavering; inequable, unequal; feculent, muddy, roiled, roily, turbid; adrift, afloat, homeless, unestablished, uninhabited; open, tentative, unadjusted, undecided, undetermined; due, outstanding, owing, unpaid; perturbed, troubled, unnerved.

unshackle *vb* emancipate, liberate, loose, release, set free, unbind, unchain, unfetter.

unshaken *adj* constant, firm, resolute, steadfast, steady, unmoved.

unshapen *adj* deformed, grotesque, ill-formed, ill-made, ill-shaped, misshapen, shapeless, ugly, uncouth.

unsheltered *adj* exposed, unprotected.

unshrinking *adj* firm, determined, persisting, resolute, unblenching, unflinching.

unshroud *vb* discover, expose, reveal, uncover.

unsightly *adj* deformed, disagreeable, hideous, repellent, repulsive, ugly.

unskillful, unskilful *adj* awkward, bungling, clumsy, inapt, inexpert, maladroit, rough, rude, unhandy, unskilled, unversed.

unskilled *adj* inexperienced, raw, undisciplined, undrilled, uneducated, unexercised, unpracticed, unprepared, unschooled; unskillful.

unslaked *adj* unquenched, unslacked.

unsleeping *adj* unslumbering, vigilant, wakeful, watchful.

unsmirched *adj* undefiled, unpolluted, unspotted.

unsociable *adj* distant, reserved, retiring, segregative, shy, solitary, standoffish, taciturn, uncommunicative, uncompanionable, ungenial, unsocial; inhospitable, misanthropic, morose.

unsoiled *adj* clean, spotless, unspotted, unstained, unsullied, untarnished.

unsophisticated *adj* genuine, pure, unadulterated; good, guileless, innocent, undepraved, unpolluted, invitiated; artless, honest, ingenuous, naive, natural, simple, sincere, straightforward, unaffected, undesigning, unstudied.

unsound *adj* decayed, defective, impaired, imperfect, rotten, thin, wasted, weak; broken, disturbed, light, restless; diseased, feeble, infirm, morbid, poorly, sickly, unhealthy, weak; deceitful, erroneous, fallacious, false, faulty, hollow, illogical, incorrect, invalid, ill-advised, irrational, questionable, sophistical, unreasonable, unsubstantial, untenable, wrong; dishonest, false, insincere, unfaithful, untrustworthy, untrue; insubstantial, unreal; heretical, heterodox, unorthodox.

unsparing *adj* bountiful, generous, lavish, liberal, profuse, ungrudging; harsh, inexorable, relentless, rigorous, ruthless, severe, uncompromising, unforgiving.

unspeakable *adj* indescribable, ineffable, inexpressible, unutterable.

unspiritual *adj* bodily, carnal, fleshly, sensual.

unspotted *adj* clean, spotless, unsoiled, unstained, unsullied, untarnished; faultless, immaculate, innocent, pure, stainless, unblemished, uncorrupted, undefiled, untainted.

unstable *adj* infirm, insecure, precarious, top-heavy, tottering, unbalanced, unballasted, unreliable, unsafe, unsettled, unsteady; changeable, erratic, fickle, inconstant, irresolute, mercurial, mutable, vacillating, variable, wavering, weak, volatile.-*also* **instable**.

unstained *adj* colorless, uncolored, undyed, untinged; clean, spotless, unspotted.

unsteady *adj* fluctuating, oscillating, unsettled; insecure, precarious, unstable; changeable, desultory, ever-changing, fickle, inconstant, irresolute, mutable, unreliable, variable, wavering; drunken, jumpy, tottering, vacillating, wobbly, tipsy.

unstinted *adj* abundant, ample, bountiful, full, large, lavish, plentiful, prodigal, profuse.

unstrung *adj* overcome, shaken, unnerved, weak.

unstudied *adj* extempore, extemporaneous, impromptu, offhand, spontaneous, unpremeditated; inexpert, unskilled, unversed.

unsubdued *adj* unbowed, unbroken, unconquered, untamed.

unsubmissive *adj* disobedient, contumacious, indocile, insubordinate, obstinate, perverse, refractory, uncomplying, ungovernable, unmanageable, unruly, unyielding.

unsubstantial *adj* airy, flimsy, gaseous, gossamery, light, slight, tenuous, thin, vaporous; apparitional, bodiless, chimerical, cloudbuilt, dreamlike, empty, fantastical, ideal, illusory, imaginary, imponderable, moonshiny, spectral, unreal, vague, visionary; erroneous, fallacious, flimsy, groundless, illogical, unfounded, ungrounded, unsolid, unsound, untenable, weak.

unsuccessful *adj* abortive, bootless, fruitless, futile, ineffectual, profitless,

unavailing, vain; ill-fated, ill-starred, luckless, unfortunate, unhappy, unlucky, unprosperous.

unsuitable *adj* ill-adapted, inappropriate, malapropos, unfit, unsatisfactory, unsuited; improper, inapplicable, inapt, incongruous, inexpedient, infelicitous, unbecoming, unbeseeming, unfitting.

unsuited *adj* unadapted, unfitted, unqualified.

unsullied *adj* chaste, clean, spotless, unsoiled, unspotted, unstained, untarnished; immaculate, pure, stainless, unblemished, uncorrupted, undefiled, untainted, untouched, virginal.

unsupplied *adj* destitute, unfurnished, unprovided.

unsupported *adj* unaided, unassisted; unbacked, unseconded, unsustained, unupheld.

unsurpassed *adj* matchless, peerless, unequaled, unexampled, unexcelled, unmatched, unparagoned, unparalleled, unrivaled.

unsusceptible *adj* apathetic, cold, impassive, insusceptible, phlegmatic, stoical, unimpressible, unimpressionable.

unsuspecting *adj* confiding, credulous, trusting, unsuspicious.

unsuspicious *adj* confiding, credulous, gullible, simple, trustful, unsuspecting.

unsustainable *adj* insupportable, intolerable; controvertible, erroneous, unmaintainable, untenable.

unswerving *adj* direct, straight, undeviating; constant, determined, firm, resolute, staunch, steadfast, steady, stable, unwavering.

unsymmetrical *adj* amorphous, asymmetric, disproportionate, formless, irregular, unbalanced.

unsystematic, unsystematical *adj* casual, disorderly, haphazard, irregular, planless, unmethodical.

untainted *adj* chaste, clean, faultless, fresh, healthy, pure, sweet, wholesome; spotless, unsoiled, unstained, unsullied, untarnished; immaculate, stainless, unblemished, uncorrupted, undefiled, unspotted.

untamable *adj* unconquerable.

untamed *adj* fierce, unbroken, wild.

untangle *vb* disentangle, explain, explicate.

untarnished *adj* chaste, clean, spotless, unsoiled, unspotted, unstained, unsullied; immaculate, pure, spotless, stainless, unblemished, uncorrupted, undefiled, unspotted, unsullied, untainted, virginal, virtuous.

untaught *adj* illiterate, unenlightened, uninformed, unlettered; ignorant, inexperienced, undisciplined, undrilled, uneducated, uninitiated, uninstructed, untutored.

untenable *adj* indefensible, unmaintainable, unsound; fallacious, hollow, illogical, indefensible, insupportable, unjustifiable, weak.

untenanted *adj* deserted, empty, tenantless, uninhabited, unoccupied.

unterrified *adj* fearless, unappalled, unawed, undismayed, undaunted, unscared.

unthankful *adj* thankless, ungrateful.

unthinking *adj* careless, heedless, inconsiderate, thoughtless, unreasoning, unreflecting; automatic, mechanical.

unthoughtful *adj* careless, heedless, inconsiderable, thoughtless.

unthrifty *adj* extravagant, improvident, lavish, prodigal, profuse, thriftless, wasteful.

untidy *adj* careless, disorderly, dowdy, frumpy, mussy, slatternly, slovenly, unkempt, unneat.

untie *vb* free, loose, loosen, unbind, unfasten, unknot, unloose; clear, resolve, solve, unfold.

until *adv, conj* till, to the time when; to the place, point, state or degree that; • *prep* till, to.

untimely *adj* ill-timed, immature, inconvenient, inopportune, mistimed, premature, unseasonable, unsuitable; ill-considered, inauspicious, uncalled for, unfortunate. • *adv* unseasonably, unsuitably.

untinged *adj* achromatic, colorless, hueless, uncolored, undyed, unstained.

untiring *adj* persevering, incessant, indefatigable, patient, tireless, unceasing, unfatiguable, unflagging, unremitting, unwearied, unwearying.

untold *adj* countless, incalculable, innumerable, uncounted, unnumbered; unrelated, unrevealed.

untouched *adj* intact, scatheless, unharmed, unhurt, uninjured, unscathed; insensible, unaffected, unmoved, unstirred.

untoward *adj* adverse, froward, intractable, perverse, refractory, stubborn, unfortunate; annoying, ill-timed, inconvenient, unmanageable, vexatious; awkward, uncouth, ungainly, ungraceful.

untrained *adj* green, ignorant, inexperienced, raw, unbroken, undisciplined, undrilled, uneducated, uninstructed, unpracticed, unskilled, untaught, untutored.

untrammeled *adj* free, unhampered.

untried *adj* fresh, inexperienced, maiden, new, unassayed, unattempted, unattested, virgin; undecided.

untrodden *adj* pathless, trackless, unbeaten.

untroubled *adj* calm, careless, composed, peaceful, serene, smooth, tranquil, undisturbed, unvexed.

untrue *adj* contrary, false, inaccurate, wrong; disloyal, faithless, perfidious, recreant, treacherous, unfaithful.

untrustworthy *adj* deceitful, dishonest, inaccurate, rotten, slippery, treacherous, undependable, unreliable; disloyal, false; deceptive, fallible, illusive, questionable.

untruth *n* error, faithlessness, falsehood, falsity, incorrectness, inveracity, treachery; deceit, deception, fabrication, fib, fiction, forgery, imposture, invention, lie, misrepresentation, misstatement, story.

untutored *adj* ignorant, inexperienced, undisciplined, undrilled, uneducated, uninitiated, uninstructed, untaught; artless, natural, simple, unsophisticated.

untwist *vb* disentangle, disentwine, ravel, unravel, unwreathe.

unused *adj* idle, unemployed, untried; new, unaccustomed, unfamiliar.

unusual *adj* abnormal, curious, exceptional, extraordinary, odd, peculiar, queer, rare, recherché, remarkable, singular, strange, unaccustomed, uncommon, unwonted.

unutterable *adj* incommunicable, indescribable, ineffable, inexpressible, unspeakable.

unvarnished *adj* unpolished; candid, plain, simple, true, unadorned, unembellished.

unvarying *adj* constant, invariable, unchanging.

unveil *vb* disclose, expose, reveal, show, uncover, unmask.

unveracious *adj* false, lying, mendacious, untruthful.

unversed *adj* inexperienced, raw, undisciplined, undrilled, uneducated, unexercised, unpracticed, unprepared, unschooled; unskillful.

unviolated *adj* inviolate, unbetrayed, unbroken.

unwarlike *adj* pacific, peaceful.

unwarped *adj* impartial, unbiased, undistorted, unprejudiced.

unwarrantable *adj* improper, indefensible, unjustifiable.

unwary *adj* careless, hasty, heedless, imprudent, incautious, indiscreet, precipitate, rash, reckless, remiss, uncircumspect, unguarded.

unwavering *adj* constant, determined, firm, fixed, resolute, settled, staunch, steadfast, steady, unhesitating.

unwearied *adj* unfatigued; constant, continual, incessant, indefatigable, persevering, persistent, unceasing, unremitting, untiring.

unwelcome *adj* disagreeable, unacceptable, ungrateful, unpleasant, unpleasing.

unwell *adj* ailing, delicate, diseased, ill, indisposed, sick.

unwept *adj* unlamented, unmourned, unregretted.

unwholesome *adj* baneful, deleterious, injurious, insalubrious, noisome, noxious, poisonous, unhealthful, unhealthy; injudicious, pernicious, unsound; corrupt, tainted.

unwieldy *adj* bulky, clumsy, cumbersome, cumbrous, elephantine, heavy, hulking, large, massy, ponderous, unmanageable, weighty.

unwilling *adj* averse, backward, disinclined, indisposed, laggard, loath, opposed, recalcitrant, reluctant; forced, grudging.

unwind *vb* unravel, unreel, untwine, wind off; disentangle.

unwise *adj* brainless, foolish, ill-advised, ill-judged, impolitic, imprudent, indiscreet, injudicious, inexpedient, senseless, silly, stupid, unwary, weak.

unwitnessed *adj* unknown, unseen, unspied.

unwittingly *adv* ignorantly, inadvertently, unconsciously, undesignedly, unintentionally, unknowingly.

unwonted *adj* infrequent, rare, uncommon, unusual; unaccustomed, unused.

unworthy *adj* undeserving; bad, base, blameworthy, worthless; shameful, unbecoming, vile; contemptible, derogatory, despicable, discreditable, mean, paltry, reprehensible, shabby.

unwrap *vb* open, unfold.

unwrinkled *adj* smooth, unforrowed.

unwritten *adj* oral, traditional, unrecorded; conventional, customary.

unwrought *adj* crude, rough, rude, unfashioned, unformed.

unyielding *adj* constant, determined, indomitable, inflexible, pertinacious, resolute, staunch, steadfast, steady, tenacious, uncompromising, unwavering; headstrong, intractable, obstinate, perverse, self-willed, stiff, stubborn, wayward, willful; adamantine, firm, grim, hard, immovable, implastic, inexorable, relentless, rigid, unbending.

unyoke *vb* disconnect, disjoin, part, separate.

unyoked *adj* disconnected, separated; licentious, loose, unrestrained.

upbraid *vb* accuse, blame, chide, condemn, criticize, denounce, fault, reproach, reprove, revile, scold, taunt, twit.

upheaval *n* elevation, upthrow; cataclysm, convulsion, disorder, eruption, explosion, outburst, overthrow.

uphill *adj* ascending, upward; arduous, difficult, hard, laborious, strenuous, toilsome, wearisome.

uphold *vb* elevate, raise; bear up, hold up, support, sustain; advocate, aid, champion, countenance, defend, justify, maintain, vindicate.

upland *n* down, fell, ridge, plateau.

uplift *vb* raise, upraise; animate, elevate, inspire, lift, refine. • *n* ascent, climb, elevation, lift, rise, upthrust; exaltation, inspiration, uplifting; improvement, refinement.

upon *prep* on, on top of, over; about, concerning, on the subject of, relating to; immediately after, with.

upper hand *n* advantage, ascendancy, control, dominion, mastership, mastery, preeminence, rule, superiority, supremacy, whip hand.

uppermost *adj* foremost, highest, loftiest, supreme, topmost, upmost.

uppish *adj* arrogant, assuming, haughty, perky, proud, smart.

upright *adj* erect, perpendicular, vertical; conscientious, equitable, fair, faithful, good, honest, honorable, incorruptible, just, pure, righteous, straightforward, true, trustworthy, upstanding, virtuous.

uprightness *n* erectness, perpendicularity, verticality; equity, fairness, goodness, honesty, honor, incorruptibility, integrity, justice, probity, rectitude, righteousness, straightforwardness, trustiness, trustworthiness, virtue, worth.

uproar *n* clamor, commotion, confusion, din, disturbance, fracas, hubbub, hurly-burly, noise, pandemonium, racket, riot, tumult, turmoil, vociferation.

uproarious *adj* boisterous, clamorous, loud, noisy, obstreperous, riotous, tumultuous.

uproot *vb* eradicate, extirpate, root out.

upset *vb* capsize, invert, overthrow, overtumble, overturn, spill, tip over, topple, turn turtle; agitate, confound, confuse, discompose, disconcert, distress, disturb, embarrass, excite, fluster, muddle, overwhelm, perturb, shock, startle, trouble, unnerve, unsettle; checkmate, defeat, overthrow, revolutionize, subvert; foil, frustrate, nonplus, thwart. • *adj* disproved, exposed, overthrown; bothered, confused, disconcerted, flustered, mixed-up, perturbed; shocked, startled, unsettled; beaten, defeated, overcome, overpowered, overthrown; discomfited, distressed, discomposed, overexcited, overwrought, shaken, troubled, unnerved. • *n* confutation, refutation; foiling, frustration, overthrow, revolution, revulsion, ruin, subversdion, thwarting.

upshot *n* conclusion, consummation, effect, end, event, issue, outcome, result, termination.

upside down *adj* bottom side up, bottom up, confused, head over heels, inverted, topsy-turvy.

upstart *n* adventurer, arriviste, parvenu, snob, social cimber, yuppie.

upturned *adj* raised, uplifted; retroussé.

upward *adj* ascending, climbing, mounting, rising, uphill. • *adv* above, aloft, overhead, up; heavenwards, skywards.

urbane *adj* civil, complaisant, courteous, courtly, elegant, mannerly, polished, polite, refined, smooth, suave, well-mannered.

urbanity *n* amenity, civility, complaisance, courtesy, politeness, smoothness, suavity.

urchin *n* brat, child, kid, ragamuffin, rascal, scrap, squirt, tad.

urge *vb* crowd, drive, force on, impel, press, press on, push, push on; beg, beseech, conjure, entreat, exhort, implore, importune, ply, solicit, tease; animate, egg on, encourage, goad, hurry, incite, instigate, quicken, spur, stimulate. • *n* compulsion,

desire, drive, impulse, longing, pressure, wish, yearning.

urgency *n* drive, emergency, exigency, haste, necessity, press, pressure, push, stress; clamorousness, entreaty, insistence, importunity, instance, solicitation; goad, incitement, spur, stimulus.

urgent *adj* cogent, critical, crucial, crying, exigent, immediate, imperative, important, importunate, insistent, instant, pertinacious, pressing, serious.

urinal *n* chamber, chamber pot, lavatory, pot, potty, jordan, toilet.

urinate *vb* make water, pee, pee-pee, piddle, piss, stale, wee.

usage *n* treatment; consuetude, custom, fashion, habit, method, mode, practice, prescription, tradition, use.

use *vb* administer, apply, avail oneself of, drive, employ, handle, improve, make use of, manipulate, occupy, operate, ply, put into action, take advantage of, turn to account, wield, work; exercise, exert, exploit, practice, profit by, utilize; absorb, consume, exhaust, expend, swallow up, waste, wear out; accustom, familiarize, habituate, harden, inure, train; act toward, behave toward, deal with, manage, treat; be accustomed, be wont. • *n* appliance, application, consumption, conversion, disposal, exercise, employ, employment, practice, utilization; adaptability, advantage, avail, benefit, convenience, profit, service, usefulness, utility, wear; exigency, necessity, indispensability, need, occasion, requisiteness; custom, habit, handling, method, treatment, usage, way.

useful *adj* active, advantageous, available, availing, beneficial, commodious, conducive, contributory, convenient, effective, good, helpful, instrumental, operative, practical, profitable, remunerative, salutary, suitable, serviceable, utilitarian; available, helpful, serviceable, valuable.

usefulness *n* advantage, profit, serviceableness, utility, value.

useless *adj* abortive, bootless, fruitless, futile, helpless, idle, incapable, incompetent, ineffective, ineffectual, inutile, nugatory, null, profitless, unavailing, unprofitable, unproductive, unserviceable, valueless, worthless; good for nothing, waste.

usher *vb* announce, forerun, herald, induct, introduce, precede; conduct, direct, escort, shepherd, show. • *n* attendant, conductor, escort, shepherd, squire.

usual *adj* accustomed, common, customary, everyday, familiar, frequent, general, habitual, normal, ordinary, prevailing, prevalent, regular, wonted.

usurp *vb* appropriate, arrogate, assume, seize.

usurpation *n* assumption, dispossession, infringement, seizure.

usury *n* interest; exploitation, extortion, profiteering.

utensil *n* device, implement, instrument, tool.

utility *n* advantageousness, avail, benefit, profit, service, use, usefulness; happiness, welfare.

utilize *vb* employ, exploit, make use of, put to use, turn to account, use.

utmost *adj* extreme, farthest, highest, last, main, most distant, remotest; greatest, uttermost. • *n* best, extreme, maximum, most.

Utopian *adj* air-built, air-drawn, chimerical, fanciful, ideal, imaginary, visionary, unreal.

utricle *n* bladder, cyst, sac, vesicle.

utter[1] *adj* complete, entire, perfect, total; absolute, blank, diametric, downright, final, peremptory, sheer, stark, thorough, thoroughgoing, unconditional, unqualified, total.

utter[2] *vb* articulate, breathe, deliver, disclose, divulge, emit, enunciate, express, give forth, pronounce, reveal, speak, talk, tell, voice; announce, circulate, declare, issue, publish.

utterance *n* articulation, delivery, disclosure, emission, expression, pronouncement, pronunciation, publication, speech.

utterly *adv* absolutely, altogether, completely, downright, entirely, quite, totally, unconditionally, wholly.

uttermost *adj* extreme, farthest; greatest, utmost.

V

vacant *adj* blank, empty, unfilled, void; disengaged, free, unemployed, unoccupied, unencumbered; thoughtless, unmeaning, unthinking, unreflective; uninhabited, untenanted.

vacate *vb* abandon, evacuate, relinquish, surrender; abolish, abrogate, annul, cancel, disannul, invalidate, nullify, overrule, quash, rescind.

vacillate *vb* dither, fluctuate, hesitate, oscillate, rock, sway, waver.

vacillation *n* faltering, fluctuation, hesitation, inconstancy, indecision, irresolution, reeling, rocking, staggering, swaying, unsteadiness, wavering.

vacuity *n* emptiness, inanition, vacancy; emptiness, vacancy, vacuum, void; expressionlessness, inanity, nihility.

vacuous *adj* empty, empty-headed, unfilled, vacant, void; inane, unintelligent.

vacuum *n* emptiness, vacuity, void.

vagabond *adj* footloose, idle, meandering, rambling, roving, roaming, strolling, vagrant, wandering. • *n* beggar, castaway, landloper, loafer, lounger, nomad, outcast, tramp, vagrant, wanderer.

vagary *n* caprice, crotchet, fancy, freak, humor, whim.

vagrant *adj* erratic, itinerant, roaming, roving, nomadic, strolling, unsettled, wandering. • *n* beggar, castaway, landloper, loafer, lounger, nomad, outcast, tramp, vagabond, wanderer.

vague *adj* ambiguous, confused, dim, doubtful, indefinite, ill-defined, indistinct, lax, loose, obscure, uncertain, undetermined, unfixed, unsettled.

vain *adj* baseless, delusive, dreamy, empty, false, imaginary, shadowy, suppositional, unsubstantial, unreal, void; abortive, bootless, fruitless, futile, ineffectual, nugatory, profitless, unavailing, unprofitable; trivial, unessential, unimportant, unsatisfactory, unsatisfying, useless, vapid, worthless; arrogant, conceited, egotistical, flushed, high, inflated, opinionated, ostentatious, overweening, proud, self-confident, self-opinionated, vainglorious; gaudy, glittering, gorgeous, showy.

valediction *n* adieu, farewell, goodbye, leave-taking.

valet *n* attendant, flunky, groom, lackey, servant.

valetudinarian *adj* delicate, feeble, frail, infirm, sickly.

valiant *adj* bold, brave, chivalrous, courageous, daring, dauntless, doughty, fearless, gallant, heroic, intrepid, lion-hearted, redoubtable, Spartan, valorous, undaunted.

valid *adj* binding, cogent, conclusive,

efficacious, efficient, good, grave, important, just, logical, powerful, solid, sound, strong, substantial, sufficient, weighty.

valley *n* basin, bottom, canyon, dale, dell, dingle, glen, hollow, ravine, strath, vale.

valor *n* boldness, bravery, courage, daring, gallantry, heroism, prowess, spirit.

valorous *adj* bold, brave, courageous, dauntless, doughty, intrepid, stout.

valuable *adj* advantageous, precious, profitable, useful; costly, expensive, rich; admirable, estimable, worthy. • *n* heirloom, treasure.

value *vb* account, appraise, assess, estimate, price, rate, reckon; appreciate, esteem, prize, regard, treasure. • *n* avail, importance, usefulness, utility, worth; cost, equivalent, price, rate; estimation, excellence, importance, merit, valuation.

valueless *adj* miserable, useless, worthless.

vandal *n* barbarian, destroyer, savage.

vandalism *n* barbarism, barbarity, savagery.

vanish *vb* disappear, dissolve, fade, melt.

vanity *n* emptiness, falsity, foolishness, futility, hollowness, insanity, triviality, unreality, worthlessness; arrogance, conceit, egotism, ostentation, self-conceit.

vanquish *vb* conquer, defeat, outwit, overcome, overpower, overthrow, subdue, subjugate; crush, discomfit, foil, master, quell, rout, worst.

vapid *adj* dead, flat, insipid, lifeless, savorless, spiritless, stale, tasteless; dull, feeble, jejune, languid, meager, prosaic, prosy, tame.

vapor *n* cloud, exhalation, fog, fume, mist, rack, reek, smoke, steam; daydream, dream, fantasy, phantom, vagary, vision, whim, whimsy.

variable *adj* changeable, mutable, shifting; aberrant, alterable, capricious, fickle, fitful, floating, fluctuating, inconstant, mobile, mutable, protean, restless, shifting, unsteady, vacillating, wavering.

variance *n* disagreement, difference, discord, dissension, incompatibility, jarring, strife.

variation *n* alteration, change, modification; departure, deviation, difference, discrepancy, innovation; contrariety, discordance.

variegated *adj* checkered, dappled, diversified, flecked, kaleidoscopic, mottled, multicolored, pied, spotted, striped.

variety *n* difference, dissimilarity, diversity, diversification, medley, miscellany, mixture, multiplicity, variation; kind, sort.

various *adj* different, diverse, manifold, many, numerous, several, sundry.

varnish *vb* enamel, glaze, japan, lacquer; adorn, decorate, embellish, garnish, gild, polish; disguise, excuse, extenuate, gloss over, palliate. • *n* enamel, lacquer, stain; cover, extenuation, gloss.

vary *vb* alter, metamorphose, transform; alternate, exchange, rotate; diversify, modify, variegate; depart, deviate, swerve.

vassal *n* bondman, liegeman, retainer, serf, slave, subject, thrall.

vassalage *n* bondage, dependence, serfdom, servitude, slavery, subjection.

vast *adj* boundless, infinite, measureless, spacious, wide; colossal, enormous, gigantic, huge, immense, mighty, monstrous, prodigious, tremendous; extraordinary, remarkable.

vaticination *n* augury, divination, prediction, prognostication, prophecy.

vault[1] *vb* arch, bend, curve, span. • *n* cupola, curve, dome; catacomb, cell, cellar, crypt, dungeon, tomb; depository, strong-room.

vault[2] *vb* bound, jump, leap, spring; tumble, turn. • *n* bound, leap, jump, spring.

vaunt *vb* advertise, boast, brag, display, exult, flaunt, flourish, parade.

veer *vb* change, shift, turn.

vegetate *vb* blossom, develop, flourish, flower, germinate, grow, shoot, sprout, swell; bask, hibernate, idle, stagnate.

vehemence *n* impetuosity, violence; ardor, eagerness, earnestness, enthusiasm, fervency, fervor, heat, keenness, passion, warmth, zeal; force, intensity.

vehement *adj* furious, high, hot, impetuous, passionate, rampant, violent; ardent, burning, eager, earnest, enthusiastic, fervid, fiery, keen, passionate, sanguine, zealous; forcible, mighty, powerful, strong.

veil *vb* cloak, conceal, cover, curtain, envelop, hide, invest, mask, screen, shroud. • *n* cover, curtain, film, shade, screen; blind, cloak, disguise, mask, muffler, visor.

vein *n* course, current, lode, seam, streak, stripe, thread, wave; bent, character, faculty, humor, mood, talent, turn.

velocity *n* acceleration, celerity, expedition, fleetness, haste, quickness, rapidity, speed, swiftness.

velvety *adj* delicate, downy, smooth, soft.

venal *adj* corrupt, mean, purchasable, sordid.

vend *vb* dispose, flog, hawk, retail, sell.

venerable *adj* grave, respected, revered, sage, wise; awful, dread, dreadful; aged, old, patriarchal.

venerate *vb* adore, esteem, honor, respect, revere.

veneration *n* adoration, devotion, esteem, respect, reverence, worship.

vengeance *n* retaliation, retribution, revenge.

venial *adj* allowed, excusable, pardonable, permitted, trivial.

venom *n* poison, virus; acerbity, acrimony, bitterness, gall, hate, ill-will, malevolence, malice, maliciousness, malignity, rancor, spite, virulence.

venomous *adj* deadly, poisonous, septic, toxic, virulent; caustic, malicious, malignant, mischievous, noxious, spiteful.

vent *vb* emit, express, release, utter. • *n* air hole, hole, mouth, opening, orifice; air pipe, air tube, aperture, blowhole, bunghole, hydrant, plug, spiracle, spout, tap, orifice; effusion, emission, escape, outlet, passage; discharge, expression, utterance.

ventilate *vb* aerate, air, freshen, oxygenate, purify; fan, winnow; canvass, comment, discuss, examine, publish, review, scrutinize.

venture *vb* adventure, dare, hazard, imperil, jeopardize, presume, risk, speculate, test, try, undertake. • *n* adventure, chance, hazard, jeopardy, peril, risk, speculation, stake.

venturesome *adj* adventurous, bold, courageous, daring, doughty, enterprising, fearless, foolhardy, intrepid, presumptuous, rash, venturous.

veracious *adj* reliable, straightforward, true, trustworthy, truthful; credible, genuine, honest, unfeigned.

veracity *n* accuracy, candor, correctness, credibility, exactness, fidelity, frankness, honesty, ingenuousness, probity, sincerity, trueness, truth, truthfulness.

verbal *adj* nuncupative, oral, spoken, unwritten.

verbose *adj* diffusive, long-winded, loquacious, talkative, wordy.

verdant *adj* fresh, green, verdure, verdurous; green, inexperienced, raw, unsophisticated.

verdict *n* answer, decision, finding, judgement, opinion, sentence.

verge *vb* bear, incline, lean, slope, tend;

approach, border, skirt. • *n* mace, rod, staff; border, boundary, brink, confine, edge, extreme, limit, margin; edge, eve, point.

verification *n* authentication, attestation, confirmation, corroboration.

verify *vb* attest, authenticate, confirm, corroborate, prove, substantiate.

verily *adv* absolutely, actually, confidently, indeed, positively, really, truly.

verity *n* certainty, reality, truth, truthfulness.

vermicular *adj* convoluted, flexuose, flexuous, meandering, serpentine, sinuous, tortuous, twisting, undulating, waving, winding, wormish, wormlike.

vernacular *adj* common, indigenous, local, mother, native, vulgar. • *n* cant, dialect, jargon, patois, speech.

versatile *adj* capricious, changeable, erratic, mobile, variable; fickle, inconstant, mercurial, unsteady; adaptable, protean, plastic, varied.

versed *adj* able, accomplished, acquainted, clever, conversant, practiced, proficient, qualified, skillful, skilled, trained.

version *n* interpretation, reading, rendering, translation.

vertex *n* apex, crown, height, summit, top, zenith.

vertical *adj* erect, perpendicular, plumb, steep, upright.

vertiginous *adj* rotatory, rotary, whirling; dizzy, giddy.

vertigo *n* dizziness, giddiness.

verve *n* animation, ardor, energy, enthusiasm, force, rapture, spirit.

very *adv* absolutely, enormously, excessively, hugely, remarkably, surpassingly. • *adj* actual, exact, identical, precise, same; bare, mere, plain, pure, simple.

vesicle *n* bladder, blister, cell, cyst, follicle.

vest *vb* clothe, cover, dress, envelop; endow, furnish, invest. • *n* dress, garment, robe, vestment, vesture, waistcoat.

vestibule *n* anteroom, entrance hall, lobby, porch.

vestige *n* evidence, footprint, footstep, mark, record, relic, sign, token.

veteran *adj* adept, aged, experienced, disciplined, seasoned, old. • *n* campaigner, old soldier; master, past master, old-timer, old-stager.

veto *vb* ban, embargo, forbid, interdict, negate, prohibit. • *n* ban, embargo, interdict, prohibition, refusal.

vex *vb* annoy, badger, bother, chafe, cross,

distress, gall, harass, harry, hector, molest, perplex, pester, plague, tease, torment, trouble, roil, spite, worry; affront, displease, fret, irk, irritate, nettle, offend, provoke; agitate, disquiet, disturb.

vexation n affliction, agitation, chagrin, discomfort, displeasure, disquiet, distress, grief, irritation, pique, sorrow, trouble; annoyance, curse, nuisance, plague, torment; damage, troubling, vexing.

vexed adj afflicted, agitated, annoyed, bothered, disquieted, harassed, irritated, perplexed, plagued, provoked, troubled, worried.

vibrate vb oscillate, sway, swing, undulate, wave; impinge, quiver, sound, thrill; fluctuate, hesitate, vacillate, waver.

vibration n nutation, oscillation, vibration.

vicarious adj commissioned, delegated, indirect, second-hand, substituted.

vice n blemish, defect, failing, fault, imperfection, infirmity; badness, corruption, depravation, depravity, error, evil, immorality, iniquity, laxity, obliquity, sin, viciousness, vileness, wickedness.

vicinity n nearness, proximity; locality, neighborhood, vicinage.

vicious adj abandoned, atrocious, bad, corrupt, degenerate, demoralized, depraved, devilish, diabolical, evil, flagrant, hellish, immoral, iniquitous, mischievous, profligate, shameless, sinful, unprincipled, wicked; malicious, spiteful, venomous; foul, impure, debased, faulty; contrary, refractory.

viciousness n badness, corruption, depravity, immorality, profligacy.

vicissitude n alteration, interchange; change, fluctuation, mutation, revolution, variation.

victim n martyr, sacrifice, sufferer; prey; cat's-paw, cull, cully, dupe, gull, gudgeon, puppet.

victimize vb bamboozle, befool, beguile, cheat, circumvent, cozen, deceive, defraud, diddle, dupe, fool, gull, hoax, hoodwink, overreach, swindle, trick.

victor n champion, conqueror, vanquisher, winner.

victorious adj conquering, successful, triumphant, winning.

victory n achievement, conquest, mastery, triumph.

victuals npl comestibles, eatables, fare, food, meat, provisions, repast, sustenance, viands.

vie vb compete, contend, emulate, rival, strive.

view vb behold, contemplate, eye, inspect, scan, survey; consider, inspect, regard, study. • n inspection, observation, regard, sight; outlook, panorama, perspective, prospect, range, scene, survey, vista; aim, intent, intention, design, drift, object, purpose, scope; belief, conception, impression, idea, judgement, notion, opinion, sentiment, theory; appearance, aspect, show.

vigilance n alertness, attentiveness, carefulness, caution, circumspection, observance, watchfulness.

vigilant adj alert, attentive, careless, cautious, circumspect, unsleeping, wakeful, watchful.

vigor n activity, efficacy, energy, force, might, potency, power, spirit, strength; bloom, elasticity, haleness, health, heartiness, pep, punch, robustness, soundness, thriftiness, tone, vim, vitality; enthusiasm, freshness, fire, intensity, liveliness, piquancy, strenuousness, vehemence, verve, raciness.

vigorous adj lusty, powerful, strong; active, alert, cordial, energetic, forcible, strenuous, vehement, vivid, virile; brisk, hale, hardy, robust, sound, sturdy, healthy; fresh, flourishing; bold, emphatic, impassioned, lively, nervous, piquant, pointed, severe, sparkling, spirited, trenchant.

vile adj abject, base, beastly, beggarly, brutish, contemptible, despicable, disgusting, groveling, ignoble, low, odious, paltry, pitiful, repulsive, scurvy, shabby, slavish, sorry, ugly; bad, evil, foul, gross, impure, iniquitous, lewd, obscene, sinful, vicious, wicked; cheap, mean, miserable, valueless, worthless.

vilify vb abuse, asperse, backbite, berate, blacken, blemish, brand, calumniate, decry, defame, disparage, lampoon, libel, malign, revile, scandalize, slander, slur, traduce, vituperate.

villain n blackguard, knave, miscreant, rascal, reprobate, rogue, ruffian, scamp, scapegrace, scoundrel.

villainous adj base, mean, vile; corrupt, depraved, knavish, unprincipled, wicked; atrocious, heinous, outrageous, sinful; mischievous, sorry.

vindicate vb defend, justify, uphold; advocate, avenge, assert, maintain, right, support.

vindication *n* apology, excuse, defense, justification.

vindictive *adj* avenging, grudgeful, implacable, malevolent, malicious, malignant, retaliative, revengeful, spiteful, unforgiving, unrelenting, vengeful.

violate *vb* hurt, injure; break, disobey, infringe, invade; desecrate, pollute, profane; abuse, debauch, defile, deflower, outrage, ravish, transgress.

violent *adj* boisterous, demented, forceful, forcible, frenzied, furious, high, hot, impetuous, insane, intense, stormy, tumultuous, turbulent, vehement, wild; fierce, fiery, fuming, heady, heavy, infuriate, passionate, obstreperous, strong, raging, rampant, rank, rapid, raving, refractory, roaring, rough, tearing, towering, ungovernable; accidental, unnatural; desperate, extreme, outrageous, unjust; acute, exquisite, poignant, sharp.

virago *n* amazon, brawler, fury, shrew, tartar, vixen.

virgin *adj* chaste, maidenly, modest, pure, undefiled, stainless, unpolluted, vestal, virginal; fresh, maiden, untouched, unused. • *n* celibate, damsel, girl, lass, maid, maiden.

virile *adj* forceful, manly, masculine, robust, vigorous.

virtual *adj* constructive, equivalent, essential, implicit, implied, indirect, practical, substantial.

virtue *n* chastity, goodness, grace, morality, purity; efficacy, excellence, honesty, integrity, justice, probity, quality, rectitude, worth.

virtuous *adj* blameless, equitable, exemplary, excellent, good, honest, moral, noble, righteous, upright, worthy; chaste, continent, immaculate, innocent, modest, pure, undefiled; efficacious, powerful.

virulent *adj* deadly, malignant, poisonous, toxic, venomous; acrid, acrimonious, bitter, caustic.

visage *n* aspect, countenance, face, guise, physiognomy, semblance.

viscera *n* bowels, entrails, guts, intestines.

viscous *adj* adhesive, clammy, glutinous, ropy, slimy, sticky, tenacious.

visible *adj* observable, perceivable, perceptible, seeable, visual; apparent, clear, conspicuous, discoverable, distinct, evident, manifest, noticeable, obvious, open, palpable, patent, plain, revealed, unhidden, unmistakable.

vision *n* eyesight, seeing, sight; eyeshot, ken; apparition, chimera, dream, ghost, hallucination, illusion, phantom, specter.

visionary *adj* imaginative, impractical, quixotic, romantic; chimerical, dreamy, fancied, fanciful, fantastic, ideal, illusory, imaginary, romantic, shadowy, unsubstantial, utopian, wild. • *n* dreamer, enthusiast, fanatic, idealist, optimist, theorist, zealot.

vital *adj* basic, cardinal, essential, indispensable, necessary, needful; animate, alive, existing, life-giving, living; paramount.

vitality *n* animation, life, strength, vigor, virility.

vitiate *vb* adulterate, contaminate, corrupt, debase, defile, degrade, deprave, deteriorate, impair, infect, injure, invalidate, poison, pollute, spoil.

vitiation *n* adulteration, corruption, degeneracy, degeneration, degradation, depravation, deterioration, impairment, injury, invalidation, perversion, pollution, prostitution.

vituperate *vb* abuse, berate, blame, censure, denounce, overwhelm, rate, revile, scold, upbraid, vilify.

vituperation *n* abuse, blame, censure, invective, reproach, railing, reviling, scolding, upbraiding.

vivacious *adj* active, animated, breezy, brisk, buxom, cheerful, frolicsome, gay, jocund, light-hearted, lively, merry, mirthful, spirited, sportive, sprightly.

vivacity *n* animation, cheer, cheerfulness, gaiety, liveliness, sprightliness.

vivid *adj* active, animated, bright, brilliant, clear, intense, fresh, lively, living, lucid, quick, sprightly, strong; expressive, graphic, striking, telling.

vivify *vb* animate, arouse, awake, quicken, vitalize.

vixen *n* brawler, scold, shrew, spitfire, tartar, virago.

vocabulary *n* dictionary, glossary, lexicon, wordbook; language, terms, words.

vocation *n* call, citation, injunction, summons; business, calling, employment, occupation, profession, pursuit, trade.

vociferate *vb* bawl, bellow, clamor, cry, exclaim, rant, shout, yell.

vociferous *adj* blatant, clamorous, loud, noisy, obstreperous, ranting, stunning, uproarious.

vogue *adj* fashionable, modish, stylish,

trendy. • *n* custom, fashion, favor, mode, practice, repute, style, usage, way.

voice *vb* declare, express, say, utter. • *n* speech, tongue, utterance; noise, notes, sound; opinion, option, preference, suffrage, vote; accent, articulation, enunciation, inflection, intonation, modulation, pronunciation, tone; expression, language, words.

void *vb* clear, eject, emit, empty, evacuate. • *adj* blank, empty, hollow, vacant; clear, destitute, devoid, free, lacking, wanting, without; inept, ineffectual, invalid, nugatory, null; imaginary, unreal, vain. • *n* abyss, blank, chasm, emptiness, hole, vacuum.

volatile *adj* gaseous, incoercible; airy, buoyant, frivolous, gay, jolly, lively, sprightly, vivacious; capricious, changeable, fickle, flighty, flyaway, giddy, harebrained, inconstant, light-headed, mercurial, reckless, unsteady, whimsical, wild.

volition *n* choice, determination, discretion, option, preference, will.

volley *n* fusillade, round, salvo; blast, burst, discharge, emission, explosion, outbreak, report, shower, storm.

voluble *adj* fluent, garrulous, glib, loquacious, talkative.

volume *n* book, tome; amplitude, body, bulk, compass, dimension, size, substance, vastness; fullness, power, quantity.

voluminous *adj* ample, big, bulky, full, great, large; copious, diffuse, discursive, flowing.

voluntary *adj* free, spontaneous, unasked, unbidden, unforced; deliberate, designed, intended, purposed; discretionary, optional, willing.

volunteer *vb* offer, present, proffer, propose, tender.

voluptuary *n* epicure, hedonist, sensualist.

voluptuous *adj* carnal, effeminate, epicurean, fleshy, licentious, luxurious, sensual, sybaritic.

vomit *vb* discharge, eject, emit, puke, regurgitate, spew, throw up.

voracious *adj* devouring, edacious, greedy, hungry, rapacious, ravenous.

vortex *n* eddy, maelstrom, whirl, whirlpool.

votary *adj* devoted, promised. • *n* adherent, devotee, enthusiast, follower, supporter, votarist, zealot.

vote *vb* ballot, elect, opt, return; judge, pronounce, propose, suggest. • *n* ballot, franchise, poll, referendum, suffrage, voice.

vouch *vb* affirm, asseverate, attest, aver, declare, guarantee, support, uphold, verify, warrant.

vouchsafe *vb* accord, cede, deign, grant, stoop, yield.

vow *vb* consecrate, dedicate, devote; asseverate. • *n* oath, pledge, promise.

voyage *vb* cruise, journey, navigate, ply, sail. • *n* crossing, cruise, excursion, journey, passage, sail, trip.

vulgar *adj* base-born, common, ignoble, lowly, plebeian; boorish, cheap, coarse, discourteous, flashy, homespun, garish, gaudy, ill-bred, inelegant, loud, rustic, showy, tawdry, uncultivated, unrefined; general, ordinary, popular, public; base, broad, loose, low, gross, mean, ribald, vile; inelegant, unauthorized.

vulgarity *n* baseness, coarseness, grossness, meanness, rudeness.

vulnerable *adj* accessible, assailable, defenseless, exposed, weak.

W

waddle *vb* toddle, toggle, waggle, wiggle, wobble.

waft *vb* bear, carry, convey, float, transmit, transport. • *n* breath, breeze, draught, puff.

wag[1] *vb* shake, sway, waggle; oscillate, vibrate, waver; advance, move, progress, stir. • *n* flutter, nod, oscillation, vibration.

wag[2] *n* humorist, jester, joker, wit.

wage *vb* bet, hazard, lay, stake, wager; conduct, undertake.

wager *vb* back, bet, gamble, lay, pledge, risk, stake. • *n* bet, gamble, pledge, risk, stake.

wages *npl* allowance, compensation, earnings, emolument, hire, pay, payment, remuneration, salary, stipend.

waggish *adj* frolicsome, gamesome, mischievous, roguish, tricksy; comical, droll, facetious, funny, humorous, jocular, jocose, merry, sportive.

wagon *n* cart, lorry, truck, van, waggon, wain.

wail *vb* bemoan, deplore, lament, mourn; cry, howl, weep. • *n* complaint, cry, lamentation, moan, wailing.

waist *n* bodice, corsage, waistline.

wait *vb* delay, linger, pause, remain, rest, stay, tarry; attend, minister, serve; abide, await, expect, look for. • n delay, halt, holdup, pause, respite, rest, stay, stop.

waiter, waitress n attendant, lackey, servant, servitor, steward, valet.

waive vb defer, forgo, surrender, relinquish, remit, renounce; desert, reject.

wake[1] vb arise, awake, awaken; activate, animate, arouse, awaken, excite, kindle, provoke, stimulate. • n vigil, watch, watching.

wake[2] n course, path, rear, track, trail, wash.

wakeful adj awake, sleepless, restless; alert, observant, vigilant, wary, watchful.

wale n ridge, streak, stripe, welt, whelk.

walk vb advance, depart, go, march, move, pace, saunter, step, stride, stroll, tramp. • n amble, carriage, gait, step; beat, career, course, department, field, province; conduct, procedure; alley, avenue, cloister, esplanade, footpath, path, pathway, pavement, promenade, range, sidewalk, way; constitutional, excursion, hike, ramble, saunter, stroll, tramp, turn.

wall n escarp, parapet, plane, upright.

wallet n bag, knapsack, pocketbook, purse, sack.

wan adj ashen, bloodless, cadaverous, colorless, haggard, pale, pallid.

wand n baton, mace, truncheon, scepter.

wander vb forage, prowl, ramble, range, roam, rove, stroll; deviate, digress, straggle, stray; moon, rave. • n amble, cruise, excursion, ramble, stroll.

wane vb abate, decrease, ebb, subside; decline, fail, sink. • n decrease, diminution, lessening; decay, declension, decline, failure.

want vb crave, desire, need, require, wish; fail, lack, neglect, omit. • n absence, defect, default, deficiency, lack; defectiveness, failure, inadequacy, insufficiency, meagerness, paucity, poverty, scantiness, scarcity, shortness; requirement; craving, desire, longing, wish; destitution, distress, indigence, necessity, need, penury, poverty, privation, straits.

wanton vb caper, disport, frisk, frolic, play, revel, romp, sport; dally, flirt, toy, trifle. • adj free, loose, unchecked, unrestrained, wandering; abounding, exuberant, luxuriant, overgrown, rampant; airy, capricious, coltish, frisky, playful, skittish, sportive; dissolute, irregular, licentious, loose; carnal, immoral, incontinent, lascivious, lecherous, lewd, libidinous, light,

lustful, prurient, salacious, unchaste; careless, gratuitous, groundless, heedless, inconsiderate, needless, perverse, reckless, wayward, wilful. • n baggage, flirt, harlot, light-o'-love, prostitute, rake, roué, slut, whore.

war vb battle, campaign, combat, contend, crusade, engage, fight, strive. • n contention, enmity, hostility, strife, warfare.

warble vb sing, trill, yodel. • n carol, chant, hymn, hum.

ward vb guard, watch; defend, fend, parry, protect, repel. • n care, charge, guard, guardianship, watch; defender, guardian, keeper, protector, warden; custody; defense, garrison, protection; minor, pupil; district, division, precinct, quarter; apartment, cubicle.

warehouse n depot, magazine, repository, store, storehouse.

wares npl commodities, goods, merchandise, movables.

warfare n battle, conflict, contest, discord, engagement, fray, hostilities, strife, struggle, war.

warily adv carefully, cautiously, charily, circumspectly, heedfully, watchfully, vigilantly.

wariness n care, caution, circumspection, foresight, thought, vigilance.

warlike adj bellicose, belligerent, combative, hostile, inimical, martial, military, soldierly, watchful.

warm vb heat, roast, toast; animate, chafe, excite, rouse. • adj lukewarm, tepid; genial, mild, pleasant, sunny; close, muggy, oppressive; affectionate, ardent, cordial, eager, earnest, enthusiastic, fervent, fervid, glowing, hearty, hot, zealous; excited, fiery, flushed, furious, hasty, keen, lively, passionate, quick, vehement, violent.

warmth n glow, tepidity; ardor, fervency, fervor, zeal; animation, cordiality, eagerness, earnestness, enthusiasm, excitement, fervency, fever, fire, flush, heat, intensity, passion, spirit, vehemence.

warn vb caution, forewarn; admonish, advise; apprise, inform, notify; bid, call, summon.

warning adj admonitory, cautionary, cautioning, monitory. • n admonition, advice, caveat, caution, monition; information, notice; augury, indication, intimation, omen, portent, presage, prognostic, sign, symptom; call, summons; example, lesson, sample.

warp *vb* bend, bias, contort, deviate, distort, pervert, swerve, turn, twist. • *n* bent, bias, cast, crook, distortion, inclination, leaning, quirk, sheer, skew, slant, slew, swerve, twist, turn.

warrant *vb* answer for, certify, guarantee, secure; affirm, assure, attest, avouch, declare, justify, state; authorize, justify, license, maintain, sanction, support, sustain, uphold. • *n* guarantee, pledge, security, surety, warranty; authentication, authority, commission, verification; order, pass, permit, summons, subpoena, voucher, writ.

warrantable *adj* admissible, allowable, defensible, justifiable, lawful, permissible, proper, right, vindicable.

warrior *n* champion, captain, fighter, hero, soldier.

wary *adj* careful, cautious, chary, circumspect, discreet, guarded, heedful, prudent, scrupulous, vigilant, watchful.

wash *vb* purify, purge; moisten, wet; bathe, clean, flush, irrigate, lap, lave, rinse, sluice; color, stain, tint. • *n* ablution, bathing, cleansing, lavation, washing; bog, fen, marsh, swamp, quagmire; bath, embrocation, lotion; laundry, washing.

washy *adj* damp, diluted, moist, oozy, sloppy, thin, watery, weak; feeble, jejune, pointless, poor, spiritless, trashy, trumpery, unmeaning, vapid, worthless.

waspish *adj* choleric, fretful, irascible, irritable, peevish, petulant, snappish, testy, touchy; slender, slim, small-waisted.

waste *vb* consume, corrode, decrease, diminish, emaciate, wear; absorb, deplete, devour, dissipate, drain, empty, exhaust, expend, lavish, lose, misspend, misuse, scatter, spend, squander; demolish, desolate, destroy, devastate, devour, dilapidate, harry, pillage, plunder, ravage, ruin, scour, strip; damage, impair, injure; decay, dwindle, perish, wither. • *adj* bare, desolated, destroyed, devastated, empty, ravaged, ruined, spoiled, stripped, void; dismal, dreary, forlorn; abandoned, bare, barren, uncultivated, unimproved, uninhabited, untilled, wild; useless, valueless, worthless; exuberant, superfluous. • *n* consumption, decrement, diminution, dissipation, exhaustion, expenditure, loss, wasting; destruction, dispersion,

extravagance, loss, squandering, wanton; decay, desolation, destruction, devastation, havoc, pillage, ravage, ruin; chaff, debris, detritus, dross, excrement, husks, junk, matter, offal, refuse, rubbish, trash, wastrel, worthlessness; barrenness, desert, expanse, solitude, wild, wilderness.

wasteful *adj* destructive, ruinous; extravagant, improvident, lavish, prodigal, profuse, squandering, thriftless, unthrifty.

watch *vb* attend, guard, keep, oversee, protect, superintend, tend; eye, mark, observe. • *n* espial, guard, outlook, wakefulness, watchfulness, watching, vigil, ward; alertness, attention, inspection, observation, surveillance; guard, picket, sentinel, sentry, watchman; pocket watch, ticker, timepiece, wristwatch.

watchful *adj* alert, attentive, awake, careful, circumspect, guarded, heedful, observant, vigilant, wakeful, wary.

watchword *n* catchword, cry, motto, password, shibboleth, word.

waterfall *n* cascade, cataract, fall, linn.

watery *adj* diluted, thin, waterish, weak; insipid, spiritless, tasteful, vapid; moist, wet.

wave *vb* float, flutter, heave, shake, sway, undulate, wallow; brandish, flaunt, flourish, swing; beckon, signal. • *n* billow, bore, breaker, flood, flush, ripple, roll, surge, swell, tide, undulation; flourish, gesture, sway; convolution, curl, roll, unevenness.

waver *vb* flicker, float, undulate, wave; reel, totter; falter, fluctuate, flutter, hesitate, oscillate, quiver, vacillate.

wax *vb* become, grow, increase, mount, rise.

way *n* advance, journey, march, progression, transit, trend; access, alley, artery, avenue, beat, channel, course, highroad, highway, passage, path, road, route, street, track, trail; fashion, manner, means, method, mode, system; distance, interval, space, stretch; behavior, custom, form, guise, habit, habitude, practice, process, style, usage; device, plan, scheme.

wayfarer *n* itinerant, nomad, passenger, pilgrim, rambler, traveler, walker, wanderer.

wayward *adj* capricious, captious, contrary, forward, headstrong, intractable, obstinate, perverse, refractory, stubborn, unruly, willful.

weak *adj* debilitated, delicate, enfeebled, enervated, exhausted, faint, feeble, fragile, frail, infirm, invalid, languid, languishing, shaky, sickly, spent, strengthless, tender, unhealthy, unsound, wasted, weakly; accessible, defenseless, unprotected, vulnerable; light, soft, unstressed; boneless, cowardly, infirm; compliant, irresolute, pliable, pliant, undecided, undetermined, unsettled, unstable, unsteady, vacillating, wavering, yielding; childish, foolish, imbecile, senseless, shallow, silly, simple, stupid, weak-minded, witless; erring, foolish, indiscreet, injudicious, unwise; gentle, indistinct, low, small; adulterated, attenuated, diluted, insipid, tasteless, thin, watery; flimsy, frivolous, poor, sleazy, slight, trifling; futile, illogical, inconclusive, ineffective, ineffectual, inefficient, lame, unconvincing, unsatisfactory, unsupported, unsustained, vague, vain; unsafe, unsound, unsubstantial, untrustworthy; helpless, impotent, powerless; breakable, brittle, delicate, frangible; inconsiderable, puny, slender, slight, small.

weaken vb cramp, cripple, debilitate, devitalize, enervate, enfeeble, invalidate, relax, sap, shake, stagger, undermine, unman, unnerve, unstring; adulterate, attenuate, debase, depress, dilute, exhaust, impair, impoverish, lessen, lower, reduce.

weakness n debility, feebleness, fragility, frailty, infirmity, languor, softness; defect, failing, fault, flaw; fondness, inclination, liking.

weal n advantage, good, happiness, interest, profit, utility, prosperity, welfare; ridge, streak, stripe.

wealth n assets, capital, cash, fortune, funds, goods, money, possessions, property, riches, treasure; abundance, affluence, opulence, plenty, profusion.

wean vb alienate, detach, disengage, withdraw.

wear vb bear, carry, don; endure, last; consume, impair, rub, use, waste. • n corrosion, deterioration, disintegration, erosion, wear and tear; consumption, use; apparel, array, attire, clothes, clothing, dress, garb, gear.

wearied adj apathetic, bored, exhausted, fagged, fatigued, jaded, tired, weary, worn.

weariness n apathy, boredom, ennui, exhaustion, fatigue, languor, lassitude, monotony, prostration, sameness, tedium.

wearisome adj annoying, boring, dull, exhausting, fatiguing, humdrum, irksome, monotonous, prolix, prosaic, slow, tedious,

tiresome, troublesome, trying, uninteresting, vexatious.

weary vb debilitate, exhaust, fag, fatigue, harass, jade, tire. • adj apathetic, bored, drowsy, exhausted, jaded, spent, tired, worn; irksome, tiresome, wearisome.

weave vb braid, entwine, interlace, lace, mat, plait, pleat, twine; compose, construct, fabricate, make.

wed vb contract, couple, espouse, marry, unite.

wedding n bridal, espousal, marriage, nuptials.

wedlock n marriage, matrimony.

ween vb fancy, imagine, suppose, think.

weep vb bemoan, bewail, complain, cry, lament, sob.

weigh vb balance, counterbalance, lift, raise; consider, deliberate, esteem, examine, study.

weight vb ballast, burden, fill, freight, load; weigh. • n gravity, heaviness, heft, tonnage; burden, load, pressure; consequence, efficacy, emphasis, importance, impressiveness, influence, moment, pith, power, significance, value.

weighty adj heavy, massive, onerous, ponderous, unwieldy; considerable, efficacious, forcible, grave, important, influential, serious, significant.

weird adj eerie, ghostly, strange, supernatural, uncanny, unearthly, witching.

welcome vb embrace, greet, hail, receive. • adj acceptable, agreeable, grateful, gratifying, pleasant, pleasing, satisfying. • n greeting, reception, salutation.

welfare n advantage, affluence, benefit, happiness, profit, prosperity, success, thrift, weal, wellbeing.

well[1] vb flow, gush, issue, jet, pour, spring. • n fount, fountain, reservoir, spring, wellhead, wellspring; origin, source; hole, pit, shaft.

well[2] adj hale, healthy, hearty, sound; fortunate, good, happy, profitable, satisfactory, useful. • adv accurately, adequately, correctly, efficiently, properly, suitably; abundantly, considerably, fully, thoroughly; agreeably, commendably, favorably, worthily.

wellbeing n comfort, good, happiness, health, prosperity, welfare.

welter vb flounder, roll, toss, wallow. • n confusion, jumble, mess.

wet vb dabble, damp, dampen, dip, drench,

moisten, saturate, soak, sprinkle, water.
• *adj* clammy, damp, dank, dewy, dripping, humid, moist; rainy, showery, sprinkly. • *n* dampness, humidity, moisture, wetness.

whack *vb, n* bang, beat, rap, strike, thrash, thump, thwack.

wharf *n* dock, pier, quay.

wheedle *vb* cajole, coax, flatter, inveigle, lure.

wheel *vb* gyrate, revolve, roll, rotate, spin, swing, turn, twist, whirl, wind. • *n* circle, revolution, roll, rotation, spin, turn, twirl.

whet *vb* grind, sharpen; arouse, awaken, excite, provoke, rouse, stimulate; animate, inspire, kindle, quicken, warm.

whiff *vb, n* blast, gust, puff.

whim *n* caprice, crotchet, fancy, freak, frolic, humor, notion, quirk, sport, vagary, whimsy, wish.

whimsical *adj* capricious, crotchety, eccentric, erratic, fanciful, frolicsome, odd, peculiar, quaint, singular.

whine *vb* cry, grumble, mewl, moan, snivel, wail, whimper. • *n* complaint, cry, grumble, moan, sob, wail, whimper.

whip *vb* beat, lash, strike; flagellate, flog, goad, horsewhip, scourge, slash; hurt, sting; jerk, snap, snatch, whisk. • *n* bullwhip, cane, crop, horsewhip, knout, lash, scourge, switch, thong.

whipping *n* beating, castigation, dusting, flagellation, flogging, thrashing.

whirl *vb* gyrate, pirouette, roll, revolve, rotate, turn, twirl, twist, wheel. • *n* eddy, flurry, flutter, gyration, rotation, spin, swirl, twirl, vortex.

whit *n* atom, bit, grain, iota, jot, mite, particle, scrap, speck, tittle.

white *adj* argent, canescent, chalky, frosty, hoary, ivory, milky, silver, snowy; gray, pale, pallid, wan; candid, clean, chaste, immaculate, innocent, pure, spotless, unblemished.

whole *adj* all, complete, entire, intact, integral, total, undivided; faultless, firm, good, perfect, strong, unbroken, undivided, uninjured; healthy, sound, well. • *adv* entire, in one. • *n* aggregate, all, amount, ensemble, entirety, gross, sum, total, totality.

wholesome *adj* healthy, healthful, invigorating, nourishing, nutritious, salubrious, salutary; beneficial, good, helpful, improving, salutary; fresh, sound, sweet.

wholly *adv* altogether, completely, entirely, fully, totally, utterly.

whoop *vb* halloo, hoot, roar, shout, yell. • *n* bellow, hoot, roar, shout, yell.

whore *n* bawd, courtesan, drab, harlot, prostitute, streetwalker, strumpet.

wicked *adj* abandoned, abominable, depraved, devilish, godless, graceless, immoral, impious, infamous, irreligious, irreverent, profane, sinful, ungodly, unholy, unprincipled, unrighteous, vicious, vile, worthless; atrocious, bad, black, criminal, dark, evil, heinous, ill, iniquitous, monstrous, nefarious, unjust, villainous.

wide *adj* ample, broad, capacious, comprehensive, distended, expanded, large, spacious, vast; distant, remote; prevalent, rife, widespread. • *adv* completely, farthest, fully.

wield *vb* brandish, flourish, handle, manipulate, ply, work; control, manage, sway, use.

wild *adj* feral, undomesticated, untamed; desert, desolate, native, rough, rude, uncultivated; barbarous, ferocious, fierce, savage, uncivilized; dense, luxuriant, rank; disorderly, distracted, frantic, frenzied, furious, impetuous, irregular, mad, outrageous, raving, turbulent, ungoverned, uncontrolled, violent; dissipated, fast, flighty, foolish, giddy, harebrained, heedless, ill-advised, inconsiderate, reckless, thoughtless, unwise; boisterous, rough, stormy; crazy, extravagant, fanciful, grotesque, imaginary, strange. • *n* desert, waste, wilderness.

wilderness *n* desert, waste, wild.

willful *adj* cantankerous, contumacious, dogged, headstrong, heady, inflexible, intractable, mulish, obdurate, obstinate, perverse, pig-headed, refractory, self-willed, stubborn, unruly, unyielding; arbitrary, capricious; deliberate, intended, intentional, planned, premeditated.

will *vb* bid, command, decree, direct, enjoin, ordain; choose, desire, elect, wish; bequeath, convey, demise, devise, leave. • *n* decision, determination, resoluteness, resolution, self-reliance; desire, disposition, inclination, intent, pleasure, purpose, volition, wish; behest, command, decree, demand, direction, order, request, requirement.

willing *adj* adaptable, amenable, compliant, desirous, disposed, inclined, minded; deliberate, free, intentional, spontaneous, unasked, unbidden, voluntary; cordial, eager, forward, prompt, ready.

willingly *adv* cheerfully, gladly, readily, spontaneously, voluntarily.

wily *adj* arch, artful, crafty, crooked, cunning, deceitful, designing, diplomatic, foxy, insidious, intriguing, politic, sly, subtle, treacherous, tricky.

win *vb* accomplish, achieve, acquire, catch, earn, effect, gain, gather, get, make, obtain, procure, reach, realize, reclaim, recover; gain, succeed, surpass, triumph; arrive; allure, attract, convince, influence, persuade. • *n* conquest, success, triumph, victory.

wind[1] *n* air, blast, breeze, draught, gust, hurricane, whiff, zephyr; breath, breathing, expiration, inspiration, respiration; flatulence, gas, windiness.

wind[2] *vb* coil, crank, encircle, involve, reel, roll, turn, twine, twist; bend, curve, meander, zigzag. • *n* bend, curve, meander, twist, zigzag.

winding *adj* circuitous, devious, flexuose, flexuous, meandering, serpentine, tortuous, turning, twisting. • *n* bend, curve, meander, turn, twist.

windy *adj* breezy, blowy, blustering, boisterous, draughty, gusty, squally, stormy, tempestuous; airy, empty, hollow, inflated.

winning *adj* alluring, attractive, bewitching, brilliant, captivating, charming, dazzling, delightful, enchanting, engaging, fascinating, lovely, persuasive, pleasing, prepossessing; conquering, triumphant, victorious.

winnow *vb* cull, glean, divide, fan, part, select, separate, sift.

winsome *adj* blithe, blithesome, bonny, buoyant, charming, cheerful, debonair, jocund, light-hearted, lively, lovable, merry, pleasant, sportive, winning.

wintry *adj* arctic, boreal, brumal, cold, frosty, icy, snowy.

wipe *vb* clean, dry, mop, rub. • *n* mop, rub, blow, hit, strike; gibe, jeer, sarcasm, sneer, taunt.

wisdom *n* depth, discernment, farsightedness, foresight, insight, judgement, judiciousness, prescience, profundity, prudence, sagacity, sapience, sense, solidity, understanding, wiseness; attainment, edification, enlightenment, erudition, information, knowledge, learning, lore, scholarship; reason.

wise *adj* deep, discerning, enlightened, intelligent, judicious, penetrating,

philosophical, profound, rational, seasonable, sensible, sage, sapient, solid, sound; erudite, informed, knowing, learned, scholarly; crafty, cunning, designing, foxy, politic, sly, subtle, wary, wily.

wish *vb* covet, desire, hanker, list, long; bid, command, desire, direct, intend, mean, order, want. • *n* behest, desire, intention, mind, pleasure, want, will; craving, desire, hankering, inclination, liking, longing, want, yearning.

wistful *adj* contemplative, engrossed, meditative, musing, pensive, reflective, thoughtful; desirous, eager, earnest, longing.

wit *n* genius, intellect, intelligence, reason, sense, understanding; brightness, banter, cleverness, drollery, facetiousness, fun, humor, jocularity, piquancy, point, raillery, satire, sparkle, whim; conceit, epigram, jest, joke, pleasantry, quip, quirk, repartee, sally, witticism; humorist, joker, wag.

witch *n* charmer, enchantress, fascinator, sorceress; crone, hag, sibyl.

witchcraft *n* conjuration, enchantment, magic, necromancy, sorcery, spell.

withdraw *vb* abstract, deduct, remove, retire, separate, sequester, sequestrate, subduct, subtract; disengage, wean; abjure, recall, recant, relinquish, resign, retract, revoke; abdicate, decamp, depart, dissociate, retire, shrink, vacate.

wither *vb* contract, droop, dry, sear, shrivel, wilt, wizen; decay, decline, languish, pine, waste.

withhold *vb* check, detain, hinder, repress, restrain, retain, suppress.

withstand *vb* confront, defy, face, oppose, resist.

witless *adj* daft, dull, foolish, halfwitted, obtuse, senseless, shallow, silly, stupid, unintelligent.

witness *vb* corroborate, mark, note, notice, observe, see. • *n* attestation, conformation, corroboration, evidence, proof, testimony; beholder, bystander, corroborator, deponent, eyewitness, onlooker, spectator, testifier.

witty *adj* bright, clever, droll, facetious, funny, humorous, jocose, jocular, pleasant, waggish; alert, penetrating, quick, sparkling, sprightly.

wizard *n* charmer, diviner, conjurer, enchanter, magician, necromancer, seer, soothsayer, sorcerer.

woe *n* affliction, agony, anguish, bitterness, depression, distress, dole, grief, heartache, melancholy, misery, sorrow, torture, tribulation, trouble, unhappiness, wretchedness.

woeful *adj* afflicted, agonized, anguished, burdened, disconsolate, distressed, melancholy, miserable, mournful, piteous, sad, sorrowful, troubled, unhappy, wretched; afflicting, afflictive, calamitous, deplorable, depressing, disastrous, distressing, dreadful, tragic, tragical, grievous, lamentable, pitiable, saddening.

wonder *vb* admire, gape, marvel; conjecture, ponder, query, question, speculate. • *n* amazement, astonishment, awe, bewilderment, curiosity, marvel, miracle, prodigy, surprise, stupefaction, wonderment.

wonderful *adj* amazing, astonishing, astounding, awe-inspiring, awesome, awful, extraordinary, marvellous, miraculous, portentous, prodigious, startling, stupendous, surprising.

wont *adj* accustomed, customary, familiar, habitual, ordinary, usual. • *n* custom, habit, practice, rule, usage.

wonted *adj* accustomed, common, conventional, customary, everyday, familiar, frequent, habitual, ordinary, regular, usual.

wood *n* coppice, copse, covert, forest, greenwood, grove, spinney, thicket, woodland.

word *vb* express, phrase, put, say, state, term, utter. • *n* expression, name, phrase, term, utterance; account, advice, information, intelligence, message, news, report, tidings; affirmation, assertion, averment, avowal, declaration, statement; conversation, speech; agreement, assurance, engagement, parole, pledge, plight, promise; behest, bidding, command, direction, order, precept; countersign, password, signal, watchword.

wordy *adj* circumlocutory, diffuse, garrulous, inflated, lengthened, long-winded, loquacious, periphrastic, rambling, talkative, tedious, verbose, windy.

work *vb* act, operate; drudge, fag, grind, grub, labor, slave, sweat, toil; move, perform, succeed; aim, attempt, strive, try; effervesce, ferment, leaven, rise; accomplish, beget, cause, effect, engender, manage, originate, produce; exert, strain; embroider, stitch. • *n* exertion, drudgery, grind, labor, pain, toil; business, ment, function, occupation, task;

action, accomplishment, achievement, composition, deed, feat, fruit, handiwork, opus, performance, product, production; fabric, manufacture; ferment, leaven; management, treatment.

workman *n* journeyman, employee, laborer, operative, worker, wright; artisan, craftsman, mechanic.

world *n* cosmos, creation, earth, globe, nature, planet, sphere, universe.

worldly *adj* common, earthly, human, mundane, sublunary, terrestrial; carnal, fleshly, profane, secular, temporal; ambitious, groveling, irreligious, selfish, proud, sordid, unsanctified, unspiritual; sophisticated, worldly-wise.

worry *vb* annoy, badger, bait, beset, bore, bother, chafe, disquiet, disturb, fret, gall, harass, harry, hector, infest, irritate, molest, persecute, pester, plague, tease, torment, trouble, vex. • *n* annoyance, anxiety, apprehensiveness, care, concern, disquiet, fear, misgiving, perplexity, solicitude, trouble, uneasiness, vexation.

worship *vb* adore, esteem, honor, revere, venerate; deify, idolize; aspire, pray. • *n* adoration, devotion, esteem, homage, idolatry, idolizing, respect, reverence; aspiration, exultation, invocation, laud, praise, prayer, supplication.

worst *vb* beat, choke, conquer, crush, defeat, discomfit, foil, master, overpower, overthrow, quell, rout, subdue, subjugate, vanquish.

worth *n* account, character, credit, desert, excellence, importance, integrity, merit, nobleness, worthiness, virtue; cost, estimation, price, value.

worthless *adj* futile, meritless, miserable, nugatory, paltry, poor, trifling, unproductive, unsalable, unserviceable, useless, valueless, wretched; abject, base, corrupt, degraded, ignoble, low, mean, vile.

worthy *adj* deserving, fit, suitable; estimable, excellent, exemplary, good, honest, honorable, reputable, righteous, upright, virtuous. • *n* celebrity, dignitary, luminary, notability, personage, somebody, VIP.

wound *vb* damage, harm, hurt, injure; cut, gall, harrow, irritate, lacerate, pain, prick, stab; annoy, mortify, offend. • *n* blow, hurt, injury; damage, detriment; anguish, grief, pain, pang, torture.

wraith *n* apparition, ghost, phantom, spectre, vision.

wrangle vb argue, bicker, brawl, cavil, dispute, jangle, jar, quarrel, squabble, spar, spat. • n altercation, argument, bickering, brawl, contest, controversy, jar, quarrel, squabble.

wrap vb cloak, cover, encase, envelop, muffle, swathe, wind. • n blanket, cape, cloak, cover, overcoat, shawl.

wrath n anger, choler, exasperation, fury, heat, resentment, indignation, ire, irritation, offence, passion, rage.

wrathful adj angry, enraged, exasperated, furious, hot, indignant, infuriated, irate, mad, passionate, provoked, rageful.

wreak vb execute, exercise, indulge, inflict, work.

wreath n chaplet, curl, festoon, garland, ring, twine.

wreathe vb encircle, festoon, garland, intertwine, surround, twine, twist.

wreck vb founder, shipwreck, strand; blast, blight, break, devastate, ruin, spoil. • n crash, desolation, destruction, perdition, prostration, ruin, shipwreck, smash, undoing.

wrench vb distort, pervert, twist, wrest, wring; sprain, strain; extort, extract. • n twist, wring; sprain, strain; monkey wrench, spanner.

wrest vb force, pull, strain, twist, wrench, wring.

wrestle vb contend, contest, grapple, strive, struggle.

wretch n outcast, pariah, pilgarlic, troglodyte, vagabond, victim, sufferer; beggar, criminal, hound, knave, miscreant, rascal, ruffian, rogue, scoundrel, villain.

wretched adj afflicted, comfortless, distressed, forlorn, sad, unfortunate, unhappy, woebegone; afflicting, calamitous, deplorable, depressing, pitiable, sad, saddening, shocking, sorrowful; bad, beggarly, contemptible, mean, paltry, pitiful, poor, shabby, sorry, vile, worthless.

wring vb contort, twist, wrench; extort, force, wrest; anguish, distress, harass, pain, rack, torture.

wrinkle[1] vb cockle, corrugate, crease, gather, pucker, rumple. • n cockle, corrugation, crease, crimp, crinkle, crumple, fold, furrow, gather, plait, ridge, rumple.

wrinkle[2] n caprice, fancy, notion, quirk, whim; device, tip, trick.

writ n decree, order, subpoena, summons.

write vb compose, copy, indite, inscribe, pen, scrawl, scribble, transcribe.

writer n amanuensis, author, clerk, penman, scribe, secretary.

writhe vb contort, distort, squirm, twist, wriggle.

written adj composed, indited, inscribed, penned, transcribed.

wrong vb abuse, encroach, injure, maltreat, oppress. • adj inequitable, unfair, unjust, wrongful; bad, criminal, evil, guilty, immoral, improper, iniquitous, reprehensible, sinful, vicious, wicked; amiss, improper, inappropriate, unfit, unsuitable; erroneous, false, faulty, inaccurate, incorrect, mistaken, untrue. • adv amiss, erroneously, falsely, faultily, improperly, inaccurately, incorrectly, wrongly. • n foul, grievance, inequity, injury, injustice, trespass, unfairness; blame, crime, dishonesty, evil, guilt, immorality, iniquity, misdeed, misdoing, sin, transgression, unrighteousness, vice, wickedness, wrongdoing; error, falsity.

wroth adj angry, enraged, exasperated, furious, incensed, indignant, irate, passionate, provoked, resentful.

wrought adj done, effected, performed, worked.

X

xanthous adj blonde, fair, light-complexioned, xanthic, yellow.

xiphoid adj ensiform, gladiate, sword-like, sword-shaped.

Xmas n Christmas, Christmastide, Noel, Yule, Yuletide.

X-ray n roentgen ray, r^ntgen ray.

xylograph n cut, woodcut, wood engraving.

xylographer n wood engraver.

xylophagous adj wood-eating, wood-nourished.

Y

yap vb bark, cry, yelp. • n bark, cry, yelp.

yard n close, compound, court, courtyard, enclosure, garden.

yarn n anecdote, boasting, fabrication, narrative, story, tale, untruth.

yawn vb dehisce, gape, open wide. • n gap, gape, gulf.

yearn *vb* crave, desire, hanker after, long for.

yell *vb* bawl, bellow, cry out, howl, roar, scream, screech, shriek, squeal. • *n* cry, howl, roar, scream, screech, shriek.

yellow *adj* aureate, gilded, gilt, gold, golden, lemon, primrose, saffron, xanthic, xanthous.

yelp *vb* bark, howl, yap; complain, bitch, grouse. • *n* bark, sharp cry, howl.

yet *adv* at last, besides, further, however, over and above, so far, still, thus far, ultimately. • *conj* moreover, nevertheless, notwithstanding, now.

yield *vb* afford, bear, bestow, communicate, confer, fetch, furnish, impart, produce, render, supply; accede, accord, acknowledge, acquiesce, allow, assent, comply, concede, give, grant, permit; abandon, abdicate, cede, forgo, give up, let go, quit, relax, relinquish, resign, submit, succumb, surrender, waive. • *n* earnings, income, output, produce, profit, return, revenue.

yielding *adj* accommodating, acquiescent, affable, compliant, complaisant, easy, manageable, obedient, passive, submissive, unresisting; bending, flexible, flexile, plastic, pliant, soft, supple, tractable; fertile, productive.

yoke *vb* associate, bracket, connect, couple, harness, interlink, join, link, unite. • *n* bond, chain, ligature, link, tie, union; bondage, dependence, enslavement, service, servitude, subjection, vassalage; couple, pair.

yokel *n* boor, bumpkin, countryman, peasant, rustic.

yore *adj* ancient, antique, old, olden. • *n* long ago, long since, olden times.

young *adj* green, ignorant, inexperienced, juvenile, new, recent, youthful. • *n* young people, youth; babies, issue, brood, offspring, progeny, spawn.

youngster *n* adolescent, boy, girl, lad, lass, stripling, youth.

youth *n* adolescence, childhood, immaturity, juvenile, juvenility, minority, nonage, pupillage, wardship; boy, girl, lad, lass, schoolboy, schoolgirl, slip, sprig, stripling, youngster.

youthful *adj* boyish, childish, girlish, immature, juvenile, puerile, young.

Z

zany *adj* comic, comical, crazy, droll, eccentric, funny, imaginative, scatterbrained; clownish, foolish, ludicrous, silly. • *n* buffoon, clown, droll, fool, harlequin, jester, punch.

zeal *n* alacrity, ardor, cordiality, devotedness, devotion, earnestness, eagerness, energy, enthusiasm, fervor, glow, heartiness, intensity, jealousness, passion, soul, spirit, warmth.

zealot *n* bigot, devotee, fanatic, freak, partisan.

zealous *adj* ardent, burning, devoted, eager, earnest, enthusiastic, fervent, fiery, forward, glowing, jealous, keen, passionate, prompt, ready, swift, warm.

zenith *n* acme, apex, climax, culmination, heyday, pinnacle, prime, summit, top, utmost, height.

zero *n* cipher, naught, nadir, nil, nothing, nought.

zest *n* appetite, enjoyment, exhilaration, gusto, liking, piquancy, relish, thrill; edge, flavor, salt, savor, tang, taste; appetizer, sauce.

zone *n* band, belt, cincture, girdle, girth; circuit, clime, region.

zymotic *adj* bacterial, fermentative, germinating.